ARMY OFFICERS IN ARAB POLITICS AND SOCIETY

ARMY OFFICERS IN ARAB POLITICS AND SOCIETY

ELIEZER BE'ERI

PRAEGER · PALL MALL

1970

Published in the United States of America in 1970 by Frederick A. Praeger, Inc., Publishers
111 Fourth Avenue, New York, N.Y. 10003

Published in Great Britain in 1970 by Pall Mall Press
5, Cromwell Place, London, S.W. 7

Published in Israel by Israel Universities Press, Jerusalem, 1969

This book is a revised and updated edition of הקצונה והשלטון בעולם הערבי *(He-Ketzuna we-ha-shilton ba'olam ha-'aravi)*, published by SIFRIAT POALIM, Tel Aviv, 1966

Translated from the Hebrew by Dov Ben-Abba

Library of Congress Catalog Card Number: 68-54318

SBN: 269 67062 9

This book has been composed and printed at the Keter Publishing House, Ltd., Jerusalem, Israel, 1969.

PREFACE

HISTORIANS, SOCIOLOGISTS and political scientists have paid until recently scant attention to the army in politics; it is only during the last decade that this has become the subject of systematic study. The reason for this neglect is not difficult to explain. In the developed countries of Europe and the United States the army did not play any major role in contemporary politics before 1914; the appearance of the Man on Horseback such as General Boulanger was a rare exception. Military dictatorship played an important role in Eastern Europe after the First World War; it was regarded somewhat optimistically as a passing phase, an aspect of general backwardness. Nor did the rise of fascism and Communism stimulate interest in the study of the army, for with all the importance military affairs assumed in these regimes the political role of the military was on the whole insignificant. (Spain and Japan were the major exceptions.) Since the nineteen fifties problems of national defence have prominently figured in public discussions in the West, the army has assumed a far more important role than before in the Soviet Union and China, and in most developing countries political power has passed, directly or indirectly, into the hands of the military. These developments have given a powerful stimulus to the study of the function of military structures on the historical and sociological level. Eliezer Be'eri's book is an important contribution to this literature and at the same time a most welcome addition to the historiography of the Middle East since the Second World War. There is a long tradition of military rule in the Middle East; the recent history of the area is an almost uninterrupted chain of military coups. The Iraqi army repeatedly intervened in politics in the nineteen thirties, Syria followed in 1949 and Egypt in 1952.

Since then almost every Arab country has been subject to military rule; in some places this has resulted in relative stability; elsewhere (Iraq, Syria) the plots and counterplots have continued to this day. All the military regimes have been strongly nationalist; some have carried out social reform. Attempts to define them in the traditional European categories of "left" and "right" are not, however, very helpful, quite apart from the fact that there are significant political differences between the military élites in the varius countries. Some of their inspiration is obviously populist in character, but there are also fascist influences and the Islamic impact should not be underrated. It would be highly misleading, moreover, to ignore in the assessment of this phenomenon non-ideological factors such as personal ambition, and, as in the case of Syria, ethnical origin. All this makes the study of the army in Middle Eastern politics both a complicated and a challenging task, and Mr. Be'eri's pioneering book, rich in detail, is shedding much new light on recent Arab politics. Written in difficult conditions, this study shows admirable detachment from the current partisan controversies engulfing Arab-Israeli relations.

It gives me great personal pleasure to be the first to welcome the publication in English of this labour of love. I first knew Ernst Bauer, as Be'eri then was, many years ago when the Middle East, and the world in general faced a crisis even more dangerous than the present. Our preoccupations were different in those days. Little did we dream of writing books and prefaces.

Boston–London, May, 1969 Walter Laqueur

FOREWORD

THIS IS A new version of *Ha-ketzuna we-ha-shilton ba'olam ha-'aravi* which was published in Hebrew by *Sifriat Poalim* (Workers' Book Guild—Hashomer Hatzair) in 1966. In certain places the text has been shortened, or the arrangement and presentation of some issues altered; some minor errors, which were pointed out by reviewers, have been corrected; some new evidence on earlier events and new literature have been taken into account. The main differences are additions pertaining to the events between Spring, 1966, and Autumn, 1967, including the Six-Day War of June, 1967 and its immediate aftermath. The developments considered terminate with two events which can be regarded as the termination of an epoch—the suicide of Marshal 'Āmir and the deposition of Marshal Sallāl. Some observations and evaluations have been checked and amplified through extensive talks with Egyptian, Jordanian and Syrian officers who were prisoners of war in Israel in June and July, 1967.

This book is a work by a Jew and an Israeli about political events and social processes in the contemporary Arab world. The relations between the two peoples are marred by conflict, and those seeking peace have thus far had no success. I make no pretense at having written as a neutral observer who is in no way involved or has no opinion about the disputed matters; even had I desired this, the reader would not have believed me. Contemporary history which tends to regard the struggles of the times from the eternal heights of absolute truth is generally less objective than that stemming from a professed position and a clear-cut point of view obvious to both the writer and reader alike.

Every type of research, whether approached from a so-called objective, neutral standpoint or a definite position, can abuse the facts, choose them arbitrarily, or err in the relative importance attributed to matters of minor or major significance. The greatest stumbling block is to confuse the boundaries between factual description, the analysis of processes and historical evaluation. I have endeavoured to show the facts as they really are and elucidate the nature of the processes. However, I have not refrained from making evaluations nor from coming to certain conclusions. At the same time, I have made an effort to distinguish between description, analysis, conclusion, and evaluation.

The book contains much criticism, sometimes strong, of various phenomena in Arab life and particularly of instances of the interference of the officer corps in politics. Some readers will argue that this is an expression of hidden animosity. But the opposite is true. The criticism is based on the assumption that whoever performed the act which was criticized could also have acted otherwise. There is no greater arrogance than the "tolerant" understanding of a certain phenomenon in another people which is denounced at home; this is thought to be the attitude of the enlightened and progressive individual towards the deplorable condition of someone else who happens to be backward. But actually this is only an overbearing form of contempt.

Several of the book's chapters are contemporary history, and it may well be asked if the time has already come for writing the annals of modern officers' movements when the writer does not have access to the archives of the countries concerned, and before they have been made available to anyone else. And, to be sure, in certain matters, it has been impossible to ascertain details thoroughly. Nevertheless, it cannot at all be assumed that these matters will ever be absolutely clear. Even the researcher to whom all the archival material will be available will not find much in it concerning the underground Arab officers' movements, and what he does reveal will have extremely relative value. Because of the nature of the movements and the habits of their members, no minutes were kept of meetings, no letters were exchanged, and no diaries were kept. Moreover, should the reports of the Arab secret services and certain foreign states be published, they would consist of a hodgepodge of account, conjecture, rumour, suspicion and vilification. The main sources for studying the movements of Arab officers are the statements of the coup plotters themselves, which were extensively published, after their accession to power, in memoirs, speeches, newspaper interviews, and testimony at trials. These descriptions are in all probability not objective. Even if some writer wished to present a true account, his memory of the past would undoubtedly have been influenced by the relations between himself and his colleagues or opponents at the time of writing. Furthermore, the biographers and historians were not always interested in relating only the truth and the whole truth. Their historiography was interwoven with propaganda and served as one of the means of disseminating opinion and inculcating certain evaluations. There is, consequently, no way of investigating the historic truth in these matters other than by a comparative analysis of all extant material in the full awareness of its limitations and in the knowledge that the revelation of numerous additional objective, authoritative information in the future is not very likely. In all these respects, there would seem to be no basic difference between a study made now and one that may be carried out in the future, either in Israel or elsewhere.

Arabic proper names have been transliterated according to the University of London *Bulletin of the School of Oriental and African Studies,* except in a few constantly recurring names, such as Nasser. Geographical names have been rendered as in J. Bartholomew's map *Middle East and Near East.*

I should like to express my thanks to all those friends who helped me, intellectually and materially, in my research and in writing this book. Some have asked not to be named personally, but I would like at least to record my gratitude to the institutions which allocated research grants, and the staff of which have given me access to most valuable materials and information: the Hebrew University of Jerusalem; Tel Aviv University and the Reuven Shiloah Research Center; the Archives and Intelligence Branch of the Israel Defence Forces; the Research Department of the Ministry for Foreign Affairs; Beth David Salomons Trust; the General Federation of Labour in Israel (the Histadrut); the photo archives of the newspapers *Ha'aretz* and *Bamakhaneh;* the Hashomer-Hatzair Kibbutz Movement and its Seminar at Givat Haviva; and above all, to my own kibbutz, Hazorea.

Hazorea, June, 1969 — Eliezer Be'eri

CONTENTS

INTRODUCTION

THE THEORY OF "THE NATURAL COURSE"

"The first condition for progress is political stability. We, like you, borrowed western parliamentarism. It did not work."

General Ayub Khan, President of Pakistan,
in a speech in Cairo, November 7, 1960.

"The army is the way to social progress. There new political classes are created which surge forward impatiently to break national patterns which have grown outmoded."

L'Orient, Beirut, April 5, 1962.

INTRODUCTION

THE THEORY OF "THE NATURAL COURSE"

On November 17, 1958 Khartoum Radio broadcast the first announcement by the Sudanese Chief of Staff Ibrahīm 'Abbūd about the coup d'état which had been carried out during the night.

In many respects 'Abbūd's proclamation was just another example of the numerous instances of "communiqué number one" (*bayān raqm waḥad*) which generally signals that another military coup d'état has taken place in any of the Arab countries, like the customary *pronunciamento* issued by Latin-America insurrectionists. The one thing remarkable in the statement published by the Sudanese Chief of Staff was the expression in it of a general political philosophy.

In gloomy colors, the announcement described the crisis which had lately been afflicting the country, and then went on to say: "Thus, in the natural course of events, the country's army and security forces rose to put an end to that chaos."[1]

The military coup was defined as "the natural course".

The announcement made by the Chief of Staff gave expression to a widely held opinion: A military coup d'état and the establishment of a military dictatorship were regarded as the natural course of political development in the contemporary Arab states.

This was the opinion of many in Sudan and in other Arab countries, and of many outside observers of the Arab political scene as well. For were not governments established and headed by army officers then ruling in Egypt, in Syria and in Iraq—the leading Arab countries of the Middle East? In Lebanon, also, a civil war had ended three months before in the election of the Chief of Staff, Shihāb, as President.

For this is a common occurrence in modern Arab states: A group of army officers organizes an underground movement, seizes power in a military coup and rules directly for a shorter or longer period, generally with-

[1] Amīn Sa'īd, *Ta'rīkh al-'arab al-ḥadith*, part 15, *Al-jumhūriyya al-'arabiyya al-muttaḥida*, vol. 2 , Cairo 1960, 195.

out handing over the conduct of affairs of state to an elected government.

The first coup of this sort in modern Arab history occurred in Iraq in 1936, and since then numerous coups and attempted coups by officers have taken place in most of the Arab countries of the Middle East. In April 1949 a Syrian journalist had already written that Za'īm's coup of March 30 had been "a natural result" of the situation in the country,[2] and since then there has been a growing tendency to accept the theory that military coups really are "the natural course" in contemporary Arab history.

This theory has been assiduously cultivated and spread by all the propaganda and indoctrination of existing officer governments. Nasser, expressing confidence that the end of the kings of Saudi Arabia and Jordan was at hand, and wishing to force the issue, took it for granted that it would be army officers who would depose Sa'ūd and Husayn; in his speech at Port Said on December 23, 1962, several weeks after Sallāl's coup in Yemen, he predicted that "a Saudi Sallāl and a Jordanian Sallāl" would appear to oust the kings.[3] Rule by army officers is regarded as a historic necessity.

Nasser also formulated the programmatic basis of the theory which assigned army officers the historic role of the revolutionary avant-garde in the Arab world. In his *Philosophy of the Revolution* he explains that after the failure of the Egyptian revolution of 1919, "the state of affairs . . . singled out the army as the force to do the job. The situation demanded the existence of a force set in one cohesive framework, far removed from the conflict between individuals and classes, and drawn from the heart of the people: a force composed of men able to trust each other, a force with enough material strength at its disposal to guarantee swift and decisive action. These conditions could be met only by the army . . . It was not the army which defined its role in the events that took place; the opposite is closer to the truth. The events and their ramifications defined the role of the army."[4] In another place in the same work, he writes, "Was it necessary for us, the army, to do what we did on July 23, 1952? . . . Why did our army find itself obliged to act in the capital of the motherland instead of on the frontiers? . . . We felt to the depths of our beings that this was our soldier's duty and that if we failed to discharge it, we would be failing in the sacred trust placed in us."[5] In the same spirit Qassim said in 1960

[2] Ghassān Tuwaynī, *Manṭiq al-quwwa,* Beirut 1954, 66.

[3] *Al-Ahrām,* Cairo, 24 December 1962.

[4] Jamāl 'Abd al-Nāṣir, *Falsafat al-thawra,* 10th impression, Cairo (1954), 27–9; Gamal Abdul Nasser, *Egypt's liberation,* Washington, D.C., 1955, 42–3.

[5] *Ibid.,* Arabic, 19–20; English, 30–2.

that the army "would not have launched this revolution had our brothers outside the army been able to wring their rights by force of peace. But they had been overcome and were enfeebled."[6] Countless expressions of this thesis can be cited from the writings and sayings of Arab officer politicians.

This view of the historic role to be played by the Arab officer class has been advanced outside the Arab world as well. Kingsley Martin's remark in the *New Statesman* is typical: "There comes a time in technically backward states when national sentiment makes colonialism impossible, or at least unprofitable, and when the people's consciousness of the gap between their own poverty and the wealth of the industrial West and its colonial hangers-on is so widespread that feudalism is doomed. In Arab countries the only force then able to carry out the necessary revolution is the army . . ."[7] This is only a more sophisticated version of the "natural course" theory of 'Abbūd and Nasser and Qassim.

D. Rustow offers a variation of the same opinion. He sees officer rule as a historical continuity: "The Middle East, more than any comparable world region, has been subject to military invasions throughout history. Most states of the region, down to the present, have been established by conquest; most of the recent changes of regime have been effected by military action. The region's traditional culture rests upon a religion that accords great prestige and legitimacy to the military. And the direct and indirect impact of modernity upon the traditional culture further tended to enhance the leading role of the armed forces and their officer corps. Against this background, it is clear that the prominent and decisive role of the military on the current Middle Eastern scene is not a momentary lapse from normal constitutional practice but conforms to ample historic precedent. Conversely, it is the occasional spells of peaceful constitutional government by civilians—as in Turkey from 1922 to 1960, in Lebanon from 1945 to 1958, in Israel since 1948—which must be seen as the exceptional situations."[8] This is a daring and oversimplified generalization. At the same time, Rustow is cautious in evaluating the nature of the officer rule: "The ultimate success of a military regime depends on its skill in allowing or promoting the rise of effective civilian institutions that will render future military intervention superfluous—in short, in forseeing a set of political rules whereby clubs no longer will be trumps."[9] While from his standpoint it would appear that until now military rule has not

[6] *MER* 1960, 232.

[7] *The New Statesman,* London, 16 February 1962.

[8] Dankwart A. Rustow, 'The military in Middle Eastern society and politics', in Sidney Fisher, ed., *The military in the Middle East,* Columbus, Ohio, 1963, 9.

[9] *Ibid.,* 19.

fulfilled its role in history, Rustow's view should, nevertheless, be bracketed with all those who consider military coups "the natural course" and officer rule a historical necessity in the modern Arab world.

Three assumptions underly these views: 1) the Arab world exists in a deep crisis of underdevelopment and transition which can be overcome only by a revolutionary change in the social structure and political regimes; 2) there is no force other than the officer class ready to implement the necessary changes; 3) the officers have the ability to effect this transformation. Each one of these assumptions should be examined separately; even if one of them is acceptable, it does not automatically follow that the others are also substantiated.

No one disputes the first assumption. The peoples of Asia and Africa are now deeply aware of their economic, social and political backwardness compared with advanced capitalism and developing socialism, and they know that there are no prospects of catching up with these countries or even reducing the gap between them if a radical transformation of their lives does not take place. Eighty years ago, Jamāl al-Dīn al-Afghānī was already asking, "The Christian religion is based on making peace, and kindness prevails in everything; it calls for the abolition of blood feuds and the renunciation of power . . . whereas Islam is based on an aspiration to victory, might, conquest and boldness, and negates every law which conflicts with its precepts . . . however, the condition of the Muslims at this time is shocking . . . it is amazing that it was precisely the Christians who invented Krupp's cannons and the machine gun before the Muslims . . . what help provided by history guided the Christians and advanced them . . . and what evil afflicted the Muslims and pushed them back?"[10] In 1930 Shakīb Arslān asked the same question in its classical form in his articles entitled "Why have the Muslims lagged behind and why have others progressed?"[11] To this day, this question has preoccupied Muslims and Arabs. And if there were in the past statesmen and thinkers among them who hoped for a rebirth through slow, gradual evolution, today all of them are convinced that their only hope is revolution. The word "revolution" has become the catchword of all the desires for liberation and progress in Arab political thinking, and there is no more honored title for an Arab than the designation "revolutionary".

[10] Al-'urwa al-wuthqā, 3 April 1884, quoted in Al-Sayyid Jamāl al-Dīn al-Afghānī wal-Shaykh Muḥammad 'Abduh, *Al-'urwa al-wuthqā wal-thawra al-taḥrīriyya al-kubrā,* Cairo 1957, 257–7.

[11] Quoted from *al-Manar,* Cairo, in Wilfred Cantwell Smith, *Islam in modern history,* Princeton 1957, 54.

The second assumption of the theory of the natural course states that the political factor designed to liberate the Arab world from outside dependence and internal degeneration is the officer class. This thesis is the mainstay of all the explanations of Arab officer coups as a historic necessity. The extreme adherents of this view have developed an ideology which maintains that the historical role which the doctrines of Marx and Engels assign to the working class and the Communist Party as its advance guard is, in the Arab states, destined for army officers with associations of Free Officers as their front rank. *The Communist Manifesto* has been supplanted by *The Philosophy of the Revolution.*

This approach facilitates the understanding of events which have occurred and the frequency of certain phenomena. In these countries there was not even a single instance of an attempt to carry out a social revolution, whereas military coups have been occurring with great frequency.

In the newly independent Arab states there existed a power vacuum into which the officers were drawn. The traditional ruling class of big landowners and members of the liberal professions originating from it and acting in its service is no longer capable of maintaining power in its hands. Their opposition to the processes of economic, national and social development clearly indicates that their power has grown outdated. But who is to succeed them? The middle class is still weak, poor in capital, experience and initiative, and lacks an independent political leadership with a clear and comprehensive ideology. Many of the intellectuals continue to cling to the interests of their landowning ancestors. The working class, mostly rural-born, is still small in numbers, disunited and inexperienced, with no deeply rooted class consciousness and little professional knowledge. The workers' struggle is paralyzed by the large numbers of unemployed villagers ready at any time to take the places of the strikers. And the millions of fellaheen are impoverished and spiritually and politically in thrall to their exploiters. Which class, what popular force is capable of establishing a regime that would ensure stability as well as development?

Attempts were made in a number of Arab countries to organize the state along the lines of a European parliamentary democracy. This system itself came to grief and collapsed in many European countries, and in the Arab world it quickly degenerated. It may be claimed that parliamentarism was not given sufficient time to consolidate and adapt to the special conditions of Arab society; it may be argued that whatever supplanted it is no better or even worse. However, the failure of Arab parliamentarism, or what was presented as parliamentarism, still stands.

It is no wonder, then, that any crisis in an Arab country is liable to shake the very foundations of the state. Power seems to lie around in the streets unclaimed. It is at such times that the officers regard themselves destined to save the country from chaos. For by its definition and nature, the army is a national body representing the people as a whole without factional considerations. It is the best organized and most efficient force in the country, versed in deeds and not in idle debate, possessing the monopoly of physical power without undue hesitation in using it.

In explaining the events which occurred in Egypt in the summer of 1952, Aharon Cohen writes, "When the old rulers are no longer able to hold on to power, the middle class too weak to seize it, and the working class not yet matured for this task, officers fill the political vacuum which has been formed."[12] Rustow suggests a slightly different definition, "It is not entirely accurate to think of the army as filling a vacuum; rather it moves in to break a stalemate."[13] The essential distinction between both figures of speech, a vacuum and a stalemate, is not great; both apply to the same kind of a crisis, the same kind of solution.

This is a common and also reasonable explanation. It can be substantiated by numerous, compelling arguments; the most cogent one is the fact that in Iraq, Syria and Egypt, other elements have time and again failed to seize or maintain power whereas groups of officers have succeeded. Nevertheless, the assumption concerning the revolutionary mission of the officers requires a more careful scrutiny. Does a relatively large number of cases of this sort constitute a rule applicable to the entire Arab world in the period from the 1930's to the 1960's? Was what occurred inevitable? Will the trend indicated in the recent past also persist in the future or will it grow weaker or perhaps stronger? What do the various groups of insurrectionist officers in different countries and at varying times have in common, and what is unique to each one?

The frequency of coups shows that they are not just a chance phenomenon. However, frequency itself is not per se sufficient proof that there were not and do not now exist other forces, besides the officers, who can effect a change in the traditional regime. Obviously the army has the advantage of possessing unequalled power, a highly developed hierarchical organization, and the ability to act swiftly; unlike a political party, it does not need the consensus of many persons acting voluntarily in order to oust or install a government. However, is this sufficient for assuming that other forces do not exist at all? Was not the military dictatorship in Sudan—which came into power in 1958 as a consequence of "the natural course"—deposed in 1964 by a popular uprising of civilians after it had become corrupt? In

[12] Aharon Cohen, *Ha'olam ha'aravi shel yameynu,* Merhavia 1958, 261.

[13] Rustow, 12.

Latin America underdevelopment and the need for revolutionary changes are very similar to those in the Arab world, and there, too, coups are very frequent; then Fidel Castro appeared, and Cuba is evidence that other forces and other ways also exist. However, no mechanical analogy can be drawn between Cuba and the Arab countries or between Sudan and Egypt or Iraq.

At any rate, one fact is clear: whether or not one accepts the assumption that the accession of officers to power is the only possible way out of the crisis of a governmental vacuum or a stalemate, or whether one cautiously refrains from seeing it as the embodiment of a historical *necessity*, the phenomenon can certainly not be regarded as only a historic *accident*.

The third assumption of the theory of the natural course contends that the officers, in addition to being destined to fill a power vacuum, are also competent and capable of bringing about necessary revolutionary transformations in Arab society.

This assumption can find support in Arab history. Beginning with the reforms in the Ottoman army in the early years of the 18th century, the military sphere was the first and oldest in Muslim countries to come in contact with western civilization. The officers were the vanguard of westernization. The Ottoman sultan in the 19th century and the Imam of Yemen in the 20th could still forbid the teaching of the heretical theory that the earth revolves around the sun. Their power and authority were not impaired by the lack of physicians, on the contrary. However, when the machine gun referred to by Afghānī was invented in the west, they could not forego acquiring it and learning how to use it for the purpose of securing their power against external and internal foes. They could stubbornly seal off their countries to the penetration of European science and politics, but they were not able to renounce the acquisition of the cutting edge of western civilization. In the course of the 19th century, between Napoleon's expedition to Egypt and the First World War, most of the European and American teachers and instructors invited to Turkey and Egypt taught military science, and the number of Turkish and Egyptian officers sent for advanced study to France, England and Germany was constantly increasing. They not only studied military tactics and technology but also acquired general knowledge, and they were influenced in matters of culture and politics; they were particularly affected by the ideas of nationalism and were impressed by the power of the constitutional state. The officers became the bearers of the doctrines of reform and of modern nationalism. Foremost in the movements for progress exemplified by the Young Turks' revolution of 1908, the establishment of the Turkish secular republic of Atatürk and the Egyptian revolt of Aḥmad 'Urābī in 1881 were army officers.

However, the situation after World War II is not what it was before World War I. The state's monopoly of military power has remained in the hands of officers; in a number of Arab countries it was handed to them for the first time after the abolition of colonial rule. But the officer corps no longer possesses the monopoly of modern education and nationalism. New social groups have appeared and multiplied whose training and aspirations and prospects all point to breaking the chains of tradition. These comprise officials and executives, technicians, and members of liberal professions—the new middle class. All over the world, and particularly in the Middle East, they are salaried employees. They have no prospect of, and consequently, no interest in, acquiring the ownership of the enterprises and institutions in which they are employed. It is in their interest that these institutions and enterprises should be owned by the state, which, in any case, already owns a considerable portion of them, and that they themselves should be the ruling elite in the country. M. Halpern thoroughly explores the rise of this "salaried middle class" as "the most active political, social and economic sector from Morocco to Pakistan." [14]

What place do the officers occupy in this alignment? Halpern regards them as an important part and an eminent representation of "the new salaried middle class," as the possessors of outstanding qualities for advancing the social revolution in the Middle East. "The more the army was modernized, the more its composition, organization, spirit, capabilities, and purpose constituted a radical criticism of the existing political system. Within the army, modern technology was eagerly welcomed and its usefulness and power appreciated. By contrast, the political system showed greater inertia, inefficiency, skepticism, and greed in utilizing the products of modern science . . . Within the army, a sense of national mission transcending parochial, regional or economic interests, or kinship ties seemed to be much more clearly defined than elsewhere in society. As the army officer corps came to represent the interests and views of the new middle class, it became the most powerful instrument of that class. The army's great strength lay in the kind of men who joined it, in the opportunity at their disposal, and the weakness of competing institutions. In contrast to most Mid-Eastern political parties, armies are disciplined, well-organized, and able to move into action without securing the voluntary consent of their men. In contrast to modern Mid-Eastern bureaucracies, armies are less likely to diffuse responsibility within the hierarchy and are more prone

[14] Manfred Halpern, *The politics of social change in the Middle East and North Africa,* Princeton 1963, 52.

to rebel against the status quo. This combination of discipline and defiance remains almost unique among Mid-Eastern organizations . . ."[15]

Halpern regards the officer corps and its political activity as one of the obvious manifestations of modernization. But it is still necessary to examine the thesis that the social character of the officers and their historical function is one and the same "from Morocco to Pakistan"; to ascertain whether or not the numerous different groups of officers which have appeared in the Arab political arena during the last generation were all expressions of the same trend; and to ask whether or not they always advanced society. The officers' advantages in strength and organization, and concentrated power at the disposal of a handful, is a blind instrument just as likely to serve negative goals as positive ones. In the last analysis, the historical role of the officers who became the heads of states should be evaluated by their actions—the proof of the pudding is in the eating.

Moreover, even if we assume that between 1950 and 1960 there was no way out of the crises in Egypt and Iraq except by the accession to power of the Free Officers in both countries, we shall still not be able to determine why and for whose benefit Nasser emerged victorious in his dispute with Naguib, nor why, in the rivalry between Qassim and Arif, at first the former, and four and one half years later, the latter, had the upper hand. The theory of the natural course, like every deterministic outlook, is liable to distract us from an intensive and extensive exploration of these and similar questions.

"The natural course" is a term borrowed from biology, as are many other political concepts which have become current in the 20th century, such as living-space, struggle for survival, and co-existence. It implies organic growth based on immanent laws and inherent causality in social life and in history just as in nature. However, a more accurate analogy would be a comparison of moves in politics and chess: In any given situation, not all moves are possible; only a certain few may be made and arbitrariness is out of the question. However, there is always a choice between a number of different possible moves—the better ones leading to victory, and others weakening one's position. It sometimes happens that a certain move which appears to be the way out of a difficult situation and leads to a momentary advantage will turn out to be the wrong choice as the game advances. Arab colonels tend to think that they are also champions on the political chess-board. They doubtlessly play with valuable pieces. However, their game itself should be reviewed and analyzed.

[15] *Ibid.*, 258–60.

PART ONE

THE STRUGGLES OF THE OFFICERS FOR POWER

"No man who knows the East is astonished at anything."
R.F. Burton, 1879.*

* R.F. Burton, in a letter to Ch. Chaillé-Long, 14 June 1879, quoted in Ch. Chaillé-Long, *My life in four continents,* London 1912, vol. 2, 420.

1. IRAQ FROM 1936 TO 1941

IN OCTOBER 1932 Iraq was accepted as a member of the League of Nations and the British Mandate was terminated. It was the first modern Arab state to achieve independence. It was also the first to experience a military coup d'état.

On October 29, 1936, at half past eight in the morning five fighter planes of the Royal Iraqi Air Force appeared over the skies of Baghdad and scattered leaflets.

The leaflets were signed by Brigadier Bakr Ṣidqī as "Chief of the National Reform Force".

Bakr Ṣidqī was of Kurdish origin. He had served as an officer in the Ottoman army and had been active in the Arab national movement before World War I.[1] He achieved prominence in the Iraqi army in 1933 when he planned and supervised the suppression of the Assyrian revolt and ordered the slaughter of the non-combatant population.[2] In 1935 he commanded the troops which suppressed the Middle Euphrates uprisings. His cruelty passed for courage, and he was promoted from colonel to brigadier.[4] In 1936 he was commander of the 2nd Division at Kirkuk. In October, while Chief of Staff Ṭaha al-Hāsihmī was on leave in Turkey, Bakr Ṣidqī was appointed Acting Chief of Staff.

The Acting Chief of Staff took advantage of his temporary post to carry out a military coup d'état. He established a precedent to be followed many times in Arab Politics.

The leaflets dropped from the planes were addressed to "The noble people of Iraq", and contained the following declaration: "The patience of the Iraqi army, comprising your sons, has been exhausted as a result of the situation from which you have been suffering owing to the conduct of the Government, whose sole object has been to promote its own personal interests with complete disregard for the welfare of the population. The

[1] Majid Khadduri, *Independent Iraq*, Second edition, London 1960, 107.

[2] Stephen Hemsley Longrigg, *Iraq*, 1900 *to* 1950, London 1953, 235.

[3] Fritz Grobba, *Männer und Mächte im Orient*, Göttingen 1967, 147.

army, accordingly, has requested His Majesty the King to dismiss the Cabinet and form a new one composed of sincere men under the leadership of Ḥikmat Sulaymān . . . "[5]

An hour later the King sent for the British Ambassador and consulted with him. Shortly afterward the cabinet met in emergency session under the chairmanship of the King with the British Ambassador present part of the time. Among the ministers present were Prime Minister Yāsīn al-Hāshimī, Foreign Minister Nūrī Sa'īd, and all the other ministers who happened to be in the capital at the time except for the Minister of the Interior Rashīd 'Ālī al-Kaylānī, who had decided to remain at his ministry in order to ensure quiet and maintain security. During the cabinet meeting the Premier-designate, Ḥikmat Sulaymān, handed the Chamberlain of the Royal Court a letter addressed to the King. The signatories were Bakr Ṣidqī and Brigadier 'Abd al-Laṭīf Nūrī, commander of the 1st Division, which was stationed in Baghdad. The letter resembled the leaflets in style and content but added an ultimatum. The army demanded that the new Prime Minister be appointed "within three hours" or else the army would "fulfill its duty in the public interest."[6] The leaflets were typewritten;[7] but the revolt was well organized. On the pretext of autumn maneuvers army units under Bakr Ṣidqī's command had taken up positions the preceding day at Qara Ghan, 80 miles north of Baghdad, and at Balad-Ruz, 55 miles to the north-east. During the night both units entered Ba'quba, 35 miles from the capital, occupied the town, cut telephone and telegraph connections with Baghdad and prepared to advance on it. As soon as the planes made their appearance over Baghdad, officers began to distribute the rebel proclamations in various sections of the city.

The government was taken completely by surprise. The Chief of Staff had not found it necessary to interrupt his vacation in Turkey and take back the army command from Bakr Ṣidqī. Nūrī Sa'īd, the Foreign Minister, was ready to leave for Saudi Arabia that very day to continue the negotiations that were in progress at the time.[8]

At half past eleven, when the ultimatum expired, five planes again flew over Baghdad under the command of Major Muḥammad 'Alī Jawwād, commander of the air force. This time they did not drop leaflets; they dropped four bombs, one of them close to the Prime Minister's office, and one near Parliament House, killing seven passers-by. But this show of

[5] Khadduri, 86.

[6] *Loc.cit.*

[7] 'Abd al-Razzāq al-Ḥasanī, *Tā'rīkh al-wizārāt al-'irāqiyya,* 8 vols., Sidon, 1933–1955, vol. 4, 1940, 186.

[8] *Al-Balāgh,* Cairo, 2 November 1936.

force proved superfluous, for Yāsīn al-Hāshimī had already submitted his government's resignation. That same day the King entrusted the formation of a new government to Ḥikmat Sulaymān and at five o'clock that afternoon Bakr Ṣidqī marched at the head of a victory parade through the streets of Baghdad in the style of Mussolini's march on Rome.

Like the dropping of the bombs the murder of al-Hāshimī's Minister of Defense, Major-General Ja'far al-'Askarī, was superfluous from the rebels' point of view. The most respected figure in the Iraqi army, Ja'far had been commander during the First World War of the Sharifian Arab army, the army of the "Great Arab Revolt" against the Turks in the Hejaz. He had served as Minister of Defense in the first Iraqi government in 1920 and later had twice been Prime Minister. His wife was Nūrī Sa'īd's sister and his own sister was Nūrī's wife. His two brothers, 'Alī Riḍā and Taḥsīn, had also been officers in the Sharifian army and had later occupied important administrative and diplomatic positions in Iraq. Many regarded Ja'far al-'Askarī as "the Father of the Iraqi army". Armed with a letter signed by the King authorizing him to conduct negotiations, Ja'far went at noon on the day of the coup to meet Bakr Ṣidqī at his camp near Baghdad. When he learned that the Minister of Defense had arrived, Bakr decided to have him killed. At first he called for volunteers among the officers who were with him, but when none came forward, he personally ordered four of them to shoot Ja'far. The body was buried without ceremony in an open field. This murder was to have far-reaching consequences.

The army was represented in the new government by a single person—Brigadier 'Abd al-Laṭīf Nūrī, who received the defense portfolio. Bakr Ṣidqī himself chose to remain outside the cabinet, and in fact was above it. He became Chief of Staff.

The government of Ḥikmat Sulaymān differed from the previous governments not only in the way it was formed but also because for the first time it included leaders of the Left. Kāmil Chadirchi, the outstanding figure of Iraqi socialism, became Minister of Economic Affairs and Public Works. Most of the power in the government lay with the "al-Ahālī" ("The People") group which was a meeting ground for socialists and liberal reformers, and what they had in common with the Bakr Ṣidqī officer group was the determination to free the country from dependence on Britain.

The new government was on the face of it a broad coalition of progressive leaders supported by high army officers, a sort of popular front such as existed at the time in France. The "al-Ahālī" group itself was composed of diverse factions, from the left wing headed by 'Abd al-Qādir Ismā'īl, who later became a communist, to opposition bourgeois democrats. In 1934 secret tentative contact was made between the group and Bakr Ṣidqī and

‘Abd al-Laṭīf Nūrī.[9] The main link between “al-Ahālī” and the officers and other opposition groups was Ḥikmat Sulaymān, who had previously been leader of the “al-Ikhā” Party, which had demanded revision of the Anglo-Iraqi treaty of 1932. He was of Turkoman origin, the younger half-brother of Marshal Maḥmūd Shawkat, who, as head of the Ottoman 3rd Army, had conquered Istanbul in April 1909 and put down the revolt against the Young Turks and deposed Sultan ‘Abd al-Ḥamīd.[10] The idea of a military revolt was never far from the thoughts of Ḥikmat Sulaymān. But he could hardly be called a representative of the progressive forces, as he owned estates encompassing more than twenty thousand acres.[11]

If Ḥikmat Sulaymān or “al-Ahālī” thought they would receive help from the army to form a popular front government, they were mistaken. The timing and planning of the revolt were the work of Bakr Ṣidqī alone. On October 23, a week before the appointed day, he admitted ‘Abd al-Laṭīf Nūrī, the commander of the 1st Division, into the conspiracy and shortly afterwards Ḥikmat Sulaymān as well and it was only at the final stage, three of four days before putting his plans into effect, that he confided in the leaders of “al-Ahālī.”[12] The new government came to power through a violent coup on the part of the army, and anyone who imagined that the army’s role would be limited to effecting the change of government was to be quickly disillusioned. Less than two weeks later, on November 10, the Prime Minister received a letter from the Minister of Defense, Brigadier ‘Abd al-Laṭīf Nūrī, containing a demand—almost a command—that all ministers instruct their subordinates to conduct themselves “with fairness and courtesy” in their dealings with the public. This in itself was a wise and proper step, but coming in the form of a directive to the Prime Minister from the Minister of Defense, it was a demonstrative act showing who was now really in charge in the country.[13]

The early hopes for sweeping social change soon gave place to bitter disappointment. Reform programs such as nationalization of certain industries, distribution of state lands to peasants, and sanctioning of trade union activities—all of which were contrary to the will of Bakr Ṣidqī—could not be realized. On June 19, 1937, the members of “al-Ahālī” resigned from the government. All those in Iraq and elsewhere who had regarded Bakr Ṣidqī’s government as the first Arab government to aim for social

[9] Khadduri, 72–3.

[10] Irfan Orga, *Phoenix ascendant,* London 1958, 37; Vernier, 77.

[11] ‘Abd al-Fattāḥ al-Yāfī, *Al-ʿIrāq bayna inqilābayn,* Beirut 1938, 18.

[12] Khadduri, 81.

[13] Al-Ḥasanī, 274–5.

improvement proved to be mistaken, even though genuinely progressive elements were included in it. Bakr Ṣidqī had readily used them to seize power and to conduct affairs of state, and he had even learned from them, but he was not prepared to share power and certainly not to hand power over to them. The military coup had given birth to a military dictatorship.

Bakr Ṣidqī turned out to be a dictator bent on power and pleasure. It is typical of the atmosphere under his rule that in April 1937, Parliament proposed to erect a statue of him in the name of the state,[14] and only when it became clear that revulsion to the proposal was widespread, did Bakr announce that he was not interested in such a token of esteem. In his family circle demoralization was rife. His third wife (he had been twice divorced), an Austrian dancer, he sent abroad, and it was said that he intended to divorce her, too, and marry a royal princess.[15] After his downfall, Muḥsin Abū Ṭabīkh, an outstanding tribal leader, wrote that Bakr Ṣidqī had tried to enlist his support in his plans to exile the King and assassinate a number of political leaders.[16] There is no proof that such a plan existed, but it is difficult to assume that Muḥsin Abū Ṭabīkh's detailed story was pure fabrication.

The Iraqi coup of 1936 was the first of its type. A perceptive British observer recognized it immediately as "an innovation of the most startling kind." He noted that "Military successes over Shi'a tribesmen in the Middle Euphrates, over the Yazidis in the north, and the like, have given to the army an assurance the bounds of which are not perceptible."[17] Thus what occurred here represented a new departure with far-reaching consequences.

The Bakr Ṣidqī coup was typical of many that followed, both in their organization and in the course they took. The way in which the military dictatorship met its end was also typical—it was overthrown by a coup of other military officers.

Government by army officers can succeed only if the officer corps is united, and Bakr Ṣidqī did not achieve this unity. Many senior officers were against him for a number of reasons. One was the memory of Ja'far al-'Askarī and his assassination. Bakr Ṣidqī's mistreatment of officers—no less than civilians—and the dissolute life which he and his family led added to the growing discontent. A third factor was nationalistic and ideological opposition. The Iraqi officer corps of those days to some extent reflected the deep divisions which cut across Iraqi society and the state, conflicts

[14] *Ibid.*, 252.

[15] Ṣalāḥ al-Dīn al-Ṣabbāgh, *Fursān al-'urūba fī āl-'Irāq,* Damascus 1956, 89.

[16] Muḥsin Abū Ṭabīkh, *Al-mabādī' wa-al-rijāl,* Damascus 1938, 105–22, quoted in al-Ḥasani, 268–72.

[17] K. Williams in *Great Britain and the East,* London, 5 November 1936, 643.

between Sunni and Shi'i and between Arabs and Kurds. Bakr Ṣidqī was of Kurdish origin. It is true that the coup was carried out together with the Arab 'Abd al-Laṭīf Nūrī, but it was soon obvious that Ṣidqī had no intention either of sharing political power or of instituting collective leadership by army officers. Khadduri is of the opinion that he had no specifically Kurdish ambitions, but Grobba is quite sure that he wanted to set up a Kurdish state.[18] In any event, he dismissed Arabs from positions of command in the army and from civilian posts and replaced them with Kurds. He did not favour the pan-Arab ideology of the Arab-Iraqi officers whose banner was "an Arab Iraq", but supported instead the principle of "Iraq for the Iraqis," which suggests a bi-national character for the state and reservations toward aspirations for Arab unity. In the sphere of practical politics these reservations found expression in a policy of strengthening ties with Turkey. Ḥikmat Sulaymān, the Prime Minister, who was a Turkoman, was also suspected by the Arab nationalists of excessive friendliness toward Turkey. Not only was he the half-brother of Maḥmūd Shawkat but he had himself been educated in Istanbul. In 1935 he spent several months in Turkey and on his return cited Atatürk's regime as the ideal model.[19]

The growing opposition did not go unobserved by Bakr Ṣidqī. Fearing for his life he took special precautions and never slept two nights in succession in the same place. But all his devices were in vain.

On August 10, 1937 Bakr Ṣidqī set out for Turkey to observe army maneuvers. On August 11 he stopped over in Mosul for a few hours rest, remaining at the airport for security reasons. As he was relaxing there with a few friends, a certain Sergeant Muḥammad Ṣāliḥ Tal-'Afarī suddenly appeared and shot him. His friend and collaborator, Jawwād, the commander of the air force, was also killed.

The assassination was well planned. The conspirators were seven officers headed by Colonel 'Azīz Yāmulkī, President of the Officers' Club at Mosul. The plotters may also have received help from abroad. Ṣabbāgh, one of the seven officers, writes in his memoirs: "All the Arab governments encouraged us to bring about the end of Ḥikmat Sulaymān's government."[20] Although he does not explain what form the encouragement took, it should not be assumed that his statement is mere exaggeration. Nowhere else in the whole of the lengthy book does he mention any case of support from outside Iraq.

[18] Khadduri, 107; Ṣabbāgh, 17, 42; al-Yāfī, 44; Grobba, 158–9.

[19] Khadduri, 75–6.

[20] Ṣabbāgh, 67.

The conspirators were not content with deposing Bakr Ṣidqī; their object was to set up a government that would be dependent upon them. When they were summoned to trial in Baghdad two days after the assassination, their response was revolt. On August 14, Brigadier Amīn 'Umarī, commander of the division stationed in Mosul, declared: "The army has raised a revolt in order to protect its innocent officers . . . we have severed our relations with Baghdad."[21] Bakr Ṣidqī's supporters in the capital wished to put down the rebellion, but they quickly discovered that the army commanders in Sulaimaniya and Kirkuk in the north and in Diwaniya in the south were on the side of the rebels. Brigadier Sa'īd Takrītī, the commander of the 3rd Division in Baghdad, joined them on the pretext of preventing civil war and ensuring army unity. Ḥikmat Sulaymān saw that the fate of his government had been decided, and on August 17 he resigned. The same day a new government was formed.

The new Prime Minister, Jamīl Madfa'ī, wanted to establish two principles: To prevent intervention by army officers in matters of policy, and "to lower the curtain" on the events of the recent past, that is to say, to amnesty those involved in the assassinations of both al-'Askarī and Bakr Ṣidqī. The second principle was realized, but not the first. The curtain was lowered, but behind it officer intervention in political life continued and in fact increased.

The Madfa'ī government remained in office more than fifteen months—an unusual phenomenon in Iraq. The outward appearance of stability was deceptive, however. In 1938 a group of officers joined forces and prepared to become the decisive factor in the state. They were known as "The Seven." It included five of the seven officers who had planned the assassination of Bakr Ṣidqī.

The most determined of them was Ṣalāḥ al-Dīn Ṣabbāgh, now lieutenant-colonel and Chief of Operations on the General Staff. He was born in 1899 in Mosul. His family originated from Damietta in Egypt; his grandfather had gone to Sidon in Lebanon; at the end of the nineteenth century his father moved to Mosul where he went into business and also became a landowner. Ṣalāḥ al-Dīn went to school in Mosul and then to secondary school in Beirut. In 1914, he entered the Military Academy in Istanbul and in 1917, served on the Macedonian and Palestinian fronts as a second-lieutenant in the Ottoman army. Later he served in Fayṣal's army in Syria and from 1921 in the Iraqi army. In 1924 he was sent on military courses first to India and then to England. His first wife, the mother of his eldest son, was English. She died two years after they were married.[22]

[21] Khadduri, 122.

[22] Ṣabbāgh, 18–22, 58, 62, 242.

Lieutenant-Colonel Maḥmūd Salmān was born in Baghdad in 1898. He was a lieutenant in the Ottoman and later in the Syrian army. From 1925 he served in the Iraqi army and was aide-de-camp to King Fayṣal and King Ghāzī. His unit was the cavalry which later became the Armored Corps. He also qualified as a pilot and was later commander of the air force.[23]

Kāmil Shabīb was lieutenant-colonel in the infantry. Born in Baghdad in 1895, he had been like his comrades a lieutenant in the Ottoman and Syrian armies and served in the Iraqi army from its establishment in 1921. On his mother's side he was related to the distinguished al-Wādī family.[24] He was the weakest character of Ṣabbāgh's group.

Lieutenant-Colonel Fahmī Sa'īd was born in Sulaimaniya in 1898. His father was a member of the 'Anbak tribe of the Middle Tigris and his mother was Turkish. His wife was a relative of Nūrī Sa'īd. Fahmī Sa'īd had also served as an officer in the Ottoman, Syrian and Iraqi armies. Of the group of officer politicians he was the one with the stormiest temperament.[25]

'Azīz Yāmulkī was the chief plotter of Bakr Ṣidqī's assassination. In 1938 he still belonged to the group of officer politicians, but by 1939 his influence had diminished and in 1940 he left the group. In 1938, he was a colonel in command of the motorized transport services. His father, "Nimrod" Muṣṭafā Pasha, was President of the Ottoman Military Court which sentenced Atatürk to death. His uncle, 'Azīz Pasha, was the Sultan's secretary. Colonel Yāmulkī was born in 1893 and although he was a Kurd, his education was virtually that of a Turk. When in 1958 he gave evidence in one of the trials in the "People's Court", he asked and received permission to read his testimony from a prepared script because "his Arabic was not good."[26]

These five, who had worked together even before the assassination of Bakr Ṣidqī, were joined by two officers of higher rank—Ḥusayn Fawzī and Amīn 'Umarī. Ḥusayn Fawzī was promoted to lieutenant-general and made Chief of Staff after Bakr Ṣidqī. His father was Kurdish and his mother Arab. He did his best to steer a course of neutrality among the various rival factions in the army, siding with whomever appeared the strongest.[27] Amīn 'Umarī, also a non-political figure, was in command of the division in Mosul when Bakr Ṣidqī was murdered there. Whether

[23] *Ibid.*, 25.

[24] *Ibid.*, 23, 79; Khadduri, 209.

[25] Ṣabbāgh, 22, 56–8, 61, 113.

[26] *Ibid.*, 77; Longrigg, 51; *Maḥkamat al-sha'b, Muḥākamāt al-maḥkama al-'askarīyya al-khaṣṣa*, vol. 6, Baghdad 1959, 2384–7.

[27] Ṣabbāgh, 17, 275; Khadduri, 130.

as a result of pressure or because he identified himself with the avengers of his mentor, al-'Askarī, he refused to hand over the assassins to the authorities in Baghdad and threw in his lot then and for the future with the conspirators. He was a son of the most distinguished family in Mosul. In 1935 he published *The History of the War in Iraq, 1914–1918* in three volumes. In 1938 he was promoted to lieutenant-general and made commander of the 1st Division in Baghdad.[28]

The cohesion of this group naturally did not escape the notice of the government, which tried to forestall further active intervention of the officer politicians in political affairs. It achieved the reverse.

On October 30, 1938 Madfa'ī reshuffled his cabinet and gave the defense portfolio, which until then he had held himself, to Ṣabīḥ Najīb. Ṣabīḥ Najīb was a veteran army officer. He had been a cadet in the Military Academy in Istanbul and a member of *"al-'Ahd,"* the secret association of Arab officers in the Ottoman army, and in 1914 had joined Fayṣal's army in Syria. When Fayṣal became King of Iraq, Ṣabīḥ Najīb was named his aide-de-camp. Later he became Inspector-General of the Police. From that position he went over to the foreign service serving first in the legation in Berlin, then successively as minister in Turkey, Iraqi representative to the League of Nations, and Director-General of the Foreign Ministry.[29] In his new post as Minister of Defense he tried to impose government authority over the army. As a former army officer with more time for his ministry than had Madfa'ī—who had devoted most of his energies to the duties of the premiership—Ṣabīḥ Najīb used to intervene personally in a great many matters. This angered the officers: "He used to summon senior officers to report to him as minister in the way a private soldier is made to report for duty."[30] But the Seven were more opposed to his objectives than to his high-handedness. He did not acknowledge them as sole representatives of the army but tried to elevate the status of others instead. As a result, Ṣabbāgh accused him of breaking "the oath he swore to us in his own house . . . The new Minister of Defense let us down and used methods of 'divide and rule'," the same methods favoured by the British, since "Ṣabīḥ loves the British."[31] The Seven finally decided to overthrow the Madfa'ī government.

Ṣabbāgh enumerates seven reasons for the decision, among them "the failure of the Government to support the revolt in Palestine"—a claim

[28] Ṣabbāgh, 17–8; al-Yāfī, 58, 67.

[29] Al-Yāfī, 142; A. Al-Marayati, *A diplomatic history of modern Iraq,* New York 1961, 206.

[30] Al-Ḥasanī, 183.

[31] Ṣabbāgh, 69.

repeated ever since by every Arab leader who attacks his rivals. But the decisive reason was the fear that Madfa'ī and Ṣabīḥ Najīb would weaken the position of the Seven, a fear that was doubtless well founded.

In December 1938 the Seven heard that the government was preparing to retire a number of officers. On December 23 they sent Lieutenant-Colonel Sa'īd Yaḥyā Khayyāṭ to the Minister of Justice to find out if the rumor were true, and when he came back with the information that it was, they decided to act.[32] The next day the military forces in Rashid Camp near Baghdad were mustered and prepared to take the capital. The threat of military action sufficed to overthrow the government. That evening Yāmulkī announced to the Prime Minister that the army would revolt if he did not resign. Madfa'ī immediately informed his colleagues of his resignation and on the following day, December 25, a new government was sworn in.

For the third time a group of officers had imposed its will on Iraq, determining not only who should be deposed but also who should replace him. This was to be Nūrī Sa'īd.

In view of the conflicts between Nūrī and these officers, which later came to light and which made them mortal enemies, it is strange that Ṣabbāgh and his collaborators should have chosen him for the premiership in December 1938. Several years later, Ṣabbāgh blamed himself for not having taken the advice of King Ghāzī who was against Nūrī's becoming premier. The truth of the matter is that they forced him on the King and the country and that Nūrī Sa'īd, now appointed Prime Minister for the third time, acceded to power through a military coup–or at least the threat of one.

Nūrī Sa'īd, like many of the Iraqi leaders between the two world wars, also started out as an army officer. In 1910, at the age of 21, he graduated from the Military Academy in Istanbul and fought as an Ottoman officer in the Balkan War of 1912. In 1914 he joined "al-'Ahd," and, deserting the same year from the Ottoman army, made his way via Cairo to Basra.[33] In November Basra was conquered by the British and he was taken prisoner. In 1915 he was sent to a prisoner-of-war camp in India where he remained until December of the same year, when he came to Cairo and enrolled in the Arab forces fighting on the side of the Allies. His activities in the years 1914 and 1915 remained obscure; it may be that he then intended to achieve Arab rights by fighting on the side of the Turks.[34] Be that as it may, in 1916 he arrived in the Hejaz, and during the course of the war rose to the position

[32] Al-Ḥasanī, 182.

[33] Lord Birdwood, *Nuri As-Said,* London 1959, 11–22.

[34] Elie Kedourie, 'Réflexions sur l'histoire du royaume d'Irak', *Orient,* Paris, No. 11, 65.

of Chief of Staff under the Commander-in-Chief of the Sharifian army who was his brother-in-law, Ja'far al-'Askarī. He took part in the conquest of Damascus and later with the rank of major-general became the first Chief of Staff of the Iraqi army under al-'Askarī as Minister of Defense. Between 1922 and 1924 he himself served as Minister of Defense and in 1930 became Prime Minister for the first time. He was to hold this post no less than thirteen times. In al-Hāshimī's government, which was toppled by the Bakr Ṣidqī revolt, he was Foreign Minister. On the day of the coup he sought asylum in the British Embassy from where he was flown to Egypt. He returned to Iraq at the time of the Madfa'ī government.

Nūrī Sa'īd's pro-British orientation was already abundantly clear in December 1938, no less the bitterly anti-British attitude of the Seven, yet the officers insisted on his appointment as Prime Minister.[35] What had brought about this strange partnership?

One common basis was enmity toward Bakr Ṣidqī's men who were still in the army. While Nūrī longed to avenge the death of Ja'far al-'Askarī, his friend and brother-in-law, Sabbāgh feared the vengeance of Bakr's followers as a result of his assassination. Ṣabīḥ Najīb's plans to retire several of the followers of the Seven and to promote their opponents in their place was regarded as a warning to both Nūrī Sa'īd and to the Seven and this brought them closer together.

Another factor in Nūrī's association with the Seven was his old rivalry with Jamīl Madfa'ī. Nūrī had been obliged to resign from the premiership in October 1932; since then he had been allotted no more than the foreign ministry portfolio in several governments, and with time his wish to return to the premiership grew stronger. He judged that only with the help of the Seven could he achieve his aim, and he further calculated that in due course he would be able to rid himself of his dependence on them as well.

The motives of the Seven in allying themselves with Nūrī Sa'īd, apart from a common enmity toward Bakr Ṣidqī's supporters, are less clear. Perhaps Nūrī managed to outwit them in the secret negotiations they held before the dismissal of the Madfa'ī government; in that case it is not hard to understand that later, realizing they had been deceived, they bore a deadly hatred for him.

The Minister of Defense in Nūrī Sa'īd's government was Ṭaha al-Hāshimī, another veteran army man who rose from service in the Ottoman and Sharifian armies to the top echelon of the military and political life of Iraq. He was the brother of Yāsin al-Hāshimī, the Prime Minister who was deposed in the Bakr Ṣidqī revolt and who died in exile a few weeks later.

[35] Ṣabbāgh, 95.

Up to the time of the revolt Ṭaha al-Hāshimī had been Chief of Staff of the army for fifteen years. He was the only officer with the rank of general, the highest in the Iraqi army. The senior officers, not excluding the Seven, respected him as their teacher and leader and as an honest man. His links with Nūrī Sa'īd were based on common views and on personal friendship, whereas he was brought close to the Seven by their joint hatred of Bakr Ṣidqī's supporters. He was the principal go-between in the secret contacts which preceded the coup of December 1938. Later, when the rift between Nūrī and the Seven deepened he tried to reconcile them again. When he could no longer be the friend of both sides, he aligned himself with Nūrī Sa'īd; even then the Seven continued to regard him with respect. In the opinion of Ṣabbāgh, Ṭaha was "bewitched" by Nūrī.[36]

On December 24, when Nūrī was "requested" to form a government, he made a show of declining, on the pretense that he was opposed to the intervention of the military in politics. Only when he was told by Emir Zayd, uncle of the King, in the presence of the Speakers of both houses of Parliament, that the King appointed him not on the wishes of the army but in accordance with the constitution, did he find it "fitting" to accept.[37] All this was not only an act. Nūrī wished it to be understood that he was not merely a lackey of the Seven, even though the service they had performed in dismissing the previous government was far from distasteful to him. The Seven naturally held a different view. Ṣabbāgh even relates that there was a specific agreement between his group and Nūrī that would "give the army the right to have its say in all that concerned the resignation of any government, the establishment of a new one and the decision as to its premier."[38] In any event, as Prime Minister, Nūrī held secret consultations from time to time with the officers who had put him in power. And it did not take long before the latter again openly intervened in politics.

On April 4, 1939, King Ghāzī was killed in an automobile accident. The question then arose as to who would be named regent for the infant crown prince—Emir Zayd, brother of King Fayṣal I, or Emir 'Abd al-Ilāh, nephew of Fayṣal and brother of Ghāzī's widow. Zayd was 41 and 'Abd al-Ilāh 26. It is possible that Ṣabbāgh and his comrades thought that they could more easily mold the young Emir to their wishes as they were already on friendly terms with him. The Seven insisted on 'Abd al-Ilāh's being appointed regent and according to the testimony of Ṣabbāgh, "the army was the firm hand which resolved that complication."[39] And that is really the way it happened. For the second time in three months the Seven placed in power

[36] *Ibid.*, 133.
[37] Al-Ḥasanī, 189.
[38] Ṣabbāgh, 133.
[39] *Ibid.*, 83.

a man who very shortly afterwards became their deadly enemy, and Ṣabbāgh and his friends reflected retrospectively: "Those unfortunate officers—they are candles that burn to provide light for others."

This intervention on the part of the officers caused no conflict with the Prime Minister, as Nūrī Sa'īd also wanted 'Abd al-Ilāh. The incident nevertheless demonstrated that the officers were prepared to impose their will wherever it seemed to them imperative to do so. Another crisis, with fresh cause for intervention, was not long in coming.

In September 1939, the Second World War broke out, adding to the problems and disputes that already existed in Iraq. By the terms of the 1930 treaty, Iraq was obliged to enter on the side of Britain if the latter were involved in war. More important than any clause of the treaty was the fact that in 1939 Iraq was in many ways still under British rule. For this very reason many Iraqis may have tended to sympathize with Germany. Nazi propaganda operated with greater persistence and with greater success in Iraq than in any other Arab country; it was not for nothing that the Mufti of Jerusalem chose Baghdad in October 1939 as his haven and base of operations. However, the supporters of Britain were also more steadfast and devoted in Iraq than in other Arab countries, and Nūrī Sa'īd was foremost among them.

On the outbreak of the conflict Nūrī proposed that Iraq declare war on Germany, whilst others favoured neutrality. They compromised by breaking off diplomatic relations with Germany and the well-connected and influential German Minister Grobba had to leave Baghdad. The controversy between the pro-Germans and the pro-British went on.

One of the complicated problems that ensued concerned the fate of German nationals in Iraq. The government interned them and later handed them over to the British, a move which the opposition severely criticized. Various emergency regulations which restricted civil liberties and created shortages, the lightning victory of Germany in Poland, British impotence in the face of her enemies in Europe, and the Soviet-German partnership in the winter of 1939–40—all these doubtless added fuel to the blaze of Nazi propaganda.

On January 18, 1940, Rustum Ḥaydar, Minister of Finance, was assassinated. Together with Ṭaha al-Hāshimī he had been the main supporter of Nūrī. The murder was an act of personal revenge on the part of an official who had been dismissed for corruption but Nūrī decided to exploit the fact that the assassin was a Nazi sympathizer and put him on trial together with a number of opposition leaders. The military court was obliged to acquit them. In the meantime, the position of the government was undermined and weakened.

In mid-February Nūrī Sa'īd decided to resign. He proposed as his successor Rashīd 'Ālī-al-Kaylānī, and suggested that Ṭaha al-Hāshimī continue as Minister of Defense and that he himself become Minister for Foreign Affairs.

Once again there occurred the strange phenomenon of an Iraqi politician advocating the raising to power of one who would shortly stand revealed as his mortal enemy. Ṣabbāgh had made Nūrī Prime Minister and 'Abd al-Ilāh Regent, and now Nūrī wanted to hand the premiership to Rashīd 'Ālī. What motivated him to take so strange a step?

Rashīd 'Ālī al-Kaylānī was a descendant of 'Abd al-Qādir al-Kaylānī, a twelfth century philosopher, one of the great theological scholars and mystics of Islam and founder of the Qādirī Order which to this day extends throughout Islam from Mauretania to India. His tomb in Baghdad, looked after by the family, is revered as a holy place, and members of the Order make it a center of pilgrimage. Apart from his distinguished ancestry Rashīd 'Ālī possessed the attributes of learning and talent. In 1933, he was Prime Minister for the first time. In 1939 he was Chamberlain of the Royal Court, a position of great influence, particularly as the King was an infant and the Regent a weak-charactered youngster of twenty-six; moreover it was a position free from the strain of direct responsibility. Nūrī Sa'īd knew that Rashīd 'Ālī did not wholeheartedly support his pro-British policy. By placing him at the head of the government he not only intended to broaden its base but hoped also to force Rashīd 'Ālī to show his hand. If he would support the British he could not oppose Nūrī in the future; if he were anti-British, then he could be brought to grief and his influence destroyed in good time.

On February 14, 1940, Nūrī Sa'īd met the officers and told them of his plan. They were astonished and shocked. Fahmī Sa'īd expressed his violent opposition and said to Nūrī: "You know very well how prime ministers are made. We have made many enemies, needlessly, in the process. There is no former minister, or supporter of a former minister, who is not our enemy. Haven't we enough trouble with the supporters of Bakr Ṣidqī? . . . the axe may fall on my head and on the heads of all of us, except you—you will always find a safe place."[40]

In the next two days there were more consultations as opinion among the officers was divided. Nūrī's resignation from the premiership was definitely decided upon. But Ḥusayn Fawzī, the Chief of Staff, Amīn al-'Umari, commander of the 1st Division, and 'Azīz Yāmulkī not only approved the handing of the premiership to Rashīd 'Ālī but demanded that

[40] *Ibid.*, 122–3.

	Sept. 7, 1952		April 17, 1954		Sept. 26, 1956		March 6, 1958	
	First government under Naguib's premiership		First government under Nasser's premiership		Egyptian government after the adoption of the constitution		First U.A.R government after union	
	O	C	O	C	O	C	O	C
President			1		1		1	
First vice-president								
Prime Minister	1		1					
Vice-presidents							2	
Members of presidential council								
Deputy prime ministers		1						
Ministers of central government							4	4
Ministers of Egyptian government		14	7	11	5	13	1	9
TOTAL	1	15	9	11	6	13	8	13
Percentage of officers	Above the government stood the Revolutionary Command Council, composed of officers only				32		38	

O= officers
C= civilians

In the governments during the period of union with Syria in 1958 and 1961 only Egyptians are enumerated. Whoever filled more than one governmental function is listed only once.

GYPTIAN GOVERNMENTS

g. 17, 1961	Sept. 29, 1962		March 25, 1964		Oct. 2, 1965		Sept. 10, 1966		June 19, 1967	
.R govern- t after the ition of the) regional tive councils	First Egyptian government under ‘Alī Sabrī’s premiership		Second government under ‘Alī Sabrī’s premiership		Government under Zakariyyā Muḥī al-Din’s premiership		Government under Muḥammad Ṣidqī’s Sulaymān’s premiership		Government under Nasser as president and prime minister	
C	O	C	O	C	O	C	O	C	O	C
	1		1		1		1		1	
			1		1		1			
	1		1		1		1			
	5		3		3		3		3	1
	3	2								
			3	8	2	6	3	1		
13	5	19	5	17	9	13	10	12	14	9
13	15	21	14	25	17	19	19	13	19	10
50	42		36		47		59		65	

the appointment of Nūrī Sa'īd and Ṭaha al-Hāshimī to any post in the cabinet be vetoed.

On February 18, the government resigned; the same day a vote was taken among the officers. Fawzī, 'Umarī and Yāmulkī were in the minority. Against them were Ṣabbāgh, Fahmī Sa'īd, Shabīb, Salmān and Ismā'īl Nāmiq, commander of the 3rd Division. There were apparently two more officers belonging to this circle who agreed with the majority but did not attend the meeting; they were Ibrāhīm Rāwī, commander of the 4th Division, and Lieutenant-Colonel Sa'īd Yaḥyā Khayyāṭ.

The minority did not accept the majority decision, particularly since one of the three was Chief of Staff and one was commander of the division stationed in the capital. According to Ṣabbāgh it was agreed among the officers "that our votes would be free, without regard to position or rank and without regard to military usage which leaves decisions to the commanding officer and imposes discipline on subordinate officers. Each one present would be entitled to one vote . . . thus the view of the majority of those present is the view of the army."[41] But the senior officers of the Iraqi army had learned to disregard the rule of law over the past three years, and the Chief of Staff did not feel that a decision made by his subordinates was binding on him if it did not suit him. He told the Regent that the army was opposed to the inclusion of Nūrī Sa'īd and Ṭaha al-Hāshimi in the new government. Knowing, however, that Ḥusayn Fawzī was not speaking for the majority of the officers, the Regent did not accept his counsel. Rashīd 'Ālī, meanwhile, was unwilling at that stage to become involved in entanglements and declined to accept the premiership.

The officers' ambition to make and break prime ministers led to a rift in their own ranks. On February 21, 'Umarī placed his 1st Division at Washāsh Camp west of Baghdad on a stand-to alert, and Ṣabbāgh's supporters reacted by doing the same—the 3rd Division at Rashīd Camp south of Baghdad, commanded by Nāmiq, was also readied. It was presently found that the 2nd Division at Kirkuk and the 4th at Diwaniya under the commands of Amīn Zakī and Ibrāhīm Rāwī respectively were on the side of Ṣabbāgh. Under the circumstances the Regent invited Nūrī Sa'īd to resume the premiership and the latter immediately agreed. His first acts were to retire the three officers who wanted to remove him and to promote friends of Ṣabbāgh to take over their commands. Amīn Zakī took over from Fawzī as Chief of Staff and Kāmil Shabīb received command of the 1st Division in place of 'Umarī.

In the highly charged discussions and complex machinations of those

[41] *Ibid.*, 133.

days Ṣabbāgh's personality stood out prominently, and after the disposal of 'Umarī, Fawzī, and Yāmulkī, there was no one left to challenge his leadership of the officers who were maneuvering and fighting in the field of politics. The British officers in Iraq, whose intelligence service kept them informed of all that went on in the country, coined the expression "The Crowned Golden Square"—with Ṣabbāgh, Salmān, Shabīb and Fahmī Sa'īd as the square and Ṭaha al-Hāshimī as the crown. In March 1940 Ṭaha al-Hāshimī tried to eliminate what he felt to be Ṣabbāgh's excessive influence and transferred him from the post of Chief of Operations on the General Staff to commander of the 3rd Division. This transfer did not please Ṣabbāgh but it was not enough to weaken his influence. The 3rd Division was after all stationed in Baghdad, and in establishment and equipment it was the strongest of the four Iraqi divisions, with all senior command positions in the hands of Ṣabbāgh's friends.

However, Nūrī Sa'īd had not abandoned his plan to give the premiership to Rashīd 'Ālī and thus make him share responsibility for the pro-British policy which was unpopular with the people. To succeed in this second attempt to carry out his plan he had to persuade Rashīd 'Ālī that it was right for him to be Prime Minister and to convince the "Golden Square" that Rashīd 'Ālī would not turn against them. For this complex task Nūrī Sa'īd needed to enlist the services of a highly respected personality, a leader renowned throughout the Arab world for his consistent nationalism, well-versed in Iraqi affairs but not himself Iraqi and thus freed of suspicion of office-seeking. And there was surely none so bountifully endowed with all these rare qualities as the Mufti of Jerusalem. He accepted the task of mediation and persuasion and carried it out successfully. It seems that the Mufti had old connections with Rashīd 'Ālī. He appreciated the fact that in 1930 Rashīd 'Ālī was a member of the "al-Ikhā" Party, which was strongly opposed to the Anglo-Iraqi treaty. With the officers, too, he had connections "going back several years," according to Ṣabbāgh.[42] Rashīd 'Ālī and Ṣabbāgh did not actually meet and talk before March 1940, yet at their first conference, arranged by the Mufti, it became clear that there was a meeting of minds between them and also between them both and the Mufti.[43]

On March 31, 1940, less than six weeks after his earlier resignation and reappointment, Nūrī Sa'īd again resigned together with the entire cabinet, and the same day Rashīd 'Ālī was appointed in his place.

Ṣabbāgh quickly saw that Rashīd 'Ālī al-Kaylānī was indeed a man after

[42] *Ibid.*, 218.

[43] *Ibid.*, 136–8.

his own heart. Among his first acts as Prime Minister he ordered weapons for the army from Italy and Japan which Britain could not or would not supply.[44] He did this without asking or even informing the British. Nothing will so ensure loyalty to a prime minister on the part of the army commanders as the supply of arms.

At the same time other events occurred which brought the relationship between the "Golden Square" and Rashīd 'Ālī from cautious cooperation to full alliance. These other events occurred very far from Iraq though they were very close to the hearts of Iraq's leaders. In April 1940, Hitler took Denmark and Norway by blitzkrieg, in May he overran the Low Countries and in June he conquered France. Italy entered the war.

It seemed that England—the England they so hated—could not hold out for long. On June 21 the Mufti sent a secret message from Baghdad to von Papen, the German Ambassador in Ankara, in which he expressed, "in the name of the Arab nation everywhere," feelings of "the greatest happiness and the most profound gratitude" at the victories of Hitler, "the great leader and teacher."[45] And if his words were not truly in the name of the entire Arab nation, they were certainly written on behalf of Rashīd 'Ālī and Ṣabbāgh and their comrades. But they were not yet able to reveal their intentions openly; even though the British lion seemed to be in its death-throes in Europe, it could still inflict damage in Iraq. To various questions put by Rashīd 'Ālī and the Mufti concerning the possibility of coming out openly against the British, the four officers gave a clear military answer: A campaign against the British was not to be thought of unless the Iraqi army had, in addition to the equipment it then possessed, "another fifty modern medium tanks, fifty more light tanks, anti-tank weapons, and an up-to-date air force capable of maintaining two hundred planes in constant readiness for action."[46]

Thus in 1940 even the most extreme of the pro-Axis officers could suggest no more than the renewal of diplomatic relations with Germany, and that not openly. On the other hand, Nūrī Sa'īd proposed breaking off relations with Italy. He also suggested sending two of Iraq's four divisions to the front—to the Balkans or to Libya—and he hinted to Ṣabbāgh that he would command the force. The officers rejected this proposal vehemently.

The declared policy of Rashīd 'Ālī's government, like that of its predecessor, was loyalty to the Anglo-Iraqi treaty. Behind the scenes, however, far-reaching negotiations were already taking place with the Germans.

[44] *Ibid.*, 139–40.

[45] Khadduri, 179; Heinz Tillmann, *Deutschlands Araberpolitik im Zweiten Weltkrieg*, Berlin (DDR) 1965, 128–30.

[46] Ṣabbāgh, 140.

The principal go-between was the Mufti, and the Germans knew that he spoke not only for the government but also for the leaders of the army.[47] At one point—it was the autumn of 1940—even Nūrī Sa'īd sought contact with the Germans. He may have wished to secure whatever advantages he could for himself and his country no matter what happened; he may have wanted to find out what his rivals were up to; perhaps both reasons prompted him.[48] Fortunately for him, however, the Germans were not prepared to establish contact with him. Apart from this one defection, Nūrī Sa'īd's orientation was consistently pro-British, whether it meant hostility to the Nazis or hostility to the Soviets. On the other hand, Rashīd 'Ālī and the rest of the pro-German nationalists of Iraq were more and more influenced by the Mufti during the summer of 1940. The quarrel that resulted from the opposing factions became an open rift at a session of the Supreme Defense Council in July or August 1940 (none of those who reported the incident remenbered the exact date).[49] The council comprised the Prime Minister, the Ministers of Defense and Foreign Affairs, and several other ministers and senior army officers. Ṣabbāgh and Shabīb were not members of the council, but they were invited to this meeting at the suggestion of Nūrī Sa'īd, since Ṣabbāgh was "thoroughly familiar with the matter from its beginnings."[50] Nūrī put forward two proposals: Severing diplomatic relations with Italy, and granting Britain facilities for military concentration and movement in Iraq. A very excited argument developed and the chairman, Defense Minister Ṭaha al-Hāshimī, had to adjourn the meeting. The excitement was caused mainly by a memorandum from Ṣabbāgh, presented in the name of the General Staff, which was read out at the meeting. Ṣabbāgh strongly supported the attitude of Rashīd 'Ālī to the apparent surprise of Nūrī, who until that moment had never thought that the Four would oppose him. After the meeting no further word was ever exchanged between Nūrī Sa'īd and Ṣabbāgh. The rift was overt and final.

This course of affairs was not unknown to the British. On instructions from London the British Ambassador inquired at the Iraqi Foreign Ministry as to the government's intentions regarding its relationship with the Axis countries, and when the reply proved excessively vague, he stated, at the end of November, that the Prime Minister of Iraq no longer enjoyed the confidence of the British Government. In London, Lord Halifax, "while fully cognisant of the gravity of the step," confirmed that the statement

[47] Lukasz Hirszowicz, *III rzesza i arabski wschód,* Warsaw 1963, 109–59.

[48] Majid Khadduri, 'General Nuri's flirtation with the Axis powers', *MEJ,* September 1962, 328–36; 'Uthmān Kamāl Ḥaddād, *Ḥarakat Rashīd 'Ālī al-Kaylānī,* Sidon 1950, 16–7.

[49] Khadduri, *Independent Iraq,* 192–3; Ṣabbāgh, 154–6.

[50] Ṣabbāgh, 145.

made by the Ambassador expressed the attitude of his government.[51] Considerable pressure from the British and the Regent was brought to bear on Rashīd 'Ālī to resign. Rashīd 'Ālī refused to go, and once again the four officers added their weight to his side. They threatened army intervention if the Prime Minister were forced to resign, and the Regent submitted. However, on January 30, 1941 Rashīd 'Ālī learned that a majority of the Iraqi parliament also opposed him, and that a vote of no-confidence was to be expected. He demanded that the Regent dissolve parliament and proclaim new elections. This time, Rashīd 'Ālī's scheming was frustrated. The Regent did not sign the order, surreptitiously leaving the capital and going to Diwaniya where the 4th Division under Ibrāhīm Rāwī was stationed. Rāwī was connected with Sabbāgh's circle and also with the royal house and Nūrī Sa'īd. He was one of the Ottoman officers of Iraqi origin who in the First World War had joined the Sharifian army. He became the personal aide of Emir 'Alī, father of the Regent 'Abd-al-Ilāh.[52] He was basically a non-political person and in January 1941, he was the only divisional commander on whose loyalty the Regent could rely.

As soon as it became known that the Regent had left Baghdad, a joint meeting was held of the cabinet, Chief of Staff Amīn Zakī and the "Golden Square". Some said that there should be no hesitation, even if it meant civil war. Fahmī Sa'īd said something that was both simple and significant: "The army is a mute instrument in the hands of the government—provided it is a national government not subject to the influence of foreigners and provided that the army and the people have the assurance that the good of the country rather than the good of the foreigners is the guiding principle of the government."[53] Naturally, as far as he was concerned, there was never any doubt as to who was faithful to the national interest. If, nevertheless, any doubt should arise, it would be for the army to decide who was loyal and who a traitor. Ṣabbāgh was even more outspoken. "The army cannot permit foreign troops, armed to the teeth, to roam the country, while it stands by without reacting, fulfilling only the role of police and gendarmerie for the benefit of the barbarian armies, shedding the innocent blood of the free populace in order to ensure the safety of those who trample its honor underfoot." And as to any resignation on the part of Rashīd 'Ālī, he said, "Nothing of the sort must take place. Iraq is blessed with a stout-hearted army. Such a thing would be contrary to the commandments of Muḥammad

[51] Khadduri, 194.
[52] Ṣabbāgh, 18, 95.
[53] *Ibid.*, 200–202.

and the soul of the Arab." Ṣabbāgh's conclusions were however not so extreme as his harangue. After all the blustering he advised Rashīd 'Ālī to resign. "Let the Regent have his way," he said, "let the government resign. After that we shall see what will happen. There is still Allah to watch over our country and a nation to defend it."

At this same meeting Rashīd 'Ālī announced his intention of resigning, and those present composed his letter of resignation. It was a strongly worded declaration which accused the Regent of surrendering to foreigners.

Ṣabbāgh's attitude with its aggressive reasoning but mild conclusions was a tactical withdrawal made at an inopportune moment with the object of redeploying his strength with greater effect at a more suitable time. Then and there he laid plans for the continuation of the struggle. He was not unaware of the fact that he was gambling not only with the fate of his country but with his own personal fate and that of his comrades. That is why he appealed to the meeting, "The Regent and his entourage are directing their maneuverings against us, the soldiers, and not specifically against you, the ministers. The British will not rest as long as we are at the head of the army . . . we shall be expecting a direct attack on us, designed to remove us from the army . . . but we swear we shall not permit that to happen. Will you then support us as we now support you?" And he relates that the ministers answered, "So be it, we swear it."

Ṣabbāgh, however, placed no reliance on the oath of loyalty of ministers who had that very moment been forced to resign, and took steps to ensure that the new prime minister would be one chosen by him. The Regent wished to appoint Muḥammad al-Ṣadr, Speaker of the Senate. The Four made it known that this appointment would mean civil war and demanded the appointment of Ṭaha al-Hāshimī. In the face of this threat of al-Ṣadr withdrew his candidacy and himself proposed Ṭaha al-Hāshimī, who was appointed.

The Four regarded Ṭaha al-Hāshimī as closer to them than any of the other notables who were not out-and-out supporters of Rashīd 'Ālī. He was the "Crown" of the "Crowned Golden Square". When he became Prime Minister at their behest, they also considered him dependent on them in carrying out his duties. Ṭaha al-Hāshimī himself wanted to bring about a conciliation between the Four and the Regent and to find common ground between the Mufti and Nūrī Sa'īd.

The main points of dissension where the question of rupture of diplomatic relations with Italy and the position of the Four Officers, and it was no longer possible to distinguish between the two problems or to put off a decision one way or the other. The contacts with Germany, which had begun under the aegis of Rashīd 'Ālī as Prime Minister, continued under

Ṭaha al-Hāshimi.[54] Pressure from Britain to break off relations with Italy became stronger—and stronger, too, grew the opposition of the Four to such a course.

At the end of March Ṭaha, who was also Minister of Defense, issued orders that Kāmil Shabīb be transferred from command of the 1st Division to that of the 4th.[55] Shabīb was the weakest of the Four. The 1st Division was stationed in the capital while the 4th was stationed in Diwaniya in the south and was also the weakest of the Iraqi divisions. The significance of the order was clear and left no doubt as to what the next step would be. It would be the shifting of Ṣabbāgh, the strongest of the Four, from the command of the 3rd Division, the strongest division, stationed in the capital, to the command of the 2nd Division in Mosul. Shabīb, after consulting with his comrades, refused to comply with his transfer order. Ṭaha was willing to cancel the order in return for an assurance from the Four that they would not intervene in political affairs in the future. But they decided once and for all to get rid of their rivals as well as those sitting on the fence.

On the eve of April 2, close to midnight, Amīn Zakī, Chief of Staff, and Fahmī Sa'īd, commander of the armored forces, came to the Prime Minister's home and informed him that the army in the capital had been alerted and the palace of the Regent surrounded; they forced him under threats to sign a latter of resignation. The officers intended by the same method to force the Regent to appoint Rashīd 'Ālī as Prime Minister. The Regent managed to slip away from the palace under cover of darkness although it was already surrounded by the army, and with the help of the American Legation reached Habbaniya the next day. From there he was flown to Basra and later to Transjordan. Nūrī Sa'īd had also had the prudence to escape from Baghdad in time and joined the Regent in Amman.

On six occasions between October 1936 and March 1941 officer groups were the decisive factor in deposing and appointing prime ministers in Iraq by use of force or by open threat of force; their intention was similarly effective in the appointment of the Regent after the death of King Ghāzī. First came the group of Bakr Ṣidqī, then the Seven headed by Yāmulkī, and after them the "Golden Square" of Ṣabbāgh. Yet up to the end of March 1941 the constitution was upheld at least for appearances' sake through all the changes that took place. Now that the Regent was no longer there to be coerced or threatened by army commanders, even this last pretence fell away. On April 3 Chief of Staff Amīn Zakī announced that "the army

[54] Hirszowicz, 163; Tillmann, 190, 194.
[55] Ḥaddād, 100.

has instructed Rashīd ʻĀlī al-Kaylānī" to set up "a Government of National Defense."[56] A few days later Rashīd ʻĀlī called Parliament together to place, as it were, the seal of approval on the new situation. It was unanimously resolved to depose the Regent and to appoint in his place Sharif Sharaf, a member of the royal family. Later, after the fall of Rashīd ʻĀlī, it was decided that all these procedures had no legal basis. According to the constitution only the Regent was empowered to invoke Parliament; moreover, less than half the members of Parliament had been present and those who were present were not free to vote according to their conscience.

Rashīd ʻĀlī's government was overwhelmingly dependent on the army commanders—and on the Mufti. The controlling body was a seven-man secret committee formed on February 28, 1941. In his memoirs Ṣabbāgh gave only their underground code names, "Pseudonyms for important persons whose real names I am not able to divulge at present, holders of high positions in the active and political forces of Iraq, Palestine and Syria."[57] Now their identity is clear beyond doubt.[58] Moreover, Grobba, the former German Minister in Iraq, now responsible for Iraqi affairs in the Foreign Ministry in Berlin, had already on August 27, 1940 recorded the existence and membership of a secret "Committee for Cooperation among the Arab Countries" in Baghdad. Its chairman and members were exactly the same as those of the 1941 committee with the addition of two representatives of the King of Saudi Arabia and two Syrians, one of them Shukrī Quwatlī.[59]

The Committee of 1941, consisting of Iraqis alone with the sole exception of the Mufti, was unequivocally pro-German. It was not merely a body for consultation and cooperation but bound to action and discipline by "a mighty oath," each "swearing by Allah that the words of the oath would be a light to guide his footsteps in all he did, that he would exert all his strength for the redemption of Arab lands . . . and that Muṣṭafā be our organizer and president, who must be obeyed."[60]

"Muṣṭafā", the President of the Committee, was the Mufti. The other members were three officers, Ṣabbāgh, Fahmī Saʻīd and Maḥmūd Salmān, and three civilians: Yūnis Sabʻāwī, an extreme pan-Arab nationalist and admirer of Hitler, whose *Mein Kampf* he had translated into Arabic, and who had served as Minister of Economic Affairs in Rashīd ʻĀlī's government; Nājī Shawkat who in 1940 as Minister of Justice in Rashīd

[56] *Ibid.*, 102; Khadduri, 213.

[57] Ṣabbāgh, 218.

[58] Khadduri, 164–5.

[59] Tillmann, 127.

[60] Ṣabbāgh, 218.

'Ālī's government had conducted secret negotiations with von Papen, the German Ambassador in Turkey (in Rashīd 'Ālī's government of 1941 he was Minister of Defense); and Rashīd 'Ālī, the Prime Minister.

The setting up of Rashīd 'Ālī's government in April 1941 about a month after the formation of the secret committee and the fact that this had been done in the form of a coup "at the army's request" were of great significance. April 1941 was one of the critical months of World War II during which the Germans conquered Yugoslavia and Greece and had advanced in North Africa as far as Sollum on the Egyptian border. The direction of their military attack pointed to the Middle East and their victories filled the hearts of their friends in Baghdad with hope and daring. The British, on the other hand, resolved to strengthen their position in Iraq.

On April 28 the British Ambassador announced that on the next day two thousand British soldiers would arrive in Basra from India. Rashīd 'Ālī declared that his government would not agree to their landing until British battalions which had arrived earlier left the country. Both sides knew perfectly well that the British would not accept this condition and on April 29 the British soldiers disembarked at Basra. On May 1, the Iraqi army placed the British Royal Air Force base at Habbaniya, 50 miles west of Baghdad, under siege. The small British force there—less than three thousand strong, half of them Assyrian levies—did not wait for the Iraqi force to make up its mind to attack. At dawn on May 2 British planes took off from Habbaniya to bomb Iraqi positions. The Anglo-Iraqi war had begun.

At last Ṣabbāgh had achieved his wish—open war against the British foe. Ṣabbāgh was more extreme than Rashīd 'Ālī and the Mufti. In the very first week of the war Turkey offered to mediate, and on May 8 she proposed a compromise that included British recognition of the Rashīd 'Ālī government and Iraqi agreement to the landing of British troops in its territory. Rashīd 'Ālī was disposed to agree, but Ṣabbāgh opposed the compromise and threatened to shoot him. Rashīd 'Ālī threatened to resign but this time the Mufti mediated and dissuaded him from taking this step.[61] All thought of compromise was dropped and the war continued. The Golden Square had once again succeeded in forcing the hand of the government and the country, but for the last time.

The Mufti and Rashīd 'Ālī had long been in contact with the German government. Since the summer of 1940 secret emissaries had conducted negotiations on political and military Iraqi-German cooperation with both the German Ambassador in Ankara and the Foreign Ministry in

[61] Ḥaddād, 120–2; Khadduri, 228.

Berlin. The actual outbreak of war in Iraq had, however, not been coordinated with Germany. Ribbentrop, the Foreign Minister, had always urged that Baghdad's relations with the British be forced into an open crisis, but the army command, which carried greater weight, was far more cautious. Hitler himself was preparing the invasion of Russia and was not interested in opening up another new front. On April 30, 1941, he fixed June 22 as B—("Barbarossa")—day, the date of the assault against the Soviet Union. The outbreak of hostilities in Iraq two days later was not according to his plans, but after the fighting had begun, on May 3, he gave orders to move aircraft to Iraq, and three weeks later in his order of the day of May 23 he placed "special importance" on the Iraqi uprising in tying up British forces and shipping and in particular in the encouragement it provided for the Arab nationalist movement in the entire Middle East—"Our Allies against the British."[62] German intervention of a practical nature, however, had limited potential. In the few weeks before the attack on Russia (which took place on June 22), the Germans were not able to spare much of their strength for a distant campaign of doubtful outcome, and in fact Hitler looked upon the war in Iraq as nothing more than a diversionary activity. The Germans sent 30 planes, as well as advisers, pilots, and technicians to Mosul via the airfields of Syria, where the Vichy French were still in control, and a consignment of aviation fuel, arms, and ammunition arrived by rail through Turkey. Assistance in the form of infantry and armored forces were out of the question. However, the British forces in Iraq were also very meager and it was not possible to reinforce them to any significant extent; the British were pinned down in the rugged campaigns of Crete and the Western Desert. On May 8 Wavell, the British Supreme Commander in the Middle East, proposed that "a political solution be sought in all possible ways" in Iraq, but Churchill insisted on the total defeat of the pro-German government in Baghdad.[63] The British transferred a few fighter planes to Iraq from Egypt and sent a motorized brigade, together with a battalion of the Transjordan Arab Legion, across the desert from Palestine and Transjordan.

In this situation the Iraqi army was of decisive importance. In the middle of May Ṣabbāgh, then commander of the western front disposing two divisions and an armored brigade, was still saying that his army was able to hold out for three months until large-scale reinforcements could arrive from the Axis powers. But he did not believe his own boastful words. Three times during May he had a "nervous breakdown," according to the Mufti's

[62] Hirszowicz, 211, 233; Tillmann, 205–7, 215–33.

[63] Churchill, *The Second World War,* vol. 3, 1950, 231.

secretary, an eyewitness.[64] The Iraqi army was routed. The commanders showed neither initiative nor ability, and the non-commissioned officers and men were completely without fighting spirit. The 4th Division in the south did not lift a finger, and the 2nd Division in the north initiated no action. The majority of the civilian population, or, at least, the politically active elements of the urban population in Baghdad, enthusiastically backed the anti-British war. The military rulers of Iraq after 1958 always glorified the events of May 1941 as a great national uprising. It was, however, the army, and first and foremost its leaders, who suffered a swift and humiliating defeat. On May 29 Rashīd 'Ālī and the military and civilian leaders of the regime, about forty of them altogether, fled to Iran. On May 31 the British army entered Baghdad and the following day the Regent returned. On June 4 the British entered Mosul. The Iraqi army was totally defeated. The British suffered only slightly more than one hundred casualties. The Iraqi casualties were 497 dead, 686 wounded, 548 missing and more than a thousand taken prisoner.[65]

It is hard to find an explanation for the walk-over victory over the Iraqi army but the fact is indisputable. One reason may have been the excessive politization of the officer corps. The activism of the officer politicians brought them victories over the politicians in their own country and even over rival officers in their own army, but it made the army weaker. They turned the army from a force serving the state into a tool in the struggle for hegemony within the state, and in that way the foundations of both state and army were undermined. And what happened in Iraq in 1940 repeated itself in Iraq and in Syria some twenty years later.

Rashīd 'Ālī, Ṣabbāgh, the Mufti and their fellows fled, but the spirit of the alliance between the extremist Arab nationalists and Nazism gave rise to still another storm. On June 2 and the morning after, during the brief transition period between the collapsing government and the new regime, a pogrom against the Jews took place. The number killed was between 156 and 179. Hundreds were injured and hundreds of Jewish houses and shops were looted. There are grounds for believing that the riots were instigated by Yūnis Sab'āwī, the last of Rashīd 'Ālī's ministers to leave the capital and perhaps the first in terms of extremism. Among the inflamed rabble many army men and police were seen. Across the Tigris bridges a stream of empty-handed people flowed eastward, and a mob laden with plunder streamed in the opposite direction.[66] At that time

[64] Ḥaddād, 112, 115, 122.

[65] C. Buckley, *Five ventures,* London 1954, 33, 36.

[66] Eliyahu Agassi, 20 *shana la-pra'ot bi-yehudey Bagdad,* Tel Aviv 1961, 10–4; Khadduri, 245; Freya Stark, *Dust in the lion's paw,* New York 1962, 114–6.

the Jewish community numbered 120,000 out of a total of 660,000 inhabitants of the city. Not all the Muslim population took part in the pogrom, and there were even some who concealed Jews and saved their lives and property. This was not the first outbreak of murder and pillage in Baghdad during an interregnum period. In March 1917 when the Turks left and the British came in, the mob rioted and looted bazaars and shops. But at that time human life was safe, and nobody differentiated between property owned by a member of one community and that of another. This modern distinction had been taught them by the Mufti.

The leaders of the vanquished regime fled to Iran. Rashīd ʿĀlī and the Mufti went from there to Germany. Amīn Zakī, Maḥmud Salmān, Kāmil Shabīb and several of the civilians were arrested in August 1941 in Teheran and handed over to the British, who interned them in Rhodesia for the duration of the war. In January 1942 the leaders of the movement were tried in absentia by a military court in Baghdad. Of the officers, Ṣabbāgh, Zakī, Salmān, Shabīb and Fahmī Saʿīd were sentenced to death. Amīn Zakī's sentence was commuted to life imprisonment with hard labor, in view of the fact that he was influenced by the others. In the spring of 1942 some of those convicted were handed over to the Iraqis, and new trials were held in their presence. On May 4 Fahmī Saʿīd and Maḥmud Salmān were again sentenced to death and hanged the next day. Amīn Zakī was sentenced to five years' imprisonment. Kāmil Shabīb was handed over to the Iraqis in April 1944, sentenced, and hanged on August 16. Qāsim Maqsūd, who commanded the 2nd Division in northern Iraq during the war, died in prison.

Ṣabbāgh managed to hide before they came to arrest him. Masquerading as a Dervish he wandered for some months in Iran, and at the beginning of April 1942 crossed the Iranian-Turkish frontier near Maku, not far from the Soviet border. In Turkey he asked for asylum as a political refugee. The Turks arrested him but refused to comply with the Iraqi government's request for his extradition. In the summer of 1945, after the war was over, the Turks agreed to regard him as a criminal offender, convicted of threatening the Regent. In September 1945 they handed him over to the British at the Syrian border. Again he succeeded in escaping but was recaptured several days later. On October 16, 1945 he was hanged in Baghdad. While in the Turkish prison he wrote his memoirs, which were published in Lebanon in 1956. This work has proved an important source of information regarding the events in Iraq in the years 1936 to 1941 and a key to understanding the outlook of the Iraqi officer politicians.

2. EGYPT DURING THE SECOND WORLD WAR

THE SECOND Arab country in which army officers tried to determine policy was Egypt.

On May 16, 1941 ʻAzīz ʻAlī al-Maṣrī deserted in an Egyptian military plane in an effort to reach the German forces then in Libya. This earned him the epithet "the Egyptian Hess"—Rudolph Hess, Hitler's deputy, had succeeded in flying to Scotland six days earlier. However, while Hess's adventure was an attempt to pave the way for peace negotiations *with* Britain, al-Maṣrī wanted to bring his country into the war *against* Britain. While Hess acted, so far as is known, as an individual and on his own initiative, al-Maṣrī was the head and emissary of an organized body. Further, the British were taken completely by surprise when Hess landed in their country, while al-Maṣrī was expected by the Germans. Although Hess reached the place he was heading for and al-Maṣrī did not, both failed in their missions. The simultaneity of timing of the two flights was quite fortuitous. But the timing of al-Maṣrī's flight to coincide with the thirty-days' war in Iraq was not at all the result of chance.

ʻAzīz ʻAlī al-Maṣrī was at that time in his sixties, a celebrated, almost legendary figure throughout the Arab world.[1] He was the son of a mixed Arab-Circassian mercantile family. His great-grandfather had migrated from Basra in Iraq to the Caucasus and there married the daughter of a distinguished Circassian family. His grandson, ʻAzīz ʻAlī's father, went from the Caucasus to Istanbul and later to Cairo, where ʻAzīz was born. At the age of ten ʻAzīz ʻAlī was sent to Istanbul for his education, and at the age of twelve he was admitted to the Ottoman military boarding-school. He was commissioned in 1901, and in 1904 graduated from a staff officers' course with distinction. Among his instructors were German officers and they had a profound influence on him. Until 1907 he served in the Balkans with the rank first of captain and then of major, distinguishing himself in

[1] On al-Maṣrī's life before 1941: M. Khadduri, 'Azziz Ali Misri and the Arab nationalist movement', *St. Anthony's Papers, No. 17*, London 1965; G. Antonius, *The Arab awakening*, London 1938, 155; Khadduri, 'General Nuri's flirtations with the Axis powers', *MEJ*, vol. 16, 3; *al-Ahrām*, 21 July 1965.

military actions in putting down revolts. At the time of the Turkish revolution he was one of the foremost members of the "Committee for Unity and Progress". He played a key role in the reconquest of Istanbul from the counter-revolutionaries in 1909. His hope then was that the Young Turks would also grant freedom to the Arabs and that a bi-national Turkish-Arab Kingdom would arise on the model of Austria-Hungary. But when he became aware of the fact that the Young Turks were even more zealous of Turkish supremacy than the Sultan, he began to work against them. In 1909 he was one of the founders of the secret Arab society "al-Qaḥtaniyya," comprised of civilian intellectuals and army officers. Tough and fiery-tempered as he was, his views did not remain secret, and in order to avoid an open crisis he was transferred in 1910 at his own request to Yemen, where he took part in the suppression of the revolt of the Imam Yaḥyā. When the revolt came to an end, al-Maṣrī volunteered to fight against the Italian invaders in Libya. His opponent Aḥmad Jamāl (the commander of the Ottoman army in Syria and Palestine in the First World War) later admitted that in Libya "he distinguished himself most exceptionally in the defence of Benghazi, where he served with Enver and Mustapha Kemal (Atatürk)." [2] In 1913, he returned to Istanbul where he became one of the founders of "al-'Ahd", a secret society of Arab officers in the Ottoman army. Most members of the society were Iraqis; a few were Syrians and Palestinians. In February 1914 he was arrested and in April was sentenced to death at a trial held behind closed doors, even though the prosecution was unable to produce evidence of his guilt. The case aroused a wave of protest in Egypt, Syria, and also in Europe. In the London *Times* there appeared four leaders calling on the Turks to desist from what they termed "neither more or less than judicial murder," which was likely to have repercussions on Turkish-Egyptian relations, "and most certainly not only on the relations between Turkey and Egypt." [3] Thanks to the pressure which was brought to bear, al-Maṣrī was released six days after he was sentenced to death and allowed to leave for Egypt, where he was welcomed as a national hero. When the war broke out, the British Governor, Lord Kitchener, asked him to join the fight against Turkey. But al-Maṣrī, although he had quarrelled with the Turks, was not prepared to fight against them. Moreover, he had always been against British rule and influence in Egypt and the Middle East, while he greatly admired the Germans. As early as the beginning of 1916 he cherished thoughts of making contact with Germany who, he hoped, would persuade Turkey to grant the Arabs autonomy within the framework

[2] Ahmed Djemal Pascha, *Erinnerungen eines türkischen Staatsmannes,* München 1922, 60–3.
[3] *The Times,* London, 9 April 1914.

of the Ottoman Empire. Only after the British had promised the Arabs independence in the MacMahon letters and after Sharif Ḥusayn of Mecca had raised the standard of rebellion, did he join the Arab revolt. In September 1916 he was appointed Chief of Staff of the Sharifian army on the recommendation of the British and despite reservations on the part of Sharif Ḥusayn himself. And, indeed, differences of opinion between him and Ḥusayn soon became apparent. When Ḥusayn gave orders for an attack on the city of Medina, where the main Turkish strength in Hejaz was concentrated, al-Maṣrī opposed the whole plan. He was all for revolt within the Ottoman Empire but not in favor of a war to split it, and he still preferred Germany to Britain as an ally. He resigned, and before the year 1916 was out he was back in Cairo. From there he intended to go to Switzerland en route to Germany. He was allowed to go to Spain, where he remained until the end of the war, and then he did go to Germany, staying there for nearly four years. In 1922, when Egypt obtained independence, he returned but was not accepted for military service. In the years which followed he had no permanent occupation until 1935 when he was, for a time, the companion of Crown Prince Fārūq, who was then studying in England. But the master and the pupil differed too greatly in their characters, and al-Maṣrī did not remain with Fārūq for long. His family life was also disappointing. In the nineteen-twenties he married a young American girl who was lecturing at the American University in Cairo. In 1939 they were divorced.

Al-Maṣrī remained true to his old love, Germany, and in 1938 he visited the Third Reich as an emissary of anti-British circles, negotiating for a secret supply of arms.[4] In the summer of 1939; when the pro-German 'Alī Māhir became Prime Minister of Egypt, he appointed al-Maṣrī Chief of Staff of the army. But as he rose with 'Alī Māhir, so did he fall with him. 'Alī Māhir was obliged to resign in June 1940; on August 1 al-Maṣrī had to take sick leave and was retired for good.

In the spring of 1941 al-Maṣrī was looking forward to a German victory. He was not the only Egyptian officer to entertain such hopes, but only among the youngest of them could a group of men with the courage to band together be found. The boldest of them was Anwar al-Sādāt.

Sādāt was only twenty-three years old at the time, yet he had extensive connections among junior officers and political circles. He was a graduate of the officers' course at the military academy which ended in February 1938. In that course and in the following two which were conducted in 1938

[4] Hirszowicz, 70 (H. is mistaken in describing al-Maṣrī as Inspector-General of the Egyptian army); Tillmann, 25–7.

a number of young cadets met who were destined to become leaders of their country. Among them were Nasser, Zakariyyā Muḥī al-Dīn, Jamāl Sālim and ʻAbd al-Ḥakīm ʻĀmir. Before they joined the army, while yet pupils in high school, they had been active in political youth organizations and parties or strongly influenced by them. There were two main organizations. "The Muslim Brethren" and "Miṣr al-Fatāt" ("Young Egypt"). The Brethren under the leadership of Ḥasan al-Bannā fostered a mystic Islamic zealotry together with an extremist nationalism, hatred of the imperialist nations—primarily England—and an hostility to every progressive western cultural influence. "Miṣr al-Fatāt," led by Aḥmad Ḥusayn, promoted secular Egyptian chauvinism under the direct influence and imitation of Italian Fascism and German Nazism.

In the spring of 1941 Anwar Sādāt was in contact with both organizations and with his officer comrades. His activities were facilitated by his being at the time communications officer at the El Maʻadi base near Cairo.[5] Apparently one of his contacts there was Maḥmūd Labīb, an older officer and retired major who had spent several years in Germany before the war and was one of the leaders of the terrorist "Secret Organization" of the Muslim Brethren.[6] Contacts with a group of young officers in the Egyptian air force proved of particular importance to him, and among them was ʻAbd al-Laṭīf Baghdādī.[7]

Sādāt writes in his memoirs: "We established contact with the German Command in Libya and we worked with them in complete harmony."[8] Their main activity was collecting information on the deployment of British troops in Egypt for German intelligence. Baghdādī also writes in his memoirs about arms acquisitions, ordnance factories and the setting up of a lathe for turning out hand-grenades. According to the historian Amīn Saʻīd, "a large quantity of arms and a hundred thousand 'molotov cocktails'" were prepared, and it was even "decided to set up a 'military government' which would take over the country and join the Germans in the fight against the common enemy."[9] Whether a large quantity of arms was assembled or only a single lathe; whether they had already "reached a decision" on the establishment of an officer government, or whether they

[5] Anwar El Sadat, *Revolt on the Nile,* London 1957, 27.

[6] Ahmed Abul-Fath, *L'affaire Nasser,* Paris 1962, 177; Arabic: Aḥmad Abū al-Fatḥ, *Jamāl ʻAbd al-Nāṣir,* Beirut (1962), 174; Ishak Musa Husaini, *The Moslem Brethren,* Beirut 1956, 173–4.

[7] ʻAbd al-Laṭīf al-Baghdādī, 'Mā qabl al-ḍubbāt al-aḥrār', in: *Hādhihi al-thawra, Cairo* 1953.

[8] Sadat, 34.

[9] Amīn Saʻīd, *Ta'rīkh al-ʻarab al-ḥadīth,* vol. 13; *Al-thawra,* Cairo 1959, 26.

had so far engaged only in espionage—there is no doubt at all that an underground organization of officers did exist.

In May 1941 the conspirators felt that the time had come for some action of a demonstrative character. Hitler was enjoying success. In April Yugoslavia and Greece had surrendered. On May 2 the war in Iraq had begun, and a new star—Rommel—played a trail across the Western Desert. On March 31 he unleashed his first offensive and on April 14 he took Sollum. The Germans were already on Egyptian soil and were approaching the Suez Canal from two directions. In the words of Sādāt, "1941 was a tragic year for Britain, but for Egypt, it was a year of hope."[10] Al-Maṣrī and his comrades decided to take some real action which would demonstrate to both friend and foe that in Egypt, too, there was a force active on the side of the Axis. They wanted to help Germany and at the same time to make the future victors regard Egypt as an ally entitled to her rights, like Iraq, and not a conquered country like Greece.

In deciding what to do they had to consider that a direct confrontation, as had happened in Iraq, was not possible as the British army was many times stronger and the nationalist force much weaker than in that country. It was therefore decided that al-Maṣrī would defect to the Germans. Apparently those Egyptian officers already appreciated the importance of the propaganda effect of such a move.

The Germans approved the idea. The first two plans—one to take al-Maṣrī on board a German submarine in Lake Burullus and the other to fly him from the Khaṭāṭba airfield half-way between Cairo and Alexandria—were discarded as completely impracticable. A third plan was tried but came to grief. The Germans, who knew Egypt better than the Egyptian officers, suggested that a German plane with British markings should be waiting at a certain hour on a level area at Jabal Rozza in the Western Desert, 47 miles west of Cairo. However, al-Maṣrī's car broke down on the way and the driver could not coax it into starting. The passenger did not reach his rendezvous and the German plane returned to its base without him.[11] Finally al-Maṣrī decided to fly from the Cairo airfield of Al Maza in an Egyptian military plane, accompanied by two Egyptian air force pilots. Once again the plan failed. On May 16 as the plane was taking off, it struck a post and crashed. Passenger and pilots were unharmed and escaped only to be caught and arrested two weeks later.[12]

The pilots were Major Ḥusayn Dhū al-Fiqār Ṣabrī, duty officer at the airfield on that day, and Second-Lieutenant ʻAbd al-Munʻim ʻAbd al-Ra'ūf,

[10] Sadat, 34.

[11] John W. Eppler, *Rommel ruft Kairo,* Gütersloh 1959, 27.

[12] Sadat, 36–8.

the same officer who had accompanied al-Maṣrī to Jabal Rozza.[13] Both were later to occupy key positions in the Free Officers' movement.

A year passed, and in the summer of 1942 Rommel mounted his second offensive in the Western Desert. On June 20 he took Tobruk and by the end of the month reached El Alamein, only 186 miles from Alexandria. Nazi supporters in Egypt prepared for his coming. Swastikas were to be seen in many places and the staff of the British Embassy in Cairo began to burn documents to prevent them from falling into enemy hands. On July 24 the Foreign Office representative who accompanied Rommel's Afrika Korps requested instructions concerning relations with Egypt in view of the impending invasion. Two days later the Foreign Office secretary, von Weizsäcker, transmitted information which reveals Germany's evaluation of the different forces then active in Egypt: "The Egyptian masses are to be regarded as generally uncritical and politically disinterested", the real partner for future collaboration with the Axis is King Fārūq "whose attitude is thoroughly pro-German and anti-British"; as to the Egyptian army, there are strong sympathies for Germany among the young officers but the army as such is "powerless" and will presumably "remain passive" if the Germans enter Egypt.[14]

However, some of the young nationalist Egyptian officers had made up their minds not to remain passive spectators. Once again there were cases of Egyptian pilots making off to join the Germans. On July 7 an air force officer defected and the next day a flight sergeant followed suit.[15] Their names were not published, but it seems that the officer was Lieutenant Aḥmad Sa'ūdi, whom Baghdādī describes as having fled at that time. He was apparently shot down by the Germans who mistook him for an enemy when he was about to land at Mersa Matruh airfield, then held by them.[16] He later died. Another pilot who tried to defect in 1941 or 1942 was Second-Lieutenant Ḥasan Ibrāhīm,[17] who was also destined to become a leader of the Free Officers.

Baghdādī tells in his memoirs of two other officers who were connected with the underground movement in the army: Major 'Izzat of the infantry who worked together with Sādāt in 1942, and Lieutenant Muḥammad Wajīh 'Abaẓa of the air force. In 1953 'Abaẓa was a lieutenant-colonel in

[13] Georges Vaucher, *Gamal Abdel Nasser et son équipe,* Paris 1959, 124; A.W. Sansom, *I spied spies,* London 1965, 70–5.

[14] Tillmann, 380–1; also 260, 297.

[15] 'La Bourse Egyptienne' and 'Egyptian Gazette' of 2 February 1943, quoted in : *Yalqut hamizrah hatikhon,* Jerusalem, January 1943, 26–8.

[16] Baghdādī, *loc. cit.*; *al-Muṣawwar,* Cairo, 28 August 1953.

[17] J. and S. Lacouture, *Egypt in transition,* London 1958, 132.

the air force and later occupied important posts in the "Liberation Rally." In 1960 he was governor of the Al-Buḥayra district and in 1964 governor of the Aswan district.

Sādāt's underground activities continued during the whole of this period. The twin forces which motivated him in 1941—opposition to the British and support of the Axis—proved to be even stronger in 1942. On February 4, 1942 the British forced King Fārūq to dismiss Sirrī and to appoint Naḥḥās as Prime Minister in his stead. This intervention in Egypt's internal affairs was vital in that critical stage of the war but it was done in a repugnant manner. The humiliation to the King caused offense and resentment in many quarters which rankled for years. On the battlefields that spring the armies of the Axis continued to be triumphant. In the Far East the Japanese astonished the world with their victories. In Russia the Germans were eminently successful, as they were in the Western Desert. Could a man like Sādāt sit idly by at such a time? In June and July 1942 he gathered intelligence for two German agents who had infiltrated into Cairo at the end of May, bringing a radio transmitter with them. One of them was a native of Cairo whose step-father had been an Egyptian judge. Rommel was much interested in the activities of these agents—but their messages never reached his headquarters. The two radio operators in Libya who were to maintain contact with them were taken prisoner by the British, and Admiral Canaris, chief of German intelligence, feared that the code was known to the enemy and that therefore no further credence could be given to information arriving by this means. Apart from that, the spies in Cairo hardly used their transmitter at all. They indulged in riotous living and were loath to put themselves in danger; the large amount of money (forged) that they had brought with them was squandered on dancing girls and prostitutes—until they were caught. Sādāt relates that they were arrested the following day "after I found them, blind drunk, with two Jewish girls." In fact only one of the girls was Jewish, and she was not a prostitute but a member of a Jewish underground organization detailed to capture Nazis.[18] The capture of the two German spies also led to the exposure of the Egyptian pro-German underground. Two days later Ḥasan 'Izzat was apprehended and on the following day Sādāt was caught. In prison they rejoined al-Maṣrī and other comrades. Once again their efforts had proved vain, but not for lack of devotion or courage on the part of the Egyptian underground.

Sādāt also mentions Muḥammad Wajīh Khalīl as being a member of his organization. Khalīl, then a captain, served with his friend Nasser in

[18] Sadat, 48–9; Sansom, 128–30; Eppler, 201–16; Hans von Steffens, *Salaam,* Neckargemünd 1960, 213–43.

1941 in the El Alamein region. In 1942 he visited Sādāt in detention and told him that his comrades were taking care of his family. In the Palestine War he was in command of the company which attacked Yad Mordekhai and several weeks later, in July 1948, he fell in the fighting at Negba.[19]

Another active member of this conspiratorial group was cavalry Second-Lieutenant Aḥmad Maẓhar. In 1941 he reconnoitered the Burullus Lake area in order to examine the plan for al-Maṣrī's escape by submarine.[20] After the takeover in 1952 he was commander of the Armored Corps. In the nineteen-sixties he became a film actor.[21]

Al-Maṣrī, 'Abd al-Ra'ūf and Ṣabrī were released from prison in 1942 upon giving their word of honor that they would refrain from subversive activities, but Sādāt remained in camp in Al-Minya Province until he escaped in November 1944.[22]

On February 1, 1943 Prime Minister Naḥḥās said in Parliament, "I have watched with great sorrow and bitterness certain trends that have attempted to influence the army and its authority, and spread despondency in the country, which could have resulted in serious disorder, could indeed have caused revolution and the collapse of law and order, endangering the country's existence and future."[23] The war was still on, and Naḥḥās' remarks were uttered in an apologetic tone and in answer to the question why al-Maṣrī had been arrested. Twelve years after these events Sādāt wrote: "I still think that if ill-luck had not so dogged our enterprise, we might have struck a quick blow at the British, joined forces with the Axis and changed the course of events."[24] To write, ten years after Hitler's demise, of delivering a decisive blow to the British is naive—to say the least. The unavailing endeavors of a number of officers testify to their passionate support of Hitler and their confidence in his victory. In the history of the war these adventures were only marginal events. But their importance in the antecedents of Nasser's Egypt is great.

Of these twelve officers one, 'Izzat, was not heard of after the war. Three of them, Labīb, Sa'ūdī and Khalīl, died before 1952. Four of the remaining eight later became founder members of the ten-man committee of the Free Officers' Association in 1949. They were Baghdādī, Sādāt, 'Abd al-Ra'ūf

[19] Sadat, 52; Lacouture, 131–2; 'Abd al-'Azīz al-Batshatī, *Shuhadā'unā al-dubbāṭ fī ḥamlat Falasṭin,* Cairo 1949, 21.

[20] Anwar El Sadat, *Geheimtagebuch der ägyptischen Revolution,* Düsseldorf 1957, 58; Vaucher, 124.

[21] *Ākhir sā'a,* Cairo, 10 March 1965.

[22] *Yalqut hamizrah hatikhon, loc. cit.*; Sadat, *Revolt,* 55.

[23] *Yalqut,* February 1943, 27.

[24] Sadat, *Revolt,* 38.

and Ḥasan Ibrāhīm. The other four also occupied important positions in republican Egypt. Hence there exists an uninterrupted continuity in leadership from the alliance with German National Socialism in the early nineteen-forties to the Arab socialism of the sixties.

Whereas the Iraqi insurrectionists of 1958 and 1963 have sometimes stressed that their movement was the successor to the uprising of 1941 and its pinnacle of triumph, in Egypt today the pro-German underground during World War II is played down, both because it was a complete failure and because Nasser's role in it was insignificant. It should not be assumed that his ideas at the time were any different from Sādāt's; but the Nasser personality cult does not sanction giving publicity that could enhance the prestige of other persons. Similarly, little mention is now made of rallying to the side of Hitler, particularly since the men who were active in that cause are now leaders of the state. It is clear, however, that although the importance of this chapter in Egypt's history is not stressed, there is no regret nor even reservations about it; from time to time it is even recalled with glory. Sādāt's books of the 1950's exude pride over his activities as Hitler's agent. Nasser, in an interview with the editor of the neo-Nazi German newspaper *Deutsche National- und Soldaten-Zeitung in* April 1964—a month before Khrushchev's visit to Egypt—vaunted the fact that, in World War Two, "our sympathies were with Germany. The Speaker of our Parliament, for example, (meaning Sādāt) was put in prison for his pro-German sympathies." In order to curry favor with the Nazis of 1964 he exonerated Hitler for the genocide of the Jews. "Surely nobody still accepts the lie of six million murdered Jews. Even the simplest man in the street here does not believe it."[25] And the link between words and deeds, between the past and the present, is evident. In the 1950's cooperation between German Nazis and these Egyptian officers, now lords of the land, was renewed, and it continued into the 1960's. German officers and Nazi propagandists and scientists have found in Nasser's Egypt not only asylum but also employment in their professions. Egypt is one of the countries in which they are encouraged to continue their activities, particularly their war against the Jewish people.

[25] *Deutsche National- und Soldaten-Zeitung,* München, 1 May 1964.

3. THE DORMANT YEARS

INITIAL assaults by the nationalist officers in Iraq and Egypt ended in failure and disappointment. Months later the very circumstances of their activity were radically altered. The winter of 1942–43 brought decisive changes. Hitler was defeated at El Alamein and at Stalingrad. The mighty Axis armies were forced to retreat and the hopes of the young Arab officers and nationalists that they would witness a speedy destruction of Great Britain and the Soviet Union collapsed. Those hated by al-Maṣrī and Sādāt, by the Mufti and Ṣabbāgh—Churchill and Stalin, even Naḥḥās and Nūrī Sa'īd—were favored with success after success. Moderate, traditional Arab nationalism with a pro-British orientation achieved an easy, brilliant triumph. "Egypt was spared the disasters of the war," in the words of the Wafd slogan—and at the same time she became a partner to victory. Without having fired a single shot in the war, she became in 1945 one of the charter-members of the United Nations. Syria and Lebanon achieved independence with the help of Britain who was interested in pushing out France; and they, too, became charter-members of the United Nations as sovereign states. The same happened in the case of Iraq. The Arab League, founded that same year at the inspiration of the British, appeared to the Arabs to be the first great step toward their unity. The officers who between 1939 and 1942 linked the fate of their movement to the "anti-imperialism" of Mussolini and Hitler were in 1944–48 unable to point to any sucess, nor were they able to see any prospect for their ideology in the near future. Their opponents had stolen their thunder. Their ideology failed to arouse sympathy in the population in the mid-1940's. During this period there was intensive propaganda for the idea or, at least, the slogan of democracy. This was generally interpreted to mean a parliamentary government based on elections and parties with a cabinet responsible to the legislature; separation of legislative, executive, and judicial authorities; particularly separation of governmental from military powers; and the subservience of the army to a government which was responsible to the electorate. The ideas of the officer politicians moved in an entirely different direction. To be sure, the fine ideals of democracy in no way materialized, and in the meantime the number of people who contended that democracy did not suit the conditions of the Middle East increased. But many of those critical of formal democracy did not in those years turn in the direction of nationalist thinking. On the contrary, they became socialists. The impressive victories of the Soviet Union were associated with socialism and served as a powerful stimulus to left-wing intellectuals and trade-unionists, who intensified their activities. When in July 1946 the government clamped down on the Egyptian left wing, in Cairo alone there were 200 arrested—many of them journalists, labor leaders and others. More than 10 periodicals were suppressed and scores of arrests were made in Alexandria and various provincial towns.[1]

Between 1942 and 1948 everyone in the Arab East mouthed democratic or socialist slogans, and officer politicians were forced to lie low.

A parallel to this phenomenon can be found in Latin America, a part of the world noted for its frequency of coups and military dictatorships. There, too, the interference of army officers in political life diminished in the years close to the end of World War II when democratic slogans were flourishing throughout the world. Six of the 20 Latin American republics, embracing a sixth of the continent's population, were under military rule in 1928. In 1936 the military were in power in half of the states comprising half of the population. But in 1947 this held true for only seven countries. Subsequently, army interference and coups increased once more, and by 1954 military dictators ruled thirteen of these countries.[2]

The Arab officer politicians were unable to act during this dormant period, but they did not change their views. Later, when they rose to power, they openly emphasized the continuity between the officers' movements of the early 1940's and those of the 1950's. Sādāt, who personifies this continuity in Egypt, wrote in 1956 that the 1941 Iraqi revolt "was the first sign of liberation in the Arab world."[3]

If Sādāt and his views were to gain favor a new shock would have to electrify the nation, to lay bare the weakness of the regime and shake the foundations of power in the Arab countries. It was not long before that shock came—on the battlefields and in the hearts of the Arab fighters in Palestine. In 1948 seven Arab countries sent troops into Palestine to thwart the establishment of the State of Israel; and they lost the war. Their defeat

[1] *Yalqut hamizrah hatikhon,* Jerusalem. July–August 1946, 102–4; Walter Z. Laqueur, *Communism and nationalism in the Middle East,* New York 1956, 43–6; Aharon Cohen, *Temurot mediniyot ha'olam ha'aravi,* Merhavia 1959, 93.

[2] Ed. Lieuwen, 'Militarism and politics in Latin America', in John J. Johnson, ed., *The role of the military in underdeveloped countries,* Princeton 1962, 131–2.

[3] Sadat, *Revolt,* 35.

could not be disguised; it was all the more painful since it mercilessly exposed the impotence of all those countries and armies compared with tiny Israel, which they had never even recognized as a state. Arab public opinion could no longer wriggle out of recognizing that there was something corrupt within their countries.

In August 1948 the influential Beirut historian and thinker, Qusṭanṭīn Zurayq, published a brochure entitled *The Significance of the Catastrophe*. Since then numerous Arab books and articles have been available which analyse the internal problems brought out into the open by this external conflict.

Zurayq's brochure starts with a bitter statement, "The defeat of the Arabs in Palestine is not a mere setback or a slight transitory misfortune. It is a catastrophe in the full sense of the word, one of the most difficult experiences which has befallen the Arabs in the course of their long history." In the same inexorable manner in which he pointed out the facts Zurayq then attempted to trace their sources, and discovered them in the Arab internal political and social system. "The victory which the Zionists achieved is not the superiority of one people over another, but rather the pre-eminence of one system over another. It stems from the fact that Zionism is deeply rooted in modern life, while we for the most part are remote from life and take no part in it; that they live in the present and in the future, while we continue to be immersed in the dreams of the past and are content with a pride in antiquity."[4] He concludes that Arab life needs radical, internal reform which means, among other things, "progressive, revolutionary action" and "a true leadership."[5] Today, after much critical and self-searching material of this nature has been published in the Arab countries, these statements sound almost commonplace. In 1948, however, this was startlingly new. Its significance lay also in the fact that this new thinking did not concern itself with generalities but with concrete events and institutions. It clearly expressed what in wide circles had been painfully experienced and suddenly realized.

In the Arab countries the Palestinian War filled the function which Marx had in 1855 ascribed to war generally in his brilliant formulation: "This is the uplifting aspect of war; it tests a nation. Just as mummies instantly fall apart when exposed to the atmosphere, so war pronounces a death sentence on all institutions that no longer possess vitality."[6] This holds especially true for a lost war, which so often creates what Lenin called a revolutionary situation.

[4] Qusṭanṭīn Zurayq, *Ma'nā al-nakaba,* Beirut 1948, 42.

[5] *Ibid.,* 51.

[6] Marx-Engels, *Werke,* Berlin (DDR) 1961–63, vol. 11, 522.

The Arab fiasco in Palestine in 1948 was primarily a military one. Paradoxically, it bolstered the esteem and self-confidence of the armies in Arab life. Military defeat was explained away as being an inevitable outcome of social grievances, not as a cause but rather an effect, and the beaten soldiers returned from the front not as culprits but as victims of the national misery. Moreover, they generally came to the realization that Zionism and Israel could not be vanquished through propaganda or diplomacy or by guerrilla and partisan tactics; the only instrument of power in the Arab states was their regular armies. The self-confidence of the officers enabled them to regain the prestige lost by the statesmen and party politicians some of whom had used the occasion for war profiteering—while troops had paid the price of war with their lives. Soldiers returning home from the front were disillusioned and embittered and no longer heeded authority. In the general confusion they were not disposed to self-criticism but placed the blame for what had happened elsewhere. They glossed over military shortcomings in order to indulge in more political criticism. For the officers returning from the front criticism of national grievances served as an excuse for vindicating their own professional and personal honor.

The Palestine War fostered political renaissance for extreme Arab nationalism as well. Among liberal Arabs war enthusiasm was quite lukewarm; few were active in the war effort and none volunteered. The communists were against the war and in the fall of 1948 they distributed an illegal leaflet issued by the Iraqi, Syrian, and Jordanian parties together with the Israeli communists, demanding a suspension of hostilities.[7] Ardent activists were to be found among right-wing fanatics; they were the moving force in most of the propagandist, organizational and military undertakings. The veteran Arab Nazi-supporters met again in the small quarters of the Arab regular and irregular forces. Among them were the Jerusalem Mufti; Fawzī Qā'uqjī; Iraqis who had fought against Britain in 1941; Muslim Brethren; members of the fascist party "Young Egypt"; and Egyptian officers who had at one time worked for Rommel. They were joined by non-Arab fascist volunteers; Yugoslav Muslims who had fought with the Hitlerite partisans of Pavelitch in World War II and did not dare to return home; former German soldiers seeking new adventures and wishing to continue the war against the Jews; and English fascist deserters. The Palestine War not only provided the shock which shook the foundations

[7] Eliezer Be'eri, 'Ma'ase be-Ahmad wa-Butrus', *Al Hamishmar,* Tel Aviv, 14 September 1958; Aharon Cohen, *Yisrael we-ha-'olam ha'aravi,* Merhavia 1964, 427; Maḥmūd al-Dara, *Al-qaḍiyya al-kurdiyya wa-al-qawmiyya al-arabiyya fi ma'arakat al-'Iraq,* Beirut 1963, 137.

of traditional Arab regimes but also gave the Arab extreme right the opportunity of once again appearing on the political stage and playing a leading role.

Nearly all the Syrian, Egyptian, Jordanian and Iraqi officers who have been staging coups since 1949—whether or not they succeeded is here irrelevant—fought on the Palestine front in 1948. It was these very people who were influenced by the fiasco in Palestine, goaded by their rebellious past, their experiences at the front and the general confusion and shock.

It is useless to ask what would have happened in the Arab world if it had not been for the Arab defeat of 1948. Perhaps some other event or process would have laid bare the crisis in the Arab world with equal brutality and provoked similar reactions; perhaps forces other than those which burst into the open after 1948 would have emerged and assumed control. In all events, it is a fact of history that what happened in Palestine served as a catalyst to reactivate the officers and bring them to power. Nor is it mere chance that officers participating in coups make innumerable promises to conquer Israel and restore the losses of 1948.

The first Arab state in which the crisis developed into a military dictatorship was Syria.

4. SYRIA FROM 1949 TO 1954

On November 24, 1948 Dr. Adīb Naṣṣūr wrote in the Damascus daily, *Alif Bā',* "It is hardly possible to find a man in the country who is satisfied. Each person one meets has some complaint to make. The ministers grumble, the leaders are angry, the members of parliament denounce, the university teacher is critical and the man in the street makes accusations." [1] Within the Chamber of Deputies, which had been elected a year previously, a similar state of affairs prevailed. None of the parties commanded a majority in the House. The material differences dividing the factions were not great but their capacity and willingness to cooperate were minimal. And now the humiliation of the Arabs in the Palestinian War came out into the open. The Syrian army, it is true, had not suffered defeat to the extent of the Egyptian army. It had even occupied some points of what had been Mandatory Palestine and which had been allocated to Israel under the United Nations' decision of November 1947. However, there had been no victory. The common Arab defeat was also Syria's.

During the winter of 1948-49 the Syrian army acquired increasing importance in the life of the country. On November 30, 1948 the demonstrations marking the first anniversary of the UN resolution on Palestine turned into anti-government riots; on December 2 a state of emergency was declared, and the army called out to restore order. The officer corps sensed that the life of the government depended upon them. In March 1949 the High Command demanded an increased military budget but the government either could not or would not comply. It was even rumored that the army allocation would be reduced. On March 20 the Chief of the General Staff, Colonel Ḥusnī Za'īm, called a secret meeting of army leaders at Quneitra and it was decided that the military would take over matters into its own hands. [2]

On March 27 Naṣṣūr wrote in *Alif Bā',* "I write these lines so that the

[1] Adīb, Naṣṣūr, *Qabla fawāt al-awān,* Beirut 1955, 15.

[2] Bashīr al-'Auf, *Al-inqilāb al-sūrī,* Damascus (c. 1949) 10–1; Ghassān Tuwaynī, *Manṭiq al-quwwa,* Beirut 1954, 25.

officers and men may know that in these bitter days the thoughts of many Syrian citizens turn to the army, some of whose feelings they share." [3] Three days later Za'īm carried out Syria's first military coup.

Naṣṣūr's article reflected the feelings of army officers and of a section of Syrian public opinion in those "bitter days." "The army has been compelled to maintain an armistice with an enemy that has not been victorious," he wrote further, "and there are soldiers who are being charged with profiteering, with having been neglectful of their duties or with having almost been guilty of treason . . . The Syrian army was sent into the battlefield without proper equipment . . . Courage made up for the inadequate training and arms . . . If there were a handful whose conduct was not that of brave soldiers defending the flag, there were hundreds of officers and men who risked their lives at the front, who gave everything for the motherland and received nothing in return . . . And now I will tell you the naked truth: Mother Syria cannot save Southern Syria. The strength of the Syrian Republic is not commensurate with the place it occupies among the Arabs; it is not in keeping with the aspirations of her sons and the awakening of her thinkers. In the light of this fact the duty of the state and the function of the army have become clear. It is the duty of the state to regard the army as its first national institution, to give priority to its needs over all others and to give precedence to the virtues of the soldier over all other civic virtues. The function of the army is to advance rapidly and steadily in strength, ability and organization . . . to carry out its mighty mission." [4]

It is not material whether Naṣṣūr sensed or was even aware of the imminent military coup, whether his article was inspired by the insurrectionists to prepare the ground or whether it was pure coincidence that he wrote his article three days before the establishment of the dictatorship. The article reveals and voices the despair of Syrian civilians, the loss of their self-confidence, their eagerness for an energetic leadership and their belief that the army alone was capable of saving them.

If, in the spring of 1949, many Syrians sought a strong leader in the person of a soldier, their wishes were fulfilled. But the stability Syria longed for did not prevail. On the contrary, the officer politicians undermined the foundations of the state to an even greater extent than the political parties and the civilian leaders had done. They rose and fell in rapid succession, like fireworks on the night of a popular holiday. Each rose to prominence, shone briefly—for a moment illuminating the darkness with many lights and colors to the applause of an enthusiastic crowd—descended rapidly

[3] Naṣṣūr, 30–2.

[4] *Ibid., loc. cit.*

and was extinguished, as yet another rose in his stead. They came and went in rapid succession—Za'īm, Shīshaklī, Bizrī, Sarrāj, Naḥlāwī, Zahr al-Dīn, Atāsī, Ḥarīrī, Ḥāfiẓ, Jadīd—these are only the ten best known. Each was Syria's strongman . . . for a day.

Ḥusnī Za'īm was the first. He was born in 1894 in Aleppo, the son of a learned shaykh and a Kurdish mother. Circassian blood ran in his veins. After military training in Turkey he was commissioned as a second-lieutenant in the Ottoman army and posted at Medina in 1917. He spent the end of the First World War in a prisoner of war camp in Egypt. In 1920 he joined the French army in Syria and by 1941 had risen to the rank of lieutenant-colonel. Politically he was fiercely anti-British. He hated Emir 'Abd-Allāh of Transjordan and the Mufti of Jerusalem was his friend. The Mufti's hatred for the British stemmed from pan-Arab nationalism; Za'īm's stemmed from devotion to France. In 1941 he fought against British and Free French forces which conquered Syria, then under the Vichy Administration. He was assigned the task of organizing guerrilla activities against the invaders. After the surrender he refused to lay down his arms and fled—but the Vichy government publicly announced that he had embezzled large sums entrusted to him. He was arrested by the Free French and sentenced to ten years in prison. After serving two and a quarter years of his sentence, he was released on condition that he settled in Lebanon. He was allowed to return to Syria only in 1946. In 1947 he was appointed Inspector-General of Police and in 1948 Chief of the General Staff of the army.[5]

The coup was meticulously planned and carried out with dispatch, without encountering any resistance. At two o'clock in the morning of March 30, 1949 army units surrounded Damascus and entered the city. Within an hour they had occupied the centers of the civil government, the police and public services. President Shukrī Quwatlī, Prime Minister Khālid al-'Aẓm and the rest of the cabinet were arrested. In the morning "Communiqué No. 1" announced that the Army Command, "with its national devotion, . . . had been compelled to take the administration temporarily into its own hands," in order "to prepare the ground for true democratic government." The people were called upon to maintain order, while any attempt to resist would be "ruthlessly and immediately put down." Other proclamations

[5] Al-'Auf, 1–2; Muḥammad Kurd 'Alī, *Mudhakkirāt*, Damascus 1948–49, vol. 3, 905; Alfred Carleton, 'The Syrian coups d'état of 1949', *MEJ*, January 1950, 7–8; Lily Abegg, *Neue Herren im Mittelost*, Stuttgart 1954, 84; Wolfgang Bretholz, *Aufstand der Araber*, Wien 1960, 213; Moshe Zeltzer, *Aspects of Near East society*, New York 1962, 143; Patrick Seale, *The struggle for Syria*, London 1965, 43.

forbade the carrying of arms and imposed a curfew. At noon Za'īm held a press conference at which he promised to establish a new government of civilians and officers and to hold elections.[6]

The new regime soon developed into an open dictatorship. Early in April the Chamber of Deputies was dissolved and all legislative and executive authority was transferred to Za'īm. Ḥusnī Barāzī set up a new government, but on April 17 Za'īm assumed the premiership himself. All members of his cabinet were civilian but they had no real authority. In the first week of June, a law was promulgated providing for the election of a president, defining and extending his powers, and providing and calling for a referendum to approve the law. None of the members of the government had been consulted in its drafting.[7] The Communist Party was outlawed immediately after the coup while other political parties were dissolved on May 29. Needless to say, a referendum held on June 25 approved the Presidency Law and Za'īm, the only candidate, was duly elected. Ninety per cent of the electorate voted and of these, 99 per cent favored Za'īm. On the next day a new government under Ḥusnī Barāzī, comprising six civilians with Brigadier 'Abd-Allāh 'Aṭfa as Minister of Defense, took office. Za'īm invested himself with the rank of marshal—which had not existed previously in Syria. He soon began to display signs of megalomania. His personality and regime, which had at first enjoyed public favor, now became the butt of mockery and hatred.

A particularly bad impression was left on Syrian public opinion by his treatment of Auṭūn Sa'āda, the leader of the SSNP *(Syrian Social Nationalist Party)* known also as the PPS *(Parti Populaire Syrien)*. The SSNP, founded in 1932, advocated the establishment of a secular and totalitarian "Greater Syria," denying Syria's and Lebanon's Arabism and the ideas of Arab nationalism and unity in general. This well-organized party was one of the major political groups in Syria and Lebanon; Sa'āda himself was an ingenious leader and a prolific author.[8]

Sa'āda fled to Syria in June 1949 after an abortive coup in Lebanon. Za'īm at first received him as his personal guest, and then suddenly, on July 6, extradited him to Lebanon where he was executed two days later. Sa'āda had many opponents in Syria. The right wing hated him for his repudiation of Arabism, while the left fought him because of the explicit fascist character of his party. But Za'īm's breach of faith was denounced

[6] Al-'Auf, 15–35.

[7] Fatḥ-Allāh Mīkhā'īl Ṣaqqāl, *Min mudhakkirāt ḥukumat Za'īm,* Cairo 1952, 81.

[8] Labib Zuwiyya Yamak, *The ideological foundations, structure and organization of the Syrian Social Nationalist Party,* Ann Arbor, Mich., 1966, *passim*; Seale, 64–72.

generally as a betrayal of the Arab tradition of hospitality and asylum to the fugitive and also as a violation of modern international practice regarding political refugees. Indeed, Arab politicians looked at the affair in a somewhat personal light. Should they be threatened in their own countries with jail or the gallows and succeed in fleeing across the border into a neighboring country, they would like to rest assured that nothing would happen to them. As in Latin America, this is a type of life insurance for any leader or plotter. In view of the frequent and sharp fluctuations in Arab political life, it is vital to every Arab politician that the principle of political asylum remain sacrosanct.

His crimes and follies notwithstanding, Za'īm had his good qualities, too. He was the first of the Arab officer politicians to entertain plans for social reform. On the day before his death he said: "Give me five years and I will make Syria as prosperous and enlightened as Switzerland."[9] Two of the reforms he introduced proved to be of lasting value. He abolished the private administration of family waqfs—religious endowments, the revenues of which are allocated to the descendants of their founders—thereby removing a religious-juridical obstacle to the agrarian reforms which he envisaged. Also Syria was the first Arab country to grant the franchise to women. At first this right depended upon literacy; but before the space of a year was out, this restriction, too, had been removed. This was a decisive first step as it meant a break with Islamic tradition. Za'īm, who modelled himself upon Atatürk, hoped to separate Church and State. One plan which remained unrealized was to have personal documents stamped with Syrian nationality alone without religious-communal affiliation.[10]

The sympathy and support which Za'īm's policies of secularization could have secured in progressive circles were lost because of his foreign policies. His strong attachment to France led him to oppose Britain and her Arab sympathizers, Iraq and Jordan. At the same time he strengthened his ties with Egypt, Saudi Arabia and Turkey. On April 21, 1949 he flew to a meeting with King Fārūq. He invited Turkish officers to train and reorganize the Syrian army, as if the bitter quarrel over Alexandretta did not exist. He reinforced his ties with France with the ratification of a monetary agreement. It was even rumored that his intentions toward Israel differed from those of other Arab governments and that he wanted to settle the Arab refugees in Syria.[11] These reports might well have been circulated with libellous intent, as this is the usual charge of Arab leaders when reproaching political

[9] Ṣaqqāl, 145.
[10] *Ibid.,* 151.
[11] Yaacov Shimoni, 'Suria bein ha-hafikhoth', *Hamizrah Hehadash,* vol. I, 21–7.

opponents with treason, but it is quite possible that he did have unconventional ideas on this question. The power that stood to gain most from Za'īm's Syria was not France, the declining, traditional rival of Britain in the Middle East, but the United States, the rising power. In May 1949 an agreement was reached with the American Tapline Company, granting it the concession to construct its large-gauge pipeline from Saudi Arabia to the port of Sidon in Lebanon.[12]

Within a few weeks of his ascent there was hardly a person in Syria whom Za'īm had not offended. Conscious of the growing tide of resentment against him, he began to fear for his life. He was fully aware that others, too, could use the army to stage a coup. The main danger to his regime and policies came from Arab nationalist elements within the army. For this reason he began to rely increasingly on Kurdish and Circassian units which he stationed in the central region after dispatching Arab regiments to the Israeli border.[13] All these maneuvers were, however, to prove ineffective.

The commander of the First Brigade, which was stationed on the Israeli frontier, Brigadier Sāmī Ḥinnāwī, together with his officers, among whom were several Druze adherents to the SSNP, plotted Za'īm's downfall.[14] On August 14 at half past three in the morning, his residence was surrounded by armored cars of the First Brigade, and after a brief show of resistance his guards surrendered and he was arrested. Prime Minister Barāzī was taken into custody. Both were brought before a court-martial headed by Ḥinnāwī, sentenced to death and summarily executed. In their "Communiqué No. 1," the insurrectionists harangued Za'īm's presumption, viciousness, lawlessness and disregard for national tradition. As usual, the army swore "before God and history" to leave the administration of the country in due time to its civilian leaders.[15]

A new star had risen in the Syrian firmament. Ḥinnāwī was born in 1898 in Idlib in north-western Syria, of mixed Kurdish-Arab parentage. Like his predecessor he began his military career in the Ottoman army and later served in the Syrian gendarmerie and in the Special Forces of the French administration. In the Palestine War he was a colonel and commanded the brigade which captured Mishmar ha-Yarden and Tel-'Azīziyāt.

Ḥinnāwī introduced an innovation into the technique of military coups, which has since become standard practice: The establishment of a committee

[12] Benjamin Shwadran, *The Middle East, oil and the great powers,* New York 1955, 332–4.

[13] George Lenczowski, *The Middle East in world affairs,* Ithaca, N.Y., 1956, 296.

[14] Seale, 63–5.

[15] Aḥmad 'Isa al-Fīl, *Sūriya al-ḥadītha fī'l-inqilāb al-awwal wa'l-thānī,* Damascus 1949, 233.

of officers which constituted the supreme legislative, executive and judicial authority in the country. This committee constituted the outward expression and the quasi-constitutional legitimation of the military dictatorship. Prior to the Egyptian army coup of 1952 the term "revolution" was not yet fashionable. What was later called the "Revolutionary Command Council" was termed the "Supreme War Council." This Council, comprising ten members, was established on the day of the coup under the chairmanship of Ḥinnāwī, who was now Chief of the General Staff. The other members were a colorful crew:

Colonel Bāhīj Kallās, 42, a Christian from Hama, Za'īm's former Chief of Staff and his right-hand man;[16]

Colonel 'Alam al-Dīn Qawwāṣ, 41, an Alawi from Antakia in the Alexandretta region, who had served in the French Syrian army, had fought with the Vichy forces and in the Palestine War and was also a Freemason;[17]

Lieutenant-Colonel Amīn Abū-'Asāf, 34, a Druze, who played an important role in all Syrian coups in 1949. He had been wounded in Palestine in 1948. Still a captain in April 1949, within less than a year he had risen to the rank of brigadier;[18]

Captain Maḥmūd Rifā'ī, 36, from Damascus. In 1936 he was in Germany studying electrical, automotive and aeronautical engineering. From 1940 to 1945 he was a lieutenant in paratroop and commando units in the Hitlerite army, serving on the Russian and African fronts and in operations against partisans in Greece and Yugoslavia. He compiled German-Arabic military dictionaries and married a German. At the end of the war he was taken prisoner by the British but returned to Syria in 1946 and joined the air force with the rank of captain. On the outbreak of the Israel-Arab war he joined Qā'uqjī's "Liberation Army," serving as the commander's aide-de-camp. Subsequently he returned to the air force.[19]

The five other members of the "Supreme War Council" were Captains Khālid Jādah, Ḥasan al-Ḥakīm, Muḥammad Diyāb, Muḥammad Ma'arūf, and 'Iṣām Muraywid.[20]

On the day after the coup and the establishment of the Supreme War Council, a temporary civilian government was installed under the aged Hāshim Atāsī who had been President of the Syriān Republic from 1936 to 1939. Khālid al-'Aẓm, the Prime Minister who had been deposed by Za'īm,

[16] *Hamizrah Hehadash,* vol. I, 162; vol. 2, 159.

[17] *Man huwa fī Sūriya,* Damascus (1951), 624.

[18] *Man huwa,* 506–7; *Hamizrah,* vol. 1, 76, 316; *al-Jundī,* Damascus, 15 May 1949.

[19] *Man huwa,* 319–20.

[20] *Hamizrah,* vol. 1, 76, ; *al-Fīl,* 234.

that it had been "forced" to carry out a coup "out of concern for the integrity and peace of the country and for the preservation of the republican regime . . . that the army has no other purpose; and that it announces that it will leave the country's affairs in the hands of its legally elected personalities and will under no circumstances interfere in political matters." At this point a highly significant concluding statement was appended: The army "will under no circumstances interfere in political matters unless the integrity and survival of the country demand it."[24] In other words, the politicians could play politics as much as they liked but only on condition that their views did not differ from the opinions of the officer politician who at the moment happened to be "the army." And this held true while Shīshaklī was in power.

Adīb Shīshaklī was born at Hama in 1909 into a family of members of the liberal professions, some of whom had already been active in the Arab national movement in the Ottoman period. At the age of 20 he began serving in the French Syrian army. In 1948 he was a captain who commanded troops in Qā'uqjī's "Liberation Army" in eastern Upper Galilee. He returned a military failure but a hero in the mirror of Syrian propaganda. In the first coup he was one of Za'īm's assistants. Za'īm appointed him Inspector-General of Police and Public Security and promoted him to the rank of colonel. As time went on, Shīshaklī no longer saw eye to eye with Za'īm and was transferred to Aleppo as commander of the military district. He was particularly incensed against Za'īm for handing Anṭūn Sa'āda back to Lebanon. Shīshaklī had in the past been a member of the SSNP and was still interested in that party.[25] That is why he willingly joined the plot against Za'īm and played an important role in the second coup. Ḥinnāwī had appointed him commander of the First Brigade garrisoned in Damascus and with the help of this unit he later carried out the third coup.

One of the powers behind Shīshaklī in the coup was his cousin and friend from his home town, Akram Ḥawrānī. He, too, already had considerable experience in weaving plots and taking part in coups. His family had been well-to-do landowners from Hama, but while he was still a child, the money was squandered and they became poor. After this he became a bitter enemy of anyone of his own former social class who lived by exploiting the region's tenant farmers. The villagers of the Hama region were agriculturally the most advanced in Syria and socially the most exploited, and Ḥawrānī became the supporter and organizer of rebellions among them. In 1939 at the age of 25 he became leader of a group of young men from

[24] *Hazīmat tāghiya,* Damascus (1954?), 11.
[25] Abegg, 56; al-'Auf, 113; al-Fīl, 65.

Hama which was partly a youth movement and partly a band of mischief-makers hailing from prominent families. A number of them chose military careers and in the 1950's became central figures among Syrian officer politicians. Ḥawrānī studied law. In keeping with the fascist spirit of the times, these young men found expression for their anti-imperialism and anti-feudalism in the doctrines of Anṭūn Sa'āda. At first they apparently did not distinguish between this ideology and pan-Arab nationalism. In 1941 Ḥawrānī and several members of his group participated in Rashīd 'Ālī's rebellion in Iraq. On his return he was imprisoned for a time. In 1947 he entered the Chamber of Deputies as a socialist. In 1948 he fought in Palestine as a volunteer. In the spring of 1949 he supported Za'īm: He drew up the first communiqués of the coup on March 30.[26] On April 3 he was appointed a member of the "Committee for Investigating the Weak Points of the Previous Period."[27] Collaboration with Za'īm did not prevent Ḥawrānī, like many others, from serving Ḥinnāwī. In Atāsī's government, formed the day after the overthrow of Za'īm, he was Minister of Agriculture. When Ḥinnāwī's pro-Iraqi tendency became clear, Ḥawrānī placed himself at the head of the opposition and on December 17 presented the minority motion for the preservation of the republican regime. When this failed he began to plan the third coup together with Shīshaklī, in whose government he served as Minister of Defence.

Ḥawrānī not only survived Za'īm and Ḥinnāwī but also Shīshaklī. He was the only one of all the Syrian leaders, both civilian and military, who was always at the top in all the coups and changes which occurred in Syria between 1949 and 1962. Like a cat he always fell on his feet. In 1950 he founded the "Arab Socialist Party." At the end of 1953 it merged with the "Arab Renaissance Party", *al-Ba'th* (which means "reanissance") to form the "Arab Socialist Renaissance Party."

The Ba'th Party was founded in the early 1940's by Michel 'Aflaq and Ṣalāh al-Dīn al-Bayṭār. On April 5, 1949 'Aflaq, as president of his party, sent a letter to Za'īm promising his support. This was the first public statement from a Syrian party expressing satisfaction with the coup. Simultaneously, the letter stressed the need for "assuring the general freedoms defined in the constitution."[28] It was not long, however, before 'Aflaq turned to the opposition. Za'īm had him arrested and did not release him until he declared that he would stop his political activities. After Za'īm's downfall, 'Aflaq no longer considered himself bound by his declara-

[26] Seale, 18, 38–40; Gordon H. Torrey, *Syrian politics and the military,* 1945–1958, Ohio State University Press 1964, 104; al-Fīl, 33.

[27] Al-'Auf, 146.

[28] *Ibid.,* 163–4.

tion and joined Ḥinnāwī's government as Minister of Education. In the Constituent Assembly elections held in November 1949 the Ba'th suffered a serious defeat. The party put up only 10 candidates in the entire country, and only one was elected. 'Aflaq himself was defeated and resigned from the government, and his party joined the opposition. During Shīshaklī's regime they adopted a vigorous opposition stand from the very beginning.

Shīshaklī learned from the experience of his two predecessors that excessive concentration of power in the hands of one man and undue public prominence would only endanger his regime as well as his personal safety. To be arrested in his home at night would mean the overthrow of his whole government. He preferred to remain in the background and to assign the affairs of state and the army to others, thus making them partners interested in the regime's survival. He retained only the job of Deputy Chief of Staff, outwardly a modest position, dealing with the appointment and transfer of officers. Yet the journalist Ghassān Tuwaynī knew immediately how to analyze the new situation. On December 23, 1949 he wrote in the Beirut *al-Nahār*: "The third Syrian coup has further complicated the crisis in government . . . the first coup forced a certain regime on the state, the policies of which the army officially and openly directed. Then came the second coup and set up a government and left it to the people to decide freely who would promulgate the country's constitution and delineate its national policy. But this coup . . . has restricted the freedom of those elected by the people and has laid down a policy without its leaders or commanders being bound by any constitutional or pseudo-constitutional responsibility."[29] Shīshaklī wanted Atāsī as President and was in favor of establishing a parliamentary government; at the same time he demanded Ḥawrānī's appointment as Minister of Defense, if not Prime Minister, while the majority of deputies in the Constituent Assembly belonged to the People's Party whose leaders strongly opposed Ḥawrānī. As a result, a government came into being which was shaky from the outset.

After a week of feverish activity, a government headed by Khālid al-'Aẓm, the Prime Minister ousted by Za'īm's coup, was formed on December 27. The People's Party, the largest faction in the Assembly, yielded premiership, reconciled itself to Ḥawrānī's appointment as Minister of Defense, and contented itself with four out of ten ministers. The government managed to stay in office, despite constant internal crises, for a period of five months. At the end of May 1950 it resigned. A week later a government was formed under the leadership of Nāẓim al-Qudsī of the People's Party, to which most of the ministers belonged. The Minister of Defense was once again

[29] *Tuwaynī,* 53.

an army officer, Brigadier Fawzī Silū, one of Shīshaklī's men and obedient to him, though older and of higher military rank. In 1948 when Shīshaklī was still a captain, Silū was already a colonel. Za'īm promoted him to brigadier, and on becoming President, appointed him Chief of Staff. When Ḥawrānī was Minister of Defense, Silū (who was of Kurdish extraction) served as the Ministry's Director-General.

In the second half of 1950 the cohesiveness of the officer corps began to come apart. Shīshaklī's intentions were vague and rumors circulated that he had changed his views and become a supporter of union with Iraq. The Hashimite governments, especially Jordan, intensified their subversion in Syria, winning over several officers to their side. As the officers' confidence in each other diminished, the dictator's grip tightened. Transfers, dismissals, and court-martials on charges of conspiracy became more frequent. At the end of July 1950 the Commander-in-Chief of the Air Force, Colonel Mūḥammad Ḥasan Nāṣir, was murdered. The murderers were not found, but many were convinced that they were emissaries of Shīshaklī. Nāṣir had supported Za'īm and had been a follower of Shīshaklī but had quarreled with him. He was an Alawi, and the murder raised a storm in his community; they were in any event embittered by the dismissal of the Alawi Qawwāṣ, who had been one of the leaders of Ḥinnāwī's group. On October 11 there was an attempt to murder Shīshaklī. The attackers were ostensibly Palestinian and Syrian pan-Arab extremists from the Jerusalem Mufti's circle, and once again many officers and civilians were arrested. In 1951 the situation was chaotic. In theory a parliamentary regime existed, but only the negative aspects of parliamentarism could be seen. There was no majority party in the Chamber of Deputies, the numerous factions could not cooperate, and there was mistrust within each group. In practice the country was ruled by a military junta which was ridden with suspicion and intrigue. Prime Minister al-Qudsī, who tried to limit the army's influence, was compelled to admit failure and in March 1951 he resigned. A number of cabinets rose and fell in succession, and the regime increasingly became one of personal dictatorship.

In October 1951 the United States, Great Britain and France proposed that a joint Middle Eastern Command be formed, and that the countries of the region be enlisted on the side of the western bloc in the cold war. Political public opinion in the Arab world overwhelmingly rejected the plan as a low trick for renewed imperialist domination. They were strongly influenced by the stand taken by the Egyptian Wafd government which immediately rejected the proposal and reacted to the pressure of the western powers by abrogating the 1936 Anglo-Egyptian Treaty. In Syria, as usual, opinions were divided. In Ḥasan al-Ḥakīm's government an open dispute broke out, while public opinion on the whole was actively opposed to joining the western camp. Shīshaklī did not clarify his views. His inclination was unmistakably pro-western, but he did not wish to identify himself with the pro-western leaders of the People's Party since they were against army interference in domestic politics.

The tensions between the rival forces worsened when a dispute of another nature came to a head at that time: The Minister of the Interior, Rashād Barmada, demanded that the gendarmerie be transferred from the army's command to the authority of his ministry, as was the case with the police. The army, of course, did not agree and several left-wing circles were against this move. Since the days of the French Mandate the gendarmerie had been organized along military lines as a mobile unit equipped with machine guns and armored cars.

The mounting social ferment in a number of rural areas lay behind the dispute over the gendarmerie. In the districts of Homs and Hama there had been uprisings of landless peasants and tenant farmers in 1951. They had refused to pay rent to the landlords and demanded that the land be distributed among the villagers who worked it. One of the major supporters of this movement had been Akram Ḥawrānī, whose influence centered at Hama. He probably hoped that his alliance with the improverished peasants would enable him to take revenge on feudal adversaries in his election district and would win him support among peasants, workers and intellectuals in the entire country. At about this time closer ties were established between his party and 'Aflaq's Ba'th, and the groundwork was laid for the union of 1953. The landlords, whose principal representatives in Parliament were the People's Party, sought to transfer the gendarmerie to the Ministry of the Interior and to use them in suppressing the peasants. The army officer corps, which was permeated with anti-feudal influences, was not considered loyal enough for this.

On November 10, 1951 Ḥasan al-Ḥakīm resigned, and for nearly three weeks the government crisis remained unresolved. On November 28 President Atāsī made a bold and desperate effort to resolve the impasse by appointing Ma'rūf Dawalībī to head a government whose members belonged mainly to the People's Party and who were known for their determination to put an end to army interference.

The reverse happened. Less than twelve hours after the new government was established, the ministers were imprisoned. Syria experienced its fourth coup d'état—the second by Shīshaklī. On November 29, 1951 a new "Communiqué Number 1" was issued, concise and crude this time with no flowery phrases about the return of the army to barracks nor about freedoms and a constitution. "The leadership of the General Staff informs the honored Syrian people that the army has assumed control of the country's security and requests the population to preserve peace and quiet, make the army's task easier, and keep track of its activities without fear or excitement; and anyone who will be misled into undermining security is warned against the strictest retaliation."[30] It was signed by Shīshaklī as Chief of Staff. Within a few days the President resigned, Parliament was dissolved, and Silū appointed President and Prime Minister.

Although Shīshaklī ruled absolute, some of his earliest measures included a number of social and economic reforms. Taxes on high incomes were increased and some indirect taxes reduced. State lands, which landlords had taken possession of illegally, were to be returned to public ownership and distributed among landless peasants. These reforms had been on the agenda for a long time but the People's Party had prevented their implementation. When the party was eliminated from power, Shīshaklī grasped at these reforms as an open valve to strong social ferment. In the winter of 1950–1951 there was drought, the 1951 crop was low, and by autumn the peasants' bitterness had reached the point of rebellion. By means of social reform Shīshaklī wanted to gain sympathizers and supporters among the leaders of the parties competing with the People's Party. At first he actually succeeded. Ḥawrānī's Arab Socialist Party gave Shīshaklī its full support in December. 'Aflaq's Ba'th followed in its footsteps, albeit with reservations. However, at the beginning of 1952, when both Shīshaklī's western orientation and the dictatorial nature of his regime had become apparent, the two parties changed their position. The Ba'th united its dissident factions and became one of the most outspoken opponents of the dictator.

After outlawing all political parties in April 1952, Shīshaklī founded the "Arab Liberation Movement" as a tool of power. In July 1953 a referendum approved the presidency of Shīshaklī as well as a new constitution which granted the President wide powers. By means of pressure and falsification the participation of 87 per cent of the electorate was secured, and of these more than 99 per cent voted "yes". But the fact that the regime was based only upon the brutal force of the army escaped no one: Shīshaklī constantly stepped up the reign of terror. Hundreds of people were arrested and tortured for subversion and attempts to organize conspiracies. There is no telling which or how many of these attempts were real. However, Shishaklī could not harm his strongest opponents who were the leaders of the outlawed parties. These men met on July 4, 1953 at Homs, the seat of the Atāsī family's power, where they signed a National Pact to overthrow

[30] *Hazīma*, 24.

the dictator. The signatories included the leaders of nearly all parties and trends.[31]

In October 1953 elections to the Chamber of Deputies were held in accordance with the new constitution and the winners were naturally the candidates favored by Shīshaklī; but the ballot was quite scanty. In Damascus and Aleppo less than 20 per cent of the electorate voted and official figures were not published. This passive restistance became active several weeks later.

It began with a trifle: At the beginning of December a play was presented at the American Secondary School in Aleppo which one of the students regarded as being offensive to Arab honor. This set off a chain of events, beginning with a demonstration, followed by a clash with the police, a students' strike, solidarity demonstrations in Damascus, the closing of schools, more clashes in Damascus, then a solidarity strike of lawyers. In the general upheaval and in the face of government intransigence, the play incident was like a stone thrown into the water which led to the formation of waves of unrest expanding in all directions. At the end of January 1954 a number of political leaders were detained and two were placed under house arrest: These were the former President of the Republic, the octogenarian Hāshim Atāsī, and Sulṭān al-Aṭrash, the leader of the Druze and hero of the anti-French revolt of the 1920's. The Druze on their mountain forcibly opposed the implementation of the order, and when troops were sent against them, rose up in a general insurrection. Martial law was proclaimed in most Syrian districts. In the Druze Mountain area the army acted in full force and with much cruelty. Villages were shelled and bombed from the air; less than a hundred soldiers and Druze fighters fell in battle but hundreds of civilians were killed.

Shīshaklī's regime came to an end in February 1954.[32] As he had risen, so he fell—by military coup. While he concentrated on the campaign against the Druze in the south, army units stationed in the north mutinied. On the morning of February 25, 1954, Colonel Fayṣal Atāsī, Chief of Military Operations in the Aleppo area, arrested his superior, Brigadier 'Umar Tamar-Khān, and assumed command himself. At the same time he proclaimed that he no longer recognized the authorities in Damascus. He was soon joined by troops stationed in the Jazira, bordering Iraq, under the command of Amīn Abu-'Asāf, and by units in the central area, under Maḥmūd Shawkat. At noon that day Muṣṭafā Ḥamdūn broadcast over Aleppo Radio that the army in the north had dissociated itself from

[31] Seale, 134.

[32] *Ibid.*, 141–143; Torrey, 241–4.

Damascus for as long as Shīshaklī stayed in power. In the afternoon the officer in command of the troops on the Druze Mountain, Lieutenant-Colonel 'Umar Qabbānī, joined the rebels. Only the troops in Damascus still took orders from Shīshaklī, but he could not trust them. Shawkat Shuqayr, the Chief of Staff, at first remained loyal, but his qualms soon became evident. Shīshaklī surveyed the situation, found it hopeless and announced his resignation. That same day he left for Beirut and two days later he was granted political asylum by King Sa'ūd. In 1960 he emigrated to Brazil where he became the owner of a rice plantation. He was assassinated by a Syrian Druze on September 27, 1964.

After Shīshaklī's flight some members of his entourage tried to save the regime and their own position on the pretext that it was the President only who had resigned. At their head was Dr. Ma'mūn Kuzbarī, Speaker in Shīshkalī's Chamber of Deputies, who proclaimed himself Acting President. But their effort was doomed from the outset. In the streets of Damascus demonstrations were already in progress against Shīshaklī and his collaborators, and in a series of clashes more than 30 people were killed.[33] Shawkat Shuqayr had in the meantime gone over to the rebels and Kuzbarī's presidency came to an end within two days.

On February 27 at Homs, Shuqayr met the seven members of the "Provisional Army Council" headed by Maḥmūd Shawkat, and on the following morning Shawkat made the following announcement over Damascus Radio:

"In view of the fact that the circumstances preventing the continuation of the legitimate Government and the exercise of the powers of His Excellency, the President of the Republic, Mr. Hāshim Atāsī, no longer exist, the leadership of the General Staff of the Syrian Army announces that the legal situation has been restored and that the Army, which is the army of the nation and the defender of the honor of the State, has returned to its barracks, in order to carry out its duties as set forth in the Constitution, and places itself at the disposal of the administration of the President of the Republic and the legal Government."[34]

This proclamation was unprecedented in the annals of modern Arab countries: Military leaders who had just seized power declared their intention to hand over the reins of government to elected civilian political leaders, and not "in due course" but immediately, and moreover, actually did so! On the same day political leaders met at Homs and resolved to regard as null and void all legislative measures adopted from the date of

[33] *Keesing's Contemporary Record,* London 1954, 13463.

[34] *Hazīma*, 101.

Shīshaklī's coup in November 1951. Atāsī was restored to the presidency and a decision was taken to hold general elections within a period of three months. In March 1954, after five years of successive military dictatorships, parliamentary government was restored. It lasted for four years, until, at the beginning of 1958 political leaders again placed the government in the hands of soldiers—the architects of the union with Egypt.

After Shīshaklī's fall Syria was no longer the country it had been before Za'īm rose to power. The vicissitudes of government had been of a transitory nature, leaving only a few scars on the body politic, and the major changes which had meanwhile occurred had little to do with the rise and fall of military regimes.

The biggest change was in the economic life of the country which brought Syria substantial prosperity and economic expansion. In the early fifties Syria was the only Arab country in which the rate of agricultural and industrial output was considerably higher than the increasing rate of population. The following table reflects the advance registered in major branches of the Syrian economy:[35]

AREA AND PRODUCTION OF SELECTED PRODUCTS IN SYRIA
(Thousands of hectares and thousands of metric tons)

		1945	1950	1954	1955	1956
Area	Wheat	750	992	1314	1463	1531
	Barley	348	416	543	614	712
	Cotton	18	78	187	249	272
Production	Wheat	415	830	965	438	1051
	Barley	248	322	635	137	462
	Cotton (ginned)	4	36	80	84	93
	Cotton yarn	1.7	5.5	6.9	7.8	8.0
	Cement		68	249	265	325
	Sugar		8	36	45	50

(1955 was a year of severe drought)

Virtually the only important measure in economic affairs taken by the military governments of 1949-54 was the abrogation, in March 1950, of the customs union with Lebanon. The union had proved to be favorable only for the Lebanese economy which thrived on free trade. It had prevented the granting of adequate protection to Syria's expanding industry. Most economic expansion in Syria in this period, in agriculture as well as in

[35] United Nations, Department of Economic and Social Affairs, *Economic developments in the Middle East,* 1945 to 1954, New York 1955, 183; *Economic developments in the Middle East,* 1956–1957, New York 1958, 87–90, 116–7.

industry, was the fruit of private enterprise. Merchants who had amassed wealth during the Second World War invested considerably in both light industry and agriculture. By purchase or lease they acquired hundreds of thousands of dunams in the north-east of the country where the annual precipitation fluctuates between 200 and 400 millimeters. For centuries these areas had been grazing land for Bedouin herds; now they were brought under mechanized extensive cultivation for grain-growing. Because of the nature of the area, however, cultivation has assumed a speculative character. Problems of maintaining the natural fertility of the soil also arose, for cultivation now exposed it to wind erosion. In the second half of the 'fifties the pace of economic expansion slowed down, but on the whole previous achievements were retained. The large sums invested came, as stated, largely from private sources with public investment constituting in 1950–1956 less than one-third, and sometimes less than one-quarter of the total sum invested in the national economy.

Economic prosperity and the strengthening of the modern capitalistic sector in both agriculture and industry intensified the class struggle. In town and country the class consciousness of the proletariat grew stronger, and within the context of the political ferment in the Arab world it gave birth to many odd organizational and ideological combinations. During the period of Shīshaklī's rule extremist parties grew in membership and influence, especially the SSNP and the Ba'th. Under the dictatorship the aggressive opposition and vocal radicalism of these two parties were enough to win them strong influence.

The Ba'th firmly established itself within the officer corps in this period, partly because many of Ḥawrānī's followers from Hama joined the army.

A new type now appeared on the public stage—the party officer politician. A large number of officers began to engage in politics, not as individuals or members of officers' groups inspired by more or less nebulous political ideas and prompted by personal ambitions, but as overt or covert members of political parties. Most of the officers who owe allegiance to a party are not organized members but rather sympathizers. But even officers who are organized members of political parties must not be regarded as representatives of their respective parties in the army who carry out the party's orders obediently. If the officer politicians possess one trait in common, it is their lack of discipline. The principle of loyalty and discipline, which is basic to their profession as soldiers, took on a distorted, relativistic character. They believe themselves entitled to exact blind obedience from their subordinates without being obliged to obey their superiors in matters where they differ politically. This relativism determines their attitude not only toward the supreme authority of the army and the state but also toward the institutions and leaders of the parties to which they belong. Party affiliations also vitiate the capacity of the officer corps to operate as a corporate entity, for its members owe allegiance to rival groups and parties. Syrian officer politicians could combine to bring about the fall of Shīshaklī but they were incapable of creating an effective and stable officer administration to replace him. This may have been one of the reasons why they preferred to hand over the responsibility of government to parliamentary leaders.

The officers who headed the insurrection against Shīshaklī can be grouped into three main political factions: pro-Iraqis, Ba'thists, and members of the SSNP. Fayṣal Atāsī can be regarded as representing the pro-Iraqi orientation. On the day before the insurrection he was in Beirut where he met the Iraqi military attaché. In 1956, too, Baghdad regarded him as an ally.[36] Amīn Abū-'Asāf was also pro-Iraqi and, moreover, in command of the area bordering Iraq. He was active in all the regimes in Syria established by military coups but played his most important role when Ḥinnāwī consolidated his policy of rapprochement with Iraq. His transfer to Jazira when Shīshaklī was in power was actually a demotion.

Two members of the Provisional Military Council during the insurrection against Shīshaklī belonged to the Ba'th—Muṣṭafa Ḥamdūn, and 'Adnān Māliki. Both were to play prominent roles in future events in Syria.

The SSNP representative in the group which expelled Shīshaklī was Ghassān Jadīd. More will be told of him later.

Although they worked together against Shīshaklī in February 1954, these officers realized that they could not maintain this unity to govern the country. The politization of the officer corps inevitably led to political diversity and, consequently to the attenuation of its political influence. Military dictatorship had reduced itself to an absurdity.

But the officers had no intention of returning passively to barracks and refraining from intervention in politics. Their lust for power was too strong. Constantly before them was the impressive example of officer administration in Egypt which, at the time of Shīshaklī's fall, had already achieved stability and whose prestige was rising steadily throughout the Arab world. And the Ba'thist officers received more from Cairo than moral encouragement alone.

Essentially, the excessive politization of the Syrian officer corps reflected general conditions in the country. Syria is a country of extreme diversity in its natural features, in the composition of its population, and in its economic and intellectual life. Syrians do not tend toward conformism and their

[36] *Maḥkamat al-sha'b,* vol. 1, Baghdad 1959, 291, 299.

public life has always been alert and animated. It has been said with considerable justification that whoever rules in Cairo rules Egypt; however, he who rules Damascus does not necessarily rule Aleppo or the Druze Mountain, the plains of Jazira or the Alawi Mountain. Syria's diversity can be her blessing, but it also can be her bane. In all events centralized, uniform government on a narrow basis, however strong it may be, cannot hope to endure in Syria. Shīshaklī learned this lesson in 1954. So did Nasser in 1961.

5. THE FREE OFFICERS' MOVEMENT IN EGYPT

THE EGYPTIAN coup of July 1952 differed in several respects from the previous coups in Iraq and Syria: It has established for an extended period a stable government unparalleled in the present-day Middle East; the new Egyptian regime, unlike the previous officer governments in Iraq and Syria, has implemented permanent social change; it has raised the status of Egypt in the Middle East and the rest of the world. In the preparations which preceded it as well as in its achievements, and the nature of the men who brought it about, the Egyptian coup was a new phenomenon. It was the work of a secret political society where the members were all officers of medium and low rank.

When Bakr Ṣidqī carried out his coup in 1936 he was a brigadier and Acting Chief of Staff; the Seven who got rid of Bakr Ṣidqī in 1937 had the support of the commanders of two of the four Iraqi divisions; in December 1938 when he overthrew al-Madfa'ī's government, Ṣabbāgh was Chief of Operations on the General Staff, and the members of his group held other key positions in the army; Ḥusnī Za'īm was Chief of Staff in 1949; Ḥinnāwī was a brigadier in August 1949, the commander of an armored brigade and actually an emissary of the General Staff; Shīshaklī in December 1949 was a member of the General Staff and commander of an armored brigade. However, the members of the Egyptian Free Officers' Association were either lieutenant-colonels or majors in July 1952; only one of them was a colonel and commander of an infantry battalion. The one exception was Naguib, a major-general, but though close to the Association, he was not a member. All the Iraqi and Syrian officers listed above were born before 1900 and grew to young manhood in the Ottoman period. The Egyptian Free Officers were members of another generation, all of them born between 1917 and 1922. Naguib, born in 1901, and Shīshaklī, born in 1909, fall between the two generations.

The biggest difference between the Egyptian officers and those who organized previous coups in Iraq and Syria is in the movement's organizational structure. To understand this one must go back to the period of World War II and even before it.

The principal source describing the early phases of this movement are the memoirs of Anwar Sādāt in which truth and fantasy intermingle.

Sādāt established an exact date and place for the movement's founding[1]—the night before January 15, 1939 at Jabal Sharīf near Manqabād in Upper Egypt. At the time there were four second-lieutenants serving in the large garrison who had been accepted at the Military Academy in the spring of 1937 and had been commissioned in the fall of 1938: Ṣādāt, Jamāl 'Abd al-Nāṣir (Nasser), Zakariyyā Muḥi al-Dīn, and Aḥmad Anwar (who became commandant of the military police after the 1952 coup and ambassador to Spain in the 1960's). It was Nasser's 21st birthday. Sādāt relates: "At the beginning of 1939 the officers of Manqabād founded a secret revolutionary society dedicated to the task of liberation." Its members resolved to "fight imperialism, monarchy and feudalism . . . to establish a strong and free democracy . . . The way lies before us—revolution."

The young officers probably threw a party in honor of their comrade's birthday and also discussed politics. What was said of Egyptian youth after the war also applied to these young men in the period preceding it: "When no organizations for cultural and recreational purposes had yet been established, nor clubs where young people of both sexes could meet, participate in discussions, and take an interest in music and motion pictures, Egyptian youth seeking distraction from its immediate preoccupations were confined by their intellectual and material conditions . . . solely to the stormy domain of politics."[2]

At least one of the second-lieutenants at Manqabād was not new to politics. Nasser already had a past rich in intensive activity in political organizations and among his classmates in high school. His name was mentioned in the press when he was 17: In November 1935 he participated in a stormy anti-British demonstration in Cairo and was wounded in the forehead by a British police officer's pistol bullet.[3] At this time, by his own admission, he was a member of Miṣr al Fātāt ("Young Egypt"), the greenshirted fascist party. Its 1933 platform defined "our aim: To put Egypt above everything, a mighty empire comprising Egypt and Sudan, in an alliance with the Arab states and leading Islam."[4] In the "Ten Commandments" of 1938 a member is obliged, among other things, "only to buy

[1] Anwar El-Sadat, *Revolt on the Nile,* London 1957, 13–14; Georges Vaucher, *Gamal Abdel Nasser et son équipe,* Paris 1959, 109.

[2] Raoul Makarius, *La jeunesse intellectuelle d'Egypte au lendemain de la deuxième guerre mondiale,* Paris-La Haye 1960, 9.

[3] *Al-Jihād,* Cairo, 14 November 1935; *Ākhir sā'a,* Cairo, 10 March 1965.

[4] *The Sunday Times,* London, 17 June 1962 (interview); Nasser's speech at Helwan, *al-Ahrām,* Cairo, 20 November 1965.

from an Egyptian, only to wear what was made in Egypt, and only eat Egyptian food . . . Scorn what is alien with all your soul and be zealous in your nationalism to madness!"[5] It may be assumed that the conversations of the young officers at Manqabād were conducted in this spirit and that they all shared the same views.

Sādāt describes the conversation at Manqabād as if in 1939 the group were already advocating the exact slogans of official Egyptian ideology of 1955. Hatred of the British and imperialism no doubt also existed then but there was no anti-monarchist ideology. Even in January 1952 the Free Officers did not yet display any sign of this. In 1939 young Fārūq was still the adored symbol of nationalist Egyptian youth, and it was not "a free, strong democracy" which was their goal. In the 1930's, it may be recalled, the term "democracy" was a word of opprobrium in the dictionary of every movement under any fascist influence whatsoever.

The young men who met at Manqabād were dispersed to various posts in Egypt and Sudan. Nasser was transferred to Khartoum where he met 'Abd al-Ḥakīm 'Āmir and the two became friends. They had known each other previously when 'Abd al-Ḥakīm had been a cadet at the Military Academy in the class after Nasser's and for a time Nasser had been his instructor.[6]

That group of lieutenants was not then unique in the Egyptian army nor the most active. It was not organized and engaged in no concrete activities. It is important only as one of the chapters in the prehistory of the Free Officers. During World War II only the group of 'Azīz al-Maṣrī and the pro-German underground were conspicuous and active. The link between them was Anwar Sādāt.

After the defeats and failure of the insurrectionist officers in Iraq and Egypt who had linked their movements with Nazi Germany and the frustration of their hopes in a German victory, the rebellious movements in the Arab armies experienced lean years. Nevertheless, the officers continued to foster their political ideas and contacts.

Of these ties, those with the Muslim Brethren grew in importance parallel to the steady rise of the Brethren's influence during the 1940's. Here, too, the chief contact man was Sādāt, the versatile conspirator par excellence. He relates[7] that he met the Brethren's leader, Ḥasan al-Bannā, for the first time when he was establishing connections with 'Azīz al-Maṣrī, at a celebration of the Prophet's birthday at the beginning of April 1941. The con-

[5] J. Heyworth-Dunne, *Religious and political trends in modern Egypt,* Washington, D.C., 1950, 104; *al-Ṭalī'a,* Cairo, No. 3, 155–8.

[6] Vaucher, 93.

[7] Sadat, 26–8.

nections continued from that time until Sādāt's arrest in the summer of 1942. While Sādāt was in prison, his place as contact man with the Muslim Brethren was taken by 'Abd al-Mun'im 'Abd al-Ra'ūf, the pilot who tried to desert together with al-Maṣrī and was arrested and also released with him in the spring of 1942, when he gave his word of honor that he would cease his subversive activities. 'Abd al-Ra'ūf became increasingly interested in the Brethren until he identified himself with them completely both ideologically and organizationally. He may have been influenced through being the scion of a family known for its devoutness to Islam; his grandfather had been a shaykh at al-Azhar.[8] He was one of the founders of the terrorist "Secret Organization" of the Muslim Brethren[9] and one of its three commanders at the beginning of the 1950's.[10]

Between 1945 and 1947 most of the officers who were later to become members of the Executive Committee of the Free Officers' Association served in various units in the vicinity of Cairo. They maintained close ties, exchanged views and gained adherents among their comrades. During this period more officers became interested in or joined Nasser's group, including Kamāl al-Dīn Ḥusayn, an artillery lieutenant and former member of the Muslim Brethren;[11] Ṣalāḥ Sālim, an infantry captain, a talented young fanatic who in a short time became one of the central figures in the group; Tharwat 'Ukāsha, a captain in the Armored Corps and a brother-in-law of Aḥmad Abū al-Fatḥ, editor of the Wafd daily *al-Miṣrī*;[12] Khālid Muḥī al-Dīn, a lieutenant in the Armored Corps and Zakariyyā Muḥī al-Dīn's young cousin, a socialist and later a member of the communist HADITU *(Democratic Movement for National Liberation)*.[13] Sādāt also became active again. In November 1944 he succeeded in escaping from detention camp, hid for a while and then appeared openly without fear of arrest. In 1945 he worked as a truck driver, held a job as a newspaperman, served once again as contact man between the officers and the Muslim Brethren and participated in terrorist activities. While his part in the murder of Amīn 'Uthmān on January 5, 1946, is not completely clear, it is known that he played a major role in it. Several days later he was again arrested and remained in prison until the end of 1948.[14]

[8] Ishak Musa Husaini, *The Moslem Brethren*, Beirut 1956, 105.

[9] Kamāl Kīra, *Maḥkamat al-sha'b*, Vol. 1, Cairo (1955), 48.

[10] *Ibid.*, 72.

[11] P.J. Vatikiotis, *The Egyptian army in politics*, Bloomington 1961, 48; J. and S. Lacouture, *Egypt in transition*, London 1958, 135.

[12] Ahmed Abul-Fath, *L'affaire Nasser*, Paris 1962, 2; Arabic: Aḥmad Abū al-Fatḥ, *Jamāl 'Abd al-Nāṣir*, Beirut, (1962), 9.

[13] Walter Z. Laqueur, *Communism and nationalism in the Middle East*, New York 1956, 48.

[14] *Ibid.*, 135; Robert St. John, *The Boss*, New York 1960, 55–6; *al-Ahrām*, 3 December 1947.

The Palestine War had a profound influence on the ideas of these young officers. The aims of the war, the prevention of the establishment of a Jewish state and the conquest of existing areas of Jewish settlement were unqualifiedly supported by them. Five years later, Nasser wrote in the *Philosophy of the Revolution,* citing Aḥmad 'Abd al-'Azīz, commander of the Egyptian volunteers in Palestine, that "the biggest battlefield is in Egypt."[15] However, these words are not to be construed as implying reservations about fighting the Zionists. 'Abd al-'Azīz meant that the most dangerous enemy of the Egyptian army was the rotten regime at home and that triumphing over Egypt's internal weakness was a prerequisite for conquering the Jewish foe—and that is what Nasser understood him to mean. Their hatred of Israel is in itself beyond doubt. On May 15, 1948 there was no one among them who, even in his heart of hearts, denounced Fārūq for ordering them to war. On the contrary, some of the officers wanted to volunteer for Qā'uqjī's "Liberation Army" five months earlier, and if it occurred to them to violate discipline, it was only to make Egyptian manpower and equipment available to the Arab fighters before Egypt's official intervention. When Nasser emphasizes that the principal battle is in Egypt itself and simultaneously boasts of his comrades' volunteering even before May 1948 and of their bravery in the war, there is no contradiction in his statements.

Baghdādī relates that he was sent on an official mission to Damascus in a military airplane in the winter of 1947–48 and there he contacted Qā'uqjī. "I saw it as my duty as an Arab that we should do something for the future of Arabism and the liberation of Palestine."[16] Together with Ḥasan Ibrāhīm he planned the organization of an air force under Qā'uqjī's command to consist of 15 Spitfires and three Dakotas. They hoped to enlist pilots among their comrades of 1941–42. At the same time, Nasser offered his services and those of his friends to the Mufti who was then living in Cairo.[17] However, the Mufti refused to accept Egyptian officers without the approval of their government.

A number of Egyptian officers requested permission from the Minister of War to volunteer. On April 20, 1948 they were granted leave from the army to volunteer for Palestine. The group consisted of 11 officers headed by Aḥmad 'Abd al-Azīz; his title was "General Commander of the Volunteer Forces on the Southern Palestine Front." He was then 40 years old, one of the

[15] Jamāl 'Abd al-Nāṣir, *Falsafat al-thawra,* 10th impression, Cairo n.d. (1954?), 13; Gamal Abdul Nasser, *Egypt's liberation,* Washington, D.C., 1955, 22.

[16] 'Abd al-Laṭīf Baghdādī, 'Mā qabl al-ḍubbāṭ al-aḥrār', in: *Hādhihi al-thawra,* Cairo 1953, 188–9.

[17] Nasser, English, 91; Arabic, 63–4.

most popular and talented of the Egyptian officers with much influence over his students at the school for battalion commanders where he taught military history. On August 23, 1948, he was shot to death erroneously by an Arab sentry near Gath while traveling from Beersheba to Migdal-Ashkalon. It was he who said "The biggest battlefield is in Egypt"; apparently while he was in Palestine his eyes opened and he became aware of the corruption in Cairo. However, until he went off to war there is no trace, either in his acts or his letters, of any opposition sentiment. The Free Officers, who admired him and after his death held him up as a model patriot and soldier, would certainly not have omitted revelations of his interest in their ideas, if there had been any. He was of an aristocratic family, the son of an army brigadier, and until the spring of 1948 had no quarrel with the regime in which he lived and under which he had achieved success.[18]

The only person from Nasser's and Sādāt's circle who was in Aḥmad 'Abd al-'Azīz's group was Kamāl al-Dīn Husayn, then a captain. He commanded the artillery of the Egyptian volunteers.

The rest of Nasser's comrades did not stand out and did not even want to be conspicuous in the spring of 1948. Nasser tells in his memoirs that in April 1948, an attempt was made to carry out a military coup, and the political police kept suspected officers under surveillance. To allay suspicion they met infrequently.[19]

On May 15, 1948, Nasser, 'Āmir, Ṣalāḥ Sālim, Zakariyyā Muḥī al-Dīn and others of their friends were sent to the front. The lieutenants of 1939 were now captains and majors. In 1949 when these officers returned from the war, they were not the same men that had left. Their opinions had not changed but had become intensified. Their self-confidence had increased and their criticism of the regime had grown. On their return to Cairo, they were received as victors, though in their hearts they were not taken in by the hypocrisy of the victory celebrations for they knew that the Egyptian army had been defeated. But they considered themselves heroes. At Negba and Faluja they had realized that the force which is conscious of its mission is the one which triumphs. Their inability to capture Negba did not prevent them from thinking about taking the capital Cairo but rather spurred them on to do so.

In the summer of 1949 the idea of founding a secret revolutionary organization ripened. This turn of events was certainly influenced by the military coups taking place in Syria during these months. By the end of

[18] Abū al-Ḥajjāj Ḥāfiẓ, *Al-Baṭal Aḥmad 'Abd al-'Azīz,* Cairo 1961, 82, 183 ff; Muḥammad 'Abd al-'Azīz al-Batshatī, *Shuhadā'unā al-ḍubbāṭ fī ḥamlat Falasṭīn,* Cairo 1949, 12–9.
[19] *Ākhir sā'a,* 9 March 1955.

1949 the Free Officers' Association was organized. Until then it had existed only as an amorphous movement; from now on it operated as an organized body. Between 1949 and 1952 the Free Officers were not the only group of its kind in the Egyptian officer corps. But after it succeeded everyone was interested in stressing its importance only: Its own members tried to consign other groups to oblivion and members of other organizations tried to appear a posteriori as if they had hardly differed from those who had in the meantime become the masters of the country. In fact the distinctions between the various groups were blurred. Each consisted of a nucleus surrounded by a periphery, and a number of officers were in touch with more than one group.

The largest of these groups was ostensibly the officers' organization of the Muslim Brethren. It was headed by Maḥmud Labīb, "General Agent of the Muslim Brethren for Military Affairs." He also commanded the Brethern's terrorist "Secret Organization."[20] These two fields of activity were interrelated. Labīb was no longer on active army service, hence in 1948 he could be styled "General Commander of the Muslim Brethren Battalions for Saving Palestine."[21] He died in December 1951. The identity of most of the officers in the Muslim Brethren remains secret. They showed no interest in revealing themselves either during Fārūq's reign or under Nasser's regime.

Anwar Sādāt also headed a group of his own.[22] Like Labīb he was not on active service at the time—he was re-accepted only in 1950. However, he continued to maintain ties with his fellow officers, including Nasser and 'Azīz al-Maṣrī, as well as with the Muslim Brethren. Eventually his group merged with the Free Officers' Association.

Yet another group was that of Captain Muṣṭafā Kamāl Ṣidqī of the Armored Corps, the fourth husband of the dancer, Taḥīyya Karyūkā.[23] Sādāt writes that his was "a terrorist group of 23 officers and NCO's which was extremely active."[24] Ṣidqī served in intelligence in 1946 and 1947. At the beginning of 1948 he joined the volunteers in Palestine,[25] apparently with the Muslim Brethren. He was involved or suspected of being implicated in many of the political assassinations that took place between 1948 and 1952. In 1949 he was sentenced by court-martial to seven years' imprison-

[20] Kāmil Sharīf, *Al-Ikhwān al-muslimūn fī ḥarb Falasṭīn,* Cairo 1951, 198–9; Kīra, 33, 139; Husaini, 173–4.

[21] *Al-Ahrām,* 20 December 1951.

[22] Keith Wheelock, *Nasser's new Egypt,* London 1960, 5.

[23] Lacouture, 142.

[24] Sadat, 74.

[25] *Al-Ahrām,* 10 January 1952.

ment and cashiered from the army for the illegal possession of arms and explosives. Some time later he was amnestied by the King and returned to the army; it was rumored that Fārūq had succeeded in winning over Ṣidqī and his men for his "Iron Guard."[26] In April 1951 he was severely reprimanded for attacking the Chief of Staff in the press and was transferred from the Armored Corps to the Frontier Force at El Arish, and later to an oasis which he was forbidden to leave without a special permit. In August 1954 after the officers' accession to power, he was sentenced to five years' imprisonment on the charge of communism.[27] This adventurer had established ties everywhere.

Opposition sentiment among young Egyptian officers came to light in a conversation that took place on June 14, 1948 between a young Egyptian officer and the writer. Although the circumstances were unusual—the officer had been taken prisoner three days earlier by Israeli troops near 'Aslūj—the Egyptian could express himself frankly, voicing vehement anti-Israel opinions as well as extreme anti-government views on Egyptian affairs. The contents of the conversation were written down by the writer immediately afterwards partly verbatim. Thus these statements can be considered contemporary testimony which cannot be said for most material about that period; what is available is retrospective, and thus objectively and subjectively biased.

The officer was Second-Lieutenant Muḥammad Aḥmad Ḥasan of the First Battalion of Anti-tank Artillery, the 25-year-old son of a Cairo police officer. He called himself an adherent of the extreme right. In 1947 he was placed under arrest for a month under suspicion of participating in the attacks on the life of Naḥḥās. By order of the King, he was later released with several other officer suspects. He did not say whether or not there was any justification in the charge; at any rate, in principle he did not mind acts of individual terror against leaders who were thought to be pro-British. On his reputed ties with terrorist extremists he spoke with some pride, adding that he knew Amīn 'Uthmān's assassin. Amīn 'Uthmān who had been a former Minister of Finance, a Wafdist, pro-British in the extreme, was murdered on January 5, 1946. One of the arrested suspects was Anwar Sādāt. The murderer, Ḥusayn Tawfīq, was sentenced in 1947 to life imprisonment; at the end of June 1948, two weeks after the conversation described, he escaped from prison. In 1956, after years of exile in Jordan, he returned to Egypt and got a job in the General Petroleum Organization. In August 1966 he was once again sentenced to life imprisonment, this time

[26] Sadat, 96.

[27] Laqueur, 48, 315; Mohammed Naguib, *Egypt's destiny,* New York 1955, 210.

for alleged subversive activities against Nasser.[28] Muḥammad Aḥmad Ḥasan thought of himself as a follower of Miṣr al-Fātāt or the Muslim Brethren. He saw no difference in the two organizations, convinced that "they have the same principles," and were kept apart only by "personal ambitions." Neither did he see any difference between the Wafd and the government, at that time headed by Nuqrāshī and the Sa'adist Party. All, he thought, needed to be pushed into more determined nationalist initiative, and that, he said, was what the young intellectuals were doing. However, he admired Fārūq: "The King is above everything," he said in a way that others have said[4] *Deutschland, Deutschland über alles.* He had strong reservations about the left. Partiality for the Soviet Union would only bring about a new imperialism. He called the pro-communist newspaper *al-Jamāhīr* "a lying paper." He had once begun to read some of Marx's writings but had not continued. However, the works of Nietzsche and Spengler had interested him a great deal. Most of all he hated the British, to whom he attributed Egypt's defects and weakness. The Sudanese question would be solved by war. To the British he also ascribed a decisive part in the formation of the surprising, great Jewish power which he had encountered in Palestine. "They were the ones who brought you (the Jews) here and supplied you with money and arms." But in the war, "the Arabs will be victorious, God willing"—the last words *"in shā'a Allāh"* were not uttered as a platitude but with emphasis and faith. After the victory the Arabs in the country would govern by free elections. At the same time he spoke contemptuously of the Palestinian Arabs. He and his comrades had come to fight for their liberation but they had had no contact with the local people and he suspected them all of being "a fifth column. The Jews have corrupted them with hashish, wine and women."

The words of the captured young officer can be regarded as a typical expression of sentiments and views then prevalent among an important part of the Egyptian officer corps, as became apparent later. These opinions are close to the "philosophy" formulated several years afterwards in Nasser's book.

Muḥammad Aḥmad Ḥasan was freed in 1949 and continued to serve in the army. In 1956 he became a major and commander of the National Guard in the Suez Canal region; in 1964 he was a colonel.[29]

When the Free Officers' Association was founded at the end of 1949, they took a decisive step by forming an Executive Committee. This first con-

[28] *The Jewish Observer and Middle East Review,* London, 7 January 1966; *al-Ahrām,* 20 August 1966.

[29] *Al-Ahrām,* 19 August 1956; 9 December 1964.

sisted of five members and was expanded to ten after a short time. The first five members were Nasser, Kamāl al-Dīn Ḥusayn, Ḥasan Ibrāhīm, Khālid Muḥī al-Dīn and ʻAbd al-Munʻim ʻAbd al-Ra'ūf. The second group of five consisted of Jamāl Sālim, Ṣalāḥ Sālim, ʻAbd al-Ḥakīm ʻĀmīr, ʻAbd al-Laṭīf Baghdādī and Anwar Sādāt.[30] Those who were absent from the committee included Tharwath ʻUkāsha, Yūsuf Manṣūr Ṣiddīq and ʻĀlī Ṣabrī. Ten out of these 14 officers were majors; two—Jamāl Sālim and Yūsuf Manṣūr Ṣiddīq—were lieutenant-colonels; two—Ḥasan Ibrāhīm and Khālid Muḥī al-Dīn—were captains. All were between the ages of 28 and 32, with the exception of Yūsuf Manṣūr Ṣiddīq who was 39.

These young men were not unknown officers who rose to fame only after the 1952 coup. Among one hundred captains promoted to the rank of major in November 1948, there were four who in the summer of 1946 were still lieutenants. Three out of these four exceptionally promoted were on the Executive Committee of the Free Officers—ʻĀmir, Ṣalāḥ Sālim and Kamāl al-Dīn Ḥusayn. Three others, Nasser, Baghdādī, and Zakariyyā Muḥī al-Dīn, were awarded decorations at the end of the Palestinian War. Ṣalāḥ Sālim had the honor of being the first Egyptian officer to be sent to Gaza after the raising of the siege of the Faluja pocket; his picture appeared on page one of *al-Ahrām* on March 1, 1949. Anwar Sādāt was renowned for his adventures in the pro-German underground during World War II and with the terrorist nationalist groups afterwards.

Five of the young officers had the distinction of being graduates of the Staff College: Nasser, Salāḥ Sālim, Zakariyyā Muḥī al-Dīn, ʻĀmir and ʻUkāsha were graduates of the ninth course of the Staff College held from September 1946 to May 1948, the only one of its kind conducted between 1945 and the fall of 1948. Of the thousand officers of suitable rank eligible for the course, only 26 were accepted.[31] Most of the other graduates of that course, beside the five already mentioned, had brilliant military and political careers then and later: ʻAbd al-Muḥsin Kāmil Murtajā became in 1963 the commander of the Egyptian forces in Yemen and in 1966 the commander of all Egyptian land forces; Muḥammad Ṣidqī Sulaymān was appointed Prime Minister in September 1966; and Kamāl Henrī Abādīr was appointed his Minister of Communications.

In 1950 Nasser was chosen President of the Free Officers' Association. Among the members stationed in the capital a "base" was established consisting of Nasser, ʻĀmir, and Zakariyyā Muḥī al-Dīn.

[30] Anwar al-Sādāt, *Qiṣṣat al-thawra kāmila,* Cairo 1956, 51–2; Amīn Saʻīd, *Tā'rīkh al-ʻarab al-ḥadīth,* Vol. 13, *Al-thawra,* Cairo 1959, 26–8.

[31] *Majallat kulliyyat arkān al-ḥarb al-malakiyya,* Cairo, August 1951, 25.

According to Sādāt, the Association was built on the cell system and organized in five sections—enlistment and training of manpower, security, terrorism, propaganda and economics, i.e., financing activities and helping the members' families. He says that this structure was already introduced in 1945.[32] In practice, however, the sectional structure remained only on paper and was not implemented.

In October 1950 the first proclamation of the Free Officers appeared and in October 1951 the first number of the *Voice of the Free Officers* was printed.[33] This leaflet was mimeographed in 700 copies and sent to officers by mail. The editors were Nasser, Khālid Muḥī al-Dīn, Ḥasan Ibrāhīm and Anwar 'Ubayd.

Decisive in the development of the Free Officers' Association was their relationship with other political bodies. The problem arose already in 1949 and stayed with the group in one form or another ever since. Relations with mass organizations close to them—the Muslim Brethren until 1954 and the Syrian Ba'th in 1958 and 1963—have always caused them much concern.

The Muslim Brethren were interested in incorporating this group into their ranks and making it subservient to their authority. Several Free Officers also favored union with the Brethren or close cooperation with them or dual membership. However, the Free Officers decided that their association should be an independent society, whose members should be subject only to its discipline. 'Abd al-Ra'ūf, who disagreed with this principle and felt closer to the Brethren, left the Association in 1951, and he may not have been the only one to do so. While the Free Officers were an underground movement, they did not allow their members to belong to other political organizations, and when they became the rulers of Egypt—and for a time also of Syria—they did not tolerate an organization that was not headed by one of their number. Before the coup, they facilitated and even encouraged the fostering of ties with various political organizations and even cooperation with them; however, they opposed all identification with them, either collective or individual. Nasser, the cleverest and most far-seeing among them, understood early that only uncompromising opposition to tendencies of "double loyalty" could make the Free Officers the sole ruling factor in the country. He did not ignore the power of the Muslim Brethren nor the convergence of its thinking and aims to those of his circle. That was precisely the reason why he considered the establishment of a clear-cut boundary between them a necessity. He realized that

[32] Sadat, *Revolt,* 70–2.

[33] Aḥmad 'Aṭiyyat-Allāh, *Qāmūs al-thawra al-maṣriyya 1954,* Cairo 1954, 63, 88.

in the end, only one of the two organizations could survive, with the other either being swallowed by it or disbanded at its order. He even understood that despite the closeness of views, the ultimate aims were not identical. He and his comrades were first of all Egyptian nationalists. For the Muslim Brethren the nationalistic factor was only one expression of zeal for Islam, a basic ingredient but no more. The officers knew that Islam is cosmopolitan where relations between Muslim peoples are concerned, but particularistic where inter-communal relations within a country are involved. Nationalism, on the other hand, would lead to secularization. Both the officers and the Brethren continuously sought points of identity between Egyptian or Arab nationalistic principles and Islam; when contradictions appeared they tried to compromise. But when there was no longer room for compromise, they made different decisions. In 1950 Nasser did not yet see these problems clearly but he felt their depth.

Until the end of 1951 the Free Officers calculated that they could not stage a coup before 1955.[34] However, in the winter of 1951-1952 Egypt shook with a social ferment that hastened developments. Revolution was just around the corner and if not the officers, perhaps someone else would have carried it out.

In October 1951 the western powers exerted pressure on Egypt to become a member of a joint Mediterranean Command. The Wafd government rejected the proposal and, moreover, announced the nullification of the 1936 Anglo-Egyptian treaty with Egyptian consent to the maintenance of British bases in the Suez Canal region and to the Condominium in Sudan. Fārūq was proclaimed "King of Egypt and Sudan." A mass struggle began; meetings and demonstrations were organized and acts of sabotage against installations of the British army in Egypt and attacks on their troops were carried out, mostly in the Canal region. As early as October "Liberation Battalions" *("fidā'iyyūn")* were organized with the cooperation of all parties—Muslim Brethren, communists, army and police officers. At its head was old 'Azīz al-Maṣrī who personified hatred of the British. Tens of thousands of Egyptian workmen vacated their jobs in British army camps. Armed clashes became more frequent and serious, culminating in a battle between Egyptian police and British troops on January 25, 1952 at Ismailia when more than forty Egyptian policemen were killed. On the next day, "Black Saturday," disturbances broke out in Cairo so stormy that the center of the city went up in flames.

During these three months of struggle led by the Wafd and the Muslim Brethren, the part played by the Free Officers was neither conspicuous nor

[34] Naguib, 89; Sādāt, *Qiṣṣa,* 56.

decisive. They filled two functions: training volunteers and supplying them with arms and ammunition. Contacts were maintained chiefly by Nasser, on the one hand, and 'Abd al-Qādir 'Awda, Deputy Supreme Guide of the Brethren, and Ḥasan 'Ashmāwī, one of the volunteer leaders, on the other. One of the Free Officers, Captain Ṣalāḥ Hadāyat, a demolition expert, helped to prepare a big mine in January 1952 for the purpose of blowing up a ship in the Suez Canal and blocking it.[35] The plan was not carried out. (Ten years later, Hadāyat was appointed Minister for Scientific Research and Director of Atomic Enterprises.) The Egyptian army and Free Officers did not participate in guerrilla tactics which led to direct clashes with British forces. The government and the officers decided to avoid involving the army in the fight to prevent "repetition of the Palestine disaster which was caused by Egypt entering a war without adequate preparation for battle. And if the Palestine disaster of 1948 was limited in scope, occurring outside Egypt, the involvement of the Egyptian army in a war with the British in 1951–52, before completing its preparations, would be catastrophic."[36] This is how a semi-official historian of republican Egypt explains the inactivity of the officers during those months. Aḥmad Abū al-Fatḥ provides another explanation, but not a contradictory one: In the winter of 1951–1952 Nasser doubted whether there was any point in the anti-British struggle. He concentrated his attention on internal matters.[37] The prerequisite to the expulsion of the British would have to be the overthrow of the King's regime. Fārūq, once the idol of Egyptian youth and still the symbol of the country's honor in 1948, was loathed in 1951 for he had come to represent corruption.

During this period of mass anti-British struggle the group of Free Officers was small in number and therefore played an insignificant part in the storm then raging in Egypt.

The existence and power of the Free Officers could be seen in the elections to the Executive Committee of the Officers' Club held every December. The candidate for the Club's presidency for 1952 was Ḥusayn Sirrī 'Āmir, an officer intensely hated by the Free Officers, and not only by them. He had been in the Frontier Force, one of the most respected units, and in 1949 its Chief of Staff. He took advantage of his position to enrich himself: He sold abandoned British weapons which could be found in abundance in the Western Desert, to the Egyptian army; stories were circulating that he engaged in the sale and smuggling of hashish and that he sold state lands.

[35] Kāmil Sharīf, *Al-muqāwama al-sirriyya fī qanāt al-Suwīs, 1951–1954*, Cairo 1957, 218, 312; Abū al-Fatḥ, 184–92.

[36] 'Abd al-Raḥmān al-Rāfi'ī, *Muqaddimāt thawrat 23 yūliyū sanat 1952*, Cairo 1957, 107–8

[37] Abū al-Fatḥ, *loc. cit.*

When the scandal was uncovered in 1950, 'Āmir was expelled from the Frontier Force. However, it was precisely this man whom the King favored, possibly because he was a partner in his deals. In August 1951 he was promoted to the rank of major-general, returned to the Frontier Force and appointed its commander.[38]

The Free Officers resolved to turn the Club elections into a showdown and put up another candidate to oppose 'Āmir, Major-General Muḥammad Najīb (Naguib). He was the antithesis of 'Āmir. While 'Āmir was notorious for his corruption, Naguib was respected for his honesty. On his breast he bore the figure three to show that he had been wounded thrice on the Palestine front, where he had served as a brigadier. He was not a member of the Free Officers but shared many of their opinions and had for some time maintained contact with them, especially through 'Abd al-Ḥakīm 'Āmir who had been his operations officer in Palestine and again in 1951.

When it became clear that the King's candidate had no prospect of being elected, Fārūq forbade the balloting. However, on December 31 about 350 officers met and decided to proceed with the elections, which were held on January 6, 1952.[39] The candidates were Naguib, 'Āmir, and two other men. There are various accounts of the number of participants in the elections and the results, but according to all of them, Naguib received 80 per cent of the votes.

In addition to Naguib, the Club's Executive Committee was elected as proposed by the Free Officers. Of its 15 members, two were on the Association's Executive Committee (Lieutenant-Colonel Zakariyyā Muḥī al-Dīn and Flight-Major Ḥasan Ibrāhīm); two were members of the Association (Lieutenant-Colonel Aḥmad 'Ubayd and Major Jamāl Ḥamād); two were either members of or ideologically close to the Association (Lieutenant-Colonels Rashād Muhannā and Anwar 'Abd al-Laṭīf). The other nine (two brigadiers, six lieutenants-colonels and one lieutenant) also enjoyed the confidence of the Free Officers, although one of them (Brigadier Ḥasan Hishmat) was arrested by them on the night of the coup six months later.[40] Another new and highly significant feature on the composition of this Executive Committee was the rising strength of the junior officers. Of the fifteen only two were above rank of lieutenant-colonel.

The Free Officers emerged from their first public showdown strengthened and encouraged. They had shown that theirs was the only one among the different officers' groups capable of planning and carrying out a serious political operation.

[38] Naguib, 83, 87, 95.

[39] Rāfi'ī, 106; Vaucher, 250; Anṭūn 'Asāf, *Al-qā'id Muḥammad Najīb,* Cairo 1953, 40.

[40] Vatikiotis, 63–4; Rāfi'ī, 106; Naguīb, 106.

On January 7, the day after the elections at the Officers' Club, an attempt was made on the life of Ḥusayn Sirrī 'Āmir, the unsuccessful candidate for the presidency. As he drove home at ten o'clock that evening, he was greeted by 17 sub-machine-gun bullets fired at him at close range.[41] His assailant was Nasser. In the *Philosophy of the Revolution* Nasser writes, "we decided that a certain man should cease to exist."[42] A few years later he no longer concealed that the intended victim had been Ḥusayn Sirrī 'Āmir—perhaps because it was no longer a secret anyhow. He even revealed that the "Free Officers decided on a policy of assassination of the regime's leaders."[43] In his book Nasser touchingly relates how he was pursued by "the sounds of screaming and wailing" after he had fired at his victim, how he had not been able to sleep all night, and how relieved he had felt the next morning when he read in the papers that the man he had wanted to kill the night before had been saved.[44] Would he really have written that way had he succeeded in carrying out his intention? The strong impression aroused by this exhibition of conscience is dispelled by the fact that Nasser concealed that two of his shots had struck 'Āmir's driver, Aḥmad Mūsā. His bullets had missed a corrupt general and had wounded an innocent corporal.

Political murder was a common event in Egypt in 1948-1952 and the Free Officers were not opposed in principle to individual terror. After their accession to power they supported the planning and implementation of political assassinations, naturally not in Egypt but in rival Arab states. However, after the failure to kill 'Āmir, they decided that that was not the way to their goal. They may also have learned from the futility of the assassinations carried out by the Muslim Brethren, that by means of individual terror one can only get rid of persons but not overthrow a regime, much less establish a new one. A military coup was planned as the sole means of action.

One of the plans envisaged at the beginning of 1952 set the date of the coup for November of the same year, at the opening session of Parliament, which would be accompanied by considerable public ferment that could be useful to the plotters.[45] However, the course of events in the spring and summer of 1952 dictated a faster tempo.

The mass outbreak on "Black Saturday" at the end of January was the angry expression of a profound social and national crisis. Government circles were startled when they saw that the struggle of the populace was

41 *Al-Ahrām,* 9, 10 January 1952.

42 Nasser, English, 53; Arabic, 36.

43 *The Sunday Times,* 17 June 1962.

44 Nasser, English, 54–6; Arabic, 37–9.

45 Tharwat 'Ukāsha, 'Mādhā ḥadatha laylat 23 yūliyū', *al-Ahrām,* 23 July 1960.

becoming more intense and would not end with the evacuation of British troops from Egypt if it were permitted to continue, and they decided to curb it. The Wafd government was dismissed but stability was not restored. Between the end of January and the end of July there were five cabinet crises and changes of government, or to be more exact, there was one continuous government crisis. The King would not allow the formation of a government which would reflect the people's national and social desires, and a government carrying out the King's wishes could not stand up against the inflamed parties and aroused public opinion. Egypt's old regime was dying. The Free Officers were only one of the forces which regarded themselves as its potential successors, and not exactly the strongest of them. But they had the advantage of being able to act quickly and to muster a powerful force concentrated in a few hands. All the other organizations were only able to act by propelling masses of people into action. The activity of the officers was founded on the inaction of mass public bodies and even on their muzzling and suppression. Nevertheless, the Free Officers did not disparage the various parties and political organizations. They strengthened their contacts with them, if only to find out their intentions or to neutralize them.

In addition to the Muslim Brethren, the officers maintained ties with the communists and the Wafd. The chief liaison with the communists was Khālid Muḥī al-Dīn, ideologically, and perhaps also by affiliation, a member of the communist HADITU. Through him, Nasser met their representatives, and they may also have regarded him as one of their sympathizers or even members. According to Abū al-Fatḥ, they had Nasser listed under the underground name of "Maurice" and membership number 117.[46] The chief contact man with the Wafd was Tharwat 'Ukāsha; Nasser met quite often with his brother-in-law, Aḥmad Abū al-Fatḥ, the editor of *al-Miṣri*, who served in the first days after the coup as his adviser and spokesman, as did later Muḥammad Ḥasanayn Haykal. From him Nasser received the information on July 21 which made him decide on the eve of the 23rd for the coup. Concurrently Nasser maintained ties with other Wafdists, managing to conceal from each his connections with the others and succeeding in giving each one the impression that he was in his confidence. He was able to learn their views and plans without divulging his own intentions, and he knew how to concentrate the affairs of the Free Officers' Association in his own hands without the role he played there becoming known outside that movement. This has been one of his outstanding talents:

[46] Abū al-Fatḥ, 217-8; French, 204–5.
[47] *Ibid.*, Arabic, 29–35; French, 16–27.

He has known how to gain the confidence of many while he trusted only a few.

The victory of the Free Officers in the elections at the Officers' Club also attracted the attention of non-Egyptian elements, especially the American intelligence service.[48] The officers themselves were interested in fostering ties with them in order to make sure that when the time came the coup would not encounter hostile outside intervention. From the point of view of the officers the United States was the most suitable country with which to initiate foreign relations. Not only did they then consider the USA the greatest power, but at the time Washington had no interest in preserving the status quo in Egypt; throughout the Middle East the Americans were striving to reduce the British share of petroleum revenue and to limit their political influence while preventing Soviet penetration. Contact with Americans was maintained by 'Alī Ṣabrī who was then a major in the air force. He possessed a number of qualities which suited him for this role: his keen mind, his aristocratic family background, and his position as chief of air force intelligence.[49] At a cocktail party held in Alexandria on July 19, the Saturday preceding the coup, several Free Officers indicated to their American colleagues that it was their intention to oust Fārūq, and were astonished at the American reaction—which was encouraging.[50] On July 23 at four in the morning 'Alī Ṣabrī informed the deputy air attaché at the American Embassy that the coup had taken place and gave assurances in the name of the new rulers that the safety and property of foreigners in Egypt would not suffer.[51] This was their first diplomatic step.

There are discrepancies in the membership figures given for the Free Officers. Sādāt of course, goes all out. He reports that in 1947 "Our Society now numbered more than one thousand officers,"[52] by which he meant more than one-third of the officer corps. However, the leaflet *The Voice of the Free Officers* was mimeographed in only 700 copies in October 1951, as mentioned above. The Lacoutures write that at the outbreak of the coup the Free Officers consisted of "about 250 members."[53] In 1958 Khālid Muḥī al-Dīn recounted that there were only 70.[54] Nasser said in 1962 that among "the 300 officers in Cairo who were our absolute supporters," there were

[48] A. Tully, *CIA-the inside story,* New York 1962, 102–4.

[49] Anouar Abdel-Malek, *Egypte, société militaire,* Paris 1962, 208; Naguib, 108.

[50] Tully, 102–4; Lacouture, 154; Lily Abegg, *Neue Herren im Mittelost,* Stuttgart 1954, 41.

[51] Lacouture, 149.

[52] Sadat, 84–5.

[53] Lacouture, 192.

[54] Wheelock, 6.

many who for security reasons could not be allowed to participate in the coup and that "Ninety officers with only small arms were all that were available to take over a nation."[55] If Sādāt's exaggeration is discounted, the discrepancies in the various figures are not as great as they appear at first sight. There was a tight nucleus of 10 to 15 veteran Free Officers. Associated with these were a few dozen loyal men who could be depended upon and who could be assigned duties; each of these kept in touch with one or two of the members of the Executive Committee without having any knowledge of the details of the society's structure and program or the names of its members. Between January and July 1952 this group grew and attracted a periphery of sympathizers. The borderline between these circles was fluid, particularly between the sympathizers and the entire officer corps. Of the members who could be definitely said to belong to the Association before the coup, the names of a little more than fifty officers are known.

Naguib made a pithy remark about the ideology of the officers in 1955 when discussing the differences between himself and Nasser and his "philosophy". He said, "Perhaps since neither of us is a philosopher, it would be better to call it the 'psychology' of the Revolution."[56] Another interpretation in the same spirit was offered in 1959 by one of the outstanding personalities of the Free Officers, 'Abd al-Qādir Ḥātim: "The method employed by the leader of the Revolution . . . was one of phases, of trial and error; completing one phase, the Revolution put itself in readiness and laid down the rules of the coming phase."[57] And if that was the case in 1955 and 1959, it must have been all the more so between 1948 and 1952. The Free Officers were determined opposition nationalists but they had no clearcut ideology. This can be seen in their proclamations prior to the coup: A proclamation of 1951 states, "The Executive Committee of the Free Officers demands that the army's function should be the achievement of the country's independence, and it will not permit the army to be used for the destruction of nationalist movements . . . the army has value only in a strong, liberated country. We demand arms for the army from all countries which sell us weapons, either from the East or West . . . We demand that the people be granted all the freedoms, since the people cannot struggle against imperialism when it is chained by laws which limit its freedom." When Fārūq's son was born on January 16, 1952, ten days before "Black Saturday," and a large military parade was planned in honor of the event, the Free Officers denounced this "joke" and the utilization of the army for a

[55] *The Sunday Times,* 17 June 1962.
[56] Naguib, 191.
[57] 'Abd al-Qādir Ḥātim in the preface to *Qaḍiyyat al-thawra fī 7 sanawāt,* Cairo 1959.

matter which had nothing to do with it; however, this proclamation is not to be regarded as indicating an anti-monarchist position in principle— on the contrary, the birth of an heir to the throne is termed "a blessed event." It says further, "You, who are accumulating wealth from the sweat of the people to spend on purposes which will not benefit it . . . You, who are leading the country to a gaping abyss in order to satisfy egotistic aspirations, it is to you that this is addressed; let it be a warning to you, perhaps you will return to the honest path . . . and you, officers, always be alert to what is being prepared for your army and your country, and do not budge one bit for your rights!" At the end of January, after "Black Saturday," a proclamation addressed to the officers warned them against "traitors among Egyptians" who sought to make use of the army for suppressing the people when its mission is to combat the external enemy. "The homeland is in danger . . . rally to the Free Officers, and thus you will triumph, you and the people of which you are an inseparable part."[58] Another proclamation at the time, in a mimeographed text written by hand, states: "Officers! You may be sure that the disaster which befell the country in the Palestine War will teach those responsible a lesson so they will pay attention to the army and its training and arming and keep it away from illusory appearances such as the participation in celebrations and the putting up of decora-

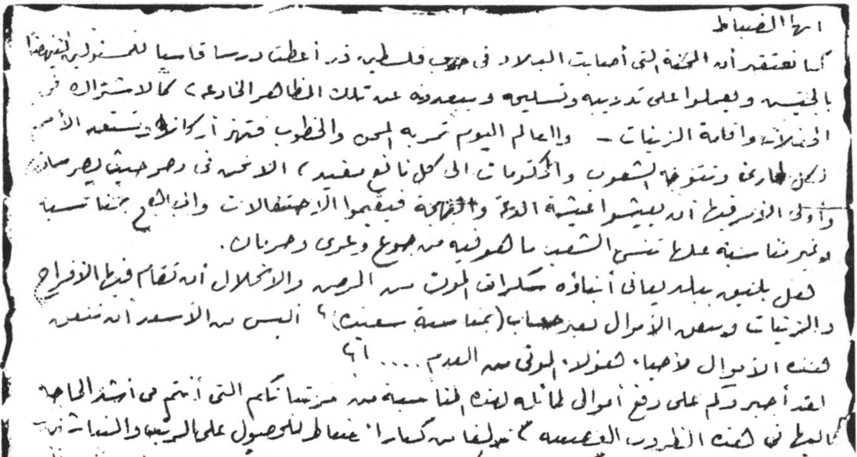
أيها الضباط
كنا نعتقد أن المحنة التي أصابت البلاد في حرب فلسطين قد أعطت درسا قاسيا للمسئولين فينتبهوا
بالجيش ويعملوا على تدريبه وتسليحه ويبعدوه عن تلك المظاهر الخادعة كالاشتراك في
الاحتفالات وإقامة الزينات — والعالم اليوم تسوده المحن والخطوب فتهتز أركانه [illegible]
[illegible]

The mimeographed hand-written proclamation

[58] Sa'īd, 29–31.

tions—at this time when disasters and painful experiences have come to the world, when its foundations are tottering, when the nations are preparing for any evil eventuality, and when peoples and governments are appealing to anyone who can be of use to them. But here in Egypt its masters and leaders are living a life of pleasure and staging celebrations and parties on every occasion and when there is no occasion: are they possibly forgetting the people and its condition, the hungry, naked and the wretched people?"[59]

These proclamations clearly indicate what was bothering the Free Officers: The degradation of the army at the front and back home, the country's lack of independence, the extravagances of the aristocracy, and the terrible poverty of the people. However, in all these proclamations there are no concrete demands regarding domestic or foreign affairs, except for those connected with the position and mission of the army. In fact, in 1952 army affairs became a bone of contention in the political struggles that preceded the coup; and the crisis, now coming to a head over the appointment of a Minister of War was the direct cause of the seizure of power by the Free Officers.

After "Black Saturday," the Wafd government was ousted. The governments of 'Ālī Māhir and Hilālī could not remain in control, and on July 2nd the King asked Ḥusayn Sirrī to form a new government. Sirrī wanted to appease the officer corps, which was seething with unrest, with the suggestion that Naguib be appointed Minister of War. Had his suggestion been accepted, matters may have followed a different course. As things happened Fārūq in his obdurate stupidity took a firm stand against the appointment, and Sirrī took the war portfolio himself. The officers' bitterness mounted.

Some time before this one of the Free Officers, Captain Ḥasan 'Allām, had been seen with a pamphlet of the Association by someone who turned out to be a palace informer.[60] On July 13 he was brought before a court-martial and sentenced to death. On July 15 the King ordered the dissolution of the Officers' Club Executive Committee and the transfer of its members to various posts in rural areas far from the capital.[61] The Free Officers now began to fear not only for their position but also for their personal safety. They completed preparations for their coup. Sirrī in the meantime saw no possibility of continuing in his post and presented his government's resignation on July 20. The King once again asked Hilālī to form a government, and on July 21 Aḥmad Abū al-Fatḥ learned that the new Minister of

[59] *Al-Muṣawwar*, Cairo, 24 July 1964.

[60] Sadat, 97 (Sadat writes erroneously "lieutenant").

[61] Vatikiotis, 66; Rāfi'ī, 146–7; *al-Miṣri*, 23 January 1953; Sādāt, *Qiṣṣa*, 74.

War was to be Ḥusayn Sirrī ʻĀmir, the bitter enemy of the Free Officers, the man who half a year earlier had miraculously been saved from Nasser's bullets and who knew that the unknown assailant had come from among the opposition officers. When Abū al-Fatḥ found out about the designated appointment, he hastened to inform Nasser of it through ʻUkāsha. At the same time the Free Officers heard that on July 24 Ḥasan ʻAllām was to be executed. Nasser thereupon set the early hours of the following night, July 23, as the date of the coup.[62] Actually, when Hilālī presented his new government to the King at Alexandria (where the court and the government spent the summer), he was surprised to learn that Fārūq had appointed Colonel Ismāʻīl Shīrīn Minister of War. Shīrīn was a scion of Muḥammad ʻAlī's family; he had received his title to military rank as the husband of Fawzīyya, Fārūq's sister.[63] To the officers Shīrīn's appointment was Fārūq's most vulgar provocation—and his last. When the new government was sworn in at Alexandria, the Free Officers in Cairo had already completed their preparations for a coup, and ten hours later they were in control of the country.

[62] Abū al-Fatḥ, 25–6; French, 19.

[63] *Al-Ahrām,* 29 March 1949; Vatikiotis, 66.

6. THE FREE OFFICERS' RULE IN EGYPT

WHEN THE date of the coup was set for the end of July 1952, it so happened that all the members of the Committee of the Free Officers' Association were either staff officers or stationed outside Cairo. The commanders of units garrisoned in the capital therefore had to be included in the planning and execution of the plot. Colonel Aḥmad Shawqī, commander of the 13th Battalion, considered a top-notch unit and later called the "Liberation Battalion," was prominent among them; so was Lieutentant-Colonel Yūsuf Manṣūr Ṣiddīq, commander of a medium machine gun company. The two units acted decisively on the night of the coup. They were responsible for the occupation of General Staff headquarters and the arrest of the Army High Command.[1]

In mid-July the Association's Committee was expanded. Of the 10 original members, nine remained; the one who had left was 'Abd al-Mun'im 'Abd al-Ra'ūf. Now four members were added: Yūsuf Manṣūr Ṣiddīq; Zakariyyā Muḥī al-Dīn, one of the old-timers in the group who until then had for some reason or other not been on the Committee; Ḥusayn al-Shāfi'ī, a lieutenant-colonel in the Armored Corps; and 'Abd al-Mun'im Amīn, a lieutenant-colonel in the artillery.[2] These 13 officers together with Naguib later constituted the Revolutionary Command Council.

One of the details involved in the preparations for the coup was the selection of a man who would represent the officers to the people and the outside world. The leaders of the Free Officers were all lieutenant-colonels or majors 35 years of age or younger who thought it necessary that a senior officer be head of state. They first thought of 'Azīz al-Maṣrī. However, the old warrior declined the role. Nor did the young officers urge him over much; his publicly known pro-German past, his stubbornness and hastiness left room for fear that he would be more of a burden than a help. The second man they tried to interest was Major-General Aḥmad Fu'ād Ṣadiq. From November 1948 Ṣādiq had commanded the Egyptian forces in

[1] Muḥammad Najīb, in *Hādhihi al-thawra,* 14.

[2] Naguib, *Egypt's destiny,* 101; Keith Wheelock, *Nasser's new Egypt,* London 1960, 14.

Palestine and was considered as having conducted himself honorably there. He was avowedly pro-British[3] and at the same time an old adversary of the Wafd. Now and then he displayed sympathy for the Muslim Brethren[4] and the Free Officers. Ṣalāh Sālim negotiated with him and promised him the post of chief of staff. At the same time a rumor reached him that the King was about to appoint him to the same position, to which he had been aspiring for a long time, and he preferred the prospect of a royal appointment to the promises of young officers. The rumor was without foundation, and the Free Officers did not contact him again; so he lost out all round.[5] The man eventually chosen and who agreed to assume leadership was Naguib. The elections at the Officers' Club proved his

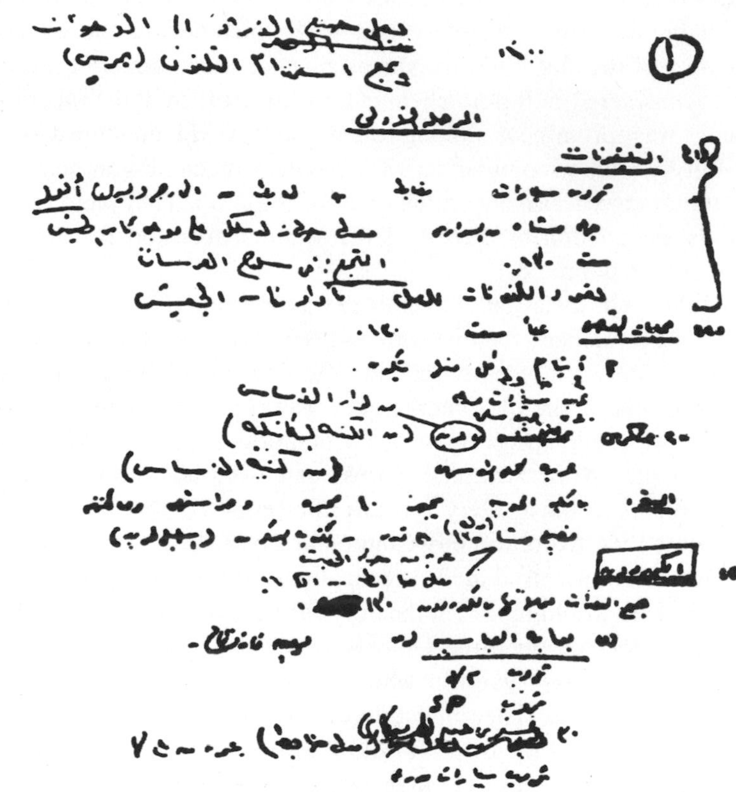

The operational plan

[3] *Al-Ahrām,* 30 August 1940.

[4] Sharīf, *Al-Ikhwān,* 170–2; Mohammed Naguib, *Egypt's destiny,* New York 1955, 31; *Hamizrah Hehadash,* vol. 2, 151.

[5] Naguib, 30.

popularity in the officer corps, and in closer association with him the Free Officers became convinced that he was their man. They did not then know that they would have a hard struggle to get rid of him again.

The operational plan for seizing power was drawn up by ʻAbd al-Ḥakīm ʻĀmir; Zakariyyā Muḥī al-Dīn made additions, and with slight changes it was finally approved by Nasser.[6]

At a meeting in the apartment of Khālid Muḥī al-Dīn on July 22 at 4 p.m., H-hour was set for one a.m. The conspirators dispersed, each one setting about his duties. At seven in the evening Saʻad Tawfīq, an officer in intelligence, informed Nasser that the General Staff had learned of a suspicious movement among the officers and had been summoned to an emergency meeting that night. Nasser and ʻAmīr tried to get in touch with their comrades to advance the time of action but they could no longer reach them. As it turned out, events happened faster than planned, and the meeting of the General Staff became a trap in which the Free Officers were able to catch all the army chiefs in one swoop. At midnight a company of the 13th Battalion under the command of Aḥmad Shawqī and an armored car company commanded by Yūsuf Nanṣūr Ṣiddīq attacked General Staff headquarters. In a brief exchange of fire two soldiers were killed, one from each side, and two were wounded. The guard then surrendered. Yūsuf Manṣūr Ṣiddīq and ʻAbd al-Ḥakīm ʻĀmir, followed by several soldiers, entered the meeting room of the General Staff with drawn pistols and demanded the surrender of all present. At first the Chief of Staff, Ḥusayn Farīd, refused and fired three wild shots from behind a partition before handing over his weapon. With him, a dozen major-generals and brigadiers were arrested. A successful coup was executed with a speed and ease its planners had not imagined.

Further army units under the command of Free Officers simultaneously seized strategic points in Cairo—the telephone exchange, the airport, and the railroad station; nowhere did they encounter resistance. At 1:30 Ḥusayn al-Shāfiʻi's tanks took over the radio station; at about the same time Jamāl Sālim assumed command of the garrison at El-Arish, and his brother Ṣalāḥ of the forces at Rafah. At three in the morning Naguib was brought to army headquarters from his house to become Commander-in-Chief of the Armed Forces. At 7.30 a.m. Cairo Radio broadcast his first communiqué on behalf of the army to the Egyptian people and the world. The communiqué had been drafted by ʻĀmir and Nasser; the announcer was Sādāt.[7]

[6] Tharwat ʻUkāsha, ʻMādha ḥadatha laylat 23 yūliyū', *al-Ahrām,* 23 July 1960.

[7] I. and S. Lacouture, *Egypt in transition,* London 1958, 147–9; ʻAbd al-Rahmān al-Rāfiʻī, *Thawrat* 23 *yūliyū,* Cairo 1959, 19–24; *The Sunday Times,* 17 June 1962; Anwar al-Sādāt, *Qiṣṣat al-thawra kāmila,* Cairo 1956, 93.

Did or did not Naguib know of the plan for the coup? This question became controversial after 1954. Actually he did and did not know. He knew about the Free Officers' movement but was not a member; he supported it and had its backing without having any knowledge of its organization or plans. On July 20 Nasser and ʻĀmir paid him a visit to tell him about the plan for the coup and the part reserved for him; however, they found two other guests in his house on whom they could not rely, Lieutenant-Colonel Ḥatāta and the newspaperman Muḥammad Ḥasanayn Haykal, so they did not broach the subject they had come to talk about.[8] During the next two days they avoided Naguib in order not to arouse the government's suspicions. On the night of the coup Naguib was at home. But when two officers came to invite him to the headquarters of the new regime he was not surprised. The Minister of the Interior had telephoned him earlier from Alexandria to ask him about troop movements in the capital, and Naguib had been sufficiently informed to know how to make an appropriate calming and misleading reply.

The surprising ease with which they seized power did not blind the Free Officers to the difficulties that lay ahead of them, and they at once started to consolidate their newly captured positions. Their first aim was to prevent outside intervention. At 4 a.m. ʻAlī Ṣabrī informed the American Embassy of the turn of events and assured them that the life and property of foreigners would be safe. The Americans, who were neither surprised nor disappointed by this turning point in Egyptian policy, extended considerable help during the first critical days by persuading the King to capitulate and to leave and by dissuading the British from supporting him.[9] A Soviet definition of the Free Officers from the year 1952 characterizing them as "a group of reactionary officers connected with the United States,"[10] is an over-simplification. But who knows how events would have developed without that American assistance.

Their second act was the formation of a new government. The officers assigned this task to ʻAlī Māhir. This was one of their most adroit tactical moves. The appointment of a prime minister still required the King's confirmation. ʻAlī Māhir was one of the most distinguished and talented representatives of the Egyptian aristocracy. Fārūq had appointed him Prime Minister half a year previously, after Black Saturday, and could not oppose his appointment now. On the other hand, ʻAlī Māhir was known to be vehemently anti-British. He had been Prime Minister at the outbreak

[8] Sādāt, 77–8.

[9] Adelbert Weinstein, *Das neue Mekka liegt am Nil,* Wiesbaden (1959 or 1960), 91.

[10] *Bolshaya Sovetskaya Entziklopedia,* vol. 15, 1962, 460.

of World War II and had been forced to resign for his unfriendly attitude toward the Allies. When the Germans were approaching Egypt, he was considered the leader of their Egyptian sympathizers and in February 1942 was placed under house-arrest. In the spring of 1952 he had also resigned from the premiership after a month in office as he had been tougher than the King toward the British. ʻAlī Māhir and the officers each believed that the other would serve as an obedient tool; the officers were right.

The officers' third step was the ousting of Fārūq, who was in Alexandria. After the seizure of Cairo and assuring the loyalty of the troops at Rafah, the officers easily made themselves masters of Alexandria. The question that now arose was what to do with the King. The officers argued the matter the whole night through. Within their small circle they conducted themselves in a democratic fashion, adopting decisions by free vote. Two views were advanced in the debate on Fārūq: That he should be made to stand trial or to be compelled to abdicate in favor of his infant son, the Crown Prince, and to leave the country. The majority voted for the second proposal and Fārūq went into exile. On August 2 a three-man Regency Council was appointed. This consisted of Prince ʻAbd al-Munʻim of the royal family, Dr. Barakāt, a jurist and former President of Parliament, and Colonel Rashād Muhannā, a prominent figure in the army.

From this stage on, the history of the Free Officers is identical with the general history of Egypt and this work is not concerned with a survey of all its phases and details. To clarify the nature of the officers' interference in Arab political life this study must concentrate on examining specific aspects of the problem. Of particular interest are the relations between the officers and other political organizations and questions concerning the special form and content of the officers' policies.

The first question of major significance is whether or not a revolution took place in Egypt in 1952. This is not a matter of terminology but rather of essence.

On July 23, 1952 and for some months later, the Free Officers had not yet begun to use the term *thawra* ("revolution") which later became the glorious official designation. The first communiqués spoke of an "awakening" (*nahḍa*) and of the "blessed movement of the Army." A decoration awarded in August 1952 to all the officers and non-commissioned officers who were on active service on July 23 was called "The Liberation Medal." A regulation dated November 13 established that any ruling by the commander-in-chief of the armed forces "as head of the army

[11] Rāfiʻī, *Thawra,* 24–6.

movement" would have legal validity.[12] The same formula is repeated in a decree dated January 18, 1953 which outlawed political parties.[13] Only the provisional constitution of February 1953 speaks of powers held by "the commander of the revolution."[14] In the same month, the phrase "Revolutionary Command Council" appears for the first time.

The common factor shared by a revolution and a coup or *putsch* is the overthrow of a regime by violence or threat of violence. The difference is that a coup is a single act and a revolution is a continuous movement. In a coup the principal feature is a change of government; in a revolution this is merely one of the phases, generally not the first and never the last. A coup is an occurrence, a revolution an era. A coup brings about a change in personnel; a revolution brings about basic changes in the structure of society, in relations between classes and in the form of government. And the principal difference between a coup and a revolution is in the role played by the people. In a coup the people remain passive, like spectators watching a play; they approve or condemn the acts and those who carried them out, even applauding and waxing enthusiastic, but they do not participate in the deed. In a revolution, however, the people—large segments of them, even masses—function as leading actors and chief movers. The revolutionary political leadership stands at the head of the movement, defines its goals and organizes it and at the same time remains close to the masses, relies on them, and impels them to action. The conquest of the Bastille *preceded* changes in the French constitution; workers' strikes and the seizure of lands by peasants came *before* the overthrow of the Tsar.

In the Egypt of 1952 there was revolutionary ferment. The mass outburst of Black Saturday in January, the violent struggle for the evacuation of the British bases and the frequent government crises were clear evidence of this; and the movement of the Free Officers was also one of its expressions. Moreover, the class struggle in town and country was becoming more and more acute. In 1951 there were 49 workers' strikes.[15] In the second half of 1951 there were several uprisings of peasants who demanded ownership of the large estates they were cultivating, and in a number of instances the rebellions were quelled only by bloodshed.[16] The forces which controlled the communications media and public opinion maintained a con-

[12] *Ibid.,* 63–4.

[13] *Ibid.,* 74.

[14] Sa'īd, 57–8.

[15] Lacouture, 125.

[16] Gabriel Baer, *A history of landownership in modern Egypt, 1800–1950,* London 1962, 221–2; Rāshid al-Barāwī, *Haqīqat al-inqilāb al-akhīr fī Miṣr,* Cairo 1952, 92, 189; M.Ḥ. Haykal, *al-Ahrām,* 2 June 1961.

spiracy of silence about the struggles of the workers and peasants, and only fragmentary accounts came to the knowledge of the public and to history. But whoever wanted to listen could hear subterranean rumblings in 1952 that announced an approaching volcanic eruption.

What, on the day after the coup, was the attitude of the Free Officers to the workers and peasants and to the inchoate revolutionary ferment among the masses? They could summon the population to action, to organize itself and participate actively in shaping the new Egypt; and they could immobilize the masses. As in most other matters they had no crystallized, clear view on this basic issue. But the test was not long in coming.

Three weeks after the coup a strike broke out in the weaving plant of the Misr Company in Kafr al-Dawār near Alexandria, in which 10,000 workers were employed. On the evening of August 12 the workers on night shift gathered in front of the managers' office and proclaimed a strike. They demanded an increase in wages which then ranged from 12-15 piasters per day; an increase in the annual leave with pay, then only four days; recognition of their union; and the dismissal of two members on the managerial staff. Most of the demands had been presented by the workers several months before but they had always been put off on flimsy pretexts. Now they believed that a new era had begun and they did not want to give in any longer. A few days earlier the management of the neighbouring Anglo-Egyptian weaving plant Bayda had accepted similar demands by its workers. The Misr workers cheered Naguib, the army, and the Revolution —they were already talking in terms of a revolution. However, the plant's management was not willing to negotiate and called the police to disperse the workers. The police began to use force, the workers defended themselves by throwing stones and the police opened fire. The workers set two office buildings on fire and proclaimed a sit-down strike. The next morning troops were brought from Alexandria and used their weapons. After a serious clash the workers were forced to leave the plant. Two soldiers and a policeman as well as several workers—they have been estimated at three, five or six—were killed; there were more than twenty wounded. Two hundred workers were arrested.

The summoning of police and soldiers and the shooting may possibly be explained away as measures adopted in haste or without the knowledge of the Free Officers and without intention of laying down a policy. If the officers had felt that in the flow of events and because of lack of experience, they had unwittingly been dragged into an anti-labor position, they could still have rectified the error. However, they continued to clamp down hard. They set up a summary court-martial with no right of appeal under 'Abd al-Mun'im Amīn, one of the leaders of the Free Officers. On August 18, five days after the arrests, sentences were already passed. Of 31 workers 15 were acquitted. Two, Muṣṭafā Muḥammad Khamīs and Muḥammad Ḥasan al-Baqrī were sentenced to death. Six were given sentences of 10 to 15 years with hard labor; five, five to eight years; three, one to three years. The pronouncement of Khamīs' death sentence was used by the authorities to demonstrate the character of the new regime. The correspondent of the London *Times* reported: "There was an impressive show of force by the military, many hundreds of soldiers being present. About 1,000 workers from the Misr plant and other factories in the neighborhood lined the three sides of the factory football ground, with armed troops facing them and tanks in the background."[17] Khamīs was made to stand in the center of the field. A major read the sentence over a loudspeaker and a lieutenant-colonel read a special announcement by Naguib.

Even at this stage the officers still had a chance to prove they were not against the workers. It was up to them to confirm, lighten or cancel the death sentences. Once again they consulted and argued for many hours. Khālid Muḥī al-Dīn, Nasser and 'Āmir suggested that Khamīs and al-Baqrī be spared execution. But the verdicts were confirmed by the majority. Naguib even had Kamīs brought to him in Cairo for a talk and promised to save his life if he would reveal who was behind the strikers. Khamīs kept silent—apparently he had nothing to tell: The stories of agitation and attempted communist revolution which had been spread in connection with the strike had been invented; a spontaneous movement of workers had demanded their rights and believed in all innocence that the victory of the Free Officers would mark the beginning of an era of freedom. But on September 8 Khamīs and al-Baqrī were hanged.[18]

The incident at Kafr al-Dawār demonstrated the attitude of the Free Officers to every independent fighting movement, and especially to the workers' movement. They did not disregard the distress and demands of the workers and peasants and even made efforts to improve their lot, but whatever they did was *for* them and not *together with* them. Spontaneous activity and free organization were neither encouraged nor even tolerated.

A year and a quarter later Nasser wrote in his *Philosophy of the Revolution* in a tone of lament and apology that during the Revolution, with the exception of him and his comrades, there had been no one in Egypt who was concerned with the common good, that all had merely been selfish sycophants, and that the picture that emerged looked dark and ominous

[17] *The Times,* London, 19 August 1952.

[18] Naguib, 172–4; Lacouture, 165–6; Wheelock, 15–16; *The Times,* London, 14 August 1952; *Hamizrah,* vol. 4, 32.

and produced in him "a psychological crisis."[19] He made no mention of Kafr al-Dawār in his book. However, his statements are not to be dismissed as just arrogant hypocrisy. Not only do they contain a measure of truth, if not the whole truth—but they allude to the principal problem of the officers' rule: In order to consolidate their power and carry out their plans, the active participation of large public bodies is necessary. However, a regime like this cannot or will not or dare not allow any group of people to display initiative or independence. It therefore stifles all activity. This is its inherent dialectic contradication.

The incident at Kafr al-Dawār lay at the crossroads. If a good government is, as stated by Lincoln, "of the people, by the people, and for the people," it can be a debatable, and it is a debated point whether or not the government established in Egypt in 1952 was *of* the people and *for* the people, but it is clear as daylight that it was not *by* the people.

Before the coup the Free Officers' Association ramified ties with various public bodies but did not collaborate with them. After seizing power the officers utilized these connections to bolster their regime, and as it entrenched itself more firmly, they proceeded to liquidate the other organizations, with no exception. They began with the parliamentary parties and ended with the Muslim Brethren.

The officers had no contact with the masses on the day of the coup. The public remained passive and were not called upon to demonstrate or take part in any other way in the establishment of the new government. On July 25 demonstrations were explicitly forbidden. The coup of July 1952 undoubtedly inaugurated a new period of basic political change and major social transformation in Egypt. But no revolution took place. The officers did not stand at the head of a revolution—on the contrary, they prevented it although they donned the mantle of revolutionaries. When King Faruq sailed from Alexandria on July 26, they honored him with a 21-gun naval salute. The workers of Kafr al-Dawār who cheered the Revolution were mowed down with bullets and their leaders sent to the scaffold.

The Free Officers made up their minds to consolidate their power against any other force, against the right no less than against the left. Breaking the power of the workers was a relatively simple task—it was the elimination of a potential rival, either as a partner or as an adversary. Breaking the back of the right involved a contest with a mighty foe, with the traditional bearers of power. The first act in this struggle consisted of a purge in the armed forces, followed by the elimination of political parties and introduction of agrarian reform.

[19] Nasser, *Egypt's liberation*, 33–9; Arabic, 22–5.

The ousting of the heads of the army was the principal act on the night of the coup itself. Personnel changes were continued, and in a short time nearly all the top brass was replaced. More than 400 officers were cashiered, most of the colonels and all men of higher rank, with the exception of Naguib and Brigadier Muḥammad Ibrāhīm. Of the dismissed men, several were put on trial and most of them were retired. Their posts were not filled particularly by the leaders of the Free Officers. These men devoted themselved to their political jobs and handed out promotions to other officers on whom they could rely and who were professionally competent. In this way the leaders of the Free Officers managed to secure the loyalty of large numbers of officers while, at the same time, they were successful in raising the standard of the army.

With the parties the officers played a cat and mouse game. Immediately after the coup the party leaders hastened to congratulate the army movement and proclaim their support of its aims. Whether they believed that in this way they could put one over on the officers and that in the end things would remain as they were, or whether they thought that in this way they would save the existence of the party system and their personal political status—in either event, they miscalculated. The officers had entirely different intentions. On July 31, the parties were ordered "to purge their ranks" as the army had done. This demand was a clever stratagem. On the surface it amounted to recognition of the parties, but in practice it established their dependence on the new regime, and even cast a bone of contention into their internal workings. The party leaders could not oppose the principle of the purge, especially after their previous contemptible declarations of loyalty. After they fell into the trap by pledging to purge their ranks, quarrels and conspiracies erupted within each party about who should be purged; while from without, the pressure for expediting the purges and expanding them was increased. If they would not purge themselves, the government threatened to do it. On September 8 a new law pertaining to political parties was published making their existence contingent upon approval of their principles and leaders by the government. The old parties hastily improvised new platforms—the Wafd defined itself as a "democratic, socialist political party," and the Sa'adists, the party of the industrialists, called itself "The Democratic Socialist Party." This farce only added several nails to the parties' coffin lids. The only party which tried to put up a fight was the Wafd, that large popular force with a generation-long tradition of standing up to the British and the royal court and with a ramified political machine. The personality of Muṣṭafā Naḥḥās became a bone of contention with the officers. The officers demanded his dismissal while the Wafdist press came out with headlines such as "There is no Wafd without Naḥḥās,"[20] who himself proclaimed, "No power except Allah and the Egyptian people can eliminate me."[21] The pathetic declaration that there was no Wafd without Naḥḥās was true, and that was just why the officers demanded his dismissal; but Naḥḥās' statement that the officers could not get the better of him was an empty boast. Naguib went on a campaign tour of several days through the towns of the Delta where Naḥḥās was born and which was the traditional stronghold of the Wafd, and he was enthusiastically received. The Wafdists themselves began to debate the question of Naḥḥās, and on October 6 he became the "honorary president" of the party—politically he was finished.

Naḥḥās had not come out of power with clean hands; his wife and her relatives had taken gross advantage of his high position to accumulate as much money and property as they desired. He had opposed agrarian reform. Nevertheless, he had symbolized the Egyptian struggle for independence and had been an old opponent of the King and he was the leader of the largest party. His ousting did not represent a transition to sounder democracy but a tightening of the noose of dictatorship. The right-wing leadership of the Wafd was eliminated from the political arena not for the purpose of clearing the way for more progressive elements but in order to put an end to a popular movement. The next step, which was taken on January 16, 1953, was the outlawing of all parties and the confiscation of their property. A week later, half a year after the coup, the "Liberation Rally" was founded.

The most important act against the right was agrarian reform. This law, published on September 9, will be discussed later. Compared with the agrarian reform in Japan after World War II—not to mention those in the Peoples' Democracies—the Egyptian reform was very moderate in its instructions and modest in scope. However, it succeeded in breaking the social basis of power of the class which had until then ruled the country. This was one of its aims—not the only one but a principal one, and it was achieved to the full. The previous landlords remained wealthy but their status was basically changed. Before this, they had owned the wealth and controlled all opinion in "their" villages while leading a pampered life in the city with their income and the constant increase in the value of their property almost authomatically assured; they had been members of parliament and men with titles—and all this had passed, never to return. Agrarian reform, together with other acts by the officers, immobilized as a political force the big landowners' class.

[20] *Hamizrah,* vol. 4, 31.

[21] Wheelock, 18; *The Jewish Observer,* 2 September 1952.

After the political elimination of the royal family, the army top brass, the landlords and the parties, as well as the strangling of incipient movements of workers, there was no longer any doubt as to who the exclusive rulers of Egypt were. As is the custom in military coups, the Free Officers promised that when the time came they would return to barracks. In the first communiqué of July 23 they proclaimed that "the army is now acting for the homeland within the confines of the constitution."[22] A communiqué of July 25 declared that all acts of the army "are of a temporary nature. All those in positions of leadership in this blessed movement will return to their regular duties the moment they are convinced that the country is in reliable hands."[23] Similar statements were made about convoking parliament at the beginning of 1953, the holding of elections in the near future, etc. Actually, developments moved on a diametrically opposite tack. In principle, three courses were open to the officers: The gradual transfer of power to others; sharing it with another element; or strengthening their own exclusive domination. They chose the third course—and not because they had no other choice.

The government formed by 'Alī Māhir on the day after the coup consisted entirely of civilians. They resigned on September 7. The Prime Minister and most of the other cabinet members refused to approve the proposed plan for agrarian reform and were ordered to leave. The new government which was formed the same day was headed by Naguib, who also became Minister of War and of the Navy and continued to serve as Commander-in-Chief of the Armed Forces. Tens of former party leaders were arrested.

In June 1953, on the day the republic was proclaimed, important changes were made in the composition of the government. Naguib, now President, also remained Prime Minister. Beside him, there were three other officers in the cabinet: Nasser as Deputy Prime Minister, Baghdādī as Minister of War, and Ṣalāḥ Sālim as Minister of National Guidance and Minister of State for Sudanese Affairs. 'Āmir was promoted from major to major-general and made Commander-in-Chief of the Armed Forces. In October two more officers joined the government: Jamāl Sālim as Minister of Transport and Zakariyyā Muḥī al-Dīn as Minister of the Interior, in control of large establishments of police and secret police; he held on to this control either as minister, Vice President, or Prime Minister from then till September 1966.

In April 1954 a new government was formed. Nasser became Prime

[22] Rāfi'ī, *Thawra,* 25.

[23] Lacouture, 156.

Minister and the number of officers in the cabinet—with the exception of Naguib, who remained President—rose to eight. The new officer ministers were Shāfi'ī, Ḥasan Ibrāhīm, and Kamāl al-Dīn Ḥusayn.

In September 1956 after the ratification of the new constitution, the heads of the regime doffed their uniforms and formally became civilians. Only 'Āmir remained in the army. However, neither the nature of the personalities nor of the regime changed. The trend to appoint officers as cabinet members continued. In all the Egyptian governments after 1952 from a quarter to a half of the ministers were always officers. What is more important, all of the top leaders were invariably officers.

However, the occupation of ministerial posts was only one of the manifestations of power by the Free Officers, and not especially the decisive one. Until the summer of 1956 it was not the government which was the determining institution in the state. Every major decision was made by the Officers' Committee. The provisional constitution of February 1953 established that "The commander of the Revolution fulfils the functions of supreme sovereignty in the Revolutionary Council, especially by those acts which he deems necessary for defending the Revolution and the regime based on it and for carrying out its aims, and through exercising the right of appointing and dismissing ministers." [24]

The composition of the Officers' Committee after the coup was never made public and apparently it was not fixed. There was talk of nine members.[25] These would be the men on the founding committee of 1949, without 'Abd al-Mun'im 'Abd al-Ra'ūf who had gone over to the Muslim Brethren. Several other officers, including Naguib, participated in some of the sessions. Half a year later, in January 1953, the Committee called itself the "Revolutionary Command Council" (RCC). The composition of this council was not made public. According to various accounts in the Egyptian press,[26] it at first had 14 members. Their names appeared for the first time as signers of the proclamation of the republic on June 18, 1953.[27] There were 12 at the time as two had in the meantime been expelled.

In June 1956 the RCC was abolished. The duplication of the RCC and the government was no longer necessary. Outwardly power was transferred to civilian patterns and the army's intervention had come to an end. In fact it affixed the final seal to the domination of Egypt by a group of officers whose sole leader was Nasser. He was far above the others in talent and

[24] Sa'īd, 57–8.

[25] Lacouture, 163; R. Crossman, 'Egypt's nine just men', *New Statesman*, London, 17 January 1953.

[26] E.g., *al-Muṣawwar*, 27 March 1953.

[27] *Al-Ahrām*, 19 June 1953.

force of personality, in shrewdness and lust for power. Anyone standing in his way was eliminated.

Absolute power was not attained without violent struggle. Victory over all elements in the population who were remote from the Free Officers in their character and outlook was achieved with relative ease. The major difficulties emerged in the struggles among the officers themselves and in the fight with the mass organization which was closest to many of them—the Muslim Brethren. Opposition to the policy and rule of Nasser came from various quarters and had diverse and even contradictory aims; but in the political battles of 1953 and 1954 all his rivals met on one front—until all of them were vanquished.

The first to be eliminated was Rashād Muhannā. Born in 1909, Muhannā represented the transition phase between the generation of Naguib, born in 1901, and that of Nasser, born in 1918. He came from a wealthy family of landowners, officers and members of the liberal professions.[28] He was a prominent figure in the Egyptian army. At the Royal Military College at Sandhurst he excelled.[29] His views were close to the Muslim Brethren. In 1947 he was placed under arrest for suspected organization of a conspiracy in the army.[30] In 1951 he was attracted to the Free Officers, who were interested in taking him into their circle, and in January 1952 he was elected to the Committee of the Officers' Club. But his loyalty was in doubt. In February he was let in on the plans for the coup; as an artillery colonel he was assigned an important part in it. However, he was suddenly transferred to El-Arish, and later the Free Officers learned that he had been posted there at his own request and that he could therefore not be trusted. After the success of the coup, he hastened to come out in support of it and appeared an extremist in his demand for Fārūq's expulsion. On July 30 he was appointed Minister of Transport in 'Alī Māhir's government and on August 2 one of the three members of the Regency Council. (According to the constitution only a member of the royal family or a former minister could serve as regent, and he received the cabinet appointment only to qualify him for the regency.)

The Free Officers hoped that the position of regent would satisfy Muhannā's ambitions and retain his loyalty without his having much influence in the country and the army. However, he was not content to be a mere figurehead and began to act as if he was taking the King's place. Moreover, he openly opposed the policies of the Free Officers and criticized agrarian reform. On October 14 he was dismissed. He was granted an

[28] Sadat, *Revolt,* 101; *al-Ahrām;* 19 February 1962 (obituary).

[29] Abegg, 43.

[30] Naguib, 16–7

annual pension of E£ 1,500, and a few days later he once again enjoyed freedom of movement and was offered an ambassadorial post.[31] But he had no desire to leave the country and continued to voice reactionary ideas. On January 16, 1953 he was again arrested and in March sentenced to life imprisonment in a secret trial held by the RCC sitting as a court-martial. The charge was an attempt to organize a revolt in the army. Several years later he was released for health reasons.

It was not long before the dismissals and secret court-martials reached the core of the Free Officers themselves. The first to be eliminated was Lieutenant-Colonel Muḥammad Ḥasan Damanhūrī, one of the outstanding members of the Association, who had served in the important post of governor of the Western Desert. On January 17, 1953 he was arrested and three days later sentenced to death by the RCC. The sentence was later commuted to life imprisonment. His younger brother, Captain Ḥasan Rif'at Damanhūrī, was arrested with him and tried. He was sentenced to five years' imprisonment and expelled from the army. The Damanhūrīs were charged with plotting within the army, and the semi-official historian of the regime called it "the most dangerous conspiracy since the Revolution took place."[32] There is no proof that the conspiracy actually existed. But Damanhūrī was critical of the dictatorship, he voiced his opinions, and that was reason enough for throwing him into prison.

The next to be ousted was Yūsuf Manṣūr Ṣiddīq who, together with 'Āmir, had arrested the army leaders on the night of the coup. In January 1953 he was a member of the RCC, and in March he was one of the 21 lieutenant-colonels to be promoted to full colonel status and was given command of an infantry regiment.[33] This was in compensation for his elimination from politics: He had already been expelled from the RCC a month earlier. Shortly afterwards he left Egypt for France. On his return to Cairo in 1954 he was placed under house-arrest. The circumstances of his dismissal are not clear but the reasons are evident. He was a leftist and according to the communist "Democratic Movement for National Liberation" one of its members. He said in March 1954—when to admit communism was tantamount to committing suicide—that he did not lean toward communism but neither did he oppose it.[34]

The second member of the RCC to be promoted to colonel in March 1953 was 'Abd al-Mun'im Amīn and apparently in his case, too, the promotion

[31] Sādāt, *Qiṣṣa,* 147.

[32] Rāfi'ī, 94.

[33] *Al-Ahrām,* 19 March 1953.

[34] *Al-Miṣrī,* Cairo, 26 March 1953; Lacouture, 47–8, 265; Anouar Abdel-Malek, *Egypte, société militaire,* Paris 1962, 208.

was connected with his political demise. In the summer of 1953 he was no longer on the RCC. He later served as ambassador to the Netherlands and West Germany. At the end of the 1950's he was living in Cairo as a retired major-general.[35] He had no desire to tighten the dictatorship and was forced to resign.

Next among the prominent officers to be ousted was Aḥmad Shawqī, the man who had commanded the 13th Battalion which captured the General Staff on the night of the coup. He later became commander of the Cairo military district. Shawqī differed from Nasser's friends in origin, age, character and outlook. He was born in 1907, the son of a well-to-do pasha from ʻAli Māhir's family, and liked to enjoy life without strictly observing Islamic precepts. He held liberal views and this drew him close to Naguib. In July 1953 he angered Nasser by deciding to accompany Naguib on a pilgrimage to Mecca; everyone knew that Shawqī, who was indifferent to religion, had a political demonstration in mind. On his return he was asked to resign all his posts. His ousting heralded an open clash with Naguib. Several months later Shawqī was tried by a military court headed by Baghdādī and was sentenced to ten years' imprisonment for "inciting officers to mutiny in the army." He was later released for health reasons.[36]

Another year of crisis was 1954. The opposition to Nasser's leadership grew on three fronts. There were four contending forces: Nasser and most of the members of the RCC, the Muslim Brethren, Naguib backed by people with liberal tendencies, and the left headed by Khālid Muḥī al-Dīn.

For a year and a half the Muslim Brethren was the only mass organization—with the exception of the official Liberation Rally—which was allowed to conduct activities openly. Immediately after the coup those Brethren who were imprisoned were released. The investigation of Ḥasan al-Bannā's assassination was reopened, and on the anniversary of his death Naguib visited his grave.[37] He also participated in the celebrations conducted by the Brethren in honor of the Prophet's birthday.[38] It was explicitly established that the ban against political parties did not apply to them.[39] The organizational ties between the Brethren and the Free Officers were of long standing and a strong ideological bond connected them. The ideology of the Brethren was one of the basic influences that shaped the views of the officers. Nasser, however, had long realized that despite the closeness to each other, their aims were not identical, and he was strict

[35] *Who's who in UAR and the Near East* 1959, Cairo, 1959, 264.

[36] Wheelock, 39; Lacouture 145, 154; Rāfiʻī, 103.

[37] *Al-Ahrām,* 13 February 1953.

[38] *Al-Ahrām,* 3 December 1952.

[39] Rāfiʻī, 74.

about maintaining the distinctions between the officers and the Brethren. But, in the first year after the coup the Free Officers hoped for full support of the Brethren; and even if they had so wished, they could not have treated them as they treated the other parties. For their part the Brethren saw a prospect of the Free Officers' making their plans bear fruit. Each of the two bodies wished and hoped that the other would be its agent, and it was precisely for this reason that a rift between them finally appeared.

The quarrel which had latently developed during the underground period came out into the open right after the coup. On the night of July 25, 1952, Nasser was visited by the leaders of the army officers who belonged to the Muslim Brethern, 'Abd al-Mun'im 'Abd al-Ra'ūf and Major Abū al-Makārim 'Abd al-Ḥayy, who requested that he equip them with weapons.[40] Their request was of course turned down—Egyptian officers had always preserved the monopoly of arms within the army. Instead of receiving arms, the Brethren were invited to nominate three of their number for ministerial posts in the new government formed in September. They had hoped for more or had wanted the power to pull strings behind the scenes, and they therefore demanded assurances that policies and new laws would be laid down only with their approval. On receiving a negative answer, they decided not to participate in the government. Ḥasan al-Baqūrī, one of their leaders, who had joined the government as Minister of *Waqfs* (religious endowments) on his own accord, was expelled from the ranks of the Brethren.[41] Nevertheless, both sides tried to avoid open conflict. But the breach could not be prevented for long.

The problem of relations between the Free Officers and the Muslim Brethren had caused dissension among the Free Officers before the coup; in 1953 it gave rise to bitter discussion and factional strife among the Brethren. Huḍaybı, the "Supreme Guide," favored compromise, but against him crystallized an extremist wing, headed by 'Ashmāwī, who wanted to restore the Brethren's militant character. In the autumn of 1953 the discord reached the point of reciprocal dismissals. It was clear to both factions that the honeymoon of the Brethren and the officers had long been over; the argument centered on ways in which to react.

On January 11, 1954 there was a violent clash between students belonging to the Brethren and others of the Liberation Rally. At a meeting on the campus of Cairo University in memory of the student members of the Brethren who had been killed in the winter of 1951-52 in the anti-British

[40] *Al-Ahrām*, 20 November 1965 (Nasser's speech at Heluan); Kāmil Sharīf, *Al-muqāwama al-sirriyya fī qanāt al-Suways 1951–1954*, Cairo 1957, 216.

[41] M.I. Husaini, *The Moslem Brethren*, Beirut 1956, 114, 131.

struggle in the Canal region, the Brethren denounced Nasser as a dictator and a lackey of imperialism.[42] Nasser struck back hard. On January 15 the Muslim Brethren were outlawed and their leaders arrested. A protest demonstration by the Brethren on the following day was dispersed by troops who opened fire. It was announced that secret arms caches belonging to the Brethren had been discovered.

As relations between the officers and the Brethren collapsed, a breach with the third factor in the struggle over the character of the regime, Naguib, appeared. The decision to outlaw the Brethren had been taken and proclaimed without consulting Naguib, who was then President of the Republic, President of the Revolutionary Council, Prime Minister, and Commander-in-Chief of the Armed Forces. On February 25 he resigned from all his duties. (This was the same day on which Shīshaklī fled from Syria.)

The unseen struggle between Naguib and Nasser which came out into the open at the end of February had been going on for more than six weeks between the outlawing of the Brethren and Naguib's resignation.

After the final expulsion of Naguib, the officers stressed that from the beginning they had only intended to make use of him as their liaison with the outside world, and it is difficult to ascertain how much truth there is in this. It may be assumed that here, as in so many other matters, they had had no clear-cut policy. After the coup Naguib's personality and tremendous popularity were great assets to the new regime. Naguib did not regard himself as only a figurehead. He was, however, confronted by Nasser.

These two personalities differed not only in age—they were a generation apart—but also in character. There is an incident which throws light on Naguib's character. Several days after the coup, on one of his trips through Cairo, he passed the military prison where the former army chiefs were kept. He told his driver to stop, visited the prisoners and promised them that a fair trial would be held and that those whose innocence could be proved would be released. With simplicity and gentle ways he won over the masses. In the government and the RCC he regarded himself as being foremost among equals. Nasser, however, could not rest until it was clear that he came first and that all the others were equal only to one another.

The two men differed in outlook. Naguib wanted a gradual transition to parliamentary government; Nasser believed it necessary to tighten the dictatorship, and the majority on the RCC shared his view. On various occasions throughout 1953 Naguib no longer concealed his dissatisfaction with various measures adopted and with the disregard for his authority. He believed that the nation could go forward guided by a leadership which

[42] *Hamizrah Hehadash,* vol. 5, 110, 198.

was broadly based and represented diverse interests and opinions. Nasser was a fanatic nationalist. He did not believe that the Egyptians would be able to overcome their own weaknesses or their external enemies unless, like a fighting army, they were arrayed under one commander. To the people Naguib was a father figure while Nasser was then "Big Brother", in the Orwellian sense.

The outlawing of the Muslim Brethren behind his back was a blatant insult to Naguib who took his case to the RCC. There he demanded that a decision for which he was responsible as President should not be adopted without his prior consent and that a decision by the majority of the Council against his opinion should not be proclaimed in his name. "It was not the same as demanding the right of unlimited veto. I was simply asking for a limited veto, that could be overridden on condition that the Council did so openly." He did not wish "to be compelled to accept the sole responsibility for decisions adopted secretly by the Council against my best judgement."[43] His opponents later represented this position as aspiration to personal dictatorship. This was not his intention nor the meaning of his demands. However, the controversy was a basic one and there was no longer room nor desire for compromise. The RCC under the leadership of Nasser and Ṣalāḥ Sālim rejected Naguib's demands and he resigned. His resignation was accepted, and upon its publication Naguib was immediately placed under house-arrest.

At this point the fourth contending factor, the left under the leadership of Khālid Muḥi al-Dīn, entered the fray.

Khālid Muḥī al-Dīn was the youngest member on the RCC—he was then 31—and at the same time one of the veterans among the leaders of the Free Officers. When the Association's Committee was founded in 1949 he was among the first five to be appointed. He was a communist and may have been a member of the "Democratic Movement for National Liberation." Nevertheless, he managed to preserve his status as a member of the RCC until the beginning of 1954, thanks to his cousin Zakariyyā Muḥī al-Dīn, Minister of the Interior and head of the secret police. He also considerably influenced his fellow officers in the Armored Corps, and it was among them that the first group in support of Naguib was organized.

On hearing of Naguib's resignation, 40 Armored Corps' officers rebelled. The public was excited and in a dither. The Sudanese government sent an official delegation to Cairo to demand assurances for the personal safety of Naguib, who was popular in Sudan where he was born and had served for many years. The Frontier Force, too, whose commander Naguib

[43] Naguib, 191, 215.

had been until the autumn of 1951, threatened to rally to his side. Those who were against the military dictatorship—the Muslim Brethren and the communists, bourgeois elements and workers, old-time Wafdists and students—all demanded Naguib's return.

On the evening of February 26 Nasser retreated and agreed to Naguib's return to the presidency. The next morning Naguib was persuaded by Khālid Muḥī al-Dīn to withdraw his resignation, and both assumed that Khālid would be prime minister. Shortly after Khālid left Naguib's house, which was still sourrounded by troops, Naguib was kidnapped by two officers of the military police who drove him out to the desert, not with friendly intentions. However, at Nasser's order he was released. At noon he dispatched a letter to the RCC, intended for publication, in which he acknowledged the authority of the RCC and "its leader" and his acceptance of "the invitation of the Revolutionary Council to return to the presidency of the parliamentary Egyptian republic."[44] The highly significant expression "the parliamentary Egyptian republic" had not been agreed upon with the RCC. They had only agreed upon Naguib's restoration to the presidency and no more than that. Nasser who, two days earlier, on Naguib's resignation had taken over all his duties, remained prime minister.

The public accepted the solution to the crisis as a victory for Naguib. When he returned to the Palace of the Republic on the morning of February 28 a huge crowd in festive mood—according to numerous witnesses the largest throng that had ever gathered in Cairo—came to congratulate him. On making their way to the Palace a group of students formed a demonstration and decried Nasser. The police opened fire on them, killing three and wounding ten. When the survivors reached the Square of the Republic, they waved a banner—a cloth dipped in blood of one of the slain students—and the crowd became more and more inflamed. From the throng there emerged 'Abd al-Qādir 'Awda, one of the extremist leaders of the Muslim Brethren, and joined Naguib on a balcony of the palace. It was only after he had spoken that the crowd dispersed. It turned out that the demonstration had been organized by the Brethren. Once again they proved their power and organizational skill. However, they would not have succeeded had a large section of the public not been aroused.

On the next day Naguib, too, suffered a defeat—far from Cairo. On March 1 he flew to Khartoum for the opening ceremony of the Sudanese parliament. The journey had been planned for some time, and the timing of his resignation on February 25 may have been calculated to exert greater pressure on the RCC, who could not overlook his considerable popularity

[44] *Ibid.*, 225–7; Rāfi'ī, 117–8.

in Sudan. However, when Naguib and Ṣalāh Sālim reached Khartoum airport on March 1, they were met by an anti-Egyptian demonstration consisting of ten thousand people, some of them spearbearers from the south, organized by the *Umma* Party. Tens of people were killed in clashes between the demonstrators, their opponents and the police. Naguib and Sālim were forced to return to Cairo as they had come. It has not been proved whether or not the British helped to organize the demonstrations. The British commander of the Khartoum police was one of those killed.

Nasser took advantage of Naguib's brief absence and his rebuff at Khartoum to deal a counter-blow, despite his agreement that no revenge would be taken after the crisis. He did not aim the blow against Naguib directly. On March 2, 118 Muslim Brethren, communists and Wafdists were arrested. In the army, too, several officers were dismissed. Naguib could not take up cudgels for the communists and the Muslim Brethren, but neither did Nasser gain popularity from his new acts of oppression. For a while Naguib had the upper hand. On March 5, the RCC decided to hold elections in June and to abolish press censorship. On March 8, Naguib again became chairman of the RCC and Prime Minister. Prisoners were released, and various public bodies and party organizations began to function again. It seemed possible that Egypt would return, or advance, to democracy, but in fact confusion reigned. Nasser and his associates had only yielded on the surface. Actually they refrained from doing anything that would facilitate an orderly transition to another regime, and they wanted to prove that without them the country would succumb to chaos. On March 25 the RCC adopted a "final decision" to disband shortly, to permit the parties to reorganize and to conduct elections.

The "final" decision was, however, far from final. Immediately after their quasi-defeat, Nasser's supporters took the initiative. Rumors circulated to the effect that the Revolution was in danger and that the parties, pashas and corruption were about to return. On March 26 a number of strikes broke out in support of the return of the RCC. The first strikers were army officers; the leader of the strike was 'Abd al-Ḥakīm 'Āmir. After them came the Cairo Transport Workers' Union. All transport in this city of millions stopped in order to clear the streets for demonstrations on behalf of the RCC. Two days later the strikes spread to other parts of the country. Naguib symbolized a front of heterogenous forces which he did not know how to direct, while Nasser controlled two powerful groups—the officer corps and the labor unions. The officer corps had no desire to give up its favored position and the power it gained during the RCC's regime, and through dismissals and promotions Nasser and 'Āmīr had succeeded in securing its loyalty. The Cairo workers were organized within the Liberation

Rally under the leadership of Major Ṭu'ayma of the Free Officers. And even if they were not fully reconciled to the dictatorship, they were still less interested in the return of the Wafdists. Moreover, what could a bus driver do in a strike proclaimed simultaneously by the head of the union, the leader of the Liberation Rally, and the Minister of Transport?

Two days after his apparent triumph it was clear that Naguib had lost the battle. On March 29 Ṣalāḥ Sālim announced that the RCC, "in response to popular demand," had revoked the decisions of March 5 and 25 and that it would conduct the affairs of the country in a "transition period" until January 1956. All the parties were outlawed with the exception of the Muslim Brethren. In the weeks that followed, the arrests and trials of statesmen, officers and journalists once again gathered momentum. On April 17 Nasser again became prime minister, two additional members of the RCC became ministers and Naguib remained president only.[45]

In April 1954 Khālid Muḥī al-Dīn was expelled from the RCC and banished to Europe. His dismissal finally sealed the suppression of the left.

In the summer of 1954, Anglo-Egyptian negotiations took place on the evacuation of British bases in the Suez Canal region. The evacuation agreement was signed on October 19. Egypt's foremost national aspiration for 72 years was fulfilled. Throughout the world the agreement was presented as the greatest achievement of the new Egyptian government. But in Egypt there was strong opposition, for there was a fly in the ointment. Article 4 of the agreement provided that "in the event of an armed attack by an outside power on any country which at the date of signature of the present agreement is a party to the Treaty of Joint Defence between Arab League States signed in Cairo on April 13, 1950, or on Turkey, Egypt shall afford to the United Kingdom such facilities as may be necessary in order to place the base on a war footing and its effective operation."[46] In other words, Nasser signed an agreement that in the event of a third world war Egypt would once again be under British occupation. This article, together with the entire agreement, was abrogated by the British invasion of 1956, but in 1954 its unambiguous meaning was to tie Egypt to the west. The Muslim Brethren, the communists, and the Wafdist left once again conducted a vigorous campaign against the agreement, denouncing it as a betrayal. On October 26, when Nasser was addressing a mass meeting at Alexandria, Maḥmūd 'Abd al-Laṭīf, a member of the Muslim Brethren, fired eight pistol shots at him at close range. He missed and was arrested on the spot.

[45] Lacouture, 179–95; Wheelock, 27–36; Rāfi'ī, 104–35; *Hamizrah,* vol. 5, 195–9, 286–7.
[46] J.C. Hurewitz, *Diplomacy in the Near and Middle East,* Princeton 1956, vol. 2, 384.

Nasser seized upon this assault to settle accounts with the Muslim Brethren. Their organization was outlawed and their leaders arrested, tortured, and sentenced. Seven were sentenced to death and hanged.

On November 4, the officers' newspaper *al-Jumhūriyya* published a photostatic copy of a letter sent to Nasser by 'Abd al-Qādir 'Awda, Deputy Supreme Guide of the Muslim Brethren, the man who on February 28 had spoken at Naguib's side from the balcony of the Palace of the Republic. The letter had been written in prison on October 28. 'Awda suggested to Nasser that the "old friendship" between the Brethren and the officers be renewed and that they put an end to the quarrel "which was only one year old." He addressed Nasser as "my brother," and the newspaper added that the two had met "more than twenty times." The trials of the Brethren disclosed many more details of the long-standing ties between them and the Free Officers.[47] But the old friendship was no longer of help to 'Awda, who was sentenced to death and hanged, just as it was not held against Nasser. Instead, Naguib was publicly accused of maintaining secret ties with the Brethren, and on November 14 he was relieved of his duties, this time for good. He was then placed under house-arrest. In 1966 he died, a broken and forgotten man.[48]

For years there was no element in Egypt that could have threatened Nasser's power. He was victorious in the dramatic struggles of 1954 partly because he had no ties with the reactionary circles of the past that surrounded Naguib, and especially because he was the cleverest tactician of them all and had the army behind him.

In 1954 Nasser wanted to demonstrate that Egypt had to choose between dictatorship of the RCC and chaos. He did not believe in a third alternative—the gradual transition to a democratic regime. He convinced many people both in Egypt and abroad that the third alternative was not feasible; but he did not prove it. At any rate, the dramatic events of 1954 showed that under the mantle of the dictatorship forces were astir within the population—right-wing and left-wing, constructive and destructive, dynamic and wayward.

By the beginning of 1955 all accounts between the RCC and its opponents had been settled, and only a few matters within the Council itself remained to be straightened out. Of the 14 original members ten remained. Of these, two more, the Sālim brothers, were expelled in 1955.

Ṣalāḥ Sālim resigned in August, 1955 after the failure of the Sudanese policy for which he was responsible.[49] Was that the only reason? Ṣalāḥ

[47] Kamāl Kira, *Maḥkamat al-Sha'b,* vol. 1, Cairo (1955), 42–4, 49–50, 58.

[48] *Al-Manār,* Amman, 4 August 1966.

[49] Rāfi'ī, 164.

Sālim was an old member of the group, a fanatical nationalist, and next to Nasser its outstanding personality. Could Nasser have feared personal competition? There had never been basic differences between them. Ṣalāḥ Sālim might again have occupied a position among the leadership, but he fell ill, and died in 1962.

His step-brother Jamāl was a man with progressive ideas, the intellectual among the Free Officers. He fathered the idea of Agrarian Reform. At first he had also been in charge of its implementation, but already in January 1953 he was eliminated from any activity in this sphere. He remained on the RCC but was not given any important duties. In November 1955 he was appointed Deputy Prime Minister and Minister of Transport, but in the government formed in June 1956 he was no longer a minister. He was assigned the task of organizing government administration [50]; since then his name has not been mentioned. He appeared at his brother's funeral as a private citizen to whom everyone showed respect. Politically his career had ended long ago.

Who were the victors?

The character of the leadership as it stabilized was reflected in the composition of the government formed at the end of June, 1956 after the ratification of the constitution and the election by referendum of Nasser as President.

On the Committee of the Free Officers' Association of 1949 there were ten members; nine of them were on the RCC of 1953. 'Abd al-Mun'im 'Abd al-Ra'ūf had been dismissed and five other members added. Of these 14 officers, six were ministers in the 1956 cabinet and three occupied senior posts without the rank of minister: Nasser—President; Baghdādī—Minister for Municipal and Rural Affairs and Minister of State for Planning; Zakariyyā Muḥī al-Dīn—Minister of the Interior; Shāfi'ī—Minister for Social Affairs and Minister of Labor; 'Āmir—Minister of War; Kamāl al-Dīn Ḥusayn—Minister of Culture and Education. Ḥasan Ibrāhīm was appointed to the Commission for National Planning. Sādāt handled the affairs of the Islamic Conference and Jamāl Sālim was appointed inspector of the civil service organization. The appointment of Ḥasan Ibrāhīm and Sādāt to secondary functions meant that they had ceased to belong to the top leadership—to which they returned several years later. For Jamāl Sālim it was the last phase before the complete liquidation of his political career.

A number of facts stand out:

All the old-time leftists were eliminated: Khālid Muḥī al-Dīn, Yūsuf

[50] *Ibid.*, 221.

Manṣūr Ṣiddīq, 'Abd al-Mun'im Amīn and Jamāl Sālim. Ousted together with them was Naguib. Of those remaining in the top leadership all had at some time between 1935 and 1955 been associated in one form or another with organizations of the extreme right. Nasser and Ḥasan Ibrāhīm had been members of the fascist *Miṣr al-Fatāt* in their youth.[51] Sādāt, Baghdādī and Ḥasan Ibrāhīm had been active in 1941–42 in the pro-Nazi underground. And at the end of the 1940's and the beginning of the 1950's all had been associated, at times closely, with the Muslim Brethren. To be sure, the group of officers surrounding Nasser had never stagnated and had gone through many stages in its political, organizational and ideological development, but it would be a mistake to dismiss those early ideological ties and political acts as the sins of youth. The men who at 35 were the leaders of the nation were not children at 30 nor infants at 25. It is not merely chance that all the leftists were eliminated and that in Nasser's Egypt Nazi experts in propaganda, secret police organization and missiles found asylum and employment. Even the argument that the Egyptian and Nazi officers were linked not by common positive aims but by hatred of common enemies—the British and the Jews—does not minimize the nature of the partnership. On the contrary, the search for a "solution" to the question of the Jews and of Israel occupies a central position in the thoughts and deeds of both the Nazis and of Nasser.

Another conspicuous feature in the composition of the top Egyptian leadership as it crystallized in 1956 is the elimination of all those who were more than one year older than Nasser. Those allowed to remain were all born between 1917 and 1921; Nasser was born in January 1918. Naguib (born in 1901), Yūsuf Manṣūr Ṣiddīq (1910) and 'Abd al-Mun'im Amīn (1912) were all gotten rid of. Of course, the principal reasons for their dismissal were political; but the elimination of older rivals also helped strengthen Nasser's position as supreme leader.

The absence of Christians among these officer politicians is also striking. The Free Officers before the coup and the officers who were assigned central functions in the government, the army, the economy and the administration after their accession to power were all Muslims.

The Free Officers considered themselves part of the Egyptian intelligentsia. Ṣalāḥ Dasūqī, one of the Free Officers who fulfilled important functions after the coup and was governor of Cairo district from 1960 to 1965, wrote, "The army revolution of July 23 was by its very nature a revolution of intellectuals."[52] By origin and inclination the officers really were very

[51] Aḥmad 'Aṭiyyat-Allāh. *Qāmūs al-thawra al-maṣriyya* 1954, Cairo 1954, 58,

[52] *Al-Ahrām,* 12 June 1961; Abdel-Malek, 196.

close to the intelligentsia of young lawyers, physicians, engineers, writers and journalists. However, their victory was not just "a revolution of intellectuals." The intellectual and social life of Egypt was in a ferment, a broad, multicolored spectrum of many currents contending for the mind of the people and for influence in the country. The Free Officers represented only one of the colors in the spectrum and persons representing other shades, nearer to red, who had injected themselves into their ranks were eliminated at an early date.

The Free Officers were a part of the rightist, nationalist wing within the Egyptian population and intelligentsia. It is not by chance, of course, that among those in uniform this wing was represented in greater proportion than among the intellectuals in general. In the officer corps, even among the Free Officers, there were men with liberal, socialist, and communist views. If before the coup they had little influence and after the seizure of power even less, when the regime generally became stabilized it was completely eliminated. Nasser's "Arab Socialism" of the 1960's, which will be discussed later, is not the sequence of a liberal, socialist or Marxist ideology, but a further evolution of a rightist, nationalist one.

To what extent was the top leadership which crystallized in 1956 consolidated and united?

For the next years this group of ruling officers was to manifest an exceptionally strong cohesiveness. Nasser, 'Āmir, Zakariyya Muḥī al-Dīn, Sādāt and Ḥasan Ibrāhīm had already become friends in about 1940 when they were young second-lieutenants. For 25 years they remained together in the underground and in government leadership. Kamāl al-Dīn Ḥusayn and Baghdādī were also old-timers. Al-Shāfi'ī, who had been induced to join the Free Officers' Association in the first half of 1952, was considered a veteran in 1956. From then until 1963 these eight men filled positions as President, Vice-President, Supreme Commander of the Armed Forces, and speaker of the National Assembly. They were solidly united in their views and deeds. In the history of political bodies there are not many examples of such consecutive stability.

In the middle of the 1960's, however, this compact group began to disintegrate. In March 1964, when the formation of a new government was announced, the public suddenly became aware of the fact that Baghdādī and Kamāl al-Dīn Ḥusayn had been relieved of all duties. Shortly before, both were still Vice-Presidents and Baghdādī was Nasser's first deputy; in official announcements his name was always mentioned directly after the President's. He stood out as an astute politician and an excellent administrator. Since then, both these outstanding leaders have disappeared. Rumors, naturally contradictory, have it that they have been imprisoned or put under house-arrest, that their properties had been confiscated, and that they had again been released. They were seen in public only at the funerals of deceased relatives in August 1964, October 1965 and January 1966.[53]

More important and more obscure than their personal fate is the question of why they chose or were compelled to resign. No explanation was ever offered either by them or by those remaining in power. It may well be, though it is not certain, that both were against Egypt's massive intervention in Yemen—Baghdādī because he feared the consequences to the country's economy and the inevitable deterioration of its relations with the west, and Kamāl al-Dīn Ḥusayn because he would have left Egypt free for the fight against Israel. It is also possible that one or both disagreed with Nasser's socialism.

In January 1966 Ḥasan Ibrāhīm's resignation was announced, again without explanation. He was the weakest of the leaders; nevertheless, until then he was one of the five Vice-Presidents.

In their place 'Alī Ṣabrī, one of the veterans of the Free Officers, now rose to top prominence. Until August 1957 he had been one of Nasser's advisers as director for political affairs in the president's office. In August 1957 he was given ministerial rank, serving as Minister of State for Presidential Affairs, and in September 1962 he was appointed Prime Minister. Although in 1952 'Alī Ṣabrī had been the liaison officer between the Free Officers and the Americans, and was responsible for Egyptian-American relations[54] in the early days of the new regime, in the middle sixties he appeared as the protagonist of a radical anti-American, socialist and leftist orientation in Egyptian domestic and foreign politics. His main rival was to be Zakariyyā Muḥī al-Dīn, who succeeded him as Prime Minister in October 1965. Zakariyyā Muḥī al-Dīn was suddenly relieved of the premiership after only 11 months in office, in September 1966, and was replaced by the politically colorless Ṣidqi Sulaymān. It was rumored that Zakariyyā Muḥī al-Dīn himself learned of his resignation only when he heard it announced over the radio. As usual, no official or semi-official explanation for the dismissal was forthcoming. He continued as a Vice-President, but for the first time in fourteen years without being chief of police. When on June 9, 1967, Nasser announced his resignation, he named Zakariyyā Muḥī al-Dīn as his successor as President, and after Nasser's swift return to office, Zakariyyā Muḥī al-Dīn was virtually his first deputy. His rival 'Alī Ṣabrī entrenched himself in 1967 mainly in his key-position

[53] *Al-Nahār,* Beirut, 26 October 1965; *Falasṭīn,* Jerusalem (Jordan), 21 January 1966.
[54] K. Wheelock, 218; Abdel-Malek, 54.

as secretary of the Socialist Union. The rivalry for power and for direction of Egypt's politics became fiercer. 'Ālī Ṣabrī stood for ever closer cooperation with the Soviet Union, Zakariyyā Muḥī al-Dīn stressed the importance of a new rapprochement with the USA; the former advocated strong socialist measures in economics, the other the need for more democracy, and so on. It is impossible to ascertain to what extent the rivalry between them reflected the clash between opposite political and ideological orientations, and to what extent it was merely the struggle for power of two overambitious politicians. The round of 1967 was won by 'Alī Ṣabrī. When in March 1968 a new Egyptian government was installed, Zakariyyā Muḥī al-Dīn disappeared altogether, and 'Alī Ṣabrī was more firmly entrenched in his position as secretary of the first Arab Socialist Union.

The dramatic events of June 1967 revealed the true nature of Egypt's regime and rulers. In May Nasser lost his restraint and reason. For years, at least since the bitter lesson of the Sinai War of 1956, he had advocated a policy of avoiding an immediate confrontation with Israel. His fundamental enmity was unwavering, and many times he said, as in his interview on the American Columbia Radio and Television Station on July 13, 1965: "War is the only solution for the Palestine problem."[55] But in actual politics he was guided by the conviction that war against Israel should be waged only after certain conditions had been achieved: 1) clear military superiority of the Arabs, 2) realization of Arab unity, 3) isolation of Israel from the western powers. Clearly those conditions did not exist. But driven by Syrian activist agitation, by bad Soviet advice and by emotions prevailing over reason, he provoked war. The closing of the Straits of Tiran, the demand to the United Nations to withdraw its Emergency Force from the Egyptian-Israeli borders, the massive concentration of large Egyptian armored and infantry forces in advanced positions in the Sinai Peninsula and other words and deeds at the end of May and the beginning of June all meant war. If there was ever any war which could not have been a surprise to anyone it was the war which broke out on June 5, 1967. As Nasser himself said insolently on May 22: "If the Jews want war, we say to them: You are welcome *(ahlan wasahlan)*, we are ready."[56] Perhaps he wanted only to bluff. But his bluff was called and the outcome was catastrophic for Egypt. In less than three days the air force and the armored corps were destroyed, the Gaza Strip and the Sinai Peninsula lost, the Suez Canal put out of action, more than ten thousand soldiers and 1,500 officers killed and 500 officers and 4000 soldiers made prisoners of war.

[55] *Al-Jumhūriyya,* 14 July 1965.

[56] *Al-Ahrām,* 23 May 1967.

For years Nasser had been the sole director and spokesman for Egypt's external policies, and he could not evade accepting responsibility for the defeat. Moreover, it seems that on the morning of June 9th, after the magnitude of the defeat had become clear, Nasser had *nolens volens* to attend a meeting at the headquarters of the armed forces with Marshal 'Āmir, most of the high commanders of the army, air force and navy, and the Minister of War. There he had to face an almost united front of critics who blamed him for the debacle and demanded more or less openly that he resign. And so he announced his resignation in his speech to the nation and to the whole Arab world on the evening of that day.

The mouthpiece and evidently the most resolute of Nasser's critics on that morning was Shams al-Dīn Badrān, the Minister of War[57]. Badrān, more than ten years younger than Nasser, represents a new generation of Egyptian army officers. He was a captain when the officers became rulers of Egypt in 1952, and from then on he worked chiefly in 'Abd al-Hakīm 'Āmir's office, rising to prominence there. In August 1962, at the Arab League meeting after Syria's secession from the UAR, Amīn Nafūrī of Syria related that Badrān had strong influence on Nasser personally.[58] In the government of September 1966 he was appointed Minister of War, and immediately afterwards his powers were greatly enlarged.[59]

After Nasser announced his resignation, Marshal 'Āmir, Minister of War Badrān and six of the seven full generals *(farīq awwal)* followed suit. Other high-ranking officers resigned or were pensioned off in the next few days. The only full general who did not resign was Muḥammad Fawzī, who became the new Commander-in-Chief of the Armed Forces.

Nasser began his speech on the evening of the 9th of June shortly before 7 o'clock; the announcement of his resolution to resign came only at the end of his speech. But popular demonstrations demanding his return to the presidency and leadership had already begun to fill the streets of Cairo before he made that announcement—clear proof that they were not spontaneous at all. On the other hand, Nasser's adversaries, who were concentrated mainly in the Army Command, made a strong effort to disperse the demonstrations at once—by sounding an air-raid alarm and by opening heavy anti-aircraft fire, far heavier than any released during the days of the war.[60] But the alarm was of no avail, neither against Israeli planes which were not near Cairo just then, nor against the demonstrations of

[57] *Al-Nahār,* Beirut, 7 September 1967.

[58] *Al-Ayyām,* Damascus, 28 August 1962.

[59] *Al-Jumhūriyya,* 12 October 1966.

[60] Eric Rouleau, Jean-Francis Held, Jean et Simone Lacouture, *Israel et les Arabes, le 3e combat,* Paris 1967, 152; *al- Nahār,* Beirut, 7 September 1967.

loyalty to Nasser and identification with him, which became more and more massive and enthusiastic. They had been triggered off by activists of the Socialist Union but they would never have succeeded to such a degree had they not been backed by intense popular feeling. It was like the detonation of a large mine. Somebody had to light the fuse, but the ignition of the fuse alone would not have caused so big an explosion without the charge of dynamite. When on the next day Nasser returned to the presidency it was indeed in response to vigorous popular demand.

It was not just the charisma—that undefinable quality of leadership—or the effect of a prolonged personality cult that produced such a strong reaction on the part of the Egyptian masses. People feared that with collapse of false hopes and illusions they would lose everything if the adored leader disappeared too. Nasser had become the father, and the father-image emerges not only when a strong personality wants to impose his authority upon others; its emergence is conditioned also on the existence of a demand for guidance and authority on the part of the quasi-children. Eric Rouleau reports a most significant incident: A Cairene, who in the morning had cried for Nasser's resignation and in the evening for his return, said: "For us Nasser is like some sort of a father; you can be angry with your father and curse him, but you will not be content when he wants to go away. I felt myself totally forlorn."[61] Arnold Hottinger put it otherwise. He wrote then from Beirut: "The occupation of the Egyptian masses' mind with their hero seems to make them forget all other troubles; it is like a drug, without which they cannot do."[62] The similes of the child dependent on his father and the addict dependent on his drug are rather different; but their meaning, the phenomenon itself which they indicate, is one and the same. Indeed: "Failures cannot diminish his (Nasser's) hold on the masses, because their adherence is not based on reality."[63]

On the morning of June 10 Nasser announced his compliance with popular demand and his return to the presidency. He could have made his return conditional on the return of his first deputy and his closest friend, Marshal 'Āmir, to his post. Nobody would or could have opposed him then. But he let 'Āmir fall—he was to be the scapegoat for the catastrophe. His resignation was accepted, sometime later he was put under house-arrest, and finally he was driven to suicide.

'Abd al-Ḥakīm 'Āmir was more than one of Nasser's very few friends, his comrade since 1938 and the father-in-law of his young half-brother.[64]

[61] *Israel et les Arabes, le 3e combat,* 137.

[62] *Neue Zürcher Zeitung,* 12 June 1967.

[63] H.E. Tütsch, *Facets of Arab nationalism,* Detroit 1965, 91.

[64] *Al-Akhbār,* 8 July 1964.

One instance may exemplify their amity: ‘Āmir's father, Shaykh ‘Alī ‘Āmir, the headman of the village of Isṭāl in Minya Province, died on February 4, 1960. The Marshal was then, in the days of the union with Syria, in Damascus, and could not attend his father's funeral, being occupied with the severe fighting raging then at Tawafīq on the Israeli border. But Nasser made the journey to the funeral, and when the Marshal's brothers told him that he, the President, should not have made the trip of more than 120 miles from Cairo, he replied: "‘Abd al-Ḥakīm's father is like my father."[65] This was the sole and single visit which Nasser paid to any of the thousands of villages in Egypt between 1952 and 1968. In his speech of November 1967 Nasser said of ‘Āmir: "I have lost the man most close to me."[66] But he himself had abandoned him.

The top commanders of the Egyptian army and air force were not better and not worse than the other leaders of the country, the ministers, the politicians or the economists; they were not more and not less inefficient than their subordinates, and not more and not less corrupt than the ideologists or propagandists. But they were made the scapegoats for the disaster. All but one of the highest ranking officers, the Marshal, the generals, many of the lieutenant-generals and major-generals were dishonorably discharged. Their representative was, naturally, ‘Āmir.

No wonder, then, that throughout the Egyptian officer corps spread deep feelings of humiliation and resentment. Not only were they beaten by the enemy; not only were many hundreds of them killed, wounded or taken prisoner. The blame for the disaster was also laid upon them by the country's leaders in mufti, those who had suffered and sacrificed less in training and fighting and whose responsibility for all that had happened was no lighter than theirs. In a sweeping purge more than 400 senior and medium-rank officers were dismissed, put under house-arrest and otherwise humiliated.[67] Towards the end of the year some of them were put on trial before military courts.

After the announcement and the acceptance of his resignation, ‘Āmir left Cairo on June 10 and went to his home village in Minya Province. He stayed there four days, then returned to Cairo. From then on his house became the meeting place for many officers who had been sacked as well as some civilians, and served as the center for their deliberations on Egypt's plight. Their resentment against the injustice done to them, in their view, and their ideas on the repair of the country's evils crystallized in the demand to reinstall the Marshal in his former position. The *spiritus rector* of their

[65] *Al-Ahrām,* 6 February 1960.
[66] *Al-Ahrām,* 24 November 1967.
[67] *Al-Nahār,* 7 September 1967.

meetings was Shams al-Dīn Badrān; another prominent officer was Lieutenant-Colonel Jalāl Huraydī, who in September 1961 was the commander of the parachutists who had to put down the Syrian secession, and lastly, the commander of the commando forces. 'Āmir himself seems to have remained rather passive for weeks, neither resolutely opposing the government's adversaries nor openly supporting them. At the end of August it was officially stated that there had been a conspiracy centered in 'Āmir's house and around his person, and that arms and military or para-military guards had been assembled there. No real proof for these accusations has been produced. Since September 1967 many stories and details have appeared in the Egyptian and foreign press about the events which ended with 'Āmir's death, a good deal of them naturally contradictory and tendentious, and the truth of what happened is still unclear on many points, especially on two questions: Had there really been a conspiracy with definite plans and aims of action, and did 'Āmir commit suicide or was he murdered?

At all events, tension existed and mounted and came to a climax on the eve of Nasser's departure for the fourth Arab summit conference at Khartoum on August 29. On the evening of August 25 Nasser invited 'Āmir to his house. It is not known what they said to each other in their long talk; but they did not come to an agreement, and eventually Nasser told his friend that he had to put him under house-arrest. Simultaneously with this quasi-friendly meeting at Nasser's home 'Āmir's house was surrounded and searched and scores of former officers were arrested.[68] Some days later, on September 4, there appeared in *Al-Ahrām* a short official announcement of 'Āmir's house-arrest and Badrān's imprisonment, and the crisis was in the open.

The events on the last day of 'Āmir's life and his death seem to have been mainly as stated in the Egyptian semi-official version.[69] His "last testament" published by *Time*[70] does not prove the contrary, even if it is accepted as authentic.

On Wednesday, September 13 at 10 minutes past 6 p.m., General Muḥammad Fawzī, the Commander-in-Chief of the Armed Forces, and Lieutenant-General 'Abd al-Mun'im Riyāḍ, his Chief of Staff, came to 'Āmir's house to invite him to testify before a military committee of enquiry. Considering his former rank and position they came personally to him to deliver the summons. 'Āmir refused to leave the house with them, and at 6.40 he went for some minutes to his bedroom. When he returned

[68] Eric Rouleau, *Le Monde*, 30 August 1967.

[69] e.g., *Ākhir Sā'a*, 20 September 1967.

[70] *Time*, New York, 15 December 1967.

to the drawing-room, Riyāḍ, who was waiting for him, remarked that 'Āmir was very nervous and was chewing something. Suddenly 'Āmir's behavior became unnatural, and when asked if he was tired, he said that he had swallowed poison, wishing to put an end to everything. 'Āmir was taken at once to the military hospital and given the appropriate treatment to save his life. Later in the evening his condition improved, and on the next day, Thursday morning, he was transferred to a hospital for convalescence. Two military officials were charged with supervising his health. Most of the day 'Āmir rested and slept. At 6.15 p.m. he went to the bathroom, and after some minutes, one of his attendants found him there unconscious on the floor. He had again swallowed poison, this time a very strong one, which had been hidden in an intimate place on his body. At half past six he was dead.

The news of 'Āmir's death came as a shock and suprise to all. The next day at 11 a.m. his body was taken out of Cairo and the funeral took place that afternoon at the family's estate at Isṭāl. Only at 10 in the evening, 27 and a half hours after his death, did Radio Cairo broadcast the official announcement and inform the Egyptian people and the world of his suicide. The announcement was followed by recitations from the Quran and religious cantations.

Many people questioned whether 'Āmir had killed himself. Truly, political murder is quite frequent among the Arabs, and suicide most uncommon. Yet most Egyptians were convinced that he had taken his life by his own hands. And perhaps they could see something symbolic in this suicide, a reflexion of the common reaction of the Arabs to the catastrophe of 1967: An attitude of self-destruction, a man—or a people—driven to suicide, not by a real or imaginary enemy, but by his best friend.

7. SYRIA SINCE 1954

THE FOUR years between the fall of Shīshaklī in February 1954 and the union with Egypt in February 1958 were marked by parliamentary rule in Syria. Freedom was granted to political parties and the press, elections were conducted and governments were formed according to parliamentary process. Actually election results, parliamentary voting and government decisions were not always determined in strict accord with constitutional regulations; but if there ever was an Arab parliamentary and democratic state in which parties and classes contested freely, it was Syria in the years between Shīshaklī and Nasser. Only internal stability was not attained during those four years: Freedom granted to various elements produced endless conspiracies and constant disorder. The variegated communal and class patterns, the animated public life in Syria, unceasing attempts at intervention by other Arab countries, and the pressures and influences of the powers in the Cold War all acted in concert to undermine the foundations of the state. Just as Shīshaklī's government can be cited as proof that a military dictatorship must become corrupt and collapse and cannot lead to the advancement of a country like Syria, so can the period of parliamentary rule in Syria bolster the view that a free play of forces in an Arab country brings it to the brink of anarchy and to loss of independence.

Much of Syria's instability stems from excessive "concern" for her welfare and future on the part of other Arab countries, particularly Egypt and Iraq. In many inter-Arab rivalries Syria serves as a prime objective. A history of inter-Arab relations during the last thousand years could almost be presented as a series of struggles for the control of Damascus, "the heart of the Arab nation." In the 1950's the rivalry over Syria was interwoven with the efforts of the powers to enlist the Middle Eastern states in the Cold War. In Syria neutrality had the upper hand. This was the logical consequence of democratization, accompanied by a rise in the prestige and influence of Egypt who, since the Bandung Conference in 1955, had placed herself at the head of the neutralists in the Middle East. The influence of the pro-western Hashimite countries, Iraq and Jordan, declined in Syria; and the hitherto serious conflicts with Turkey, which was strongly pro-western, became more acute.

The officers who participated in the coup that expelled Shīshaklī delivered the government into the hands of civilian politicians and returned to their barracks. However, their withdrawal from the political scene was only temporary: they were no longer able to abstain from the play of politics either as leading actors on the stage or as those pulling strings behind the scenes—and the laxity of civilian rule was more than usually tempting. At the end of 1956, less than three years after the ousting of Shīshaklī, the cautious London *Times* concluded that Syria was once more "subject to a military dictatorship." [1] However, conflicting interests and views split the officers and the officer politicians were no more capable of joint action than were the deputies in parliament.

Several groups of these officers were active in exile, mainly in Beirut. There they planned coups in liaison with Shīshaklī and leaders of the *Syrian Social Nationalist Party* (the SSNP), and especially with emissaries of the Iraqi government. The Iraqi army's General Staff supported their plans and supplied them with money and arms. The principal contact with the Iraqis in 1955 and 1956 was Muḥammad Ṣafā. In 1948 Ṣafā had been a battalion commander in Qā'uqjī's army in Palestine. Later, with the rank of colonel, he served as military attaché in France and the United States. He was a follower of the SSNP and was dismissed from the army by Shishaklī in December 1952. He fled to Iraq from where he lead a "Free Syrian Movement" which aimed to bring Syria into the Hashimite pro-western camp. In June 1954, after Shīshaklī's fall, he slipped into Syria and was arrested on the charge of attempting a coup. In 1955 he once again divided his time between Baghdad and Beirut. Together with the Iraqi General Staff he planned the organization of a "Free Syrian Army". The plan came to light at the trials of Nūrī Sa'īd's army chiefs in the People's Tribunals of Qassim and Mahdāwi: In a secret camp in Turkey or Cyprus an army was to be trained to invade Syria. The plan was worked out in detail, including the establishment of brothels in the training camp to discourage soldiers from venturing outside and violating secrecy. [2]

Without Iraqi aid Muḥammad Ṣafā's adventures would have been quite unimportant, and even so they remained merely an episode. Among the Syrian officers themselves an opposing current, the Ba'thists, were gaining

[1] *The Times*, London, 28 November 1956; S.E. Finer, *The man on horseback*, London 1962, 150.

[2] *Maḥkamat al-sha'b, Muḥākamāt al-maḥkama al-'askariyya al-khāṣṣa*, vol 1, Baghdad 1959, 64, 299; Patrick Seale, *The struggle for Syria*, London 1965, 263–82; *Hamizrah Hehadash*, vol. 4, 279, vol. 5, 299, vol. 6, 58.

in strength in the mid-1950's. In the parliamentary elections held in September 1954 the Ba'th received 22 out of 142 seats, compared with one out of 114 in 1949. Always a minority-party, it nevertheless succeeded in expanding its influence in the country far beyond its actual power, especially in the army. Prominent among the Ba'thist officers in 1954 was 'Adnān Mālikī, one of the leaders of the conspiracy that overthrew Shīshaklī. He was born in Damascus in 1918 and served in the army from 1939. In the Palestine War, he was wounded in the battle of Mishmar ha-Yarden. He was a close associate of Za'īm who promoted him to the rank of lieutenant-colonel. Later Mālikī quarreled with him and was sent off to France to study. In the Shīshaklī period he directed educational activities in the army. His Ba'thist views did not remain secret and he was retired in December 1952. In 1953 he was imprisoned for a time. After the expulsion of Shīshaklī he became, at the age of 36, chief of operations with the rank of colonel. He was regarded by many as the man of the future and for this reason the enemies of the Ba'th decided to get rid of him. On April 22, 1955 he was assassinated in Damascus while watching a soccer match between Syrian and Egyptian army teams. The killer, who immediately took his own life, was a sergeant in the military police and an agent of the SSNP.[3]

Just as the attempted assassination of Nasser in October 1954 was the pretext for a swift, cruel campaign of suppression against the Muslim Brethren in Egypt, so the murder of Mālikī was followed by persecution of the SSNP. A large show trial was held and the party was outlawed. Lieutenant-Colonel Ghassān Jadīd was denounced as the organizer of the murder. He, too, had been a member of the Provisional Military Council which had ousted Shīshaklī. However, apart from hatred of the dictator, the SSNP and the Ba'th had nothing in common, and in 1954 antagonism between them reached a peak. At the beginning of 1955 Ghassān Jadīd was dismissed from the army for his connections with the American Embassay and for causing agitation among soldiers. He fled to Lebanon. Mālikī's assassin was an Alawi like Jadīd and came from the same village. After Māliki's murder Jadīd was sentenced to death in absentia. When the Lebanese government did not respond to the extradition demand, Syrian intelligence agents tried to kidnap him. Failing to carry this out, they settled accounts with him in a simple fashion. On February 19, 1957 he was shot dead in a Beirut street.[4]

After Mālikī's murder the prestige and influence of 'Abd al-Ḥamīd Sarrāj mounted. Sarrāj was born in Hama which was also the home town

[3] *Al-Mālikī, rajul wa-qaḍiyya,* Damascus 1956, *passim*; *al-Jundī,* 15 May 1949.

[4] *Hazīmat ṭāghiya,* Damascus (1954?), 101; Seale, 240; *Hamizrah Hehadash,* vol. 7, 136–7.

of his associates Ḥawrānī, Shīshaklī, Ḥamdūn and Qanūt. While studying at the Homs Military College in 1947 he was greatly influenced by the personality and pan-Arab opinions of Jamāl Fayṣal, then an instructor at the College. (During the union with Egypt Fayṣal was to become the commander of the UAR Armed Forces in Syria.) Sarrāj's views, like Fayṣal's, were very much like those of the Ba'th, but neither of them became a member of the party. In 1955 Fayṣal became head of the personnel department on the General Staff and Sarrāj became chief of intelligence. Sarrāj flooded the country with a network of agents and perfected the functioning of his office so skillfully that it was said of him that he could hear the sound of an ant walking anywhere in Syria. Despite the fact that he was not a member of the party, he was accepted as head of the Ba'thist officers. It was his ambition to become chief of staff but he never achieved this. His intrigues aroused distrust among all non-Ba'thist elements, and the power which he managed to concentrate in his hands gave rise to suspicion that if he were granted added authority, an open military dictatorship would be restored. In July 1956 the Chief of Staff, Shawkat Shuqayr, was forced to resign. Shuqayr, a Druze from Lebanon, regarded an officer's mission as being more a professional military function than a political one. The Ba'thist officers combined forces with the right-wing officers to get rid of him. But Sarrāj, to his great disappointment, was not made Shuqayr's successor; Tawfīq Niẓām al-Dīn, a conservative officer and scion of one of Syria's most aristocratic wealthy families, was nominated for the post. A year later, in August 1957, Niẓām al-Dīn was also forced to resign because of differences with Sarrāj and his clique who appointed, promoted, and dismissed officers in accordance with their own political considerations. However, Sarrāj's aspirations were once again frustrated and 'Afīf Bizrī was appointed chief of staff. The Ba'th despaired of becoming the dominant force in the country and in the army—its leaders realized that if new parliamentary elections were to be held, the party would increase its representation slightly but continue to remain in the minority. For this reason the Ba'th and Sarrāj banked heavily on union with Egypt.[5]

The new Chief of Staff was no more to the right than the Ba'th, on the contrary he was an out-and-out leftist. 'Afīf Bizrī was attracted to the socialists and communists while attending courses in France. In the summer of 1955 he was still a lieutenant-colonel, but two years later he was a major-general. Many, both supporters and opponents, labeled him a communist and he probably was a regular party member. In the autumn of 1957 a

[5] G.H. Torrey in S.N. Fisher, ed., *The military in the Middle East,* Columbus, Ohio, 1963, 60–8.

number of Ba'thists, in explaining the differences between them and Bizrī, said that he was "more left-wing" and had less reservations regarding the Soviet Union. Emphasis on the link with the USSR makes it clear why he was selected as chief of staff. The Minister of Defense at the time was Khālid al-'Aẓm, a millionaire industrialist who boasted of his friendship with Khrushchev. The Ba'thists, despite their real or imagined left-wing tendencies, were anti-Soviet; Michel 'Aflaq, their ideologist, was, like many former communists, a foe of communism and communists. Al-'Aẓm, a capitalist by class and outlook, favored a type of peaceful co-existence among states with different economic and political systems—which ran parallel to Khrushchev's view—and regarded Moscow's economic and political aid as a guarantee of Syria's independence against the pressures of her pro-western neighbors as well as Egyptian pan-Arabism. For this reason he preferred Bizrī to Sarrāj.

At the end of 1957 panic took possession of Syria. Her neutralist policy isolated her from her neighbors, all of whom—Lebanon, Turkey, Iraq, Jordan and Israel—were in one way or another tied to the west and hostile to her. Fears mounted of an invasion by any one of them, given American encouragement. At the same time many held the opinion that the communists were gaining power inside Syria. These people mistook the shadows of mountains for the mountains, with the results that both inside and outside Syria the prevailing view was that the country was on the verge of becoming a Peoples' Democracy dependent on the Soviet Union. Moreover, all agreed that the country's confused leaders lacked any talent for mutual cooperation. Therefore they solved the problem by "fleeing forward" to union with Egypt. From Damascus' instability they fled to the stability of Cairo; from the fear of communism to the solid anti-communism of Nasser; and from the loneliness of Syrian independence to Arab unity.

Syria's union with Egypt is the rare example in modern history of a complete voluntary union of two non-neighboring countries taken at the initiative of the smaller. It was the result of temporary circumstances and did not last long, but it also had deep roots in Syria's public consciousness and history. Damascus was always the principal object of every Arab aspiration to establish a great united state; it was also the active center from which ideas of union radiated. That the Ba'th grew in Syria was primarily due to the mystic pan-Arab ideology of "One Arab nation with an eternal mission." In the mid-1950's this eternal mission was personified in Nasser. The new Egyptian leaders identified themselves with and defined themselves as Arabs, elevating Arab nationalism to the foremost plank on their propaganda platform. In that period Nasser's foreign policy scored one brilliant success after another, ranging from the termination of Egypt's protracted struggle to force the British to leave and to give up their military bases to withstanding the pressures and temptations of joining the Baghdad Pact. It secured a profusion of military aid from the USSR, nationalized the Suez Canal and won a political victory over the combined forces of Britain, France and Israel who attacked Egypt in 1956. In the words of the saying, "nothing succeeds like success." Egypt's prestige soared.

The initiators of proclamations and resolutions in the Syrian parliament that prepared the way for union were the Ba'thist leaders. Practical measures to implement it were initiated both by Ba'thist and non-Ba'thist army leaders. On January 12, 1958 Chief of Staff Bizrī, without the knowledge of the government, flew to Cairo with 13 other senior officers who comprised the entire Army Command, to meet Nasser and suggest immediate union. Only two army leaders remained in Damascus—Deputy Chief of Staff Nafūrī and Sarrāj, chief of intelligence. At a time that synchronized with their colleagues' flight to Egypt, they informed the government of the purpose of the flight and demanded help with its speedy materialization.[6] Negotiations between the Syrians and Egyptians lasted less than three weeks, and on February 1 the "United Arab Republic" (UAR) came into being. Egypt and Syria were no longer separate politically but only geographically.

There are several conjectures as to why Bizrī joined the advocates of union and placed himself at their head. However, it is clear that he hoped for some measure of Syrian autonomy within the UAR. Consequently, he was one of the first to be persuaded to resign—as early as March 22.

Nasser responded to the Syrian initiative with hestitation. Upon the Syrians' entreaties, however, he made it a condition of union that Syria allow him to dictate to her and that she renounce everything that characterized her regime politically. Egypt's organizational and governmental systems were transplanted to Syria as if she were one of its provinces. All political parties were forced to disband and were outlawed. The Ba'th hoped that they would be permitted to continue in existence as a party and even cherished the hope that they would be allowed, in the guise of national union, to function as the ruling party. For it had been the Ba'th that had promoted union; furthermore, its leaders had a highly developed lust for power. For a long time they had been very close to power without holding any, and now they wanted to enjoy its benefits. However, this moor had done his work and it was indicated that he should go. Nasser was not prepared to share power with another popular force in Syria any more than in Egypt. He had never identified himself with the Ba'th, and,

[6] Seale, 320; *Orient,* no. 20, 1959, 205–16.

as in the case of the Muslim Brethren, he knew that groups with similar ideas could be most dangerous rivals. The excessive ambitions of the Ba'thists after unification increased his suspicions. Later, in a speech delivered in 1963, he accused them of wanting to "transform Syria into their private estate."[7] The Ba'thist leaders became ministers but not as representatives of their party; and from the date of the establishment of the UAR their powers were gradually and consistently reduced. The days of turbulent party activity were over, to be supplanted by the rigid stability of a police state.

The UAR government in Syria was essentially government by officers. Syrian ministers, both civilian and officers, were added to the top-level governing group of Egyptian officers. Syrian officers who at the beginning of the UAR regime were given ministerial posts or important command positions in the army were in the following three categories: Ba'thists, like Ḥamdūn; Ba'thist sympathizers, such as Sarrāj; and non-Ba'thist supporters of Arab unity like Jamāl Fayṣal. 'Afīf Bizrī, the Syrian Chief of Staff, had to resign three weeks after the establishment of union, and the command of the UAR armed forces in Syria was handed to Jamāl Fayṣal. In the first UAR government with its central and regional institutions there were 14 Syrian ministers, of whom four were army officers. In the various shifts of personnel and reorganizations which took place during the period of union the proportion of officers among the Syrians steadily rose. In February 1958 two out of every seven Syrian ministers were officers; in August 1961, two out of five. More strikingly significant is the fact that the veteran Ba'thist minister officers were eliminated. Muṣṭafā Ḥamdūn and 'Abd al-Ghanī Qanūt resigned at the end of December 1959 together with the civilian Ba'thist ministers Akram Ḥawrānī and Ṣalāh al-Dīn Bayṭār. Half a year earlier the Ba'th had already suffered a serious defeat. At the elections to the National Union in July 1959, only 200 out of 9,445 elected representatives were party members.[8] In the 1954 elections to the Syrian Parliament the Ba'th secured 15 percent of the seats; in the three years elections and the union with Egypt its influence mounted—but one year and a half after the establishment of the UAR it was left with only two per cent. In fact only candidates approved by the authorities were permitted to stand. It was clear that Nasser wanted to get rid of the Ba'th. This was not difficult for in 1959 the Syrian's disappointment with the union with Egypt could already be felt; many citizens regarded the Ba'th as initiator of the liquidation of Syrian independence and it was convenient for Nasser to have it serve as a scapegoat.

[7] *Al-Ahrām,* 23 July 1963.

[8] *MER* 1960, 497.

In the spring of 1960 rumors were circulating that two additional Syrian officer ministers, Amīn Nafūrī and Aḥmad 'Abd al-Karīm, had resigned, and in the beginning of May their resignation was officially published. Nafūrī was one of the few officers who had begun military service as an ordinary private. In Za'īm's period he was promoted from lieutenant to captain and company commander; in the 1950's he rose rapidly until in August 1957, on Bizrī's appointment as chief of staff, he became a brigadier and deputy chief of staff. In Shīshaklī's time he was close to the latter's "Liberation Movement" and later was attracted to the Ba'th but did not identify himself with it. He was believed to have pro-western tendencies and even ties. Either because of this or because of his close relations with the Ba'th, and perhaps both, a rift appeared between him and Nasser. Aḥmad 'Abd al-Karīm's views throughout the 1950's resembled Nafūrī's, but unlike the latter he requested leave when Bizrī was appointed chief of staff.[9]

In place of the outgoing officer ministers other Syrian army officers who were nonpartisan and unreservedly devoted to Nasser were appointed: Colonels Akram Dīrī, Aḥmad Hunaydī, Ṭu'ma 'Awdat-Allāh and Jādū 'Izz al-Dīn. The only Syrian officer who kept a ministerial post throughout the period of union was Sarrāj. He not only succeeded in rising with the Ba'th when it was in the ascendant and in leaving it when it fell into disfavor in Nasser's eyes, but he concentrated increasingly wide powers into his hands until he became a sort of deputy president in the Northern Region. From October 1959 'Abd al Ḥakim 'Āmir had begun to supervise UAR policy in Syria; in September 1960 he was replaced by Sarrāj, who was Regional Prime Minister, secretary of the National Union, Minister of the Interior and controlled the police and the ramified security services. Some commentators considered the granting of the numerous powers to Sarrāj a personal victory for him in his rivalry with 'Āmīr, while others regarded it as the granting of more autonomy to Syria in view of growing disappointment and restiveness. In any case Nasser could be sure of Sarrāj's loyalty. Sarrāj was not supported by any major public element in Syria; his power depended on his readiness to serve as the tool of the UAR President, and Nasser found it convenient to have his work in Damascus done by a man born in Hama and not by an Egyptian.

Some have claimed that Egypt had also made Syria an economic colony of hers, a market for her industrial products, in the hope that Egyptian merchandise which was cheaper because of lower wages would also supersede Syrian goods on the domestic market. An examination of the balance

[9] Torrey, *loc cit.*; *MER* 1960, 499; *Hamizrah Hehadash,* vol. 9, 204; *al-Jundī,* 15 May 1949.

of trade does not confirm this contention.[10] In monetary and customs matters the two countries were not united. If Egypt had intentions of exploiting Syria, she did not carry them out, either because of the short duration of union or for other reasons. The years of union were a period of serious economic crisis for Syria and this fact contributed greatly to the Syrians' disappointment in the dream of Arab unity as it materialized. Actually the causes of the crisis were not of man's making. From the winter of 1958-59 Syria suffered five years of drought. The average wheat crop was 68 kg. per dunam in 1957 and 90 kg. in 1958 but was 35 kg. in 1959, 43 kg. in 1960 and 36 kg. in 1961. The barley crops declined even more precipitously.[11] Syria depends more than any other Middle Eastern country on the quantity of winter precipitation; she derives special benefit from the blessing of a rainy year and suffers much more from the curse of drought. She was not afflicted with the protracted drought because of the Egyptians, and if the union had succeeded in other matters, the drought would not have shaken it. But since the union's political and national foundations were weak, the economic crisis was an additional culminative factor against it.

Opposing the various centrifugal forces in Syria stood the apparently solid foundation of the union—the army. But a dangerous breach appeared in the ranks of the officers. We shall cite a number of the statements included in the declaration made by 'Abd al-Karīm Zahr al-Dīn, the new Syrian Chief of Staff, at a press conference held on October 2, 1961, four days after dissolution of the union. Even if what he had to say was one-sided and perhaps inaccurate, it no doubt reflected the feelings of the Syrian officer class; on other occasions even harsher statements were made. He pointed to the decisive role played in the establishment of the union by "the Syrian Arab officers who suckled the milk of union in their cradles, grew up in its light, and believed in it as they believed in God. But this spirit was extremely remote from the mentality of our southern brothers. This was the beginning of the events which harmed the union and perverted its sanctity; they started in connection with the army. From the first day, we wanted to manifest the union by exchanging officers between Syria and Egypt; our young men went to the South full of energy and brimming with feeling for the Arab cause—and what came to us from Egypt? This is the point of departure which lays bare all the perversions and sins which were later committed in the name of the union. They sent us officers who had specialized in spying before learning about any other activity. They came

[10] *Economic development in the Middle East, 1959–1961,* New York 1962, 79–81, 160.
[11] *Ibid.,* 100, 108.

to us in the spirit of secret police officers and not in the spirit of nationalism in which we received them nor in the feelings of Arab brotherhood which bring forth friendship and mutual confidence between men. These men began spreading like an octopus through various institutions, stuck their tentacles into everything and made themselves supreme in all matters. Rule and order demand strict observance of rank and military regulations at work, in appointments and in establishing contacts but these men disregarded them. Instead of contacting the Army High Command and their superior officers, the Egyptian rulers contacted their own officers directly, depite the fact that the latter's ranks and duties were inferior to their commander's. They controlled all the sensitive positions in the headquarters of the First (Syrian) Army and at the headquarters of the units. But our high-ranking officers who were stationed in Egypt discovered themselves behind empty wooden desks with no authority or power." Whenever warnings and complaints were heard about violation of established military practices, the Syrian officers were accused of regionalism and "organized general dismissals began; from day to day the number grew of those dismissed in various ways—by transfer to the Foreign Ministry and the army administration or through retirement . . . in this way confidence and friendship between the northerners and southerners disappeared, as if our southern brothers had wanted this hatred to spread and grow. The situation resembled the state of affairs in the mandatory period—a sort of imperialism . . . in the unification of laws logic demands that the best version be chosen. But our brothers from the South never had any such intention. They imposed their law by force. No one from the First Army took part in preparing the military law which was published, printed and distributed just as it was prepared, written, and publicized—in the south."[12]

At the meeting of the Arab League at Shtura in August 1962 the Syrian spokesman, Amīn Nafūrī, reiterated these charges and added numerous details: "More than 1,100 Syrian officers and 3,000 NCO's were dismissed from the army and 500 Syrian officers transferred to Egypt . . . without work for them in their new posts except for reading the newspapers every day . . . In place of the Syrian officers more than 2,300 Egyptian officers were sent to Syria, where a man with the lowest rank received a salary of at least 800 Syrian pounds a month as compensation, paid from the Syrian treasury, in addition to his basic pay."[13] He also claimed that the Syrian Air Force's flight school at Homs was transferred to Egypt. Whereas before union, he said, 20 to 30 flight officers graduated each year, during

[12] Ṣalāḥ al-Dīn al-Munajjid, *Sūriyya wa-Maṣr . . . wathā'iq wa-nuṣūs,* Beirut (1962), 111–4.
[13] *Al-Ayyām,* Damascus, 28 August 1962.

the three years of union only five Syrian completed flight officers' courses in Egypt. Egyptian officers who seduced Syrian girl students were not court-martialed but sent back to Egypt.

There may have been exaggerations in these charges, although the Egyptians never producted facts to refute them, but they do demonstrate how grievances and feelings of discrimination accumulated among the officers to the extent that Egyptian domination recalled the mandatory period and was considered "a sort of imperialism."

The strength of a dictatorial regime is also the source of its weakness. The maximal concentration of power in the hands of a few and the silencing of all criticism lead to a state of affairs in which the government can no longer either know or properly assess the importance of hostile elements. Otherwise Nasser would have been more careful in the summer of 1961 before adding a direct attack against the most basic interests of the Syrian middle class to his suppression of party and workers' organizations and the degradation of officers and intellectuals. However, that is just what he did. The nationalization ordinances and the other socialist laws of July 1961 played a different role in Syria than they did in Egypt. The middle-class opposition to these measures stemmed from unconcealed reactionary class interests, but it could also have emerged as a form of national opposition. Nationalization in Egypt operated primarily as Egyptianization, as the transfer of enterprises and capital from the ownership of foreigners to Egyptian ownership. Issawi found that among 1,007 names of stockholders with more than E£ 10,000 of shares in 148 companies which were nationalized in July 1961 and whose identity could be determined, only 55 per cent were Muslim Egyptians. Six per cent were Copts, and all the others held foreign nationality or were Syrians. If it were at all possible to determine the distribution of capital, it would certainly become clear that the Egyptian share was less than half. Moreover, 22 per cent of these stockholders were Syrians and Lebanese; i.e., the Syrians even owned a fairly large proportion of Egyptian stocks.[14] In 1961 banking, insurance and wholesale trade in Egypt were to a large extent still in foreign hands as were also (less conspicuously) industry and transport. In Syria, however, such branches of the economy were run mostly by its own middle class which in the 1950's displayed a great deal of economic momentum. If in Cairo and Alexandria the significance of the laws of July 1961 was primarily Egyptianization of foreign capital, in Damascus and Aleppo it was also possible to define them as Egyptianization—but of Syrian capital.

At the same time rumors abounded in Syria that Egyptian and Syrian

[14] Charles Issawi, *Egypt in revolution,* London 1963, 89–90.

currencies were about to be united, and that the prospective conversion rate between the two currencies would prove disadvantageous to the Syrian region.[15]

It is impossible to judge the relative importance of each of the diverse elements that together led to the secession of Syria from Egypt, but the juxtaposition of the dates of the nationalization laws of mid-July and the secession coup at the end of September 1961 clearly shows how influential the bourgeois Syrian class was. Among other circles, too, there was hardly anyone left in Syria who supported union, either among the peasants or the workers or among the intellectuals and army officers.

Syria's secession from the UAR was brought about by an army officers' coup.

The Syrian officers who carried out the coup in 1961 had as early as 1959 begun to discuss the evils of the union regime, and in 1960 they contacted the Jordanian government.[16] One of those who maintained contact between the officers, business men and Jordanian representatives was Khālid Jāda, a retired lieutenant-colonel, who had been a member of Ḥinnāwī's pro-Hashimite Supreme War Council in 1949. The few statements published later convey the impression that they had begun to discuss action at the beginning of 1961. But the talk remained quite general; no organization was crystallized nor plan of operation worked out until one or at the most two days before the coup.[17]

At that time a crisis in the relations between the Syrians and the Egyptians broke out on an entirely different issue—around 'Abd al-Ḥamīd Sarrāj. Sarrāj was the last of the Syrian leaders to remain in the highest UAR echelons until the summer of 1961. In the UAR government which was formed on August 17 when the regional governments were abolished, he was one of the seven Vice-Presidents, with the portfolio of internal affairs. A month later there were sharp differences between him and 'Abd al-Ḥakīm 'Āmir. On September 21 both were called to Cairo for talks with the President, and on September 26 the public heard that Sarrāj had resigned and that his resignation had been accepted. On the same day Sarrāj returned to Damascus. 'Āmir went too—and two days later both were arrested by the officers who had dissolved the UAR. 'Āmir's intelligence and security agents must at the time have concentrated their attention on Sarrāj and the possible reactions to his resignation, with the result that a third party was able to surprise by coup. The surprise was absolute.

[15] Muḥammed S. Nabulsi, 'Problems of integrating the monetary systems of Egypt and Syria under the UAR regime', *Middle East Economic Papers,* 1964, Beirut (1964 or 1965), 75.

[16] M.Ḥ. Haykal in *al-Ahrām,* 4 May 1962.

[17] *MER* 1961, 610–4.

At 4 a.m. on September 28 two columns of troops entered Damascus—an armored column arrived from Qaṭana in the southwest and the Desert Guard under the command of Lieutenant-Colonel Ḥaydar Kuzbarī reached the capital from Dumair in the east. In Damascus they were joined by the garrison commanded by Brigadier 'Abd al-Ghanī Dahmān. Within half an hour army headquarters, the broadcasting station and the airport were seized. The commander of the First Army in Syria, Lieutenant-General Jamāl Fayṣal, a Syrian, was arrested in his house. 'Āmir, too, was arrested. According to one version he was arrested at army headquarters, where he had hurried on hearing about unusual activity; according to another version he was arrested at home. Jamāl Fayṣal's deputy, Major-General Anwar al-Qāḍī, an Egyptian, was arrested too. Before his arrest he had time to command an Egyptian major in an artillery brigade at Quṭaifa, north-east of Damascus, to hurry to the capital to suppress the uprising. The major bypassed the brigade's Syrian commander, who was asleep at his home in Damascus, ignored the protests of the duty officer, and issued an order to move on the capital. The soldiers were told of an Israeli surprise attack. On the way to Damascus the brigade was met by its commander who had been informed of events. He sent the men back to base and the Egyptian officers were arrested.[18]

This story is typical of the events of the day in most of Syria. The struggle was not between separatists and unionists or between socialists and reactionaries but simply between Syrians and Egyptians. The only people who had demonstrated in Damascus that morning in support of the UAR were Palestinian refugees. Communiqué No. 21 issued by Syrian army headquarters on October 1 explicitly mentioned "foreigners and refugees" who had participated in the demonstrations for the purpose of overthrowing "our power" and threatened to arrest them and expel them from Syria.[19] It was only in northern Syria that Syrian army commanders remained loyal to the UAR for some hours. It became clear at noon that the commander of the northern district at Aleppo, Brigadier Ḥikmat Jamīl al-Dāya, and the commander in Latakia, Colonel Kāẓim Zaytūna, opposed the rebels. From noon until nine o'clock in the evening Aleppo Radio denounced the uprising. But officers siding with the Damascus rebels took Aleppo, too. In the evening Colonel Fayṣal al-Ḥasan, commander of the second training base, led 200 soldiers in the capture of the Aleppo radio station. Shortly after, Latakia fell to the rebels. Details of these incidents are not known, but apparently fighting broke out between pro- and anti-UAR units. At

[18] The best documented and most detailed account of the break-up of the UAR is given in *MER* 1961, 605–23.

[19] Al-Munajjid, 104.

any rate, by midnight UAR rule belonged to the past throughout Syria.

Only four of the rebellion's leaders need to be mentioned: Brigadier 'Abd al-Ghanī Dahmān, commander of the Damascus garrison; air force Brigadier Muwaffaq 'Aṣāṣa who was acting commander of the air force that day and succeeded in grounding all the Egyptian pilots in Syria; Lieutenant-Colonel 'Abd al-Karīm Naḥlāwī, the chief of Marshal 'Āmir's bureau in Syria; and Lieutenant-Colonel Ḥaydar Kuzbarī, commander of the Desert Guard, a cousin of Dr. Ma'mūn Kuzbarī, Prime Minister of the first government after the secession and a representative of the wealthy middle class.

On September 28, 1961 the union of Syria and Egypt came to an end. However, it is not clear whether or not the Syrian rebels had intended absolute secession. They may only have wanted to obtain military and political autonomy for Syria and abolish nationalization while yet preserving the framework of union. It is unlikely that any document antedating the day of secession will be found that would give an inkling of their intentions. The sixteen communiqués broadcast from Damascus that day[20] leave room for both interpretations. "The Revolutionary Supreme Headquarters of the Armed Forces" refrained from naming the country liberating itself from dictatorship and corruption; they mentioned neither Syria nor the UAR. Its flag is the "banner of Arabism," and Arab unity was not said to have failed but to have been perverted. A clear demonstration of independence and secession did not come until late at night—Damascus Radio ended its broadcasts with the old Syrian anthem. At 7.30 a.m. on September 29 the radio announced that the Revolutionary High Command had asked Dr. Ma'mūn Kuzbarī to form a new government, and in the announcement made several hours later on the composition of the new government, the country was for the first time called "The Syrian Arab Republic" (before union the country was called "The Syrian Republic").

If the rebels' intention had been autonomy within the union, it would by then have become clear that this was the last thing to which Nasser would agree. He confronted them with the choice of surrender or secession. Whoever heard his two speeches of September 28 could have entertained no doubt that he had been surprised and deeply shocked. Nevertheless, he was not ready for any compromise, either in the hope that the uprising would fail, or with the understanding that any retreat under the pressure of revolt was likely to shake the structure of the regime in Cairo as well—a matter he considered to be worse than the loss of Syria.

'Āmir's reaction was different. From what he saw in Damascus he

[20] *Orient*, no. 19, 1961, 177–91.

believed that it would be possible to save the union by granting certain concessions to the Syrian officers. From eight o'clock in the morning of September 28 negotiations took place between the rebels and 'Āmir, Jamāl Fayṣal and the officer ministers of the UAR government (all prisoners at headquarters). At 1.30 there was a broadcast of communiqué No. 9 in which the Revolutionary High Command declared that its goal was "to defend and preserve the attachment of the Arabs for each other," that it had no intention of "endangering the victories which had already been achieved by Arab nationalism"; that it had explained to "Marshal 'Āmir the problems and aims of the army" and that in full understanding he had "made the necesary decisions to safeguard the unity of the armed forces of the United Arab Republic. Thus army matters have been restored to their normal course." The communiqué again spoke of the UAR and of 'Āmir as "the Vice-President of the Republic and the Supreme Commander of the Armed Forces," and created the impression that agreement had been reached. However, the communiqué was not broadcast in the name of 'Āmir who would not sign it without authorization from the President. He was permitted to communicate with him by wireless, and it then became clear that Nasser was against compromise. Nasser's intransigence, his unwillingness, and perhaps his inability, to make a compromise, cost him Syria.

At about 2 p.m. when Nasser's reply arrived, it was learned in Damascus that in the meantime support for the uprising had spread in most of the Syrian provinces. At 3.15 communiqué No. 10 cancelled the previous one. 'Āmir was flown to Cairo. The secession was final.

Cairo, however, was preparing for military action to suppress the revolt in Syria. This had been decided upon that morning on the assumption that northern Syria had not rebelled. Orders were issued to naval and commando units to leave for Latakia and Aleppo. The commander of the commando troops advance company was Major Jalāl Huraydī. In the early afternoon he was personally briefed by the President and supplied with one million Syrian pounds. But when he was already on the way, there was no longer any doubt that the whole of northern Syria, too, was then in rebel hands, and Nasser cancelled the military plans. An order was broadcast to Huraydī not to open fire but he apparently did not receive it. At midnight he parachuted down to the airfield at Latakia with 13 officers and 105 men. During the drop the men in the company scattered over a wide area and did not assemble until daylight; they then found themselves surrounded by Syrian troops and surrendered. Two months later they were returned to Egypt.

Developments in Syria after the secession from the UAR resembled the events that followed the ousting of Shīshaklī in 1954. A government of civilian statesmen was formed and elections took place two months later. Although no activity by political parties had been officially allowed, the Constituent Assembly elected on December 1, 1961 surprisingly resembled the one elected in the fall of 1954; 42 per cent of the deputies were independents or the representatives of Bedouin tribes (in 1954 they constituted 47 per cent); the largest party was once again the People's Party with 22 per cent of the seats (21 per cent in 1954); 14 per cent were members of the National Party (13 per cent), and 14 per cent were Ba'thists (15 per cent).[21] The rest were Muslim Brethren or followers of the SSNP. The three governments in the first half year after the secession all worked for a gradual and consistent elimination of the heritage bequeathed by the period of union. The laws of agrarian reform were changed to the detriment of the peasants; nationalization acts were cancelled; instead of establishing closer relations with the Soviet Union, economic collaboration with West Germany was increased. A highly significant turning point occurred in the sensitive sphere of inter-Arab relations: During the entire 1950's, since the fall of Ḥinnāwī in December 1948, Egypt had the upper hand in the perennial struggle between Cairo and Baghdad over Damascus. Now after Damascus had freed itself of Cairo, a rapprochement with Iraq got under way. In the middle of March President al-Qudsī met Qassim at Rutba on the Syrian-Iraqi frontier, and their joint announcement of March 16, 1962 proclaimed far-reaching political and military coordination.

Trends in the new Syrian government both in domestic and foreign affairs were not likely to bring stability to the country, and Egypt exerted herself to the utmost to add to the ferment. All her organs of propaganda unremittingly and vehemently attacked the rulers in Damascus as reactionaries, separatists and traitors.

As in the post-Shīshaklī period the Syrian officers at first wanted to operate from behind the scenes and prevent their personal aspirations and political views from flaring into open dissension. On the day after the secession an officer who had not until then been active in politics was appointed commander-in-chief of the army. He was Major-General 'Abd al-Karīm Zahr al-Dīn, a 48-year-old Druze, who in the period of union had been director of the department of equipment and supply in Syria. His appointment was also calculated to allay the apprehensions of the Druze, who were not happy to have as Prime Minister Dr. Kuzbarī who in the past had worked with their inveterate enemy, Shīshaklī.

However, the army could not long remain aloof from politics, even for

[21] *MER* 1961, 502.

appearances' sake, and six months to the day from the secession there was yet another military coup. A new period of military dictatorships had begun.

On March 28, 1962, the Army High Command announced that it had assumed control. The Assembly was dissolved, the government dismissed and a curfew imposed. The President resigned. More than a hundred leading officials, including the Premier and all the ministers, with one exception, were arrested.

The coup was carried out by the same officers who had headed the secession coup of September 28, 1961: Naḥlāwī, Dahmān, 'Aṣāṣā, 'Abd-Rabbu, and Hindī.[22] For the sake of emphasizing continuity, the coup's announcement was labelled "Communiqué No. 19" as a sequence of the 18 communiqués released at the end of September. The only leader of the secession coup who was not asked to participate this time was Ḥaydar Kuzbarī, the prominent representative of capitalist interests and of rapprochement with Jordan and Saudi Arabia. On March 29 he was arrested. In their proclamations the rulers now denounced capitalists, speculators and separatists.

The High Command in Damascus paid lip service to the slogans of union and socialism but had no intention of putting them into practice. However, in a number of other centers, especially in the north, there were officers who looked forward to the restoration of union. When they realized the true intentions of Damascus they were surprised and defiant. The dissidents were headed by Colonel Jāsim 'Alwān, the commander of the Aleppo garrison. On March 31 Aleppo rebelled against Damascus. 'Alwān had restored to active service a number of officers who had been relegated to the retired list after the secession from the UAR. The UAR flag was then raised over the fortress at Aleppo, and in the first three days of April "the UAR broadcasting station in Aleppo" came on the air in the name of the "Free Officers' Movement."

The Homs garrison was split. An exchange of fire between the rival factions ended when troops from Palmyra, which was loyal to Damascus, entered the city. On the morning of April 2 riots also started in Damascus. Unionist students demonstrated with the UAR flag and pictures of Nasser. The army opened fire on them, killing a few, and a curfew was re-imposed. Meanwhile the war of communiqués between Aleppo and Damascus continued and grew more acute; Aleppo called for help from Egypt, and the struggle threatened to turn into a full-fledged civil war. On the morning of April 3 airplanes from Damascus appeared over Aleppo. Then came

[22] *Al-Ḥayāt,* 3 April 1962.

the turning point. Confronted by the danger of civil war, a few of the Aleppo officers retreated; commanders of the army units in the town were not prepared to go all the way with ʻAlwān, while the extremists he had just returned to the army were not yet able to seize positions of command. At noon negotiations were started between Aleppo and Damascus under pressure from the moderates, and the extremists again started to doff their uniforms. A compromise was reached in the afternoon, and at 6 p.m. Damascus was able to announce that the situation in Aleppo had returned to normal and that peace had been restored to the country.

The compromise was a mutual undertaking to carry out resolutions of the "Homs Convention." With the danger to the army's unity in mind, the heads of the rival officer factions, the President and a number of former Prime Ministers met at Homs on April 1 to find a way out of the tangle. They decided that extremist officers from both sides, the anti-Egyptian faction and the Union group, should leave the army. A civilian government should once again be formed, but it would not be responsible to the Assembly, which would not be reconvened. In other words, the army would not relinquish its supervisory and command position and the cabinet would have the status of a government of experts. The succeeding days and weeks were permeated with the spirit of these decisions.

On the morning of April 3 seven officers, leaders of the September and March coups, were flown to Switzerland; they were Brigadiers Dahmān and ʻAbd-Rabbu and Colonels Naḥlāwī, Hindī, Rifāʻī, ʻAsalī and Ḥājj ʻAlī.[23] Until the previous day some of the offices they held were: Commander of the Damascus region, Chief of Operations on the General Staff, and various other leading military posts. Now they were civilians in exile who lived in hope of appointments in the Ministry for Foreign Affairs or an opportunity to return to the army and the domestic political arena.

ʻAlwān, too, had to leave that afternoon. He did not go abroad but went underground. He handed over the Aleppo command to Colonel Lu'ay al-Atāsī, an officer who until then had maintained a position of neutrality among the rival groups of officers while in command of the Deir ez-Zor region. In the following year he was one of the central figures among the Syrian officer politicians.

On April 4 Zahr al-Dīn, who had remained commander-in-chief, carved several new appointments for the top army brass. Brigadier Nāmiq Kamāl, who was away studying in the USSR at the end of the union period, was promoted to major-general and became chief of staff. On April 13 President al-Qudsī returned to his office, and three days later a new government

[23] *Al-Ḥayāt,* 4 April 1962.

was sworn in. Zahr al-Dīn, who had given himself the defense portfolio, defined it as "a government of technicians." Prime Minister Bashīr al-'Azma and several other ministers were taken from the medical faculty of the University of Damascus.[24] Syrian policy during Zahr al-Dīn's regime was succinctly formulated in a communiqué broadcast on the morning of April 2: "General headquarters of the armed forces of the Syrian Arab Republic announces that the High Command favors unity with the liberated Arab countries headed by Egypt, providing that this unity be established on proper foundations, that the country's honor and existence be safeguarded by preventing the recurrence of past mistakes, and providing that these foundations be subject to a free plebiscite."[25] In other words, they paid lip service to Arab unity and acknowledged Egypt as the leader of the Arab world, but opposed factual unification, particularly with Egypt. The promise of a plebiscite remained unhonored. On social and domestic problems the government made pious remarks without carrying them out. The 1958 agrarian reform law was restored but altered to benefit the landlords.[26] Statements were made again and again about nationalization of the "Company of the Five," the country's largest capitalist and industrial enterprise, but in the meantime it failed to change hands. In September 1962 Khālid al-'Aẓm, the "Red Millionaire," became Prime Minister, and relations with the Soviet Union became closer as the rift with Egypt deepened. Strikes, demonstrations, resignations and dismissals of ministers, and arrests and releases from jail succeeded each other intermittently in the course of the entire year. Extremist bodies from all sides intensified their activity—the Muslim Brethren, communists, "Unionists," Nasser's adherents and the anti-Nasser faction of the Ba'th headed by Akram Ḥawrānī. The Cairo propaganda department seized upon every outbreak and difference of opinion to denounce the "isolationist, reactionary" regime. And Egypt used more than propaganda to stir up trouble.

At the beginning of 1963 against the background of everybody's struggle against everybody else, some officers once again attempted to carry out a minor coup. On January 1 Zahr al-Dīn promoted himself to the rank of lieutenant-general. At the same time the High Command planned a series of promotions, transfers and dismissals of officers. The cashiered officers included Naḥlāwī and those of his friends who had been exiled with him

24 B. Vernier, 'Le rôle politique de l'armée en Syrie', *Revue de la politique étrangere,* Paris 1965, no. 5, 486.

25 Radio Damascus, 2 April 1962.

26 E. Garzouzi, 'Land reform in Syria', *MEJ,* vol. 17, 88–90; *Economic developments in the Middle East, 1961–1963*, New York 1964, 26.

in April and were still loyal to him; they were to receive appointments in the foreign service. When he learned of the dismissals, Naḥlāwī suddenly returned from exile to Damascus on January 9 with three of his friends. Their arrival was a signal that a major and three captains in the 70th and 72nd brigades at Qaṭana and a number of other junior officers in the vicinity of Damascus should present several demands, including the reinstatement of Naḥlāwī and his friends to active service, the dismissal of Zahr al-Dīn and an edict stating that Khālid Bakhdāsh, the communist leader, should not be permitted to return to Syria. The Damascus Army Command alerted units whose loyalty was certain. Concurrently—the authorities did not know whether it was connected with this tension—high school pupils and university students demonstrated, either at the initiative of the Muslim Brethren or of the Unionists, at Der'a and the University of Damascus. There was rioting at Ṣanamayn where more than 20 persons were injured. On the evening of January 13 frontiers with Lebanon and Jordan were closed for fear of outside intervention. On the same evening representatives of the rebels were called for a meeting with the President. Officers representing the High Command, Akram Ḥawrānī, and 'Iṣām al-'Aṭṭār, who lead the Muslim Brethren, were present. The session lasted until daybreak. Eventually Naḥlāwī's men were persuaded that their demands and threats were untenable. By the afternoon of January 14 tension eased. Naḥlawī and his followers had to leave the country, as they had done in April. All four became counselors in Syrian embassies—Naḥlāwī at Bonn, Hindī at Prague, Rifā'ī at London, and Fakhrī 'Umar at Bern. Twenty-four officers on active service who had supported them were arrested.[27]

Zahr al-Dīn and al-Qudsī, who had sought a middle path between the extreme adherents of Nasser and his sworn enemies, once again had the upper hand. Less than a month later, on February 8, 1963, Arif and the Ba'th carried out their coup in Iraq and Qassim fell to the triumphant cheering of Nasser. For Syria this was the prelude to the Ba'thist military coup of March 8.

Overnight Iraq was transformed from Egypt's bugbear to her ally. Syria found herself isolated and within the country all opposition unionist circles raised their hopes and rejoiced. The government's laxity sharpened the differences between the President and Prime Minister as well as those within the army command. Al-Qudsī and al-'Aẓm differed as to whether they should reconvene the Constituent Assembly which had been dissolved by the army the previous March. Army leaders were divided between

[27] *MEJ*, 1963, 36; *al-Ḥayāt*, 15–17 January 1963, 14 March 1964; *al-Jarīda*, Beirut, 15 January 1963; *al-Nahār*, Beirut, 18 January 1963.

those who favored and those who opposed the plan to transfer dozens of officers to new duties.[28]

One of the candidates for transfer was Brigadier Ziyād Ḥarīrī. He was to have been posted to Baghdad as military attaché and to give up his post as "commander of the front," i.e., the army on the Israeli frontier where the main body of the Syrian forces were concentrated. Upon his refusal to obey the transfer order he was classed as a rebel. Ḥarīrī of Hama, Akram Ḥawrānī's brother-in-law,[29] was close to the Ba'th but not a party member; his principal motive was personal ambition and he held no clear-cut political views. After his break with the High Command in Damascus, he became the head of the March coup's planners and executors. His most important associate was Rāshid Quṭaynī, who was also not a party man. Quṭaynī had been military attaché in Jordan until the February transfers when he was appointed chief of intelligence on the General Staff.[30]

Another important leader of the conspirators was Brigadier Muḥammad Ṣūfī who commanded the Homs garrison.

The coup was initially planned for March 7. But at the last moment Quṭaynī and Ṣūfī withdrew from the plot as they feared that the government had been informed and that it had no chance of success. Then Harīrī resolved to act on his own one day later and Quṭaynī re-joined him. They informed a few other officers and the Ba'th leadership of their plan.[31]

At daybreak on March 8, 1963 rebel forces advanced on the capital from three directions. The strongest column with heavy tanks and anti-aircraft guns came from the "front" under the command of Brigadier Tawfīq al-Shāwā. Special emphasis was placed on anti-aircraft weapons as it was feared that the air force under the command of Brigadier 'Aṣāṣa would vigorously oppose the coup. At 4 a.m. the column reached Damascus where Ḥarīrī and Quṭaynī were waiting. After a brief exchange of fire, army headquarters was taken and immediately afterward the remaining strategic points in the city fell into rebel hands—this was the routine pattern of military coups in Damascus. The commander of the Damascus region, Brigadier Jamīl Fayāḍ and the commander of the military police, Lieutenant-Colonel 'Uthmān al-Jīrūdī, joined the rebels, and military police were sent to arrest the deposed commanders and ministers in their homes. Khālid al-'Aẓm succeeded in finding asylum in the Turkish Embassy near his house; he had already had some experience of coups—in his capacity as Prime Minister he had been arrested on the night of Za'īm's

[28] *Al-Ḥayāt,* 14 March 1963.

[29] *Al-'Amal,* Beirut, 27 June 1963.

[30] *Al-Ḥayāt,* 9 March 1963.

[31] Malcolm Kerr, *The Arab cold war, 1958–1964,* London 1965, 58.

coup in 1949. ʿAṣāṣa's effort to send out the air force against the coup failed, as the NCO's at the Dumair military airfield overrode the commander of the base, Colonel Haytham Muhā'inī, and did not permit the Migs to take off. At 6.30 the new Revolutionary Council met for the first time, and at 6.45 communiqué No. 1 of the "National Council of the Revolutionary Headquarters" was broadcast.[32] As soon as news of the coup broke, Cairo and Baghdad expressed enthusiastic support for it.

The coup was meant to end the period of isolation and reaction. The first communiqué began with a declaration that opened wide horizons: "In the name of God and Arabism. Since the beginning of history Syria has been fulfilling its positive function in the struggle under the banner of Arabism and Arab unity. Arab Syria and its people have never recognized the boundaries of its country and only acknowledge the frontiers of the greater Arab homeland. Even Syria's national anthem does not contain the word 'Syria' but glorifies Arabism and the heroic war of all the Arabs." After denouncing reaction, which took advantage of the errors of union with Egypt and created "the catastrophe of separation," the communiqué concluded with the statement that the army was always alert to these facts and that its officers and command invariably endeavored "to encourage the voice of the Syrian people. This morning, the command carried out a revolutionary movement and assumed power."[33]

In the communiqué of the morning neither the Baʿth nor socialism had yet been mentioned. The only active revolutionary force was the army and the only slogan to which emphasis was given was Arab unity. The Baʿth and its leaders and socialist ideology appeared at noon, but only after the army had completed the job of seizing power. A debate was at once started as to who was entitled to take credit for the revolution and its triumph. On March 14 Quṭaynī announced in Cairo that the army alone had planned and carried out the revolution "with no connection with any civilian body whatever."[34] On the other hand, Michel ʿAflaq claimed in an interview with a *Le Monde* correspondent that he had taken part in the preparations for the February and March revolutions in Iraq and Syria and that "the Baʿth party had organized both."[35] These contradictory versions are both of doubtful value as historic evidence. As in other debates of this sort, the intention was less to establish past merits than to determine future prerogatives. ʿAflaq did not deny that the executive body had been the army,

[32] *Qiṣṣat al-thawra fī al-ʿIrāq wa-Sūrlyyā,* Beirut (1963), 56–7; *al-Ḥayāt,* 14 March 1963.
[33] *Orient,* no. 34, 1963, 181-2.
[34] *Bi-Sarāḥa, makhādir muḥādathāt al-waḥda,* Cairo 1963, 11; *Arab Political Documents,* 1963, Beirut (1964), 77.
[35] *Le Monde,* Paris, 21 March 1963.

but he wished to present the army as the emissary of the party with the latter as the guiding authority.

Apart from unionist officers, nonpartisan groups and the Ba'th, a number of other elements appeared to present their demands. They were "*The Socialist Unity Movement*," "*The Arab Nationalist Movement*" and "*The United Arab Front*."[36] All these advocated unconditional restoration of union. The Ba'th wanted a union in which it would be the dominant power in Syria, and it also aspired to closer relations with Iraq, to serve as a counterweight to the great Egyptian power and Nasser's strong personality. Matters were further complicated as the Ba'th itself was divided. Akram Ḥawrānī's faction was denounced as anti-unionist and on the day of the coup Ḥawrānī was arrested, so that only 'Aflaq's faction appeared to speak for the party. Furthermore, each of the party's groups was divided into a civilian branch and a military one.

On the basis of the power, the prerogatives and the demands of the various elements, "The National Council of the Command of the Revolution," the highest authority in the state, was set up in the afternoon of March 8, and on the following day the new government was formed. The Revolutionary Council consisted of 17 men. The names of 12 of them, seven officers and five civilians were made public. Of the officers only one was definitely a Ba'thist, Muḥammad 'Umrān, and he was promoted from major to colonel.[37] The government consisted of 20 ministers, half of them members of the Ba'th, including Prime Minister Ṣalāh al-Bayṭār. There were only two officers among the ministers, but they held key posts: Lieutenant-Colonel Sāmī al-Jundī, who was promoted to brigadier, became Minister of Defense; and Colonel Amīn al-Ḥāfiẓ, a veteran Ba'thist who was recalled from Argentina where he had been serving as military attaché, was appointed Minister of the Interior with the rank of brigadier.

Lu'ay al-Atāsī was appointed commander-in-chief of the army, and several days later also President of the Revolutionary Council. He was in a strong position by dint of having attended the Homs Convention and because of his suppression of the 'Alwān uprising in Aleppo in April 1962. However, Zahr al-Dīn did not leave him in the Aleppo command for long; he was considered a Unionist and sent to the United States as military attaché. In January 1963 he was recalled to Damascus, ostensibly to give evidence at the trial of the Aleppo rebels. When his testimony failed to satisfy the country's leaders, he was incarcerated in the Al-Mezze prison. He was released on the morning of March 8 and on the same day jumped

36. Kerr, 60–1.

37 *Cahiers de l'Orient contemporain*, Paris 1963, 91.

three grades from colonel to lieutenant-general. He was a young man—36, which was Nasser's age when he got the upper hand of Naguib—and acceptable to various elements inside and outside Syria: The Atāsī family represented the best in Syrian nationalist tradition. At the same time he represented closer relations with Egypt; his wife was a native of Cairo, the daughter of a wealthy merchant from Homs who was a relative of the Atāsī family and had been living in Egypt from the early 1920's. Lu'ay al-Atāsī had served in Egypt as assistant to the Syrian military attaché in the days before union and had completed a course for staff officers there. During the period of union he commanded a brigade in the vicinity of Alexandria. Before that he had gone to France to study and in 1962 he was in the USSR. He also had ties with the United States: Two of his brothers lived there, one of them a student of engineering.[38]

Ḥarīrī became chief of staff and Quṭaynī his deputy. Naturally they, too, were promoted.

As in Iraq the new regime had on its banner the triple slogan "Union, Freedom, Socialism," and it was not for nothing that "Union" came first. The restoration of union with Egypt, this time together with Iraq, seemed around the corner. In less than a week, on March 14, delegates from the three countries met in Cairo under the chairmanship of Nasser to discuss union. However, numerous difficulties arose and the talks lasted a month. On April 17 a tripartite pact was published. In fact, only the establishment of a federal union, to be implemented in stages, was announced. But it was received with tremendous enthusiasm throughout the Arab world, especially in Syria and Iraq. None of these hopes materialized and it was precisely Syria, who had always been the most active and the most sought-after in all matters pertaining to Arab unity, who in the summer was once again at loggerheads with Egypt, and in the winter with Iraq as well. The mutual suspicions of Nasser and the Syrian Ba'thist leaders were stronger than their readiness to make concessions for the sake of union. Struggles between Syria and Egypt and among the Syrians themselves broke out immediately and the Syrian army again became the principal bone of contention.

The first outbreak had already occurred before the end of April. The pro-Nasser Unionists in Aleppo, their traditional center of power, were disappointed because unification had not taken place immediately. They tried to rush matters and the army commanders there revolted. Headquarters in Damascus was able to nip that movement in the bud. However, a number of Ba'thist officers were not satisfied with the measures taken and on April 27 two battalions of the 72nd Armored Brigade, whose com-

[38] *Qiṣṣa*, 56-7; *Ākhir Sā'a*, 3 April 1963; *al-Nahār*, 18 January 1963.

manders were Ba'thists, moved from Kiswa on Damascus to demand the dismissal of 47 Nasserist officers. After negotiations it was agreed that the battalions would return to base and the dismissal demand would be executed —and that is what happened. The cashiered officers included an air force major-general, Nūr-Allāh al-Ḥājj Ibrāhīm; the Minister of Defense, Lieutenant-General Muḥammad Ṣūfī; and the Deputy Chief of Staff, Major-General Quṭaynī.[39]

In the nine years since the ousting of Shīshaklī the Ba'th had at times been close to ruling Syria. Now for the first time the struggle for control of the army, the country's center of power, had ended in a clear victory for the party and it resolved to consolidate and extend its conquest. The first obstacle, and therefore to be eliminated, was Ziyād Ḥarīrī, the ambitious officer around whom the non-Ba'thists had clustered. It was he who had carried out the coup of March 8. He was chief of staff, and in the new government which had been formed on May 13 the Minister of Defense as well. Differences appeared when he opposed two of the Ba'thist demands: A change in the agrarian reform law which reduced the area a farmer was permitted to hold even more than the 1958 law; and dismissals and new appointments of numerous officials and officers.[40] On June 20 Ḥarīrī went to Algeria on a goodwill mission and the Ba'th took advantage of his absence. The Revolutionary Council published a new agrarian reform law and discharged 27 officers from the police and 13 from the army. Ḥarīrī—a major-general, Chief of Staff and Minister of Defense—was posted as military attaché to the United States with instructions to leave Algiers immediately for his new appointment via Paris. The dismissed officers refused to obey the order and the evening of June 25 Ḥarīrī suddenly returned from Algeria to Damascus with the Prime Minister and the rest of the members of the delegation. That night and on the next two days the Revolutionary Council, with Ḥarīrī's participation, held a series of meetings. The civilian and military leaders of the Ba'th now spoke of a conspiracy that had come to light, and the Minister of Information in an interview with a correspondent of *al-Hayāt* spoke of "the dismissal of 800 officers from the army and the appointment of 900 others to replace them."[41] Tension mounted, both sides drew up army units and clashes between them began. Emissaries from the Iraqi Ba'th and army attempted to mediate in order to prevent a civil war. They tried to persuade Syrian Ba'thist leaders to forego some of their dismissal demands, and they made Ḥarīrī understand that if

[39] Kerr, 107; *al-Anwār*, Beirut, 3 May 1963; *al-Siyāsa*, Beirut, 3 May 1963; *al-Hayāt*, 4 May 1963.

[40] *Hamizrah Hehadash*, vol. 14, 237; *al-Ḥayāt*, 26 June 1963.

[41] *Al-Ḥayāt*, 28 June 1963.

an armed fight broke out Iraq would intervene against him. Ba'thist officers turned out to be in control of the army units inside and around the capital, the armored brigades and the air force. Ḥarīrī was forced to yield. On July 7 he was placed under house-arrest and on the following day banished to Vienna.

Now a new star appeared over Syria—Amīn al-Ḥāfiẓ. Directly after Ḥarīrī's ouster on July 10 he became Minister of Defense with the rank of major-general. He was already Deputy Prime Minister, Minister of the Interior and acting military governor. In 1961 al-Ḥāfiẓ studied in the USSR and after the secession he was for a short while head of the army's training branch. When differences arose between him and the leaders at the time, he was sent as military attaché to the Soviet Union and later to Argentina, from where he was recalled on the day following the coup of March 1963. In the struggle against Ḥarīrī he was the tough one, toughness bordering on cruelty being conspicuous in his character and actions. He comes from a poor Aleppo family and is a declared Ba'thist party member.

On July 1, 1963 an announcement proclaimed the establishment of the Syrian "National Guard," a para-military party organization, as a further step in the strengthening of Ba'thist rule. Its commander was Ḥamad 'Ubayd, a lieutenant-colonel, who had been sentenced to life imprisonment in January for his part in the Aleppo revolt of the previous April. The Ba'th also tried to transform the regular army into a party instrument. There was talk of members taking an oath of allegiance to Ba'th doctrine and leadership. The slogan an "ideological army" became an official precept from July 1963 on. In practice this meant ever-recurring dismissals of scores of officers, first non-Ba'thists and later Ba'thists adhering to a faction other than the one momentarily in power.

Unionists understood that the end of their hopes was at hand. They made another desperate effort to alter the course of events—on July 18 they tried to carry out a military coup in Damascus. This time the rebels acted in broad daylight. At 10.15 a.m. four Migs attacked army headquarters and several minutes later a number of small infantry units—including the Signal Corps and military police—captured army headquarters and the adjacent radio station. Simultaneously broadcasts ceased as a result of internal sabotage by one of the technicians. Aiding the army rebels were civilians, particularly discharged officers, soldiers and Palestinian refugees. The rebel leaders were Jāsim 'Alwān and Muḥammad Jarrāḥ, a cashiered major-general, who during union had directed general security in Syria. The purpose of the uprising was the restoration of union, as in the Aleppo rebellion of April 1962, and the rebels had grounds for anticipating active Egyptian intervention if their movement spread. At first they had some success; the major in charge of the headquarters guard ordered his men to withdraw. However, headquarters officers led by Amīn al-Ḥāfiẓ took up sub-machine-guns and repulsed the attack. At the same time they called out loyal troops to seize strategic centers in the capital, and they imposed a curfew. Fighting in Damascus lasted until 2.30 p.m. The use of tanks, artillery and airplanes caused numerous casualties; according to various estimates the number of those killed in Damascus ranged from 170 to 800.[42]

The rebels who were caught were sentenced on the same day by special court-martial, and on the following day at noon Colonel Hishām Shabīb, commander of the signal corps, five of his NCO's and four civilians were executed. Two hours later two NCO's from other units were shot. Since the killing of Za'īm in 1949 this was the first time in the history of the numerous Syrian military coups that death sentences were carried out. The trials and executions that included one woman lasted a further two days. The hunt for escaped conspirators and trials of arrested persons continued for a long time, but no more death sentences were passed. 'Alwān and Jarrāḥ, who were sentenced to death in absentia and later arrested, were amnestied in 1964 and allowed to leave for Egypt.

Al-Ḥāfiẓ had triumphed again. Two measures, the logical outcome of his victory, followed. On July 22, the eve of the Egyptian national holiday, Nasser announced the dissolution of the tripartite pact. On the same day Lu'ay al-Atāsī resigned as President of the Revolutionary Council and barricaded himself in his house. His resignation was accepted on July 27, and al-Ḥāfiz became President of the Revolutionary Council—the dictator of Syria—for two and a half years.

The Ba'th's rivals in Syria were vanquished. However, the country did not attain stability. Egyptian propaganda attacks and subversion continued, and the war of vilification between Cairo and Damascus attained an all-time high. Al-Ḥāfiẓ said at a press conference in Damascus on November 21, 1963: "We find ourselves constrained . . . to ask whether the leaders in Cairo know what their propaganda organs are doing? If they do know, they are committing a crime; if they do not, their crime is even worse . . . If they do not stop this, I shall be forced to say that the very shoes of a Syrian soldier are worth more than the heads of many of those cowards and are capable of crushing their heads if they insult his dignity and honor."[43]

What became increasingly more serious than the strife with Egypt were the internal struggles, particularly within the Ba'th. Of secondary importance were the differences between the factions of 'Aflaq and Ḥawrānī. Ḥaw-

[42] *Cahiers,* 1963, 234–5; *Keesing's Contemporary Review,* 1963, 1958, 2; *al-Ḥayāt,* 19 July 1963; W. Vogel, 'Die Syrische Armee', *Truppenpraxis,* Darmstadt, May 1964, 331.

[43] *Arab Political Documents,* 1963, Beirut 1964, 480–1.

rānī even stopped paying lip service to the cause of union with Egypt and was no longer regarded a member of the party. The struggle within the party between its military and civilian branches assumed extremely serious proportions, 'Aflaq, the ideologist, and Bayṭār, the Prime Minister, each regarded himself the highest authority for laying down policy. Al-Ḥāfiẓ and his fellow officers, however, considered only soldiers as being capable and possessing the authority to decide on important matters. A similar tug-of-war between officers and Ba'thist party leaders took place in Iraq at this time, and what happened in Baghdad between March and November 1963 influenced Damascus to a degree unheard of for generations. In Iraq the November struggle ended in a complete defeat for the Ba'th in favor of the army. In Syria, the party's birthplace and center, it was impossible to achieve such an unambiguous outcome. Whereas Ārif had succeeded in outlawing the party, the regime in Syria remained Ba'thist, and from November 1963 relations between the two countries became progressively worse.

On November 12, during the Ba'thist military crisis in Iraq, Bayṭār resigned and on the following day al-Ḥāfiẓ became Prime Minister in addition to his other powers. On April 25, 1964 a new provisional Syrian constitution was published.[44] It established explicit constitutional patterns for the supremacy of the "National Council of the Revolutionary Command:" It constitutes "the legislative authority and supervises the activities of the executive authority;" it chooses its president and appoints and dismisses the government, which is responsible to it. On May 13 Bayṭār once again became Prime Minister. Under the new constitution there was no longer the shadow of a doubt who the master was and who was his assistant.

However, at that time al-Ḥāfiẓ needed Bayṭār's help as the representative of a wider public. In the previous two months an extremely serious political and economic crisis had broken out. Capitalists smuggled their money to Lebanon, prices soared and numerous enterprises closed or reduced their activities. At the same time, both as one of the reasons for the crisis and as its result, relations sharpened between the Ba'thist factions and throughout the agitated country over the means to be adopted for overcoming the crisis; some demanded nationalization while others advocated that it was private initiative that should be encouraged. At the end of March a number of mysterious arms raids on police stations in Aleppo and Damascus announced the approaching storm which broke out in Hama on April 9.[45] Its direct cause is not clear; it may have been due to a

[44] *Al-Ba'th,* Damascus, 27 April 1964; *Hamizrah Hehadash,* vol. 14, 197–204.
[45] *Al-Akhbār,* Cairo, 8 April 1964.

mass demonstration staged by the town's population in protest against the sentence of a year's imprisonment meted out to a student at the 'Uthmān Hawrāni Secondary School. He had erased, from the classroom blackboard, Ba'thist slogans written by the teacher.[46] The demonstration was dispersed by soldiers and police who used firearms, and a number of people were wounded or killed. The protest, however, did not cease but became more intense and assumed new forms.[47] On April 10, which was a Friday, the preachers of Hama's mosque fiercely attacked the Ba'th in their sermons. The most active force among the opponents of the government seem to have been the Muslim Brethren. On Saturday, there were demonstrations on the streets and clashes with security forces in which at least one student was killed. On Sunday Hama went on strike and stores were closed. Amīn al-Ḥāfiẓ went to Hama personally to order the release of the boy arrested on Thursday and indemnity payment to the parents of the boy killed on Saturday. But on Tuesday April 14 extremely severe clashes broke out again. Apparently soldiers were fired upon from the al-Sulṭān Mosque. In the ensuing fights, a number of soldiers were killed and the mosque was shelled by artillery. The number killed in Hama on that day certainly exceeded 60. Ten days later al-Ḥāfiẓ, when asked about the casualties at Hama, declared at a press conference: "On our side there were 20, of which five were killed, and among the civilians about 40 to 50 and perhaps 60 at the most, if new victims are discovered under the ruins."[48] At this stage the movement, which had become a rebellion, spread to other towns. On April 24 Damascus witnessed a demonstration in support of the government, but two days later the local merchants and shopkeepers declared a general strike against it. The strikes and disorders continued until April 30. At Homs and Aleppo the unrest was high. In Damascus the National Guard opened closed shops by force. A decree was published which made the closing of a shop by its proprietor "without legitimate reasons" a crime punishable by 20 years' imprisonment with hard labor plus the confiscation and nationalization of the shop.[49]

The rebellion in Syria during April 1964 was the first large movement of civilians against a military dictotorship. Although a single battalion of troops can disperse a demonstration of tens of thousands, a strike is a civilian weapon which can immobilize the power of the military. Not for nothing did al-Ḥāfiẓ react with excessive severity to the shopkeepers' refusal to sell their merchandise. But it was possible to break the mutiny

[46] *Al-Jarida,* Beirut, 15 April 1964.

[47] *Chronicle of Arab Politics,* vol. x, no. 2, Beirut (1964), 178–185.

[48] *Al-Ḥayāt,* 25 April 1964.

[49] Jean-Pierre Viennot, 'Le Ba'th entre la théorie et la pratique', *Orient,* no. 30, 26.

because of its reactionary and limited class nature and its undefined general political character. Socialistic-Unionistic elements and the Muslim Brethren, Nasserists and foes of nationalization had acted, but without a clear and common program, and the government could appear as the defender of the interests of the workers and intellectuals.

These shocks afforded al-Ḥāfiẓ enough reason for reinstating Bayṭār as Prime Minister in May; the new constitution and the actual balance of forces gave assurance that the borderline between the real ruler and the second-in-command would not be obscured. At the same time, al-Ḥāfiẓ was promoted to lieutenant-general. Debates, intrigues and conspiracies continued among the Ba'thists throughout the summer months. On October 3 Bayṭār once again presented his resignation, and on the following day, al-Ḥāfiẓ was again President and Prime Minister.

Al-Ḥāfiẓ's right-hand man at the decisive stages of his ascendancy was Muḥammad 'Umrān, an Alawi and old-time Ba'thist. In Zahr al-Dīn's time he had been dismissed from the army but on the morning of the coup in March 1963 he was recalled to duty.[50] He was appointed to the Revolutionary Council and to the delegation sent to Cairo to discuss union; he was promoted from major to lieutenant-colonel and placed in command of the 5th Brigade at Homs.[51] In June 1963 he commanded the 70th Armored Brigade, the strongest unit in the Syrian army. His rise through the ranks was rapid, and in November 1963 he became a major-general. In January 1964 when al-Ḥāfiẓ attended the summit meeting of the heads of Arab states, and in November 1964 when he went to Paris for an operation, 'Umrān took his place. But neither did this alliance last. The first differences of opinion between them had already appeared in the autumn of 1963. 'Umrān, who in the past had been one of Akram Ḥawrānī's supporters, became his greatest opponent in 1962, and in 1964 he was against all of al-Ḥāfiẓ's feelers to effect a reconciliation with him. Instead he favored reconciliation with socialist and Nasserist elements as well as allotting more influence to civilians in managing the affairs of the Ba'th and the state. At the end of 1964 al-Ḥāfiẓ rejected 'Umrān's proposals, and the latter had to resign from the government and the army. In accordance with accepted practice he was sent abroad, and on December 14 was appointed ambassador to Spain.[52]

The man who replaced 'Umrān—and who also had a part in his fall—was Ṣalāh Jadīd, the Chief of Staff. He, like 'Umrān, is an Alawi and he, too, had risen from major to major-general between March and November

[50] Radio Damascus, 8 March 1963.

[51] *Al-Ḥawādith,* Beirut, 17 May 1963.

[52] Vernier, 498; *al-Ḥayāt,* 30 June 1963; *al-Nahār,* Beirut, 9 December 1964.

1963. He is a younger brother of Lientenant-Colonel Ghassān Jadīd, the SSNP leader who was assassinated in 1955, but, unlike him a Ba'thist of long standing. In February 1963 he was still a retired colonel, kept out of the service because of his political affiliation. After the March coup he returned to the army and in November 1963 he became a major-general and chief of staff.[53] His principal partners in the struggle against 'Umrān were two Druze officers, Ḥamad 'Ubayd and Salīm Ḥāṭūm. 'Ubayd had been sentenced to ten years' imprisonment for his participation in the Aleppo rebellion of March 1962.[54] After the March 1963 coup he was released, rose quickly through the ranks and became the commander of the National Guard and then the commander of the armored brigade at Qaṭana.[55] Ḥāṭūm had in 1964 and 1965 been the commander of a commando battalion guarding the district containing army headquarters and the radio station in Damascus; the history of Syrian military coups has taught that control of these installations is the key to control of the entire country.

'Umrān may have hoped that Alawi communal solidarity would prevent Jadīd from abetting his dismissal. But he was mistaken. They belong to different Alawi tribes: 'Umrān is a member of the "Tailors" *(khayyāṭūn)* and comes originally from the village of al-Mukharram, east of Homs; Jadīd is one of the "Smiths" *(ḥaddādūn)* from the region of Latakia.[56] Moreover, 'Umrān aspired to straighten out difficulties with Egypt and to the increasing participation of civilians in conducting Syrian affairs; these had also been the ambitions of 'Aflaq and Bayṭār. Jadīd, however, adopted an extreme position both in the controversy with Egypt and in his socialist radicalism. The two logical conclusions of this attitude were that in 1965 Jadīd and his colleagues aimed to establish closer relations with China; and knowing how limited the popular base of their policy was, they opposed 'Umrān's intentions of disbanding the military committee of the party and softening the dictatorial nature of the regime. In this anti-Egyptian extremism Jadīd could have found partners in Akram Ḥawrānī and his comrades, but his extremism regarding nationalizations and socialism and his disparagement of the civilian leaders prevented closer relations between him and Ḥawrānī.

In his rise and his ousting of Ḥarīrī, Lū'ay al-Atāsī and 'Umrān, Amīn al-Ḥāfiẓ made considerable use of the assistance of Alawi and Druze Ba'thist officers. But being himself a Sunni Muslim, he did not want the

[53] *Al-Anwār,* Beirut, 17 December 1964.
[54] *Al-Ḥayāt,* 18 January 1963.
[55] *Al-Nahār,* 16 December 1964.
[56] Vernier, 466; *al-Ḥayāt,* 12 December 1965.

two minorities to achieve real supremacy and began to limit their influence in 1965. That is one of the reasons for the dispute which broke out between him and Jadīd in the summer of 1965. But the principal reason was a change in the political orientation of al-Ḥāfiẓ. What sometimes happens to a leader who succeeds in overcoming his adversary occurred in his case: After his triumph, the victor carries out the policy of the vanquished. Al-Ḥāfiẓ realized that he could only prevent Syria's complete isolation in the Arab world and the government's internal collapse by adopting a moderate line toward Egypt and by suspending further nationalizations. Only by compromising with the necessities of life did he succeed in holding power for more than two years, a longer time than all preceding military dictators, with the exception of Shīshaklī.

In the early months of 1965 numerous enterprises were nationalized. Most of them were completely nationalized and part of them to the extent of 90 per cent or 75 per cent of their capital. The nationalization angered small businessmen and artisans no less than the big capitalists, and only a few regarded it as beneficial to themselves or the national economy. In addition to a number of enterprises employing several hundred workers the government also nationalized a series of small workshops—a soap factory employing three men, etc. This resulted in bureaucratic red tape and nothing else. At the beginning of July, 27 pharmaceutical firms were restored to private ownership, and from then on socialism was once again declared to be a long-range goal and not an immediate policy. In rural areas the government adopted a more moderate and more consistent policy; the activities of agrarian reform continued at a slow pace and with success.

In foreign policy, too, al-Ḥāfiẓ had to oppose Jadīd's line, especially in matters of inter Arab relations and anti-Israel activism. Already in the period of union with Egypt the Ba'thist chiefs accused the other Arab leaders of treacherous appeasement toward Israel and demanded immediate war. At three summit conferences the heads of the Arab states, under the leadership of Nasser, reached a more realistic, uniform position. The Egyptians at war in Yemen and the Iraqis fighting in Kurdistan did not let the Syrians drag them into a meaningless war in 1965; and unable to follow up his extreme anti-Israel propaganda with deeds, al-Ḥāfiẓ was compelled to moderate its tone.

The differences between Jadīd and al-Ḥāfiẓ were already apparent in May,[57] and from then on became progressively worse. At the beginning of September Jadīd was dismissed from his post as chief of staff. He then entrenched himself in his position as secretary of the "regional" (Syrian)

57. *Al-Ḥayāt,* 5,6 May 1965.

leadership of the Ba'th, which in contrast with the "national" (all-Arab) leadership, had become the stronghold of the extremists. In December 1965 the breach between them widened. The direct cause was the attempt of Lieutenant-Colonel Muṣṭafā Ṭallās, commander of the army at Homs and one of Jadīd's men, to dismiss a number of officers loyal to al-Ḥāfiẓ.[58] Al-Ḥāfiẓ grasped at the opportunity to cashier Ṭallās, and within a few days 'Umrān was returned to Syria, the all-Arab leadership of the Ba'th disbanded the "regional" leadership, the Zu'ayyin government was forced to resign, and on January 2, 1966 a new government headed by Bayṭār was established. At its formation it was heralded as a civilian government. And to be sure, of its 26 members—the largest number of cabinet ministers in all Syrian governments—only two were army officers, fewer than in previous governments. However, these two were the two strong men in the cabinet: Muḥammad 'Umrān, Minister of Defense, and Major-General Mamdūḥ Jābīr—who in previous governments had served as Minister of Defense and Minister of Public Works—as Minister for Prime Minister's Affairs. Bayṭār's government came to power as the result of the victory of one group of officers over a rival group. In this way, Bayṭār's brand of Ba'thist leaders was able to exploit the internal breach in the ranks of the officer politicians, while al-Ḥāfiẓ took advantage of the growing public opposition to the political adventures of the officers in order to get rid of the rival faction.

The Bayṭār-'Umrān government remained in power for less than two months. On February 23, 1966 Jadīd's group carried out a coup and ousted President al-Ḥāfiẓ and the government.

Since 1963 the Ba'thist military regime in Syria had been professing the slogan of the "ideological army." And the slogan was actually applied; the Ba'thist officers seized all the command positions and whoever was not or did not become a Ba'thist was dismissed. At the overpoliticization of the officer corps, two additional trends became predominant: Most of the politically affiliated officers joined the extreme, leftist and activist faction of the Ba'th; and officers coming from the minority groups—especially Alawis, Druze and some Yazidis—rose to the fore in a much greater proportion to their number and importance in the population of the country as a whole. Among the civilian members of the party, the Sunni Muslims, supporting the moderate faction, constituted a majority, whereas among the officer politicians they were a minority.

The party organ by which the extremist faction ruled in 1965 was the "regional," i.e., the Syrian leadership, theoretically subordinate to the

[58] *Ibid.*, 1 January 1966.

all-Arab "national" leadership. In December 1965 the moderate faction won out over the extremists; al-Ḥāfiẓ dismissed Zu'ayyin's government which the extremists controlled, 'Aflaq and 'Umrān returned to political leadership, and in January 1966 Bayṭār's government was formed. The next inevitable and logical step was the ousting from the army of the officers belonging to Ṣalāḥ Jadīd's group. Anyhow, the strong position of the members of the minorities had for a long time been a thorn in the flesh of al-Ḥāfiẓ the Sunni. And thus in the third week of February 1966 he prepared an order concerning the dismissal from the army of 30 officers of Jadīd's men.[59] And as is often the case in the history of military coups, the government's dismissal plans convinced the candidates to be ousted that they had nothing to lose, and they decided to act.

A strong ideological and political formulation of the controversy was given in a lecture delivered by Michel 'Aflaq in one of the sub-branches of the Ba'th in Damascus on February 18. The lecture was published in full in the Beirut *al-Ḥayāt* of February 25. It was tantamount to a declaration of war on Jadīd's faction and implied that al-Ḥāfiẓ's men were no longer looking for a way to compromise. 'Aflaq accused the rival faction of "degenerating to regional separatism." The all-Arab leadership alone is "the true leadership of the party, for the Ba'th is a unitary party, and the all-Arab leadership has in mind the supreme interests of the Arab nation, whereas other leaders digress to regional interests." He also flung at his adversaries the charge that they "demonstrated unheard-of ideological sterility" and that "they do not even possess a minimal education." Commenting on their turning to communism and Marxism, 'Aflaq stressed the contradictions in principle between the ideas of the Ba'th and Marxism, which "provides no answer for our national problems. The local communists dissociate themselves from nationalism and oppose it, and similarly they also dissociate themselves from Arab unity." Moreover, Marxism is connected with the "world communist movement," and during World War II "the communist parties demanded that the Arabs keep quiet about French and English imperialism, because the French and British were the allies of the Soviets; and this position was a betrayal of the nation's aims." That group assumed control of the party in Syria against its rules, for "of the nine civilian members in the disbanded regional leadership, seven joined the party only after the revolution (of March 1963)," and what is most important, "they gained the leadership of the party and the government by means of the military group." In the end, 'Aflaq demanded a "return to fundamentals and a thorough-going reform of the party," and frankly

[59] *Ibid.,* 26 February 1966.

said, "A part of our members in the army degenerated to the state of factionalism and domination of the party and the people, opportunism and self-interest . . . we wish to reform the duties of the army by preventing army men from forming a cohesive bloc at the core of leadership in the party or the government. If the party should select one of its military members for its leadership he will not remain a soldier but will become a party man and a popular leader and he cannot possibly retain his military position. There is no true revolutionary party in the world whose leaders are military commanders continuing in command of their units. However, here we had some men who simultaneously served in the party leadership, as ministers in the government, and as commanders in the army." For this reason 'Aflaq insisted that once and for all an end should be put to army interference in politics.[60]

At this time a controversy broke out over elections to the regional leadership of the Ba'th. At first the date was set for February 20, but when al-Ḥāfiẓ realized that his group would not secure a majority until various dismissals were carried out, he prevented the elections from taking place. The dispute became more acrimonious and violent debates between the leaders of the rival factions took place in public. Half a week before the coup, on February 19, *al-Ḥayāt* reported that "the Bayṭār government is in effect paralyzed," citing as one of the principal reasons, "Jadīd's men are retaining their control of the army."[61]

Another development which apparently impelled Jadīd to execute the coup were rumors that Muḥammad 'Umrān, the Minister of Defense, had secretly flown to Cairo and met with Nasser. For closer relations with Egypt had long been 'Umrān's principal aim, whereas Jadīd considered this treason. There is no confirmation of 'Umrān's flight, but in his speech on the evening of February 22 Nasser avoided attacking Syria and the Ba'th. It was a long speech, the occasion was the anniversary of Egypt's union with Syria in 1958, and Nasser's tone in other matters was polemic, which it had not been for a long time—but he did not attack Syria.

While Nasser was delivering his speech in Cairo, final preparations for the coup were being completed in Syria.

As usual, commando units entered the capital at night to converge on general staff headquarters, the radio station and the residences of the country's leaders. Paratroopers under the command of Salīm Ḥātūm came from Kharsata, a suburb of Damascus, and a column of tanks commanded by 'Izzat Jadīd clattered out of Qabun Camp. When Ḥātūm's paratroopers

[60] *Ibid.*, 25 February 1966.
[61] *Ibid.*, 19 February 1966.

turned on al-Ḥāfiẓ' house at dawn they encountered strong resistance and a prolonged battle followed. Al-Ḥāfiẓ assumed personal command of the guard of 120 soldiers of the Desert Force, and, as in the suppression of 'Alwān's insurrection in July 1963, he fought bravely with weapon in hand. There were dead and wounded on both sides and al-Ḥāfiẓ' men surrendered only after he was injured. A battle was also fought for the "Guest Palace" in Damascus, and there were clashes elsewhere in the country. This was no doubt the bloodiest of the numerous Syrian coups since 1949.

At 6.20 a.m. communiqué No. 1 was broadcast. It informed the people and the world that the government in Damascus was overthrown—"The Provisional Regional Leadership" of the Ba'th proclaimed a curfew throughout Syria. Five minutes later communiqué No. 2 was broadcast, announcing the closing of the frontiers and harbors and airports. At 6.30 a communiqué was broadcast announcing the arrest of the leaders of the defeated government. Ten minutes later an announcement was made concerning suspension of the constitution and the appointment of Major-General Ḥāfiẓ Asad as Minister of Defense and of Aḥmad Suwaydānī as chief of staff and the latter's promotion from colonel to major-general.

These two appointments demonstrated in what direction the new regime was headed. Ḥāfiẓ Asad is one of the Alawi Ba'thist officers who quickly rose to the top. At the beginning of 1963, when he was 33 years old, he was still a major; in 1964 a lieutenant-colonel; and in December of the same year, when Jadīd had the upper hand, he was suddenly promoted to major-general.[62] Of greater importance is the fact that he commanded the air force since 1963; the air force was the most active supporter of the insurrectionist officers in February 1966. Aḥmad Suwaydānī is a Sunni, but like his Alawi comrades and in contrast to most of the Sunni officers, he is of rural origin. At the beginning of 1965, at the age of 33, he served as chief of intelligence, but after Jadīd was ousted as chief of staff, he was transferred to a lesser post. He is known as a Marxist, a definite sympathizer of the Viet Cong and China, where he went on an extended visit, and the head of the group of "Ideological Officers." Until February 1966 he made use of his substantial influence in the army and the party behind the scenes; he had the reputation of being taciturn and was nicknamed "Sphinx" by his comrades.[63]

From 7.30 on Damascus Radio broadcast—and thus also invited—telegrams expressing support of the coup. The first came from the army

[62] *Al-Nahār,* 5 July 1963, 25 February 1964; *al-Hayāt,* 24 February 1966.

[63] *Al-Jarīda,* Beirut, 3 August 1965; *al-Ḥayāt,* 24 February 1966; *al-Ṣafā,* Beirut, 20 November 1966.

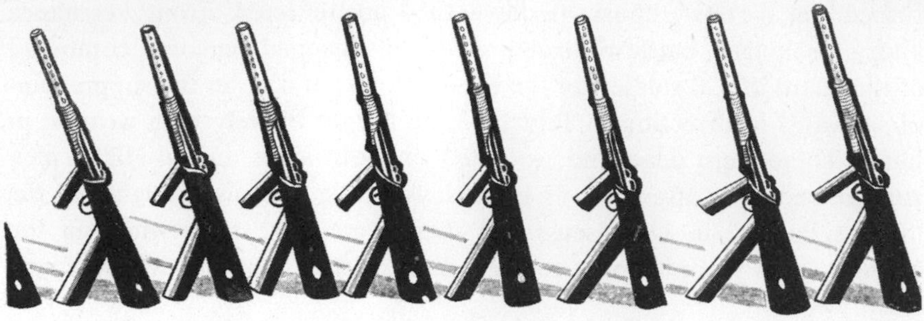

"The new Syrian government", a cartoon in *al-Nahār* of Beirut, 2 March, 1966

units, but the wires were few in number, and even these from tiny units were broadcast several times. For many hours no expression of support arrived either from Aleppo and the north or from the southern front. In the neighboring countries, broadcasts from Aleppo and the south were picked up which denounced the coup. In the north the insurrectionists encountered active resistance by army units and by civilians, headed by Aḥmad Abū Ṣāliḥ from Aleppo, a member of one of Bayṭār's former cabinets, and by Ḥamad ʻUbayd.[64] ʻUbayd, the Druze, the old rival of Jadīd, the Alawi, and like him a typical Baʻthist officer politician, had been Minister of Defense in Zuʻayyin's government of September 1965; he was then also promoted from colonel to major-general. But the resistance to the coup was short-lived. When there was no further doubt that the coup had been victorious in the capital, there was no longer any sense in resisting nor prospect of success in doing so. A large majority of the Syrian population was not enthusiastic about Jadīd's accession to power, but neither had there been much sympathy for al-Ḥāfiẓ; there was no one interested in or ready to fight for one Baʻthist military faction against another.

Within a few days life in Syria returned to its customary course, and on March 1, a new government was formed. As others had done before him, Jadīd himself preferred to remain outside the government, and, in fact, above it, and to maintain his hold on the leadership of the party as its secretary. Dr. Nūr al-Dīn Atāsī was appointed President of the Republic, Dr. Yūsuf Zuʻayyin again became Prime Minister, and Dr. Ibrāhīm Mākhūs Minister for Foreign Affairs. All three are physicians, under 40 years of age, and represent the urban Sunni civilian intelligentsia. The new government was most anxious not to appear as an open military dictatorship, but the cabinet was now reduced from 26 to 20, and the number of officer ministers again increased from two to four.

[64] *Al-Ḥayāt,* 18, 24 December 1966.

The new government was the most extreme leftist of all previous and present regimes in Syria and in all the Arab countries. Its radicalism was conspicuous in many spheres. In the ideology and ubiquitous propaganda of the Ba'th, the Marxist tone predominated. For a time, encouragement was given to "Workers' Battalions" under the leadership of Khālid al-Jundī in which the influence of the Chinese "Red Guards" was apparent. Nationalization and agrarian reforms were once again intensified. For the first time a member of the Communist Party became a member of the cabinet—Samīḥ 'Aṭiyya was appointed Minister of Transport.

Syria's 1966 radicalism was the most obvious in foreign affairs. The regime received the recognition and support of the USSR and established closer relations with it; an agreement was signed for large-scale Soviet support in implementing the great enterprise of the Euphrates dam.

In its relations with Israel, too, in 1966 Syria took an extreme line, officially adopting the theory of an Arab "People's War", and supported with propaganda, training and operational assistance the acts of terrorist organizations such as "al-Fatḥ" inside Israel.

In one basic sphere, that of relations with Egypt, Jadīd was compelled to deviate from his previous line of thinking and action to follow in the footsteps of al-Ḥāfiẓ. The Syrian regime of 1966 became too isolated in the Arab world and needed a crutch, which it found in Egypt, not without the mediation of the Soviet Union. In November 1966 a defense agreement was signed between Syria and Egypt. In theory, the agreement assured Syria of Egyptian aid in case of attack; in practice, the agreement required Syria to curb her extreme activism and refrain from provocative acts, chiefly against Israel, liable to involve Egypt in a war at an inopportune time. However, a government without sufficiently broad backing among the population, self-confidence, internal cohesiveness and stability could not allow itself to moderate the extremist slogans and provocative deeds which it had previously encouraged.

The instability of the Syrian regime in 1966 and its dependence on the army are demonstrated by the shocks it suffered from the abortive military coup in September. The conspiracy was headed by an officer who several months earlier had been Salāḥ Jadīd's right-hand man—Salīm Ḥāṭūm.

Jadīd and Ḥāṭūm together had ousted al-Ḥāfiẓ in February. Scarcely a week had passed before the press published the first reports of a dispute between them; the leaders of two groups, having cooperated in the liquidation of the previous regime, were now heading in different directions.[65]

Jadīd accused Ḥāṭūm of ideological inconsistency and being hasty

[65] *Al-Ḥuriyya,* Beirut, 28 February 1966.

where practical matters were concerned thus causing excessive bloodshed in the February 23 coup.[66]

To the extent that Jadīd and Ḥāṭūm were the leaders of factions, the alternating cooperation and disputes between them amounted less to cooperation and disputes between ideological currents or ambitious men, than to representatives of different communities. Jadīd was an Alawi and Ḥāṭūm a Druze; and in 1966 most of the Alawi Ba'thist leaders supported Jadīd and most of the Druze, Ḥāṭūm.

On December 30, 1966, *al-Ḥayāt* published a list of 89 Syrian officers who had been expelled from the Ba'th and the army. The list came from *al-Ni-ḍāl*, a confidential publication distributed only to the leaders of the Ba'th branches. In the case of a number of cashiered officers, among them many Alawis and Druze, the charges against them were noted, the most conspicuous being "communal clannishness" (*takattul ṭā'ifī*).[67]

One of Ḥāṭūm's relevant arguments against Jadīd was that he had allowed foreign, hostile elements, both communist and rightist, to infiltrate the Ba'th, while loyal leaders like al-Ḥāfiẓ were expelled. Apparently, he also suggested releasing al-Ḥāfiẓ from prison. Instead, Jadīd prepared to cashier Ḥāṭūm from the army.

In August 1966 Ḥāṭūm held the rank of major and commanded a commando battalion in Harsata Camp; he was only 29 years of age. He was joined by another Druze officer, Colonel Ṭalāl Abū 'Asalī, 37 years old, the commander of a brigade on the Syrian-Israeli "front."[68] Fahad al-Shā'ir also cast in his lot with them. Al-Shā'ir, like them a Druze, was older and of higher rank; he was a major-general formerly in command of the "front" and deputy chief of staff. In the March 1966 coup he did not take a clear-cut stand in favor of Jadīd, and at the beginning of August he was dismissed.[69] By the end of the month he had kept his rank and reputation, but had no military force under his command.

Already at the beginning of August Ḥāṭūm and Abū Asalī began to move their units toward the capital in order to arrest Salāḥ Jadīd. They had hoped for the support of Ḥāfiẓ Asad, Minister of Defense and commander of the air force, but when this failed they cancelled the coup for the time being.[70] However it was no longer possible to conceal their differences.

At this time Jadīd's most loyal supporter appeared in the guise of the leader of the "Workers' Battalions", Khālid al-Jundī, who encouraged the

66 *Al-Muḥarrir*, Beirut, 3 March 1966.

67 *Al-Ḥayāt*, 30 December 1966.

68 *Falasṭīn*, Jerusalem, 16 September 1966; *al-Ḥayāt*, 8 September 1966.

69 Radio Amman, 6 August 1966.

70 *Al-Ḥayāt*, 7 September 1966.

most extreme socialist and anti-imperialist nationalists. Arms were distributed to the "Workers' Battalions".

The controversy came to a head when on September 8 Ḥāṭūm and Abū 'Asalī arrested President Nūr al-Dīn Atāsī and Chief of Staff Aḥmad Suwaydānī at the "front." Evidently, Ṣalaḥ Jadīd was also arrested at his home in Damascus.[71] However, the attempt to seize power failed when Ḥāfiẓ Asad threatened to send the air force against Ḥāṭūm and the Druze, and when the "Workers' Battalions" in Damascus prepared to march against Ḥāṭūm's forces which had started to advance on the capital.

In the evening of September 8 a curfew was imposed on Damascus and a number of arrests made. Apparently, a secret agreement was reached between the contending factions for the mutual release of arrested leaders. That night and on the morning of September 9 several violent clashes took place between rival military units. The number of casualties is not known.

The position of Ḥāfiẓ Asad was significant. Although it was no secret that he had numerous reservations concerning Jadīd's policies, ultimately in all the trials of 1966 he always backed him and opposed his rivals.

Salīm Ḥāṭūm and his comrades fled on the morning of September 9 to seek political asylum in Jordan. They were accompanied by 12 officers, six NCO's, three privates and one civilian. On the following day Ṭalāl Abū 'Asalī fled to Jordan with six lieutenants.[72] During the next few days several other groups of fugitives arrived in Jordan. Additional groups continued to arrive, and in a few days several hundred Syrian soldiers and civilians, most of them Druze, had fled to Jordan.

At the time of the Six-Day War in June 1967 Salīm Ḥāṭūm, together with Major Badr Jum'a, returned to Syria—either in order to join the battle against Israel, as they stated, or in order to organize a new conspiracy, as they were accused of. Anyhow, they were arrested; on June 24 they were court-martialed and on June 26, executed.

Following the attempted coup of September 1966, the Jordanian government was accused of organizing and financing it. One of the principal accusers was Ṭalāl Abū 'Asalī, himself one of the attempted coup's leaders and refugees to Jordan. He remained in Jordan only two weeks; on September 26 he arrived in Beirut "on a personal visit", fleeing from there four days later to Cairo where he sought asylum.[73] He spoke vehemently of Jordanian and Saudi Arabian conspiracies against Syria, but could supply no facts or details.

[71] *Ibid.*, 10, 13 September 1966; *Jewish Observer and Middle East Review*, 23 September 1966.
[72] Radio Amman, 10, 11 September 1966.
[73] Radio Cairo, 1 October 1966.

There is no doubt that other Arab countries have always evinced interest and have intervened to a great extent in Syrian internal affairs. But the Syrians themselves are extremely active in their public life and associations. Absorbed in their ideological, class, communal and personal quarrels, they are more the manipulators of foreign support in their internal affairs than they are the instruments of others. For some time Syria wielded the greatest influence in general Arab politics and in the Palestinian question—and other states had to pay a heavy price for it. By encouraging Palestinian terrorist groups in word and deed, by embracing officially the theory of an immediate and "popular war" against Israel, by inciting Arab mass hysteria against her, the Syrian government was the most decisive single factor which provoked the Six-Day War of June 1967. But in the war itself this most hostile and activist of all Arab states tried to remain quite inactive and to leave the job of fighting to others, the Syrian army itself carrying out only some belated and quite symbolic acts of aggression. Nevertheless, after having beaten the Egyptians and the Jordanians, the Israeli air and ground forces went to war against the Syrians. The "ideological army" did no better than the other Arab armies. The Syrian officer corps in particular, so frequently purged for political reasons and weakened by mutual factional and communal mistrust, revealed itself as morally and professionally worthless. It proved to be less competent than the Syrians who had encountered the Israelis in various clashes between 1947 and 1963. The Syrian officers had learned much about fighting each other and their country's civilians, but not how to take on another army. Contemporary Syrian history can serve as an outstanding example of the plain fact that officer politicians are both bad officers and bad politicians.

8. IRAQ SINCE 1958

IRAQ was the first Arab country to achieve independence—in 1932—and also the first to experience military coups and dictatorships—in 1936. During the four and a half years from Bakr Ṣidqī to Rashīd ʻĀlī, groups of officers played the decisive political role in the country. Their interference undermined its stability and finally embroiled Iraq in a disastrous war. For the next 17 years her leaders managed to prevent army officers from interfering in politics at a time when military coups were succeeding one another in Egypt and Syria. Until the summer of 1958 Iraq seemed the most stable of the large Arab countries. However, Nūrī Saʻīd's regime collapsed suddenly in July 1958 and relative stability was succeeded by absolute confusion. Groups of officers carried out subversive activities, competing with each other in incessant struggles, while the political upheavals flooded the country with rivers of blood. It was not the officers alone who were engaged in these disturbances; from time to time political parties and communal and national groups were active in mass movements. But the important decisions were always made either by or among officers.

The peculiar nature of Iraqi society is reflected in these upheavals. In general Egypt can be described as the land of homogeneity, Syria as a country of heterogeneity, and Iraq as the land of antagonism. The internal life of Egypt is characterized by moderation, that of Syria by tensions and that of Iraq by extremism. Iraq has tall mountains counterpassed by spacious deserts and immense river valleys. She is blessed with abundant water resources and petroleum as are few countries in the world, but her population lives in squalor. The inhabitants are divided into various linguistic, ethnic and religious minorities, with pronounced tensions existing for generations between Sunnis and Shiʻis, Arabs and Kurds, and Muslims and Christians. In public life political currents appear in Iraq in extremist form; and extreme trends find more supporters there than in other Arab countries. Islamic fanaticism and secularism; pan-Arabism and separatism; fascism and communism; xenophobic anti-imperialism and slavish attachment to England; hatred of Zionism verging on genocidal anti-Semitism and the acceptance of a dynamic and influential participation of Jews in economic and political life—a land of contrasts and extremes. It is not by chance that the struggles in Iraq were so often accompanied by acts of cruelty and bloodshed.

In the decade between the Palestine War and Qassim's coup there were in Iraq a number of foci of opposition to Nūrī Sa'īd's regime. One of them was among army officers. Very little is known about the initial stages of their conspiracy; taking into account the personalities and character of these men—many of whom are no longer alive—and the circumstances of their activity, it is unlikely that much more will be learned in the future. What is known was for the most part brought out by various testimonies during Arif's trial held in December 1958 in the Special Military Court.[1] The trial was conducted in camera, but a record of the proceedings was published in full in 1959. The court had not yet become "Mahdāwī's Circus"; the accused was able to defend himself and argue his case and the testimony presented was relevant.

Three factors influenced Iraqi nationalist officers in the late 1950's. The first was the strong anti-imperialist movement in the country and the underground or semi-underground activy of opposition parties of the right and left. The second factor was the impressive example of Syrian and Egyptian officer politicians who had acted with daring and succeeded in seizing power. The underground Iraqi officers called themselves Free Officers, after their Egyptian counterparts. Nasser's brilliant successes and his heading of the opposition to Nūrī Sa'īd's policies were a spur to action. The third factor was the Iraqi army's tradition of interfering in politics recalled by the memory of Bakr Ṣidqī, Ṣabbagh's Golden Square and the like. Qassim and Arif often referred to the war in May 1941 as a glorious episode in the history of the country and the army. They themselves had at the time been junior officers and had taken part in the military actions. Qassim had also somehow been involved in Bakr Ṣidqī's movement. Bakr Ṣidqī's friend and principal partner, Muḥammad 'Alī Jawwād, the commander of the air force who was murdered together with him at Mosul, was Qassim's cousin. After the murder, Qassim, who was then a lieutenant, was transferred out of his unit and sent to Diwaniya in the south.[2]

The first meeting of the opposition officers which was reported took place in the summer or fall of 1956 in Baghdad at the home of Colonel Ismā'īl 'Ārif's brother.[3] (The name 'Ārif is very common in Iraq and various people bearing it do not belong to the same family.) Qassim was

[1] *Maḥkamat al-sha'b, Muḥākamāt al-maḥkama al-'askariyya al-khāṣṣa,* vol. 5, Baghdad 1959, *passim.*

[2] 'Abd al-Raḥmān al-Jadda, *Thawrat al-za'īm al-munqidh,* Baghdad 1960, 17–8.

[3] *Ibid.,* 23–6.

invited but did not attend for reasons of caution. Nevertheless, word leaked out and he was summoned to a talk with Nūrī Sa'īd. He succeeded in dispelling the suspicions about him but his friend Ismā'īl 'Ārif was placed under surveillance for a while.

On October 25, 1956, a joint Egyptian-Syrian-Jordanian military command was formed; Jordanian-Iraqi negotiations about the stationing of Iraqi troops in Jordan had already been conducted previously, and an Iraqi brigade had been concentrated at H3, a petroleum pipeline pumping-station in the desert near the Jordanian border. After Israel, France and Britain invaded Egypt, the Iraqi army entered Jordan on November 3 at the request of the Amman government and established quarters at H 4. This was the 19th Brigade under the command of Brigadier 'Abd al-Karīm Qāsim (Qassim). In mid-December the brigade returned to Iraq, and after the stormy events of those weeks Qassim and his circle began to think about an impending coup.[4]

Qassim's group was not the only one of its kind. Another group, apparently larger, comprising about a dozen officers, was headed by Brigadier Muḥī al-Dīn 'Abd al-Ḥamīd, the senior in age (42) and rank. The most outstanding man in his group was Nājī Ṭālib, also a brigadier. Until 1956 he was military attaché in England, and later, chief of the training section on the General Staff.

At first, neither of the two groups knew of the other's existence. The man who established contact between them was Colonel Waṣfī Ṭāhir, a member of 'Abd al-Ḥamīd's group. Waṣfī Ṭāhir was Nūrī Sa'īd's aide-de-camp, and was thus able to move in many circles and obtain much information. For the sake of appearances Qassim also cultivated the friendship of Nūrī Sa'īd and the Crown Prince and so, in the name of amity and loyalty, underground bonds were established. Waṣfī Ṭāhir started negotiations between the groups, and in the spring of 1957 they joined forces.[5]

This combined organization of officers was headed by Qassim. Even people who had known him well for years did not cease to wonder how he had reached a position of leadership. He was distinguished neither for his family, education nor oratorical ability. His nationalistic zeal, courage, puritanism, and fairness toward his men are not enough to solve the riddle of the secret of the man's power. When he stood at the head of the state, he displayed inordinate talents as a tactician as well as consistent, obdurate pursuit of his principal aims, but his personality remained an enigma.

[4] *Maḥkamat al-sha'b,* vol. 5, 1987.

[5] *Ibid.,* 1786–91, 2085–8; S. Jargy, 'Une page de l'histoire de la révolution irakienne: Le procès Aref', *Orient,* no. 12, 1959, 85–6.

'Abd al-Karīm Qāsim was born in Baghdad on December 21, 1914. His father owned a small farm near the capital; his grandfather owned a leather shop in town; one of his father's brothers had been an Ottoman military officer. According to some sources, his mother was of Kurdish extraction. In 1931 Qassim completed his studies at a Baghdad high school and worked as a teacher for one year. In the fall of 1932 he enrolled in the military academy, and in 1934 became a second-lieutenant. In 1935 he participated in quelling a tribal revolt in the Euphrates region. As a relative of Muḥammad 'Alī Jawwād, he was considered a member of Bakr Ṣidqī's group and was transferred to Diwaniya in 1937. In 1940, he was accepted for a staff officers' course, and in 1941 took part in the fighting against the British. In 1945 he became a major, distinguishing himself by bravery in battles with Kurdish rebels. From May 1948 to June 1949 he was in Palestine. He fought in the battle for the Gesher police station and later became a battalion commander at Kafr Qassem with the rank of lieutenant-colonel. He was one of the few Iraqi officers who gained the sympathy of the local Palestinian Arabs. In 1950 he went to England to study, and in 1955 became a brigadier.[6]

Just as puzzling as his personality were Qassim's relations with Arif. 'Abd al-Salām 'Ārif was born in Baghdad on March 21, 1921, the son of a shaykh. There was nothing distinctive about his army service. In 1948 he took part in the battle for Jenin. He was impulsive, knew how and loved to make speeches, and was strict about religious observance; in all this he was the opposite to Qassim. However, for some reason, strong ties of friendship bound these two from 1956. There is conflicting information as to which of the underground groups of officers Arif belonged at the time. In any case, at the beginning of 1957 Qassim proposed his admission to the united organization of Free Officers. The others, however, were against this, arguing that the man was unreliable. After lengthy debate, Arif was accepted and sworn in during April 1957 on Qassim's personal responsibility for his loyalty. The two grew closer; Qassim regarded Arif as a man he could trust, and Arif spoke of Qassim as if he were his father.[7]

Political discussion among the Free Officers at the time focussed on many problems. Muḥī al-Dīn 'Abd al-Ḥamīd testified at Arif's trial: "We assessed the organizations supporting us and the forces against us and the possible situations that could arise . . . We thought about economic and financial matters and about the possibility that imperialism could undermine the revolution by economic means several days or months after its success,

[6] Al-Jadda, 20–5, 31–5, 60–7; Benjamin Shawadran, *The power struggle in Iraq,* New York 1960, 40–3; B. Vernier, *L'Irak d'aujourd'hui,* Paris 1963, 148.

[7] *Maḥkamat al-sha'b,* vol. 5, 224–37, 252, 1976–89, 2004.

through our currency, for instance, which was linked to the Sterling Bloc, etc." To Mahdāwī's query whether they had also discussed the question of Arab unity, he replied: "We did not discuss the matter of federal union or unity . . . I only remember that we spoke about asking them [the UAR] for help [after the coup] in their broadcasts and their press and in granting the Republic recognition."[8] Obviously he pretended not to remember whatever would have been undesirable to bring up in that courtroom, and Mājid Amīn later related that a three-day discussion on Arab unity had taken place. Even before the coup, there had been no general agreement on the question which later became the principal cause of differences among the officers. They were all strongly influenced by Nasser's successes and propaganda. Some of them regarded themselves as carrying on the tradition of the Golden Square, the 1941 rebellion, and the ultra-nationalistic pan-Arab aspirations, and maintained ties with the right-wing Istiqlal Party.[9] Others were close to the National Democratic Party and were under the influence of its left-wing views and of communist ideology, and their enthusiasm for Nasser was mixed with suspicion of his aspirations for Egyptian expansion and with reservations concerning the anti-democratic nature of his regime. The three-day long debate among the Iraqi Free Officers ended in a compromise: it was decided that after seizing power, they would first ensure internal Iraqi Kurdish-Arab unity; after a transition period, a plebiscite would be held on Arab union or federation. Thus, a compromise formula had been found that both the advocates and opponents of union with Egypt could accept. On acceding to power, Qassim acted in accordance with this policy; but the controversy which remained undecided was like a mine that Nasser did not hesitate to detonate.

A committee in charge of planning the coup was formed among the officers in Baghdad under Qassim's supervision. One proposal called for the capture of al-Falluja (west of Baghdad), in May 1958, by a brigade which would then advance on the capital. Another plan required the coup to be carried out on the 25th anniversary of the staff officers' college at Rashid Camp in June 1958.[10] The plan put into operation on July 14, 1958 was Operation Hawk *(ṣaqr)*.[11]

On July 14 circumstances were almost ideal for a coup. Civil war in Lebanon was at its peak; several days earlier President Chamoun had

[8] *Ibid.*, 1990–1.

[9] Maḥmūd al-Dara, *Al-qaḍiyya al-kurdiyya wal-qawmiyya al-'arabiyya fī ma'rakat al-'Irāq,* Beirut 1963, 140.

[10] *Ibid.,* 141.

[11] *Maḥkamat al-sha'b,* vol. 5, 2059; Robert Murphy, *Diplomat among warriors,* New York 1964, 413; Waldemar J. Gallman, *Iraq under General Nuri,* Baltimore 1964, 205.

announced that he would not seek re-election, and the governments of Iraq and Jordan were considering direct intervention in Lebanon in order to check mounting UAR influence. King Fayṣal, Crown Prince ʿAbd al-Ilāh, and the Prime Minister of the Hashimite Federal Union, Nūrī Saʿīd, were preparing to fly to Istanbul on July 14 at 8 a.m. for a conference of the Baghdad Pact leaders and the attention of the security institutions was concentrated on the arrangements for the ceremony at Baghdad airport. It was decided at the same time to transfer a brigade of the Iraqi army to Jordan within the framework of the Hashimite Union and in connection with events in Lebanon. The 20th Brigade of the Third Division was selected for this duty; the commander of the third battalion of this brigade was ʿAbd al-Salām Arif. It was stationed at Jalaula on the Iranian frontier, about 100 milles north-east of the capital, and on its way to Jordan it had to pass through Baghdad on the night of July 13. The commander of the Third Division, Major-General Ghāzi Dāghistānī, was summoned to Baghdad on July 13; acting in his place as divisional commander was the senior brigade commander who commanded the 19th Brigade, ʿAbd al-Karīm Qassim. This brigade and divisional headquarters were located at Baʿquba, the same town from which Bakr Ṣidqī had started out to capture the capital 22 years previously. The marching order to the 20th Brigade was accompanied by another most important item—the issuance of ammunition. Since 1955 ammunition had not been issued to Iraqi army units with the exception of fixed quantities supplied before maneuvers or operations. Brigadier Nājī Ṭālib, one of the leaders of the Free Officers who was then head of the training branch of the General Staff, saw to it that on July 13 abundant ammunition was drawn from the stores. When the brigade passed through Baʿquba, Arif arrested the battalion commanders and assumed command of the brigade. At three in the morning his column of armored vehicles reached the Fayṣal Bridge over the Tigris in Baghdad; there the units dispersed to seize the broadcasting station, railroad depot and principal government buildings. The unit advancing on the royal palace encountered resistance from the guard. During a pause in the exchange of fire the King and Crown Prince ʿAbd al-Ilāh went outside to negotiate and were immediately killed. The troops and the large crowd that had meanwhile collected stormed the palace and killed most of the royal family. After ʿAbd al-Ilāh was beheaded his body was tied by the feet to a car and dragged through the streets; this was the Iraqi way of treating traitors (on some occasions they were dragged along still alive). Nūrī Saʿīd managed to hide in the city. On the following day he tried to slip away, dressed as a woman; a child in the street recognized him, he was mobbed and killed. The building of the British Embassy was burned down.

Many persons associated with the regime lost their lives and property.

Was there any cooperation between the Free Officers and party representatives, or other civilians, in preparing and carrying out the coup? The officers maintained numerous ties, sometimes important ones, with opposition leaders of the right and left and were deeply influenced by their political outlook. The leaders of the parties also knew that the secret society existed, but they had no detailed knowledge of its organization. Two years later one of the leaders of the Communist Party related, "I still remember the day of July 12th, 1958, when we were informed that the date of the revolution had been set for the 14th. The party then issued a terse proclamation dated July 12 and bearing no signature in order to mislead the authorities in case it fell into the hands of the police; it did not clarify the principal goal for which it was printed." [12] The proclamation warned against putting one leader or another into the forefront and called for "intensified political vigilance." It was distributed among party members on the night between the 13th and 14th of July. For party members and sympathizers it was tantamount to instructions from the leadership to support an imminent rebellion without the exact plan being known.

Five days after the coup, Qassim held his first press conference. When asked if civilians had participated in preparing it, he replied: "We know everyone of them. We know who is loyal and who is a traitor. That is why the officers' organization was formed as it was and not on the basis of cooperation with the parties. The loyal ones are our partners in the struggle." [13] Qassim thus also alluded to previous mutual connections and to future cooperation; nevertheless, he strongly emphasized the priority of the officers—they, and they alone, would determine who was loyal and who a traitor.

Already on July 14 a presidential Council of the Republic and a government were formed. Qassim became Prime Minister and Acting Minister of Defense, and Arif was Deputy Prime Minister and Minister of the Interior. The rest of the cabinet consisted of another soldier, Brig. Nājī Ṭalib as Minister of Social Affairs, and twelve civilians. The Minister of Finance was Muḥammad Ḥadīd, Vice-President of the left-wing National Democratic Party, which had already in 1936, in the time of Bakr Ṣidqī and Ḥikmat Sulaymān, fulfilled an important function. The Minister of Economics was Dr. Ibrāhīm Kubba, a Marxist, mistakenly considered communist by many. The Minister of Development was Fu'ād Rikābī, a Ba'thist, and the Minister of National Guidance was Ṣiddīq Shanshal, one of the leaders

[12] Al-Dara, 142–3; *Ittiḥād al-sha'b,* Baghdad, 20 July 1960.
[13] *Al-Ahrām,* 20 July 1958.

of the right-wing, pan-Arab, anti-imperialist Istiqlal (Independence) Party. The Minister of Public Works and Transport was Bābā 'Alī, the son of Shaykh Maḥmūd from Sulaimaniya, the leader of the Kurdish revolt who had proclaimed himself "King of Kurdistan" in 1922. All the opposition and anti-imperialist forces emerged from the underground and worked together, even sharing responsibility in the new government. They were united by hatred of the old regime, but their plans for building a new Iraq differed and their interests conflicted. Who could decide which one would predominate?

If a revolution differs from a coup d'état in two essential features—the active participation of the masses as opposed to their passivity, and the continuity of change as opposed to one singular event—then July 14, 1958, heralded the beginning of a genuine revolution. But the Iraqi revolution cannot, of course, be compared to the French, Russian or Cuban revolutions. Here, from the outset and throughout most of its phases, the officers remained always the decisive factor in the revolution. Four parties succeeded in activating a considerable segment of the population—the Communist Party, the National Democratic Party, the Istiqlal, and the Ba'th; each of them also found loyal adherents among the officers, and each of them had at one time been close to gaining power and imposing its authority on the army. But in the decisive showdown the officers always had the upper hand. And when the officers, who were members or sympathizers of a party, were faced with a decision to whom to be loyal and obedient—the party or the army—most of them chose the army; those who did not were liquidated politically and even physically. Under Qassim, as under Arif, revolutionary Iraq was always an unmistakable military dictatorship.

July 14, 1958 was a turning point and not only in Iraq. In addition to abolishing the monarchy in Baghdad, Qassim also removed the keystone of the Baghdad Pact. Suddenly an imminent possibility appeared—for some a great danger, for others a mighty prospect—of Iraq's joining the UAR, with Jordan and Lebanon also being swept along by the current of events. On July 15 United States marines landed in Lebanon, and two days later airborne British forces were flown to Jordan across Israel. As in the fall of 1956 there were fears that the tension in the Middle East might spark off a world war. However, a few months later, war threatened to break out between the UAR and Iraq; the civil war in Lebanon had ended and the country's independence preserved; and King Ḥusayn had saved his throne.

Relations with the UAR were the first political issue with which Qassim had to deal and they remained the focal point of Iraq's external and internal struggles for some time. In July 1958, half a year after the union of Syria and

Egypt, the UAR was at the peak of its prestige in the Arab world. With the fall of Nūrī Sa'īd, it seemed that Nasser's last great rival had been eliminated.

The Iraqi coup surprised the UAR as it did the rest of the world. Certainly Cairo and Damascus knew of an underground movement in the Iraqi army, and perhaps something of Qassim as well, but not much more. On July 14, 1958, Nasser was Tito's guest in Yugoslavia. On hearing the first accounts on the radio at 6.17 a.m., 'Āmir, his deputy, sent the following order to Jamāl Fayṣal, commander of the army in Syria: "Try contacting revolutionary army headquarters in Baghdad. It is desirable to let them know in some way that we shall support any movement whose aim is the liberation of the Iraqi people. We are expecting explicit instructions from the President." At 6.22 a.m., the control tower at Damascus airport concontacted the control tower in Baghdad. Communications were interrupted however, and were later renewed through the police at Mosul. At 8.23, 'Āmir informed Jamāl Fayṣal: "I have received an order from His Excellency the President, at Brioni, to extend to the revolution in Iraq every possible assistance."[14] Two Egyptian lieutenant-colonels were at once dispatched to Baghdad, and a few days later, a shipment of rifles, hand grenades and shells followed.

In Baghdad Qassim's victory was welcomed as a victory for Nasser, who was the most popular leader in Baghdad at the time. A German newspaperman, who arrived in Baghdad on July 19, in the UAR's first military airplane, together with the Iraqi delegation which was returning from a meeting with Nasser in Damascus, described the atmosphere when the aircraft reached the landing strip: "When the soldiers of the Iraqi army discerned the red, white and black markings on the wing tips of the two-motored plane, an electric spark seemed to have been ignited. Like madmen they rushed after the airplane which was still rolling at a speed of a hundred miles per hour, waving their rifles and dancing. When we stopped, 500 or 600 people gathered around the plane. Tens of singers began singing jubilantly and the crowd joined in. Bayonets were drawn and raised, hundreds of people applauded, others embraced each other and suddenly a cry was heard which again united the people who were milling, leaping and moving in dance rhythm, a cry which welded them together into one army-like unit. The cry was 'Nasser'. This was followed by an enthusiastic shout, 'We are your soldiers, Gamal.' The officers were yelling together with all the others . . . The heat at the airport had reached 115°F in the shade and 138° in the sun. The shirts of the frenzied soldiers were as

[14] Amīn Sa'īd, *Tā'rīkh al-'arab al-ḥadīth,* vol. 13, *Al-Thawra,* Cairo 1959, 246–7.

wet as rags, but the excitement at the sight of the military airplane from Damascus had overcome human fatigue on that afternoon."[15]

The delegation which met Nasser in Damascus on July 19 was headed by Arif. An agreement was signed on behalf of both republics which emphasized their close solidarity on international matters and their resolve to take immediate, positive steps to advance the economic and cultural cooperation between the two that would "maintain constant contact and consultations between both countries in all matters pertaining to them."[16]

A surprising feature of this agreement was the absence of a single word about Arab unity, even as a general, historical aim. Qassim acted according to the policy which had been laid down by the Free Officers even before the coup: To strengthen first and foremost Iraqi independence and internal unity, and to postpone to a later date the controversial question of Arab unity. Qassim had apparently never been enthusiastic about Arab unity, and in the summer of 1958 he was already aware of the nature of the Egyptian-Syrian union. It seems that the establishment of the UAR not only gave encouragement and momentum to the aspirations for unification throughout the Arab World, but also revealed the meaning of Egyptian pan-Arab policy in actual practice. It was by that time obvious that what had been attained in Syria was more Egyptian domination than unity. Qassim wanted independence for Iraq. This was made clear in his statements at a press conference held several days after the delegation returned from Damascus: "I am grateful to the UAR which was the first country to recognize the Iraqi Republic; my brother Jamāl 'Abd al-Nāṣir was then away from his country, and the whole world was taken unaware by the surprise operation of that night, which had been organized so well that no one was aware of its advent, not even our friends. We shall undoubtedly collaborate with the UAR in foreign policy as we shall with every country that wants to work together with us on the basis of reciprocal relations and, above all, for the good of the people."[17] Thus he admires Nasser as a brother, not as the "leader of Arab nationalism," and not as his elder brother either. He stresses Iraq's independence in every plan and action, and thanks the UAR specifically for its recognition of the Iraqi Republic as an independent state.

Arif intended otherwise. He was under Ba'thist influence at the time although he had never been a member of the party. He also wished to fulfill personal ambitions by appearing as a loyal adherent of Arab unity. At his

[15] Adelbert Weinstein, *Das neue Mekka liegt am Nil,* Wiesbaden (1959 or 1960), 19–20.

[16] *Documents on international affairs,* 1958, London 1962, 304.

[17] J. Heyworth-Dunne, 'Partis politiques et gouvernement dans l'Irak d'aujourd'hui', *Orient,* no. 15, 1960, 80.

meeting with Nasser in Damascus he signed the agreement in Qassim's spirit, and at the same time betrayed him. Secretly he promised the UAR's leaders that he would work even against Qassim for Iraq's joining the Union. On his return from Damascus he delivered speeches throughout the country, heaping praise on Nasser and scarcely mentioning Qassim. At the same time the Egyptian press began to criticize Qassim's policies, at first in the form of gentle warnings against the increase of communist influence in Iraq.

Arif acted methodically. On July 14 the officers were already discussing who would be Iraq's new representative to the United Nations, and looking to the army for a candidate. Waṣfī Tāhir proposed Brigadier Ismā'īl 'Ārif, one of the leaders of the Free Officers, but 'Abd al-Salām Arif suggested an intelligence major, Ṣāliḥ Mahdī 'Ammāsh, for the post. 'Ammāsh, who became important on Qassim's fall in 1963, was a member of the Ba'th and the head of its military organization.[18]

On September 12 Arif was "relieved" of his post as deputy commander-in-chief of the armed forces; on September 30 he was also dismissed from his position as Deputy Prime Minister and Minister of the Interior and appointed ambassador to West Germany. But he refused to leave Iraq. On October 11, Qassim convened a meeting of the leaders of the Free Officers and the commanders of the four divisions in the Iraqi army at the Ministry of Defense in order to persuade Arif to accept the proposed mission and prevent an open crisis. Qassim, Arif and brigadiers Fu'ād 'Ārif and Aḥmad Ṣāliḥ 'Abdī met privately for several hours. Arif gave various reasons for his refusal—the state of his father's health, concern for his numerous children and his reluctance to leave his friend and leader Qassim. Qassim, on the other hand, pointed out Arif's factiousness and demanded that he leave the country for at least three weeks. At eleven o'clock 'Abdī went to another meeting. In the course of the conversation, Fu'ād 'Ārif turned to the window for a breath of air and suddenly heard Qassim shouting, "What are you doing, 'Abd al-Salām?" Turning around, he saw Qassim grasping Arif's hand which held a drawn pistol. Refuting the charge that he wanted to murder Qassim, Arif claimed that he wished to commit suicide. Qassim did not believe him and replied, "If you want to take your own life, why do it at my place?" But he was prepared to forgive him. Fu'ād 'Ārif also left the room, leaving Qassim and Arif alone. Several minutes later, Qassim came out to the other leaders and told them that Arif had agreed to go to Bonn. On the following morning Arif flew to Germany—for one day.

[18] *Maḥkamat al-sha'b,* vol. 5, 2035, 2171–4, 2277; M. Ḥ. Haykal in *al-Ahrām,* 18 November, 1963.

For three weeks he roamed around European capitals and on November 4 he returned to Baghdad. The next day, he was arrested and on November 27 his trial began. The charge and the prosecution's testimony were concerned only with his attempt to murder Qassim on October 11; the political controversy was mentioned only incidentally. He was even acquitted of the charge of conspiracy but was sentenced to death for his attempt to murder Qassim. Nevertheless, the court recommended leniency out of consideration for his previous meritorious accomplishments. At first, Qassim delayed the carrying out of the sentence, then commuted it to life imprisonment; in November 1961 Arif was released and his military rank restored. The story goes that Qassim sometimes visited him in prison.

About the time of Arif's trial another important secret trial was held in the supreme military court, the "People's Court." It was that of Rashīd 'Ālī al-Kaylānī. Since the failure of the 1941 uprising Rashīd 'Ālī had been in exile at first as the guest of Hitler in Germany and Mussolini in Italy and later in Saudi Arabia. Qassim quashed the sentence against him and his colleagues, the 1941 uprising was proclaimed a national uprising, and already in mid-July, Rashīd 'Ālī was invited to return to Iraq. However, Qassim did not hurry to issue a passport for him, and he did not return to Baghdad until September 1. He was then given a reception befitting a national hero. On his return he immediately renewed his political activity, appearing as an advocate of Arab unity and as reactionary opposed to agrarian reform. At his trial he argued in his own defense that he was not against the reform itself, but that he had suggested that uncultivated land be distributed to landless peasants before the expropriation of landlords' property. The significance of the position he took was clear: The first agrarian reform measures had at the time aroused considerable tension and even led to violent clashes between peasants and landlords, especially in the south. Rashīd 'Āli emphasized that at his age and in failing health he had no possibility or intention of gaining conspicuous position in the life of the country; he wished only to serve as a unifying point for all reactionaries. He was also accused of maintaining contacts abroad, meaning the UAR. He, too, was sentenced to death and later pardoned. Several other Ba'thist officers and civilians were arrested with him, including Ṣāliḥ Mahdī 'Ammāsh, and the Ba'th Party was outlawed in Iraq.

Rashīd 'Ālī's trial aroused a great deal of interest in the Arab world. In the UAR Qassim's regime was increasingly criticized as being un-Arab, isolationist, cosmopolitan *(shu'ūbī)* and communist-directed. In December 1958 Nasser unleashed an ideological attack against communism that

[19] *Hamizrah Hehadash,* vol. 10, 82–3; Vernier, 154.

led to a serious debate between him and Khrushchev. In January 1959 a new wave of arrests of communists got under way in Egypt and Syria. Whereas in the debate with the communists the UAR preserved the rules of courtesy, the attacks on Qassim were completely uncurbed and the vilification was accompanied by subversive activities. Three quarters of a year after the elimination of Nūrī Sa'īd, relations between Cairo and Baghdad were as tense as they had been in his time, and perhaps even more so, and the UAR once again agitated for the overthrow of the Iraqi government.

In March 1959 Qassim's right wing and pan-Arab opponents staged an uprising at Mosul. Mosul had on several occasions been Baghdad's contender for the title of principal city in the country, in a way similar to the relationship of Aleppo to Damascus in Syria. The proximity of Kurdish regions nurtured nationalist extremism among the Arab population, and commercial ties with relatively close Syria intensified pan-Arab trends. The commander of the Mosul garrison, the 5th Brigade of the 2nd Division, was in the spring of 1958 Colonel 'Abd al-Wahhāb Shawwāf—a son of the Grand Mufti of Baghdad, a rightist and an advocate of Arab unity.[20] The divisional commander was Brigadier Nāẓim Ṭabaqjalī; his views and those of several other officers in the north were similar to those of Shawwāf. Testifying at Arif's trial in December 1958, Ṭabaqjalī tried not to implicate the defendant and adopted an attitude of, "I am a soldier and don't understand anything about politics." Asked what he thought of Arif's propaganda for Arab unity, he replied evasively, "It was premature."[21] Qassim obviously suspected him, and in January 1959 it was decided to transfer him to the command of the 4th Division whose officers were loyal to Qassim. Ṭabaqjalī did not agree to the transfer and announced that he preferred to go on pension, but in the end he remained commander of the 2nd Division.[22]

A mass meeting of the Iraqi Peace Movement was scheduled to take place on March 6 in Mosul—perhaps because it was the center of the right-wing. The Director of Railroads, Major-General Ṣāliḥ Zakī Tawfīq, considered a communist, granted special facilities to those attending the Mosul meeting, and on March 8 about a quarter of a million people, including many communists, gathered there. Both sides prepared for a fight. The meeting itself passed peacefully but demonstrations continued. On March 7 a number of clashes occurred and a curfew was imposed. On March 8 some members of the Peace Movement pulled down a picture of

[20] *Maḥkamat al-sha'b,* vol. 6, 1959, 2924–30; Vernier, 156.
[21] *Maḥkamat al-sha'b,* vol. 5, 2317.
[22] Amīn Sa'īd, *Tā'rīkh al-'arab al-hadīth,* part 15: *Al-Jumhūriyya al-'arabiyya al-mutahida,* vol. 2, Cairo 1960, 363–6.

Nasser in a café. Troops were sent to disperse them and bloody disturbances began. The intervention of the troops was planned in advance by the local command as a provocation, and the Baghdad government reacted at once by announcing Shawwāf's dismissal and ordering his arrest. Shawwāf proclaimed a revolt, called for Qassim's overthrow and ran up the UAR flag in Mosul.[23] For two days bitter fighting raged in the city and its environs. Bedouin from the Shammar tribes in the Syrian desert came to the aid of the rebels; their leader, Shaykh Yāwir al-'Ujayyil, mobilized his men in defense of the feudal order under the banner of war against the Kurds and infidels. The Kurds, on their part, streamed from their villages to join the left wing in a war against what they termed reactionary, pan-Arab nationalism. The UAR supported the rebels in its broadcasts and, evidently, had the uprising continued, she would have intervened militarily. The army in the central region of the country, however, remained loyal to Qassim, and on March 9, Shawwāf went on the defensive. He was wounded in an air attack on his headquarters and brought to a military hospital. His enemies made their way inside threatening him; he shot at them with his pistol and they killed him.[24] On March 10 the revolt petered out. A number of rebels succeeded in escaping to Syria. A wounded officer died there of his injuries and his funeral was conducted as a great anti-Iraqi demonstration. In Baghdad the funeral of the lawyer Qāzanjī, one of the leaders of the Peace Movement who had been killed in Mosul, turned into a stormy demonstration against Nasser. Nearly 200 officers were cashiered from the army, including 70 colonels and brigadiers.[25] The number of victims of the revolt reached hundreds, if not thousands. The legacy of hate and vengeance it left behind smoldered on like glowing coals which any gust of wind could whip into flames.

The most active organized public body which stood by Qassim in suppressing Shawwāf's rebellion was the Iraqi Communist Party. In the weeks to come, he was forced to rely on it more and more, and its influence continued to mount throughout the country and in the army. Colonel Fāḍil 'Abbās Mahdāwī, Qassim's cousin and the president of the People's Court, and Colonel Mājid Amīn, the prosecutor in the same court, took part in a communist demonstration on April 24. At the same time Soviet-Iraqi ties grew closer and reciprocal visits and exchanges of delegations increased. In April, Soviet ships brought to Basra hundreds of Kurds who were returning from exile in the USSR. Iraq seemed to be on the verge of be-

[23] *Maḥkamat al-sha'b,* vol. 18, 1961, 7211; *Hamizrah Hehadash,* vol. 10, 229–30; Vernier, 157.
[24] *Al-Ḥayāt,* 28 March 1963.
[25] *Al-Ahrām,* 27 April 1959; *Hamizrah Hehadash,* vol. 10, 372.

coming the first People's Democracy in southwest Asia. This was the opportune moment for the communists, but they did not take advantage of it—or did they not want to accede to power?

On April 29 the Iraqi Communist Party published a proclamation in connection with the First of May in which it demanded "to participate in the responsibility for the government, together with the representatives of other loyal democratic parties and forces."[26] Qassim replied in a speech on May Day, "Parties do not help the country at this time but place it in a delicate situation. Certain people asked me to found a party that would liberate the country from all other parties and organizations. I answered them that the entire people is my party . . . that I am the people's party and that all of us are Allah's party."[27]

So passed the First of May. Since Qassim's speech did not explicitly negate the communists' demand, they continued to nurture hope for several more days. In this way the initiative slipped from their hands, and Qassim, the adroit tactician, launched a counterattack. At the beginning of May he appealed to the parties to consider exigencies of national unity and to renounce for the time being their individual aspirations. This position was supported by the leadership of the National Democratic Party, a reformist, liberal faction, that feared the competition of the growing communist power and even thought that Qassim intended to follow its line. On May 20, they published an announcement in their newspaper *al-Ahālī* declaring their intention to suspend activity during the transition period as Qassim had requested on the assumption that the government would implement most of the reforms it had demanded.[28] A minority had reservations about the announcement and the party split. Three days later, the communists were also forced to retreat. On May 23, *Ittiḥād al-sha'b* published an announcement in a special edition that "The Iraqi Communist Party renounced its demands for participation in the government for the sake of national unity and makes it obligatory on all its active members to honor this decision."[29] Qassim showered compliments on the communists for their patriotic stand—and continued to work against them. A purge of communist officers in the army and police began in the second half of June; at first a few officials were transferred from key positions to respectable positions of lesser importance (for example, the capital's Chief of Police was given administrative duties at national headquarters), but later there were dismissals and finally arrests.

[26] *Ittiḥād al-sha'b,* 29 April, 1959.

[27] *Orient,* no. 10, 1959, 197.

[28] *Hamizrah Hehadash,* vol. 10, 374; Vernier, 162.

[29] Vernier, *loc.cit.*

Qassim's policy was logical. He had never been a communist or a Marxist, and although he was indifferent to religious observance, he was convinced that a communist regime was not possible in a Muslim country. He relied on the Communist Party during the crisis of March, 1959, because he had no choice; he had no intention of becoming its tool. When its power increased beyond all expectation, he decided to clip its wings, and when it ceased to give him full support, he wanted to settle accounts with it. His policy regarding the Soviet Union was similar. He utilized its support to free Iraq from dependence on Britain and the West, but he was extremely careful not to become dependent on it. His arms purchases were in line with his policy: He equipped a number of units with Soviet armaments and at the same time continued to outfit others with British weapons. The air force had flights of Mig's and Hunters; the armor in one brigade consisted of Soviet T-54 tanks and in another of British Centurions.

It is more difficult to understand the policy of the Communist Party. It did not aspire to power but only to a position in the government, and when its wishes were not granted, it retreated without a fight. Why did it yield? Perhaps it did not feel strong enough to contend with the "one and only leader". Perhaps Qassim had threatened that if it did not yield, he would take up cudgels against it and use the rightists to destroy it and its members. Or it may have been advised by Moscow not to rush matters.

Two months after their retreat, in July 1959, the communists again endeavored to take the initiative. They chose a time when their position was already weak and a method which was unscrupulous and criminal—the massacre of the Turkomans in Kirkuk. On July 13, on the eve of the celebrations of the Revolution's anniversary, the Communist Party renewed its demand for participation in the government. On the same day, Qassim announced the formation of a new government consisting of six army officers and 11 civilians, including the communist Dr. Nazīha Dulaymī; she was the first woman minister in an Arab or Islamic country, and was asked to join the government more as a woman than as a representative of her party. The Kirkuk massacre was one of the reactions to the slap in the face which Qassim gave the communists.

The Turkish-speaking Turkomans are one of the important Iraqi minorities despite their small number—less than 100,000 altogether. Their chief center is Kirkuk, where they occupy an important position as storekeepers and as officials of the government and the oil company. At the end of the 19th century the Ottoman authorities entrusted them with a function similar to that of the Circassians in Transjordan—they encouraged this loyal, stable element to settle on the frontier of the Bedouin regions between the Arab tribes of the desert and the Kurdish tribes in the mountains.

For generations the Kurds have regarded them as foreign invaders. In recent times their hatred was intensified by the Turkomans' obvious sympathy for Atatürk's Turkey which is anathema to the Kurds, as well as by class conflict between the Kurdish tribesmen and the Turkoman urban storekeepers and office workers. In the summer of 1959, during the rapprochement between the Kurds and the communists and the cooling-off of relations between the governments of Baghdad and Ankara, class and communal conflicts took the form of a bitter political clash. Both Kurds and communists regarded the Turkomans as the personification of reaction. The July 14 celebrations in Kirkuk suddenly turned into violent demonstrations against Turkomans and in the next few days there was a wholesale massacre. About a hundred persons were buried alive. Members of the "United National Front", of the Iraqi Communist Party, of the Kurdish Democratic Party and the left-wing faction of the National Democratic Party, Kurdish tribesmen who had flocked to the city, and men and officers of the 2nd Division all took part in acts of murder, robbery and torture. The riots were not spontaneous. Concurrently with the outbreaks in Kirkuk, Turkomans were also attacked in Nasiriya in the south and at Samarra. The disturbances spread throughout the country and were suppressed several days later by the army.[30]

The extreme aggressiveness of the communists at Kirkuk may have been induced by two Chinese emissaries who had spent some time in the region. Both were Muslims, Burhan Shahidi, President of the Chinese Islamic Society, and since the Bandung Conference of 1955, the principal representative of China in the Arab countries, and Ma-Kin, who had come to Iraq to negotiate a Sino-Iraqi cultural agreement. At Qassim's demand the Chinese ambassador to Baghdad was later replaced.[31]

If there were need of further evidence that the communists had played a role in the Kirkuk massacre, it was supplied by the testimony of the Communist Party itself. After a meeting of the Central Committee, *Ittiḥād al-sha'b* published a lengthy announcement by the party which contained severe self-criticism: "After the Revolution, our party made special efforts to correct certain extreme practices of the population without always adopting a basic decision on this matter . . . it must be said that apparently certain elements had infiltrated the population for the purpose of exploiting its emotional agitation and occasionally directing it to acts of sabotage. Part of the population adopted lynch methods, the torture of prisoners, robbery, and attacks on the rights and freedoms of innocent citizens;

[30] Vernier, 167–71; *Hamizrah Hehadash,* vol. 11, 77–8.

[31] Vernier, 266–7. F. Joyaux, 'La politique chinoise au Moyen-Orient', *Orient,* no. 40, 1966, 31.

such methods are incompatible with the united revolutionary struggle against the enemies of the Republic."[32]

The self-criticism could barely repair the loss of prestige and influence of the Communist Party after the atrocities of Kirkuk. The extreme right again went over to the attack, this time playing up the religious angle. Posters in the form of questions and answers on matters regarding Muslim religious law began to appear, e.g., "Is it permissible to purchase meat from a butcher whose father is a communist?" The reply, of course, was "No".[33]

Qassim once again appeared as the "one and only leader" able to save the country from chaos, and in his customary manner, after defeat of the left, he again dealt the right a blow. On August 12 a special high military court began hearing the cases of 23 officers and civilians accused of participating in Shawwāf's revolt. Verdicts were announced on August 16 and 19; four civilians and 13 officers were sentenced to death, including Brigadier Nāẓim Ṭabaqjalī and Colonel Rif'at al-Ḥājj Sirrī. The communists vociferously demanded that the sentences be carried out—thus hoping to divert attention from their setback at Kirkuk. Qassim, as usual, delayed his decision, but on September 20, Ṭabaqjalī and the other condemned men were executed.[34] The UAR's hatred and malevolence surged up again, and on October 7, Ba'thists tried to assassinate Qassim as he rode through Baghdad's main thoroughfare. His chauffeur was killed and Qassim was seriously injured, but he survived. A wave of arrests and persecutions again swept Iraq.

In his speech of July 14, 1959, Qassim promised that within half a year, on Iraqi Army Day on January 6, 1960, the activity of political parties would be allowed. On that day, the Law of Associations went into effect which permitted the establishment of parties and their activity—providing that the party's aims would be compatible with the country's independence and unity, the republican regime, etc, and would be approved by the Ministry of Interior. On the day for submitting applications, two Iraqi communist parties suddenly appeared—the traditional one, headed by Zakī Khayrī, and another, headed by Da'ūd Ṣā'igh, an opportunist representing only a small communist faction. Ṣā'igh's party was approved on the following day, and later the Minister of Interior claimed that he could not approve two parties with the same name. The Communist Party submitted a new application in the name of "The Unity of the People" *(Ittiḥād al-sha'b)*, the name of its newspaper. After some delay the application was finally

[32] *Ittiḥād al-sha'b*, 29 August, 1958.
[33] S. Kahle, "The Kassem era as I saw it", *Contemporary Review*, London, April 1963, 179.
[34] *Hamizrah Hehadash*, vol. 11, 77.

rejected on February 22.[35] By resorting to legerdemain, Qassim wanted to split the Communist Party and force it underground at one fell swoop.

But Qassim defeated his own purposes—he lost the support of the left wing without diminishing the enmity of the right. His maneuvering of the rival forces pushed all of them into the opposition while the propaganda and subversion of the UAR continued unabated. Nasser could not forgive Qassim for wanting to establish in Iraq an officer regime like the one in Egypt without accepting Egyptian leadership. Qassim's only support remained the army. Emile Tūmā, the Israeli Arab communist ideologist, wrote in 1962 that "The Iraqi July revolution differed from the Egyptian one . . . not by its aims but by its nature, . . . the masses in it were not just a tool of the bourgeoisie but participated in the revolutionary activity under the leadership of their Communist Party, and for this reason, it was to a certain extent able to introduce greater changes in the government. From the outset it was clear that the army was not alone in the fray."[36] But already in 1960, the army was the sole ruler, not with but against the masses, and Qassim's regime was a clear-cut military dictatorship engaged chiefly in trying to ensure its own existence. Its survival from 1960 to 1963 posed a riddle which remains unsolved.

In the spring of 1961 more trouble appeared—the Kurds revolted.

The seal of the Iraqi Republic in Qassim's time bore an Arab sword intertwined with a Kurdish dagger, a symbol of the brotherhood of both peoples. In the provisional Iraqi constitution of July 27, 1958, article two declared that "the Iraqi state is an integral part of the Arab nation" but article three qualified it with the statement that "Arabs and Kurds are considered partners in this nation and their national rights within the unity of Iraq are recognized by this constitution."[37] This allusion to a bi-national regime was a revolutionary innovation. Furthermore, in the provisional constitution, in contrast to the previous one, Arabic was not designated as the only official language in the country. The Kurdish leader Mullā Muṣṭafā Barazānī returned from exile in the Soviet Union on October 6 and was received with great honor; the house of Nūrī Sa'īd was given him for his living quarters. In its first year the Kurds were among the strongest supporters of the Republic.

Various factors brought the Kurds closer to Qassim: opposition to the Baghdad Pact—collaboration of Iraq, Turkey and Iran could always help in suppressing the Kurds; opposition to the union of Iraq with the UAR; and friendship with the USSR and the communists. The Kurds were

35 *MER* 1960, 237–9.

36 Emīl Tūmā, *Thawrat* 23 *tammūz fī 'aqdihā al-awwal,* Haifa 1962, 77–8.

37 *The Middle East* 1962, London 1962, 142.

Qassim's loyal helpers in suppressing Shawwāf's rebellion and they hoped that he would keep his promise to them—or what they thought he had promised: administrative autonomy in Iraqi Kurdistan, a Kurdish university and schools, and economic development of their region, especially by constructing roads (a necessary condition for marketing the fruit and other agricultural produce of the remote mountain regions before they rotted). However, either because he was unable or unwilling, Qassim did not fulfil the hopes which the Kurds had pinned on him. After turning against the left, he was not interested in encouraging any element considered pro-communist. By its nature a military dictatorship is opposed to the idea of autonomy to a section of the population. The economic stagnation which actually existed in the whole of Iraq, was interpreted by the Kurds as a continuation of discrimination against their own regions. After the honeymoon between Qassim and the Kurds, relations between them cooled. Qassim, as was his practice, tried his luck with a policy of divide and rule. From the summer of 1959 he began to display signs of friendship to the leaders of the Zibārī tribe, the traditional enemies of the Barazānīs in their contest for the leadership of the Kurds. Here, too, he only managed to deepen the rift between former friends without securing the effective support of new ones.

The disappointment in Qassim strengthened the hands of those Kurds who demanded far-reaching political concessions. On October 19, 1960 the Kurdish newspaper *Khabāt,* the organ of the Democratic Party of Iraqi Kurdistan, appeared in Baghdad with an article that stated: "Article two of the constitution established that Iraq is part of the Arab nation. This is a statement more sentimental in nature than scientific or rational. The word 'Iraq', as we all know, is current today in two senses. First of all, it means both geographically and historically a country much smaller than the present-day Iraq. Secondly, as a political term, it refers to a country created after World War I by the union of a large part of historical Iraq and a part of southern Kurdistan, sometimes called Shahrizur or the Vilayet of Mosul, according to the administrative divisions of the Ottoman state, on the ruins of which the Iraqi state was established for the purpose of satisfying the aspirations of British imperialism which wanted to lay its hands on the country's resources, especially oil, and secure control of the route to India. Therefore, Iraq cannot be considered a part of the Arab nation either in the political sense of the word, as meaning a state, or in the geographical sense . . . The people of the Iraqi Republic, comprising Arabs, Kurds and other national minorities, cannot be a part of the glorious Arab nation. Such an idea makes no sense. It suffices to speak of the Kurds, a race actually going as far back in history as the Arabs, in order to demonstrate that this contention does not dovetail with the facts . . . Kurdistan was never regarded as part of the Arab lands, neither in part nor as a unit and not the portion included in the Iraqi state. Throughout history, it sometimes happened that Kurdistan either wholly or in part found itself in an Islamic state, as was the case with respect to many Muslim countries. Nevertheless, Kurdistan was not considered a part of the Arab lands . . . It is enough to consider the historical facts and concrete reality which clearly show that the eternal Iraqi Republic consists of a part of the Kurdish nation, whose country is Kurdistan, and a part of the Arab nation, whose country is the great Arab homeland . . . "[38]

The editor of *Khabāt* was Ibrāhim Aḥmad, then the secretary-general of the Democratic Party of Iraqi Kurdistan. A lawyer from Sulaimaniya,[39] he represented the Kurdish urban intelligentsia and the modernistic, socialist or communist, wing of Kurdish nationalism. Barazānī, a feudal shaykh from northern Iraq, represents its traditionalistic and tribal aspects. The two leaders have for years been the two poles of Kurdish nationalism in Iraq, mostly cooperating, sometimes rivalling.

A few days after the appearance of the article in *Khabāt,* Mullā Muṣṭafā Barazānī went to Moscow as a guest of the Soviet government to attend the celebrations of the October Revolution. In January 1961 he returned to Iraq. At first he stayed in Baghdad; in the spring he went to Barazan, and not long afterwards the uprising started.[40]

At first the Baghdad government attempted to describe the battles in the north as inter-tribal quarrels and police actions to establish order; but in September Qassim had to admit publicly that he was fighting a rebellion. The announcement of the revolt was made simultaneously with the report that it had been suppressed by the army—the first of many victory announcements whose worth stood in inverse ratio to their frequency. In the last two years of Qassim's rule and life, a large part of his army was pinned down in a cruel war against the Kurds, and the protracted struggle without victories continued to weaken his position among the Arabs.

Qassim also became involved in purposeless dispute in Kuwait. In June 1961 Kuwait was granted independence, and Qassim at once renewed an old Iraqi demand for the annexation of the shaykhdom. Concentrations of Iraqi troops on the Kuwaiti border led to the landing of British and Saudi Arabian forces to defend it. The Arab League unanimously rose up against Iraq, and in the middle of August it was agreed that Arab troops would replace the British units. On September 23 Saudi, Egyptian, Jordanian

[38] *Orient,* no. 17, 1961, 189-91.
[39] *MER* 1960, 250.
[40] *MER* 1961, 279–88; David Adamson, *The Kurdish war,* London 1964, 97–8.

and Sudanese contingents, together about 4,000 men, took over their positions. Qassim's stand brought about one of the rare instances of unanimity of opinion and action among the Arab states.[41]

Some relief was afforded to Qassim on Nasser's failure in Syria and the dissolution of the UAR in September 1961. In the controversy between Nasser and Qassim, Damascus, "the heart of Arabism", decided in the latter's favor. In 1962 Syria became the principal target of Egypt's propaganda attacks, relations between Syria and Iraq improved and Iraq was no longer as isolated as she had been the previous year.

Qassim yearned sincerely to liberate his fellow countrymen from their poverty and dependence and was imbued with a mystic faith in his mission. He wanted to unite the Iraqis in the building of their future. But instead the differences among the Iraqis widened until they were united almost solely in their opposition to him and his regime. Three days before his death, *Le Monde* published a report by E. Saab, who had had a long conversation with Qassim on the night of January 31. This is how he described him; "He looked very nervous. He relaxes by means of a wretched handkerchief which he constantly squeezes in his left hand supporting a shoulder paralyzed since its piercing by the bullets of assailants. He was miraculously saved in the attack of 1959, but it nevertheless left deep marks on him. He emerged from it weakened. The man whom I met again for the first time since June 1959 may not have lost any of his energy, but there are wrinkles on his tanned face and they express anxiety. 'Two or three hours of sleep are enough for me,' he says, 'That's the way it has been for four years already. If I allow myself too much sleep, I feel guilty. There is too much to do and life is too short.'"[42] Ten days later he was no longer alive.

The defeat of Nūrī Sa'īd liberated the antagonistic forces in Iraqi society. Freedom meant first of all the freedom of every communal and political group to conduct a struggle against its rivals. Qassim wanted to consolidate his regime by accepting the support of different groups at various times without being dependent on any of them. His maneuvers succeeded in weakening all of them but at the same time he weakened his own position and made himself universally hated. Once the primal source of his power, the army became the exclusive basis of his regime. And when a large part of the officers turned against him, his doom was sealed.

Many of the officers who had carried out the coup of 1958 and had been in command of the principal units of the army at the beginning of the Republic had already retired or been dismissed before 1960. The rift with

[41] *MER* 1961, 117–40.

[42] *Le Monde,* Paris, 5 February, 1962.

Arif at the end of 1958, the great purge among the army officers after the Shawwāf munity in the spring of 1959 (especially in the 2nd Division), and later the dismissal of pro-communist officers left a heavy residue of opposition to Qassim among the officers. The group of officers who had been in top level government positions since July 1958, remained loyal to him until the end. But this group had become isolated from the rest of the officers as well as from the population.

As mentioned above, the setback suffered by his great rival Nasser, in Syria in September 1961, afforded Qassim a breathing spell. But a year after secession from the UAR, Syria was no longer a serious counterweight to Egyptian pressure and influence. The weakness of the Damascus regime, as opposed to the stability and renewed momentum of the Egyptian government and the latter's unceasing propaganda against separatism once again served to intensify pan-Arab sentiments in Iraq. Ba'thist influence spread among officers in Syria and Iraq. It was often claimed that American agents had also encouraged Qassim's overthrow. King Ḥusayn of Jordan, who had no interest at the time in annoying them, said in September 1963, "I know for certain that the coup in Iraq on February 8 was supported by American intelligence."[43]

The most suitable day for a military coup in an Arab country is Friday, especially during the month of the Ramadan. The day Qassim's regime was overthrown was Friday, February 8, 1963, and it coincided with the 14th of Ramadan (so that the figure 14 appears in the names of the two Iraqi revolutions: the "Revolution of July 14" and the "Revolution of Ramadan 14").

The coup was planned as a combined military operation. The principal objectives were the radio station and the Defense Ministry's building complex in Baghdad, where Qassim lived and worked. It was like a fortress inside a city; three infantry battalions were permanently stationed there and 18 anti-tank and anti-aircraft guns had been set up.[44] The insurrectionists' base was at Habbaniya, where the 4th Division and armored and aircraft units were stationed. H-hour had been set for 9 a.m. Perhaps because most coups had taken place at dawn, Qassim was used to working in his office until 5 a.m., but during daylight his vigilance relaxed. 9 o'clock in the morning, especially on a Friday in Ramadan, was a time for rest and sleep. Qassim was sleeping at the time in his mother's house. At 8.30, a number of young rebel officers burst into the house of Brigadier Awqātī, commander of the air force and a communist, and killed him in front of his children.

[43] M. Ḥ. Haykal, *al-Ahrām,* 27 September, 1963.
[44] Muḥammad Wajdī Qandīl, in *Ākhir Sā'a,* Cairo, 13 February 1963.

At the same time, light tanks from Habbaniya arrived at the broadcasting station in Abu-Ghurayb, west of the capital, and suspended its operation. At 9 o'clock Hunters appeared over Baghdad and began to bomb the Ministry of Defense with rockets. The commander of the operation was Captain Mundhir Windāwī who was in one of the airplanes. Mig 17's came over in a second wave. After launching rockets, the airplanes strafed the Ministry of Defense with machinegun fire and then attacked the aircraft lined up on the ground at the Rashid camp. Encamped here was the 19th Brigade, which had been Qassim's until 1958 and which included most loyal units of all the armed forces. A little later the rebels seized the broadcasting studios in the capital and quickly announced the coup and the death of Qassim. However, Qassim himself appeared in town and even received an ovation as he hurried from his mother's house to the Ministry of Defense, where he took command of the defenders. Rebel armor and paratroopers, who had in the meantime reached Baghdad, surrounded the fortified complex of buildings and heavy fighting, involving considerable losses on both sides, developed. From his headquarters Qassim appealed to the troops in Rashid Camp for help. Their loyalty was already undermined, and only some of the units left for the city. There they encountered rebel armored cars, and in the exchange of fire were worsted. Most of the troops in Washash Camp northwest of Baghdad joined the rebels, and officers who showed signs of opposition were arrested. Ba'thist groups of the National Guard also joined rebellious army units; it is not clear whether they had had any advance knowledge of the planned coup.

At the last moment, Qassim was left with only a single ally—the communists. The head of his Intelligence, Ṭaha Shaykh Aḥmad, appealed to them for help and they went out into the streets and demonstrated. Officers loyal to Qassim opened arms stores and handed out weapons and ammunition to them. The communists well knew that the anti-Qassim rebels were their bitter enemies and old accounts between them and Qassim were forgotten. In the morning, they distributed a mimeographed proclamation in the party's name with the headline: "To arms—to suppress the conspiracy of imperialism and reaction!" The proclamation sounded the alarm: "Our national independence is in serious peril. The achievements of the Revolution are in serious peril. Ruthlessly destroy the treacherous plotters! Take arms from the police stations and wherever you find them, and attack the plotters, the agents of imperialism! . . . "[45]

However, the population was not ready to back Qassim any longer.

[45] *Al-Nahār,* Beirut, 15 February 1963; *Arab Political Documents,* 1963, Beirut (1964 or 1965), 21.

Ba'thists attacked and the communists were forced to defend themselves. The decisive factor was the army, and there, too, Qassim had fallen into disfavor. Even the 19th Brigade abandoned him. At noon, the Ministry of Defense remained the only center of military opposition, and communist pockets of resistance in the workers' districts were cut off from it. The radio had already been in the service of the rebels for several hours, and all the Egyptian stations were repeating their announcements and enthusiastically supporting them.

The rebels were headed by 'Abd al-Salām Arif. He was no longer on active service, and in order not to arouse suspicion, he slept at home on Thursday night. At 8 in the morning he went to Abu-Ghurayb, from where he and Colonel Aḥmad Ḥasan al-Bakr drove in a tank at the head of an armored column to Baghdad. In the evening Qassim contacted Arif by telephone, informing him that he was prepared to capitulate provided that he would be permitted to leave the Ministry of Defense in his army uniform and go abroad. Arif demanded unconditional surrender, and later related that he had told Qassim that he would not allow him to be another Tshombe and that Iraq would not be a Congo. Qassim knew what awaited him and continued to resist.

On Saturday morning the air attack against the Ministry of Defense was renewed, and paratroopers, under the command of Colonel 'Abd al-Karīm Muṣṭafā Nuṣrat, charged and advanced, fighting from room to room. At noon the last two hundred defenders surrendered. Qassim gave up when he ran out of ammunition for his pistol. Together with his two friends, Mahdāwī and Ṭaha Shaykh Aḥmad, he was taken to the radio station, where he met Arif again. It may not only have been Qassim who thought that Arif would repay him for the favor of four years ago and spare his life. But before an hour had elapsed, he was shot dead together with his two friends.

The account of his last conversation with Qassim which Arif gave several days later is certainly not accurate, but it sheds light on the victor's character. If the story has a purpose, it is to enhance the prestige of the narrator. However, the account does not throw favorable light on Arif.He related, "Qassim was sitting in the corner across from Mahdāwī and between them were Ṭaha Shaykh Aḥmad and Kan'ān Khalīl Sālim. I entered the room and with me were the members of the National Council, the Prime Minister and the other members of the government, and several of the Revolution's officers. From my pocket I drew out a copy of the sacred Quran, the same volume on which we swore in the July 1958 Revolution to keep the covenant, not to betray principles and to work for the unity of Arab nationalism. I held the Quran and said to 'Abd al-Karīm Qassim, 'For the sake of truth and history, I am asking you in the presence of the National Council and our brother officers—swear on this sacred book, are you the one who drew up the plan of the July 14th Revolution?' Qassim did not say a word. I raised the book again and asked him, "Can you swear to me by this sacred Quran that you knew the details of July 14?' And I asked further, 'Also swear on this sacred Quran that you prepared the first announcement of the July 14 Revolution or that you have its original draft in your possession.' Qassim kept quiet and I asked once more, 'Abd al-Karīm Qassim, will you swear by the sacred Quran that the July 14 Revolution did not protect Arab unity? Wasn't there an agreement? Wasn't there an oath taken on the sacred Quran that the aim of the Revolution is Arab unity? You swore on the Quran in front of everybody that that was the holy agreement among us concerning the aim of the Revolution! I grasped the sacred book and said, 'I swear before truth and history that I drew up the first announcement of the July 14 Revolution. 'Abd al-Karīm Qassim read it, and as far as I remember, and I hope I'm not mistaken, after the reading it we shifted one word either to come earlier or later in the text. Here is this announcement, this is the original draft, and Qassim has no copy in his possession. You have absolute freedom, Qassim, to answer or correct what I have said. I swear that I shall fast if I have lied by the sacred Quran.' But Qassim did not say anything. Then I asked him, 'Why did you lie about Nasser? How did your conscience allow you to accuse Jamāl 'Abd al-Nāṣir of treason and of plotting against you knowing that it is a false charge and that he told me that he wishes you well and that he always would say to me "Qassim is your brother from years back, and the good of the people demands that there should be no discord between you, that you should be tolerant toward him and treat him in the best possible manner." Still you say that Nasser plotted against you, when the truth of the matter is that it was you who conspired against Nasser.' And then I asked him, 'Why did you attack the staff of the UAR Embassy and trump up charges against them? Did you really imagine that the UAR would be disturbed by such conduct and return all its people from Iraq and close its embassy in Baghdad? Wasn't that your intention? But Allah lives, and the UAR has never severed its ties with Iraq. Why did you work against Arabism and Arab unity, 'Abd al-Karīm?' And now 'Abd al-Karīm Qassim spoke and said, 'This is not true. I love Arab nationalism, and I organized the convention of the foreign ministers of the Arab states in Baghdad. I turned to the Islamic and Arab countries.' I said to him, 'I'm sorry to say that it is not so. Your calls were always against Arabism, unity and Islam. You are a cosmopolite *(shu'ūbī)* and against Arab nationalism.' At this point Qassim wanted to defend himself and spoke of his deeds as a ruler in domestic matters when everything was tottering. The words came out weak and confused from his trembling mouth. He was saying, 'I exerted myself on behalf of the poor. I built thousands of small houses for the poor.' In reply I said to him, 'No, 'Abd al-Karīm Qassim. Your government was not a government of the poor; it was a government of princes, a government of your brother "Prince" Ḥāmid and the other princes among your relatives and cronies. You tell the people that you own nothing except the shirt on your back, when with my own eyes I saw the special wing you added to the Ministry of Defense which put Monaco or the island of Capri in the shade; why did you lie to the people and make fun of them?'"[46]

With praise for himself and jeers at his vanquished rival Arif wanted to establish his place in history. But he achieved Balaam's results, for in his story it was Qassim's statements about his concern for the poor that honor the man who uttered them. And in fact the slum dwellers and workers of Baghdad fought Arif and the Ba'th for two days.

After Qassim's murder, a view of his crushed body in all its horror was shown on television. This served to encourage the massacre carried out all over Iraq; in the scope and cruelty it exceeded all those that had preceded it in the country. Communists or people denounced as such were the main victims. The Ba'thist National Guard was the worst destructive force, and wherever it encountered serious opposition the army was called in.

The new government was formed of two elements, army officers and leaders of the Ba'th together with a number of nonparty ministers, chiefly experts. The Ba'thists occupied important posts: 'Alī Ṣāliḥ al-Sa'dī was Deputy Prime Minister and Ṭālib Ḥusayn Shabīb Minister for Foreign Affairs. As in Qassim's governments, the army officers were a minority—eight out of 22—but occupied key positions. Arif became President and was promoted to the rank of marshal; his brother, Colonel 'Abd al-Raḥman 'Ārif, became a brigadier and the commander of the 5th Armored Division. Colonel Aḥmad Ḥasan al-Bakr became a brigadier and Prime Minister. Ṣālih Mahdī 'Ammāsh, who in 1958 had been head of the Ba'thist military organization, jumped four grades from lieutenant-colonel to lieutenant-general and was appointed Minister of Defense. The new Chief of Staff was Ṭāhir Yaḥyā, one of the older Free Officers; in July 1958 he had been appointed inspector-general of the police, and after Rashīd 'Ālī al-Kaylānī's trial, he had been retired; now he was promoted from colonel to major-general. The commanders of all five army divisions were replaced by men loyal to Arif. Nearly all the officers who now attained high-ranking positions

[46] *Al-Ahrām*, 17 February, 1963.

had been dismissed from the army at the end of Qassim's period and most of them had been involved in the Shawwāf revolt.

A National Council of the Revolution which ranked higher than the government was also formed, but the number and names of its members were not made public. It, too, was based on the cooperation of officers and Ba'thist leaders. A short time later, it was no longer mentioned and apparently ceased to exist.

At first it seemed that Arif was a sort of Iraqi Naguib and that the strong man was the talented and cautious Prime Minister al-Bakr. Arif, however, knew how to consolidate his position, and before a year was up, al-Bakr was ousted. Nasser stood by Arif. In the critical days of Iraqi-Egyptian relations in 1963, Cairo refrained from attacking him personally, and when the two countries drew closer sang his praises.

Arif's government in 1963 was faced with the same three basic problems which had confronted Qassim's regime in 1958: relations between the officers and the civilian party leaders; relations between Iraq and Egypt; and relations between Arabs and Kurds. Party leaders who participated in the coup and government of February 1963 were not, as in 1958, the representatives of various anti-imperialist parties of the right and the left but only Ba'thists. The Ba'th wanted to be the sole guiding and deciding factor in the country. Its confidence and ambition mounted when a Ba'thist military coup also took over in Syria in March. The Iraq of Arif and the Ba'th succeeded in attaining the designation of a "liberated Arab country," and on April 17 a tripartite agreement for a federal union was signed with Egypt and Syria.

The chapter on Syria has already described how the plans and tripartite agreements for union came to be annulled and how the hostility between Nasser and the Ba'th was renewed with greater force. However, the Iraqi Ba'thist leaders, like the Syrians, resolved never to renounce power again once they had it.

In order to strengthen its influence in Iraq the Ba'th set out to win adherents among army officers and to glorify the National Guard. Until February 1963 only a few officers were organized members of the party, including 'Ammāsh and Windāwī. Many, like Arif, were close to the ideology and leadership of the Ba'th without actually belonging to it. In the summer of 1963, a number of officers joined the party; it had thereby increased its influence in the army; actually, the officers' position in the party had been strengthened.

The National Guard, which was set up at the time of the coup, at first served to spearhead the violence in the attacks against the communists. The Ba'thists' intention to transform it into a party army became progressively clearer. Its size and powers were expanded from time to time, and its commander, the 28-year-old pilot Windāwī, became one of the most influential people in the country. The National Guard was a military organization without military discipline whose mission was to terrorize the population. Its cruel and wanton acts aroused the hatred of the population, and among the officers, too, it was increasingly regarded with suspicion and considered a rival body. The existence of a well armed para-military organization with units throughout the country was the last thing the officers were prepared to tolerate. The officers were just biding their time until they could disband the National Guard, disarm its members and also eliminate Ba'thist influence in Iraq.

The Ba'th made the work of its opponents easy. As is usual in this party, profound differences and powerful personal quarrels broke out among its leaders. By the end of summer two factions had crystallized, the extremists headed by 'Alī Ṣāliḥ al-Sa'dī, and the moderates under the leadership of Ṭālib Shabīb and Aḥmad Ḥasan al-Bakr. 'Ammāsh made an effort to mediate between them but failed. The extremist wing developed a pseudo-Marxist ideology of class struggle, nationalization and party organization based on the principle of democratic centralism. Al-Sa'dī and his companions were also the most vehement in their controversy with Nasser. The moderate wing stressed the army's function as a guide and was opposed to nationalization.[47]

In September 1963, the disputes developed into an open crisis. While political questions were being discussed at several party meetings in Baghdad and Damascus, the top army brass was preparing a decisive action against the National Guard—the transfer of Windāwī to another job. Windāwī, however, refused to obey the order and remained at his post. It was not until the beginning of November that Windāwī saw that most of the officers were supporting al-Bakr and that 'Ammāsh had also stopped backing al-Sa'dī; he then gave up the command of the National Guard. However, while al-Sa'dī's position in Baghdad was being undermined, he achieved an important victory in Damascus. There, the sixth National (i.e., all-Arab) Congress of the Ba'th had been convening from September 5 to the 23. This meeting, its resolutions and new leadership marked a great advance for the extremist wing.[48]

Actually, the storms in the Ba'th, at least in the Iraqi Ba'th, were only tempests in a teapot. Al-Bakr, the head of the Ba'thist officers who opposed the extremists, prepared al-Sa'dī's ousting, and Arif, who had never joined

[47] *Al-Ḥayāt*, 14 November, 1963.
[48] *Arab Political Documents,* 1963, 438–62.

the party, supported him. On November 10 a special session of the Iraqi Ba'th was called which elected a new regional leadership—without al-Sa'di; the only one of his old loyal followers in it was Windāwī.[49] Half of its members were officers, an innovation of great significance in the annals of the party in whose institutions until then there had always been a majority of civilians. The next day the military authorities arrested al-Sa'dī—who was Deputy Prime Minister and Minister of Guidance—and exiled him with four of his friends by special army airplane to Madrid. Al-Sa'dī himself had asked to be sent to Madrid—a secure retreat from communist vengeance. Franco, too was ready to play the host to this "Marxist"; in the massacre of the Iraqi communists, he had shown his true identity.

On November 13 the Ba'thist extremists once again tried to seize power. The National Guard seized the main post office and the telephone exchange in Baghdad. Windāwī stole a jet from Habbaniya airbase and set out to bomb the president's palace just as on February 8 he had bombarded the Ministry of Defense to destroy Qassim. This time, however, the army put up a fight. The only thing that Windāwī succeeded in doing was to demolish five Mig's lined up at Rashid Camp.[50] This was the greatest military feat accomplished by any of its officers since the Iraqi air force had come into existence. Windāwī himself then fled to Syria.

The Ba'thist coup failed, but within the party the initiative passed once again to al-Sa'dī's men, who constituted the majority of the Baghdad membership. The leaders of the all-Arab party, headed by 'Aflaq and Ḥāfiẓ, came to Baghdad from Damascus and sent the leaders of the Iraqi Ba'thists' moderate wing abroad to Beirut, thus disposing only of several active civilian members but not of the officers. While the party leaders were trying to find a solution to their disputes, the officers carried out an additional coup to eliminate the Ba'th from the political arena in Iraq. On November 18 armored cars of the 5th Division under the command of Brigadier 'Abd al-Raḥman 'Ārif, the President's brother, seized Baghdad's key positions; the commander of the action was the Chief of Staff, Lieutenant-General Ṭahir Yaḥyā. A number of officers suspected of supporting the National Guard were arrested, curfew was imposed and the army threw a cordon around the National Guard's camps in Baghdad. A proclamation was issued disbanding the National Guard and announcing the formation of a new government. The order for disbanding the National Guard was also signed by 'Aflaq; perhaps he hoped to get rid of al-Sa'dī in this way.[51] The coup encountered only slight opposition. A show of force

49 *Ibid.*, 470.

50 *Al-Ḥayāt*, 14, 15, 19 November, 1963.

51 *Al-Jarīda*, Beirut, 29 February 1964.

by the army was enough to silence and immobilize the other elements.

The new government was formed, for the most part, of devout Moslems, both Sunnis and Shi'is. Its 21 members included 8 officers holding key positions. The positions of the Ba'thists deteriorated precipitously: Brigadier al-Bakr, the Prime Minister and strong man in the former government, was "promoted" to the respected but meaningless post of Vice-President; Brigadier Ḥardān Takrītī became Minister of Defense and Deputy Commander-in-Chief of the Armed Forces, but did not retain his real position of power as commander of the air force. It was not long before it became clear that leaving al-Bakr and Takrītī in the government was only a neutralizing action required by the events of the moment. In January 1964, the office of vice-president was abolished and al-Bakr was transferred to the Ministry for Foreign Affairs with the rank of ambassador—a political kiss of death—without arousing undue attention. In March 1964 the same happened to Takrītī. His position as Minister of Defense was occupied by Ṭāhir Yaḥyā, who continued to serve as chief of staff.

In November 1963 the Iraqi officer politicians were faced with the question to whom they owed allegiance and obedience—the party or the army. When it was no longer possible for them to vacillate, the overwhelming majority of those concerned, came out in favor of the army and the officers. A few, like Windāwī, decided in favor of the party and were immediately eliminated. Al-Bakr and Takrītī, whose stand was either lukewarm or hesitant, were ousted after a short transition period. Officers joining the party strengthened its influence but not its discipline, and in a party ridden with strife like the Ba'th the invetiable consequence of their becoming members was the weakening of party authority.

In February 1963 Arif needed the Ba'th. In February 1964 he no longer remembered its favors and denounced it as a treacherous, atheistic party. He promised Nasser that when he visited Baghdad "he would not find a single Ba'thist in Iraq."[52]

In the summer of 1964 remnants of the Ba'th made two more attempts to overthrow Arif. Only a few contradictory details were learned of the first plot. Evidently, the Ba'thists had planned a coup for the night of July 18. The conspiracy was discovered and tens of persons were arrested, including former officers of the army, the police and the National Guard.[53] In his speech on July 20, on the holiday commemorating the Prophet's birthday, Arif launched one of his bitterest attacks against the Ba'th; in the Iraqi press the governments of both Syria and Iran were accused of com-

[52] *Al-Akhbār,* Cairo, 17 February, 1964.

[53] *Al-Jihād,* Amman, 21 July, 1964; *al-Ḥayāt,* 2 August, 1964; *al-Muṣawwar,* Cairo, 21 August, 1964.

plicity in the plot. The charges against Iran were apparently based on the fact that the conspiracy had been chiefly concentrated in Shi'i regions south of Baghdad and its plan had included an uprising of the tribes.

The second plot was also frustrated, but only at the last minute. On September 4, at 2.30 p.m., Arif was to fly from Baghdad to the second Arab Summit Conference at Alexandria, and all the country's leaders were either going to accompany him or take leave of him at the Baghdad airport. Six Iraqi air force Mig's were to escort the President's aircraft. The pilots of these planes were Ba'thists and they had undertaken to attack the airport and everything on it at 2 p.m. and then bomb Rashid Camp and the planes stationed there. At the same time, a tank battalion under the command of Lieutenant-Colonel Aḥmad Jabūri was supposed to leave Rashid and capture the government's centers of power in the capital. The conspiracy was headed by Aḥmad Ḥasan al-Bakr.

That same morning one of the pilots divulged the plot to the authorities. Countermeasures were at once taken, the five pilots were executed, and a a new wave of arrests broke the Ba'th's remaining power in Iraq.[54]

The day after the thwarted conspiracy, on the morning of September 5, the first contingent of Egyptian troops arrived in Iraq. Three days later it reached the strength of an armored battalion and was stationed at Tājī Camp near the capital. The Egyptian force was later increased and remained in Iraq during 1965 and 1966. In the summer of 1965, it consisted of more than a thousand men and 100 tanks.[55] Initially, its purpose was to secure Arif's shaky government; afterwards it was left in Baghdad to represent Egyptian-Iraqi solidarity.

Both Qassim and Arif had started out in officers' coalitions with political parties—the former, with various anti-imperialist parties of the right and left, the latter, only with the Ba'th. What followed was similar in both cases: Instead of cooperation, there were struggles which ended in the elimination of the parties and the establishment of exclusively officers' regimes.

One of the basic distinctions between the governments of Qassim and Arif was the difference in Egypt's attitude. A brutal military dictatorship which maltreated its opponents in show trials and which was a thorn in Nasser's flesh was supplanted by a brutal military dictatorship which settled accounts with its opponents without trials and won Nasser's support.

The relations between Egypt and Iraq developed in 1963 parallel to the development of relations between Arif and the Ba'th, but in reverse. The

[54] *Al-Ḥayāt,* 8, 10 September, 1964;*Rūz al-Yūsuf,* Cairo, 26 October 1964.

[55] *The Daily Express,* 15 July, 1965.

period of cooperation between the Iraqi officers and the Ba'th was a time of rapprochement with Syria and tension with Egypt, and, as the prestige of the Ba'th declined in Baghdad, Arif's stock rose in Cairo. Arif, the pan-Arab extremist, was then interested in a union of Iraq and Nasser's Egypt. But the Nasser of Arif's time was a different man. Syria's secession from the UAR, the necessity for his reconciling himself to the existence of the governments of Ḥusayn in Jordan and Fayṣal in Saudi Arabia, his involvement in Yemen, all these had made him more cautious and restrained. He was in no hurry to form a union with Iraq. His dissociation from the war against the Kurds was one of the reasons for his rejecting the implementation of the Iraqi proposals for unification, but not the only one. He was not prepared to take on himself the responsibility for the survival of Iraq's shaky regime. An indication of this is the fact that, until the end of 1967, he had not responded to the numerous invitations to visit Baghdad.

In 1965 the question of general Arab unification, or even a union between two Arab countries only, ceased to have any immediate significance. This was very different from the situation in the summer of 1958. Then the most pressing question in the Arab world seemed to be: how much time would elapse before Iraq and Jordan and other Arab countries would follow in the footsteps of Syria and either join or be annexed by the UAR? Arab union seemed to be just around the corner. With the establishment of the Egyptian-Syrian union Nasser reached the peak of his power and influence. Then signs of decline gradually became evident. Iraq became a Republic, but Qassim preserved its independence and upset the unification efforts of Arif and Shawwāf. Civil war in Lebanon ended in the summer of 1958 with a refashioning of Lebanese sovereignty. King Ḥusayn survived his adversaries. In 1961, Syria broke away from Egypt and became her rival; this was sustained both under the clear-cut separatist regime of 1962 and the Ba'thist governments of 1963–1966. The agreement for a tripartite union of Egypt-Syria-Iraq, concluded in April 1963, was aimed at a loose federation and it went out of existence a quarter of a year later without leaving a trace. In 1964, Egypt's failure in Yemen became more obvious, and simultaneously her economic difficulties increased. In 1965 there were indications of serious political ferment in Egypt, and people were wondering not when Nasser would be President in Damascus and Baghdad, but whether his position at home was really still firm.

The three summit conferences of Arab kings and presidents in 1964 and 1965 actually re-affirmed the independence of each Arab state. The vision of Arab unity had once more receded from the realm of actual political programs and had moved yet again into the sphere of messianic hopes.

Arif's attitude towards the idea of Arab unity in general and towards the plans for union with Egypt in particular also changed. Like others before him, when he was no longer a member of the opposition but bore the responsibility for conducting the state, he had to concern himself with the concrete interests of his country, and his pan-Arab enthusiasm cooled off. No longer did he desire to share Iraq's oil revenues with Egypt.

However, not all the Iraqi nationalists, both civilian and military, abandoned plans of union with Egypt. This controversy served as a background for the events which shook Baghdad during the summer and fall of 1965.

On July 11, 1965 six ministers in Ṭāhir Yaḥyā's government resigned, including Minister of the Interior Brigadier Ṣubḥī 'Abd al-Ḥamīd and Minister of Culture and Guidance Brigadier 'Abd al-Karīm Farḥān. All the men who resigned were known for their extreme pro-Egyptian views. In accordance with Nasser's position and in sharp opposition to the views of Arif, they suggested, in February 1965, granting a measure of autonomy to the Kurds. Their suggestions were rejected, and on April 4 the Iraqi army launched a renewed offensive against the Kurds. Again war began which pinned down most of the Iraqi army in the north for months to come without leading to a showdown. At the beginning of July a new controversy came out into the open: The Nasserists demanded nationalization and other socialist measures for which Arif was not prepared, and they opposed the newly-signed agreement between the Iraqi government and the Iraq Petroleum Company, which once more extended the concession areas of the company.[56]

On July 12 six new ministers were appointed to replace those who had resigned. Ṭāhir Yaḥyā remained Prime Minister, but Arif resented his growing power and prestige and began to undermine his position. Neither did Arif wish to burn all the bridges with Cairo. Not all the pro-Egyptian officers took the extreme step of resigning; the most important among them was Major General 'Ārif 'Abd al-Razzāq, commander of the air force, who became the President's protégé at the same time that the powers of the Prime Minister were curtailed. On September 5 Ṭāhir Yaḥyā resigned, and the next day a government headed by 'Ārif 'Abd al-Razzāq was formed.

'Ārif 'Abd al-Razzāq was born in 1924 in the village of Kabīsa in the Ramadi district west of Baghdad. At the end of the 1940's he went to England for further study. After the coup of July 1958, he became commander of the air force base at Habbaniya. Following the failure of Shawwāf's rebellion in 1959, he was arrested; later he was retired, but at the end of the

[56] *Al-Ḥayāt,* 10 July, 1965.

same year was returned to the service. During Arif's coup in February 1963, he himself piloted a Hunter jet which attacked Qassim's headquarters. In November 1963, he became Minister of Agriculture and in December was appointed commander of the air force.[57]

'Abd al-Razzāq had the reputation of being moderately pro-Egyptian, and the President apparently hoped that as Prime Minister he would draw away from the extremists. However, the differences between 'Abd al-Razzāq and the pro-Egyptian ministers who had resigned in July had only been tactical ones, and on becoming Prime Minister, he began to work toward implementing their common aims. Hardly ten days after he assumed his new duties it had already become clear who sided with Arif and who was against him. Arif was preparing to leave for the third Arab Summit Conference at Casablanca; before his departure, his brother, Chief of Staff 'Abd al-Raḥmān 'Ārif, published an order relieving a number of well-known pro-Egyptian officers of their duties, including the transfer of Intelligence Chief Colonel Hādī Khammās to the position of military attaché in India and the dismissal of the Director of General Security, Colonel Rashīd Muḥsin. All the Nasserists, both avowed and secret, as well as the Prime Minister, opposed these orders as a body, and they were cancelled.[58] But the rival camps were already confronting each other, and there was no longer peace but only an armistice.

On his departure for Casablanca on September 14, Ārif appointed a number of loyal followers headed by his brother, the Chief of Staff, to assume his presidential duties in his absence. However, his opponents regarded his being away as an opportune time to depose him. The method was the customary coup d'état and the date was set for September 16.

That day, at 10 a.m., the plan was carried out in the usual fashion: Brigadier Muḥammad Majīd, Chief of Operations on the General Staff, and Colonel 'Irfān Wajdī, director of the military academy, left Abu-Ghurayb Camp near Baghdad for the radio station with a battalion of tanks. The Prime Minister and the rest of the plotters were ready in their offices, waiting for the broadcast of a communiqué announcing Arif's deposition and union with Egypt. Two officers in key positions known to be loyal to Arif were at that time summoned to the Prime Minister to be arrested: Colonel Sa'īd Ṣalībī, commander of the garrison in the capital, and Lieutenant-Colonel Bashīr Ṭālib, head of the Republican Guard. Ṣalībī did come and was arrested. Ṭālib, however, who arrived a little late, sensed the conspiracy, and from the door of the Prime Minister's office he

[57] *Ākhir Sā'a,* Cairo, 13 February, 1963; *al-Jarīda,* Beirut, 7 September, 1965; *al-Akhbār,* Cairo, 8 September, 1965.

[58] *Al-Ḥayat,* 21 September, 1965.

turned away towards his barracks. Meanwhile, the movement of the battalion which had left Abu-Ghurayb had been detected. The Chief of Staff placed his units on an alert, and Bashīr Ṭālib left with a tank battalion of his own to confront the mutinous unit. The rebels realized that they had lost the advantage of surprise and surrendered.[59]

'Ārif 'Abd al-Razzāq together with his wife and children and a number of conspirators arrived in Cairo on the same day in an Iraqi military airplane as fugitives. Arif's men either could not or did not want to prevent their departure.

The Egyptians really knew nothing of the coup and the plan to unite with them. They received the plotters as political refugees, but refrained from giving any indication whatsoever which could be interpreted as approbation of the conspirators' intentions. However, Arif was not certain that Nasser was really faithful to their alliance. When he learned of the abortive coup, he hurried back to Baghdad from Casablanca. On reaching Cairo, his airplane encountered the aircraft which had brought 'Abd al-Razzāq, and he feared that there was something amiss. To make sure that the Egyptians were not really plotting against him and that "nothing would happen to him en route", he requested that Flight-Captain Ḥusayn 'Abd al-Nāṣir should fly him back to Baghdad. Ḥusayn 'Abd al-Nāṣir, is the President's brother (from a second wife whom his father had married after the death of Jamāl's mother) and 'Abd al-Ḥakīm 'Āmir's son-in-law.[60]

Arif returned to Baghdad as a victor, but the prestige of the army, his principal support, had been undermined. Dr. 'Abd al-Raḥmān Bazzāz, a civilian statesman who had previously been ambassador in London, was appointed to head the new cabinet which was formed on September 21. One of the outstanding ideologists of Arab nationalism, he places special emphasis on the strong qualitative, historical bond between Arabism and Islam.[61] He has reservations concerning socialism, and on the issue of Arab unity he is against forcing matters.

For the first time republican Iraq had a civilian prime minister. The officers realized that they could not rule alone and would increasingly need the participation of civilian intellectuals. However, just as they could not rule alone, so they could not maintain a true partnership with anyone else. Bazzāz' government also kept very important portfolios for officers: Brigadier 'Abd al-Laṭīf Darrājī was Minister of the Interior and Major-General 'Abd al-'Aziz 'Uqaylī, Minister of Defense and Acting Minister of

[59] *Ibid.,* 18, 21 September, 1965.

[60] *Al-Akhbār,* 8 July, 1964; *al-'Amal,* Beirut, 25 September, 1965.

[61] Sylvia G. Haim, *Arab nationalism, an anthology,* Berkeley and Los Angeles, 1964, 55–8. 172–188.

Transport. Both of them had helped Qassim in 1958, had been involved in the Shawwāf rebellion of 1959, and had once more advanced in the world together with Arif after the 1963 coup.

Bazzāz' prime objectives were to assure Iraq stability, avoid extremism in either direction, bring about domestic peace between Arabs and Kurds and tone down any disputes with the Iraq Petroleum Company. He also hoped to get the military out of politics but this, too, gradually and quietly. Bazzāz, the conservative, could neither rely on popular movements nor on the power of the army, and his intentions could not be realized. Shocks continued to rock the political life of Iraq, and the country has been unable to free itself from the vicissitudes of military dictatorship.

On April 13, 1966 President 'Abd al-Salām 'Ārif was killed in a helicopter accident during a flight over southern Iraq; those who perished also included 'Abd al-Laṭīf Darrājī. On April 16 his older brother, the Chief of Staff Major-General 'Abd al-Raḥmān 'Ārif, was chosen as President in his place. On the date of his brother's death he was on an official visit in Moscow, and on learning of the accident, he hurried home. The new President displayed intelligence and courage before and after his accession, but the principal qualification which brought him to the presidency—besides being the brother of 'Abd al-Salām 'Ārif—was his being a military officer. It was not by chance that his serious rival for the office of president was another officer: Defense Minister 'Abd al-'Azīz 'Uqaylī. In the new government, also headed by Bazzāz, formed on April 18, 'Uqaylī was no longer a minister.

On June 29 Bazzāz broadcast in the name of the government a 12-point program which seriously aimed at satisfying Kurdish aspirations for autonomy and intended once and for all to put an end to the debilitating war in the north.[62] The next day Bazzāz prepared to leave for Turkey on a state visit. But he had not reckoned with 'Ārif 'Abd al-Razzāq.

After the failure of his attempted coup in September 1965, 'Ārif 'Abd al-Razzāq stayed in Egypt as one of the numerous political exiles from all parts of the Arab world supported by Nasser. However, he did not remain there long, and at the beginning of June 1966 he slipped back into Iraq where he renewed his ties for the purpose of planning a new coup, contacting, among others, Brigadier Yūnis 'Aṭṭār-Bāshā and Lieutenant-Colonel Ṣubḥī 'Abd al- Ḥamīd.

Ṣubḥī 'Abd al-Ḥamīd was Chief of Operations on the General Staff after Arif's coup in 1963 and, subsequently, Foreign Minister and Minister of Defense. In September 1965 he participated in 'Ārif 'Abd al-Razzāq's

[62] Radio Baghdad, 29 June, 1966.

abortive coup and was arrested, but was released at the end of the year. Whereas in June 1966 he was one of the former great personalities, Yūnis 'Aṭṭār-Bāshā was in an actual position of power—commander of the Fourth Division garrisoned in Mosul. He, too, is one of the officer politicians. In 1959 he was active in the Shawwāf rebellion and was sentenced to life imprisonment.[63]

The coup was scheduled for June 30, and H-hour was fixed at 3.30 p.m.

The insurrectionists operated from a number of centers: Their principal base was at Mosul where 'Abd al-Razzāq, with the help of Yūnis 'Aṭṭar-Bāshā, seized the airfield and himself piloted one of the Hunters which left to bomb the centers of power in Baghdad. Another flight of airplanes took off from Habbaniya, and armor moved out from the camp at Abu Ghurayb. There were also a number of supporters of the coup at Rashid Camp. All the forces operating in the capital and its vicinity were apparently headed by Colonel Hādī Khammās, former chief of army intelligence and 'Ārif 'Abd al-Razzāq's partner in the attempted coup of 1965.

At 3.30 p.m., the rebels succeeded in broadcasting an announcement on one of the waves of Baghdad Radio. However, the broadcast was interrupted after a few minutes.[64] The rebels had immediately encountered resistance. They had no active supporters at all among the civilians. President Arif displayed courage and presence of mind, and with the help of the Republican Guard at once threw a number of army units into action against the rebels. On landing at the Mosul airport on his return from his bombing flight, 'Ārif 'Abd al-Razzāq was arrested.[65] At 7.50 in the evening, Baghdad Radio was already announcing the failure of the attempted coup. Shortly afterwards, it began to broadcast the customary profusion of congratulatory telegrams, chiefly from army units. At night curfew was proclaimed in Baghdad, and the next day life in Iraq returned to normal. Dozens of plotters were arrested. A number fled—according to an official Iraqi announcement, 12 civilians and 13 officers, including Brigadier 'Abd al-Karīm Farḥān who in 1964 had been Minister of National Guidance, and 3 colonels.[66]

In the days that followed, many people asked whether the leaders of the extreme pro-Egyptian line had really carried out an attempted coup without either the support or knowledge of Cairo. Had 'Ārif 'Abd al-Razzāq actually left Egypt without the consent, or at least knowledge, of the

63 *Maḥkamat al-sha'b,* vol. 18, Baghdad 1962, 6879, 6902.

64 Radio Damascus, 30 June, 1966, 18.15 h.

65 *Al-Muḥarrir,* Beirut, 3 July, 1966; *al-Ahrām,* 5 July, 1966; *Ākhir Sā'a,* Cairo, 6 July, 1966; *al-Usbu' al-'arabī,* Beirut, 6 July, 1966.

66 Radio Baghdad, 2 July, 1966.

Egyptian authorities? On the other hand, they argued, it is a fact that the Egyptian force at the al-Tājī camp in Baghdad had done nothing to help the rebels. They also pointed out that Egypt usually does nothing to interfere with the movements of numerous Arab exiles who have found asylum within her border. They argued further, "It is not logical that an officer who had failed in previous attempted coups, in one of which he had served both as prime minister and minister of defense, would be selected by an outstanding leader like Nasser to be the hero of a new abortive attempt."[67]

In any case, on the morning of July 1, immediately after the suppression of the attempted coup, the Iraqi government sent a top-level political and military delegation to Cairo, apparently for the purpose of securing explanations and information.[68] Later the same day, Prime Minister Bazzāz stressed at a press conference that he was convinced that Egypt had had no part in the attempted coup, "even if those elements over which Egypt had maintained strict surveillance—a number of Ba'thists—had succeeded in escaping" from Egypt.[69] Whether or not he was really convinced or wanted to prevent further strain on his government by conducting a controversy with Egypt, his premiership was finished. On August 6 he tendered his resignation. In his letter of resignation to the President which was published, he explicity stated that he was retiring from office solely in accordance with the President's wishes.[70] In other words, the officer corps no longer agreed to allow a civilian to be prime minister, especially a person with liberal-conservative tendencies. In the letter of resignation Bazzāz emphasized that he had found a compromise solution to the Kurdish question, "the most important problem facing Iraq since its founding". The continuation of this policy was also opposed by the military.

Nājī Ṭālib, one of the old leaders of the Free Officers, was appointed prime minister. On his accession to power, the character of the regime in Iraq as a military dictatorship became again most obvious. The Iraqi officers have never been united among themselves since they took power in 1958. But their being divided into various rival factions does not mean that they would tolerate somebody else as the country's leader, not even an outstanding nationalist-conservative politician like Bazzāz. The officers have become the most privileged class in society. Their merit as servants of their nation is most questionable, yet their success in becoming their country's masters is certain.

[67] *Al-Anwār,* Beirut, 2 July, 1966.
[68] *Al-Ḥayāt,* 2 July, 1966.
[69] *Radio Baghdad,* 2 July, 1966.
[70] *Al-Ḥayāt,* 10 August, 1966.

9. SUDAN

SUDAN belongs both to Arab and to Black Africa. Of all the Arab countries it has the second largest population and is the largest in area. The distance from its border with Uganda to its frontier with Egypt is equal to the distance from the southern tip of Italy to the northern shore of Denmark.

Sudan became independent on January 1, 1956. The transition to independence came with exemplary quietness. However, the aftermath of the storms at the end of the last century still strongly influence political divisions in the country. The roots are religious and sectarian; the ramifications go as far as varying orientations in foreign policy. The two principal sects are the Mahdiyya and Khātmiyya. The Mahdī movement came as a puritanical reaction to the inroads made by a modern civilization whose representatives in the third quarter of the 19th century were Egyptian officers and governors. The Umma Party, the political organization of the Mahdiyya in the middle of the 20th century, made its peace with modernization while yet preserving national opposition to Egypt. Its opposition to Egyptian aspirations for the unification of the Nile valley brought it closer to the British, who repaid it with loyal support. The rival sect, the Khātmiyya, which is closer to orthodox Islam, is a Sufi order. By its nature, and even more because of its opposition to the Mahdiyya, it always had Egyptian backing, and in this case, too, the assistance was mutual. The Khātmiyya and a large part of the young Sudanese intelligentsia constituted the principal elements of the anti-British National Unionist Party which favored unification with Egypt—until Sudan became independent.

From the day of its independence Sudan unanimously wished to maintain friendly relations with Egypt but not to merge with it. Memories of Egyptian rule in the 19th century and fear of domination by the new regime in Egypt reinforced the desire for independence.

The young independent state encountered serious difficulties. In 1958 the hitherto stable economy became shaky when the price of cotton, the principal export item, declined on the world market. Foreign trade accounts that had shown a surplus of $62,000,000 in 1956 ended in a deficit of

$ 42 million in 1957; the decline continued in 1958. The cost of living index of the lower ranking government officials in Khartoum rose by 20 per cent in 1957.[1]

By February 1958 there was a crisis in relations with Egypt. The Anglo-Egyptian-Sudanese agreement of 1899 had set the 22nd parallel as the boundary between the two countries. However, in the 20th century, at the suggestion of Egypt, Sudan administered two regions north of this latitude, set up according to tribal populations, one along the shores of the Red Sea and the other on the Nile. But at the beginning of 1958, the Cairo government sent officials there under military protection for the purpose of preparing the plebiscite scheduled for February 21 for a vote on the Egyptian-Syrian union. The Khartoum government on the other hand assumed that inhabitants of the two regions would participate in the elections to the Sudanese parliament on February 27 as they had done on previous occasions. The diplomatic dispute became more serious, and on February 20 Sudan appealed to the Security Council, where no decision was taken. The problem was finally solved by an Egyptian withdrawal from the disputed regions. However, Cairo did not yield the principle, and as a result the Sudanese continued to regard Egypt with suspicion. Moreover, Egyptian interference in Sudanese internal affairs did not cease. In 1958 the United Arab Republic was formed and Egyptian Pan-Arabist policy reached the peak of its momentum. On July 15 'Alī Khashaba, who had four years earlier served as a major at Egyptian army headquarters in the Sudan, arrived in Khartoum as counselor at the Egyptian Embassy. Four days later he was expelled from Sudan, accused of subversive activity, and suspicion regarding Egypt grew.[2] Khashaba was not a junior official; in 1964 he served as ambassador to Algeria.

In the February 1958 elections the Umma party gained the largest number of seats, 71 out of 173, but this was not a majority. The government headed by 'Abd-Allāh Khalīl was dependent on the support of several small factions. The opposition National Unionist Party (44 deputies), led by Ismā'īl al-Azharī, enjoyed Egyptian backing. In the fall, party disputes, became more acute and the economic situation deteriorated further. Fearing that Egypt would take advantage of the internal weakness to annex the country to the UAR, 'Abd-Allāh Khalīl decided to hand over power to the army.

An additional motive for the establishment of a military dictatorship stemmed from the crisis between the north and the south. The Negro

[1] United Nations, *Economic developments in the Middle East,* 1958–1959, New York 1959, 98; *Sudan Almanac,* 1960, Khartoum 1960, 149.

[2] *Hamizrah Hehadash,* vol. 10, 67.

population of the three southern provinces, about a quarter of the country's inhabitants in an area greater than Iraq, Syria and Lebanon combined, is non-Muslim and non-Arabic-speaking. Systematic attempts to Islamize and Arabicize them, initiated in the period of Egyptian rule during the second half of the 19th century, were stopped under British rule in the first half of the 20th century and renewed with greater intensity on the eve of independence. In 1955 Equatoria Province revolted and Khartoum's authority was reestablished only after months of brutal suppression. In the summer of 1958 relations again deteriorated, and in parliament a spokesman for the south asked for southern autonomy.[3] The spokesmen for the Beja tribes in the north-east and of Kordofan and Darfur in the west also insisted on greater decentralization. As centralized government by Muslim Arab political leaders seemed improbable, an attempt was made to attain this goal by military government—the Sudanese army consisting mainly of northerners and nearly all its officers being Arabs.

'Abd-Allāh Khalīl was an army veteran, born in 1892 at Omdurman and educated at Gordon College in Khartoum, the school that for half a century had been the *alma mater* of Sudanese intelligentsia. From 1910 to 1924 he served in the Egyptian army and from then till 1948 with the Sudanese forces. He was the first Sudanese to achieve the rank of brigadier.[4] Upon retirement he devoted himself to political activity and in December 1948 was first appointed Prime Minister. Ten years later, again appointed Prime Minister, he decided to hand the government to the army.

The Chief of Staff was Ibrāhīm 'Abbūd, born in 1900 at Muḥammad Nūl, a town in the vicinity of Suwākin on the Red Sea, the son of Muḥammad bin 'Abbūd, a native of Suwākin and a judge in charge of tribal affairs. Ibrāhīm 'Abbūd also studied at Gordon College and from the age of 18 served in the Egyptian and Sudanese armies. During World War II he commanded a Sudanese unit which as part of the British army saw active service in North Africa. In 1954 he became a major-general and in 1957 a lieutenant-general. Like many of the people of eastern Sudan he was close to the Khātmiyya and pro-Egyptian, and in the mid-1950's was greatly impressed by Nasser's policies.[5]

On November 10, 1958 'Abd-Allāh Khalīl and 'Abbūd met and evidently discussed the handing over of power to the army. Six days later the two major parties came to an agreement on the formation of a coalition govern-

[3] J. Oduho and W. Deng, *The problem of the southern Sudan,* London 1963, 36–8.

[4] *Who's who in UAR and the Near East,* 1959, Cairo 1959, 238.

[5] P.M. Holt, *A modern history of the Sudan,* London 1961, 184; R.L. Hill, *A biographical dictionary of the Anglo-Egyptian Sudan,* Oxford 1951, 245; G. Vaucher, *Gamal Abdul Nasser et son équipe,* vol. 1, Paris 1959, 116.

ment in the belief that they could terminate the parliamentary crisis in the usual way. But they were too late. That night several battalions of troops entered the capital at the order of the Chief of Staff, seized government buildings and placed the ministers under arrest. As usual, one of the principal objectives was the broadcasting station. Nowhere did they encounter any resistance. On the morning of November 17 an announcement by 'Abbūd was broadcast to the Sudanese people stating that "in the natural course of events, the country's army and security forces rose to put an end to the chaos that now gripped the land".[6] Martial law was proclaimed, all parties outlawed and meetings and demonstrations prohibited. The press ban was lifted after one day.

Several days later 'Abd-Allāh Khalīl claimed that he had known in advance about the coup, but 'Abbūd denied this. Both were right. Khalīl knew of the coup and even encouraged it, but he was ignorant of its nature and its timing. He may have thought that he would remain the power behind the scenes, but 'Abbūd had seized control. 'Abd-Allāh Khalīl and Ismā'il al-Azharī were retired on pension. They were no longer allowed to participate in public affairs.[7]

The new regime established by the high command was an undisguised military dictatorship. The supreme authority for legislation, executive power and judiciary affairs was vested in the "Supreme Council of the Armed Forces" consisting of 13 officers under 'Abbūd. Second in prominence was Major-General Aḥmad 'Abd al-Wahhāb, 'Abd-Allāh Khalīl's son-in-law, an energetic man with a solid military and general education. 'Abbūd's junior by ten years, he had served before the coup as his deputy and chief of staff. He was a member of the Umma Party and was known as a vigorous opponent of Egyptian aspirations for unification of the Nile valley.

In addition to the military council, a government consisting of twelve ministers was formed. Six were members of the military council and held the most important portfolios. Most of the civilian ministers were close to the Umma-Mahdiyya circles, while the majority of the members of the military council were associated with the National Union-Khātmiyya faction. 'Abbūd wanted, and achieved, the neutralization of the traditional party-sectarian influences in order to assure the supremacy of the officer corps.

'Abbūd's first year in power was one of crises and unrest.

When officer regimes seized power in Egypt, Iraq and Syria, they could

[6] Amīn Sa'īd, *Tā'rīkh al-'arab al-ḥadīth,* vol. 15, Cairo 1959, 195.

[7] Holt, 181-2.

point out several instances of corruption in the previous parliamentary regime in order to justify their military dictatorship. This was not the case in the Sudan. The sovereign state was still young, less than three years old. To be sure, in 1958 there was a crisis in parliamentary and party relations as well as in the sphere of economics, but the achievements of the party leaders in the struggle for independence were not yet forgotten. The powerful Sudanese labor union did not give up easily. In reaction to the attitude of appeasement of some of its leaders, communist influence mounted among workers' groups and among intellectuals.[8]

Under the military dictatorship these tensions could be expressed only by a crisis in the officer corps itself. At the end of February 1959 an argument broke out between two members of the military council, Major-General Aḥmad 'Abd al-Wahhāb and Brigadier Ḥasan Bashīr Naṣr, who both belonged to the Khātmiyya but were political rivals. The intellectual Aḥmad 'Abd al-Wahhāb was considered a radical in internal and foreign affairs, while Ḥasan Bashīr Naṣr, who was less educated, showed a conservative attitude at home and a pro-Western orientation in international relations. On March 1 'Abd al-Wahhāb was arrested and three days later all members of the military council handed their resignations to 'Abbūd. At an officers' meeting the next day a new council was formed under 'Abbūd. Of the 13 members of the previous council eight remained, including 'Abd al-Wahhāb, and five left to be replaced by three new men. Three of these 11 officers belonged to the Khātmiyya, three to the Mahdiyya, the others were independent. However, Aḥmad 'Abd al-Wahhāb refused to accept the composition of the new council and would not swear allegiance to it; on March 9 he was relieved of his duties, retired and given 3,000 dunams of state land as compensation. His rival, Ḥasan Bashīr Naṣr, was promoted to the rank of major-general and made Minister of State and Deputy Supreme Commander of the Armed Forces. On the same day a new government was formed. This time 10 of its 15 members were officers (in 'Abbūd's first cabinet there were only six out of 12) and all members of the military council received ministerial portfolios.

Shortly after the March 1959 crisis a new shock jarred 'Abbūd's government. On May 22 two companies from the Eastern Command arrived from Gedaref at Khartoum on telegraphed orders that turned out to be forged. They were summoned to participate in a coup d'état but the plan failed at the outset and they were returned to base on the same day. Details of the plot were never revealed, but the names of its leaders are known. Two were

[8] André Ribaud, 'Ou en est le Soudan', *Orient,* no. 12, 1959, 40–41; K.D.D. Henderson, *Sudan Republic,* London 1965, 110; Holt, 184.

members of the military council—Brigadier ʿAbd al-Raḥīm Shīnān was one of the officers who joined the council in March and had previously headed the Northern Command; Brigadier Bashīr Aḥmad ʿAbd-Allāh Ḥāmid also became a member of the council in March and had formerly commanded the eastern front. Both were arrested and sentenced to death in September but their sentences were commuted to life imprisonment. Sixteen other officers, five enlisted men, and a number of civilians were arrested. Between May 20 and 30 a large-scale manhunt for communists and members of the "Front of the Struggle against Imperialism" was carried out. Hundreds were arrested in Khartoum, Omdurman, Atbara and elsewhere.

There was another attempt to carry out a coup against the military regime on November 10, 1959, this time by officers of junior and middle rank at the infantry school at Omdurman under the command of ʿAlī Ḥāmid. The rebels took over the school and the radio station in Omdurman, broadcast an announcement directed mainly against Ḥasan Bashīr Naṣr and seized the bridge between Omdurman and Khartoum. There their advance was checked and the rising quelled. Two days later three officers and eight civilians were brought to trial. Five of them, including ʿAlī Ḥamid, were sentenced to death and hanged on December 2; five others were given long prison terms, and one was acquitted; 17 other officers were cashiered from the army.

The conduct of the Sudanese officers in power did not differ from that of officers in other Arab countries: The early months served as a transition period—not for the officers' return to their barracks but for the purpose of tightly concentrating all decision-making power in their hands. The military dictatorship did not advance toward its own dissolution but toward the creation of a power monopoly. Among the upper echelon of officers, the expulsion of a number of strong personalities and their replacement by several weak ones led to the increasing concentration of power in the hands of the heads of the new regime.

After their success in suppressing the parties and rival groups in the army, the officers embarked on a systematic campaign against the strongest and best-organized public body in the country, the Federation of Labor Unions of the Workers of the Sudan. Upon seizing power the officers did not dare to dissolve the workers' organization and only outlawed its activities. In 1959 the union became the focal point for opposition to the dictatorship and the authorities waited for an opportunity to get even with it. In February 1960 they published new laws dealing with trade unions and labor disputes which outlawed strikes, forbade office workers to organize and permitted only separate unions to be set up in individual places of employment.

Differences of opinion arose within the unions as to the attitude and tactics to be adopted toward the government regulations. In this way the regime succeeded in splitting and atomizing the united strength of the workers' movement. In the autumn of 1960 most of the workers' organizations were already tools in the hands of the military regime.

The consolidation of the officers' regime in 1960 was facilitated by an improvement in the economic situation that year. In 1959 foreign trade once again showed a surplus of $ 10 million, and profits continued to rise at the beginning of 1960. After this, decline set in again, and 1960 ended with an only balanced foreign-trade account. In 1961 there was a deficit of $ 20 million.[9] But in the winter of 1959–60 the government did not yet feel the economic pressure. Large sums were secured in American aid and various development projects were started.

In 1960 'Abbūd's regime seemed to be a relatively stable military dictatorship that was slowly developing the economy on capitalistic lines. However, 'Abbūd did not succeed in gaining the loyalty and cooperation of the parliamentary representatives. In June 1961 well-known leaders of various leanings presented a petition to the government with the result that they were all exiled to Juba in the distant south. The exiles included 'Abd-Allāh Khalīl, Ismā'īl al-Azharī, the leader of the Khātmiyya, 'Abd-Allāh al-Mirghanī, and the secretary-general of the Communist Party Muḥammad Maḥjūb.[10]

In the southern districts the military regime speeded up Arabization and Islamization. Hundreds of Christian missionaries were expelled. Use of Latin script was prohibited and only Arabic was recognized as the language of instruction and administration. Arabic is to the southerner as alien as English or Italian, but an educated person from the south who spoke and wrote English was now considered illiterate and could not find a job. In 1960 a Christian Cultural Center was closed and its teachers were arrested because its church had a blackboard on which roman numerals were written.[11] The question may indeed be asked whether there is any sense in educating Central African tribes to become islands of Christian culture in a region where Arab-Muslim culture is spreading and in adding religious differences to racial and social distinctions. But these problems cannot be solved by coercion and suppression, especially when they are accompanied by economic exploitation and social degradation. Northerners enjoy numerous privileges in the south; they occupy government positions there,

[9] *Hamizrah Hehadash,* vol. 13, 100, 456.
[10] Radio Cairo, 11 July, 1961.
[11] Oduho, 48.

but no officials from the south serve in the north; Arabic-speaking men marry Negro women but a Negro may not take an Arab wife.

While inside Sudan 'Abbūd conducted a campaign of Arabization, in foreign policy he demonstrated the independence and uniqueness of the country vis-à-vis the other Arab states. The terminology of Arab nationalism and unity did not exist in his political dictionary. Arabization of the south was called "Sudanization". In the inter-Arab quarrels Sudan remained neutral. It is the only Arab country that never severed diplomatic relations with other Arab states and that never contracted an alliance with another Arab state.

The reason for Sudan's cautious neutral position is clear: the Sudanese realized even before the Syrians that the Egyptian version of Arab nationalism meant Egyptian domination. They had already experienced union with Egypt for six decades in the last century and they knew that in Nasser's Egypt the will to dominate had intensified. Sudan, furthermore, has a natural advantage which Cairo cannot ignore: the Nile arrives in Egypt from Sudan. Sudan can thus sabotage the basic element of Egypt's existence. The implementation of the enormous undertaking of the High Dam depends on Sudan's consent. That is why Egypt has relinquished her aspirations to expand southward. In the Cairo press and radio, perpetually occupied with affairs of nearby and distant Arab countries, little could be found on the Sudan after 1955; for months this large neighboring country appeared to be a white spot on the Egyptian map of Arab politics. Mutual suspicion coupled with unavoidable concessions produced positive results: the Egyptian-Sudanese agreement of November 1959 on the division of the Nile waters. The previous agreement, signed in 1929 between British officials for Sudan and British officials for Egypt, left room for serious grievances on both sides. But the new agreement between the governments of Nasser and 'Abbūd solved complicated technical and economic problems in a way that can serve as a model for international settlements of water disputes.[12]

After the overthrow of 'Abbūd, Muḥammad Ḥasanayn Haykal released details concerning the military regime in Sudan and its leaders. In the winter of 1960 he visited the country and talked with Major-General Ṭal'at Farīd, the Deputy Prime Minister and Minister of Information. "I told him, 'I have learned that the opposition is preparing a petition and is getting ready to present it to the government to demand its dissolution.' He said, 'What is a petition worth? Isn't it a piece of paper? Can't it be torn up like any other piece of paper?' I said, 'But it's being presented to you by

[12] Y. Shilo, 'Ha-heskem 'al haluqat mey ha-nilus beyn Mitzrayim la-Sudan', *Hanizrah Hehadash,* vol. 10, 320-5.

people behind whom there are other people.' He asked, 'Have you heard about my left foot?' The question surprised me, for, to tell the truth, I had not heard a thing about Major-General Ṭal'at Farīd's left foot; at first glance, his query seemed irrelevant to the discussion. Anyhow he added, 'I was once a famous soccer player in Britain. The spectators knew that if the ball came within range of my left foot, it was a certain goal.' I felt that there was no point to this kind of discussion and shifting to the problem which was troubling me, I said to Major-General Farīd, 'Let me ask you—why do you call what you've done in Sudan a Revolution? In my opinion, a revolution means a comprehensive social change, and I don't feel that this is what has actually happened in the Sudan. A change has undoubtedly occurred in the form of government, but this change has more the effect of a coup than of a revolution. Nevertheless you insist on using the term Revolution, why?' Once more I confess that I expected any reply but the one Major-General Farīd made. He asked, 'What is your first name?' Hesitantly and without understanding the meaning of the question, I said, 'Muḥammad. If my memory doesn't fail me, that's my name.' He said, 'Who picked this name out for you?' I said, 'If I am not mistaken, it was my father who selected the name.' He said, 'Very well. If that's the case, we are the parents of the event which took place in Sudan on November 17, and we are free to call it by whatever name we please. We have picked out the name Revolution.' I did not continue the discussion . . . "[13]

On seizing power, 'Abbūd declared that the establishment of an officers' regime is "the natural course" in contemporary Arab history, and he set up and maintained a blatant military dictatorship. Six years later 'Abbūd was overthrown in a way which was unprecedented in the annals of modern Arab military dictatorships. The unique feature is not the fall of 'Abbūd itself, for, with the exception of the Egyptian government, not one of the regimes installed by an officers' coup lasted more than four to six years, and usually much less. What is unique in 'Abbūd's overthrow is the fact that this regime was not destroyed by a military coup but by a popular uprising, and he was compelled to yield his position to civilian authority.

The Khartoum uprising took place on October 21, 1964. The first link in the chain of incidents that quickly developed into a general rebellion was a meeting of university students who criticized government policy in the south. The students demonstrated after leaving the university, and when security forces tried to disperse them, crowds joined the demonstrators. The disturbances and clashes lasted for three days, during which time six

[13] *Al-Ahrām,* 6 November, 1964.

persons were killed and 71 injured.[14] At night a curfew was imposed and during the daytime businessmen, workers and government officials went on strike. The old parties reemerged with their veteran leaders and combined with new organizations to form a National Front that demanded the withdrawal from power of the officers, the resignation of the government, the dissolution of the Supreme Council and of the Armed Forces, the restoration of the 1956 constitution, elections and a solution to the problem of the south.

Criticism of the regime found expression primarily among the intellectuals. The left increased its influence among them, and the left-wing intelligentsia had established ties with the workers' movement. During the 1940's and 1950's the labor movement in the Sudan was the strongest, best organized and most active of all Arab labor movements,[15] and the suppressive measures of the military dictatorship did not manage to destroy it. At this time the Communist Party gained adherents among the workers and the intelligentsia. The first victim in the Khartoum riots was a communist student.[16] The power of the party was not as great as it seemed at the beginning of the uprising but it was able to act as an organized body and take the initiative; it thus had a decisive voice in the formation of the National Front.

The left wing was joined by other groups that had been suppressed by the officers. These were the majority of the spiritual and political leaders and the mass of their followers.

No one rose to defend the officers' dictatorship—not even the army. The ruling officers were hated because of their arrogance, their newly acquired wealth and the corruption that had spread in their ranks. Moreover, during the crisis they were divided among themselves. 'Abbūd's deputy in the presidency and the Army Command, Major-General Ḥasan Bashīr Naṣr, the strong man in the military council, wanted to use the full power of the army for suppressing the opposition. However, he met with the refusal of many senior officers and explicit opposition from all the junior officers. He was opposed by a group of seven "neutral" officers—three major-generals, a brigadier and three colonels—who served as mediators between the army and the civilians. Their leader was Brigadier Muḥammad Idrīs 'Abd-Allāh, a relative of Ismā'īl al-Azhari.[17] He was the governor of the Kassala district in the east, and when the disturbances

[14] *Al-Jumhūriyya,* Cairo, 26 October, 1964.

[15] S. Fawzi, *The labour movement in the Sudan.* London 1957, *passim.*

[16] *Al-Jumhūriyya,* 2 November, 1964.

[17] *Al-Ḥayāt,* Beirut, 30 October, 1964.

broke out he arrived in the capital with a division of troops who did not allow the army to be used against the civilian population.

On October 26 ‘Abbūd was forced to dissolve the supreme military council and to dismiss the government. His announcement was received with cheers. But ‘Abbūd remained President, and discussions on the formation of a caretaker government were still going on between the National Front and the army. The atmosphere continued to be tense as the National Front demanded the absolute withdrawal of the army from political life. On October 28 disturbances were renewed and again there were dead and wounded. Radio and television employees at Omdurman announced a strike and ended the last broadcast with the slogan, "Long live the Sudanese people's struggle for freedom!" [18] The soldiers had to beat an additional retreat. Ḥasan Bashīr Naṣr was deprived of his military duties, and on October 30 a new government composed of civilians was formed.

Events in Sudan brought strong reactions from the Arab world, especially Egypt. At first Cairo was confused. A popular uprising against an officers' regime could have dangerous repercussions in other regimes headed by officers. However, Cairo came to the conclusion that the popular forces that had bestirred themselves in the Sudan would put an end to ‘Abbūd's pro-western policy and bring the country closer to Egypt,—a correct surmise, as it turned out. During the disturbances the embassies of the United States and Britain were attacked and rumors were spread that Egyptians had guided the course of events. These rumors were unfounded as Cairo itself was evidently surprised by the eruption of violence. Several days later Egypt adopted a clear stand on the side of the Popular Front: it was clear to the Egyptians that ‘Abbūd's regime had outlived its time, while the prospects of harnessing the new government to the Egyptian camp in the Arab world attracted Cairo very much.

‘Abbūd, who was still president, feared that Egypt would make itself master of Sudan, and he made one last attempt to avenge himself against his opponents in the army and free the country of Egyptian influence. On November 8 several officers, ranking from captain to lieutenant-colonel and known as pro-Egyptian and sons of veteran political leaders advocating unification with Egypt, were arrested by his order. [19] However, he achieved the opposite of what he wanted. The government released the imprisoned officers and in their stead arrested and banished from the capital several senior officers who had been leaders of the previous regime.

[18] Radio Cairo, 28 October, 1964.

[19] *Al-Ḥayāt,* 11 November, 1964.

On November 9 thousands of civilians staged a demonstration, asking that the army be purged of men who had supported the dictatorship.

That evening another attempt was made to restore military rule. Armored and service corps units began to move on the capital. When the news leaked out, the National Front excitedly broadcast an appeal at 11 p.m.: "The National Front ... urges all citizens to prepare themselves to go into the street immediately and to proceed to the Council of Ministers and the radio station to protect them and to demonstrate ... and proclaims immediately a general political strike—the weapon of the people—in order to safeguard the national gains."[20] Later the Communist Party claimed that it had discovered the reactionary plot and that one of its members had broadcast to the people. In any case throngs of people came out into the streets and the civilian government remained in power.

On November 15 'Abbūd resigned and his office was taken over by a presidium. Six years of officers' rule ended in a fashion entirely different from previous Arab military dictatorships.

The new civilian government in Sudan was faced with many complicated problems. In May 1965 parliamentary elections were held, and interestingly enough their results were amazingly similar to those of 1958 before the accession of the officers to power. The two traditional major political parties once again shared most of the seats. Six years of military dictatorship seemed to have left no mark: It was as if the changing events of this period had only a superficial effect on political and social relationships and were only a transitory episode in the life of the people.

A further ephemeral and inconsequential episode was the abortive military coup which took place in the night of December 27, 1966, A small group of Sudanese subaltern officers and soldiers, not more than 300 altogether, under the leadership of 24-year-old Lieutenant Khālid Ḥusayn 'Uthmān, advanced from the Khartoum military training camp towards the center of the town in order to occupy the radio station and some government buildings. On the way they were intercepted by loyal troops, disarmed and arrested without further ado.[21] On the next day other opponents of the government were arrested, mostly communists or communist-sympathizers.

The central issue in Sudanese politics at that time were the political rights of the Communist Party, and the government seized the opportunity of the attempted military coup to denounce the communists as its instigators

[20] *Al-Ahrām,* 10 November, 1964, quoted in: *Arab Political Documents,* 1964, Beirut 1965, 455; K.D.D. Henderson, *Sudan Republic,* London 1965, p. 210.

[21] Radio Omdurman and Radio Cairo, 28 December, 1966.

or even organizers and to suppress them. A year earlier, on December 9, 1965, the government had enacted a law banning the Communist Party and ousting eight deputies from the Constitutional Assembly as communists. The Communist Party appealed to the High Court and on December 22, 1966, the High Court declared the government's action unconstitutional. The following days witnessed fiery debates in the Assembly, the press and among the public, demonstrations and counterdemonstrations. In these circumstances the attempted coup served the government's argumentation. The communists on the other hand at once denied all the allegations. No connections between communists and the insurrectionists could ever be shown. The motives and the aims of the 300 insurgents remained obscure —perhaps they themselves had no clear idea what and whom they were against or for.[22]

[22] *Al-Nahār*, 6 January, 1967: *Cahiers de l'Orient contemporain, LXIV,* février 1967, 38–39; *LXV*, avril 1967, 11–14.

10. YEMEN

UNTIL the middle of this century Yemen, like Tibet, was almost completely sealed off from modern influence. It was a theocratic state under the rule of a parasitic oligarchy, which suppressed and exploited the people in the name of religious authority—the *Sayyids*, the elite of the Zaydi branch of Shiʻi Islam who are venerated as descendants of the Prophet Muḥammad. Estimated to number some 300,000 out of a total population of four and a half million, they are ruled by an Imam whose position parallels that of the Sunni caliph. Imam Aḥmad, who ruled from 1948 to 1962, was the personification of cruelty and reaction. (The following is characteristic of his regime: In 1957 the first factory, a million-dollar weaving plant, was built in Yemen. Just before construction was completed, all work was discontinued at the Imam's orders; the cotton merchants had convinced him that the processing of cotton in the country and the suspension of its sale as a raw material would cause him to lose export tax money.[1])

In 1958, after the unification of Syria and Egypt, Yemen joined the UAR as a member of the United Arab States. The union was a federation in theory and a fiction in practice, but its existence had secured Cairo's blessing for the Imam's Yemen. In December 1961, after the secession of Syria from the UAR, the federation fell apart, and Egypt "discovered" and denounced the reactionary nature of the Yemeni regime. Cairo became the center of activity for Yemeni republican exiles, and the Voice of the Arabs Radio spread their propaganda. They were headed by Dr. ʻAbd al-Raḥmān Bayḍānī, the son of a Yemeni Sunni merchant and an Egyptian mother, who was born and educated in Cairo; his wife is the sister of Anwar Sādāt. From the middle of the 1950's he has successfully played a double—or triple—game as one of the Imam's important advisers, an adherent of the "Free Yemenites" and an Egyptian agent in Yemen. At the end of the 1950's he served as Yemeni ambassador to Bonn where he also received a Ph.D. degree in political economy. After Syria's secession from the UAR and the breach between Yemen and Egypt, he went into exile in Cairo at the

[1] William R. Brown, 'The Yemeni dilemma', *MEJ*, vol. 17, 356-7.

end of 1961, and since early 1962 he has broadcast his speeches from there.[2]

Imam Aḥmad died on September 18, 1962 from wounds suffered in one of the attacks on his life. He was succeeded by his son Badr, who was believed to be inclined toward modernization and to rapprochement with Egypt, unlike his father or his uncle Ḥasan, his rival for the throne. Nevertheless, Egyptian propaganda treated him with animosity as one who was following in his father's footsteps. His regime lasted only a week. On September 26 he was overthrown by a military coup.

On his accession Badr appointed 'Abd-Allāh Sallāl as the commander of his personal guard—and virtually chief of staff of the army. Sallāl was a veteran officer who had been involved in conspiracies against Imam Aḥmad and who had suffered a great deal under his regime, but Badr had no suspicions of Sallāl's revolutionary inclinations and plans. Under the pretext of taking preventive security measures against a plot hatched by Ḥasan and his ultra-conservative followers to overthrow Badr, Sallāl got permission to bring some tanks to the capital. Towards evening on September 26 these tanks attacked Badr's palace, and a republic was proclaimed. The resistance of the palace guard was feeble, but the attackers themselves displayed little military ability. Instead of storming the building, they stopped the tanks at some distance from the palace and began shelling it with cannon. The first shells flew over the roofs without scoring any hits, and it took several hours to capture the palace. In the meantime the Imam managed to escape. Many of his men and some members of his family were killed or executed in the early days of the Republic.

The Republicans wasted no time in announcing that the Imam had been killed. His uncle Ḥasan, who as Yemen's representative to the UN was living in the United States, hurried to Saudi Arabia, proclaimed himself Imam and took command of the Royalist forces. When two weeks later it was clear beyond doubt that Badr was alive, Ḥasan, after some hesitation, recognized him, most certainly under Saudi pressure. The fact that the Imam, the holy ruler, had escaped was regarded by many of the loyal followers of the Zaydi tradition as a sign of divine intercession that lent courage to those fighting the Republic.

Ṣallāl became president, prime minister, commander-in-chief of the armed forces, and head of the Revolutionary Command Council. He was born in San'a in 1917, the son of a smith, a Zaydi of the common people with no ties of blood or marriage with any of the tribes. He attended high school in the port city of Hodeida and then entered the army. In 1936 he was

[2] Harold Ingrams, *The Yemen,* London 1963, 125; J. Heyworth-Dunne, 'Témoignage sur le Yémen', *Orient,* no. 31, 1964, 58-73.

sent to an officers' course in Baghdad together with several other Yemeni cadets—the first Yemeni officer trainees to be sent abroad for further study and the first foreign cadets to be enrolled at the Iraqi Military Academy. At least half of this group, comprising 13 cadets, were afterwards involved in conspirational and insurrectionist activities in Yemen. Among them were Ḥamūd al-Jā'ifī, Sallāl's right-hand man in the coup of 1962, the first Defense Minister of the Republic, from May 1964 to January 1965 prime minister, and in 1965 head of the Supreme Defense Council; Ḥasan al-'Amrī, who from 1965 on became prime minister several times and later one of the leading antagonists of Sallāl; and three others who had been executed or committed suicide in 1948, 1955 and 1961 after participating in various insurrections against Imam Aḥmad. The rebellious nationalist Iraqi officers with whom they studied in 1937 and 1938 (one of the instructors was Qā'uqjī) made a strong impression on the young Yemenis. After his return to Yemen, Sallāl, like his comrades, became involved in several plots against Imam Yaḥyā and Imam Aḥmad. At the beginning of the 1940's he was detained in San'a prison for three months. In 1948 he was involved in the rebellion of 'Abd-Allāh al-Wazīr against Imam Aḥmad, sentenced to death, and held for seven years under atrocious conditions. While he was in prison, books on the French Revolution and Nasser's *Philosophy of the Revolution* were smuggled to him. They strengthened his resolution, but even years later, he did not recover entirely from the injuries to his health caused by imprisonment. At Bayḍānī's initiative and through Badr's intercession he was finally released and appointed director of the port of Hodeida. In March 1962 Imam Aḥmad was wounded in an attempt on his life at Hodeida, and Sallāl was dismissed. Badr, who supported and believed in him, appointed him commander of his body guard and supervisor of the military airport. In the summer of 1962 he was placed in charge of the officers' school at Sana. When Badr became Imam he appointed Sallāl to the position which gave him the opportunity to oust him.[3]

Conspiracies and insurrections were always most common in Yemen, and with the return of the cadet group from Iraq, from 1940 on, the participation of army officers in those activities became ever more conspicuous. But before 1962 no organized and concerted activities of groups of army officers seem to have existed. There were only sporadic acts such as in January 1959 when proclamations signed by "Free Yemeni Army Officers"

[3] *Al-Kulliyya al-'askariyya al-malakiyya,* 1934–1949. Baghdad 1950, 7–8; Ingrams, 119–22, 130–1; Heyworth-Dunne, 71; *Falasṭīn,* Jerusalem, 12 January, 1964; Yael Vered, *Hafikha wa-milḥama be-Teman,* Tel Aviv 1967, 24–7; M. Wenner, *Modern Yemen,* New York 1967, 135–7.

were found in Ta'izz; but the Imam attributed enough importance to this to place the city under martial law.[4]

In September 1962, there were certainly some different conspiracies afoot in Aan'a, and it is impossible to ascertain to which extent the various conspirators knew of and assisted each other's plans. One of the most active among them was 'Alī 'Abd al-Ghanī, a young lieutenant. In the night of the coup he commanded the tanks which attacked the Imam's palace. Some weeks later he was killed in action in the civil war.[5]

The new Yemeni regime was built on two elements: Army officers like Sallāl and al-Jā'ifī, and intellectuals like Baydānī who became Prime Minister, and Muḥsin al'Aynī, Foreign Minister. But the partnership did not last. In January 1963 Bayḍānī went to Cairo and was asked to resign. In Yemen the coup produced a military dictatorship too, but this was the dictatorship of foreign troops—the Egyptian army.

The new Yemeni regime quickly secured the recognition of the Arab republican governments, the countries of the Eastern Bloc, the neutralist states and many western countries, including West Germany (on October 23, 1962) and the United States (on December 19, 1962). Yemeni exiles and emigrés in Aden and Cairo supported it, as did the Shāfi'i Sunnis in Yemen and some of the Zaydis, who believed that the time was ripe for throwing off the yoke of the Sayyids. Opposing them, was the ousted Imam who succeeded in concentrating about him several tribes in the north and east of the country, and even organized a new army. The Royalist forces were commanded by several young sons from his relatives' families who were studying abroad at American and Middle Eastern universities and who had hurried back to Yemen at the beginning of the struggle.[6] These young men fought Sallāl and his Egyptian allies—but they had no desire to restore the country to its previous condition.

The Royalist forces received considerable support from Saudi Arabia and Britain, which controlled until 1967 the shaykhdoms of the Federation of South Arabia. The first Royalist bases were in Saudi Arabia and at Beihan; at the beginning of October regular troops of the Saudi army were deployed on the Yemeni border. But the assistance which Sallāl received from outside had altogether different dimensions. Egypt at once extended considerable political, promotional and technical aid, and several days later began to send troops. The sending of Egyptian forces to Yemen was preceded by a top-level debate, the effects of which could be felt for a long time afterwards. There were some who warned against direct, open

[4] Ingrams, 108.
[5] Dana Adams Schmidt, *Yemen: The unknown war,* London 1968, 22–8.
[6] Neil McLean, 'The war in the Yemen', *Royal Central Asian Journal,* April 1964, 104.

intervention in Yemen, but the activists had the upper hand. The latter were headed by Anwar Sādāt, and Nasser supported him. He certainly had no idea what was in store for him—that it would be a long war which would pin down some of his best troops for five years under very difficult conditions on a distant front. By December 1962 the number of Egyptian soldiers in Yemen exceeded 10,000, and from the spring of 1963 there were always more than 30,000. In August 1965, just before the talks at Jedda between Nasser and King Fayṣal in an attempt to bring peace to Yemen, Egyptian forces there, according to Egyptian sources, consisted of more than three divisions with at least 60,000 men,[7] and this was to remain their number for two more years. Thousands were killed and wounded, and the expenses mounted to hundreds of millions of pounds. Sallāl's regime became almost totally dependent on the Egyptians, and for Egypt Sallāl's presidency became a major issue of its inter-Arab and international prestige. But the huge Egyptian force could not eliminate active opposition to the republican regime. On the contrary, its mere presence increased the opposition of many tribes and other circles. The Egyptian used poison gas in certain military operations and behaved as an aggressive foreign occupation army. By mid-1963 the Egyptians and Sallāl's forces controlled all the big cities and principal transport routes, the latter sometimes only during daylight. However, in the wide-open regions in the north and east the guerrilla warfare of the Zaydi tribes continued. The situation of the Egyptian army in Yemen in some ways resembled that of the French troops in Algeria in 1960.

The course of events and struggles in and around Yemen since 1963 is not the subject of our discussion, which deals with the role of the officer corps of the Arab states in determining policy, for the Yemeni army officers were not even a secondary factor in these tempestuous years. The fighting forces, as well as the partners in the political discussion, were either non-Yemeni, chiefly Egyptians and Saudi Arabians, or tribal Yemenis. The regular Yemeni army and its commanders could carry out a coup, but could not seize power. Sallāl remained the President of the Republic and was allowed to represent Yemen at the Arab summit conferences—but he had become a president without any decision-making power, and even as a figurehead was only superficially recognized by many, while others did not recognize him at all. When the regular army has no real power, its officers cannot rule. Sallāl became ever more the puppet of the Egyptians.

At the fourth Arab Summit Conference in Khartoum in August 1967 after the Six-Day War, Nasser, his army badly beaten and his country

[7] M. Ḥ. Haykal, *al-Ahrām,* 28 July 1965; McLean, 104; L. Alexandros in *Wehr und Wirtschaft,* Darmstadt, May 1966.

greatly weakened, had to promise King Fayṣal of Saudi Arabia to withdraw all Egyptian troops from Yemen. It was not the first time that the Egyptians had made such a promise, but this time they had no choice but to carry it out. In autumn 1967 Egyptian troops were left only at the port town of Hodeida, and in December 1967 the last Egyptian troops left Yemen.

One of the almost immediate results of the Egyptian withdrawal was Sallāl's downfall. Sallāl imagined that without the overbearing presence of the Egyptians his own position vis-à-vis the Yemenis would be stronger. Moreover, he intended to follow a more independent course in foreign politics, too, and this meant non-compliance with the Egyptian-Saudi Arabian compromise on Yemen which had been arrived at in the Khartoum Summit Conference. In nearly all these respects he was mistaken; the Yemenis, almost without distinction of their rival and warring factions, were all eager to get rid of him, and the Egyptians were no longer powerful enough nor even interested enough to support him.

At the beginning of November 1967 Sallāl flew to Moscow via Cairo and Baghdad for political negotiations, and to attend the festivities of the 50th anniversary of the Soviet Revolution. On November 5 at 1 a.m., while he was in Baghdad, infantry and commando forces led by some lieutenant-colonels with the authority of the Army Command surrounded Sallāl's house, the major government offices and the broadcasting station without encountering any resistance. The powers of government were given to a three-men Presidential Council, headed by 'Abd al-Raḥmān al-Iryānī, the 67-year-old distinguished Zaydi judge, who had already been republican prime minister. Its other two members were Muḥammad 'Alī 'Uthmān and Aḥmad Muḥammad Nu'mān, a liberal landowner, the leader of the Shafi'i Sunnis of Yemen. On November, 25, Nu'mān resigned, and his place took General Ḥasan al-'Amrī. Al-'Amrī had gone to Egypt for negotiations in August, 1966, when he was prime minister. But he was not officially received in Cairo, kept virtually under house-arrest there and was forced to resign. He had become the principal republican opponent to Egypt's domination in Yemen. Only after Sallāl's fall he was released from Egyptian captivity.

Sallāl was not allowed to return to Yemen and was granted political asylum in Iraq. The Egyptian government immediately recognized the new Yemeni regime. Sallāl had fallen as he had risen—by a military coup.

11. JORDAN

THE HISTORY of the Hashimite Kingdom of Jordan from its establishment in 1949 until 1962 was stormy. Here, more than in any other state, foreigners intervened, gained influence and joined forces with elements inside the country; the most active forces were the governments of Britain, the United United States, Egypt, Syria, Iraq and Saudi Arabia, as well as all-Arab political parties, particularly the Ba'th and the Muslim Brethren, who were generally directed from the centers in Syria. The Jordanian governments permitted no legal opposition; therefore all those who aspired to change the regime or its international orientation were forced to start conspiracies. These circles generally sought and found aid in governments or parties outside Jordan. Officers of the Arab Legion, the Jordanian army, played a considerable part in opposition activities, but they neither initiated nor participated in the two major acts of terror that shook the state—the assassination of King 'Abd-Allāh in 1951 and the murder of Prime Minister Hazzā' al-Majālī in 1960. Only one of the 16 men accused of the murder of al-Majālī was from the Legion: Second-Lieutenant Hishām al-Dabbās, of the Engineer Corps, a relative of one of the leaders of the conspiracy. He was one of the 11 sentenced to death, seven of them in absentia, and one of the four hanged on December 31, 1960.[1]

Several officer politicans tried to organize and carry out coups during the 1950's. These attempts were smaller in number and scope than in Syria and Iraq; and unlike them all failed. The three main reasons for their failure, in increasing order of importance, were: (a) the personalities of Kings 'Abd-Allāh and Ḥusayn, both of whom demonstrated clear thinking, courage and leadership in critical situations; (b) British command of the Arab Legion until the expulsion of the British officers in March 1956; (c) the special composition of the Legion. More than half, and later nearly half, of the officers, non-commissioned officers and enlisted men were until the 1960's bedouin, who were loyal to the King and to the Hashimite regime. Unlike officers in other Arab countries they neither

[1] *MER* 1960, 328-30.

regard themselves nor are they regarded by others as "intelligentsia in uniform." It is a significant fact that the officer politicians who appeared in Jordanian underground movements were not bedouin but were all of peasant or urban origin.

The failures of the Jordanian officer politicians resulting from a unique character of the Legion do not mean that the army does not occupy a central position in the political structure of the country. On the contrary, if it were not for the army the Hashimite regime could not hold its own in the welter of internal struggles and subversion from the outside. The definition of Jordan as a "royal military dictatorship" holds true.[2] One does, however, have to bear in mind the difference between this dictatorship and the officers' regimes in Iraq, Syria and Egypt. Although the army is the mainstay of the government, the officers do not determine policy.

Nonetheless, as mentioned above, there have been individuals and groups within the Legion who tried to seize power by coup or to overthrow the government by coordinating their activity with a civilian underground. The first of these individuals was 'Abd-Allāh Tall. The Tall family in Irbid produced several public personalities and army officers, and in 1948 'Abd-Allāh was one of the few Legion officers who could be called "an intellectual" in uniform." This may have been the reason why he was singled out by King 'Abd-Allāh. In March 1948 he was promoted to the rank of major, and two months later, at the personal request of the King, to lieutenant-colonel. In the decisive battles for Jerusalem he served as battalion commander in the Old City. In the summer he was appointed military governor and later civil governor of the Jerusalem district.

It is not clear when he fell out with the King. In his memoirs he writes that as early as the summer of 1948 he was already strongly opposed to 'Abd-Allāh's moderate policy. But the book, which appeared in Egypt in 1959, is tendentious and not entirely accurate. Anyhow, 'Abd-Allāh Tall was the King's chief emissary in his contacts with Israel, although he was already close to the Jordanian Ba'thists and extremist Palestine nationalists. By the beginning of 1949 his anti-Hashimite and anti-British views were quite consolidated. Za'īm's coup in Syria at the end of March made an impression on him and his circle, "and was a reason for advancing thinking to the stage of execution."[3] On the very next day after the coup, on April 1, 'Abd-Allāh Tall met Ḥusnī Za'īm in Damascus—ostensibly in order to deliver a letter from the King, but actually for the purpose of securing Syrian aid in deposing him. Tall relates that Za'īm agreed to imprison the

[2] S.E. Finer, *The man on horseback,* London, 1962, 2.

[3] 'Abd-Allāh al-Tall, *Kārithat Falasṭīn,* Cairo 1959, 588.

ousted King in the Deir ez-Zor Desert.[4] Tall's views did not remain secret, and in May 1949 the King transferred him from Jerusalem to London where he was given a post as military attaché. Tall refused to be put on ice politically and on June 7 he resigned. For the next three months he lived in his house at Irbid. After Za'īm's expulsion Tall hastily and covertly contacted his successor, Ḥinnāwī. However, on becoming aware of Ḥinnāwī's pro-Hashimite orientation, he turned to Egypt and secretly visited Cairo in September. He had always thought the prospect of a coup in Jordan to be dependent on outside support. On October 5, 1949 he and his family fled Jordan and after a five-day stay in Damascus settled in Cairo where he remained active for 15 years. In Damascus he met Michel 'Aflaq. In Cairo he worked first with the Mufti. In August 1951 a Jordanian court sentenced him to death in absentia for complicity in the murder of King 'Abd-Allāh. Later, when both the Mufti and the Ba'th had fallen from favor in Egypt, Tall was one of the few Jordanian and Syrian exiles in Egypt who were close to Nasser. For him Nasser's Egypt was "our great homeland; the delight of free men."[5]

The second Jordanian officer who tried to overthrow the Hashimite Kingdom, 'Alī Abū Nuwār, was born in the Jordanian town of Salt and he, like 'Abd-Allāh Tall, received promotion as the King's protégé. In 1948 he was a lieutenant in the Palestine War.[6] Later he became a member of the Jordanian delegation at the armistice negotiations held in Rhodes, attended a staff officers' course in England and served as military attaché in France. In Paris he became a friend of Tharwat 'Ukāsha, a veteran member of the Egyptian Free Officers, who was military attaché at the embassy. He also became friendly with young King Ḥusayn who was there on vacation. In November 1955 he was appointed the King's adjutant. He no doubt influenced the King's decision to dismiss Glubb and other British commanders in the Legion; and on getting rid of them in March 1956, he took command of the army in western Jordan. Three months later, in May, he became chief of staff. He was 33 then, and in half a year had risen from major to major-general. Camille Chamoun, President of Lebanon, met him in the summer of 1956 and tells that already then "he certainly made no secret of his admiration for the Egyptian dictator."[7] His leanings were also known to officers of the Legion[8], but it is not clear when he made up his mind to turn against the King. An underground organization of the Young

[4] *Ibid.*, 589.

[5] *Ibid.*, 599.

[6] 'Ārif al-'Ārif, *Al-Nakba*, vol. 6: *Sijill al-khulūd*, Sidon and Beirut 1962, 183.

[7] Camille Chamoun, *Crise au Moyen-Orient*, Paris 1963, 326.

[8] *Hamizrah Hehadash*, vol. 7, 292.

Officers' Movement in the Legion was already functioning in 1954, and in January 1956 leaflets decrying the Baghdad Pact and the Legion's British officers were distributed in the name of the "Free Officers' Association,"[9]

In the spring of 1957 the opposition in Jordan joined forces for a turbulent struggle against the regime. Glubb had already been out of office for a year. After nationalization of the Suez Canal and the evacuation of Port Said, Sinai and the Gaza Strip by Israeli, British and French troops, Nasser was at the height of his glory. For the first time a neutralist government was in power in Jordan under Sulaymān Nābulsī. It had the backing of both left-wing and pan-Arab circles. King Ḥusayn saw that power was about to slip from his hands to anti-western elements and ultimately to Nasser, and he decided to check this development in time. Early in February he ordered his government, despite its neutralist policy, to prohibit the free distribution of material from the Soviet press. Nevertheless, at the beginning of April the government decided to establish diplomatic relations with the USSR and the crisis reached a peak. At about this time, on April 7, an attempted rebellion was quelled in the army. An armored car unit began to move on the capital from Zarqa, 17 miles away. Asked what this meant, the Prime Minister and Minister of Defense replied that they knew nothing of the movement. In answer to a query, 'Alī Abū-Nuwār, the Chief of Staff, claimed that it was a training exercise and nothing more. However, Ḥusayn ordered that the armored cars be returned to base, and that is how the matter ended—for the time being.[10] On April 10 the Prime Minister suggested that the King dismiss 20 senior officials who were loyal to the monarchy. Instead the King dissolved the government.

The population reacted violently to Nābulsī's dismissal, and it was difficult to find a new prime minister who would do the King's bidding. On April 13 crowds demonstrated in Amman, shouting anti-American slogans with clear anti-Hashimite undertones. On the same day an attempt was made to carry out a military coup. Toward evening Colonel Ma'ān Abū Nuwār, a cousin of the Chief of Staff, was about to leave Zarqa for Amman with a battalion of artillery. When the Third Battalion, consisting of bedouin, learned of this, they surrounded the camp and did not let the rebels through. The hostile units did not remain static and fighting broke out between the Legion battalions; at least three officers on Abū Nuwār's side were killed and several were wounded.[11]

At midnight Ḥusayn summoned 'Alī Abū Nuwār and they drove to Zarqa together by car. On the way they met a company of bedouin from

[9] Peter Young, *Bedouin command,* London 1956, 173–4.

[10] J.B. Glubb, *A soldier with the Arabs,* London 1957, 434.

[11] *Hamizrah Hehadash,* vol. 8, 308; *MEJ,* vol. 11, 297.

the Legion hurrying to the capital to protect the King. On recognizing the passengers in the car, they cheered the King but wanted to kill Abū Nuwār. Ḥusayn ordered Abū Nuwār to return to Amman while he continued on his way to Zarqa escorted by the bedouin. He entered the camp as a victor. He drew attention to the fact that as a member of the Hashimite family he is a descendent of Muḥammad, and he castigated the rebel officers for raising their hands against one of the Prophet's sons. He did not let the matter go just at a rebuke, and more than 20 officers at Zarqa and Amman were imprisoned. According to Glubb—a statement that was certainly not unfounded—14 of them were receiving large monthly pay packets from Egypt.[12] On the next morning Ḥusayn returned to the capital at the head of a strong force consisting of bedouin units, armored cars and artillery. The leaders of the opposition were placed under house-arrest. 'Alī Abū Nuwār was dismissed as chief of staff. He was allowed to leave the country and on the same day went to Egypt via Syria and joined the Free Jordanians there.

'Alī Ḥiyārī, a fellow townsman of Abū Nuwār and of the same age, was appointed chief of staff.[13] In the course of his new position he went to Damascus where he announced his resignation only three days after his appointment. He, too, joined the exiles in Cairo. He was replaced by Ḥābis al-Majālī, who remained in office until 1965.

Ḥusayn's courage and especially the loyalty of the bedouin saved the regime for some length of time. However, several years passed before it became clear that the King's victory had been conclusive. For a long time the regime rested on feet of clay; there were recurring subversive plots and coups and on a number of occasions officers either led them or participated in them. Two of these incidents can be mentioned here.

Maḥmūd Rusān, also of Jordanian non-bedouin extraction, is a member of a large family from the district of 'Ajlūn.[14] In 1948 he was a captain and staff officer in the Fourth Battalion, which fought at Latrun.[15] In 1956 he was a lieutenant-colonel. His views resembled Abū-Nuwār's, but he fell out with him and his friends when they obtained central command posts after Glubb's dismissal, despite the fact that Rusān had been in service longer.[16] Rusān was arrested, and in June 1956 sentenced to three years' imprisonment; several other officers were sentenced with him. However, Rusān was freed, transferred to the foreign service and appointed ambas-

[12] Glubb, *loc. cit.*

[13] 'Ārif al-'Ārif, 181; Young 185.

[14] *MER* 1960, 327.

[15] *Be'eyney oyev,* Tel Aviv 1954, 123-217.

[16] *Hamizrah Hehadash,* vol. 7, 292.

sador to the United States.[17] After the Iraqi coup in July 1958 he was again arrested, together with 11 others majors and colonels and four civilians, and sentenced to 10 years' imprisonment.[18]

In May 1959 another pro-Egyptian conspiracy among Legion officers was discovered and an entire group arrested. They were headed by the Deputy Chief of Staff, Major-General Ṣādiq al-Shar'. Al-Shar', like 'Abd-Allāh Tall, was a native of Irbid. In 1948, at the age of 31, he was a captain and operations officer in the First Brigade. In 1955 he finished a course for staff officers at Camberley. On his return he criticized England for the power he claimed the Jews had there. He was not known to support 'Alī Abū Nuwār's movement, but by 1958 Ḥusayn began to suspect him. After his arrest he was sentenced to death in July 1959 but the sentence was not carried out. In the summer of 1963 he was released from prison and allowed to accept the post of military adviser in Kuwait.[19]

The Cairo exiles were organized into a Jordanian "Revolutionary Council." In the spring of 1963 its members consisted of five civilians and five officers: 'Abd-Allāh Tall, 'Alī Abū-Nuwār, 'Alī Ḥiyārī, Ṣubḥī Tūqān and Maḥmūd Mūsā.[20] Maḥmūd Mūsā attained the rank of colonel in the Legion and fled from Jordan after 1957.[21] Ṣubḥī Ṭūqān, who was born in Nablus, served as an officer in the Palestine Police until May 1948.

In mid-1963 and during the Arab summit conferences there was a rapprochement between Nasser and Ḥusayn, and the exiles in Cairo became more of a burden than a help to the Egyptian government. Nasser no longer tried to overthrow Ḥusayn, and the prospects of the Jordanian Revolutionary Council, which were flimsy anyway, completely vanished. Nasser climbed down because Egyptian attempts to dominate in most of the Arab countries had failed. King Ḥusayn, contrary to all expectations, survived his numerous rivals, and the exiled Jordanian officer politicians folded up their flag. At the end of 1964 they were amnestied and in 1965 'Abd-Allāh Tall, Abū Nuwār and Ḥiyārī returned to Jordan as repatriates and penitents. Ḥusayn could afford this generous gesture: They were no longer dangerous.

[17] *Ibid.*, vol. 8, 58.

[18] *MER* 1960, 327-8.

[19] *Hamizrah Hehadash*, vol. 10, 368; *MER* 1960, 327; 'Ārif al-'Ārif, 183; *al-usbū' al-'arabī*, Beirut, 3 August, 1964.

[20] *Sawt al-'urūba*, Beirut, 30 April, 1963.

[21] 'Abd-Allāh al-Tall, 103; Young, 62.

12. LEBANON

LEBANON differs from all other Arab countries. It is the only one in which the Muslims have no clear majority. The average per capita income in Lebanon is more than twice as high as in any other Middle Eastern country with the exception of Israel, and the inhabitants enjoy much greater social freedom and a higher cultural level. The existence of Israel contributes to Lebanon's independence, although this is not admitted. Lebanon is also the only country which derives economic benefit from the Arab boycott against Israel.[1]

Lebanon with its numerous communities has no official state religion, and political life is conducted in accordance with the unwritten National Charter of 1943. It is generally accepted that a little more than half of the inhabitants belongs to various Christian communities. The Chamber of Deputies is elected on a community basis—for every five Muslim and Druze deputies there are always six Christians, so that the total number is always a product of 11. At first there were 55, at one time 77, at another time 44, and 66, and now 99. The President is a Maronite Christian, the Prime Minister a Sunni Muslim, the parliamentary speaker a Shi'ite Muslim, and the commander-in-chief a Druze. However, it is doubtful that a Christian majority still exists. It is possible that the greater rate of natural increase of the Muslims and Druze, immigration of Syrian Muslims into Lebanon and the emigration of Lebanese Christians to lands across the sea has rendered the Christian majority a fiction. In order not to upset the status quo there has been no population census in Lebanon since 1932.

One of the underlying priciples of Lebanese life is the limited size of the army. Together with the gendarmerie, it consisted of only 10,000 men in 1965. Should the Lebanese be mobilized either through conscription or by calling for volunteers, the Christians would remain conspicuously in the minority, a prospect intolerable to them. Neither do the Lebanese harbor

[1] M. Shefer, 'Hashpa'at ha-qera' ha-kalkali ha-'arawi-yisra'eli 'al kalkalat artsot 'araw', *Hamizrah Hehadash,* vol. 14, 158–84; Michael Shefer, 'Les conséquences du boycottage arabe sur les économies arabes et israéliennes', *Les Temps Modern,* No. 253 Bis, Paris 1967, 925–67.

any illusions about the value of their army in war, even if it were larger, and they prefer to spend their money on more remunerative matters. In consequence, the officer corps and army in the Lebanon played a different role than those in other Arab countries. When it became part of internal politics, it did not tear down the constitution but acted to preserve it.

Since the evacuation of the French forces in 1946 the commander of the Lebanese army has been Major-General Fu'ād Shihāb, a scion of one of the country's most prominent Maronite families. Born in 1903, he received his general and military education in the 1920's at the military school in Damascus, the Saint-Cyr Academy, and L'Ecole Supérieure de Guerre in France. He then served with the French mandatory forces. His wife is French.

Shihāb first appeared in Lebanese internal affairs in September 1952. General political ferment had mounted against a background of severe economic crisis accompanied by unemployment and soaring prices. The prime target for criticism was President Bishāra al-Khūrī, who introduced a system of corruption and abetted the accumulation of wealth by members of his own family. On September 15 a general strike was declared to back a demand that the President resign. Prime Minister Ṣā'ib Slām also demanded al-Khūrī's resignation. On September 17 the President asked Ḥusayn 'Uwaynī to form a government. The latter consented on condition that he had the support of Shihāb and the army and could rely on the army's aid in suppressing the strike. But Shihāb made it clear that the army was not prepared to go beyond the confines of the law and that they would not spill Lebanese blood. This reply decided Bishāra al-Khūrī's fate. On September 1 at 2 a.m. he resigned. His final political move was to appoint Shihāb Prime Minister, Minister of the Interior, and Minister of Defense.

Shihāb looked upon his government only as a brief caretaker regime and even refused to be nominated a candidate for the presidency. In an announcement to the people he stated: "I took over the government in accordance with the constitution ... so that the Chamber of Deputies, which is the legal authority in the country, could elected the President of the Republic."[2] On September 23 Camille Chamoun was elected President whereupon Fu'ād Shihād resigned and returned to the army. He had assumed a political role as commander of the armed forces in an emergency and for the purpose of keeping the army out of politics.

This was also his attitude during the Lebanese civil war in 1958. Once more a crisis centered on the personality of the President. The Lebanese constitution prohibits reelection after a six-year term. Chamoun had in the

[2] *Al-Ḥayāt,* 19 September 1952.

meantime shown himself to be extremely pro-western, with undue personal ambition and a wish to change the constitution so that he could be re-elected. This was not the only reason for the civil war, but once he renounced this intention, the war ended. He was compelled to yield to internal opposition as well as to pressure from the UAR on the one hand and from the United States on the other. The Lebanese army refused to intervene in the fighting, and during the half year from March to July 1958 it was the only public element in the country that neither fired a shot nor was shot at. One of the considerations of its commander, Shihāb, must have been the desire to preserve the army's very existence. In any case, this tiny army would not have had the power to bring about a decision, and if its officers had received an order to take action, it probably would have split up like the rest of the population and fallen apart. Thanks to its nonintervention it remained the only body that wielded authority in the country, and its commander could assume the role of arbitrator, acceptable to all parties.[3] After Chamoun announced that he would not stand for the presidency again, Shihāb was elected President. He achieved this primarily as commander of the army, but unlike other officers who are heads of state in the Arab world, he was elected legally. He had said, "It is not me whom the Lebanese have elected; I only represented their inability to elect someone else."[4] These are not the words of a military dictator.

Some observers regarded the election of an army commander to the presidency as one of the ramifications of army seizures of power in Arab states. Two weeks before Shihāb's election, Qassim had made his coup in Iraq, and three months later 'Abbūd's took place in Sudan. But the similarity is only superficial: Shihāb's presidency was precisely the opposite to military dictatorship.

This was finally demonstrated in the summer of 1964 at the expiration of Shihāb's six-year term. Unlike his predecessors he was respected inside and outside Lebanon and there were many who urged him to continue in office. Had he agreed, it would have been possible to muster the two-thirds majority in the Assembly required to change the constitution. But he insisted on leaving the presidency and did so. On August 18 Charles Ḥilū was elected the fourth President of Lebanon. On September 23 he was sworn in, and Shihāb retired from public life.

Lebanon was not spared an attempted military coup along accepted Arab lines. However, the fact that it was small in scope and failed speedily

[3] Kamal Salibi, 'Lebanon and Fuad Chehab, 1958–1964', *Middle Eastern Studies,* London, April 1966, 211–26.

[4] Pierre Rondot, 'Quelques réflexions sur l'expérience politique du 'chéhabisme' au Liban', *Orient,* no. 16, 1960, 46.

demonstrated how different circumstances are in Lebanon.

The conspirators were a number of junior officers, members of the SSNP—The Syrian Social Nationalist Party. The idea of a coup first cropped up in the summer of 1961 at a meeting between Dr. ʻAbd-Allāh Saʻāda, the party's "leader" since 1960 (but not Anṭūn Saʻāda's brother), and Captain Shawqī Khayr-Allāh. The success of the Syrian officers in seceeding from the UAR at the end of September encouraged the SSNP to prepare a coup in Lebanon. As usual, military and civilian elements hoped that each would be decisive in the new regime. The plotters knew more clearly what they were against than what they positively wanted. They were anti-feudal, anti-Egyptian, anti-communist, anti-sectarian and especially opposed to an increase in Muslim influence in Lebanon. The final but absolutely illusory aim was, according to party doctrine, the establishment of a state of "Syria within its natural boundaries" consisting of Lebanon, Syria, Jordan and Iraq, based on secularism and opposed to Arab nationalism.[5] The organizational preparations for the coup, the allocation of posts to army and party units for the occupation of government buildings and the arrest of military and civilian leaders were detailed. The date was set for the night of December 30, 1961, when most of the officers would be on leave.

At 9 p.m. on December 30, Captain Fu'ād ʻAwāḍ moved his company, consisting of 90 men in 13 armored cars and nine jeeps, from Tyre to Beirut. They arrived at their destination at about 2 a.m. and were joined by Captain Khayr-Allāh and some 20 armed party members. On entering the Ministry of Defense they succeeded in occupying the ground floor, but loyal officers in the upper storey refused to surrender and alerted other forces in the town. After an exchange of fire within the building, the rebels retreated and at about 4 a.m. fled from Beirut. Other attempts to occupy strategic posts in the capital and to arrest officials also met resistance and failed. A group of 17 SSNP members, however, succeeded in arresting Brigadier Yūsuf Shumayyiṭ, the Chief of Staff, and Colonel ʻAbd al-Qādir Shihāb in their homes. They killed three soldiers and wounded two during the operation. On their retreat from Beirut the rebels took the kidnapped officers along; eventually they freed them on the road in the Matn region on the afternoon of December 31.

The rebels concentrated in the mountain village of Dik al-Mahdi, some eight miles from Beirut, the home of Asʻad al-Ashqar, one of the SSNP's Higher Council, whose house had been the party's main arms

[5] Labib Zuwiyya-Yamak. *The Syrian Social Nationalist Party, An ideological analysis,* Cambridge, Mass., 1966, *passim.*

store. The village was cordoned off by government troops. After two hours of firing some of the rebels fled, but those who remained surrendered only the next day after al-Ashqar's house had been shelled. Sporadic resistance continued in the mountains near Dik al-Mahdi until January 3, 1962. On January 1 the SSNP was outlawed in Lebanon.

There were heavy casualties. According to an official statement the number of killed mounted to 27, six of them members of the security forces, two Lebanese members of the SSNP, and 19 foreign nationals, mostly Syrians and Palestine refugees and members of the SSNP. More than 2,400 people were detained. Khayr-Allāh was arrested on January 11 in Beirut, and 'Awaḍ on January 20.[6] In November 1963 they were sentenced to death together with six others; the sentences were later commuted to life imprisonment.

The uniqueness of the Lebanese coup lies in the close cooperation of the army officers with a civilian party leadership. Why the party leaders sought the assistance of the military requires no further explanation. The officers sought the aid of the politicians less from their loyalty to the doctrines and the organizational build-up of the party than from their realistic appreciation of the Lebanese army's intrinsic weakness. Another prominent feature of the coup was the large number of non-Lebanese helping the insurgents. Among the 323 civilians named in the bill of indictment on May 9, 1962 there were 54 Syrians and 20 Palestinian refugees. Among the 21 civilians killed, 19 were non-Lebanese. One of the results of the abortive coup was the adoption of tighter measures by the Lebanese government during 1962 to keep the refugees under surveillance.

The whole coup was somehow of "farcical nature . . . The lunatic fringe aspect was strongly in evidence."[7] The episode rang down the curtain on the SSNP.

[6] Pierre Rondot, 'Le mouvement du 31 décembre 1961 au Liban', *Orient,* no. 34, 1965, 7–24; *MER* 1961, 398–404; *MEJ,* vol. 16, 1962, 200.

[7] *The Economist,* London, 6 January, 1962.

PART TWO

PATTERNS OF THE MILITARY COUPS

Hillel saw a skull floating on the face of the water. He said to it: Because you didst drown others they drowned thee, and the end of those that drowned thee will be that they will be drowned.

The Saying of the Fathers, II, 6.

1. DEFINITIONS AND CLASSIFICATION

THE SEIZURES and attempted seizures of power by Arab army officers have become so increasingly frequent during the middle third of the twentieth century that some effort to classify them by type is now indicated. Such classification might help to clarify some general questions:

Why has army rule become the conventional form of government in certain Arab countries?

Is the occurrence of military coups and officers' government to be regarded as a historic necessity?

Can any periodicity in the occurrence and in the frequency of military coups be discerned?

Which are the similarities and the peculiarities of the different coups in the various countries?

What decides if a coup succeeds or fails to achieve its aims?

All classification, of course, is bound to be somewhat schematic, emphasizing those aspects of one phenomenon common to other phenomena while disregarding those aspects that are transient or unique. This is the method pursued by any theoretical reasoning, and particularly by sociological inquiry, which seeks to determine the laws that interconnect the phenomena under investigation.

There were more than 35 coups and coup attempts by Arab army officers during the middle third of the twentieth century that lend themselves to tabulation. Several criteria determine which of them fall within the scope of our scheme.

To begin with, it is necessary to distinguish between military rule and civil government headed by a military man. A general as president does not in itself signify the existence of government by the military. Within the last hundred years—we need not refer back to earlier periods—there has been more than one instance of civil government headed by a military personage. Presidents Grant (1869–77) and Eisenhower (1953–61) in the United States, MacMahon (1873–79) in France and Hindenburg (1925–34) in Germany were former generals who rose to office after achieving military fame. However, they were elected to the presidency according to established constitutional procedure. In exercising their authority they relied on the army no more than had their predecessors in office. They did not seize power by coup, military or otherwise, and did not maintain any military rule, nor did they seek to remain in office on expiration of their term. This does not mean that these men were exemplary democrats or outstanding progressives, but neither were they military dictators. Fu'ād Shihāb, President of Lebanon from 1958 to 1964, is in this category.

The case of General de Gaulle is unique. His rise to the presidency of France in 1958 was the direct outcome of a military mutiny headed by Massu and Salan. Yet, not being on active service at the time, he held no position of command in the army. In April 1961, when Generals Challe, Zeller, Jouhaud and Salan revolted with the object of imposing upon him the will of the *colons* and the army in Algeria, he repudiated them and crushed that military revolt.

Hence a system that originates from a military insurrection does not always constitute a military dictatorship. In Syria, too, the regime that succeeded the Shīshaklī government in 1954 on the crest of a military revolt and lasted until 1958 was a parliamentary one, even though the army officers' frequent and increasing interventions determined—and distorted—matters to no small extent.

The following table of coups and abortive coups by Arab officers *does not include* the following:

a) Governments headed by military men acting in accordance with the national constitution in force at the time. For example, the premiership of Nūr al-Dīn Maḥmūd, the Iraqi Chief of Staff, from November 1952 until January 1953; Shihāb's premiership in Lebanon in 1952 and his presidency from 1958 to 1964.

b) Groupings and underground activities of officers that were not direct attempts at seizing power. For example, the pro-German underground in the Egyptian army in 1941 and 1942; and the activities of 'Abd-Allāh Tall against the Jordanian kings.

c) Preparations for military coups that were cancelled, discovered or frustrated before their scheduled date of execution and which gave rise to no action. For example, the conspiracy of the Iraqi pilots to overthrow Arif in September 1964.

d) Uprisings not initiated by army officers. For example, the popular rebellion in Jordan in December 1955 against that country's becoming a member of the Baghdad Pact; the disturbances and strikes in Syria in April 1964; the Sudanese revolt of October 1964, putting an end to the military dictatorship of 'Abbūd.

On the other hand, the table includes insurrectionist activities of officers

Egyptian Mamelukes at the end of the 18th century, based on drawings by C. Vernet

Muḥammad ʻAlī

Sulaymān al-Faransāwī
(Octave Sève)

Aḥmad ʻUrābī

The commanders of the Arab Revolt in a camp near Aqaba, 1917
The first rider on the right is Ja'far al-'Askarī, the second, Fayṣal

'Alī Jawdat al-Ayūbī, Ja'far al-'Askarī and Nūrī Sa'īd
as Ottoman officers

Ḥusayn Fawzī

Bakr Ṣidqī

Ṣalāḥ al-Dīn Ṣabbāgh

Fahmī Sa'īd

Maḥmūd Salmān

Rashād Muhannā

'Azīz 'Alī al-Maṣrī

Aḥmad 'Abd al-'Azīz

18, Kanawaty, Bacos, Alexandria, the house in which Nasser's parents lived at the time of his birth

Nasser standing between his father (left) and his uncle Khalīl Ḥusayn and his brothers Shawqī, 'Izz al-'Arab and Līthī

End of July, 1952: Baghdādī, Nasser, Kamāl al-Dīn Ḥusayn, 'Āmir, Naguib and Ḥasan Ibrāhīm

Naguib and Nasser, 1953

The Revolutionary Command Council on the day of the proclamation of the Egyptian Republic, June 18, 1953.
Sitting: Baghdādī, Nasser, Naguib, ʻĀmir, Ṣalāḥ Sālim, Sādāt.
Standing: Shāfiʻī, Khālid Muḥī al-Dīn, Jamāl Sālim, Kamāl al-Dīn Ḥusayn, Ḥasan Ibrāhīm, Zakariyyā Muḥī al-Dīn

The commanders of the Egyptian Air Force during the Six-Day War on trial before a military court, October 1967: Air Marshal General Muḥammad Ṣidqī Sulaymān, Commander of the Air Force, General Jamāl 'Afīfī, Chief of Staff of the Air Force, Major-General 'Abd al-Ḥamīd Daghīdī, Commander of the Eastern Air Region, Major-General Ismā'īl Labīb, Commander of Anti-Air Defense

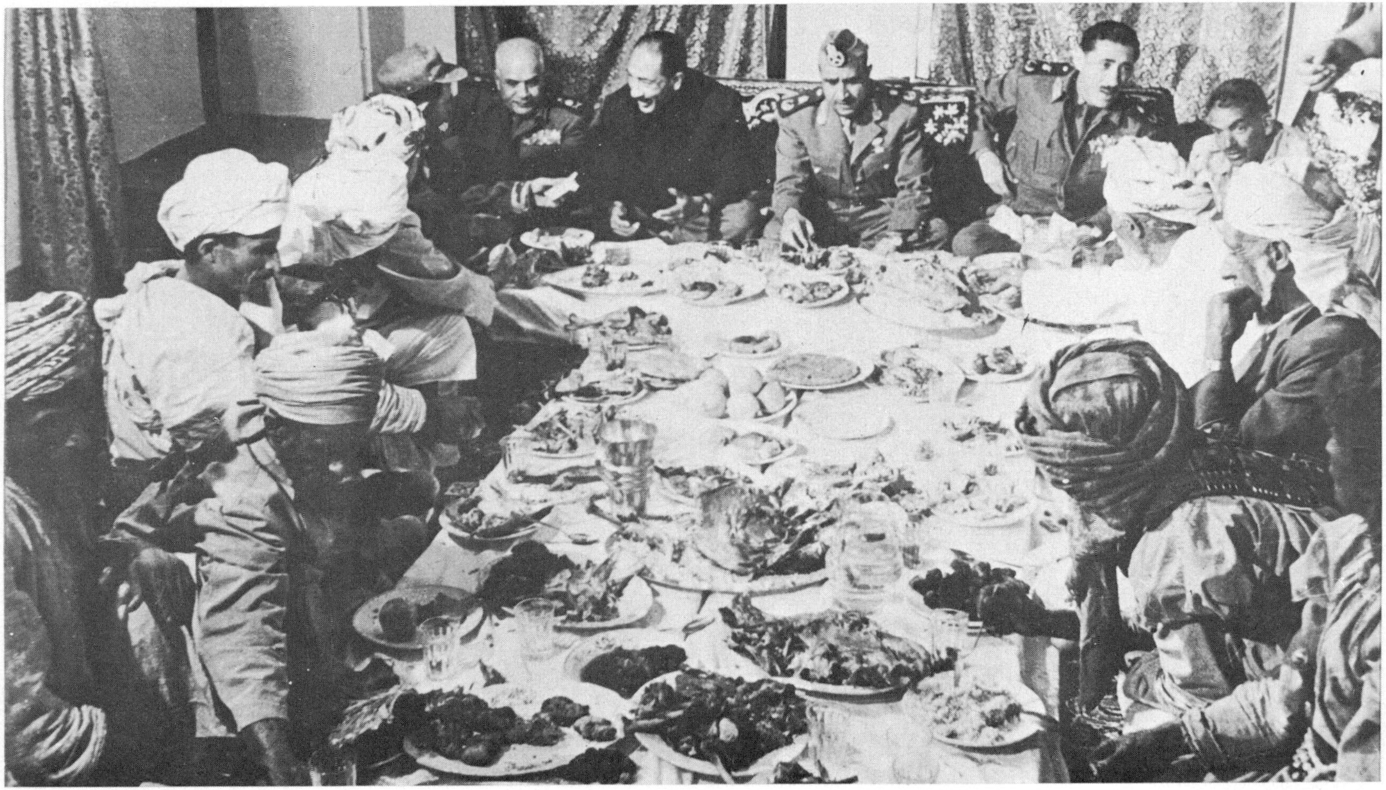

Marshal ‘Āmir, Sādāt and General ‘Alī ‘Alī ‘Āmir, the Egyptian Chief of Staff, as guests of Sallāl in San‘a, end of January, 1963

Ḥusnī Za'īm

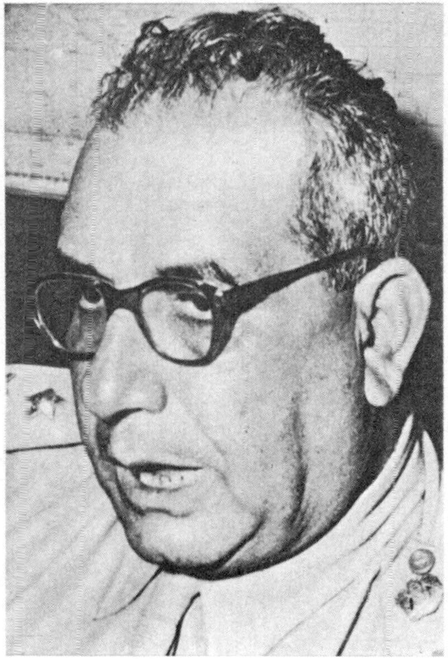

Sāmī Ḥinnāwī

Adīb Shīshaklī

Ghassān Jadīd

'Adnān Mālikī

'Afīf Bizrī

Muḥammad ʻUmrān

Ziyād Ḥarīrī

Ṣalāḥ Jadīd and Michel ʻAflaq

Lū'ay Atāsī, President of the Syrian National Council, on his arrival in Cairo with the Egyptian Prime Minister 'Alī Ṣabrī, listening to the national anthems, July 18, 1963

Amīn al-Ḥāfiẓ (saluting) and Fahad al-Shā'ir, 1964

Ḥāfiẓ Asad, 1966

Qassim and Arif, 1958

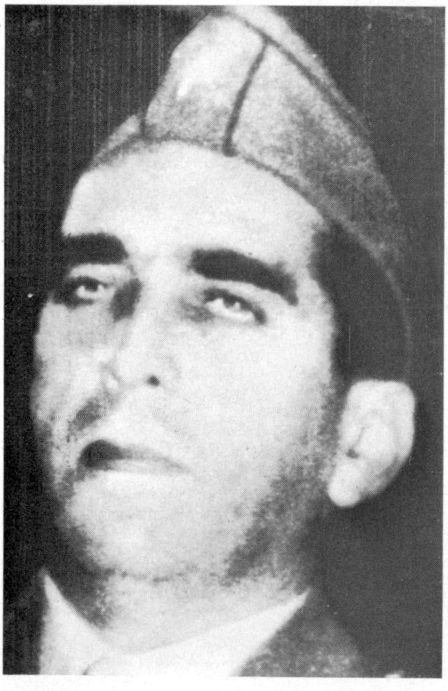

Shawwāf

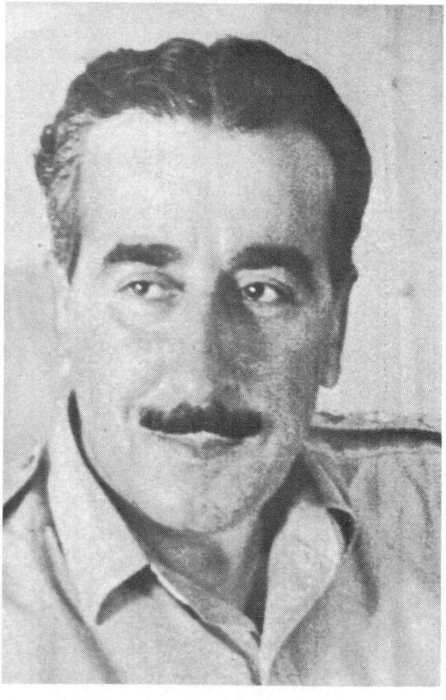

Ṭabaqjalī

'Ārif 'Abd al-Razzāq, under arrest after the failure of his coup in 1965

Mundhir Windāwī

Ṭahir Yaḥyā

Aḥmad Ḥasan al-Bakr, 1968

'Abd-Allāh Tall, 1948

'Alī Abū Nuwār, 1956

Ibrāhīm ʻAbbūd, 1958

that led to a seizure of power or succeeded in forcing the government to implement a certain policy, even though they were achieved with only a threat of military action, such as that of the seven Iraqi officers who, in 1939, compelled the political leaders to appoint ʻAbd al-Ilāh as regent. Coups and attempted coups of this sort are included in this discussion whether or not they succeeded and whether or not they were actually carried out openly or implemented without the knowledge of the general population.

Thus, the table lists *attempts of Arab army officers calculated to seize power in a coup or force a certain policy on the government whether they succeeded or failed.* These coups and abortive coups are not mere interference of officers in politics and not the utilization of military force for the sake of personal prestige. They are the utilization of military force by commanders of the entire army or certain units, and its application by violence or threats of violence for the purpose of establishing governing processes and policies against the existing constitution and in order to set up a regime in which army commanders have the supreme decision-making authority either entirely on their own or in cooperation with civilian elements.

The recurrence of Arab military coups lends one to investigate the laws governing their advent, frequency and character. However, such inquiries constantly expose one to two risks: On the one hand, an involved formulation of simple, self-evident data; and on the other hand *petitio principii*—arbitrary generalization of some facts and the ignoring of others in order to make the whole fit a theory, or, in other words, employing the sought-after conclusion as a demonstration of its own validity.

Thus, in his article on "The military in Middle Eastern society and politics" D.A. Rustow writes:

> "There is a remarkable parallel in the timing of the initial military coups in Iraq, Syria and Egypt. Iraq was released from mandate status in 1932; in 1936, General Bakr Ṣidqī performed his military coup, which in the next five years was to be followed by six others. In Syria, French occupation was withdrawn in mid-1945; in 1949 there were three successive military coups under Colonels Zaʻīm, Ḥinnāwī and Shīshaklī. In 1947 the British discontinued their wartime occupation of Egypt proper, concentrating their remaining troops in the Canal Zone; in 1952 the Free Officers seized power under General Naguib and Colonel Nasser. It is obvious that a military seizure of power by indigenous officers will not occur during foreign occupation; a colonial regime may expect mutinies as in India in 1857, but not *coups d'état*. The Middle Eastern evidence would seem to suggest that it takes four to five years after *de facto* independence

ARAB OFFICERS' COUPS AND ATTEMPTED COUPS

No.	*Date*	*Country*	*Leaders*	*Qualifications of the leaders and collaborators*	*Adversary*	*Method*	*Public reaction*	*Result*	*Objectives and Outcome*
					Up to and during World War II				
1	29 Oct 36	Iraq	Bakr Ṣidqī	Acting Chief of Staff in collaboration with *Al-Ahālī* leaders	Constitutional monarchy	Unopposed military action	Passive	Success	Moderate reforms, not achieved. Military patronage of civilian government becomes open military dictatorship
2	11 Aug 37	Iraq	Yāmulkī	Field officers	Military dictatorship	Assassination and unopposed revolt of army units	Passive	Success	Restitution of former regime and relative stability
3	24 Dec 38	Iraq	The Seven	Field officers in complicity with Nūrī Sa'īd	Constitutional monarchy	Army alert and threat of action	Passive, unaware of events	Success	Appointment of Nūrī Sa'īd to premiership
4	5 Apr 39	Iraq	The Seven	Field officers	Constitutional monarchy	Pressure and threats	Passive, unaware of events	Success	Appointment of 'Abd al-Ilāh to regency
5	21 Feb 40	Iraq	The Golden Square	General and field officers	Constitutional monarchy and rival group of officers	Split in army and alarm for action	Passive, unaware of events	Success	New government of Nūrī Sa'īd
6	1 Feb 41	Iraq	The Golden Square	General and field officers connected with the Mufti and Rashīd 'Ālī al-Kaylānī	Constitutional monarchy	Threat of army revolt	Passive	Success	New government dependent on military and civil nationalist extremists
7	3 Apr 41	Iraq	The Golden Square and Rashīd 'Ālī al-Kaylānī	Army Command and extremist nationalists	Constitutional monarchy	Unopposed military revolt	Passive and favorable	Success	Government of Rashīd 'Ālī al-Kaylānī, dependent on pan-Arab and pro-German extremists, war and defeat

No.	*Date*	*Country*	*Leaders*	*Qualifications of the leaders and collaborators*	*Adversary*	*Method*	*Public reaction*	*Result*	*Objectives and Outcome*
					After the Palestine War of 1948				
8	30 Mar 49	Syria	Ḥusnī Za'īm	Army Command	Constitutional republic	Unopposed military action	Passive	Success	Moderate reforms, rapprochement towards France, swift development towards open military dictatorship
9	14 Aug 49	Syria	Sāmī Ḥinnāwī	General staff of army and general officers	Military dictatorship	Unopposed military action and executions	Passive	Success	Domination of Military Council and the People's Party, pro-Hashimite and and pro-British international orientation
10	19 Dec 49	Syria	Adīb Shīshaklī	Command of division, in cooperation with Akram Hawrānī	Unstable parliamentary regime, dependent on the military	Military action, against feeble and short-lived opposition	Passive	Success	Gradual transition from civil government dependent on army to open military dictatorship
11	21 Nov 51	Syria	Adīb Shīshaklī	Military dictator	President and government, dependent on army, deposed	Arrests	Passive	Success	Gradual transition from civil government dependent on military to open military dictatorship
12	23 July 52	Egypt	The Free Officers' Association	Organization of field and company officers	Constitutional monarchy	Military action against feeble opposition	Passive	Success	Reforms on many spheres
13	25 Feb 54	Syria	Fayṣal Atāsī, Ḥamdūn, Gassān Jadīd, Abū 'Asāf	Commanders of army units in north and east of the country, cooperating with various parties	Military dictatorship	Military revolt	Mass demonstrations and clashes in Damascus	Success	Renewal of parliamentarianism

ARAB OFFICERS' COUPS AND ATTEMPTED COUPS

No.	*Date*	*Country*	*Leaders*	*Qualifications of the leaders and collaborators*	*Adversary*	*Method*	*Public reaction*	*Result*	*Objectives and Outcome*
14	26 Feb 54	Egypt	Khālid Muḥī al-Dīn	Field officers of Armored Corps and other left-wing officers	Revolutionary Command Council led by Nasser	Negotiations, accompanied by threats and demonstrations	Strong popular ferment, demonstrations, activities of Muslim Brethren	Success	Return of Naguib and democratization of the regime
15	26 Mar 54	Egypt	Nasser and 'Āmir	The Revolutionary Command Council and majority of officers	Naguib	Strikes and demonstrations of officers	Strikes and demonstrations	Success	Absolute rule of the RCC under Nasser's leadership
16	13 Apr 57	Jordan	'Alī Abū Nuwār	General and field officers at Zerqa	Constitutional monarchy	Preparations for military revolt	Passive	Failure	Acceptance of Egypt's external and internal politics
17	14 July 58	Iraq	Qassim and Arif	Association of field officers	Constitutional monarchy	Violent military action	Demonstrations and killing of many of the former regime	Success	Republic and fundamental changes in many spheres
18	17 Nov 58	Sudan	Ibrāhīm 'Abbūd	Army Command	Constitutional republic	Military coup encouraged by the government	Passive	Success	Continuation of former policies under open military dictatorship
19	8 Mar 59	Iraq	'Ad al-Wahhāb Shawwāf	General and field officers at Mosul	Rule of Qassim and the left	Military revolt aided by UAR	Sanguinary riots at Mosul	Failure	Union with the UAR
20	22 May 59	Sudan	'A.R. Shīnān and B.A. Ḥāmid	General officers	'Abbūd	Threat of military action	Passive	Failure	

ARAB OFFICERS' COUPS AND ATTEMPTED COUPS

No.	Date	Country	Leaders	Qualifications of the leaders and collaborators	Adversary	Method	Public reaction	Result	Objectives and Outcome
21	10 Nov 59	Sudan	Ālī Ḥāmid	Field officers	'Abbūd	Military revolt	Passive	Failure	
22	28 Sept 61	Syria	Kuzbarī, Naḥlāwī, Dahmān	General officers	Egyptian rule in Syria	Military coup	Passive and favorable	Success	Secession of Syria from UAR
23	31 Dec 61	Lebanon	Fu'ād 'Awaḍ and Shawqī Khair-Allāh	Company officers, members of the SSNP	Constitutional republic	Military revolt	Passive	Failure	Rule of the SSNP
24	28 Mar 62	Syria	Zahr al-Dīn, Naḥlāwī, Dahmān	Army Command	Constitutional republic	Arrests	Demonstrations	Success	Rapprochement towards Egypt
25	31 Mar 62	Syria	Jāsim 'Alwān	Field officers at Aleppo	Military regime	Military revolt	Demonstrations	Failure	Reunion with Egypt
26	26 Sept 62	Yemen	'Abd-Allāh Sallāl	Chief of Staff	Autocratic monarchy	Violent military revolt	Initially passive, subsequently civil war	Success	Republic, alignment with Egypt in foreign and domestic affairs
27	8 Feb 63	Iraq	'Abd al-Salām Arif	Active and retired field officers and Ba'thists	Military dictatorship of Qassim	Violent military action	Violent riots	Success	Cooperation of officers and Ba'th, massacre of communists, alignment with Egypt
28	8 Mar 63	Syria	Lū'ay Atāsī	General officers and Ba'thists	Military dictatorship	Military revolt	Demonstrations	Success	Cooperation of officers and Ba'th, alignment with Egypt and Iraq
29	18 July 63	Syria	Jāsīm 'Ālwān	General and field officers	Military dictatorship	Military revolt	Passive	Failure	Reunion with Egypt
30	13 Nov 63	Iraq	Mundhir Windāwī	General and field officers, command of the National Guard and radical wing of Ba'th	Military dictatorship	Military revolt and demonstrations	Demonstrations	Failure	Rule of radical wing of Ba'th

ARAB OFFICERS' COUPS AND ATTEMPTED COUPS

No.	*Date*	*Country*	*Leaders*	*Qualifications of the leaders and collaborators*	*Adversary*	*Method*	*Public reaction*	*Result*	*Objectives and Outcome*
31	18 Nov 63	Iraq	ʻAbd al-Salām Arif	Top level of military dictatorship	Baʻth Party and National Guard	Violent military action	Passive	Success	Elimination of political parties, inclusive Baʻth, exclusive military dictatorship
32	16 Sept 65	Iraq	ʻĀrif ʻAbd al-Razzāq	The Prime Minister and some general officers	ʻAbd al-Raḥmān Arif	Military action	Passive	Failure	Overthrow of Arif and union with Egypt
33	23 Feb 66	Syria	Ṣalāḥ Jadīd, Salīm Ḥāṭūm	Field officers and radical wing of Baʻth	Amīn al-Ḥāfiz, Ṣalāḥ Bayṭār, ʻAflaq and moderate wing of Baʻth	Military action, heavy fighting with many casualties	In some places involved in street fighting	Success	Inauguration of extremist Baʻth regime
34	30 June 66	Iraq	ʻĀrif ʻAbd al-Razzāq	General and field officers	ʻAbd al-Raḥmān Arif	Military insurrection	Passive	Failure	Repetition of attempted coup of September 1965
35	8 Sept 66	Syria	Salīm Ḥāṭūm	Field officers, most of them Druze	Radical Baʻth government	Preparations for revolt	Passive	Failure	
36	27 Dec 66	Sudan	Khālid Ḥusayn ʻUthmān	Company officers	Constitutional republican government	Military insurrection	Passive	Failure	
37	4 Nov 67	Yemen	Al-Iryānī, Aḥmad Muḥammad Nuʻmān, Muhāmmad ʻAlī ʻUthmān	Army Command	Sallāl	Unopposed coup	Passive	Success	Establishment of regime independent of Egypt, capable of ending the civil war

Company officers: Second-lieutenant, lieutenant, captain.
Field officers: Major, lieutenant-colonel, colonel.
General officers: Brigadier, major-general, lieutenant-general, general, marshal.

for civilian institutions to be sufficiently discredited and the army officers sufficiently self-confident to set the stage for the first coup."[1]

A military coup is impossible under foreign occupation and Rustow states that this is "obvious." But to rule that four or five years must elapse between independence and a first coup is quite arbitrary. It applies to Iraq of Bakr Ṣidqī in 1936 and the Syria of Za'īm in 1949. Yet to regard 1947 as the beginning of an era in Egypt is hardly consistent with the course of that country's gradually developing strength. Furthermore, if that rule were valid, military coups should also have occurred between 1950 and 1960 in Lebanon, Jordan, Libya, Tunisia and Morocco. This theory does not explain why there were no military coups in Iraq between 1941 and 1957 and why they did take place in 1958. It fails to account for the belated seizure of control of Yemen (where the coup took place after Professor Rustow's article was written) by the military of that country, so long an independent state. And it does not make clear why a successful coup was carried out in Sudan (which the writer of the article overlooked) after less than three years of independence. The theory, then, boils down to the simple fact that military coups are a common occurrence in modern Arab states and that since they are so frequent, the first coup in any given state often takes place only a short while after independence is achieved.

In the same volume Majid Khadduri submits a theory of cycles governing the changes of regime in Iraq:

> "The principal changes in government produced by violent means, military or otherwise, since independence were those of 1934, 1936, 1938, 1940–41, 1948, 1952, the abortive coup of 1956 and the revolution of July 1958. It is to be noted that these coups have recurred in a cyclical form, each cycle maturing in a two- or four-year period: the coups (tribal or military) before the war recurred in a two-year cycle; those after the war, in a four-year cycle."[2]

The events cited in this list vary in kind: Some were military coups, some tribal revolts, others were uprisings of the urban population against pro-western foreign policy. Yet Khadduri's list fails to take note of changes of regime or other crises accompanied by violence, the impact of which were no less palpable than those he mentions, especially when they happened in odd-numbered years; for example, the coup that overthrew Bakr Ṣidqī in 1937 and the Kurdish revolt of 1945. The conjectural four-year cycle following World War II is traceable between 1948–52–56, but the events of 1958 followed within two years only, and the sanguinary uprisings of

[1] Sidney Nettleton Fisher, (ed.), *The military in the Middle East*, Colombus, Ohio, 1963, 10.
[2] *Ibid.*, 41.

1959—also ignored by Khadduri—came less than a year later. Four years elapsed between the Shawwāf revolt of March 1959 and the Arif coup of February 1963—although they were by no means tranquil years—while between the coups of February and November 1963 there was an interval of just over half a year. It would appear that the cyclical structure placed upon these events represents hardly more than an arbitrary *post factum* explanation.

There is another theory in Rustow's article that attempts to identify a governing pattern of laws. He writes:

> "Armies commonly seize power on the domestic scene after defeat on the battlefield, not after victory. On this point it may be argued that the historical evidence offers too few examples to support firm generalizations; but it is surely no coincidence that Turkish victory in the War of Independence of 1919–22 was followed by thirty-eight years of military subordination to orderly civilian rule, or that Israel, the one Middle Eastern country to win any battlefield victories in recent decades, is also the only country that has not had a single military coup. Instances on the converse side are equally striking: the Ottoman Empire's defeat in the First Balkan War was followed by the so-called Sublime Porte Incident of January 1913, in which Enver, at the head of a gang of trigger-happy lieutenants, stormed the government offices in Istanbul . . . and established the dictatorship of the famous Young Turk Triumvirate of Enver, Camal, and Talât. In 1919, the defeated Ottoman army under Mustafa Kamal organized nationalist resistance in Anatolia in open defiance of the Sultan and his collaborationist ministers. Finally, the Syrian coups of 1949 and the Egyptian revolution of 1952 were in large part a response to the humiliation of defeat in the Palestine War."[3]

This theory contributes very little. It is true that the national crisis that often follows defeat in war provides fertile ground for revolutions and coups of various kinds. This is the "revolutionary situation" alluded to by Lenin. Still, not every military debacle has resulted in a military coup, not even in the Arab East; and in other parts of the world military coups have followed triumph in battle: In Paraguay, victory over Bolivia in the Gran Chaco War in 1935 was followed by the military coup of 1936, the first of a series. On the other hand, in the twentieth-century Arab states there has been no opportunity for any army to rise to power on the wings of victory in war; there have been no such victories. The fact that a certain event failed to take place in a non-existent situation proves nothing.

[3] *Ibid.,* 10–11.

2. CHARACTERISTICS AND COMPARISONS

ANY ATTEMPT to classify Arab military coups and find laws and principles governing their recurrence needs discretion and accuracy and might be premature. Our only objective in the following pages is to call attention to some noteworthy lines of development.

Careful scrutiny of the 37 actual and abortive military coups reveals certain characteristics.

What stands out is the growing frequency of these coups, including attempted ones, and also their spread to an increasingly large number of countries.

In the four and a half years from the fall of 1936 to the spring of 1941 there were seven coups, on the average one every 231 days, all in one country.

In the seven years from the spring of 1941 to the spring of 1949, the dormant period, there were no coups.

In the five years from the spring of 1949 to the spring of 1954 there were eight coups, on the average of one every 228 days, taking place in two countries.

In the four and a quarter years from the spring of 1954 to the summer of 1958 there were no coups, except the abortive coup of April 1957 in Jordan.

In the one and a quarter years from the summer of 1958 to the fall of 1959 there were five coups, on the average one every 97 days, in two countries.

In the two years from the fall of 1959 to the fall of 1961 there was a lull again.

In the two years from the fall of 1961 to the fall of 1963 there were 10 coups, on the average one every 78 days, in four countries.

In the two years from the fall of 1963 to the fall of 1965, there was again a respite.

In the two years and a quarter from the fall of 1965 to the end of 1967 there were six coups, on the average one every 130 days, in five countries.

This list does not take into account the underground activities of Egyptian officers that were launched by ʻAzīz al-Maṣrī and Sādāt in 1941 and 1942, since they did not attempt to seize power. Their inclusion in the list would not basically alter the overall picture: A first wave of activity by politically minded Arab officers from the days of Bakr Ṣidqī in Baghdad until Rommel's appearance at the gateway to Egypt, followed by a dormant period until after the Palestine War of 1948; a second wave of coups until the stabilization of Nasser's rule in Egypt and the overthrow of Shīshaklī in Syria in 1954, and then a renewed lull; and from 1958 more frequently occurring coups in more countries. Fifteen, half of the 30 coups and attempted coups after the Palestine War of 1948, took place between July 1958 and November 1963.

Syria and Iraq differ greatly from all the other Arab countries. Of the 37 coups, 14 took place in Iraq, 12 in Syria, and eleven in the other five countries on the list. Of the 25 successful coups, 10 took place in Iraq, nine in Syria, and six in the rest. The officer regime that arose in Egypt in 1952 succeeded in entrenching itself and has established a more stable government than those that preceded it. In Syria and Iraq, by contrast, each military coup has merely been a prelude to yet another military counter-coup. This political activity and strife rampant among officers have intermittently rocked these two countries and their peoples like a pendulum that swings between harsh, brutal dictatorship and between administrative disintegration.

In nearly every country where there have been successful military coups, they have been followed shortly after by additional attempts—successful or otherwise—at military counter-coups, the one leading to the other. Nor should this occasion surprise: If, under a parliamentary or quasi-parliamentary regime, with a weak government at the helm, the high road to its overthrow has led through a military coup, by the threat to employ the army's potential for brute coercion, how much more so must this be true of a military dictatorship! A military coup is then not merely the high road: It appears to be the only road.

In classifying coups and attempted coups according to those executing them, five different categories may be distinguished:

a) Coups carried out by the military supreme command. There have been ten such, designated in our tabulation as numbers 1, 8, 9, 11, 15, 18, 24, 26, 36 and 37. All were successful.

b) Coups planned and executed by officers' associations previously organized and functioning for some time in the underground, i.e., the "classic" type of coup. There have been only two such coups, the Egyptian one of July 1952 and the Iraqi coup of 1958. Both succeeded.

c) Coups carried out by a group of officers working openly in unison. Such were the three coups of the Iraqi Golden Square in 1940 and 1941. All three were successful.

d) Coups by officer groups organized solely for that purpose shortly before taking place and headed by senior officers. Seventeen such coups have been carried out, numbers 2, 3, 4, 10, 13, 16, 19, 20, 22, 27, 28, 29, 30, 32, 33, 34 and 35. Nine of these were successful; eight failed. The prospects for success or failure are, then, about equal.

e) As in paragraph d) but without the participation of senior officers. Five such coups have taken place: The activities of Khālid Muḥī al-Dīn in support of Naguib in the Egyptian crisis of spring 1954; ʻAlī Ḥāmid's movement in Sudan in November 1959; the abortive Lebanese coup at the end of 1961; ʻAlwān's uprising at Aleppo in 1962; and the abortive Sudanese coup at the end of 1966. All five failed, the first after initial success, the remaining instantly.

There can be no clear-cut delineation of these categories; these and similar classifications defy accuracy. The group of officers which carried out the secessionist coup in Syria against the UAR in September 1961 has been included in the fourth category; perhaps it could be regarded as belonging to the second category, namely, of associations organized underground and working their way toward their goal over a considerable period.

Fifteen of these coups, four out of every ten, encountered no serious or immediate opposition: Numbers 1, 2, 3, 4, 8, 9, 11, 12, 17, 18, 20, 24, 28, 31 and 37. It was this, indeed, that ensured their success. Of the 22 others that did encounter any manner of serious opposition, 11 were successful; 11 failed. A military coup's prospects for success are conditional in large measure on the element of surprise paralyzing the adversary and precluding any counter-initiative on his part. The decisive hour in a military coup is usually its first. If it fails to achieve immediate success, its prospects of succeeding at all sharply decline.

The reliance on the element of surprise for success stems from the fact that the organizers of a coup generally put into operation a bare minimum of army units, i.e., two or three battalions. Since, for the most part, they can depend on the loyalty of only a few units, surprise is the only method possible. Even where a larger number of units could be deployed, as in the case of a coup by an army supreme command, an indispensable minimum is preferred, owing to the extreme importance attached to the element of surprise which is in inverse proportion to the size of the operating force. In general it may be stated that if the loyalty of a small military force, secrecy in preparation and surprise in execution are assured, and, of course, if the existing government is shaky and unpopular, a coup may be regarded as feasible with prospects of success.

Hence there is an almost fixed procedure, with few variations, for military coups, and they are carried out according to a single blueprint: Two or three battalions or a brigade enter the capital, preferably at night, either in secrecy or on the pretext of maneuvers; within the hour companies and platoons seize army headquarters, the railroad station and airport, the central telephone and telegraph exchange, and place the government and army chiefs under house-arrest. One of the most important objectives is always the radio station, from which soon after, usually at daybreak, "Communiqué No. 1" is broadcast.

In Iraq—and only in Iraq—part of the air force has taken part in occasional coups, beginning with the coup of Bakr Ṣidqī in 1936 and on through the abortive coup against Arif in September 1964.

At times the mere concentrating of forces and threat of a coup suffice to intimidate a government into yielding to the demands of the insurrectionists. Such was the case in the coup of the Seven in Iraq in December 1938 and in April 1939. As in international relations, the aggressive party can sometimes succeed in its demands by imposing threats it has no intentions of implementing.

Those planning military coups assume that, once having secured control of the army command and civil administration centers in a surprise action and having demonstrated their determination to employ the force at their disposal when necessary and without hesitation, the commanders of the remaining military force will shrink from fighting them, whether because of clandestine sympathy with the insurgents, fear, or misgivings about the obedience of their troops. Generally, the basic assumption is that the commanders or the soldiers of any army would not overcome their aversion to opening fire on other units of the same army. When asked to suppress the Kapp *putsch* within the German army in 1920, General Von Seeckt refused, saying, "The Reichswehr does not fire at the Reichswehr." Those planning military coups are themselves free of such hesitations or inhibitions, yet take them into account as potent factors among their adversaries—and usually they do not miscalculate.

The men who carried out the military coups and established their dictatorships have learned much from one another. Bakr Ṣidqī borrowed the method of "Communiqué No. 1" from the Latin American custom of issuing a *Pronunciamento*. He modeled his victory parade in Baghdad on October 29, 1936 on Mussolini's March on Rome in 1922.

In 1949 Ḥinnāwī set up his "Supreme War Council"; since then the "Revolutionary Command Council" or "Revolutionary Council" has become the accepted pattern for concentrating legislative, executive and judiciary powers in the hands of the army officers. There have, of course, been instances in which no such council was set up. Indeed, one of Arif's charges against Qassim voiced at his trial in December 1958 was that Qassim had not set up such a council after the July 14 coup, contrary to what had been agreed among the Free Iraqi Officers when they planned the coup. After the Iraqi and Syrian coups in 1963, civilians who represented the Ba'th were included for the first time. In Iraq, the Arif coup of November 1963 brought this civilian collaboration to an end. The composition of these councils is usually secret, so that frequent reshufflings of their membership through dismissals or additions are easily made. These councils represent institutionalized arbitrariness, arbitrary administration in relation to the people as a whole and to the officer corps as well. This is rule without legitimacy, responsible to none.

Along with reciprocal influences and outright imitations between military coups in different countries, within the countries themselves there has been some continuity among those engineering the coups. It is not only the displacement of officers by officers that is so striking, but the fact that many of the officers involved in these coups were active in several consecutive ones. Of the many available examples, we cite a few: Anwar Sādāt, Ḥasan Ibrāhīm, Ḥusayn Dhu-al-Fiqār Ṣabrī and several others were active in the pro-Nazi underground in Egypt during World War II, in the Free Officers' Movement and in many stages of rule by the officers. Qassim, kinsman to Muḥammad 'Alī Jawwād, was close to the 1936 followers of Bakr Ṣidqī.[1] Mahmūd al-Durra, a young major close to Ṣabbāgh from 1939 to 1941, reappeared in 1959 in the Shawwāf revolt and again became prominent in Iraqi politics in 1963 after the fall of Qassim.[2] 'Abd al-Salām 'Ārif and Ṭāhir Yaḥyā participated in Qassim's coup, in the coups against Qassim and later against their former partners in the overthrow of Qassim. Repeated participation in various coups and even in counter-coups is common to Syrian officers as well: Shīshaklī aided Ḥinnāwī in overthrowing Za'īm; four months later he displaced Ḥinnāwī. Amīn Abū 'Asāf was active in all three Syrian coups of 1949. Muṣṭafā Ḥamdūn, who raised the banner of revolt against Shīshaklī, has been one of the central figures in the innumerable convulsions of Syrian politics. Obviously the continuity of individuals in various coups has exerted its influence on their similarity of form and character.

These officer politicians have never functioned in a vacuum. At all times they have been influenced by ideological and political cross-currents within the public at large. From time to time, they have also enlisted the cooperation of representatives of civilian political organizations in preparing

[1] 'Abd al-Raḥmān al-Jadda, *Thawrat al-za'īm al-munqidh,* Baghdad 1960, 15–8.

[2] Ṣabbāgh, 48, 60, 231; *MER* 1960, 247–8; Maḥmūd al-Dara, *Al-qaḍiyya al-kurdiyya wal-qawmiyya al-'arabiyya,* Beirut 1963, 120–1; Maḥmūd al-Durra, *Tārīkh al-'arab al-'askari,* Cairo 1961, on the book's cover; *Al-Manār,* Amman, 13 July 1964.

their coups, in carrying them out and in conducting state affairs thereafter. In their inaugural proclamations they make it their practice to pledge themselves publicly to hand over the reins of government to the duly elected leaders of the people at the opportune moment and to return to their barracks.

Civilian collaboration in military coups and governments can be divided into a number of categories. Common to all of them is the fact that in this collaboration, if and to the extent that it does exist, the military had nearly always held the initiative and made the decisions, with the civilian partner in a secondary position.

One type of military coup takes place behind the scenes, not only without the participation of any segment of the general public but without its knowledge, even after the event. Such was the displacement of the Iraqi governments in December 1938, in February 1940 and in February 1941; the appointment of ʻAbd al-Ilāh to the regency by demand of the Seven in April 1939; and such—though it failed—was the coup attempted by ʻAli Abū Nuwār in Jordan in April 1957. These interventions and coups, supposedly secret, did not lead to the establishment of undisguised military dictatorships, even when they did succeed.

A second kind is that in which officers have openly overthrown the government without the knowledge or collaboration of any public organization or non-military public body. Coups of this sort generally usher in the beginning of open military dictatorship. One third of all the Arab military coups are in this category; it is, indeed, the most widespread. Such were the coups that overthrew Bakr Ṣidqī in 1937; Zaʻīm, Ḥinnāwī and Shīshaklī in 1949; Shīshaklī's second coup in 1951; the coup of the Free Officers in Egypt in July 1952; the coups in Sudan by ʻAbbūd in 1958 and against him in 1959; and the Yemenite coup of 1962. Even when these officers did maintain fairly close relations with other political circles, as did the Egyptian Free Officers in 1952, they did not include them in planning or preparations for executing the coup.

A third type are those coups in which non-military bodies have had advance knowledge, however vague, of their imminence and in which they have participated effectively. This kind of coup is, of course, the most varied and it, too, is fairly widespread. Nearly half of the Arab military coups fall into this category. The leaders of Hikmat Sulaymān's *Al-Ahālī* group were informed in advance of Bakr Ṣidqī's intentions in the first military coup of the modern Arab states. The Iraqi coup of April 1941 was the joint act of the Golden Square and the Rashīd ʻĀlī and Muftī circles, organized as the secret committee at the end of February 1941. The coup that overthrew Shīshaklī in 1954 was carried out in close collaboration with civilians at a time of turbulence in various regions of Syria. The coup of September 1961, severing Syria from the United Arab Republic, was also carried out in liaison with civilian leaders. In the coups of February and March 1963 in Iraq and Syria the Ba'th Party played an active role, and in February 1966 in Syria one of its factions against the other. Communists and possibly other opposition groups possessed prior information on the impending coup of July 1958 in Iraq. These coups are accompanied by large scale public embroilment, and governments arising in their wake are usually composed of both officers and civilians.

This classification does not purport to be, nor can it be, absolute. The lines between one category and another are fluid, and the variations in each one, especially the third, are manifold.

Civilian collaboration generally increases after the coup. Along with the revolutionary council, a government composed mostly of civilians is also set up. But this duplication contains the seeds of conflict. The officers' council—which has placed the ministers in office and constitutes the agency dominating the executive—now begins to issue instructions to the government. If the latter complies, it becomes superfluous, its influence declines and the day is not far distant when the officers will appoint themselves and their colleagues as ministers. If the government proves dissident, the officers dismiss it. Invariably the status of the civilians in the government wanes. Thus the military coup is usually the beginning of a military dictatorship as well. The promise given by the officers to return to their barracks remains fraudulent.

A military coup need not always be followed by a military administration. S.E. Finer cites four examples of civilian regimes established through military action;[3] Napoleon III's Second Empire of the 1860's, the Turkish Republic from 1924 to 1960, Mexico since 1946, and France's Fifth Republic which is the outcome of the military uprising in Algeria in 1958, but not a military dictatorship. Nevertheless military coups have tended to produce military dictatorships, and this has been markedly so among the Arab states. Between 1949 and 1967 there were 30 military coups in six Arab states and only in two instances, both in Syria, did the officers hand over rule to civilian leaders: In 1954 after Shīshaklī's overthrow, and in 1961 after secession from Egypt. Even in these two cases the return of the officers to barracks was but a lull in their efforts to rule alone. After a brief interval their intervention in political matters grew even bolder. The first instance culminated in union with Nasser's Egypt; the second came to an end precisely after one half year with the coup of Zahr al-Dīn.

[3] S.E. Finer, *The man on horseback,* London 1962, 164.

The men who execute military coups in the Arab states are always officers. What of the ranks? What is their role and their share in these actions? After all, no military operation is conceivable without them, and if the coups have taken their toll in casualties, it is their blood that has been shed.

In Latin America there have been instances in which soldiers have disobeyed the orders of revolting commanders or of commanders opposing revolt, especially in Brazil.[4] In July 1908 Turkish generals loyal to the Sultan were shot by their soldiers when they sought to suppress the Young Turks. The revolutions in Russia and Germany toward the end of World War I were largely soldiers' revolutions.

In the history of the Arab military coups since Bakr Ṣidqī, the rank and file have always been so much potter's clay in the hands of their commanders. They have not shared in the planning, have not been asked for their opinions nor deemed to have any opinions of their own. It has always been axiomatic that the Arab soldier obeys his commander blindly, whoever the enemy, even though the commander himself may be manifesting extreme disobedience toward those to whom he has sworn allegiance. Whenever hostilities have broken out, these soldiers have fought; it may be asked whether they will fight valiantly, adroitly or shiftlessly, but never whether they will identify with the objective. Only rarely has a commander thought it necessary to offer any explanation in order to persuade doubting soldiers to obey his orders. One of these rare occasions was on September 29, 1961. An Egyptian major, wishing to transport a brigade from Qutaifa to Damascus in order to suppress the secessionist revolt against the United Arab Republic, told his Syrian troops that this sudden mobilization was for the purpose of repelling an Israeli surprise attack.[5] However, this was an exceptional occurrence under exceptional circumstances. It is not merely that the explanation was a false one. Actually this Egyptian was not the brigade commander and his order constituted a usurpation of authority. By its very nature, this was a national Syrian revolt against Egypt and the Egyptian officer was in no position to take Syrian troop discipline for granted. Another example of troops' refusing to obey their officers occurred in March 1959 in Mosul, when the NCOs, under communist influence, caused Shawwāf's rebellion to fail.

The Arab military coups, then, are officer coups and exclusively so.

The Arab East invites comparison with Latin America, and not only because of the frequency of their military coups. Disregarding for the

[4] E. Lieuwen, *Generals versus presidents,* London 1965, 75–80.

[5] *MER* 1961, 607.

moment great internal differences within these two areas and viewing them as two entities, the similarities between them are manifold and important: Both belong to the "underdeveloped" countries but to the upper stratum of that large group, which is relatively richer and more advanced economically, politically and culturally. Both are characterized by extremes of prodigal, parasitic, exploitative wealth at one end and abyssmal poverty at the other and extreme polarization in the possession of landed property. In both areas the national economy is largely dependent on the commercial export of a single or limited range of raw materials—the one exporting mainly crude oil and cotton, the other specializing in coffee, banana crops, sugar, crude oil, cotton or tin. Rapid urbanization has outpaced industrialization in both regions. There is near or complete uniformity of literary language, culture and religion in their predominant communities. Yet both are politically divided into numerous and at times antagonistic states with a tradition of fiery religious fanaticism which finds its modern expression in aggressively nationalistic, politically sectarian zealotry. In each, fully developed and active nationalist movements foster pride in an independence achieved after struggles with great and ancient empires—the Spanish, the Portuguese, the Ottoman—side by side with a deep, well-founded anxiety about the designs of the modern imperialist powers to attain political or economic domination, open or disguised. And both areas are troubled by the chronic instability of the system of government in most of their respective countries. It is no coincidence that Latin America and the Middle East are the two areas in this world most affected by military coups.

Yet, despite the similarities between these two regions and the frequency of their military coups, there is no indication of any mutual influence being exerted by these military interventions. The Arab officer politicians have time and again been subjected to influences emanating from Germany and Italy, by the memory and example of military revolt movements in the Middle East such as those of 'Urābī, of Atatürk or the Arab officer clubs in the Ottoman army. In particular, they have absorbed the influence and learned from the accomplishments of their colleagues in neighboring Arab states. But events in Latin America have never aroused special attention in the Middle East, and contacts between them are confined to the transfer of money by Lebanese emigrants in Central America to their relatives back home and the cooperation between oil-producing Arab states and Venezuela for the purpose of maintaining the price level of oil on the world market. The first Latin American regime that has evoked serious interest among the Arabs and led to the formation of strong mutual ties is the Fidel Castro regime in Cuba, which does not at all lie within the category of military dictatorships. On the other hand, the new Egyptian regime, established and dominated by army officers, made a great impression on some circles of the Argentine army, and among the young officers there are apparently many "*Nasseristas.*"[6]

The absence of mutual or acknowledged influences restricts the significance of this parallel between the two areas but does not invalidate it. The similarity in circumstances and officer intervention in the political life of Latin America and the Arab world demonstrates that in like conditions of soil and climate, though widely separated in space and time, similar plants will grow. This similarity shows that the frequency and characteristics of military coups are not random outcroppings but the product of historical circumstances. One qualification, though, has to be added: If a phenomenon is not fortuitous, it does not imply that it is rigidly predetermined and that no other would be possible in its stead. A plant flourishing in a given locality will not be the only one that can sprout, bloom and yield its fruit there. Another plant might be incapable of growing wild but would grow if sown and nurtured. The fact is that not all Latin American states have experienced military dictatorships, as is proved by Uruguay and Chile. In Costa Rica military intervention in politics was a brief, isolated episode; while in Mexico, weaned from such disturbances these many years, they are now a thing of the past. In sum, while the similarity in circumstance and appearance of military intervention in these two areas does not prove military dictatorships to be a historical necessity for either one or both, it does indicate that these are not chance occurrences.

The various forms of Arab and Latin American military coups and dictatorships show, together with their similarities, pronounced differences.

The history of intervention by the officer class in the political life of Latin America has been longer and more variegated than in the modern Arab states, and not merely because the Arab states are younger. This intervention is but one of the manifestations—although an important one—of that prolonged general lack of political stability which has plagued Latin America more than the Middle East.

The frequency of illegal and violent changes of government by military, civilian and joint civilian-military coups has engendered a different tenor of political life, as some statistics from the history of the Latin American republics will show. Bolivia achieved independence in 1824; during the 129 years till 1952, 179 coups were carried out in that country. In Honduras between 1824 and 1954 presidents changed 116 times. Between 1830 and

[6] Lieuwen, 24.

[7] *Ibid.*, 4–8; Merle Kling, 'A theory of power and political instability', in John M. Kautsky, (ed.), *Political change in underdeveloped countries*, New York 1962, 125–6; John J. Johnson, *The military and society in Latin America*, Princeton 1964, 4–5.

1895 Ecuador had 11 constitutions. In Mexico between 1860 and 1946 not a single president completed his legal term of office. During the 10 years between October 1945 and November 1955, 31 governments in 14 Latin American countries were illegally overthrown. The replacing and expulsion of ministers were even more frequent than the ousting of presidents, the overthrow of governments or the abolishment of constitutions. Nobody knows how many plots have been smashed or how many coups have failed.

In 1954 there were open or only partly disguised military dictatorships in 13 out of the 20 Latin American republics. Then for some years a process of shrinking military influences could be discerned, so that by 1960 officers were in power in only eight countries, a low figure considering the political climate there, although in itself high indeed. On the return stroke of the pendulum, however, the number of states under officer rule had risen to 14. The new wave of military coups in Latin America is not fortuitous; it is the reaction to the Cuban revolution of 1959. Castro's influence was a heady stimulus to the left in all the American countries south of the USA—and in response to it all the Latin American military coups of this period were vigorously rightist-reactionary. Accordingly, "it is no accident that both Latin American nations that have steadfastly refused to sever relations with Cuba—Mexico and Uruguay—are nations in which the armed forces are, in large part, non political."[8]

In Latin America it is said that the ultimate stage in a military career is the presidency of the republic. Politization of the army and militarization of the state have become a tradition there, the culmination of several factors all operating in the same direction. One of these is the Spanish influence. The first Spaniards arrived in the western hemisphere with Christopher Columbus in 1492, the same year in which the last of the Muslim rulers was driven out of Spain. Spanish rule in Latin America lasted for three hundred years, and its extremely powerful influence persisted long after political domination had ended. In Spain military uprisings took place at frequent intervals. It was Engels who in 1855 wrote of "the true reasons" for these revolts:[9]

"As a consequence of the long, unceasing wars against Napoleon, the various [Spanish] armies and their commanders acquired substantial political power and this, at first, endowed them with a pretorian character. From the revolutionary period there still remained in the army many energetic men; the enlistment of guerrilla fighters in the regular army

[8] Lieuwen, 101.

[9] F. Engels, 'Die Armeen Europas', in Marx-Engels, *Werke,* Berlin 1961–1963, vol. 11, 479–80.

even strengthened this element. Thus, soldiers and subalterns were still permeated with the revolutionary tradition, while their officers clung to their pretorian prerogatives."

Basing himself on this analysis, Engels arrived at the following prognostication:

"Since all the parties have employed the army as a tool, it should occasion no surprise if it takes the government into its own hands for any length of time."

And indeed, what Engels foresaw in 1855 became reality in Spain in 1874.

From the beginning to the end, Spanish rule in Latin America was invested with peculiar forms. Separated from the royal government of the mother country by thousands of miles, stationed in the vast expanse of a sparsely populated colonial territory with a paucity of communication systems, the colonial governors were, for all practical purposes, autocrats with no limitations upon their domination or arbitrariness, and with the army at their disposal their sole staff of support. No urban middle class had arisen yet to confront the Spanish knightly, feudalistic mentality with its contempt for work and craftsmanship, as had the puritan middle class of England and the United States, imbued with the ethos of labor and wealth.

The wars of independence from 1810 to 1825 ushered in a period of unrestrained violence. The military was the decisive force; but again, there was only a minimum of coordination between the embattled forces and within each only a minimum of professionalism and discipline. The young republics developed a cult of liberation heroes, and the latter were loath to beat their swords into ploughshares. Amid the chaos that prevailed until the middle of the century, they were not inhibited and felt free to indulge every whim and fancy.

After the elimination of colonial rule three pillars of Latin American society remained: The landowners, descended from the Spanish conquerors; the Church; and the army. Of these the army alone was in the ascendancy. It was imbued with the prestige of victory and had at its disposal the means of violence and the efficiency of hierarchical organization. The military could regard itself as the sole guarantor of national integrity and unity as against the strong social and racial centrifugal forces in vast areas of great distances, sparse population and poor communications.

At the same time, the factors of disintegration affected the structure of the armies themselves. The second half of the nineteenth century was characterized by the rule of the *caudillos*, the feudal military-political leaders who were the despots of their provinces and the heads of semi-private armies. The *caudillo*

"... often personified the virtues and vices, the culture and savagery, the arrogance and religiousness of his people, who, in the throes of anarchy, looked to him for political salvation ... He occupied a position somewhere between the *Hacendado* and the central government unless, as occurred often enough, he acually became the central government. Unlike the average *Hacencado*, who represented passive resistance to centralized authority, the *caudillo* was an activist, a man too ambitious to wait."[10]

This was the type of person who left his imprint on the life of these countries in the second half of the nineteenth century; and his influence continued to be felt for many years thereafter.

At the end of the nineteenth century an accelerated capitalist development of Latin America began, as the continent became a supplier of important raw materials for the world market and a large-scale capital investment area for North America and Europe. Bourgeois and proletarian classes developed in the coastal towns. The large-scale European middle-class immigration brought new attitudes and the functions and the prerogatives of the central authorities increased. Concomitant with this development and advancing technological modernization came the growing importance of the regular armies—and their officers. The latter, for the most part, were of urban middle-class origin. Though their background differed from that of the *caudillos*, their mode of existence in the state and their attitude toward the law were very similar. The tradition that might makes right now took the form of the *junta*, a clique of officers banded together for the purpose of bringing off a coup and setting up a dictatorship.

What did remain unchanged from the days of the Spanish *conquistadores* down to the times of the *juntas* was the ideological apathy. The Arab officer politicians usually aspire to develop political philosophies of their own; not so their Latin American counterparts. Of course, there have been exceptions in this respect—Perón, for example,—but they are few. Generally, these dictators pay lip service to the prevalent social, political and religious outlook, sometimes in fine-phrased, ringing Spanish rhetoric, at other times with arrogant contempt, but their driving ambition is not toward a new order but domination.

Just as the history behind them had been a longer one, so, too, the Latin American coups of the twentieth century assumed more numerous forms than the Arab coups which appear homogeneous by comparison.

An outstanding difference between Latin American and Arab coups can be seen in the respective amounts of violence and bloodshed. A coup

[10] Johnson, 39.

that fails to achieve an immediate surprise victory is liable to engender hostile engagements between the military units of the contending parties, or even civil war. Such embroilment, even when of short duration, usually takes a heavy toll of victims. This has happened more than once in Latin America. In the abortive revolt of the Argentine navy against Perón in 1955, the cost in dead and wounded rose to 1,500 within a few hours. Among the Arab states only Iraq somewhat resembles Latin America in this respect. Compared with Latin America, the Arab coups have on the whole been quite "anemic."

The frequency rate of Latin American military coups is much greater and their ration of success much smaller than in the Middle East. In Paraguay alone between 1940 and 1948 there were 26 attempted coups, all failures. The assumption that military units recoil from opening fire on other units of the same army—and this assumption lies at the basis of the Arab military coups and has contributed much to their speedy successes—does not tally with Latin American reality. Rash violence is common there in personal quarrels and public contests, and revolvers are quickly drawn from their holsters. To this must be added the peculiar tension that exists in some of these countries between various arms of the service, as, for example, between the infantry and the navy in Argentine.

The amount of violence accompanying military coups in Latin America and their development, at times, into civil war, stems from the fact that the officer politicians there are mostly associated with civilian organizations, political parties and trade unions. Civilian collaboration in the coups and dictatorships—whether as actual partners or puppet presidents—is generally on a wider scale than in the Arab world. What is equally true is that the suffering endured by civilians thought to oppose the regime is much greater. So, too, is the number of victims who fall prey to terrorism which is very often the principal means of preserving the regime—until the next coup. Among the Arab states it is again Iraq and, to some extent, Syria that remind one of the situation in Latin America.

There is also a striking personal difference between most of the military dictators in these two areas. Once having gained control of the government in Argentine, Venezuela, pre-Castro Cuba and the other Latin American states, they shed all restraints about the waste of public funds, in the personal pocketing of money and uninhibited debauchery. On being overthrown, they have succeeded in fleeing their countries and smuggling legendary sums of money out with them. By comparison, all the Arab dictators look like naive idealists. Even Adīb Shīshaklī, who departed Syria a rich man, was a well-behaved child compared to Perón, Jiménez and Batista, each of whom took many million dollars into exile.

Although the Latin American dictators have come away from their adventures with fabulous wealth, there has been no substantial change in the condition of their countries. A dictator comes, a dictator goes, and the country stands still. Herein lies the basic and most important difference between the military coups in Latin America and those in the Middle East. In the former the military coups and the mixed military-civilian coups are more frequent and more violent as well, yet at the same time they are more superficial. They are not intended to nor do they effect any fundamental change either in the domestic class alignment or in foreign policy orientation. Practically the sole exception to this was Perón during his period of domination in Argentine from 1946 to 1955 when he measurably reduced the income of the landowners. On the other hand, in Turkey and the Arab world the rise of the officers to power has resulted from time to time in great political and social transformation. Monarchies have been replaced by republics, the political rule of the great estate owners has been liquidated, agrarian reform has been inaugurated, international political orientations have been altered; and so, too, in other domains. The sum total of all these changes has not actually been a revolution: The public masses and their organizations have not been activated but rather placed under restriction; the changes themselves have not always been for the better; many problems have remained unsolved, while others have yielded their place to new ones. There can, however, be no doubt that the Arab officer politicians have brought about profound changes in their countries, which cannot be said of Latin America.

The position of the officer class in Latin America has reduced even legal civilian governments to such dependency upon it that they have been compelled to solicit its support by the most irregular methods—in other words, through bribery. In 1930 the Argentine government, by secret ordinance, requested all officers to submit accounts of their indebtedness, and these obligations were made good from the state's treasury. This deal cost the Argentine taxpayers 7,000,000 pesos.[11] The army is an acknowledged factor in Latin American politics even when it is not itself at the helm, to such an extent that military coups there are viewed as ordinary political events, like elections and administrative changeovers in other countries.

One thing, however, has transpired in Latin America which is just beginning to emerge in the Arab world, namely, that a military dictatorship becomes so thoroughly degenerate and arouses such aversion that its continued existence is no longer possible and it is forced to surrender its position to a legally constituted civilian government. The best example is Mexico.

[11] *Ibid*, 121–2.

From the accession of Porfirio Diaz to power in 1876, that country's history for 70 years was a continuous series of dictatorships, uprisings, civil wars, coups and foreign invasions, until a progressive constitutional democratic regime took over in 1946. Dictatorship had reduced itself to the absurd. In this respect, too, Latin America differs from the Arab world—or has it merely preceded it?

Chile's unique position among Latin American states deserves special mention. That country boasts, and justly so, that it has never been vanquished in battle. Three facts in its history are outstanding: a) Military victories against Spain in 1865–66 and against Bolivia and Peru in the grim war of 1879–80 resulted in Chile's annexing an area rich in natural resources. b) The high professional caliber of its army. Beginning in 1886, this army was organized and trained by German instructors along German lines, omitting none of the external trappings and professional attributes. Since then, the Chilean army has been judged as superior among Latin American armies. c) This army has abstained from interfering in politics. With the exception of the period between 1927 and 1932, which turned out to be a passing episode in the country's history, Chile's political life since independence (1818) has been conducted along constitutional lines, and certainly for the good of its people. It is the consensus of opinion that Chile is one of the most progressive of the twenty republics in the living standard of its inhabitants and in its cultural and social attainments. We do not propose hasty conjecture as to the causal relationship—which the cause and which the effect—between the Chilean army's achievements in battle and its professional level on the one hand, and its avoidance of politics on the other. In any event, there is some interconnection between these facts, and if the one has not produced the other, they certainly have exerted a reciprocally strengthening influence. In this respect it is Jordan, among the Arab countries, that reminds one of Chile both in the level of its army and in the latter's subservience to the constitutional regime.

Would a glance at a third area of military coups, the Far East, reveal similarities or reciprocal influences between officer intervention in politics there and in the Arab world?

Like the Arab states, Korea, Vietnam, Burma and Pakistan have achieved independence within the last generation, and like the Arab and Latin American states, they belong to that "third world" of underdeveloped countries, the masses of whose inhabitants, roused from a tradition of slowly changing economies and ways of life, have been cast into the vortex of the "revolution of rising expectations" entailing a loss of equilibrium between contending economic and political forces. In all these states, one of the first stable modern institutions to arise has been a strong army, strong at any rate within the array of domestic forces. As the administrations of these countries, racked by mighty centrifugal forces, become increasingly involved, it has seemed more than once that the simplest way out is to hand the government over to the army or for the latter to seize it. And actually military coups and other unconstitutional interference of the military in politics have been most frequent in all these countries in the last 20 years. This is also pertinent to Thailand, although Thailand, unlike Korea, Burma, Vietnam and Pakistan, never lost independence.

While the resemblance is patent, there is no evidence of any reciprocal influence between the officer politicians in the Far East and the Arab world. The occurrences in South Korea and South Vietnam have indeed attracted attention in the Middle East; but if the officers in those countries are in need of inspiration and models from abroad for intervening in politics, they have most probably found them in modern Japan, for which they have greater affinity in all respects.

Burma and Pakistan are ostensibly much more associated with the Arab world. Both were part of British India and acquired their independence during the same period in which various Arab states also freed themselves from British domination. Pakistan is close to the Arab world by virtue of its being an Islamic state; and Burma because, like the army-ruled Arab states, it is neutralist. In both these countries the army seized control of the government in the second half of 1958, in September and October respectively, at a time when the same thing was happening in two important Arab states, in Iraq in July and in Sudan in November. The Burmese and Pakistan coups were also similar to each other and to the Sudanese coup—but not the one in Iraq—in that they were totally free of bloodshed. In all three countries the civilian parliamentary regime had reached a crisis in the face of which the heads of state themselves requested the army chiefs to take over the government. In Burma, where mighty national and party struggles had been raging, it was the Prime Minister U Nu who approached General Ne Win with the request that the army take over the administration of the state.[12] The situation in Pakistan was characterized by the scandals in its legislature: In September 1958 the government proposed a resulution of no-confidence in the speaker, who was a member of the opposition. When the latter refused to submit this resolution to a vote, government members of the House assaulted him and, after he had fled the chamber lightly wounded, passed a resolution declaring him to be of unsound mind. The deputy-speaker of the House, a government supporter, tried to con-

[12] S. Yinam, 'Burma beyameynu', *Hamizrah,* vol. 13, 207.

duct the following session; he was set upon by opposition members and mortally wounded.[13] President Iskander Mirza thereupon declared a state of emergency, suspension of the constitution, dispersal of national and provincial parliaments and governments and prohibition of all parties; and General Ayūb Khan, Commander in Chief of the army, was appointed to carry out emergency measures. Two weeks later Ayūb Khan was appointed prime minister, and one week after that, the President resigned and Ayūb Khan took over his office too. There is, then, a marked resemblance between what transpired in Pakistan and in Sudan in the fall of 1958. One may add a few more points of similarity: For many years before he became a statesman, President Iskander Mirza was a senior officer in the army, like the Prime Minister of the Sudanese government, 'Abd-Allāh Khalīl, who summoned 'Abbūd, Commander in Chief of the army, to become the country's leader. Both Mirza and Khalīl were probably of the opinion that after a while the army would return to its barracks and once again submit to the authority of the civilian administration; and both found themselves permanently ousted.

These are parallels, interesting perhaps, but no more than that. In neither country, Sudan or Pakistan, did the events in the one arouse any interest in the other, and certainly they exerted no mutual influence. It was only when Ayūb Khan visited Egypt in November 1960 that he singled out the military dictatorship as that which he had in common with his hosts, remarking that "the first condition for progress is political stability. We, like you, borrowed Western parliamentarism. It did not work."[14] Of course, as head of a state adhering to the Central Treaty Organization, he was unable to speak in neutralist Egypt of a joint orientation in foreign policy. Likewise, he realized that stressing Islam as a foundation common to both states would be construed in Egypt only as an overture for its support of Pakistan on the Kashmir issue against India, whereas friendship with India is one of the foundation stones of Egyptian policy and support of India in its quarrel with Islamic Pakistan is the price Egypt is paying for India's support of its position on the Palestine question. When, too, the Sudanese 'Abbūd visited Pakistan in the spring of 1964 on his way to India and China, or when 'Abd al-Ḥakīm 'Āmir went in December 1966, no particular stress was laid on any affinity between the different regimes and their origins.

Ayūb Khan, 'Abbūd, 'Āmir and all the others were well-advised when

[13] Finer, 82; Khalid bin Sayeed, 'Collapse of parliamentary democracy in Pakistan', *MEJ*, vol. 13, 397.

[14] Radio Cairo, 7 November 1960.

they refrained from alluding to the roles of army officers as the founders of regimes in their respective countries. For the historical role of the officers corps had been quite different in Pakistan than in Egypt or in the other Arab countries. The Arab officer politicians have a tradition of subversive and revolutionary views and actions. In Pakistan, however, the army is "an offshoot of the British Indian Army, and therefore the oldest and most firmly-established executive institution in [the country]. After partition, when all the branches of the government apparatus had to be built from scratch, Pakistan inherited a considerable part of the elite of the British Indian Army. The army had always recruited a large number of the enlisted men and officers from the Moslem provinces of India."[15]

In Burma, unlike Pakistan or Sudan, the army restored control of the government to the civilians after a year and a half. In the spring of 1960 elections were held and U Nu again became prime minister. But there, too, the general rule apparently obtains as in most of the countries in which the military has ever held power: It is no longer willing to wean itself from the habit of government. On March 1, 1962 Ne Win carried out a coup and set up an undisguised military dictatorship. Again, one might point out some parallels, especially with Syria, but these, too, would be just parallels.

What were foreign agents doing during these military coups, and to what extent did they exert any influence?

Here one must differentiate between interference from Arab and non-Arab states. Formally, Yemen and Iraq are just as independent vis-à-vis Egypt and Saudi Arabia as they are vis-à-vis the United States and the Soviet Union. However, there is a difference, and not merely a psychological one, if a group of Arab conspirators receives arms, funds and advice from the Egyptian or Saudi military attaché or from a non-Arab embassy or oil company.

These interventions, of every kind and from many quarters, have been numerous. However, they are intrinsically difficult to reveal and even more difficult to prove. Not everything that has happened is known, and not everything told is necessarily true. Quite frequently there is a tendency to gross exaggeration in evaluating the activities of foreign agents and in estimating their importance in determining the outcome of these coups. The communist press often describes changes of regime in the Arab world as though London or Washington had decided upon them and implemented them, as though the local personalities were mere puppets in the hands of invisible foreign

[15] K.D. Newman, 'Pakistan's protective autocracy', *Pacific Affairs,* March 1959, 24, quoted in Moshe Lissak, *Modernization and role-expansion of the military in developing countries,* manuscript to be published.

wire-pullers. Thus, the Ḥinnāwī coup of August 1949 in Syria which was pro-Hashimite and pro-British was described as a British performance; the Egyptian coup of July 1952 as American; the Shawwāf revolt in Iraq in March 1959 as Egyptian. This is oversimplifying matters. There have, indeed, been connections and cases of support from time to time, and in the preceding chapter we tried to recount those that are known. In no instance, however, should one attach exaggerated importance to them. If the foreign powers were capable of establishing or removing the Arab rulers at will, they certainly would be capable of equipping their protegés with the force necessary to entrench their rule, and in that event they would retain their positions for much longer than they have for the most part succeeded in doing. King Ḥusayn was accurate in speaking of the February 1963 coup in Iraq as supported, but not engineered, by the Americans.[16] One may, furthermore, presume that even without that assistance Qassim's regime would have fallen.

The testimony in the memoirs of all kinds of secret agents should be regarded with caution. These people do their work clandestinely for years in obscurity and without publicity, as unknown individuals; to keep their name and appearance a secret is part of their jobs and their lives. It is thus understandable that, the moment they have an opportunity to open their mouths and divulge what they know after years of silence, they compensate by exaggerating the boldness of their operations and the degree of their influence. Whoever has for years succeeded in obliterating his tracks often manages to succeed in the opposite direction—in crediting himself with deeds in which his own part was really insignificant.

Generally it is true that foreign agents can operate and exert influence when there are local people who are interested in cooperating with the force in whose service they are acting. Events in Iraq from 1937 to 1940 were greatly influenced ideologically and by organizational and political aid from Germany. But even Grobba could not have accomplished much without the ambitions and arms of Ṣabbāgh, Rashīd 'Ālī and the Mufti.

The view that foreign agents determine the shifts in Arab politics is no more serious than the description of Ludendorff as the maker of the October Revolution because it was he who enabled Lenin to travel to Russia in a sealed coach. The people who are making Arab history are the Arabs themselves, even though not entirely alone. Those who are making Syrian history are Syrians, and it is the Iraqis who are making Iraqi history.

[16] Muḥammad Ḥasanayn Haykal, *al-Ahrām,* 27 September 1963.

PART THREE

THE HERITAGE OF HISTORY

"The idea of political freedom (of the individual within the group) first appeared in the Middle East at the end of the 18th century, grew and developed during the 19th, and in most of the area died out in the middle of the twentieth."

B. Lewis

1. MILITARY POWER AND THE AUTHORITY OF THE STATE

A STATE in which the elected representatives of all or most of the people determine the laws, in which the administrative apparatus is responsible to a separate legislative body and the military leaders are subject to the authority of these legislative and executive arms of government—such a state is a relatively new phenomenon in history, very rare prior to the 19th century, and, even now, more a vision than a fact in most of the world. Historically, a separation between the functions and powers of the military and the political authority generally did not exist; the head of state had either acceded to power through a military victory over an external foe or a domestic rival or had inherited power from such a conqueror and was strong enough to hold on to it. And in modern times, too, it happens, and not only in the Arab world, that a government in which the army is subject to a civilian authority vacates its position in favor of an officers' regime.

One may conclude that the subordination of the army to a supreme political authority is only an exceptional situation in history, most desirable, perhaps, but transitory, while military rule, on the other hand, is the normal condition, and seizures of power by the military the natural course, as 'Abbūd said in 1958.

The question is sometimes asked: Why should it be assumed natural for a military leader commanding an organized force to obey a king or president who is helpless without an army? However, such logic can easily be reduced to an absurdity. Just as the question is asked why a general should obey a statesman, it may also be asked why the commander of the air force should obey the chief of staff, why the commander of a tank battalion should obey a brigade commander, and so on, until the question of why ten men in a squad should obey a corporal.

It is not difficult to prove that the world is always on the brink of chaos. Subversion and coups by the army in the Arab countries, Latin America and southeast Asia have at times brought people dangerously close to anarchy. Sometimes it seems as if no political authority could exist there unless based on the threat of or the actual execution of unfettered violence.

However, human beings cannot exist on the assumption that each is a wolf to his fellow man. Man is a social being; this is not a moral postulate but a fact of human existence. Without cooperation and mutual aid, without conventional social patterns which are found even in the most primitive societies, man cannot exist.

If might is right, then history is finished. To regard the rule of violence alone as befitting man's nature and the course of history is superficial; it cannot explain why the world does not daily return to chaos.

However, even without considering thc accession of officers to power as the expression of a general historical trend, there are some who see it as the result of a specific development precisely in the middle of the 20th century, a development universal in its scope and, at the same time, particular to our period. It is possible in our day to discern a strong overall trend toward the priority of military considerations and institutions in many very different states, and, consequently, the military governments in modern Arab states may once more be regarded as the expression of a general phenomenon. This view of a general trend towards militarization was systematically developed by Harold Lasswell in his "garrison-state theory." As Lasswell himself defines it, "the simplest version of the garrison-state hypothesis is that the arena of world politics is moving toward the domination of specialty in violence."[1] Lasswell published his theory for the first time in 1937, before World War II. The appearance of atomic weapons, the supersonic airplane, missiles and subsequent developments have added validity to his ideas and focused attention on them. In our world, split between two camps of regimes antagonistic to each other in their fundamentals and aspirations, when any war is liable to become a conflict involving total risk and total destruction, considerations of security, defense and war override all other aims and activities; and those with knowledge and authority in military—and also police—matters reach the highest levels of decision making. There is no escape from a maximum concentration of power and authority, from preferring executive institutions to legislative ones, and from the supremacy of the planners and directors of the eventual war. According to Lasswell, history until World War I was dominated by a trend of progress towards a commonwealth of free peoples and individuals, led by men whose principal motives were economic productivity, businessmen in the broad, positive meaning of the word. However, the

[1] Harold D. Lasswell, 'The garrison-state hypothesis today', in Samuel P. Huntington, (ed.). *Changing patterns of military politics,* New York 1962, 51.

process of history has shifted direction and the soldier has once again come to the fore. The risk in war is no longer defeat but annihilation, and there seems to be only one way to prevent it—deterring the potential enemy by maximum power and retaliatory force and split-second readiness to react to an attack. Lasswell himself does not regard the garrison-state as an ideal, but rather as a disastrous trend of possible development. He also envisages the prospect that the very demands of modern technique and administration will themselves lead to a demilitarization of the garrison-state and that there will come into being "a truly civil garrison where anyone resembling the traditional soldier or policeman is as out of date as horse cavalry."[2] Basically, however, Lasswell considers only world unity and eternal peace an alternative to the garrison-state. As Huntington writes in his criticism, he sees the alternatives as either total peace or total war, "the unattainable or the unbearable."[3] The range of perils, external and domestic, which threaten every country can rise or decline; it may rise rapidly, even suddenly—its decline can only be gradual. Lasswell's theory contributes nothing to bringing this very difficult and very necessary prospect any closer.

Lest an attempt should be made to use this theory in order to explain and justify the seizure of power by officers in the Arab countries, one should point out the basic differences between the emergence of a garrison-state—stemming from real or imaginary military needs arising from the possibility of war with an external enemy, country and army—and between officer intervention in Arab politics which has always been in the nature of an internal struggle within the state, and sometimes within the army, and which never brought up the reason or the purpose of building up the military potential in anticipation of a conflict with an external foe. The real objective was always internal change. The defeat in the war with Israel occasionally served as an excuse for overthrowing a faltering civilian government, but the declared goal was always an internal reshuffle.

All peoples and periods have seen struggles for mastery between political and military authorities. In modern times, a world-wide trend towards renewed militarization is recognizable, as pointed out by Lasswell's theory. It serves as the background for the rise to power of officers in the Arab countries. If an atmosphere of demilitarization had prevailed throughout the world during the last thirty years, officer rule could not have spread in the Arab world and presented itself as a natural course. But the real sources of the military coups in the contemporary Arab world as a specific

[2] *Ibid,* 66.

[3] Samuel P. Huntington, *The soldier and the state,* Cambridge, Mass., 1967, 350.

phenomenon are grounded in Arab national history and in the heritage of Islamic civilization. The universal trends which can be observed in the development of relations between the general and the statesman serve as the background of modern Arab military coups, but not more than that.

Neither shall we exaggerate in evaluating the specific influence of Arab historical tradition on modern political life. There undoubtedly exists a long tradition of conquests and the regimes of military usurpers and conquerors—"the burden of history in the Middle East" as George M. Haddad has aptly called it. "Many of the old motives and attitudes have persisted and the army often still speaks for itself and for its own interests, while claiming to be the trustee of the people's welfare."[4]

But more or less similar phenomena are apparent in the histories of many other areas in the world, and historical analogies of different eras only very seldom point to any meaningful influence. The military conquest of Egypt by Arabs in the 7th century was no more a precedent for Nasser's rule than was the taking of Gaul by Julius Caesar for de Gaulle's regime.

The institution of Mamelukedom has had some influence on the development of the type and image of modern Arab army officers, and some remarks will be devoted to it in dealing with their social origins. But the prolonged rule of Mamelukes in various Arab countries of the Middle East as a form of government has been of little real importance for the emergence of military rulers in the independent Arab national states of the 20th century.

The predisposition of the body politic in the Arab Middle East for officers' seizures of power and rule is to be seen in two spheres: The specific pattern of Islamic civilization; and a number of peculiarities inherent in the historic development of Arab nationalism.

[4] George M. Haddad, *Revolutions and military rule in the Middle East: the northern tier*, New York 1965, 28.

2. THE ISLAMIC TRADITION

THE INFLUENCE of Islam constitutes both an important incentive in the officers' rise to power and an obstacle preventing them from achieving their ends. Only by clarifying this dialectic bond, can we assign the Arab officer politicians their true role in history.

The power and influence of organized religion in the 20th century is impressive in other regions as different from one another as Italy, West Germany, South America and Burma. But the influence of Islam in modern times as an emotional and political force is particularly powerful by virtue of its very nature and historic image.

From its inception, Islam has been much more than a religion in the limited sense of beliefs, rituals and precepts of behavior. It is essentially a comprehensive political and social system in which the affairs of this life are no less important than those hereafter; in the course of its history it has created a complete civilization of its own. W.C. Smith, one of the brilliant students of modern Islam, regards it and Marxism as "the world's two chief large-scale endeavours to implement a social ideal."[1] Islam wishes to make the kingdom of heaven come true on earth, in this world and in our days, not in some future Messianic Age and not at the End of Days; the organization of a people's life in accordance with the *sharī'a*, the Islamic law, and the assurance of the supremacy of the Community of the Faithful are more important for the redemption of the world than redeeming the soul of the individual. It does not maintain, as does Jesus, "My kingdom is not of this world,"[2] nor does it insist, "Not by might, not by power, but by My spirit,"[3] on the contrary: The legitimization of war and its justification as a holy war are not unique to Islam; both Judaism and Christianity preceded it in sanctifying bloodshed in God's name, and in intolerance towards unbelievers they generally surpassed it. However, the religious sanction of political power as such has remained a valid and accepted maxim in the 20th century only in Islam.

[1] Wilfred Cantwell Smith, *Islam in modern history*, Princeton 1957, 23.

[2] St. John 18:36.

[3] Zechariah 4:6.

The principle of the separation of church and state is alien and contrary to the spirit and tradition of Islam. When in 1925 Shaykh 'Alī 'Abd al-Rāziq boldly advocated in his book "*Islam and the Principles of Government*"[4] the abolition of the caliphate and the separation of civil law and the affairs of state from religious law, this was one of the outstanding manifestations of what A. Hourani called "The Liberal Age" in Arab thought.[5] The learned men of al-Azhar had good reasons for unanimously expelling the Shaykh from their ranks and disqualifying him for any religious office. Despite its great practical significance, historically 'Abd al-Rāziq's argumentation was unfounded. There is no support for the separation of church and state in the time of the Prophet Muḥammad or in any other period of Islamic history. "Important leaders and thinkers of the Christian Church (especially at the Reformation) have devoted energy and brains to working out a statement of the Christian faith in which the idea of a secular state fits, or at least with which it is compatible. They have worked out and built religious institutions (such as the church) that can function religiously in a secular society. And Christian believers have accepted these things. Christians have the kind of religious beliefs and customs and organizations that allow them to live in a secular state without ceasing to be devout Christians, and without ceasing to be loyal and effective citizens."[6] From the outset, Christianity established the principle "Render therefore unto Caesar the things which be Caesar's, and unto God the things which be God's."[7] But in historic Islam such a statement is inconceivable. The revolutionary undertaking of Atatürk, the secularization of communal and political life in Turkey, lost much of its momentum after the death of its leader; and as far as we are concerned, his example was not followed anywhere in the Arab world.

Christianity came into being as a religion of the oppressed and persecuted in a mighty empire; the state regarded them as a hostile element and they repudiated it. Islam, on the other hand, came into being as a movement founding a state, establishing a policy of its own, as a triumphant force conquering countries as much as winning souls. The center of the historical and religious consciousness of the Jews and Christians is occupied by martyrdom, either of the people or of the crucified Messiah. In Islam—with the exception of a part of the Shi'a—the center of consciousness has been occupied by the conquests and victories of the Community of the Faithful. Muḥammad was at once a prophet, a military leader and the found-

[4] 'Alī 'Abd al-Rāziq, *al-Islām wa-uṣūl al-ḥukm,* Cairo 1925.

[5] Albert Hourani, *Arabic thought in the liberal age,* London 1962.

[6] Smith, 253.

[7] St. Luke 20: 25.

er of a state. The commonest and most important title of the head of the nation in classic Islam, beginning with the Caliph 'Umar, was *Amīr al-mu'minīn*—"Commander of the Faithful." He was the caliph, the successor of Muḥammad. The caliphate "in reality substitutes the Lawgiver (Muḥammad) in as much as it serves, like him, to protect the religion and to exercise [political] leadership of the world."[8] Islam's attitude toward political and military power is not one of negation, dissociation or suspicion, but of complete affirmation. A religious value is attached to power, success and victory as such. Islam endows the army with the prestige and authority of an institution meriting divine blessing, and its heritage paves the way for military intervention which is to be regarded as most fitting and proper in the eyes of God and man.

Does modern nationalism contradict or weaken the force of traditional Islamic consciousness? At first glance it appears to do so to a considerable extent. The aim of nationalism has been to build the state on the secular foundations of common language and territory and to establish a new bond of loyalty in which the factors uniting the Arabic-speaking Muslims and Christians in Damascus are more important than those uniting Muslims from Damascus and Istanbul, who speak different languages. The national movements of the Greeks, Bulgarians, Arabs and the Turks themselves dissolved the multi-national Ottoman Islamic empire. In the Cyprus crisis of 1964 the Muslim Arabs of Egypt and Syria supported the Christian Greeks and not the Muslim Turks. Egypt, all of whose leaders are professing Muslims, is close in foreign policy to the atheistic Soviet Union but not to Pakistan, which is not only the country with the largest number of Muslims in the world but also defines itself as an "Islamic republic." Pan-Islamism, in contrast to pan-Arabism, is dead and gone. If a new great war breaks out it is difficult to imagine that Arab armies will fight each other; but it is quite possible that various countries in each of which Islam is the state religion will be in opposing camps.

Nevertheless, Islam had not ceased to exist as a political force in our time. Within the Arab countries the national awakening had not led to a weakening of Islamic consciousness and fanaticism, but to the contrary. "The modern Muslim world has accepted and espoused with fervor those aspects of nationalism that are relevant or contributory to the historic rehabilitation of Islamic society, and compatible with Islam's central precepts. It had accepted only superficially, or briefly, or not at all, those aspects that would interfere with or distract from the practical task of that

[8] Ibn Khaldūn, *Muqaddima,* tr. Franz Rosenthal, vol. 1, New York 1958, Bk. One, Ch. III. Section 23, 388.

rehabilitation. And except for the Turks, and then to only a limited degree, it has not accepted those aspects that would run counter to traditional Islamic loyalties."[9]

During the rebellion of 'Urābī in Egypt a discerning observer wrote, "In a Mohammedan country threatened by a Christian power any patriotic sentiment which may exist in the people has always a tendency to transform itself into religious fanaticism, and in Egypt at the time in question, the transformation was systematically encouraged by the nationalist leaders."[10] Seventy-five years later, in the Suez War, the battle cry of the people of Port Said in fighting the British and French was the traditional slogan of the Muslim warriors, *Allāhu Akbar,* "God is great."

The Arab national awakening in the 20th century has almost always brought with it an Islamic rival, and the triumph of nationalism in the Arab countries has usually resulted in the pre-eminence of the Muslim Sunni element in the population and discrimination against minorities. In the consciousness of the masses there is no great distinction between zeal for the native land and zeal for the Muslim "nation" *("Umma").* Even about the intellectuals Ṭaha Ḥusayn wrote, "Western life only reached a small class of people, where it had some influence on their minds but could not touch their feelings and sentiments."[11] It is a fact that every departure from the limited local sphere is accepted by large circles in the Arab world as being primarily an Islamic identification. "To list all the identification tags the regime wishes to issue to all citizens of the UAR is to render the regime's program for Arab nationalism and Arabism less realistic. If an Egyptian is to share in Egyptianism, Arabism, and Afro-Asianism, one wonders whether he would not prefer to settle for what comes naturally: being an Egyptian. This he always was. Although he has spoken Arabic for almost 13 centuries, he was never really aware of an Arab nation in the modern sense of the term. But he has always been aware, perhaps vaguely, of a Muslim community, and possibly a Muslim nation . . . Islam without Arabism has been and is possible. Can there be Arabism without Islam? To resolve this issue is no mean political task."[12]

In our day, Islam does not create effective international political ties but within every people and state it leaves its imprint on the nature of nationalism. This applies especially to Arabs and Arab nationalism.

Arabism and Islam are bound to one another with special ties which

[9] Smith, 84–5.

[10] D. Mackenzie Wallace, *Egypt and the Egyptian question,* London 1883, 103.

[11] Ṭaha Ḥusayn, *Ḥafiẓ wa-Shawqī,* quoted in Walther Braune, *Der islamische Orient zwischen Vergangenheit und Zukunft,* Bern und München 1960, 50.

[12] P.J. Vatikiotis, *The Egyptian army in politics,* Bloomington 1961, 210.

call to mind the connection between the Jewish people and Judaism. The Arabs and Islam appeared together on the stage of history. The founder of Islam was also the father of the Arab nation. In his book *"The Historic Roots of Arab Nationalism"* in (Arabic) which appeared in 1960, Dr. 'Abd al-'Azīz al-Dūrī cites statements made by al-Tha'ālibī in the 11th century, "Whoever loves the Prophet, loves the Arabs" and "Whomever God has guided to Islam knows that Muḥammad is the chosen of the prophets, and the Arabs, the chosen of the nations, and Arabic, the chosen of the languages."[13] The Arabs became a nation because of Islam, and Islam is the greatest creation of the Arab people. The vast conquests of the new religion in the 7th century were the triumphal procession of Islam, and established Arab power. When Arabs derive inspiration from memories of their past glory and yearn for its restoration, they turn to the golden age of Islamic history. The Arabic language is the tongue of divine revelation and the holy book, the language of prayer and literature of Muslims of all generations. The sites of pilgrimage for the Muslims of the whole world are in Arabia, and in prayer they face Mecca.

Islam today is not the normative framework for the group and the individual that it was a century ago. New beliefs weakened the religious faith of many to the point of indifference and heresy and created fresh ties of identification and loyalty. Yet Islam had remained a mighty public and emotional force; links with the community of Islam have remained strong even for most of those who have abandoned it as a faith. In the Arab world it has merged with nationalism, influenced it, and been influenced by it. This Arab nationalist mentality with an Islamic coloring is more self-confident and aggressive in the independent countries than when it was under foreign domination, and more so in the 1960's than in the 1920's. The liberal period in Arab thinking and politics of the 1920's has ended. Nationalism tops the scale of values, nourished by Islamic tradition and thinking. The purely religious aspect of Islam has become weakened, but the communal and political aspects have gained new momentum. And in this sense it is relevant to our discussion.

The history of Islam not only relates numerous examples of soldiers seizing power; it also shapes the views of those seeking power and predisposes those on whom it is imposed to regard the rule of officer politicians as a genuine continuation of the national tradition.

Altough the spirit of tradition buoys up the position of the officer politicians, they themselves do not aspire to revive old social forms. The officers are one of the most inveterate modernizing groups in Arab society, part

[13] 'Abd al-'Aziz al-Dūrī, *Al-judhūr al-tārīkhiyya lil-qawmiyya al-'arabiyya,* Beirut 1960, 46.

of the new intelligentsia. The officers' self-image is summed up in the phrase: We are intellectuals in uniform. They see their mission as bolstering national independence and transforming the patterns of society. And modernizing trends inevitably lead to clashes with the laws and tradition of Islam. The tradition which helped the officers in the struggle for power is a serious obstacle in its consolidation. The officers, consciously or not, are availing themselves of forces likely to cause them trouble. It is not by chance that the Muslim Brethren were at first the chief partners of the Free Officers in Egypt and later their most dangerous foes.

Among the various Arab officer politicians attitudes to Islam differ: There are fanatical Muslims, such as 'Abd al-Salām Arif; holders of moderate orthodox views, like Naguib; men indifferent to religion, like Qassim; and advocates of reforms, such as Za'īm. Nasser apparently aspires very cautiously to the neutralization of religion as a political force, although he himself is a devout Muslim. A revolutionary of secularization like Atatürk did not appear among the Arab officer politicians. They want, in varying degrees, to free themselves from the rule of Islam as a *dogma*, but all of them are anchored in Islam as a *community*.

When they achieved power, the officers in all countries adopted a number of important steps conflicting with tradition. They granted suffrage to women, and in Qassim's Iraq and Nasser's Egypt women also held cabinet posts. In Egypt the religious courts for adjudicating laws of personal status were abolished. These and similar measures are the continuation of a development which began a long time before the accession of the officers to power and which would also have progressed without them, as it has been doing in Arab countries where there are no officer governments. The most radical "separation of church and state" in an Arab country is Bourguiba's Tunis, where officers have less influence than in any other Arab land. Bourguiba has gone so far as to demand in February 1960 that the religious leaders allow workmen to eat during working hours in the fasting month of Ramadan.[14] When a debate flared up, he did not retreat from his position, and even achieved his end. And it is interesting that among his arguments Bourguiba also made use of traditional Islamic politico-religious reasoning, referring to the religious authority of a person holding political power: "As the head of an Islamic state, I, too, can speak in the name of religion."[15] Even he relied on an Islamic precept in order to abolish an Islamic law conflicting with the needs of modern society. The religious courts dealing with personal status have been abolished in Egypt, but the

[14] *Orient,* no. 13, 1960, 43–52.
[15] *Ibid,* 51.

civil courts which now sit in such cases are still handing down verdicts in accordance with religious law, whether it be Moslem, Christian or Jewish. Civil marriage, for example, does not exist. The abolition of religious courts without the abrogation of religious law has brought little change in the life of most Muslims; and for minorities, this measure actually amounts to a reduction in the autonomy of their communities. Islam sometimes exhibits considerable flexibility and generally more readiness to go along with the spirit of the times and to compromise with the trends of the regime than does Rabbinic Judaism or Roman Catholicism. Thus, religious leaders in Egypt have permitted birth control. However, in other matters the Islamic clergy continue to maintain a stubborn stand, and here, too the governments hesitate to come out against them openly. The Egyptian government has not dared to abolish polygamy. Actually, less than five per cent of Egyptian married men have more than one wife, but the question of the abolition of polygamy is of fundamental significance with respect to the position of women in society in general. For this reason, the religious leaders are against abolition, and, thus far, the government has yielded on this point despite its interest in changing the law both as a matter of principle and as part of its efforts to cope with the population explosion. In May and June 1962, Shaykh al-Ghazālī appeared as chief spokesman for reaction at the National Congress of Popular Forces in Egypt and expressed opposition to equal rights for women. When he was attacked at the convention and in articles and cartoons in the press, the students of al-Azhar demonstrated on his behalf in the streets of Cairo. Islam is thus the only force which between 1955 and 1965 has succeeded in organizing demonstrations against the Egyptian government. In Nasser's proposal for the National Charter which was discussed at the Congress, Islam was not mentioned as the state religion; but in the final version which was approved on June 30, 1962, Islam was once more defined as such. This was the only point on which Nasser saw himself forced to retreat.

The Islamic heritage has indubitably played a role of prime importance in the emergence of the officer class and its accession to power both as a helpful element and as a restraining force and will continue to do so. The problems which it poses for modern life have not yet been solved.

3. THE OFFICERS IN THE ARAB AWAKENING

THE ISLAMIC heritage serves simultaneously as a base and a stumbling block to the officers' rule, whereas modern Arab nationalism serves it both as a base and an aim.

Army officers have played a key role in Arab nationalism from its beginnings as a political movement. This holds true for Egyptian nationalism as well, which went its separate way until the middle of the 20th century. It is true that there were early mutual influences between Egyptian and Arab nationalism as exemplified by the figure of 'Azīz 'Alī al-Maṣri; but more than they were affected by each other, the Arab and Egyptian movements at the end of the 19th and the beginning of the 20th centuries were influenced by modern Turkish nationalism—and in it, too, officers played a decisive role.

The officers and their political movements took their principles and forms from nationalist movements in the west. In Turkey a group of liberal intellectuals, whose goal was constitutional reform, was organized between 1865 and 1870. These were the *Young Ottomans.*[1] Their influence fell on fertile soil in the military academy, and their coup of 1876 which deposed Sultan 'Abd al-'Azīz "was carried out by an alliance between Ottoman army and naval commanders and former grand viziers," and "the forces which they used came from the military academy."[2] This was a highly important precedent for the modern coups which have followed one another in rapid succession since then in the Ottoman Empire and the countries under its domination or influence.

We have neither evidence nor information as to how and to what extent the coup of the officers and intellectuals in Turkey in 1876 influenced 'Urābī's movement which came into being five years later in Egypt. However, the lack of evidence is no proof of the absence of influence and the proximity of time may not be accidental. In Turkey itself the *Young Ottoman* movement was the direct progenitor of the *Young Turks,* who

[1] Bernard Lewis, *The emergence of modern Turkey,* London 1961, 149 51.

[2] S. Mardin, 'Libertarian movements in the Ottoman Empire 1818–1895', *MEJ,* vol. 16, 1962, 170, 176.

formed a secret organization in 1889, on the first centennial of the French Revolution.[3] Among them, too, soldiers played a leading role.

'Urābī's revolt in Egypt resembled the *Young Ottoman* movement in Turkey in the cooperation between the intellectuals and the officers corps. In other aspects it differed. The most conspicuous feature of Egypt's national struggle was against foreign rulers—Turks and Circassians in the army, and Turks, Frenchmen and Englishmen in the economy and in politics. The struggle for internal reforms assumed in Egypt the form of a fight for national independence. Less striking, but no less important, was another difference: Without the leaders having intended it so, 'Urābī's movement became the expression of a popular uprising not only against foreign rule but also against native oppression. The correspondent of the London *Times* in Egypt at the time reported, "Arabi did not acquire and preserve his influence by terrorism, for at the commencement he had not power to injure anyone, and during the whole time of his power he never caused a single individual to be beheaded, hanged, or shot . . Nearly everybody in Egypt . . . wished to be freed not from the tyranny of military despots, but from the wholesome checks created by the Anglo-French Control, while the great mass of the ignorant peasantry wished to be liberated from the yoke of the usurers, which was the only kind of foreign influence with which they were personally acquainted."[4] It is precisely the testimony of an Englishman, advocating European supervision and intervention in the social nature of the movement which is very instructive: 'Urābī promised to cancel the debts of fellaheen and expel the usurers—many of whom were Greeks and Syrian and Lebanese Christians—and this was "one of the major factors in the popular support for 'Urābī".[5]

In the 19th century Egypt was from the point of view of modernization the most advanced Middle-Eastern country—a fact which the *Young Ottomans* clearly acknowledged.[6] The Egyptian rebellion almost assumed a revolutionary character. However, the civilian and military leaders of the movement, especially 'Urābī himself, were not outstanding individuals; they were not gifted with qualities of leadership and intellectual acumen; they did not understand the deep significance of the movement which had borne them aloft, and they did not know how to gauge the relative strength of their supporters and their adversaries. They were extreme where moderation was in order, aggressive when they could have achieved more by flexibility, and indifferent where vigorous action was required. The move-

[3] Lewis, 192–3.

[4] D. Mackenzie Waliace, *Egypt and the Egyptian question*, London 1883, 396–7.

[5] Gabriel Baer, *A history of landownership in modern Egypt 1800–1950*, London 1962, 36.

[6] S. Mardin, *The genesis of Young Ottoman thought*, Princeton 1962, 192.

ment met with utter failure. However, 'Urābī was not forgotten in Egypt, and in the memory of the next two generations his movement remained engraved primarily as a military manifestation. Naguib and Nasser frequently pointed to 'Urābī's movement as the precursor of their own and to *their* triumph as the belated victory of *his* struggle.

At the beginning of the 20th century the Turks once more outpaced the Egyptians and Arabs and again served as a source of influence and inspiration for them. The activist part of the *Young Turks* movement founded the *Committee for Unity and Progress* which carried out the revolution of 1908. This was a revolutionary political organization of army officers. It is interesting to note that the first nucleus of this committee was formed among those who more than any other group represented the close ties between the officers and the intellectuals—students of the military medical academy.[7]

For decades to come the revolution of the *Young Turks* was the prototype of many officer movements in various parts of the world and particularly in the Middle East. It was a modern nationalist movement of officers utilizing military force to effect changes in the internal political regime of the country, a movement which aroused enthusiasm and elicited support among large numbers of intellectuals and members of the middle class and which established a military dictatorship. The name "Young Turks" has become a well-known term for officer politicians throughout the world.

The 1908 revolution of the *Young Turks* exerted a very great influence on the young Arab national movement, and primarily on the young Arab officers who were then serving in the Ottoman army, the comrades, and in certain circumstances also the partners of the Turkish revolutionary officers. The Turkish revolution stimulated thinking, activity, and hopes among the Arabs. However, hopes were quickly dashed and not only the hopes of the Arabs ended in despair. "The long night of Hamidian despotism was over; the dawn of freedom had come. The constitution had once again been proclaimed and elections ordered. Turks and Armenians embraced on the streets; the age of freedom and brotherhood had come. The writings of that time reflect an almost delirious joy, which found its echoes even in the sceptical European press. The second Turkish Constitutional regime lasted longer than the first, but it, too, ended in failure, bitterness and disappointment. The dangers and difficulties at home and abroad were too great; . . . the regime degenerated into a kind of military oligarchy of the Young Turk leaders which ended only with the defeat of the Ottoman

[7] D. Rustow, 'The military in Middle-Eastern society and politics', in Sidney N. Fisher, (ed.), *The military in the Middle East,* Colombus, Ohio, 1963, 7.

Empire in 1918."[8] In the general disappointment the hopes and aspirations of the Arabs were dealt a special blow. Previously, they had been suppressed in theory by Islamic cosmopolitanism and in pratice by Turkish despotism. From now on, the new rulers intensified their tyranny and increased their discrimination against the Arabs as a concomitant of pan-Turanian nationalist doctrine. However, the national Arab awakening which came with the elimination of 'Abd al-Ḥamīd's rule in Turkey did not languish, and the bitterness born of disillusionment strengthened the aspirations for liberation. The regime of repressions drove the Arab national movement underground on the eve of World War I. It is no wonder that officers played a large part in its clandestine activities. In 1913, 'Azīz 'Alī al-Maṣrī organized the secret officers' Arab nationalist society *al-'Ahd* whose members—mostly Ottoman officers of Iraqi origin—later became the leaders of the Sharifian army and the heads of the new Iraqi state. The twelve personalities who alternatively filled the position of prime minister in Iraq between 1920 and 1944 included six members of this group, among them Nūrī Sa'īd, Ja'far al-Askarī and Ṭaha al-Hāshimī.

World War I was followed by a period of national and social revolution in all countries which had arisen from the ruins of previous empires—Russian, German, Austro-Hungarian and Turkish-Ottoman. All the Arab countries in Asia and Africa, with the exception of the Arabian peninsula, became—under diverse constitutional forms—colonies of Great Britain and France. But national movements surged like a tide among their peoples. In Egypt, Syria and Iraq there were volcanic uprisings between 1918 and 1921 which were quelled only after long, bitter struggles. This time, the awakening everywhere was headed by civilian political leaders, for local military forces were usually auxiliary troops commanded by the foreign authority and the officer corps was under strict surveillance. Members of the minority groups were systematically given preference over Muslim Arabs. Young Arabs with political or nationalist ambitions, on the other hand, selected a military career only when they could not enter the liberal professions because of lack of means. However, hardly a generation had passed before the officer once more appeared as a major active factor in the Arab political arena.

Again it was Turkey which forged ahead and set a precedent for the Arab peoples. Despite the fact that she had been conquered and degraded, Turkey bestirred herself in a national movement which achieved independence and effected basic changes in the structure of government and society—under the leadership of a soldier, Atatürk. At the beginning of the century, as

[8] Lewis, 206–7.

a twenty-year-old cadet at the military academy, Muṣṭafā Kamāl joined the *Young Turks*. He played no important role in the 1908 revolution, but during World War I he achieved distinction and became a national hero. In 1915, he commanded the division which repulsed the massive British attack on the Dardanelles. "This victory, which saved the capital from invasion, was the only really striking success won by Ottoman arms during the war."[9]

In 1919, after the defeat, he organized and directed the fierce opposition to the Greek invasion. to the subjugation of Turkey by the Allies, and to the rotten, feeble government in Istanbul. In 1923 the cosigners of the Lausanne treaty recognized Turkey's full sovereignty over all her territories. Turkey became a republic, the caliphate was abolished, secularism was proclaimed as the foundation of legal and spiritual life, and etatism of the economic system.

The examples of the *Young Turks* and of Atatürk made a profound impression on the Arab officers and became a stimulus to action when their own countries became independent. As one Arab state after another became sovereign, the army officers, emboldened, did not hesitate for long.

The leaders of the first coups in Iraq between 1936 and 1941, in Syria in 1949, and the veterans of the pro-Nazi military underground in Egypt in 1941 had all been Ottoman officers in their youth: Bakr Ṣidqī, 'Azīz Yāmulkī, Ṣabbāgh and his three comrades of the Golden Square, Ḥusnī Za'īm and Sāmī Ḥinnāwī and 'Azīz 'Alī al-Maṣrī. Multiple personal, organizational and ideological ties connected these men with the ruling officer politicians of the 1950's and 1960's, from Nasser to Arif and Sallāl. Thus, from the very beginning of the Arab national movement, the officer corps had an important part in its development. Its domination of the independent Arab countries did not come as a *deus ex machina*. It is a continuation of the political heritage of Islamic civilization and of the underground tradition of Arab nationalism.

[9] *Ibid*, 239.

PART FOUR

HISTORICAL AND SOCIAL ORIGINS OF THE ARAB OFFICER CLASS

"An officer is much more respected than any other man who has little money."

Dr. Samuel Johnson, 1776

1. THE OFFICER CORPS AS A SOCIAL FORMATION

EVER SINCE the beginnings of historiography and historiosophy, writers have concerned themselves with the relationship between heads of state and the commanders of their armies. They have examined the subject in depth and in breadth, dealing with the position of the military man in society, the struggle between statesman and soldier, and the influence of each upon the other. There exists a very large and valuable literature describing and analyzing the role of the army officer and the functions of the army in all periods and in all countries. But the nature of the officer corps itself and the social origins of its members have received but little attention. Much has been written on the politics and attitudes of the officer corps but relatively little research has been done into the officers' individual and collective social origins. At times, one can find observations such as that which appears in the important anthology on *The Role of the Military in Underdeveloped Countries* which was published in 1962: "Western scholarship had been pecularity inattentive to the sociology of armies."[1] Since then, perhaps beginning with M. Janowitz's research, increasing attention has been given to the sociological composition of the officer corps. But so far their enquiries have been confined to the armies of the highly developed western nations. Communist scholars have done no better. A Soviet social scientist wrote in 1963: "I should like to remark that we do not yet posses any study of those elements of society in the underdeveloped countries which do not fit into the concept of 'bourgeoisie' but which in many countries play a very large or even leading role. I have in mind the intelligentsia and the army."[2]

On the question of research in the Egyptian army an Egyptian Marxist wrote in 1962: "The analysis of the middle-rank groups in the army remains

[1] Lucien W. Pye, 'Armies in the process of political modernization', in John J. Johnson, (ed.), *The role of the military in underdeveloped countries,* Princeton 1962, 70.

[2] Georgiy Mirskiy, 'Creative Marxism and problems of national liberation revolution', Mirovaya Ekonomika i Mezhdunarodnyye Otnosheniya, no. 5, 1963, translated in *The Mizan Newsletter,* London, April 1964, 5.

yet to be done, both with regard to their social milieu and to their ideology at the time of the Revolution."[3] And it is not to be expected that this work will be done by Egyptians.

There would be perhaps but limited interest in studying the social background of the officer class if the army were no more than an obedient instrument in the hands of the state's leadership, carrying out its military and defense objectives and differentiating between friend and foe in foreign relations only. But what army confines its interest to such a sphere? What army can entirely refrain from utilizing its influence in internal politics when it is the largest consumer of the national budget; when it has to make constant claims on the channelizing of industry, the training of professional manpower, the locations of factories, and the organization of transport; and when in every important political and diplomatic decision security considerations must largely prevail? In countries such as the Arab states of our days, where the officer class plays a decisive part in political and social life, it becomes essential to try to elucidate the social origins of this class. And in particular the question as to who benefits from an officer regime cannot be answered without research into the social strata and family ties of these officers.

Together with the argument that the social origins of the officer class are of no interest as long as they do not mix in politics, it is sometimes claimed that they are not very important in view of the special nature and structure of the army. The officer class is, after all, a defined and closed professional and social group, relatively separated from the rest of society. Apart from monastic orders there is no comparable social body that so sets its stamp, for so much of a man's life, on every individual belonging to it. The modern professional officer class is a cohesive body with an independent, well-developed and highly-fostered group-consciousness, no less molded by its own way of thinking and scale of values, just as it keeps to its own special dress, code of regulations and judicial system. As such its psychological pressure toward assimilation is enormous. By donning his uniform the officer accentuates his membership in a collective which is separate from other sections of society, and demonstrates his desire to resemble his colleagues and to identify with them, not only in their outward appearance but in their mode of life and their mentality. It was in this spirit that C. Wright Mills wrote in his book on *The Power Elite* of the United States: "Social origins and early backgrounds are less important to the character of the professional military man than to any other high social type. The training of the future admiral or general begins early and

[3] Anouar Abdel-Malek, *Egypte, société militaire,* Paris 1962, 208.

is thus deeply set, and the military world which he enters is so all-encompassing that his way of life is firmly centered within it. To the extent that these conditions exist, whether he is the son of a carpenter or a millionaire is that much less important."[4]

Yet this is not altogether so. Although the average general is not affected by the fact that his father was either a carpenter or a millionaire to the same extent that the average lawyer would be, still the effect is there; and the effect on the captain is greater than that on the general. And more important, if the influence of background is less material in the case of the American officer of whom Mills writes, it is nevertheless very important in the case of the Egyptian or the Syrian officer. And there is more here than a question of carpenter or millionaire. In the United States Army, at least, it hardly matters if Lieutenant "X" is Protestant or Catholic, Jew or Negro, while in Syria it matters considerably to his "image" and his chances of promotion if the officer is Sunni or Druze or Greek-Orthodox.

Despite its significance, research into the social background of the officer corps remained relatively neglected—and not by chance. Janowitz, one of the first to realize its importance and the author of a comprehensive work on the nature and sociology of *The Professional Soldier,* i.e., the officer—to be sure, only the American—points to two sources contributing to this neglect. One is the object of the research, the officer corps itself, and the other the subject, the researchers themselves. The officer corps chooses to regard itself and even more to appear in the eyes of the citizenry as the standard bearer of the best in the national culture and as the body representing the nation as a whole; consequently, "no profession resists inquiry into its social origins as stubbornly as does the military."[5] As for the researchers: "In American sociology it was once widely assumed that to study military institutions was an expression of a particular political or value point of view. How many times have sociologists said to me with profound naiveté and without realizing their bias, why study the military and thereby make it better. The naiveté is based on an exaggeration of the consequences of sociological research. The bias, in that it is a distortion to believe that a more efficient military is more dangerous than an inefficient institution."[6] Of course, revealing the sources of opposition is the starting point to eliminating them.

We shall not go from one extreme position to another—from regarding the officer corps as isolated in society to ignoring its uniqueness. Every social body is more than the sum of the individuals belonging to it, and

[4] C. Wright Mills, *The power elite,* New York 1956, 192.

[5] Morris Janowitz, *The professional soldier,* New York 1960, 80.

[6] Morris Janowitz, *The new military,* New York 1964, 8.

all the more so the officer corps with its permanent and rigid structure. Eliminating the isolation does not mean dissolving the social formation.

The army officer in the twentieth century is a new social type, a member of a new social group, which has been aptly defined by Huntington: "The modern officer corps is a professional body, and the modern military officer a professional man . . . A profession is a peculiar type of functional group with highly specialized characteristics," for example, physicians and lawyers. The special characteristics of such a professional group are three in number: "Expertise, reponsibility and corporateness." "Expertise" means professional knowledge acquired by long study; "Responsibility"—carrying out a duty essential to Society; and "Corporateness" the sharing by members of a profession of a "sense of organic unity and consciousness of themselves as a group apart from laymen." "The legal right to practise the profession is limited to members of a carefully defined body." This officer corps is a new profession, a product of the nineteenth century. The medieval knight was an "aristocratic, individualistic amateur," and the officers of the European armies up to the end of the eighteenth century were "mercenaries or aristocrats." "Only in the Napoleonic Wars did the officers begin to acquire a specialized technique to distinguish themselves from laymen . . . the professional soldier as a social type is an uniquely characteristic of modern Society as is the industrial entrepreneur . . . prior to 1800 there was no such thing as a professional officer corps. In 1900 such bodies existed in virtually all major countries."[7]

Huntington's definition places much emphasis on the novelty of the modern officer corps. But does this apply in the same manner and to the same extent to the officer corps of different countries? It is evident that the characteristics of a social group in the twentieth century differ greatly from those of the eighteenth, so that it is often easier to show the new and the different than the continuity. True, the medieval knights and the officers in the Thirty Years War were not professional officers in the modern sense, yet how should one define the commanders or knights of different military organizations prior to 1800 if not as professional officers—the commanders of the Praetorian Guards in Roman antiquity, of the French Royal and Papal Swiss Guards, of the Russian Streltsi and the Japanese Samurai?

In Middle-Eastern Islamic society the profession of the officer, according to the definition of characteristics given by Huntington, is certainly not a new one. All the characteristics he gives fit the Mamelukes—the expertise, responsibility and corporateness. Moreover, the Mamelukes established important precedents of rule by a military elite.

[7] Samuel Huntington, *The soldier and the state*, Cambridge, Mass., 1957, 7–8, 17–9.

The institution of the Mamelukes existed for about a thousand years, from the middle of the ninth century until the thirties or forties of the nineteenth century. Mameluke sultans ruled in Egypt, Palestine and Syria from 1250 until the Ottoman conquest of 1516/7, and in Egypt the Mameluke emirs were masters of the land even under Ottoman sovereignty until their defeat by Napoleon in 1798. In the days of Muḥammad 'Alī, too, in the first third of the nineteenth century, they were one of the main pillars of the Egyptian army. Outside of Egypt the characteristics of the Mameluke army had a deep and lasting influence on the shape of other Muslim armies too. The Janissary battalions, the core of the Ottoman army up to 1826, were in fact a variant of the Mameluke army.

The term "Mamelukes" indicates an institution which existed exclusively in the Islamic civilization—a military elite of slaves. *"Mamlūk"* means a man who is the property of another—a slave. However, while the word *'abd* indicates a black-skinned slave (and to this day the negro is called *'abd* in colloquial Arabic) the Mameluke was a white-skinned slave whose lot was military service. Boys of Turkish, Mongolian, Gurage, Circassian or Armenian extraction—Christians or pagans, since Muslims could not be enslaved nor sold into slavery—were brought from the steppes of southern Russia, from the region of the Black Sea, the Volga and the Caucasus, to Baghdad and Cairo. There they were converted to Islam and from an early age given intensive selective training in special boarding schools to make them mounted knights. On completion of his training the Mameluke emerged a free man; he could be accepted as a cavalryman in a battalion, and the owner and the trainer of other cadet-Mamelukes.

Even after receiving his freedom, the Mameluke retained his contact with and loyalty to his former owner, and also his feelings of companionship and solidarity with his comrades from his slavery-training period and the graduation-liberation ceremony. Sons of Mamelukes could not themselves become Mamelukes nor be accepted into the oligarchy of the knights; they mingled and became one with the general population. There was naturally no lack of attempts on the part of the Mamelukes—particularly those who rose to positions of command and top rule—to name their sons their successors and found dynasties. The breakdown of the principle of nontransfer of the title and status and Mameluke by hereditary succession was one of the first factors causing the degeneration of Mameluke rule.

At the time of the flowering of this regime the Mamelukes themselves were the supreme rulers of Egypt and the lands conquered by it. On the death—sometimes by assassination—of a sultan, his successor was elected by the Mamelukes themselves from among their number. This system of choosing the strongest and the most talented from a limited oligarchy, differing from the populace in language and profession, provided a line of sultans who excelled in both military and political leadership. In the thirteenth century the Mamelukes cleared the last of the Crusaders out of Palestine and Syria and stopped Hulagu Khan's Mongolian Tartars. The victory of Quṭuz and Baybars near 'Ayn Jālūt, the modern 'En Harod, in 1260 in one of the most decisive battles of the Middle Ages saved Egypt from destruction such as had befallen Iraq two years earlier and from which she did not recover for centuries. From then on Egypt has been the stronger of those two lands competing for thousands of years for the hegemony of the Middle East. At the end of the thirteenth century and the beginning of the fourteenth the Mamelukes raised Egypt to an age of splendor in the Middle East, in economic and cultural life no less than in military power. The widely-held view of the Mamelukes as crude dictators derives from the picture they presented at the later period of their degeneracy, and ignores their great achivements in earlier times.

The Ottoman army which conquered the Mamelukes at the beginning of the sixteenth century was itself officered by a group similar to that of the Mamelukes, and the Janissaries in particular were in direct continuation of the same tradition. One of the important differences—and the decisive one from the military point of view—was the organization of the Janissaries as an infantry force equipped with firearms, while the Mameluke cavalry remained mounted, fighting with sword and lance.[8]

The Mamelukes ruled Egypt for six hundred years. They were a military elite of expert professionals, an oligarchy separate from the rest of the population, with an ingrained consciousness of its superior strength and rights. Although one should not overestimate the influence on contemporary political life of an historical phenomenon, which ceased to exist more than a hundred years ago, neither should one disregard the influence on recent developments of relationships which prevailed uninterruptedly for a thousand years—particularly in Arab and Muslim society, where even in the middle of our century traditional concepts and patterns of life steadfastly held their own against modern values and preserved their existence through adaptation. The army officer type as defined and characterized by Huntington exists as a new social type only in the societies of highly industrialized countries. In Middle-Eastern society, where there is ample and long precedence of an officer corps separate from the rest of the populace, the corporateness of the officer corps is to a great extent conditioned by its history.

The influence of previous patterns and relationships is always the source

[8] David Ayalon, *Gunpowder and firearms in the Mameluk kingdom,* London 1956, *passim.*

of conscious or unconscious imitation. On the other hand, previous patterns have often been the objects of opposition, an example to be avoided and the concept to be fought against. Thus, the phenomenon of the Mamelukes in some respects served only as a starting-point for the development of the modern officer corps in Egypt or in Turkey, and later as an institution to be uprooted in all its ramifications. Yet, even so, knowledge of it is essential for understanding the social grouping and historic development of the contemporary Arab army officer corps.

2. OTTOMAN AND TURKISH OFFICERS

THE IMAGE of the officer and the characteristics of the officer class are different in the various Arab countries. Even within each individual country considerable changes have taken place from time to time. Nevertheless, there persist certain patterns and influences, in particular external sources of influence which have affected the creation of the image of the officer in every Arab country and which are common to all Arab armies, even if the extent of this influence varies from one country to another.

The character of the modern Arab officer class derives from two main sources—the Ottoman and the European, particularly the British, German and French.

The Egyptian army of the nineteenth century bore a strong resemblance to the Ottoman army both in its structure and in the composition of its officer class. Up to the time of World War II the armies of Iraq and Syria were staffed with many officers who had begun their profession in the army of the Sultan before World War I. The Western influence, on the other hand, started with the Ottoman army itself as far back as the eighteenth century, becoming ever deeper and broader as time went on. The Egyptian army had been under direct British command ever since 1882, and its organization and training conformed to the British pattern. The Arab armies in Asia were under the British and the French since 1920. Between the two world wars many British and French officers served as military commanders and instructors in Iraq and Syria, and many Arab officers spent a long or a short period of advanced training in the military academies of England and France. After World War II the number of Arab officers attending military academies in Western Europe increased until the middle fifties. In more recent years, Egyptian, Iraqi and Syrian officers have been going to Russia, Czechoslovakia and Bulgaria for their advanced training.

One cannot consider the characteristics of the armies and the officer class in the Arab countries without noting the Turkish-Ottoman influence, though many attempts have been made to ignore it, however inconsistent this may be with historical truth, from an unwarranted feeling that some stigma attaches to such influence.The tendentious historiosophies of Arab nationalism and of British and French imperialism joined forces in the first third of the twentieth century to present the Ottoman era in a false light, making it appear as though the period of its rule was a continuous decline—a long dark age of retrogression between the golden age of the Arabs and Islam in the early Middle Ages and the Arab revival of the last two generations, as though the Sultan of Turkey had always been "The Sick Man of the Bosporus." This was not so. The period of the Renaissance in Europe, the sixteenth century, marked a flowering of civilization in Turkey too. After long generations of decline and weakness, Islam flourished again under Ottoman rule. In 1529 and again in 1683 the Ottomans stood at the gates of Vienna, and their force was not military alone. "The Ottoman Empire was the last and the most enduring of the great Islamic universal empires that ruled over the Middle East since the day when the first of the caliphs succeeded the last of the prophets."[1]

However the seventeenth century already saw the beginning of the retreat of Ottoman rule and the growing ascendancy of the European Christian states. The sphere in which Western superiority showed itself earlier and more tangibly than any other was the military sphere—in matters of equipment, in technique and in the organization of armies. The first reforms based on European examples which were introduced into the Ottoman Empire were army reforms, and the officer class was the first broad social group to come into close contact with European culture and with European scientists. The influence thus absorbed naturally did not remain confined to the military sphere. A British traveller, who was in Turkey in the middle of the nineteenth century, relates as a typical example that the cadets in the Turkish military academy not only read Voltaire's book on Charles XII, from which they had to learn for their military studies, but also read his heretical *Dictionary of Philosophy*.[2]

In 1826 the Janissary army was abolished and its personnel slaughtered, and the Baktashia Order with which it was connected was proscribed. The Ottoman army was organized anew on European lines. As the Prussian officers were at that time held to be the best in the world, and as Prussia was neither a neighbor nor a rival, a Prussian delegation was invited to Turkey to give advice and guidance on the training and organization of the army. At the head of the delegation was Captain von Moltke, who later rose to fame as the Prussian chief of staff and architect of the victories over Austria and France. The German instructors remained with the Ottoman army from 1835 to 1918. Turkish youngsters who were sent abroad

[1] Bernard Lewis, *The Middle East and the West*, London 1964, 72.

[2] Charles MacFarlane, 'Turkey and its destiny', London 1850, vol. 2, 275, quoted by Şerif Mardin, *The genesis of Young Ottoman thought*, Princeton 1962, 213.

for their military studies from 1830 onwards studied for the most part in Paris, London and Vienna.

In 1840 von Moltke and two of his colleagues gave the following instructive report to general headquarters in Berlin on the Ottoman officer class: "The weakest part of the army . . . was the officers. Two of the major-generals came from the harem of Muhammad Khusrau's palace, a third had been a porter ten years earlier and a fourth had been a galley-slave taken off a ship. There were a few talented officers among the brigadiers and colonels, and these provided the momentum that kept things going, though they received almost no help from the officers junior to them. Often very young men were made majors. They might have been narghileh-tenders or coffee-makers to some pasha, and they were immediately given command of a battalion. Captains and lieutenants were usually the more elderly men . . . none had scientific training as we know it, and few had battle experience."[3]

A British traveller of that period reports that the students in the military medical school—all of them—came from "the very poor . . . sons of common sailors, ostlers, pedlars, porters, etc., and no Turk of upper or even middle class would send his son to the school."[4] Since these days many changes have taken place in the Turkish army, but one important and basic factor remains the same: The officer class is recuited from the lower strata of society. A survey of the Ottoman army by an Austrian officer in 1870 tells us: "There exists an intimacy between the officers and the men which in other European armies would be contrary to regulations . . . This unusual state of affairs is explained by the low standard of education of the officers, most of whom are of necessity taken from the ranks, since the educated classes keep well away from service in the army."[5]

Thirty years later, at the beginning of the present century, when Muḥammad Kurd 'Alī, the Syrian publicist, fled from Damascus, the Turkish governor offered a reward "and immediate promotion from private to captain to any man in the army or police force who captured [him] dead or alive."[6]

The position of the officer in society was not of the highest. One of the reasons why Atatürk's mother was opposed to his joining the army was: "Officers have never had any money—if he became an officer, that was.

[3] Helmuth von Moltke, *Briefe über Zustände und Begebenheiten in der Türkei aus den Jahren 1835 bis 1839,* Berlin 1893, 528.

[4] Mardin, 131.

[5] (Anon.), *Die Wehrkraft des osmanischen Reiches und seiner Vasallen-Staaten im Mai 1871,* Vienna 1871, 61.

[6] Muḥammad Kurd 'Alī, *al-Mudhakkirāt,* vol. 1, Damascus 1948, 90; *Memories of Kurd Ali; a selection,* Washington 1954, 26.

He might well fail his examinations and end up as a common soldier."[7] In republican Turkey the situation has changed but little. Although during the reign of Atatürk the army was accorded considerable honor and respect, "Few, if any, sons from families of even moderate means ever thought of the military as a career . . . boys sought an education in business, engineering, law, medicine, dentistry, government service, the foreign service; anything but the army or navy. Still, there were not enough schools and only the fortunate could choose. Hence a poor boy, or a middle-class son from a more remote part of Anatolia might be able to obtain an education only in a professional military school."[8]

A typical sample of the social origins of the present-day Turkish officer class is the group of thirty-eight officers who carried out the revolution of May 1960 under Gürsel. Only twelve of them were born in the large towns of Istanbul, Ankara, Izmir and Salonika. Some came from small country towns and most, from little villages. Of the twenty-seven whose fathers' professions are known, twelve were sons of army officers, four sons of clerks and four sons of traders—the remainder were apparently sons of farmers. Several were orphaned at an early age and had to advance in life entirely on their own. One ran away from his poverty-stricken home in the western Anatolian hills and made his way, dragging himself through the freezing cold to Erzincan, where he was accepted at a military school. One had been a shepherd boy.[9]

From the time of the Janissaries to the present day, many Turkish officers came to military schools as orphan children and were trained at government expense, thus being obliged to serve the state upon graduation. Atatürk himself was in this category, the son of a customs official in Salonika who traded in timber as a sideline. The family's prospects for economic advancement were cut short with the early death of the father, and Muṣṭafā Kemāl chose the profession of army officer out of economic consideration no less than for reasons of nationalist ideology. Another typical example from World War I is the career of Irfan Orga, as described in his interesting autobiography[10]: A well-to-do family of carpet merchants was reduced to absolute penury during the war. The father, a reserve officer, was called to the colors and killed in action. The mother, now destitute, was able to save the children from starvation by getting them into the military school.

The popular social origins of Turkish officers did not create a strong link

[7] Irfan Orga, *Phoenix ascendant,* London 1958, 30.

[8] S.N. Fisher, 'The role of the military in society and government in Turkey', in Sidney N. Fisher, (ed.), *The military in the Middle East,* Colombus, Ohio, 1963, 29.

[9] *Ibid,* 31; Walter F. Weiker, *The Turkish revolution 1960–1961.* Washington 1963, 118–9.

[10] Irfan Orga, *Portrait of a Turkish family,* London 1950.

between the officer class and the public at large. It must be borne in mind that the officer had usually been separated from his family at an early age, and in many cases the family ties had been weakened before his entry into the army—indeed this had been a cause of enlistment. Within the army, both at the military schools and in officer circles, there has always prevailed a feeling of superiority and isolation of the officer class, as a group distinct from the general population in its thinking as well as in its way of life and occupation. For most of those who chose it, the military career was the gate to the world of the ruling elite, and they were absorbed by it, as always happens to careerists everywhere.

On the other hand, the popular origins of so many Ottoman and Turkish republican officers attest to an important—but only relatively seldom observed—feature of Middle-Eastern Muslim-dominated society in general: great social mobility. It is often assumed, although without reason and without much practical corroboration, that social mobility goes hand in hand with equality, as if societies of very sharp social stratification afforded a minimum of social mobility. As a matter of fact, Ottoman and Turkish society has by no means been an egalitarian one for hundreds of years; class distinctions and differences between various strata of the population determined by property ownership, income and political rights have been very sharp. At the same time, quite a large number of persons holding the highest positions in government, in the economy and especially in the army have always been men whose parents belonged to the lowest classes, judging by criteria of wealth and occupation. This phenomenon is most obvious in Turkish society, and especially in the Turkish army.[11] But it is not restricted to Turkey; it exists, although now everywhere to the same degree, in all countries which were at the time part of the Ottoman Empire.

[11] Frederick W. Frey, *The Turkish political elite,* Cambridge, Mass., 1965, 136–143; Stanislaw Andrzejewski, *Military organization and society,* London 1954, 22.

3. THE EGYPTIAN OFFICER CLASS

In the first half of the nineteenth century Egypt was the strongest power in the Middle East. The armies of Muḥammad ʿAlī had conquered vast areas of the Sudan, the Hijaz, Palestine and Syria. In 1832 and again in 1839 they defeated the army of the Sultan in Anatolia, and only the intervention of the European powers prevented them from overrunning Istanbul. In 1823 Muḥammad ʿAlī's regular army had numbered only 19 thousand men. By 1833 the infantry and cavalry together amounted to 90 thousand, with an additional 10 thousand irregulars and a navy 25 thousand strong. In 1839, the peak year, the regular land forces alone numbered more than 130 thousand.[1]

Muḥammad ʿAlī, the founder of modern Egypt, was a Turk from Kavala in Macedonia, a small port on the coast of the Aegean Sea. He came to Egypt with the Macedonian Brigade of the Ottoman army which fought the Napoleonic invasion. In 1801, at the age of thirty-two, he was already a lieutenant-colonel.

After the withdrawal of the French in 1801, chaos prevailed in Egypt. The Ottomans wanted to harvest the fruits of their victory and to stabilize their rule, the Mamelukes tried to restore the situation as it had been before the coming of Napoleon, and the British, who played an important part in repulsing the Napoleonic invasion, intended to make Egypt a British sphere of influence. In an atmosphere of quick successive changes of rule accompanied by shortages and famine, the population of Cairo was ripe for serious disturbances. They wanted to be rid of the Mamelukes, the Turks, the French and the British altogether. Muḥammad ʿAlī, at the head of his Macedonian and Albanian troops, adroitly succeeded in maneuvering between the conflicting forces and emerged ruler of the country. In 1805 the Sultan recognized him as Governor of Egypt.

Muḥammad ʿAlī took Napoleon as his model. He tried to make Egypt

[1] G. Douin, *La mission du Baron de Boislecomte (L'Egypte et la Syrie en 1833)*, Cairo 1927, p. 113; ʿAbd al-Raḥmān Zakī, *Tārīkh ūrṭat al-banādiq al-sādisa al-mushāt,* Cairo 1938; *Majhūd Miṣr al-ḥarbī,* Cairo 1952, 23, 32–3; A.V. Pawlikowski-Cholewa, *Die Heere des Morgenlandes,* Berlin 1940, 255–6.

a modern state, industrial, centralized and expansionist. Industries producing goods for the army and navy were given economic precedence. Education and medicine were similarly geared to military requirements.

Muḥammad ʿAlī sought to recruit the rank and file for his army in Black Africa, using what were in fact negro slaves. The Egyptian fellaheen he wanted to reserve for the development of agriculture and armament industries, as he was loath to place weapons in their hands. The recruitment of slave soldiers was an important motive for the conquest of the Sudan, but this source of manpower could not keep pace with the great needs of the rapidly expanding Egyptian army, particularly as many of the captured negroes succumbed to the hardships of the journey before they reached Cairo. No alternative remained, therefore, but to mobilize the Egyptian fellaheen, and from the thirties of the nineteenth century the rank and file of the army was Egyptian. But the same was not true of the officers.

The officer class in Muḥammad ʿAlī's army was made up of four basic groups: A nucleus of Mamelukes, a majority of Turks, a handful of French and Italian instructors and a minority of Egyptian Arabs.

In the first decade of Muḥammad ʿAlī's rule the Mamelukes were potentially dangerous enemies and he resolved to break their power once and for all. In 1811 their leaders were invited to a party at the Citadel in Cairo. When they were inside the gates were locked, and all of them, more than four hundred men, were massacred. The surviving Mamelukes fled to the Dongola region of northern Sudan, where they maintained an independent regime until the Egyptian conquest in 1820. Although they had been dangerous to him, the Mamelukes were necessary to Muḥammad ʿAlī. He set about attracting those who were left after the great slaughter, most of them youngsters, to serve as officers in his army. There was no longer any fear that the Mamelukes would regain power, and their training had fitted them for high positions only within the framework of the army. Both on account of their military capacity and as a counterbalance to the Turkish officers, they were given important appointments. In 1833 six of the 12 main positions of command were held by Mamelukes. The total number of Mameluke officers at that time was between three and four hundred.[2] Indeed, the enlistment of new Christian slave children from lands east and west of the Black Sea and their education in Cairo still continued during the first three decades of the nineteenth century, until the firm establishment of Russian rule in the regions from where the boys were taken.

Until the death of King Fu'ād in 1936 the language spoken at home by members of the Muḥammad ʿAlī dynasty was Turkish. When other lan-

[2] Douin, 101; Aimé Vingtrinier, *Soliman-Pasha,* Paris 1886, 101.

guages were used, they were French or Italian. The second estate of the country (after the royal court) in which Turkish origins long predominated was the army. The language of command in the Egyptian army was Turkish throughout the nineteenth century and until 1923.[3] The Turkish-speaking Turks, Circassians, Albanians and Kurds formed the majority of Muḥammad 'Alī's officers. But it was not easy to attract Turkish officers for service in Egypt, for until 1840 this meant service in an army which was fighting the Sultan. Muḥammad 'Alī used high salaries as an inducement. While private soldiers and non-commissioned officers in the Egyptian army were paid less than those in the Ottoman army, the pay of the officers was much higher. Some comparative figures are:[4]

MONTHLY PAY IN PIASTERS, 1833

(In 1833 one piaster was worth about one-third of a French franc).

Rank	*Egyptian Army*	*Sultan's Army*	*Ratio*
Private	15	20	0.75 to 1
Sergeant-Major	40	120	0.33 to 1
Second-Lieutenant	250	120	2.10 to 1
Captain	500	180	2.80 to 1
Lieutenant-Colonel	2,500	400	6.25 to 1
Brigadier	8,000	1,200	6.67 to 1

A brigadier *(amīr ālāy)* in the army of the Sultan received 60 times as much as a private. In the army of Muḥammad 'Alī he got 533 times as much as a private. In addition to his pay the officer also received larger daily rations of food and tobacco; a lieutenant two rations, a lieutenant-colonel eight and a brigadier 15. And more important than these—senior officers were at times awarded grants of land. Such land grants in some cases proved to be the beginnings of family estates, which were added to by the children and grandchildren of the original grantees. There were also cases where officers were awarded wives from the Governor's harem.

The European officers laid the foundations for modernizing the army. In 1833 more than 70 Italian officers, about 70 French and about a dozen Spaniards and Englishmen were serving in the Egyptian army.[5] The French

[3] (Anon.), *Die Wehrkraft des osmanischen Reiches and seiner Vasallen-Staaten,* Wien 1871. 87; Pierre Crabitès, *The winning of the Sudan,* London 1934, 38; W. Hardy Wickwar, *The modernization of administration in the Near East,* Beirut 1963, 12.

[4] Douin, 114.

[5] *Ibid,* 108–9.

were officers of Napoleon's army who had not found employment in their profession after the defeat of the Emperor, and who either could not or would not adapt themselves to civilian occupations. These French officers filled most of the administrative and training positions in Muḥammad 'Alī's army. The most outstanding among them was Octave Sève, otherwise known as Sulaymān Pasha al-Faransāwī (1788–1860). Sève had reached the rank of lieutenant in Napoleon's army. However, when he arrived in Egypt in 1816 he represented himself as a colonel. After proving his ability in various missions in the Sudan and Greece, and after embracing Islam, he was made chief of staff, lieutenant-general *(farīq)* and a Pasha. His son and daughters married into the most exalted families of Egypt.[6] Most of the other Europeans returned home after their period of service.

The Egyptians themselves formed the weakest pillar in the structure of the officer class. There were Egyptians and Sudanese who rose to be non-commissioned and commissioned officers—how many is not known. But the majority of these officers rose no higher than the rank of second-lieutenant or lieutenant. Very few became captains, and none at all rose higher.

In 1840 the Powers compelled Muḥammad 'Alī to reduce his army to 18,000. In the time of his successors, 'Abbās (1848–54) and Sa'īd (1854–63), its size alternately increased and diminished. Sa'īd in fact introduced a change of policy in recruiting officers. He regarded himself as an Egyptian and had no liking for the Turks. He encouraged young Egyptians, particularly the sons of village notables, to enter military schools and become officers. Egyptian officers who were commissioned before his time were promoted. Under Sa'īd at least two reached the rank of colonel *(qā'im-maqām)*.[7] It was also under his rule that Copts were commissioned for the first time.[8]

One of the two who were promoted to colonel was Aḥmad 'Urābī. He was born in 1841 in a village in the Delta to a family, originally Bedouin, who had settled there in his grandfather's day. His father was the *shaykh al-balad,* village headman, and from him Aḥmad learned to read and write. Arithmetic he learned from a Coptic moneychanger. From the age of eight until 12 he studied at al-Azhar, and in December 1854 he joined the army. Thanks to his knowledge of reading and writing he was immediately

[6] Vingtrinier, *passim*; Richard L. Hill, *A biographical dictionary of the Anglo-Egyptian Sudan,* Oxford 1951, 336; Gabriel Baer, *A history of landownership in modern Egypt, 1800–1950,* London 1962, 47.

[7] Buṭrus Abu Manna, *Egyptian officials and officers in the second half of the nineteenth century,* Jerusalem 1962. (Unpublished seminar paper, in Hebrew).

[8] Peter Meyer-Ranke, *Der rote Pharao,* Hamburg 1964, 166.

promoted to lance-corporal and appointed battalion clerk. In 1858 he was made lieutenant and in 1859 and 1860 he received several rapid promotions. By the end of 1860, at the age of nineteen, he was a full colonel. In the same year he became adjutant to Sa'īd and accompanied him on his visit to the Hijaz.[9] But when Sa'īd decreed the exemption of soldiers from the duty of fast on Ramadan, 'Urābī opposed this heresy and was for some time removed from active service.[10]

In 1856 Sa'īd introduced the system of granting officers land instead of pensions, though one-time money grants continued. When Ismā'īl came to power in 1863, he granted 150 feddans (acres) to each colonel, 200 to each brigadier and 500 feddans each to officers of still higher rank. Aḥmad 'Urābī, who inherited 8½ feddans from his father, bequeathed to his sons 570 feddans.[11]

It was in Sā'īd's day that the construction of the Suez Canal was begun, requiring abundant man power. The size of the army was drastically reduced—at one time to less than five thousand.

Ismā'īl's policy differed radically. He had grandiose aspirations for transforming Egypt into a great modern power. Accordingly he increased the strength of the army to such an extent that by the end of the seventies it again numbered more than 80 thousand.[12] Apart from exceptional cases officers were now recruited exclusively from among the graduates of military schools.[13] In order to foster the modernization of the army, Ismā'īl again resorted to the help of Western officers—this time Americans. As in France after the Napoleonic wars, so in America after the Civil War there were officers looking for employment in their profession, army men with battle experience who found it hard to adapt themselves to civilian life. Ismā'īl preferred Americans to French or British because America had no imperialistic ambitions. From 1870 to 1879 there were 54 American officers serving in the Egyptian army, among them one who had been an American major-general and three who had been brigadiers. Some were from the North and some from the Confederate army. In 1879 they were all discharged as a result of the financial crisis which struck Egypt, the only exception being Stone Pasha who was chief of staff of the Egyptian army from 1870 to 1882.[14] The American officers were not given command of

9 'Abd al-Raḥmān al-Rāfi'ī, *Al-za'īm 'Urābī,* Cairo 1952, 8–10.

10 D. Mackenzie Wallace, *Egypt and the Egyptian question,* London 1883, 67–8.

11 Baer, 20, 27, 46, 50.

12 Zakī, 9.

13 *Die Wehrkraft des osmanischen Reiches,* 82.

14 Hill, 346; Charles Chaillé-Long, *My life in four continents,* London 1912, 230–3; William B. Hesseltine and Hazel C. Wolf, *The blue and the gray on the Nile,* Chicago 1961, *passim.*

units; they were employed at headquarters in staff positions and in surveying and mapping. Several of them did splendid work in exploring and mapping the regions of the Nile sources, western Sudan and Chad.

The expansion of the army together with the new system of appointing officers exclusively from among military school graduates substantially increased the proportion of Egyptians among the officers. By the end of the period of Ismāʿīl's rule they formed a large majority. However, the Turkish-Circassian minority was unwilling to give up its privileged position and clung to the posts of top command. In the seventies several of the Egyptian officers reached the rank of brigadier, but the promotion of many others was held back. Increasingly bitter tension arose between the Egyptian and the Turkish officers; this, later, was the immediate cause of the ʿUrābī revolt. Aḥmad ʿUrābī himself, who at the age of nineteen was a colonel, received no promotion in the nineteen years that followed, and it was only after the ousting of Ismāʿīl in the summer of 1879 that he was made a brigadier. Ismāʿīl made ʿUrābī a gift of one of the slaves of his harem, who later became his wife,[15] and in February 1879 he took a favorable view of the revolt of the Egyptian officers which centred around ʿUrābī in order to get rid of Nūbār Pasha, the Prime Minister. Nevertheless Ismāʿīl, himself a Turk, did not set much store by Egyptian officers and he helped to discriminate against them.

Ismāʿīl, whose grand modernization schemes corresponded with his ambitious personality, was favored at the time of his accession by an exceptional circumstance: During the American Civil War (1861–65) cotton export from the USA to Europe was halted, and the demand for Egyptian cotton rose steeply, as did its price. The volume of export rose fourfold from 1860 to 1864, its value tenfold. But in 1865 the boom was over, and gradually it became obvious that Ismāʿīl was a spendthrift whose policy was anything but adapted to actual Egyptian conditions. In the middle of the 1870's the country was on the verge of bankruptcy. In 1875 Ismāʿīl was compelled to sell his Suez Canal shares to the British Government. In 1876 the Treasury of Egypt was put under French-British control. Two other events in 1876 accentuated the crisis: In Turkey the *Young Ottomans* obtained the first liberal constitution; and in Ethiopia the Egyptian army suffered a severe defeat in war. Thus fertile ground for the growth of a radical opposition movement was prepared. A major catalyst in its development came with the personal and spiritual influence of Jamāl al-Dīn al-Afghānī, who was active in Cairo from 1871. Yaʿaqūb Ṣanūʿa. a jounalist and playwright of Jewish origin, known by his pen-name Abū Naẓẓāra, was also

[15] Charles Royle, *The Egyptian campaigns 1882 to 1885*, London 1886, vol. 1, 32.

rather influential. He founded a secret political association, many of whose members were army officers.[16]

The 'Urābī movement began as a protest by Egyptian officers against discrimination by Turks and Circassians who headed the state and the army. Protracted delays in pay led to unrest, and when in February 1879 rumours spread to the effect that many of the Egyptian officers were to be discharged, disorder broke out. Officers attacked Nūbār Pasha, the Armenian Christian Prime Minister and Wilson, an Englishman who was a member of Nūbār's cabinet, and arrested them. They were released only after the intervention of the Khedive, who was not in the least displeased at what had taken place—he had no use for Nūbār—and the next day the latter was compelled to resign. In the eyes of the public the victory belonged to the officers.

From then on the officers movement merged with the general nationalist awakening. Even at the time of the attack on Nūbār and Wilson, cries of 'Death to the Christian dogs' were being heard—the reference being to the Armenian Prime Minister and also to the British and the French. That same year Egypt's first nationalist party was founded. Ninety-three of the 327 signatures on the party's manifesto were signatures of army officers.[17]

In 1879 Ismā'īl was deposed. His son Tawfīq ruled on behalf of the creditors and the controlling powers. The crisis worsened and once again the officer class became one of its principal centers of focus. In July 1880 the Minister of War, the Circassian 'Uthmān Rifqī, introduced a new military service law which limited the period of service for soldiers to four years. 'Urābī's men saw in this a ruse to prevent soldiers from rising from the ranks, in other words to prevent Egyptians from becoming officers. In January 1881 a number of officers presented a petition to the Prime Minister, protesting against discrimination against Egyptian officers and demanding the dismissal of Rifqī. At the head of the officers who produced the petition were 'Alī Fahmī and Aḥmad 'Urābī, commanders of the first and fourth battalions. They were arrested but immediately freed by their comrades. At the beginning of February a government was formed with Maḥmūd Sāmī al-Bārūdī—who was a sympathizer of 'Urābī—as Minister of War. Later in 1881 Tawfīq again attempted to crush the 'Urābī movement. He dismissed Bārūdī and gave orders for the battalions loyal to 'Urābī to be moved from the capital to Alexandria and the small towns of the Delta. The reaction was open rebellion. On September 9 'Urābī with 2,500 soldiers and 18 cannon surrounded the Khedive's palace and presented three demands: The formation of a new government, recall of the Chamber of

[16] Irene L. Gendzier, *The practical visions of Ya'qub Sanu'*, Cambridge, Mass., 1966.

[17] 'Abd al-Raḥmān al-Rāfi'ī, *'Aṣr Ismā'īl*, Cairo 1932, vol. 2, 218.

Notables, and an increase in the strength of the army. 'Urābī had become head of the popular nationalist movement, and Tawfīq was obliged to give way. A new government was formed and Bārūdī returned to his old position as Minister of War. In December an inaugural meeting of an elected legislative assembly was held. Tawfīq's concessions did not however bring any return to tranquility, but rather added encouragement and impetus to the nationalist upheaval. On February 5, 1882 there was another change of government. 'Urābī became Minister of War and to all intents and purposes the one man who mattered.

As usually happens when a direct representative of the officer class rises to power, 'Urābī turned his attention first to the improvement of the conditions of the officers and the army in general. Forty Turkish and Circassian officers, among them 'Uthmān Rifqī, were convicted of an attempt on the life of 'Urābī and sentenced to dismissal from the army and deportation from Egypt. Their places were taken by Egyptians. Some 400 Egyptian officers were promoted and about 150 sergeants became officers. The size of the army was increased, and pay for all ranks was raised. The junior officers in particular benefited. The pay of a second-lieutenant rose from 350 to 600 piasters a month, a rise of more than 70 per cent. A captain's pay rose from 500 to 950 (a raise of 90 per cent), a colonel's pay rose from 2,500 to 3,500 (40 per cent) and the more senior ranks received an increase of 500 piasters each, representing a rise of 5 to 10 per cent.[18] An Egyptian officer who a few months earlier lived in fear of dismissal now enjoyed higher rank, much higher pay, and prospects of further promotion. It would be wrong to assume, however, that 'Urābī ousted all non-Egyptians. Although the accusations of plotting his assassination were not actually proved, 'Urābī feared for his life, and he endeavored not to vex the Turks unnecessarily. When in 1882 101 officers were transferred to service in the Sudan—quite a normal procedure and subject to regulations which ensured return posting after three years at that hardship station—86 of them were Egyptians, nine were Circassians and six Turks.[19] Clearly there was no discrimination against the non-Egyptians, although the Circassians did try to refuse the posting.

In the meantime the nationalist movement grew in size and became more radical. The social character of the movement came to the fore, and ferment took hold of the masses in the villages no less than the intellectuals in Cairo. Farmers began to collect weapons. "An officer of the army told the peasants at Zagazig that the acres belonging to their landlords 'were theirs by right'.

[18] 'Abd al-Raḥmān al-Rāfi'ī, *Al-thawra al-'urābiyya,* second edition, Cairo 1949, 209–10, 261.
[19] *Ibid,* 259.

In a word, all the usual symptoms of revolution were prevalent in Egypt."[20] 'Urābī was closer to the yearnings of the fellaheen, the great majority of the Egyptian people, than all the leaders of Egypt who came after him, civil or military, from Muṣṭafā Kāmil to Nasser.

However, 'Urābī and his comrades were not endowed with the qualities of great politicians and did not have the ability to dominate the movement and direct its course.

On September 12 the decisive battle was fought between the Egyptian army and the British at Tell el Kebir. 'Urābī had failed as a general no less than as a politician. The following day the British entered Cairo, and so began the "temporary" subjugation of Egypt, which was to last until 1956.

On September 19, 1882 the Khedive issued a decree consisting of one short sentence: "The Egyptian army is disbanded." The next day the new Egyptian army was constituted. Its strength was limited to six thousand men and it was led by British officers. The Chief of Staff, Sir Evelyn Wood, was a major-general in the British army; in the Egptian army he became a full general and was accorded the title *Sirdār*. At the beginning of 1883 25 British officers were serving in Egypt, most of them with one or two ranks higher than they had held at home.[21] Most of the junior officers were Egyptians who had served in the old Egyptian army.

The new army engaged at once in hard fighting against the forces of the Mahdī in the Sudan. Between 1896 and 1898 the Egyptian army participated in the re-conquest of the Sudan under Kitchener. At that time the army was again strengthened. At the beginning of the twentieth century it numbered, together with the Sudanese army, 16 thousand officers and men. Of the officers in the year 1905, 63 were British and 623 Egyptian. Battalion commanders were either Egyptian or British, but the great majority of the more senior officer ranks went to the British.[22]

In the fifty years between the conquest of the Sudan and the Palestine War, from 1899 to 1948, the Egyptian army did not fire a single shot in anger (the only clashes were between the Frontier Corps and hashish smugglers in Sinai and the Western Desert). Across the world and even on the soil of Egypt itself armies of the nations fought in two world wars. During this time Egypt carried on a stubbon and protracted struggle for national independence. But the Egyptian army was neither a partner nor a factor in any of this. The army, which in the days of Muḥammad 'Alī and until the time of 'Urābī had been the main centre of power and activity in the life of the country, was between 1900 and 1945 a body bereft

[20] The Earl of Cromer, *Modern Egypt,* London 1908, vol. 1, 258.

[21] *Ibid.,* vol. 2, 467; Crabitès, 6–7.

[22] Sir Auckland Colvin, *The making of modern Egypt,* London 1906, 325–6.

of importance. Its futility was symbolic of the helplessness of Egypt, and the British succeeded in rendering it neutral even in the struggle to regain the country's independence. A young Egyptian seeking a career, if he were imbued with national consciousness and political aspirations, could see little opportunity or honor in a military life. A young man who had as his objective a life of comfort with a good income would have even greater disdain for the army with its tedium, its convenience and its restrictions. Russell Pasha, who was for many years inspector-general of the Egyptian police, described the difficulties in recruiting suitable young men to the service, and what he wrote regarding the police is equally true of the army: "For example, a young man of good family decides to enter the police as a career, and after passing through the college finds himself posted . . . to Cairo or Alexandria: he leads a pleasant and agreeable life for a year or two and then finds himself transferred to some completely uncivilized township in Upper Egypt. When the time comes for him to marry, no Cairo-bred young woman of his social status will consent to such exile, or if for family reasons the marriage is inevitable, with the husband away in the villages and the wife amusing herself in the cities, it soon comes to grief".[23] Yūsuf Najīb, father of Muḥammad Naguib, who was himself an officer, said to his sons that "the Egyptian army . . . was not all that it was supposed to be. It was not really an army at all, but rather an auxiliary corps in which Egyptians were expected to take orders from the British". When he had to decide the future of his sons Muḥammad and 'Alī, he was of the opinion, in the words of Muḥammad, that "Since I was the better student, it would be better for 'Alī to be the officer and for me to be a lawyer or an engineer. I could do more for my country in civilian clothes, he thought, than I could ever do for it in uniform".[24] Nearly twenty years later Nasser joined the army since his father did not have the means to pay the costly fees for study at university. "I went into the army as a career for financial reasons", he said in 1962.[25]

Eventually, 'Alī Naguib and his brother Muḥammad and Nasser chose military careers. No doubt it was family tradition that influenced the Naguib brothers; the officer class was the profession and social circle of their father and of their mother's family. For young men like Nasser it was one of the few openings for assured income and social ascent open to them, and despite hesitation, uniform attracted them.

During the first half of the twentieth century the distance between the officer class and the rank and file of the Egyptian army widened. In 1886

[23] Sir Thomas Russell Pasha, *Egyptian service, 1902 1946,* London 1949, 28.

[24] Mohammed Naguib, *Egypt's destiny,* New York 1955, 43.

[25] *The Sunday Times,* 17 June 1962.

the "exemption fee" to be paid by those wishing to be excused army service was fixed at twenty pounds. Certain categories of young men were automatically excused from military service on account of positions occupied by their fathers: Sons of government officials, sons of the clergy and sons of army officers. Students in institutions for religious study were also excused. Among all the rest—those who did not succeed in obtaining advance release from the hated military service—a ballot took place, though even here there were possibilities of "adjusting" the effects of chance selection. From those selected by lot many were still released for reasons of health, and the assessment of physical fitness was not always quite scrupulous. Out of 110 thousand, eligible for conscription in 1904, about three thousand were needed for service. 9,147 altogether paid the "exemption fee," a third of those due for conscription were released automatically for religious and other reasons, and 16 per cent simply did not take part in the ballot.[26] Those who were forced by the village or neighborhood headmen to enrol, so as to provide the necessary quota for the army, were the most miserable and ignorant wretches to be found in the place.

'Urābī and many officers and army chiefs in the nineteenth century rose from the ranks, but in the twentieth century the rank and file could no longer become officers. The highest rank they could now reach was regimental sergeant-major. On the other hand, the officer never began his military career in the ranks. According to the 1928 regulations only those between the ages of 16 and 21 who had matriculated from secondary school and passed medical examination were eligible for the military academy.[27] The cadet went straight into the academy and if he passed his graduation examination, he emerged an officer. Thus in the first half of this century all Egyptian officers came from families that were able to send at least one of their sons to secondary school and to keep him there until matriculation. Secondary school graduates at that time numbered less than one per cent of the relevant age group in the country. Insofar as cadets were accepted before 1928 without matriculation, these boys were not from the lower classes, but rather the less bright sons of officers or of notables who wished to facilitate their entry into the circles of the officer class.

It is hardly surprising therefore, that a deep chasm separated the officers from the men. The fact that such an army held no very honored place in the life of the nation served only to intensify the arrogance of the officers

[26] Colvin, pp. 326–8.

[27] Aḥmad 'Aṭiyyat-Allāh, *Qāmūs al-thawra al-maṣriyya 1954*, Cairo 1954, 109; Georges Vaucher, *Gamal Abdel Nasser et son équipe*, Paris 1959, 96.

vis-à-vis the men under their command—as a form of compensation for social indignity and exclusion from the political arena.

In the autumn of 1936, after the signing of the new treaty with Britain, the Wafd government took a step toward the democratization of the officer corps. It gave instructions for the doors of the military academy to be opened to young men who did not come from the families of the privileged classes. It regarded the gradual change of the character of the officer corps as an important national and social task. As a result, in the winter and spring of 1937 a number of young men were admitted who hitherto, had they applied, would not have been accepted—young men such as Nasser, a son of a minor postal official. But it would be wrong to think that from that time on all cadets were of that type. They were still only a small minority. Even Nasser, who perhaps represents the most popular stratum in the officer class, matriculated from secondary school and came from a family of some means not dependent entirely on the lowly salary of a minor official. His paternal grandfather owned a small tract of land at Bani Murra in Asyut province on which in 1898 he built a private mosque. He also built the first school in the village. Those of his sons who remained in the village inherited a small family estate. Nasser's maternal grandfather was a well-to-do building contractor and charcoal dealer in Alexandria.[28] When Jamāl was born his parents lived in the Bacos quarter of Alexandria in a single-storey five-room house.[29] In his youth he lived in Cairo with his uncle—his father's brother—Khalīl Ḥusayn, an official in the Wafq administration.[30]

The composition of the Egyptian officer class in the last years of the monarchy was, from the point of view of social and family origin, rather varied. [31] Nevertheless, a number of main source-groups are discernible. In most cases the fathers and uncles of the officers were middle-grade officials, members of the free professions, army officers, village notables and landowners, senior officials, merchants and contractors. The dividing line between these groups was of course not rigid and there was a good deal of interpenetration. Most parents and relations of the officers belonged to the middle and upper strata of the middle class, whose income derived mainly from salaries. A smaller proportion, though not an inconsiderable one, lived on rents from landed property. A very small proportion of the families were urban business people, such as shopkeepers. Thus the general

[28] Vaucher, pp. 12–5, 28–9; Joachim Joesten, *Nassr—the rise to power,* London 1960, 14.

[29] *Akhir sā'a,* Cairo, 10 March 1965.

[30] Vaucher 28–32.

[31] For a detailed analysis of the family background of a samole group see below, Appendix.

assumption that the officers came from the petite bourgeoisie is not accurate, nor does it explain much.

The origins of the Egyptian officer class become clearer if one notes that certain other social groups are not represented, or are barely represented, in officers' families. There are no representatives of the broad masses of poor tenant fellaheen, of agricultural workers, artisans, urban laborers and small shopkeepers. At the other end of the scale the large landed property-owning families, the Egyptian aristocracy, are indeed conspicuous by their absence. There were a number of eminent wealthy Egyptians in Fārūq's day whose fathers or grandfathers had been officers, yet none of them went into the army. The way from army officer to aristocrat was a one-way street. For example, the brothers Aḥmad and 'Alī Māhir, both of whom became prime minister, were the sons of Muḥammad Māhir (1854–1909) who was trained at the military academy, gazetted second-lieutenant at the age of twenty, and later rose step by step to the highest positions in the army and the civil administration.[32] Muḥammad Rātib, a Circassian who was Sirdār of the Egyptian army from 1864 to 1879 and later marshal, laid the foundations of his family's very extensive landed property. His descendants married into the family of Sulaymān Faransāwī, formerly Sève, the French-born Chief of Staff of the Egyptian army in Muḥammad 'Alī's time, and also into the royal family. By the twentieth century not one member of the family was left serving in the army.[33] In G. Baer's book *A History of Landownership in Modern Egypt,* about one hundred families are mentioned as owners of large estates in the first half of the century. Some thirty of these families "were represented in either the Lower or Upper House between 1942 and 1952 (in many cases by more than one member of the family)... Eighteen of the families provided Cabinet Ministers between 1924 and 1950."[34] But of officers these families provided none. Not a single officer appears among the entire one hundred families. As Naguib has written, their sons "were too busy enjoying their wealth to be bothered with military service."[35]

Similarly, very few Egyptian officers are sons of Muslim religious functionaries, while, by contrast, in the Iraqi army the number of officer sons of followers of religious callings is large. This is a very interesting phenomenon, and, moreover, one which has played an important part in shaping the character of the officer class within Egyptian society. In Egyptian society the shaykhs, imams, religious judges and the teachers in urban

[32] Hill, 264–5.

[33] Baer, 49, 160, 168; Hill, 269–70; *al-Jumhūriyya,* Cairo, 29 October 1954 (obituary).

[34] Baer, 143.

[35] Naguib, 14–15.

and rural traditional Islamic institutions of learning were and still are numerous. According to the classification of earners by occupation in the official Egyptian population census, the number of "religious personnel, of the various religions," more than 90 per cent of them Muslims, was as follows: In 1927 more than 61,000, in 1937 some 51,000 and 1947 more than 52,000. The number of engineers, physicians, chemists, writers and journalists, all taken together, was in 1927–12,000, in 1937–15,000 and in 1947–32,000. However, while up to the middle of the present century the number of persons with a traditional Muslim education had been much greater than those who had a modern education, only in a few instances did sons of those in the religious category become army officers. On the other hand, sons and brothers of those who had a Western-type humanities or technical training have long formed a high percentage of the officer corps. In 1936 Ḥasan al-Bannā, the Supreme Guide of the Muslim Brethern, had good reason to demand that a proportion of the appointments in the army be made available to graduates of al-Azhar. Yet his efforts were of no avail; thirty years later, in 1965, the annual al-Azhar students' conference again recommended that the university's graduates be accepted at the military academies.[36]

The social strata from which the officer class has been drawn are the same as those from which has come the intelligentsia—men of modern-type education, such as lawyers, doctors and engineers—and it has often been justifiable pointed out that the Egyptian army of the mid-twentieth century is in fact an "intelligentsia in uniform." This expression, however, like all generalizations, serves the purposes of analogy rather than of precise definition. Nevertheless, it illustrates the self-image of many if not all of these officers. The man who, because of limited means, went to the military academy instead of pursuing a more costly course of study at the university, did his best to equate his position as an officer with that of the lawyer or engineer.

However, not all the youths who chose the career of army officer did so because this was their only chance of rising in the social scale. Many chose the army when they could equally well have chosen university. It appears that these were either sons of village notables or scions of families with an army officer tradition.

A considerable number of officers were sons of village notables and *ʿumdas*. The *ʿumda* is the head of the village and government representative on the local level. According to the 1895 law—little-changed until recently—

[36] Ḥasan al-Bannā, *Mudhakkirāt al-daʿwa wal-diʿāya,* Cairo n.d., p. 237; *al-Ahrām,* 7 November 1965.

which gave legal force to a practice that had existed earlier, he has to be a landowner.[37] Sometimes he is one of the richest men in the village. He is the chief, and also representative, of all the notables and the well-to-do farmers who, unlike the large estate owners, do not live in the cities. These are the owners of fifty or hundred feddans who directly exploit the tenant fellaheen and the hired agricultural laborers. These farmers might be termed, for the sake of comparison, the kulaks of the Egyptian villages.

One officer who was the son of an *'umda* was 'Abd al-Ḥakīm 'Āmīr. His father, Shaykh 'Alī 'Āmir, who died in February 1960, was the *'umda* of Isṭāl (Minyā), and "one of the affluent."[38] His elder son took over the management of the family farm while the other sons were sent to university. 'Abd al-Ḥakīm wanted to study medicine, but for reasons of ill-health was not able to prepare adequately for the entrance examination and failed. He then enrolled in the faculty of agriculture. However, the subject did not appeal to him and a few weeks later he entered the military academy.

Many officers are sons or relatives of officers. As in other armies, the profession is in many cases something of a family tradition. For example, half the officers of the group of 14 who were members of the Revolutionary Command Council of 1953 had relatives who were also officers. Two council members, Ṣalāḥ and Jamāl Sālim, were stepbrothers, and Zakariyyā and Khālid Muḥī al-Dīn were cousins. Kamāl al-Dīn Ḥusayn was a cousin of Second-Lieutenant Jalāl Ḥajjāj, who fell in the Palestine War, and of several other officers.[39] 'Āmir was a relative of Lieutenant-General Muḥammad Ḥaydar Pasha, who had been Chief of Staff in 1948 and was later Minister of War. And Naguib was the son of a distinguished military family.

It is not only in the officer corps that family tradition decided the occupation in life. From ancient times, for generations and generations, the son has followed in his father's footsteps. Yet in the officer class of the thirties, forties and fifties of the present century, which was after all a new and expanding professional group, there were comparatively more individuals whose fathers followed occupations other than military than there have been in many other professional groups. Moreover, sons of officers, when they grew up, preferred to go in for easier and more renumerative professions, while sons of officials of medium and low grade found in the career of an army officer one of the few openings that could lead to

[37] Gabriel Baer, 'The village shaykh in modern Egypt', in *Studies in Islamic history and civilization,* Jerusalem 1961, 127–9; Saad M. Gadalla, *Land reform in relation to social development—Egypt,* Columbia, Missouri, 1962, 67.

[38] *Akhbār al-Yawm,* Cairo, 28 April 1956; *al-Ahrām,* 6 February 1960.

[39] *Al-Ahrām,* 28 October 1948 (obituary).

higher social status. As we have seen, half of the Revolutionary Council were sons and relatives of officers, while half came from families without other army officer connections. Still one cannot disregard the scope and influence of family tradition in the officer class as a social group. An instructive example is the case of the Naguib family.

The paternal grandfather of Muḥammad Naguib was a peasant with a smallholding in the village of Naḥḥāriyya in the Delta. He died young and his eldest son, the uncle of Muḥammad Naguib, later cultivated fifty-five feddans—apparently part of it family property and part rented from others. The younger brother Yūsuf, Muḥammad Naguib's father, now orphaned, completed his schooling in the village and enlisted in the army as a private. In 1896 he attracted the notice of Kitchener: He played in the army football team, and in the course of an international match he continued playing after suffering an injury. So the Sirdār had him admitted to the military academy. In 1898 as a second-lieutenant, he took part in the campaign in the Sudan, where he remained until his death in 1914. He died a captain. His wife Zahra, mother of Muḥammad Naguib, was also an orphan, fatherless from early childhood. Her father was Muḥammad 'Uthmān Ḥishmat, an Egyptian colonel who fell on January 15, 1885 in the defense of Khartoum against the Mahdī. In the same battle two of his brothers and a cousin were killed—all Egyptian officers. Yūsuf Najīb had four sons. His eldest, born of his first marriage to a Sudanese woman, became a peasant farmer in the family's home village, Naḥḥāriyya. Muḥammad followed in the steps of his father and his mother's father and became an officer, as did the third brother, 'Alī. In 1952, 'Alī was a major-general and commander of the Cairo military area. He was arrested at the time of the military coup but was later appointed Egyptian ambassador to Damascus. The fourth brother, Maḥmūd, became a veterinary surgeon and lecturer at Cairo University. One of their sisters studied medicine and became a government-employed doctor. Her husband was an army officer. Two other sisters married officials. Muḥammad Naguib's wife is the daughter of a lieutenant-colonel in the army.[40] These names are surely sufficient—though many more could be quoted—to demonstrate the type of family which carries the officer tradition, and to demonstrate also the family relationships between fellaheen, members of the free professions, clerks or officials and officers.

The national composition of the officer class in Egypt had undergone a complete change in the hundred years between the death of Muḥammad

[40] Naguib, 35–49, 61; Hill, 369; Antūn 'Assāf. *Al-qā'id Muḥammad Najīb,* second edition, Cairo 1953, 8–9, 45; Aḥmad 'Aṭiyyat-Allāh in the preface to Muḥammad Najīb, *Risāla 'an al-Sūdan,* Cairo 1954, 70–7.

'Alī and the Palestine War. Native-born Egyptians, then a small minority occupying none but the lowest ranks, are now the only element in the officer class. As for the Turks, Circassians and the descendants of the Mamelukes who still lived in Egypt, they had intermingled with the general Egyptian population. The only exception was the royal court and its wider family circle, but among them there were no army officers.

With the Egyptianization of the officer class, some Christians also attained commissioned rank. In 1949 the Christians—almost all Copts—comprised about seven per cent of the officers in the Egyptian army, which was a fair reflection of their proportion of the Egyptian population in general. However, of the 90 officers of the rank of brigadier and above, only one, a major-general in the medical corps, was a Christian. In this corps the proportion of Christians was higher than in other arms, while in the (armored) cavalry corps, the most exclusive of them all, the officers were all Muslims.

The Free Officers always insisted that the officers—and they themselves in particular—were of the masses of the Egyptian people and representative of them. This claim is justified up to a point, but it is far from accurate. Unlike court circles, the officer class was around 1950 entirely Egyptian from the national point of view. From the sociological point of view, most of the officers were sons and brothers of officials, army and police officers and middle-class members of the free professions, while some came from relatively well-to-do peasant farmers and small and medium-scale landowners, from the upper strata of the middle class and the lower and middle strata of the upper class. If by the term 'the people' one is to understand reference to those Egyptians who were not of, or related to, the few hundred families of great landowners, bankers, industrialists and big businessmen, then these officers were undoubtedly 'of the people'. If, however, 'the people' is taken to mean the 80 per cent of the Egyptian populace who own less than one feddan of land each, the urban and rural laborers, the artisans and the petty traders—then the officers were certainly not 'of the people'.

Another characterization of the officer class identifies it as to its background and outlook with the new salaried middle class.[41] Again it must be pointed out that this is a *pars pro toto* generalization which may be even misleading. The analysis of a sample group of Egyptian officers in 1948 indicates that two-thirds of their relatives were salaried employees—quite a large percentage indeed, but certainly not all of them. Moreover,

[41] Manfred Halpern, *The politics of social change in the Middle East and North Africa*, Princetown 1963, *passim*.

some of the salaried, such as high-ranking officers and senior officials, can by no means be regarded as belonging to the middle class. The links between the military and the salaried middle class are definitely strong but far from exclusive. The links connecting officers with village notables and other medium-sized agricultural estate-owners are also quite conspicuous.

Have there been any major changes in the social composition of the Egyptian officer class since 1952?

Beyond a doubt there have been important changes in Egyptian society, and this includes the army—the favored child of the new regime. The great expansion of the army inevitably brought with it a measure of democratization. The increase by several thousands in the number of officers opened the way to officerdom for young men from new and wider levels of the population. A similar effect resulted from broadening the base of the education system in the country, and the consequent increase in numbers of secondary school matriculants. To the rank and file the expansion of the army brought recruits from all levels and classes, and no longer from the poorest and most backward alone. Another positive factor was an all-round improvement in the level of training and equipment, in organization and in combat principles. It would be wise, however, not to overestimate the importance of the changes. It is true that the top level of command in Fārūq's time was removed, but the new top command really came from the same officer class. They are men who entered the service under Fārūq. While the *position* of the officer class in the life of the nation has undergone a fundamental change, its *composition* has been far less affected. The officer corps itself took care to maintain its continuity. After the Free Officers became the masters of the country in 1952, more than 400 officers were cashiered from the armed services—the great majority of the colonels and all those holding higher ranks, except Naguib and Muḥammad Ibrāhīm. The leaders of the Free Officers themselves took over only some of the positions which thus became vacant. They devoted themselves to their political tasks; in the army command they promoted other officers whom they regarded as faithful politically and qualified professionally. In this way they wisely assured the loyalty of wide circles of officers and maintained the professional standard of the service. 'Jumping' ranks, which is so frequent in the ultra-politicized Syrian army, is unknown in Egypt, with the sole exception of 'Abd al-Ḥakīm 'Āmir, who in 1953 was promoted from major to brigadier, in 1957 to lieutenant-general and in 1958 to marshal. However, an important change did take place which did not alter the composition of the officer corps as such, but enhanced the prospects of advancement in rank, pay and social standing of each individual in it. As a by-product of the enlargement of the armed forces, promotions were accelerated. The average officer of Naguib's generation, born at the beginning of the century, attained the rank of colonel *(qā'imaqām,* now *'aqīd)* at the age of 47, 26 years after being commissioned. The officers of Nasser's generation, born at the end of World War I, who were lieutenant-colonels in 1952, became full colonels at under 40 years of age after less than 20 years of service. Now, in the middle of the sixties, there are some officers who at 42 are already brigadiers. But the continuity of the officer class from the days of the monarchy has been maintained. A youngster admitted to the military academy after 1952 would by 1967 attain no higher rank than that of major, and in isolated cases that of lieutenant-colonel. All the colonels and officers of higher rank were commissioned before 1952.

The decisive test for an army is war. Fārūq's army in 1948 did not stand the trial in Palestine, and the revelation of its impotence was one of the major causes for the regime's subsequent collapse. But the Egyptian republican army which fought in Sinai and on the Suez Canal in 1956 was little different from the army of 1948. The highly-praised heroism of the defenders of Port Said was not the heroism of the officers or men of the army, but of civilians who took up arms. After an additional ten and a half years of revolutionary Egypt and Arab socialism, when Egypt and Israel again joined battle, the Egyptian army was no better, neither in morale and fighting spirit nor in professional proficiency.

One of the outstanding features of the Egyptian army, hardly changed from Fārūq's to Nasser's day, is the enormous gulf separating the officers from the ranks. In the nineteenth century many officers had risen from the ranks, but not so in the twentieth, and the chasm between officers and soldiers widened even more from 1900 to 1950. The resulting attitude of the officer towards his subordinates, ingrained over so long a period, continues to mark intra-army relations. An example from the Sinai Campaign in 1956 is typical. Some dozens of Egyptian officers who had been captured by the Israeli army were being held in one place. After the conclusion of their preliminary routine interrogation, they were permitted to ask questions and make requests. The majority asked for better prison conditions for themselves, and also showed interest in the course of the campaign; several asked what had happened to other officers of their acquaintance. Not a single one enquired about his men. Many similar phenomena could be observed again in 1967. The gap between the officers and the soldiers remains enormous. This is so not only because the officers regard strict discipline and emphasis on the hierarchy of ranks to be fundamental requirements of army life and efficiency. The deeper cause for the continued existence of the chasm is the fact that officers and soldiers stem from and represent different social classes. The officers are all sons of middle-class or well-to-do families; the majority of them are city-born, in contrast to the soldiers, who are mostly from the villages. Another remarkable difference is the fact that most of the soldiers are sons of large families and have many brothers and sisters and children, whereas the officers come from small families, with few brothers and sisters and even fewer children, from families which practice birth control. Only in very few cases do rankers become officers—as specialists in technical services, like mechanics, or clerks in the lower echelons of army administration. A man entering the army as a private becomes a sergeant-major after some 15 years of service, and then a second-lieutenant; when he gets his commission he is already 37 years old. The other officers of his rank are 15 years younger, and those of his age are already far his superiors, being lieutenant-colonels. In the officer corps as a whole these men are neither typical nor influential. In the summer of 1963 it was decided to admit to officer-training courses sergeants who had served in Yemen. Three months later the military academy was opened also to privates who had completed two years of active service; but these were exceptional cases only, and generally admission to the military academies remained conditional upon graduation from a secondary school.[42]

The character of the new Egyptian regime had led to adverse developments among the officer class, side by side with the advantages it brought. The officers have been raised to the top of the ladder of social prestige, self-esteem and political power. For many of them great opportunities have opened up for the attainment of important positions in government, in the diplomatic service and in the economic sphere with, of course, higher incomes. These opportunities have also given rise to increased lobbying on the part of aspirants, and to arrogance, rivalry and corruption. There has never yet been a dictatorship in which corruption has not been endemic, and in a dictatorship of officers it spreads first and fast among them. As a rule, such a regime succeeds in concealing the shortcomings of its profiteers, though not always. The case of Majdī Ḥasanayn is by no means an isolated one. Before the revolution he was a major, a member of the Free Officers' Association and one of the intimates of Nasser. He fathered the idea of the "Liberation Province," the development and rural settlement project in which the regime took pride. Majdī Ḥasanayn was made director of the project. He went to Europe to buy machinery (although he completely lacked the requisite technical knowledge) and became one of the prominent personalities in Egypt—until the whole grandiose scheme was seen to be a complete failure. But not before Ḥasanayn had managed to build himself a splendid house. The public censure of his wasteful expenditures reached

[42] *Al-Ahrām*, 18 August 1963; 3 November 1963; 2 January 1966.

such proportions that in the autumn of 1957 Nasser was obliged to dismiss him. In the summer of 1958, however, by now in civilian clothes, he turned up again as manager of the National Cement Company. In the summer of 1966 he was appointed ambassador to Czechoslovakia.[43]

The officer class has become the ruling class. Their prestige has grown higher and higher. Today's status symbol is the authomobile; and an astute observer of present-day Egypt had pointedly remarked: "Captains ride in luxury cars and colonels live as Pashas used to do."[44]

All this was badly shaken in June, 1967. In 1948 the army of monarchical, feudal and corrupt Egypt, badly equipped with outdated, if not defective, weapons, was able to stand firm against Israel for more than six months—now the large army of Arab socialism, equipped with quantities of excellent modern Soviet arms, was ignominiously beaten in less than a week. Now the popular anger after the defeat was largely vented against the officers of the army and the air force, many of whom were openly abused and even attacked on city streets. Nasser's reaction was quite typical: He partly gave way to the popular bitter resentment—and took the wind out of its sails by diverting it to a small and well-defined group only. The high command of the army and the air force was made the scapegoat for the defeat; about 300 officers were dismissed from the service,[45] some of them accused and convicted by military courts of criminal negligence in carrying out their duties; Marshal 'Abd al-Ḥakīm Āmir was driven to suicide. The blame for the defeat was thus apportioned quite arbitrarily; as a group the officers were no better and no worse than all other groups of the Egyptian ruling elite, and the decisions which drove Egypt into war and unavoidable defeat were Nasser's. He sacrificed a small part of the officer corps in order to save the position of the ruling class as a whole, and in it the officers' position of privilege. After a short while the officers were able to plead that a collapse of the "inner front" would be exactly the ememy's aim, and that especially in times of crisis loyalty to the established order and its representatives was the first duty of the citizen. Moreover, the massive re-equipment of the Egyptian armed forces by the Soviet Union in the second half of 1967 again enhanced the importance and the prestige of the officers. It is by no means easy to drive them out of their well-entrenched positions—at any rate on the "inner front".

43 Maḥmūd Fawzī al-Wakīl, (ed.), *Hādhihi al-thawra,* Cairo 1953, 362; Aḥmad Abū al-Fatḥ. *Jamāl 'Abd al-Nāṣir,* Beirut n.d. (1962), 179, 298–9; Keith Wheelock, *Nasser's new Egypt,* London 1960, 67–8, 94–7, 169; *al-Akhbār,* 15 July 1966.

44 Adalbert Weinstein, *Das neue Mekka liegt am Nil,* Wiesbaden n.d. (1959), p. 97.

45 Muḥammad Ḥasanayn Haykal, *al-Ahrām,* 27 October 1967.

4. THE IRAQI OFFICER CLASS

The State of Iraq, an artificial creation, was established only after World War I. At the end of the Ottoman period no such thing as Iraqi nationalism existed. The various regions of the country and its many communal groups were not united by any common aspiration. Fayṣal, who was placed on the throne to symbolize the country's unity, was a foreigner from the Hijaz and his first throne was in Syria. He came to Baghdad only after he was expelled from Damascus by the French.

In its early years the state was beset by persistent tribal revolts; clashes between Sunnis and Shi'is and between Arabs and Kurds; struggles between the British, French, Turks and Arabs over the region of Mosul, so rich in oil, and so important strategically. It was a struggle that was to continue until 1925.

The defense of the country against enemies from beyond its borders was left to the army and air force of Great Britain, the victorious power and the holder of the League of Nations mandate for the territory. To protect British army and air-force installations battalions of levies were recruited, mercenaries armed with light weapons only, consisting of natives of the non-Arab minority groups, led by British officers. Most of the rank and file were Assyrian Christians while a few were Kurds. At the end of 1921 these battalions had a total strength of five thousand but the number was later gradually reduced.

The Iraqi army was formed in January 1921. It was intended to symbolize, and, in case of need, to enforce the unity of the new state against the various centrifugal forces. Its task was an important one. The tribes and the minorities were not only rebellious, they were well armed. In the spring of 1920 an attempt was made to disarm them, and in the Baghdad and Basra districts alone fifty thousand rifles were collected. In autumn of the same year another sixty thousand were collected from the tribesmen. Nevertheless, in 1932 the King again estimated—and his estimate is regarded as a conservative one—that there were one hundred thousand rifles in the hands of the tribesmen. At that time the army and the police together had no more than fifteen thousand. The government set as its goal for the development of the army a position of strength from which it could put down two revolts in two different places at one time.[1] And indeed, since the inception of the state the main occupation of the Iraqi army has been internal policing and repression, first against tribal rebellion, then against political and class movements and also against Kurdish revolts, which assumed a nationalist political character. Only twice was the army pitted against external enemies—at the time of Rashīd ʻĀlī in May 1941 and in 1948 against Israel. All in all, it is not surprising that this army, which was the prop of the state, came to regard itself as the competent authority for the conduct of all its affairs.

Many Iraqi professional army officers, Arabs and Kurds from Baghdad and Mosul, began their career in the Ottoman army. Up to the end of the 1908 revolution the Ottoman government was cosmopolitan-Islamic, and many Syrians and Iraqis became officers and rose to high rank. Iraq was slower than Syria to take part in the Arab national awakening, and it also fell behind in economic and cultural development. Thus many sons of Baghdadi merchants saw in the position of Ottoman army officer a good way, indeed the only way, to social advancement. Every year 60 to 70 Iraqi cadets were accepted at the military academy of Istanbul.[2] One of the Iraqi officers, Muḥmūd Shawkat, the elder brother of Ḥikmat Sulaymān, commanded the Third Army. It was with this elite force that in April 1909 the counter-revolution of the Sultan was put down and the government of the Young Turks firmly established. His chief of staff at that time was Muṣṭafā Kemāl (Atatürk). Later Maḥmūd Shawkat became Minister of War and Prime Minister. He was assassinated in June 1913. Throughout this period his government was dominated by the *Young Turks* and Turkish nationalism.

Other officers of Iraqi origin became caught up in the cause of Arab nationalism. After the old-fashioned Islamic dictatorship of ʻAbd al-Ḥamīd came the modern Turkish nationalist dictatorship. The Arab intellectuals and officers, who sought the revival of their culture and national freedom, were driven to organizing secret societies. One of the more important of these was *al-ʻAhd* founded in 1914 as an officers' association. Iraqis formed a sizeable proportion of its members.

George Antonius, who for nearly twenty years was practically the sole historian of the rise of Arab nationalism, stressed the activities of these societies and their members, and glossed over the fact that they represented only a small minority of the population and a small minority even in the

[1] Majid Khadduri, *Independent Iraq,* second edition, London 1960, 34–5; Agra, *Tzevaot ha-ʻaravim bedorenu,* Tel Aviv 1948, 41.

[2] Lord Birdwood, *Nuri As-Said,* London 1959, 9.

Ottoman army. At the outbreak of World War I the Arabs formed more than a quarter of the population of the Ottoman Empire, and the army's 24,000 officers[3] included many hundreds, perhaps thousands of Arabs. By contrast, *al-'Ahd* together with the rest of the Arab societies, members and sympathizers, numbered a few dozen only. Most Arab officers remained loyal to the Sultan up to the end of the war. Among those who joined the Sharifian Arab army were very few who on their own initiative had gone over to the Sultan's enemies. Most volunteered—or were enticed into volunteering—only after being taken prisoner by the British. Of course the difference between a deserter and one taken prisoner was sometimes small, and there were cases where submission to capture was the chosen form of desertion. On the other hand there were deserters from the Ottoman army who for personal or political reasons were unwilling to fight on the side of the Allies. In 1915 Nūrī Sa'īd, who was a member of *al-'Ahd,* was one of them.

The intensity of the nationalist feeling of these officers should therefore not be over-estimated, but neither should it be dismissed. The makers of history are ever few in number but they do make history.

There is a substantial difference between the participation of Iraqis and that of Syrians in the Arab nationalist activities of the Ottoman army officers. The population of Iraq was larger than that of Syria, yet the number of Syrians in the Arab nationalist movement was greater by far than that of the Iraqis. Dawn found the names of 126 personalities who were active in the various branches of the movement before 1914. The origins of 113 of them could be traced, and of these 18 were Iraqis, and 51 Syrians. Twenty-two were Palestinians, 21 Lebanese and one Egyptian. However, of the 51 Syrian only 10 were officers and members of *al-'Ahd,* while the 18 Iraqis were all army officers.[4] The Arab Ottoman officers who joined the Sharifian army were almost all Iraqis. This was to no small extent the result of the fact that during World War I the methods of repression employed against Arab nationalism were more severe in Syria than in Iraq. The hanging of 22 Arab leaders in Damascus and Beirut in the spring of 1916 was a serious blow to the movement in Syria. On the other hand, the severity of the repressive measures used in Syria testifies to the fact that the movement in that country was stronger—and to the Turks more dangerous—than it was in Iraq. Officers of Iraqi origin who joined the Arab army did not as a matter of course serve in regions of their own country—this was not Ottoman military custom. Thus their political ideologies can hardly be regarded as

[3] M. Larcher, *La guerre turque dans la guerre mondiale,* Paris 1926, 69–72, 594.

[4] C.E. Dawn, 'The rise of Arabism in Syria', *MEJ,* vol. 16, 2, 148–50, 164.

manifestations of prevailing opinion at home. The Syrian civilian intelligentsia were closer to their city populations, yet they too had but little contact with the masses. And to the social problems of their country neither the officers nor the civilians paid serious attention. . .

Iraqi officers of the Sharifian army who came with Fayṣal and the British to the new Iraq were the main support of the state and the army. From their ranks came six of the 12 personalities who between 1920 and 1940 in turn occupied the premiership in Iraq. Among them were Nūrī Sa'īd, and Ja'far al-'Askarī and Ṭaha al-Hāshimī. Ja'far al-Askarī was Iraq's first Minister of Defense and Nūrī Sa'īd the first Chief of Staff. The heads of the first two military coups, Bakr Ṣidqī and 'Azīz Yāmulkī, were also former Ottoman officers, and so were Ṣabbāgh and his three comrades in the Golden Square.

Nūrī Sa'īd and other politician officers of his circle cast their lot from 1916 on with the British and with the Hashimite dynasty, and remained loyal to them to the end of their days. Their competitors in the contest for power, the younger generation of officers, made this alliance the main object of their attack, and they were open to any and every anti-British and anti-Hashimite influence. Such influence came in the thirties mainly from the direction of Rome and Berlin, in the fifties from Cairo, and in the sixties from Moscow.

The Iraqi officer class has always represented only certain sections of the heterogeneous population of the country. The Christians and the Jews, who up till 1950 formed rather more than five per cent of the population (they formed a much higher percentage of the urban population, from which most of the officers came), had very few representatives indeed in the officer group—those few included some Jews—and then only in the lower ranks of the medical and technical services. The Shi'i Arabs, the largest community in the country, amounting to almost half the total population, were also always represented by a small proportion only, and this proportion became smaller the higher the rank. Most of the officers, like almost all heads of government during the monarchy and the republic, were Sunni Muslim Arabs, despite the fact that Sunni Muslims constitute only about a fifth of the entire population. The Kurdish Sunnis, who are about as numerous as the Arab Sunnis, constituted in the 1920's and 1930's a large proportion of the rank and file as well as the officers. Since then their proportion has dropped. The British, who until the 1950's were the army's instructors, tried a number of times to strengthen the non-Arab Sunni element in the officer corps, but their efforts met with small and diminishing sucess. In the military academy, which was founded in 1924, tribesmen were accepted for officer training for the first time in 1927. Their training period was fixed at five years instead of the three year period usual for town-bred candidates. Nevertheless by 1930 only 11 tribesmen were to be found in the academy.[5] Ṣabbāgh, who never differentiated between Sunnis and Shi'is, complained that by the end of 1937 "more than 90 per cent of the officers who held in their hands the reins of army command were non-Arabs."[6] His statement was unfounded, however; he apparently considered all who did not share his nationalist views to be non-Arabs. Thus he wrote of Nūrī Sa'īd, with total disdain for the facts, "He is no Arab . . . he is a Turk from Konya."[7]

The social origins of the Iraqi officer class fall within three distinct categories, and in this respect there appears to have been little change from Ottoman times to the early nineteen-sixties.

One category, not found in the case of the Egyptian officers, is that of privileged and wealthy families. A number of officers come from the distinguished Baghdādī 'Umarī family which claims to descend from the Caliph 'Umar. One of these was Amīn 'Umarī, who in 1935 was brigadier and in 1941, after the Rashīd 'Ālī revolt, chief of staff. Another was Major-General Ḥusayn 'Umarī, who was involved in 1959 in the Shawwāf revolt and during Arif's rule was appointed administrative inspector of the Ministry of Interior.[8] From the Suwaydī family of Baghdad was Nājī Suwaydī, first an Ottoman officer and later an officer in the Sharifian army, who in the spring of 1930 became Prime Minister and finally one of Rashīd 'Ālī's associates. From the Dāghistānī family of Baghdad there was Major-General Ghāzī Dāghistānī, who was deputy chief of staff until July 1958. His father had been a lieutenant-general in the Ottoman army.[9] Of the Rāwī family we know the names of six officers. Among them are Ibrāhīm Rāwī, an Ottoman and later a Sharifian officer, commander of the 4th Division in 1941; and 'Abd al-Ghanī Rāwī, who in 1958 had the rank of colonel and was one of the Free Officers. In 1959 after the Shawwāf revolt he was dismissed from the army; in 1963 he was active in the March rebellion; and later he was in command of the 3rd Armored Division.[10] Najīb Rubay'ī, head of the Presidential Council in Qassim's time, was also from one of the most prominent aristocratic Baghdadi families. His brother

5 *Al-Kulliyya al-'askariyya al-malakiyya 1924–1949*, Baghdad 1950, 21.

6 Ṣalāh al-Dīn al-Ṣabbāgh, *Fursān al-'urūba fī al-'Irāq*, Damascus 1956, 72.

7 *Ibid.*, 15.

8 *Maḥkamat al-sha'b, Muḥākamāt al-maḥkama al-'askariyya al-khāṣṣa*, vol. 18. Baghdad 1962, 7210; Radio Baghdad, 19 February 1963; Ibrāhīm al-Durūbī, *Al-Baghdādiyyūn-akhbāruhum wa-majālisuhum*, Baghdad 1958, 117.

9 Al-Durūbi, 211.

10 *Maḥkamat al-sha'b*, vol. 5, Baghdad 1959, 2187; *Qiṣṣat al-thawra fī al-'Irāq wa-Sūriya*, Beirut (1963), 14–20; *al-Hayāt*, 24 November 1963.

Ḥasīb, who died in 1956, was a major-general and deputy chief of staff in charge of administration.[11] Of the Sa'adūns, the wealthiest family in southern Iraq, we know of seven officers, among them 'Abd al-Khāliq Sa'adūn, who was air attaché in London in 1959.[12] Mumtāz Sa'adūn, a captain in the air force, was the pilot of the military plane that brought 'Arīf 'Abd al-Razzāq to Cairo after his abortive coup in September 1965.[13]

A second category of officers almost entirely missing in Egypt comprises the sons of the Muslim clergy. To this belong the brothers 'Abd al-Salām and 'Abd al-Raḥman Arif as well as 'Abd al-Wahhāb Shawwāf and his brother Muḥammad, who was a major-general in the medical corps and under Qassim a minister of health. These were sons of the Grand Mufti of Baghdad.[14] Another, Nāẓim Tabaqjalī, was the son of an influential clerical family which included Muftis of Baghdad and Hilla.[15]

These two categories count for several hundred officers. The great majority of the five thousand officers who were in the Iraqi army since its inception, and are there still, come from middle-class urban families, sons of junior officials and small traders. The strata that provided so many Egyptian officers—the free professions and the well-to-do farmers—were limited in size and influence in Iraq until the middle of the century, and the part they played in the officer class was accordingly a minor one. Most Iraqi officers are from families whose livelihood is not derived from landed property or invested capital but from salaries; this officer group has no connection with any feudal or property-owing elements. For this middle-class capitalistic development does not represent a gateway to economic independence or social advancement, but a threat of proletarianization, a threat that the petit bourgeois all over the world fears more than the devil himself. This is fruitful ground for the growth of Facism in its various forms and of étatism. Economic dependence on government machinery is growing, and the control of this machinery has become a primary political objective.

As in the Egyptian and other armies, many officers in the Iraqi army are related by family ties to other officers. Nūrī Sa'īd and Ja'far al-'Askarī were double brothers-in-law—each married the other's sister. Two brothers of Ja'far—Taḥsin and 'Alī Riḍā—were officers, as was Riḍā's son, Za'īm, who in 1949 held the rank of colonel.[16] Such well-known families as Rubay'ī,

[11] Al-Durūbī, 70.

[12] *Who's who in UAR and the Near East 1959*, Cairo 1959, 260.

[13] Radio Damascus, 19 September 1965.

[14] *Maḥkamat al-sha'b,* vol. 5, Baghdad 1959, 2096; al-Durūbī, 38–40, 114–5.

[15] Al-Durūbī, 33–5.

[16] 'Abd al-Fattāḥ al-Yāfī, *Al-Irāq bayna inqilābayn,* Beirut 1938, 125; *al-kulliyya,* 132; Birdwood, 93; *al-Dalīl al-'Irāqī li-sanat 1936*, Baghdad 1936, 431.

Hāshimī, Dāghistānī, Sa'adūn and Arif furnished a number of officers. 'Abd al-Karīm Qassim once said that he was "the first army man" in his family.[17] Nevertheless, his father's brother, 'Alī Muḥammad al-Bakr, and two sons of his father's sister were officers; one of them was Muḥammad 'Alī Jawwād, the right-hand man of Bakr Ṣidqī, and the other, 'Abd al-Jabbār, was a major-general and director of military recruting under Qassim.[18] Family connections played an important part in the splitting and uniting of the various groups in the Iraqi officer class.

[17] B. Vernier, *L'Iraq d'aujourd'hui*, Paris 1963, 133.

[18] Abd al-Raḥmān al-Jidda, *Thawrat al-za'īm al-munqidh*, Baghdad 1960, 5–7, 15–17; *al-Ahrām*, 15 July 1958.

5. THE SYRIAN OFFICER CLASS

SYRIA'S HISTORY over the last fifty years has been a stormy one, and the history of her officer class even more so. Everything was subject to frequent change, starting with uniforms, continuing with language of command and ending with ties of loyalty. Between 1915 and 1966 the Syrian officer was obliged again and again to regard as his enemies those to whom he had but yesterday sworn allegiance.

In World War I dozens of Syrian Arab officers served in the Ottoman army, remaining loyal to Turkey until its defeat. From November 1918 until July 1920, during the reign of Fayṣal in Damascus, many of them served under the Syrian national flag. Later they became officers of the French mandatory government, in the "Troupes Spéciales du Levant." After the fall of France in the summer of 1940 it was the representatives of Vichy, the agents of Hitler, who ruled Syria. In June 1941, when the British and the Free French defeated the Axis in Syria, the Syrian officers were fighting alongside the Vichy French. From then up to the end of World War II they remained subject to British domination. In 1945 Syria achieved independence—and a new era of instability began. In the revolts of Za'īm, Ḥinnāwī and Shīshaklī the officer class was the main factor as well as the prime objective in the shifting ties of allegiance. In the four years that followed the rout of Shīshaklī, the officer class continued wreaking havoc upon the government, itself suffering shock and strain in the process. From 1958 to 1961 the officers were under orders from the Egypt of the United Arab Republic, and in 1961 were once again the active force in splitting the union. Since 1962 their political activity has become even more intense.

Over a period of 50 years the frequent changes in the country's leadership—many engineered by the officers—were almost always accompanied by dramatic transformations in the composition of the officer corps from general headquarters to battalion commands, by transfers from unit to unit, promotions and dismissals.

During the period of French rule a considerable military force was permanently stationed in Syria. It was an army composed mostly of troops from Metropolitan France and her North African and Black African colonies. Parallel to the army the French also maintained the gendarmerie, a paramilitary police force, for internal security. It was directed mainly against organized groups, be they criminal or political, smugglers, tribal rebels or political revolutionaries. Both the army and the gendarmerie were used by the French as instruments for suppressing nationalist movements.

The French did not encourage members of the Sunni-Muslim majority to join the armed forces, but set out instead to attract minority groups—Circassians, Alawis, Druze, Isma'īlis and Christians. This recruiting policy followed a tradition established by colonial powers in their various dependencies: The British in India recruited soldiers mainly from the Sikhs and Pathans; the Dutch in Indonesia from the Christians of Celebes; the French in Morocco from the Berbers, and so on. The colonial powers recruited at first enlisted personnel and later also officers, "from tribal groups remote from the central capital, from minority groups and especially from groups with limited independence aspirations. Frequently these groups came from economically less-developed areas and were therefore attracted by the opportunities in the army. There was also a mystical or folkloric element in some of these recruitment policies. Colonial powers believed that men recruited from more primitive areas were better fighters and less contaminated by the corruption of urbanism and western patterns. Certain of these groups did have strong military traditions, but their political reliability was a crucial factor."[1] To what extent the mixture of warlike tribal characteristics and political unreliability could be dangerous, the French were to learn in the Druze revolt which broke out in 1925 and lasted two years.

In order to suppress the revolt the French assembled a large army in Syria, some 40 thousand strong at the end of 1926. At the end of 1927, after the revolt had been put down, the French army in Syria and Lebanon, including its auxiliary forces, still numbered more than 30 thousand, and at this size it was maintained. The number of natives—Syrians and Lebanese—in the army of the French mandatory regime was gradually increased. In 1926 they were about five thousand; by 1930 they had reached 13 thousand.[2] The officer corps in mandatory Syria was always small in size. In January 1930 there were 319 officers in Syria and Lebanon, 157 of them French and 162 Syrians.[3] In 1938 out of a total of 306 officers in Syria, 88

[1] Morris Janowitz, *The military and the political development of new nations,* Chicago 1964, 52–3.

[2] Comte R. de Gontant Biron, *Sur les routes de Syrie,* Paris 1928. 147; André Bruneau, *Traditions et politique de la France au Levant,* Paris 1932, 339 40.

[3] Hans Kohn, *Nationalismus und Imperialismus im Vorderen Orient,* Frankfurt am Main 1931, 414.

were French and 218 Syrian.[4] The Syrians were almost all company officers, i.e., below the rank of major.

The army of the independent Syrian republic was at first a continuation of this same force. By the end of 1945 the army numbered 5,000, and the gendarmerie about 3,500, with 114 officers. The independent state took pains from the start to strengthen the army and steadily expanded it. By the time of the Palestine War the army was about 12 thousand strong and the gendarmerie about 4,500.[5] The size of the gendarmerie has since remained unchanged. According to the establishment as published in July 1954 it stood at 4,258, including 109 officers.[6] At the time of Za'īm the army establishment was put at 27 thousand men. To-day it stands at 60 thousand in regular service apart from reserves.[7] The number of officers must be somewhere around 3,000. A conscription law provides for two years' service, but so far it has been possible to avoid service by payment of a redemption fee of 500 Syrian pounds (about $230.00).[8]

With very few exceptions the professional officers in the Syrian army all hold certificates of matriculation from secondary schools and are graduates of the Homs Military Academy. Like their counterparts in the Iraqi and Egyptian armies, from the start they tread a different path from that of the rank and file. Graduates and academically trained persons who do not choose the army as a profession are given shortened courses for reserve officers at Aleppo, where there is also a training school for flight officers.

The high degree of politicization of the Syrian officer class and the succession of shocks to which it exposed the country and itself brought about constant changes in the composition of the officer group, particularly in its higher ranks. Those who reached the rank of lieutenant-colonel were usually out of the army after a few years. Since the Palestine War of 1948 the Syrian army has had more than a dozen chiefs of staff, and the changeover never took the form of an orderly transfer of duties but of dismissal, sometimes accompanied by violence. During the period of union the Egyptians tried to wean the officers from politics, mainly so as to improve their military effectiveness, but also with the political objective of rendering the Syrian officer corps powerless as an independent political force, and thus ensuring Egyptian supremacy. The elements which the Egyptians considered undesirable, and in particular the Ba'thists, were kept from key posi-

4 Gordon H. Torrey, *Syrian politics and the military,* Ohio 1964, 44.

5 Agra, *Tsevaot ha-'aravim bedorenu,* Tel Aviv 1948, 74–5.

6 *Hamizrah,* vol. 6, 58.

7 Torrey, 129; J. Tusan, 'Les forces armées du Moyen-Orient', *L'Armée,* Paris, September 1963.

8 W. Vogel, 'Die Syrische Armee', *Truppenpraxis,* Darmstadt, May 1964.

tions. They were transferred to Egypt, generally from positions of command to positions of administration. After the union was dissolved, the process of politicization came back with greater intensity, until in 1963 an "ideological army" was officially spoken of—in other words, exclusively Ba'thist party rule in the officer corps. Yet at no time and in no sense was unity of the officer class achieved—rather the reverse.

The constant changes and the splitting of the Syrian officer class into many conflicting factions are not the only causes of its diversity. The officer class is composed of different basic elements from a communal as well as social point of view. Nevertheless, the Syrian officer class comes much closer to reflecting the composition of the general population than does the Egyptian or the Iraqi.

The Sunni Muslim element is politically dominant in Syria and Iraq. In Egypt, where they form nine-tenths of the population, their proportion within the officer class is slightly greater than it is in the general population. In Iraq, where they form only one-fifth of the population, their proportion within the officer class is much greater than in the general population. In Syria, on the other hand, where they are two-thirds of the population, their proportion is smaller in the army—among the officers, the non-commissioned officers and the men—than in the general population. The Alawis, the Druze, the Isma'īlis and the Shi'i, who together form one-six of the population, are better represented in the army, both among officers and other ranks.

There are several reasons for the strong representation of the minority groups in the Syrian army. The first, historically speaking, is the recruiting policy of the French when they were in power; and the Alawis and Druze, on reaching positions of command, brought in their relatives and others of their community group and helped them to advance. The second cause is sociological: the Sunnis are mostly townsmen while the Alawis and Druze are villagers. Kāmil Muruwwah explained: "The townsman, however poor, is able to pay (the redemption fee) to escape the two-year military service. The villager, on the other hand, can find no such sum for his release from the obligation of military service. Moreover, compared with his position and work in the village, soldiering is an agreeable alternative. The result was that the number of Alawis in the army increased, helped by a sympathetic attitude on the part of the Druze and the Isma'īlis, who extended solidarity to their fellow minority groups. In this way the Sunnis became a minority and the village obtained the upper hand over the town."[9] The poverty in the minority areas which motivated the local population

[9] 'Siyāsī 'arabī qadīm', *al-Ḥayāt*, Beirut, 19 Decembdr 1964.

to accept conscription and fulfil their military service led the better-off among them to choose the career of army officer. Those villagers who had managed to matriculate but were not able to continue their studies at a university saw entry into the military college at Homs as a good start to social advancement and security.

Political factors also contributed to strengthening the position of the Alawis and the Druze in the officer class. At the beginning of national independence after 1945, the Arab administration tended to raise the Sunnis to key positions. However, since Za'īm's coup of 1949 the rate of political wear and tear among them was high. After each revolution some of them rose rapidly in rank, and then after the next turn of the tide were dismissed from the army, making way for others who in their turn did not last long in their positions. Members of the minority groups were less active in the sphere of political strife in the nineteen-fifties, and thus suffered less from its wear and tear. Therefore in the sixties they occupied important positions of command made vacant by the successive dismissals of the Sunnis by one side or the other. In 1963 and 1964 members of the minority groups reached the top ranks, and as good Syrians and typical Syrian officers, they too were infected with the spirit of politicization. They appeared generally—but not always—as rural rebels against urban supremacy and extremist supporters of nationalization and expropriations. The reason for this is quite obvious as one of these officers explained: "Don't expect us to eliminate socialism in Syria; for the real meaning of such steps would be the transfer of all the political, financial, industrial and commercial advantages to the towns, i.e., the members of the Sunni community. We, the Alawis and the Druze, will then again be the poor and the servants. We shall not abandon socialism, because it enables us to impoverish the townspeople and to equalize their standard of life to that of the villagers . . . What property do we have which we could lose by nationalization? None!"[10]

In the bitter struggle over Syria's position in thc Arab world vis-à-vis Egypt and Iraq—a struggle which is carried on inside Syria as well, and indeed also within the officer corps—the supporters of union and the followers of Nasser come mostly from the Sunnis, while the Alawi and Druze officers, like others of their community groups, are more in favor of Syria's independence. This parallel between community origin and political orientation should not, however, be regarded as a hard and fast rule, unfailingly establishing the attitude taken up by all factions. Even within a single minority group divisions of opinion manifest themselves in accordance with different political trends, personal rivalries, or membership of different

[10] *Ibid.*, 5 May 1966.

factions within the community group. For example there are the Lieutenant-Generals Muḥammad ʻUmrān and Ṣalāh Jadīd, both Alawis, who in 1965 were engaged in a struggle for military power within the Baʻth party and in the country as a whole. ʻUmrān is of the *Haddādīn* (Blacksmith) tribal faction in one of the Alawi villages east of Homs; Jadīd is of the *Khayyāṭīn* (Tailors) in the Latakia region.[11] ʻUmrān was all in favor of a closer relationship with Nasser's Egypt in 1964 and 1965, and Jadīd took his place at that time in the forefront of those bitterly opposed to such a rapprochement. The quarrel between them was fought in several stages and ended in February 1966 in ʻUmrān's defeat. The pro-Egyptians were unwilling to rely on the Alawis, and the Alawis did not support those who showed themselves to be pro-Egyptian—and ʻUmrān fell between the two stools. One of Jadīd's supporters was Lieutenant-General Ḥāfiẓ Asad, chief of the air force; he too was a Baʻthist and an Alawi.[12]

Later in 1966 the group headed by Jadīd also split, and Ḥāṭūm and his men tried to oust him. In the early days of September, Ḥāfiẓ Asad's attitude was all but unequivocal, and only at the last moment did he come out for Jadīd and against Ḥāṭūm. It was then generally assumed that the clinching factor was Asad's communal solidarity with his fellow Alawi, Jadīd, against Ḥāṭūm, the Druze. Correspondingly, Ḥāṭūms faction comprised a majority of Druze.

Communal divisions among the Syrian officers certainly gave rise to important political consequences. On the other hand, their influence should not be overestimated. Ṣalāh Jadīd, the Alawi, is a veteran member of the Baʻth; his brother Ghassān, who was assassinated in 1957, was one of the outstanding members of the SSNP, and so was another Alawi, a relative of the Jadīd brothers, Muḥammad Ḥasan Nāṣir, the commander of the air force who was assassinated in 1950.

The Syrian officer class is more varied in its composition than the Egyptian from the social point of view as well as in its community origins. This diversity reflects an important basic fact: The social polarization in Syria is less acute than in Egypt and Iraq. The poorest of the poor in Syria are not so wretched as the poorest of the poor in these other countries, and their most wealthy are not so rich. Moreover, in Syria the middle class of manufacturers, craftsmen, well-to-do merchants and the other bourgeois strata and also well-off farmers are stronger and more independent, relatively speaking, than in any other Arab country except Lebanon. The gulf which

[11] *Al-Ḥayāt,* 10 February 1965; *al-Jarīda,* Beirut, 13 October 1965; *The Encyclopaedia of Islam,* first edition, vol. 3, 964; B. Vernier, 'Le rôle politique de l'armée en Syrie', *Revue de la politique étrangère,* Paris 1965, no. 5, 466.

[12] *Al-Anwār,* 17 December 1964; *al-Ḥayāt,* 9 December 1964.

separates the estate owners from the fellaheen, and the traders from the academic class, is less deep. In the same way the range of social levels from which officers originate is wider in Syria.

In the Syrian officer corps are to be found sons of some of the most distinguished Sunni-Muslim families. For example, the Mardam family of Damascus gave their country a prime minister as well as several officers. 'Abd al-Raḥman Mardam was promoted to the rank of colonel in Za'īm's time.[13] At the beginning of the UAR period he retired with the rank of lieutenant-general. Tawfīq Niẓām al-Dīn who was chief of staff from July 1956 until August 1957 is a member of one of the most distinguished landowning families in the Kamishli region. Ḥaydar Kuzbarī, one of the heads of the secessionist revolt of 1961, came of a wealthy bourgeois Damascus family. From the important Atāsī family of Homs came two presidents of the republic and more than ten officers, including Fayṣal Atāsī, a leader of the rising against Shīshaklī in 1954, and Lū'ay Atāsī, who from March to July 1963 was head of the Revolutionary Council; Jawdat Atāsī, who served with the military police, later became a senior officer in the civil police and in 1964 ambassador to Moscow.

At the other end of the scale many officers, including Muslims, Alawis and Druze, come from poor families. A few of them reached high, even top military and political positions. The father of Muḥammad 'Umrān was a poor villager who sold his cow to pay for his son's education; his mother worked as a domestic helper.[14] Amīn al-Ḥāfiẓ comes from a poor family of Aleppo. Jāsim 'Alwān's parents, poor folk from Deir ez Zor, were driven from their home when he was a child and he had to fend for himself. The father of 'Abd al-Karīm Zahr al-Dīn was a tax collector in a remote village in the Druze mountains.

Between the extremes of the poor and the privileged wealthy are to be found the majority of the Syrian officers—sons of well-to-do peasant farmers, traders and members of the free professions. A large and very important group are the officers from Hama. Hama, with more than 100,000 inhabitants, is the fourth largest town in Syria. Adīb Shīshaklī was the son of a Hama family of landowners and professional men whose members had taken an active part in the Arab national movement since the beginning of the century.[15] Also from Hama came Akram Ḥawrānī who was a relative and, until 1952, the friend and partner of Shīshaklī. Ḥawrānī's leadership and power began among his own family and in his

[13] *Al-Jundī,* Damascus, 15 May 1949.

[14] Vernier, 466.

[15] Fā'iz Salāma, *A'lām al-'arab,* part 2, Damascus 1963, 6–11; C.E. Dawn, 'The rise of Arabism in Syria', *MEJ,* vol. 16, 65; *Oriente Moderno,* Roma 1937, 490; Vernier, 464.

home town and the surrounding area.[16] Prominent among the young men whom he influenced toward the Ba'th movement and whom he rallied around himself were some officers of his native town. The most important of these was 'Abd al-Ḥamīd Sarrāj. There were others, too, who were by no means small fry: Muṣṭafā Hamḍūn, a relative of Ḥawrānī, and 'Abd al-Ghanī Qanūt were both among the principal Ba'thist officers in the army from 1952 to 1957. In 1958 and 1959 they were ministers in the UAR government and in the first year following secession from Egypt they played a central role in politics. Colonel Rasmī al-Qudsī, commander of the force whose artillery, on the orders of Shīshaklī, shelled the Druze Mountain villages in January 1954, also came from Hama. Brigadier Ziyād Ḥarīrī, a leader of the revolt of March 1963 who later served as chief of staff, was also a native of Hama and brother-in-law of Ḥawrānī. Finally one may mention Bahīj Kallās, right-hand man of Za'īm who promoted him to colonel. Kallās was subsequently a major supporter of Ḥinnāwī and a member of his Supreme War Council. He is a Christian.

A survey of the Syrian officer corps, with the many coups it effected and the frequent bouleversements it suffered, may gave rise to the impression that it has little professional military worth. And indeed the battleworthiness of the Syrian army was undoubtedly impaired by these recurring and sudden changes in command, usually accompanied by far-reaching upheavals at brigade and battalion level. The heavy doses of indoctrination—actually Ba'thist politicization—in the period of the "ideological army" since 1963 made the Syrian officer even more oppressive in his thoughts and arrogant in his behavior than before, but his professional qualities were further diminished. Nevertheless, the basic cause of the weakness of the Syrian officer corps is also a source of strength. Its very diversity, which renders it susceptible to the effects of constant political shocks, mirrors its close relationship with the general public as regards class composition, communities and political parties. The lack of unity in the officer class resulting from its diverse social strata and its closeness to the people are two sides of the same coin. As a result, the distance between officers and men is less great in the Egyptian army.

In encounters with the Israeli forces in the years 1948 to 1964 the Syrian soldier has shown his fighting ability. The Syrian Brigade Group under the command of Fahad al-Shā'ir also showed its mettle in battles against the Kurds in Iraq in 1963. A German officer, who was an eyewitness to the suppression of the 'Alwān rebellion in July 1963, wrote that the Syrian army is "a well-prepared instrument—at least in parts—in the hands of a

[16] Patrick Seale, *The struggle for Syria,* London 1965, 38–40.

resolute government . . . The occupation of all strategically important points in the city of Damascus was effected quickly and without mishap as in a planned training maneuver, despite bloody battles involving artillery, armor and air power."[17] However, in the Six-Day War of 1967, when it had to confront not civilians or other army units of its own country but the Israeli army, the Syrian army's performance was almost as miserable as that of the Egyptian. This ineffectiveness must be at least partly blamed on the exaggerated politicization of the body politic in Syria in general and in the army in particular during the nineteen-sixties. Ba'th-party-indoctrination could not and did not increase the morale or the strength of the fighting force. The officer corps has been wrecked by purge after purge in succeeding changes of regimes. The frequent transfers and dismissals, quick and sudden rises in rank, and the relativeness of loyalty and discipline minimalized the military proficiency of the officer corps.

[17] Vogel, 331.

6. THE JORDANIAN OFFICER CLASS

"THE JORDANIAN Arab Army," as it has been called since 1956, was created in the autumn of 1920 as the "Arab Army" and was known abroad by its English name, "The Arab Legion." Nominally the Arab Legion was the army of the whole Arab world, but actually it was tiny in size. At first it consisted only of 5 officers, 75 mounted riflemen and 25 mounted machine-gunners. In the two years which followed its numbers were increased to 1,000 men, and by 1926 its strength reached some 1600. In 1926, when the Trans-Jordan Frontier Force (TJFF), which was under the command of the British High Commissioner, was formed, the strength of the Arab Legion was reduced to little more than half that number. In the thirties its structure was expanded very slowly. On the eve of World War II it comprised 44 officers, 3 cadets, 1,130 non-commissioned officers and men, 160 reserve soldiers and 600 civil guards. Due to its small size, the emphasis from the beginning was on fire-power and mobility and constant improvement in the standard of training and discipline. The Legion's first tests in the early nineteen-twenties—putting down the revolts of fellaheen in northern Transjordan who refused to pay taxes, and pushing back the Saudi-Wahhabi incursion in the south—resulted in utter failure, and it was only the intervention of the British Royal Air Force which saved the young Transjordanian Emirate. In May and June 1941, however, when the Legion served as an auxiliary unit to the British army in the fighting against the Rashīd 'Ālī government in Iraq and in the taking of Syria from the Vichy French, the Legion showed its capabilities. It was the only Arab army which fought on the side of the Allies in World War II, and the only one which attained its objectives. Since then, it has had the reputation of being the finest, the most highly trained and the best disciplined army in the Arab world. These qualities were again tested and proven in the Palestine War of 1948, particularly in the battles of Jerusalem and Latrun. The strength of the force, at first 6,000, rose in 1949 to 12,000 and in 1956 to 25,000.

By the middle nineteen-sixties the numbers approached 50,000, nearly 2,000 of them officers.[1]

Emir (since 1946 King) 'Abd-Allāh was until his assassination in 1951 the faithful ally—or perhaps the vassal—of the British, and this dependency was inordinately manifested in the Arab Legion. It was supported and financed entirely by the British up to 1956. The Legion was commanded until 1939 by its founder, Peake Pasha, a British officer who had served in Egypt and Sudan before World War I and, like Lawrence, in the Sharifian army during the war. In 1932 John B. Glubb joined the Legion, having previously served in Iraq. From 1933 he was second-in-command under Peake, and when the latter retired in 1939, Glubb succeeded him as Chief of Staff.

Glubb's most important and successful innovation was the organization of an all-Bedouin unit known as "The Desert Patrol." The main duties of the Legion up to the early nineteen-thirties were to uphold the authority of the State—by guarding its frontiers and ensuring internal security against raiding, rebellion, smuggling and inter-tribal feuds among the Bedouin, whether Transjordanian, Saudi or Iraqi. Until Glubb's time only farmers and townsmen were enrolled in the Legion, but they did not succeed in imposing the law of the country upon the desert. Through the Bedouin units Glubb was able to acquire psychological authority and also military control over the tribesmen. The Bedouin, when organized in their own units, also proved to be better and more loyal soldiers than the farmers. As a result, the Legion of the nineteen-thirties became mainly an army of Bedouin units.

Over a period of 35 years the British officers formed the backbone of the Legion. At the beginning they occupied all the important positions of command and held most of them even as late as 1956. On the eve of World War II they numbered 5 officers, on the outbreak of the Palestine War of 1948 37—plus 180 British sergeants—and on the first of March 1956, when Glubb was dismissed, there were 64 British officers, most of them above the rank of major.[2] The first Arab officer to attain the rank of brigadier was 'Abd al-Qādir al-Jundī. A native of Syria, he had served in the Legion since 1920 and was made deputy chief of staff in 1948. The Arab next in

[1] J.B. Glubb, *The story of the Arab Legion,* London 1948, 59, 235; J.B. Glubb, *A soldier with the Arabs,* London, 1957, 333–6, 434; C.S. Jarvis, *Arab command,* London 1942, 69; Peter Young, *Bedouin command,* London 1956, 191–3; 'Ārif al-'Ārif, *Al-Nakba,* vol. 6, *Sijill al-khulūd,* Sidon and Beurit 1962, 185; G. Lias, *Glubb's legion,* London 1956, 101–2; Benjamin Shwadran, *Jordan,* New York 1959, 201–3, 251; P.J.Vatikiotis, *Politics and the military in Jordan,* London 1967, 57–81, 137.

[2] Young, 191; Shwadran, 203, 260.

rank in 1948 was his relative Aḥmad Ṣidqī al-Jundī, at that time Colonel in command of the 4th Brigade. In April 1952 ʻAbd al-Qādir retired and Aḥmad Ṣidqī replaced him as Chief of Staff. Since 1956 the officers have all been Arabs, but the British tradition continues. Flying officers of the young Jordanian Air Force get their instruction in England, and all other officers are sent there to complete their military training. Nevertheless, British influence is gradually declining, partly through the increasing supply of American equipment and adoption of American methods and partly through general Arab influence.

One of the important features of the Legion is the relationship between the officers and the other ranks. There exists a social gap or psychological constraint, but it is not so wide as is in the Egyptian army.

The Arab Legion has always been an army of volunteers who enrolled for long-term service. Up to the middle of the nineteen-fifties most of the officers rose from the ranks, beginning as privates and rising steadily, rank by rank. Promotion was always very slow, but always open. In the middle fifties a sergeant with less than ten years' service was "very rare."[3] On the other hand many legionaires enlisted very young, sometimes at about 15 years of age, so that quite a number were officers by the age of 30 or 35. Regulations never prescribed that officers had first to serve in the ranks, and there were always some officers who on enlistment had gone straight to an officers' training course. These were in the minority, however, up to the nineteen-forties, while in the fifties they were about half, and only later did they form the majority of the newly-commissioned officers. Along with this development, officer–men relationships were generally better in the Legion than in the armies of other Arab states. Although discipline in the Legion was always extremely strict, the new recruit knew that most of the officers over him were once privates like himself, and the battalion commander knew that to-day's recruit might be a future officer.

One example of an officer who began as a private is Saʻūd Rashdān, born in the early nineteen-twenties to the north-eastern Saudi Bedouin tribe of Muṭā'ir. As a youth he somehow managed to reach Syria—a distance of more than five hundred miles—and joined the French army. In the fighting of 1941 he was taken prisoner by the Legion and joined its ranks. In 1948 he was a sergeant and a member of Glubb's personal bodyguard. In 1951, at the age of about 30, he was second-lieutenant and company commander. In 1955 he was captain and was sent on a military training course in England.[4] Later he was given command of the 9th Battalion—

[3] Young, 25.

[4] *Ibid.*, 25–6, 153–5, 202.

a Bedouin unit—and he retired from the army in the early nineteen-sixties.

A second example of an officer who began as a private is Maḥmūd Mūsā, born in 1914 in the Transjordan village of Sūm. In 1948 he was a captain and was decorated for distinguished service as a result of his bravery when in command of a company in Jerusalem. Later he was commander of the National Guard at Nablus and in 1954 he returned to the Legion as a battalion commander. In 1957 he had the rank of colonel. He took an active part in the officers' attempted coup in April of that year, and when it failed, he fled to Syria.[5]

The Bedouin form the main basis of the Jordanian officer corps, both quantitively and qualitively, but not exclusively. The first Arab officers of the Legion in the early nineteen-twenties were veteran officers of the Ottoman army, a relatively large number of them Circassians and Turkomans.[6] Later there came villagers and townsmen from Transjordan, Palestine and Syria, and in the forties, as a result of the change in the structure of the Legion introduced by Glubb, Bedouins. Of 355 officers and men of the Legion who fell in the Palestine War of 1948, 151 were Bedouin, originating from more than 20 different tribes. The tribe with the numerically greatest representation among these casualties was the Sirḥān with 55 names, while there were 21 of the Ḥuwayṭāṭ tribe, 14 of the Banū Ṣakhr and 11 Shamar.[7] Up to the middle of the nineteen-fifties many of the Bedouin in the Legion came from non-Jordanian tribes, mostly from Saudi Arabia and Iraq. Prominent among them were Shamar from Nejd, the defeated enemies of Ibn Sa'ūd. The Bedouin serve in separate battalions: In the 9th Battalion, for example, there were in 1954 about 800 Bedouin out of some 900 men. The remainder, including about 20 Christians, carried out duties for which it would be hard to find suitable men among the Bedouin—signalers and medical orderlies.[8] The Bedouin recruits did not know one letter from another when they joined the Legion, and it took many hours of training before they learned how to read the figures on the range-scale on the rifle sights. Even those who rose from the ranks to become officers could not be called—as the Arab officer class likes to describe itself—"intelligentsia in uniform."

The farmers and the townsmen are mostly to be found in the artillery regiments, in the armored, medical and engineering corps and, of course,

[5] *Ibid.,* 62, 176; 'Abd-Allāh al-Tal, *Kārithat Falasṭīn,* Cairo 1959, 103, 122; *al-Fajr al-al-jadīd,* Baghdad, 9 April 1964.

[6] Glubb, *The story,* 197; Jarvis, 70.

[7] 'Ārif al'Ārif, 185–6; (al-'Ārif enumerates erroneously 362 names instead of 355; 7 of them appear twice).

[8] Young, 24–5, 30, 79.

in the air force. Although the main strength of the Jordanian army is still its infantry, with the country's development other corps are constantly increasing in importance, resulting in a decline in the proportion and standing of the Bedouin. As throughout Arab society, wherever the Bedouin encounter the settled population, so in the Jordanian officer corps conflicts and rivalries are in evidence, often in the form of political dissension. The Bedouin are to this day more or less indifferent to the spirit of Arab nationalism. The Bedouin soldier's loyalty to his tribe has been supplanted by loyalty to his king, his army and his commanding officers. The British, and equally King 'Abd-Allāh and King Ḥusayn, never failed to appreciate the importance of this quality in the Bedouin, and indeed they exploited it to strengthen the Hashimite regime. All this gave rise to conflicts between the young non-Bedouin officers imbued with modern nationalistic spirit and the Bedouin. One of the nationalists' complaints against Glubb was that in granting commissioned rank to candidates he placed excessive importance on character and past service and did not sufficiently value an academic diploma as is customary in the Syrian army.[9]

If the farmers and townsmen of Transjordan were in King 'Abd-Allāh's day considered a danger to the Hashimite-British regime, the inhabitants of Cis-Jordan who became naturalized Jordanians in 1950 were held in even greater suspicion, and the Palestinian refugees most of all.

Even after the dismissal of the British officers, the leaders of the state were careful to restrict the entry of Cis-Jordanians and Palestinian refugees into the army, and to deny them key positions. The expansion of the army, as required by the Arab Summit Conferences of 1964, was thus delayed, for any expansion must of necessity raise the proportion and importance of these elements. Nevertheless, in the long run the Jordanian officer must come closer to the image and the outlook of his colleagues in the neighboring Arab armies. Even the Bedouin recruit of to-day is not the same as his counterpart of a generation ago; although he did not learn to read and write at home in his tribe, he has a transistor radio, he listens to broadcasts from Cairo and Damascus—and the emotional impact of the spoken word is stronger than that of the written. In this case, not seeing, but hearing is believing.

It is a fact, and a very significant one, that all Jordanian officers involved in attempted coups against the Hashimite kings were from urban or farming stock, and not a single Bedouin was ever among them. Particularly conspicuous as birthplaces of many Jordanian officer politicians, recalling the

[9] A.H. [Hottinger], 'Das Versagen der arabischen Effendis', *Neue Zürcher Zeitung*, Zürich, 19 January 1958.

example of Hama in Syria, are two small towns—Salt and Irbid. In both there is a Christian minority alongside the Muslim majority, and, as is often found in such cases, both were centers of nationalist zealotry. The two towns were the nearest urban settlements to Transjordan's neighbors—Salt to Palestine on the west bank of the Jordan, and Irbid to Syria. In the rivalry for public and economic primacy in the country they both lost to Amman when it was made the nation's capital, and against this background feelings of discrimination and an attitude of opposition were created. From Salt have come 'Ālī Abū Nuwār, 'Alī Khiyārī and Hishām 'Abd al-Fattāḥ al-Dabbās, the only Jordanian officer who took part in the assassination of Prime Minister Hazzā' al-Majālī in 1960. From Irbid or from the Ajlun district of which Irbid is the center come 'Abd-Allāh Tall, Maḥmūd Mūsā, Ṣādiq al-Shar' and Muḥmūd Rusān.

A further weakening of Bedouin preponderance resulted from the assimilation of the National Guard into the regular army. The National Guard was set up at the end of 1949 as a kind of militia for guarding the areas bordering Israel; it was composed of Palestinian villagers, and was influenced in structure by the system of the Israeli regional and settlement defences. From the military point of view the National Guard was never very effective, but it served as an organizational framework for extremist Palestinians. In 1956, while Nābulsī was the head of a leftist government, the National Guard was integrated with the Legion. The anti-Hashimite circles saw in the merger an opportunity to strengthen the pan-Arab influences in the Legion; the conservatives saw in it an opportunity to get rid of the risk inherent in the existence of a separate organization of armed Palestinians. At any rate, the National Guard was a body without real value, and nobody was against its dissolution and the transfer of its personnel and its arms to the regular battalions of the army.

Until 1967 the Jordanian army was quite different from most other Arab armies, especially from the Egyptian and the Iraqi. It was smaller in size and its equipment less modern and sophisticated, but the professional standing of its officers and men was higher and their fighting spirit, discipline and esprit de corps were stronger. To a certain extent at least these qualities can be attributed to the popular social origin of many officers and the men and the relative abstention of the officers from interference in internal politics. But even so the Jordanian army was no match for the Israeli. When it entered the Six-Day War in June 1967, following the Jordanian-Egyptian rapprochement of the previous weeks, it was routed swiftly, and Jordan's losses were the heaviest of all the Arab states.

PART FIVE

MOTIVATIONS OF THE ARAB OFFICER POLITICIANS

"Like a reconnaissance patrol, these thoughts are an effort to explore within ourselves—to discover who we are and what our role is to be in the succeeding stages of Egypt's history."

Nasser, 1953

"Our feeling that we have been falling behind has been very deep from the turn of this century and from before that; it is the principal motive of the revolutions which have successively taken place from 'Urābī until today."

R. Naqqāsh, 1958

1. THE SELF-IMAGE OF THE ARAB OFFICER POLITICIAN

THE ATTEMPT to understand the motives behind the political activities of Arab army officers is not meant to be a psychological analysis of subjective motivations or a polemic over whether a certain officer who became president is a high-minded idealist, a soldier risking his life or a power-seeking schemer. In every political individual, from the purest to the corrupt, are to be found both the aspiration to be a leader of men and ideological motives, the desire to make a vision come true even when it is only a rationalized projection of hidden psychological drives.

Nor are we interested here in asking what is the nature of a leader—is it the "charisma" of Max Weber, that enigmatic quality of leadership, or the glitter of success of some lucky adventurer? We shall try to clarify the diverse motives of the officers who are active in the Arab political sphere and their ideologies, beginning with some reflections on their self-image, or, as it has also been called, their auto-stereotype.

The appellations which the Arab officer politicians like to apply to themselves are of little use in analyzing the motives behind their activities. They are foremost among those whose self-image comprises various qualities characterized by such different epithets as "nationalistic", "revolutionary", and "socialistic". Formerly it would have been thought contradictory, like speaking of dry rain, if somebody were called a nationalist revolutionary or a revolutionary nationalist. Today this is the self-image of the adherents of many movements of Asians and Africans and American Negroes as well. But it cannot help to explain their motivations.

The modern Arab officer class is sometimes called "the armed intelligentsia," and the officers themselves define their status in society as that of "intelligentsia in uniform." The interpretation implied by such names and definitions is a positive appreciation of both the intelligentsia and the officer corps as pioneers in the national awakening and in social and spiritual advancement.

This characterization of the officers as "intelligentsia in uniform" draws attention to a very significant fact, especially important as it projects the officers' self-image. But it is far too generalized. It is therefore desirable to clarify the terms and identify the phenomena referred to.

The expression *"muthaqqaf"*, which means "intellectual" has become so common in modern Arabic that its original meaning has been blurred. Anyone who knows how to read and write and does not engage in physical labor, every teacher, clerk and official calls himself an intellectual, just as every pupils' riot is called a "students' demonstration." Before the singular noun *"muthaqqaf"* there appeared in modern Arabic usage the collective plural form *"al-muthaqqafūn,"* a translation of the French and English term "the intellectuals." As in western languages, this expression did not apply to all who had any erudition.

The western "intellectuals" were the modern rebel rationalists who burst the bonds of spiritual, in particular, religious, tradition. Opposition to the established intellectual and organizational authority of religion, militant anti-clericalism and agnosticism were fundamental parts of their outlook.

The term "intelligentsia" originated in Russia, and was coined apparently by Boborykin in the 1860's. His intelligentsia was a social group consisting of "that portion of the modern intellectual elite possessing an education equivalent to that of contemporary Western Europe which had no part in the government apparatus."[1] Only later was the meaning of the term expanded to include all members of the free professions including teachers and some officials, but the intelligentsia as a social formation does not include either the disciples or the functionaries of religious tradition—shaykhs, imams, rabbis, religious sages, priests and monks. On the contrary, it embraces those with modern education and outlook of all kinds, so long as they are western-modern. At various times it was a source of ferment and revolution—in the eighteenth century in France, in the nineteenth in Russia and in the twentieth in Asia and Africa. It is "the social group which creates modern political ideas and provides the leadership for the revolutionary movements."[2]

With the Arabs, like most other peoples, the first budding of the national movement took place among the intelligentsia. It was not by chance that the earlier proponents of the idea of the Arab awakening in the nineteenth century, beginning with the revival of culture, language and literature—at first without political aims—were Lebanese Christians, pupils of French and American missionaries.

For many Asian and African peoples, and especially for the Arabs, the

[1] H.R. Seton-Watson, 'Intelligentsia and the revolution', *Soviet survey,* London, VII-IX, 1959, 90–6.

[2] H.R. Seton-Watson, *Neither war nor peace,* London 1960, 164.

rise of a modern intelligentsia represents something of a break in the history of their spiritual life. The essence of the beliefs and objectives of modernistic intellectuals was an admission of the supremacy of western civilization and, at the same time, a call to a struggle for the preservation or the restoration of national, spiritual and political independence, in opposition to the encroachement of those same western powers. The enemy and the model were one and the same. To hold their own against the west they had to westernize. The movement which aimed to ensure the survival and independence of the national culture was based on the negation of the national tradition. At the heart of the intelligentsia lies a deep-seated feeling of ambivalence: The intellectual is torn between the desire to learn and imitate the values and way of life of the foreigners and the will to protect himself against foreign principles and to reinforce his national values. This attraction-repulsion in respect of western culture gives rise to confusion and causes profound spiritual conflict. Whoever can see the synthesis of these contradictory forces, calling for acceptance of the west culturally but its rejection politically, may have solved the dilemma for himself and others who think as he does; but should he try to rouse the public at large, he will find that their reaction derives from tradition rather than from the new spirit. A call to enlightened nationalist feeling is always liable to be taken as a rallying cry for traditional Islamic zeal. This dilemma facing the Arab intelligentsia explains many of its reservations, its inconsistent thinking, its lack of self-confidence.

By "the west" we mean that philosophy, science, technology and civilization which is now conquering the whole world and which originated in Europe at the dawn of the modern era. To the west as thus defined belong both the USA and the USSR. In all the countries of Asia and Africa, new instruments of work, transport and warfare which have been developed in the west are being pressed into use, for these nations quite rightly see that local traditional tools and methods hold them back, and they know that the ability to produce a washing-machine themselves would be a great achievement. The same applies in matters far removed from tools and methods of work—to dress, for example, which although purely an external thing, nevertheless reflects the mentality of the wearer; Negroes in Africa, who used to go naked, and Eskimos in the far north adopt the universal mode of dress which is western, from head to toe. The same is true of the sciences and the humanities, in political science, in entertainment and in the arts. In most spheres the intelligentsia, through learning from others, pioneered the Arab awakening. In this may be seen a continuation of ancient Arab and Islamic tradition. Ever since the days of the prophet Muḥammad, who based his new religion on knowledge and interpretation of the principles of Judaism and Christianity, the Muslim peoples—and particularly the Arabs and the Persians—have excelled in their readiness to receive the best of the heritage of other civilizations and their aptness in adapting it into a new entity for themselves. The present case is different, however. The westernizers in this new era, unlike the Muslims in the Middle Ages, did not learn from conquered peoples whose glory was past, but from rivals who excel them in the present, rivals who have overrun and subdued their pupils. "The intelligentsia of the early Abbassid period steeped itself in Hellenistic ways of thinking, took over Indian methods of medicine, adopted Iranian principles of administration, and in general delighted in widening its horizon and gratifying its curiosity about the world without feeling any (but occasional religious) hesitations about taking over elements of non-Arab and non-Muslim origin. The traditions from which influence would emanate were either politically dead, like Hellenism, or subjugated, like Iran, or irrelevant for the destiny of the empire, like India. The sense of the Muslims of being the master in their own house was in no way weakened by the knowledge that they were taking over the best the others had to offer. . . The completion of westernization during the last 150 years is totally different. It was the inadequacy of their power which first induced in some of the Muslim elites a readiness for reform . . . the removal of what was felt to be an inferiority . . . Can we ever become the political equals of the west unless we westernize completely."[3]

The modernism of the new oriental intelligentsia had its origins in the feeling—and in the fact—of backwardness and it has evoked, as one would expect from its nature and from the character of the west of the period, not only a drawing-closer and attraction, but also repulsion and opposition. The relationship is basically ambivalent. The west has appeared not only in the guise of a shining example, but also as a trader and a jailer, as a conqueror of lands no less than as a conqueror of hearts. In the case of many members of this intelligentsia one can discern a feeling of inferiority, in more restrained form among the Turks and Persians, who have always managed to keep their national independence, and in more obvious form among the Arabs, who have been deprived of independence for many generations and who achieved it only after intense struggles. The Arab intelligentsia had undertaken to be the leader of the people in its spiritual and political war against the foreigner by acknowledging his superiority and studying his methods. The dilemma of the Arab intelligentsia in the twentieth century arises from the difficulty that it calls at one and the same time for a national struggle and for a kind of assimilation

[3] G.E. von Grunebaum, *Modern Islam,* New York 1964, 32.

of the values and way of life of the enemy. It is not suprising, that many of these intellectuals are left irresolute, hesitating in the middle of the road. Some of them are not ready to carry through to the end with the struggle for independence, fearing the rise to power of internal reactionary, conservative forces, who from time to time impress their characteristics on the nationalist movement as it becomes a popular mass movement, the native population being tied to tradition; some hold back from drawing all the indicated spiritual and cultural conclusions from westernization in their wish to enjoy the confidence and support of these masses. The intellectual who wishes to emerge from the seclusion of his ivory tower must take into consideration the mood prevailing among the public at large and try to adapt himself to it.

One result is the ideological and political differentiation within the intelligentsia itself.

This differentiation is also the result of the decisive fact that the intelligentsia is not an independent class. It plays a central role in the upward struggles of social classes; it is the group which has the courage and the ability to formulate their theories and provide them with their ideological weapons. No less than it serves itself, it serves the whole body politic. But it does not neglect its own group interests, quite often presenting them in the guise of the general national interest. Today members of the free professions, technicians and administrators of various kinds occupy key positions in the government, the army and all branches of economic activity and they are most active in collectively and aggressively bringing their own interests to the fore, even to the point of propagating ideologies such as James Burnham's doctrine of the "Managerial Revolution." But this is no proof of the intelligentsia's class-disinterestedness.

The French intelligentsia in the eighteenth century mostly ranged itself by the side of the rising revolutionary bourgeois class, as did the Russian in the nineteenth. The Arab intelligentsia in the twentieth century is much more split in its orientation. One reason is the great variety in its strata of origin. The French and Russian intellectuals of two hundred and one hundred years ago were in major part descendants of the bourgeoisie and the petty nobility. The Arab intellectuals of the last two generations come from various levels with conflicting interests—sons of the bourgeoisie and estate owners, sons of professional men, wealthy villagers and others. And despite the great importance of the intellectual born of the ruling class who goes over to the oppressed class and provides it with ideological ammunition, this is not the only image of the intellectual. Many intellectuals remain attached to their class of origin, serving it in their own manner, yet none the less faithfully and effectively. It would only be a mistake to regard all intellectuals or so-called intellectuals as automatically aligned with the forces of progress.

The intelligentsia as such is neither progressive nor reactionary. At times it serves as the all-important forum of ideas within every progressive movement and organizes its forces. But it fulfils the same functions in reactionary groups as well. It was the intellectuals who fashioned the ideological weapons of Marxism and Nazism, of internationalism and anti-Semitism, of the kibbutz movement and the Muslim Brethren. Karl Mannheim developed an entire theory of the "socially unattached intelligentsia (freischwebende Intelligenz)" using Alfred Weber's terminology, and the quest of these unattached intellectuals "for the fulfilment of their mission as the predestined advocate of the intellectual interests of the whole."[4] But this is only an abstraction which incorrectly identifies the function of the intelligentsia in society with its own self-image and which converts a part of historical reality — disregarding the rest — into an historical and social law. There is no vacuum in society, and "the intellectual interests of the whole," like its other interests, have always been subjected to varying and contradictory interpretations, especially by the intellectuals of whatever stripe.

The officer corps has all along occupied a central position in the intelligentsia of Turkey, Egypt and the other Arab countries. By origins, customs and inclination the officers are kin to the civilian intellectuals and are indeed sometimes related to them. Their characterization as "intelligentsia in uniform" points to an important aspect of their social and psychological image.

This attachment on the part of the officer class to the intelligentsia and to modernism has its roots deep in history. Over a period of five hundred years, from the fifteenth to the nineteenth century, the military sphere was the main area of contact between the East and the West, their encounters being mainly on the field of battle, and it was in this sphere that western superiority stood out most strikingly and convincingly. It was undoubtedly from this specific area of contact that there arose the compulsion to learn the secrets of the new power.

Military science was, however, never the only, nor even the first, channel through which western civilization penetrated into the East. The Islamic armies were using firearms as far back as the Middle Ages, and the Turkish science of artillery evolved as much from native sources as from European. The first innovation brought from the west was the printing press. The first books printed in a Muslim country by the revolutionary European

[4] Karl Mannheim, *Ideology and utopia,* New York 1959, 155, 158.

method were Hebrew books, printed in Istanbul in 1493 or 1494. Refugees expelled from Spain in 1492, who found a haven in the Ottoman Empire, continued and renewed their spiritual and technical activities there. How revolutionary the introduction of printing was is shown by the fact that the printing of books in Arabic and Turkish, the languages of Islam and its holy books, was strictly prohibited up to the beginning of the eighteenth century. More than two hundred years passed between the setting up of the first Hebrew press in Istanbul and 1727, when the first Turkish press was allowed, but opposition to this act of heresy was so strong that the press had to close down again fifteen years later and was only reopened in 1784, when books began to be printed in steadily increasing numbers.[5]

After the first printing works were established in Europe in the second half of the fifteenth century, the printed word spread rapidly in books, pamphlets and leaflets among a wide range of social strata. Many people could read and write. Democratization of learning began. If the number of books and the number of copies of each book in the Turkish language remained very small until the end of the eighteenth century, it must be remembered that the number who could read Turkish was very small. How much more tardy and slow, therefore, was the influence of civilization via the printed word in the case of the Arabs. On the other hand, the innovations in the military world quickly affected a very wide circle. Army officers were not the first to be touched by the winds of modernization, but the officer class was the first social group which, as an entire group and as a group of recognized social and political standing, was influenced by the new spirit of modernism.

Endless examples could be quoted of the introduction or penetration of western technical and spiritual innovations into the systems of work and thinking of the officers. It will perhaps suffice to give some examples from the nineteenth century alone:

European instructors in military schools were the first to have direct persistent influence over whole groups of native personnel. Egyptian army officers were the first to be sent to Europe for study. The Egyptian army was the first organization in a Muslim country to introduce, in the first half of the nineteenth century, European dress. Up to 1837 education was part of the task of the Egyptian Ministry for War.[6] The army was also the first Egyptian institution to introduce compulsory education. In 1870, at the suggestion of Chief of Staff Stone, it was decided to establish a school

[5] Bernard Lewis, *The Middle East and the West,* London 1964, 41, 50–1.

[6] Jamal Mohammed Ahmed, *The intellectual origins of Egyptian nationalism,* London 1960, 10.

in every battalion. It may be that in describing the results there was some exaggeration, but it was reported that by 1874 76 per cent of the army could read and write.[7] Statistics on the subject of education which make no mention of the quality of the achievements are even today the most suspect of all statistics. Nevertheless, the attachment to learning, again found specifically in the army, is typical. Between 1865 and 1875 seven out of every ten graduates of the Egyptian civilian modern schools were taken into the army.[8]

Revolutionary movements of the intelligentsia thus found their most active and effective supporters among the officers. The Egyptian movements were in this respect no exception, neither were they the first. The standard-bearers of the Decembrist Conspiracy in Russia in 1825 were officers. It was a great and at times decisive part that was played by the officers in the *Young Ottomans* movement in Turkey in 1865, in the *Young Turks* movement at the end of the last century and the beginning of this, in the movement for the introduction of a constitution in Egypt which ended in the 'Urābī rebellion of 1881, in the Arab national societies on the eve of World War I, and in other Arab groups of fighters for independence. Modern officer movements, from Bakr Ṣidqī and Sallāl, regard themselves as continuing the same tradition.

The intelligentsia was always an active element in political struggles. The intelligentsia in uniform continued political activity with greater intensity, sometimes to a point of one-sided politicization; by the nature of their profession they could not be as active or creative as the civilian intelligentsia in such fields as research, literature or education among the general public. This trend to greater politicization was strengthened by the relationship between the rulers and the intellectual officers. These rulers, whether governors of independent states like Sultan 'Abd al-Ḥamīd, Hashimite kings in Iraq and Jordan, or foreign governors in colonial or mandatory regimes, endeavored to keep officers away from politics. They feared the modernistic spirit and the nationalist zealotry of the officers—and so thrust them into the arms of the extremist underground opposition movements. Arab intellectuals, including the officer politicians, are unacquainted with Mannheim's theory of the "free intelligentsia" and its mission: had they been familiar with it, they might have found in it a faithful description of their self-image.

In a speech delivered in 1931 Atatürk described, in typically strong terms, the intelligentsia and the officer class as a social group who bear the stan-

[7] W.B. Hesseltine and H.C. Wolf, *The blue and the grey on the Nile*, Chicago 1961, 86.

[8] J. Heyworth-Dunne, *Introduction to the history of education in modern Egypt*, London 1938, 381–2.

dard of nationalist ideology and fulfil its aims. He said "Every time the Turkish nation wished to take a step forward, it cast its eyes on the army . . . When I speak of the army, I speak of the intelligentsia of the Turkish nation—the true masters of this country . . . The Turkish nation regards the army as the guardian of its ideals."[9]

Already in 1931 the role of the officer class among the intelligentsia and the nationalist-conscious elements was overemphasized and exaggerated. Social and ideological developments among all Middle-Eastern peoples since then have broadened and diversified the ranks of the educated, and the officer class can no longer be claimed to have a monopoly of the characteristics of the intelligentsia. However, the idealization of the officer class as the perfect and almost exclusive representative of the intelligentsia persists—and not only among those who are themselves in uniform. In a discussion among seventeen Soviet experts in 1964 on the subject of "Socialism, capitalism and the under-developed countries," G. Mirskiy said that in those countries the officers are "the best-educated section of the intelligentsia, always better equipped than others with progressive ideologies" and they "struggle for the modernization of their backward countries."[10] This is not just a superficial and romantic generalization. G. Mirskiy himself was induced to revise his statement when he dealt, in 1967, with the problem of "the army and politics in the third world." There he wrote: "The ideological outlook of the military leaders is bourgeois in respect to its background and remains today the principal support of neo-colonialism. They (the military dictators in different countries of Asia, Africa and Latin America) have no taste for large-scale social changes. They also lack the necessary qualifications for leadership of a state."[11]

Indeed, in the Arab countries, as elsewhere in Asia and Africa, there are other groups of intellectuals who are much superior to the officer class in the level of their education and more advanced in their political and social mentality and ideas. The officer class can now claim precedence with regard to power alone.

[9] Quoted in G.S. Harris, 'The role of the military in Turkish politics', *MEJ*, vol. 19, 1965, 56.

[10] G. Mirskiy, 'Creative Marxism and problems of national liberation revolution', Mirovaya Ekonomika; Mezhdvnarodnyye Otnosheniya, no. 5, 1963, translated in the *Mizan Newsletter*, London, April 1964, 7.

[11] G. Mirskiy, 'The army and politics in the third world', *Literaturnaya gazeta*, Moscow, No. 32, 2 August 1967.

2. THE OFFICERS' VIEWS AS EXPRESSIONS OF ARAB NATIONALISM

THE ARAB officer politicians have no single outlook and no uniform ideology uniquely theirs. They are divided in their opinions, and their views and disputes are more or less identical with those of the civilians. The difference is that civilians win arguments by a spate of words, while the officers settle controversies by the sword. However, even if the views of the officers resemble those of civilians, not all the Arab ideological and political currents are represented among them to the same degree as among other sections of the population. Among the officer politicians there are also persons with liberal views, but their proportion is not the same as in the civilian politically aware population. Similarly, there are relatively few conservatives among them. The officer politicians are generally unwavering nationalists favoring social reforms, zealous supporters of the state's independence and prestige, and indifferent to the values of individual freedom. Their political views are to a certain extent the projection of their habits as soldiers—persons who are constantly seeking technical and organizational improvement and who are used to issuing orders; the "art of persuasion" is not their particular proficiency.

The common element in the views of the officer politicians is the general ideology of Arab nationalism. This ideology, however widespread, is far from being a well-formulated doctrine or a methodically arranged system of beliefs and opinions. One of the important ideologists of Arab nationalism, Hazem Nuseibeh, rightly remarked, "The bitter disillusionment which followed World War I impressed a stamp of pessimism, negativism, and cynicism upon the movement. The literature of Arab nationalism from this time is a bitter monotone, distinguished more by what it opposes than by what it proposes."[1]

It was to be expected that officers who constantly and knowingly deviate from the sphere of their professional functions and legal powers and strive to become a ruling elite would also develop a militaristic ideology presenting the man of war as a model individual and glorifying war as a supreme

[1] H.Z. Nuseibeh, *The ideas of Arab nationalism,* Ithaca N.Y. 1956, 55–6.

value in the life of the nation. An ideology of this sort has a time-honored tradition in Europe's political philosophy beginning with Heraclitus' saying "Struggle is the father of everything". Hegel wrote that war protects the moral health of peoples "as the movement of the winds protects the seas from becoming decay, which they would reach, were constant quiet or even eternal peace to prevail".[2] Von Moltke, a soldier, emphasized that "man's most noble virtues are only revealed in war . . . courage and abstinence, loyalty to duty and self-sacrifice at the risk of one's life".[3] Similar views can also be found in the political journalism of France and and England; and they reached their peak in Germany during the period between the two world wars when militarism gave birth to some of the most extreme nihilistic and cynical conclusions. Ernst Jünger, regarding battle as "an internal experience", wrote "War is not a human institution just as the sexual instinct is not a human institution; it is a law of nature, so that we shall never escape its magic". Accordingly "there exists only one crowd which does not look ridiculous—the army".[4] In Japan a militaristic mentality was rooted deep in an ancient tradition and in official ideology until the end of World War II. A brochure published by the Japanese War Ministry in 1934 reads "War is the father of the universe and the mother of culture".[5]

There would seem to be a basis for a militaristic ideology in Islam in the principle of the Holy War, the *Jihād*, which is a religious duty obligatory on the community of believers. In recent generations, when Islam was no longer on the offensive, attacking and expanding, but on the defensive, the concept of *Jihād* was at times given a new apologetic interpretation of a moral struggle against the individual's evil inclinations and of the people's aspirations for social reforms, but the original meaning of the principle has never disappeared. The Muslim Brethren advocate a *Jihād* for the purpose of establishing a fanatical, aggressive Islamic regime. In April 1953 Anwar Sādāt proclaimed in a Cairo mosque, "The *Jihād* is a religious duty of all Muslims".[6] The war against Israel is often spoken of as a *Jihād*.

Thus exists a basis for the growth of a militaristic Arab ideology, and the seeds of Western militarism, especially German, could have sprouted and flowered in the soil of the Islamic tradition of the *Jihād*. In fact, however, while the views of the Arab officers, as of Arab nationalism in general,

[2] Quoted in G. Ritter, *Staatskunst und Kriegshandwerk*, München 1954, 266.
[3] *Ibid.*, 27.
[4] E. Jünger, *Der Kampf als inneres Erlebnis*, Berlin 1936, 37, 56.
[5] Quoted in S.P. Huntington, *The soldier and the state*, Cambridge, Mass. 1957, 129.
[6] Al-Ahrām, 25 April 1953.

cover a broad field—not without weeds—this wild growth of militaristic ideology never took root. Pacifism never had a vogue in the spiritual life of the Arabs and neither did militarism. This should be pointed out precisely because soldiers as such have developed ramified political activities and because they were undoubtedly subjected to the powerful influences of militaristic views. Even though they belived that the army is destined to be the advance guard in modern Arab society, they did not attach intrinsic value to the image of the commanding officer. They emphasized the historic role of the officers and not their absolute supremacy. They sang the praises of their own courage, their comrades, and their heroic figures in the struggles and wars against imperialism and Israel—but without sanctifying war for its own sake. If not in their political acts, at any rate in their ideas, the Arab officers had the sense to understand that "the best soldierly tradition is the strong will to fight which also dares to strive for what appears to be impossible, since he hopes to achieve it by moral effort. . . But when the soldierly tradition became political rule, it irredeemably led to ruin. For what is the supreme virtue in a soldier is liable to be irresponsible arrogance in a statesman".[7] As we have pointed out, it is the ideology of the Arab officer politicians which is being discussed and not their methods after they seized power. In practical politics they usually acted like commanders who regard the population as subordinates in a bold operation owing obedience on pain of being considered mutineers or enemies.

In the reasons given by the officers for invading the sphere of politics, considerations of the army itself are hardly mentioned. They announce that the army assumes control for the purpose of eradicating corruption, preventing anarchy, establishing a regime based on freedom and justice, liberating the country from dependence and imperialism, advancing the cause of Arab unity and similar missions—all of them general social and political goals. These declarations do not claim that the army assumes power in an emergency in the face of a threat to the country's security by a foreign enemy. Even strengthening the country's military power is hardly ever stressed as a motivating factor; only in the declaration of the goals of the Egyptian coup of July 1952 as the fourth of its six aims mention was made of "the establishment of a strong national army". But the interests of the officers as a professional group did, in fact, lead them at times to interfere in politics: Za'īm's coup in Syria in March 1949 was provoked, among other reasons, by the government's plan to cut the military budget and dismiss officers. A stronger and much more frequent motive was the

[7] Ritter, 75–6.

self-protecting interest of officers who as members of political groups feared dismissals and penalties, e.g., the transfer of the Golden Square by Ṭaha al-Hāshimī at the beginning of April 1941. King Fārūq's order of July 15, 1952 to disband the committee of the Officers' Club together with mounting apprehension for the Free Officers' personal safety were to some extent responsible for advancing the date of the Egyptian coup to July 23. However, there are hardly any references to proper military motivations in the public explanations and ideologies of the officer politicians.

This phenomenon occurs throughout the world wherever modern military dictators and politicians are to be found—in Latin America and Southeast Asia as in the Arab states. Most of these countries are not faced with dangers stemming from problems of defense and security, and the officers cannot justify their coups by the need to resist outside enemies. In the case of Pakistan and its serious dispute with India over Kashmir, it was possible to point to the requirements of military preparedness as grounds for the officers' assumption of power; however, there, too, Ayūb Khan has cited the failure of the previous parliamentary regime as the sole cause for his military dictatorship, both when he seized power in October 1958 and throughout the entire period since then.

In the Arab world the unremitting enmity to Israel constitutes one of the very foundations of the ideology and politics of almost all political leaders. Moreover, the defeat in Palestine in 1948 was one of the strongest motives for the coups in Syria in 1949 and in Egypt in 1952. The blow suffered by five armies at the hand of a single small nation which they have not even deigned to recognize as an existing state shook the foundations of the Arab governments, destroyed the prestige of their leaders and drove them to a moral stocktaking in public. The feeling of shame burned most strongly in the hearts of the military; upon seizing power they would often proclaim that the regime they had established, and only this regime, would ensure that the "disaster of Palestine" would not recur. However, despite the overweening importance of the Palestine question in Arab political thinking, it was only a secondary argument in the officers' justifications of their coups before the Six-Day War. Their main foe was always the internal enemy. To place excessive emphasis on strengthening the army as a result of the Palestinian experience would have exposed the weakness of the Arab armies from the purely military point of view, a fact which the officers were not at all interested in revealing. There is a vast output of Arab critical literature dealing exhaustively with the defeat in Palestine which discusses extensively, and sometimes profoundly, all sorts of deficiencies and mistakes—with the exception of purely military faults and blunders. At most, the supreme command was criticized. The following is a typical statement:

"The Egyptian soldiers in all ranks demonstrated ability, endurance, and much bravery, for they were defending a cause in the justness of which they believed. However, our sons soon discovered that they were the victims of a dangerous conspiracy spun by ignorance and treachery. The high commanders, who had undertaken to draw up plans in order to assure victory, conducted the war from their comfortable offices in Cairo by means of improvisations devoid of even the least bit of professional war-making know-how. Orders were issued which the commanders and officers in the field saw no possibility of carrying out, as they were aware of the flagrant errors on which they were based; successive contradictory orders were given that stemmed from ignorance and frivolity, and the souls ascended to heaven complaining of the ignorance of the persons in authority".[8]

These words referring to the war of 1948 were written in 1952. They could equally well have been written in 1967, following the Six-Day War, and very little would have had to be altered. The fundamental realities of Arab life have changed far less than the kings and presidents. In June 1967, the souls of Egyptian soldiers again "ascended to heaven complaining of the ignorance of the persons in authority". And again the blame was laid by the persons in authority on others, this time on a certain group of high-ranking officers with Marshal 'Āmir in their forefront. The real leaders of the nations—the really responsible decision-makers, first Fārūq and then Nasser—were not ready to realize or to admit the basic faults of the regime. The main lesson which the rulers of 1967 had learned from the experience of 1948 was to intensify their efforts to prevent a recurrence of the overthrow of a leader who had failed. After 1948, the officer politicians were in opposition to the heads of the regime. In 1967 they had themselves become the rulers.

In identifying the internal enemy and diagnosing the shortcomings of the regime, the officer politicians in the forties and fifties generally displayed more courage than the other Arab ideologists and politicians. Their diagnosis was not always correct, and, in general, not original, but they dared say without hesitation what others only alluded to; and they were ready for acts from which others shrank. This is one of the sources of their power and success. Za'īm was not the first to think of granting women the franchise, but he was the first to put the idea into practice. The Egyptian Free Officers were not original in their plans for agrarian reform; but they were the first to implement them.

The point of departure of this radicalism is the awareness of the backwardness of the Arab countries. This awareness, too, was not peculiar to

[8] Rāshid al-Barāwī, *Ḥaqīqat al-inqilāb al-akhīr fī Miṣr,* Cairo 1952, 215–6.

the officers, but they felt and emphasized it more strongly. They clearly saw the weakness of the traditional Arab regime, both in their professional work—the technical inadequacy of the armies and the feebleness of their social and industrial bases—and in their personal experiences in the unfortunate wars in Iraq in 1941 and against Israel; and their underprivileged position in society propelled them to penetrating criticism. Always present in any airing of views was their consciousness of the Arab peoples' backwardness. Summarizing the consequences of the Iraqi war of 1941, Ṣabbāgh compares his country to a baby, "Small countries achieve their independence by making demands and struggling; they are like infants who are only suckled when they cry".[9] And twenty years later, the subject of backwardness and the fight against it is repeated in the speeches of Nasser. While denouncing the enemies of the Arabs—real and imaginary—he often reminds and admonishes, "Let us not forget the gap between the wealthy, advanced nations and our people and other poor, backward peoples". Speaking at the UN General Assembly in 1960, he aptly expressed this idea: "The nature of the circumstances we live in today makes a long wait unbearable to the people. Scientific progress is probably the first aspect of the surrounding circumstances. Any farmer in our country, from the extreme south in Aswan to the extreme north in Kameshli, for example, may, by means of radio and the press, observe the high standard of living of the ordinary United States citizen, or he may observe the magnificent achievements performed by the people of the Soviet Union. If this farmer should compare his condition with that of others, he would feel a surge in his breast urging him to raise his standard of living to reach the lead enjoyed by others. Our people may be told that patience is necessary and that other nations had to have it, but allow me to state here that the capacity of any generation for enduring patience is measured according to the circumstances of that generation, and not by the circumstances of others. Those who had the patience to endure crossing the sea in small boats directed by the winds differed completely from those who are able to cross it now in a few hours time by jet aircraft".[10]

The views of Arab officers politicians are thus only expressions of certain currents in general Arab nationalism. In their own eyes, too, they are the pioneers of national liberation and social reform for the entire nation. However, the positions of power which they captured have made these views extraordinarily influential.

[9] Ṣalāḥ al-Dīn al-Ṣabbāgh, *Fursān al-'urūba fī al-'Irāq,* Damascus 1956, 257.
[10] *MER* 1960, 469.

Their positions are neither steadfast nor uniform. Together with general Arab thinking they developed and changed in the course of time. We shall now discuss the main points in the views of Ṣabbāgh, who was conspicuous among the Arab officers before the fall of Hitler, of Nasser and of the Ba'thist officers.

3. ṢABBĀGH'S OUTLOOK

In His memoirs Ṣalāh al-Dīn Ṣabbāgh devoted a number of chapters to the principles in which he believed. His exposition is not systematic, and had he written in 1940 or 1941, during the period of Hitler's glory and his own political activity, he would have formulated several ideas differently than he did in 1945, when he was a persecuted exile following his movement's failure and the Nazi defeat. Nevertheless, his writings are an instructive document of the opinions and style of the man and others like him in his time.

He wrote: "I don't believe in the democracy of the English, the Nazism of the Germans or the Bolshevism of the Russians. I am a Muslim Arab, and for me there is no substitute for this among all the views and philosophies; I want no comparison or preference among them as this is sterile and meaningless, for wherever I turn, I see the foreign wolf preying upon and torturing my nation—in the Mediterranean, Oman, the Persian Gulf, in the heart of the Arabian peninsula and near the tomb of the Prophet."

"There is no more murderous wolf for the Arabs and no deadlier foe of Islam than Britain. As for the Arabs, they have been torn apart into small countries, communities and tribes that fight each other . . . If Arabs seeking freedom rise up in Palestine, Egypt, Aden, the seven shaykhdoms and Iraq, the guillotine is sharpened for them and bombers are loaded with fire. Three hundred and fifty million Muslims are still groaning under the yoke of British imperialism. The bloody 'Lion-Heart' of the Crusaders' wars was an Englishman and so was Allenby, who conquered Jerusalem and said, 'Now the Crusades are over,' and so was Gladstone, who threw the Quran into a closet and said, 'There will be no quiet in the world as long as this remains,' and so was Cromer who said, 'Only this Quran impedes civilization.'"

"If you give some attention to the location of countries and continents, and if you understand the strategic significance of the British wars, you will then see that the Arabs have no future unless the British Empire comes to an end . . ."

"If she helps Judaism and favors the National Home, she does not do so for love of the Jews, but for her own imperialistic interest. And as long as her empire exists, this interest will keep a grip on the Arab countries . . ."

"I hate Britain and everyone who walks in her ways because I am a Muslim, and Islam commands that I shall not be ruled by a person denying human ideals and principles, and because I am an Arab, and Arabism loathes a foreign army squatting on my soil, and because I am a soldier, and as a soldier I shall not consent to have a foreigner lead me . . ."

"My brother Arabs—your fathers glorified their magnificence by the nobility of spiritual qualities, for these are the marks of independence; and where do you have these qualities? Your unity has been torn to shreds, you have become divided within yourself, you have lost independence and greatness. This is your picture today: You boast of killing your sister and her lover, you do not allow your daughter to marry so that she may remain protected under your aegis—and then your brother-in-law who is fighting for your honor and religion comes to you and you do not bandage his wounds; a foreign army squats in your country and defiles everything you hold sacred and you are not horrified."[1]

Ṣabbāgh felt and thought, acted and hated as an Arab and a Muslim; for him Arabism and Islam are inextricably bound together in the past and present. Among the numerous personalities mentioned in his book either in praise or condemnation, there is no non-Muslim Arab about whom a good word is said. His fellow countrymen who are Muslims but not Arabs, the Kurds, are *a priori* and as such regarded as separatists and traitors. In his attitude toward them and the Assyrians he reveals a racialistic approach which is alien to the spirit of original Islam; he may well have been influenced by Nazism in this respect. In presenting various persons he often writes of his friends that so-and-so is "an Arab by extraction and outlook" (Ibrāhīm Rāwī), "an Arab by descent and feeling" (Maḥmūd Salmān) and about himself he proudly writes "I am an Arab on both sides of my family."[2] On the other hand, his statements about his opponents often begin with the words which he applied to Nūrī Sa'īd, "called Sa'īd, but he is not of the sons nor of the family of Sa'īd but a Turk from Konya."[3] Another, Da'ūd Ḥaydar, is rejected because "Arab blood does not flow in his veins."[4] Those of his friends who are not of Arab descent seem to need forgiveness, and Ṣabbāgh apologizes for them as he does for Amīn Zakī: "He was born in Baghdad of a Kurdish father, but he is loyal to the

[1] Ṣalāḥ al-Dīn al-Ṣabbāgh, *Fursān al-'urūba fī al-'Irāq,* Damascus 1956, 29–30.
[2] *Ibid.,* 18, 25.
[3] *Ibid.,* 15.
[4] *Ibid.,* 16–17.

Arab cause, a zealous defender of Islam and hates imperialism and its agents."[5]

Nevertheless, his attitude to the English is ambivalent. He is grateful to them for his military education which he received from British officers who served in Iraq, and he has pleasant memories of his training in England. While there, he married an Englishwoman who bore him two sons (she died two years later).[6] However in his final analysis the friendship of the English is "not sincere, it is like the politeness of a person in authority giving himself airs before a subordinate who has been humiliated." And time and time again racialism erupts: "I am sorry to say that the royal family selected an English Jew as its private physician, instead of an Arab doctor of pure blood, at a time when Palestine is groaning under Jewish Zionism . . . How will the Arabs attain their independence when their leaders act in this manner?"[7]

Ṣabbāgh's Arab and Islamic fanaticism brings him to pan-Arab nationalism. His patriotism is not Iraqi but all-Arab. His model heroes come from all parts of the Arab world—'Abd al Kārīm from Morocco, 'Abd al-Qādir from Algeria, 'Urābī and Zaghlūl from Egypt, the Mufti and 'Abū-Durra from Palestine, Yūsuf al-'Aẓma from Syria and Sharīf Ḥusayn from Hījaz.[8] It was consistent with his character that he accepted the Jerusalem Mufti as his spiritual guide and political leader.

Just as Ṣabbāgh's political and national horizons were broad, so his outlook on matters of internal politics was narrow. He was not concerned with social and economic questions. He completely lacks the aspiration for social reform which most of the officer politicians conspicuously displayed after World War II. In enumerating a number of general principles, he writes vaguely that brotherhood and justice demand "that the poor man should not go naked and hungry while his rich brother enjoys all the fine things. The countries of the Arabs are Arab property."[9] The possibility of abolishing the class system or of changing the relationship between the classes does not occur to him. He sees and criticizes the deterioration in private and public morality in Iraqi society; the reason is "alien education in our homes," and the worst consequence of personal egotism is "that it drives our people's leaders to national betrayal."[10] The remedy for every ill is a return to the principles of Islam and adherence

[5] *Ibid.*, 18.
[6] *Ibid.*, 57–8.
[7] *Ibid.*, 164.
[8] *Ibid.*, 205, 233, 237.
[9] *Ibid.*, 9.
[10] *Ibid.*, 163.

to Arab tradition. He considers a man's killing his sister and her lover in order to protect the family honor—as cited above—one of the special Arab virtues.

Ṣabbāgh did not specify how his principles could be carried out in practice in modern times. However, when he participated in practical discussion on internal politics, he unhesitatingly considered the military factor to be decisive in all matters, both in war and peace, with the exception of of judicial affairs. In all decisions relating to questions of transport, finance, irrigation, education, etc., "military consideration should prevail and army representatives have the deciding voice."[11]

Ṣabbāgh did not know how to formulate his ideas brilliantly, nor did he distinguish himself by profound thinking. The complicated question of the relationship between modern nationalism, essentially secular, which bases the state on the duty of supreme loyalty to the linguistic-territorial partnership, and loyalty to Islam, supra-national, discriminatory, and divisive within the national state, did not enter his mind at all. This is why he was able to think and write with such simplicity, unpretentiousness and self-confidence. In these respects he was representative of large segments of his nation, and this is why his memoirs are important: Not only for the description of events in which he had taken part but also as the documentation of a mentality. He expresses the opinions of the Iraqi officer politicians of his time and also of many Arabs later on. He was not aware of all the implications that proceeded from his views, so he expressed simply and even naively ideas that wiser men tried to obscure or conceal, despite the fact that their feelings and intentions did not differ much from his: Alienation from and contempt for the values of liberalism, democracy and socialism; a desire for a resolute dictatorship in internal affairs and external aggression; a passionate hatred for imperialism and animosity toward all who are not Muslim Arabs.

Anti-imperialism is the common element of most currents of Arab nationalism. The few exceptions who advocate a policy of alliances with western powers, e.g., the Hashimite kings, were never able to gain the sympathy of the masses and the support of the intellectuals for their policies, even though their personal qualities and political achievements were not one whit inferior to those of their rivals. And, indeed, the Arabs, like the other peoples of Asia and Africa, certainly have reason to hate the English and the French who maintained foreign governments in their countries and exploited their resources.

In the thinking of Ṣabbāgh and others like him, nationalism and anti-

[11] *Ibid.,* 189–90.

imperialism appear interwoven with chauvinistic xenophobia and bigoted religious fanaticism. The question is asked: What is the primal factor in his consciousness? Are Islamic fanaticism and Arab chauvinism only a traditional garb donned by modern nationalism? Or is anti-imperialist nationalism only an up-to-date expression, coined in our era, of an old, unchanging identification with the traditional system of beliefs and opinions of the Islamic state? What is temporary and transitory and what is permanent—and, in the long run, decisive—in this ideology; what is a motivating factor and what only a manifestation? It can be said that for most leaders and ideologists of Arab nationalism both factors, the modern nationalist and the traditional Islamic, are intermingled, that they are two diverse trends influencing each other and stemming from common roots. But even if this mutual influence is taken into consideration the question still remains: What is the strength and importance for each leader and ideologist of one factor in relation to the other?

Since both factors are essentially different and give rise to conflicting conclusions, the question is not only one of historical origin and psychological motives nor even only of emphasis, but a qualitative one. It has frequently happened in the Islamic world in the past century that a secular, nationalistic view formulated by an intellectual leadership was received by large sections of the population in a spirit of traditional conservatism. To a large extent this characterizes the entire history of Arab nationalism. Until World War I, it consisted primarily of limited circles of westernized intellectuals of liberal and secular outlook; it is not mere chance that Christians played such a large part in it. Between both world wars, nationalism in the Arab world became a mass movement, and large numbers of villagers and city dwellers still living under the decisive influence of tradition adopted it as their own and put their stamp upon it. In the 1920's Arab nationalism appeared as a movement which aspired essentially to westernization. In the thirties and forties it appeared more and more as a movement of resistance to westernization, not only resistance to the political control of the west but also rejection of western cultural elements and social concepts. This change, too, was influenced by many of the processes which originated not in the Arab world but, again, in Europe. The decade between the outbreak of the world economic crisis in 1929 and the beginning of World War II was marked by victories of reaction and Fascism and the defeats of the forces of progress in the spiritual as well as the political spheres. Both worldwide and internal Arab processes led to the renewed strengthening of reactionary fanaticism and traditionalism in wide Arab circles. Arab officer politicians of that period and of Ṣabbāgh's category were, as they have been wont to boast, both close to the masses and part of the intellectuals.

Espousing the desire of the masses, they zealously fought for Islam and traditional Arabism. In welcoming modern influences they were affected by the spirit of aggressive Fascist nationalism then emanating from Europe.

This is how Ṣabbāgh reached the stage of justifying Islamic polygamy,[12] and of advocating a political, military and ideological alliance with the Nazis. His thinking and activities were a characteristic expression of a sentiment prevalent among Arab officer politicians and other large classes of the Arab population in Iraq and elsewhere.

[12] *Ibid.*, 13.

4. THE PHILOSOPHY OF NASSER

BEFORE SEIZING power the Egyptian Free Officers did not promulgate general social and political views. Their proclamations were vague anti-imperialist, patriotic declarations and protests against slurs on the army and abuse of its officers. From the day of the coup, however, they have issued a ceaseless spate of ideological pronunciamentos and publications to explain their views and impress them upon the minds of millions of Arabic-speaking people throughout the world.

It is sometimes said that the Egyptian officers are not guided by any philosophy but only by a lust for power and political expediency, or, at the most, by feelings of hatred at once indistinct and aggressive, and their ideology is only a mask and rationalization for irrational drives and power-seeking interests. Such arguments are now and then articulated by their Arab foes in the unbridled style of vilification characterizing inter-Arab controversies which Nasser himself, more than any other leader, debased to the level of demagogic mud-slinging. Even sympathetic observers who try to explain the new Egypt come to the conclusion that the motivations of her leaders do not stem from a sound ideology. Thus, Wheelock writes of Nasser's neutralism that it "is not a philosophy but a blanket of morality in which he has sought to shroud his aggressive tactics."[1] Weinstein, a German officer who became a writer and who has a good understanding of the Egyptian officers, writes, "The Arab world under Nasser's leadership conducts an inter-bloc policy . . . Actually, behind the aspiration for an independent position in relation to both blocs, there stands no appropriate spiritual force. World communism is a fascinating idea . . . The West's democracy is a wonderful thing, a mighty result of wisdom, experience, and humanitarianism . . . But what is Arab nationalism? . . . It receives its drives from the complex of the Anti- . . . The swinging of the pendulum between forces is thus not only a crafty exploitation of given possibilities as they arise but also demonstrates that the Arab world does not yet have

[1] Keith Wheelock, *Nasser's new Egypt,* London 1960, 282.

a spiritual basis of its own."[2] Even Nasser and his associates have at times admitted that their system is pragmatism. In a speech delivered on July 21, 1960, the author of *The Philosophy of the Revolution* said, "We reached our ideologies as a natural outcome of our experience . . . We extracted our ideologies from the details of the events we passed through, and did not permit any ideology to force itself on us. Nor did we borrow them without the support of the facts of the events. In this way, ideologies were put to the service of life, not vice versa, because a social or political ideology is only a pattern and method for the movement, not a goal."[3] These statements recall what Eduard Bernstein said about socialism, that the movement is everything and the goal nothing.

Nasser's ideology was never fixed nor frozen. Most of the slogans he spouted in 1962 in the period of "Arab Socialism" were not yet mentioned in his statements of 1952. Arab nationalism, which was the be-all and end-all between 1956 and 1961, he did not refer to as a movement and certainly not as a value of identification in all his statements and writings before 1955. And it hardly appears in his speeches after 1961. It is easy to conclude that his ideas are only a rationalization of political stratagems. Yet the proponents of the new Egypt maintain that the ideological changes mark various stations on a straight, continuous road and that they demonstrate the precious attributes of readiness to learn from experience and of flexibility in detail while cleaving to the basic, unchanging mission.

Both the cynical view that regards changes in ideology simply as political expedients and the idealistic belief that considers them successive steps on a straight road see a *pars pro toto*; both contain an element of truth, but each alone is misleading.

Let us review the ideology of the Egyptian officers in two spheres—the national and the social—at various stages of their development. Nasser's writings and speeches can serve as a basis, for, since 1954, it was he who gave voice to all the ideological innovations; no one else expressed a new opinion in public, and whatever he said at once became state doctrine.

Whoever regards Nasser's public utterances only as demagoguery and propaganda to fit the occasion is mistaken. These are not lacking, but they are not the heart of the matter. His writings and speeches are expressions of his true beliefs and views, and this is the source of their great persuasive power. It is possible to find contradictions between any statesman's public declarations and the statements he makes in diplomatic conversations with foreign ambassadors or in reply to badgering questions thrown at him

[2] Adelbert Weinstein, *Das neue Mekka liegt am Nil,* Wiesbaden (1959–60 ?), 109–10.

[3] *MER* 1960, 467.

by journalists at inconvenient moments. Nasser's true feelings can be found in his public speeches. They are often frank monologues of detailed, thorough exposition. Proof of this is the fact that his actions suit them. Whoever wishes to understand the significance and intentions of his policies at a certain time will find them explicitly stated in his speeches of several months previous. Naturally, he is not infallible; many programs have foundered on the rock of reality, and numerous ideas have changed in the light of experience. These speeches are not prophecies for the future but faithful evidence of his motives and emotions. Whoever thinks that the goals outlined in *The Philosophy of the Revolution* are only dreams exerting no influence on life and possessing no very concrete political significance is repeating the errors of those who did not realize at the time the significance of the *Communist Manifesto* or of Hitler's *Mein Kampf.*

In his youth, until he entered the Military Academy at the age of 19, Nasser's ideas were apparently influenced chiefly by the extreme nationalism of his uncle Khalīl Ḥusayn and of "Young Egypt." In his early manhood, from 1938 to 1952, the circles of revolutionary officers contributed to his development. His ideas reached their first formulated crystallization in *The Philosophy of the Revolution.*

It is no fortuitous circumstance that the book was entitled "Philosophy." Qusṭanṭīn Zurayq emphasized in his influential work, *The National Consciousness,* that "There is no hope of an Arab national renaissance as long as it cannot draw from a national philosophy that could lend shape to its spirit, define its orientation, set up its goals, and determine its ways and means."[4] Since then, Arab nationalist thinking has constantly strived to define its contents and aims in search of its "philosophy."

The Philosophy of the Revolution was not written by Nasser alone. His ghost writer was Muḥammad Ḥasanayn Haykal.[5] However, the ideas and the principal formulations are Nasser's. The book consists of three chapters, the first two written in the summer of 1953 and the third in December of the same year.[6] But more than a quarter of a year in time separates both parts. The first two chapters are a document of unadulterated *Egyptian* nationalism. The third chapter marks the transition to *Arab* nationalism.

Egypt's national consciousness and national movement in the second half of the 19th century and the first half of the 20th were Egyptian and

[4] Qusṭanṭīn Zurayq, *Al-wa'y al-qawmī,* second ed., Beirut 1940, 19–20; Shimon Shamir, 'The question of a "national philosophy" in contemporary Arab thought', *Asian and African studies,* vol. 1, Jerusalem 1965, 1.

[5] Robert St. John, *The boss,* New York 1960, 193–4.

[6] Gamal Abdul Nasser, *Egypt's liberation,* Washington, D.C., 1955, 81; Arabic, *Falsafat al-thawra,* Cairo (1954?), 57; *Taṣrīhāt al-ra'īs Jamāl 'Abd al-Nāṣir,* Cairo (1955), 28, 63.

not Arab. Egypt did not consider herself an Arab country, and Egyptian desires for independence were to emphasize and shape Egyptian individuality not only against the British and the Turks but also vis-à-vis the Arabs in Asia. Of course, Egyptian ideologists and statesmen could not disregard the bonds of language, religion and tradition with the peoples east of Suez; but they did not regard them as a national tie nor did they believe there was any solidarity between themselves and the Arabs. They saw the relationship between themselves and the Arabs as the people of the United States look upon their relationship with the British—a common language and tradition, and even a certain amount of sympathy, but no identification. And like the attitude of the Americans to the English, this sympathy also had something of the attitude of an ambitious successful young man who does well in town towards his poor naive cousins who remained behind in the village. The general Egyptian attitude to the idea of Arab unity was expressed in the famous saying of Sa'ad Zaghlūl, the founder of the *Wafd* and Egypt's national leader until his death in 1927: "If you add one zero to another and then you add another, what will be the sum?"[7] Ṭaha Ḥusayn, Egypt's leading man of letters, in his great book, *The Future of Education in Egypt,* which appeared in 1938, developed the idea that in culture and civilization, Egypt, like Italy and France, belongs to the European and Mediterranean world based on the legacy of Hellenism rather than to the Eastern world (in which he also includes the Arabs) whose centers are India and China.[8] The Arabs are hardly mentioned in the work's two volumes.

Here and there someone in Egypt before 1940 advocated a pan-Arabism embracing also the lands of the Nile Valley. The Egyptian advance guard of the cause of Arabism were the cousins 'Abd al-Wahhāb 'Azzām and 'Abd al-Raḥmān 'Azzām, who was later to become the first secretary of the Arab League. In 1932 'Abd al-Raḥman 'Azzām wrote essays on *The Arabs, the Nation of the Future* and *Arab Unity, a Necessity for the Arabs and Happiness for Mankind.* However his articles were not published in Egypt; they appeared in the Palestine bi-weekly *Al-'Arab.* More numerous and influential than the Egyptian pan-Arabists were the proponents of a diametrically opposite view, "Pharaonism," which sought to base Egypt's national life on her pre-Islamic, Pharaonic and Hellenistic past, when the adjacent countries in Asia were at best Egyptian colonies. Extremists among

[7] Quoted many times, e.g., in Ṣāṭi' al-Ḥuṣarī, *Al-'urūba awwalan,* Beirut 1955; Anwar G. Chejne, 'Egyptian attitudes toward pan-Arabism', *MEJ,* vol. 11, 253.

[8] Ṭaha Ḥusayn, *Mustaqbal al-thaqāfa fī-Miṣr,* Cairo 1938, vol. 1, 28–63.

[9] *Al-'Arab,* vol. 1, Jerusalem, 27 August 1932, 15 October 1932.

them even suggested severing the linguistic tie between Egyptians and Arabs by transforming the spoken Egyptian dialect into a written language.

The Arabs in Asia, too, then regarded Egypt as a separate, non-Arab country; even extremist pan-Arabists did not include her in the countries which should compose the united Arab state. A typical example: when 'Uthmān Kamāl Ḥaddād, the Mufti's secretary, held secret negotiations in Berlin in August 1940 on a comprehensive German-Arab alliance, Grobba, the German negotiator, wrote a memorandum on Ḥaddād's proposals which spoke expressly of "countries recognized as Arab countries" on the one hand, and of Egypt and Sudan separately.[10] At the same time the official Supreme Defense Council in Baghdad surveyed, according to Ṣabbāgh, the political and military situation in "Egypt and the Arab countries."[11] The Arab countries in Asia, from Syria to Oman, were regarded as one region, and Egypt as another neighboring but separate one.

During the century from Moḥammad 'Alī's withdrawal from Palestine in 1841 to the founding of the Arab League in 1945, Egypt—including all her governments and opposition factions—interested herself but little in what went on east of Suez. Her aspirations to advance beyond her frontiers were directed southwards, to the Sudan. The conquest of various parts of that immense region which had begun in 1820 continued in stages until the end of the 1870's and extended Egyptian power to the sources of the Nile in Uganda. Egypt did not renounce her aspirations in Sudan when it became independent, after the Mahdī's revolt, from 1881 to 1895, nor following its conquest by the British, nor during the period of the Anglo-Egyptian condominium in the first half of the 20th century. Egypt's leading nationalist slogan was "Union of the Nile valley," and in October 1951 Fārūq was proclaimed "King of Egypt and Sudan." When the Free Officers acceded to power three-quarters of a year later, they did not change this orientation. In the official yearbook published on the first anniversary of the coup in July 1953, the frontispiece shows a symbolic map of the Nile valley without a border between Egypt and Sudan and with Cairo and Khartoum marked by two hearts; the caption says "Two hearts through which one Nile flows."[12] In the platform of the "Liberation Rally" of January 1953 the evacuation of the British forces from Egypt and Sudan and Sudan's right to national determination head the "national aims." Friendship with the Arab peoples and strengthening the Arab League are sections in the chapter on "foreign aims."[13] On the day of the proclamation

[10] Majid Khadduri, *Independent Iraq,* second ed., London 1960, 184–5.

[11] Ṣabbāgh, 142.

[12] *Hādhihi al-thawra, kitāb al-'ām al-awwal,* Cairo 1953, frontispiece.

[13] *Al-Ahrām,* 16 January 1953.

of the republic in June 1953 the soldiers took an oath of allegiance to the army "inside and outside the borders of the Nile valley."[14] The first two chapters of *The Philosophy of the Revolution* also speak in the name of Egyptian, not Arab, nationalism. The goal of the movement is defined as "an Egypt free and strong."[15] The homeland is Egypt, the people is Egyptian, the nation is Egyptian. Describing his thoughts during the Palestine War, Nasser writes, "We were fighting in Palestine, but our dreams centered on Egypt. Our bullets were aimed at the enemy in his trenches before us, but our hearts hovered over our distant country, which we had left to the care of the wolves."[16] Even when he was fighting devotedly for the Arabs, he did not regard their homeland as his. And the Arabs themselves are mentioned in this part of the *Philosophy* just once—in the course of a brief survey of Egyptian history: "It fell to Egypt that she should be the geographical crossroads of the world. So often were we a channel for the invader! So often were we the prize of covetous adventurers! . . . It is not possible to disregard the Pharaonic history of Egypt, the interaction of Greek culture and our own, the Roman invasion and the Islamic conquest which brought in its wake waves of Arab immigration. I believe that we must also dwell at length on our history through the Middle Ages, since it was the vicissitudes of that period which contributed so much to what we think and how we act today."[17] That is all he has to say about the Arabs—"waves of immigration in the Middle Ages" mentioned in the same breath as "invaders" and "adventurers," Greeks and Romans. How these statements differ in spirit from the pan-Arab temper of Salāḥ al-Dīn Ṣabbāgh's book! Ideal personalities were for Ṣabbāgh leaders from the whole Arab world. On the other hand, the figures which Nasser mentioned on two occasions in 1954 as the spiritual fathers of his movement are all Egyptians who paid no attention to Arab nationalism: 'Umar Makram, Aḥmad 'Urābī, Muṣṭafā Kāmil, Muḥammad Farīd and Sa'ad Zaghlūl.[18]

Illuminating and characteristic are the books which interested Nasser. Vaucher listed in the library of the Military Academy in Cairo the books which Nasser read when he was a cadet there in 1937 and when he was an instructor there between 1943 and 1946.[19] The list of 97 works contains books like Dale Carnegie's *How to Win Friends and Influence People.* Several fields of interest are conspicuous: Military theory (36 books),

[14] *Al-Ahrām,* 24 June 1953.
[15] Nasser, *Liberation,* 49; Arabic, 33.
[16] *Ibid.,* 21; Arabic, 12.
[17] *Ibid.,* 61–2; Arabic, 42.
[18] *Taṣrīḥāt al-ra'īs Jamāl 'Abd al-Nāṣir,* Cairo 1955, 12–3, 48.
[19] Georges Vaucher, *Gamal Abdul Nasser et son équipe,* Paris 1959, 97–103.

history of wars in the Middle East from Napoleon to World War I (14), the biographies of generals and statesmen (16), and matters pertaining to Egypt and Sudan (12). Only a single volume on the list deals with questions of the Middle East and the Arab world at present—that of Professor Alfred Bonné (of the Hebrew University of Jerusalem), *The Economic Development of the Middle East.*[20] He certainly also read books in addition to those from the Military Academy, especially in Arabic. But this list of books demonstrates clearly that his national consciousness was Egyptian.

The turning point from Egyptian to Arab nationalism becomes apparent in chapter III of *The Philosophy of the Revolution.* Nasser says that in the two previous chapters, "the emphasis has been on time. I therefore feel that 'place' is claiming its right to be examined."[21] It becomes clear to him that the Egyptians are surrounded by three circles in which they must concentrate and conduct their activities, Arab, African and Islamic. "Can we fail to see that there is an Arab circle surrounding us—that this circle is a part of us, and we are a part of it, our history being inextricably part of its history . . . Can we possibly ignore the fact that there is an African continent which Fate decreed us to be part of, and that it is also decreed that a terrible struggle exists for its future—a struggle whose results will be either for us or against us, with or without our will? Can we further ignore the existence of an Islamic world, with which we are united by bonds created not only by religious belief, but also reinforced by historic realities?... Among these circles there can be no doubt that the Arab circle is the most important, and the one with which we are now closely linked . . . So far as I can recall, the first glimmers of Arab awareness began to steal into my consciousness when I was a student in secondary school. I used to go out on a general strike with my comrades every year on the second of November[22] to protest against the Balfour Declaration which Britain had made on behalf of the Jews, giving them a national home in Palestine, thus tyrannously wresting it from its rightful owners." At first he could not understand his zeal for "a country I had never seen," but gradually things grew clearer, and "the result was that when the Palestine crisis [of 1948] began, I was utterly convinced that the fighting there was not taking place on foreign soil, nor was our part in it a matter of sentiment. It was a duty necessitated by self-defense."[23]

The sincerity of these statements should not be doubted. We have seen how in Nasser's words in the first part of his book the focus of identifica-

[20] Alfred Bonné, *The economic development of the Middle East,* Jerusalem 1943.
[21] Nasser, *Liberation,* 82; Arabic, 58.
[22] In the original version as well as in the English translation is written erroneously: December.
[23] *Ibid.,* 85–90; Arabic, 58–63.

tion, even when he was fighting in Palestine, is Egypt and only Egypt. Now he writes of indissoluble historical ties with the Arab world. However, in this new view, also, Egypt is the center and the Arab world is a circle revolving around her. The ideas and terms of "Arab nationalism", "Arab unity" and "the Arab nation" are not yet mentioned.

Nasser likens the position of Egypt in the Arab circle as well as in the other two circles to a role wandering in the region in search of a hero to perform it. He recalls Pirandello's play *Six Characters in Search of an Author*, "And I do not know why it seems to me that this role, exhausted by its wanderings, has at last settled down, tired and weary, near the borders of our country and is beckoning to us to move . . . since no one else is qualified to play it. Here let me hasten to say that this role is not one of leadership. It is rather a role of interaction with and responsibility to all the abovementioned factors. It is a role such as will spark this tremendous power latent in the area surrounding us."[24]

The hero-figure may be Egypt, the Free Officers, or the author himself, or the words may have been written from the beginning with a triple meaning in mind. As for the role, it is perfectly clear despite Nasser's apologetic denial that it means leadership. In the years since he wrote these words he has left no room for doubt that the Arab world must regard Egypt as the exclusive leading country, and himself personally as the sole absolute helmsman.

The ideology of the three circles and the Arab orientation of the last part of *The Philosophy of the Revolution* and the shift from Egyptian to Arab nationalism stem from a number of sources. Nasser mentions two of them in his work. One is the will 'to create a mighty force in this region" and the aspiration for a strong country by global standards. He lists three "main sources of our strength": The ties among "a community of neighboring peoples"; "our land itself and its position on the map—that important strategic position"; and oil.[25] Obviously, oil is located far from Egypt, and the other power factors carry weight on the scales of international policy only as the components of a large political entity. Nasser was aware of a fact to which he also alluded in his book—that the power of Egypt and the Arab countries does not reside either in their military or economic strength but in their nuisance value to the military and economic power of distant countries in Western Europe. This was his trump card (until the circumstances of global and geographical strategy involving oil changed in the sixties) and thanks to his ability to play it boldly he achieved many of his successes in world politics in the second half of the fifties.

[24] *Ibid.*, 87–88; Arabic, 61–62.
[25] *Ibid.*, 106; Arabic, 74–75.

Another source of his conversion to Arab orientation was his passionate hatred of Zionism and Israel. It is a fact that Arab nationalism as well as those currents in Egyptian nationalism by which Nasser was influenced were always violently opposed to Zionism. This enmity has served to bring Egyptian and Arab nationalism closer together and still serves as a prime unifying factor among Arabs everywhere. British imperialism has also made important contributions towards encouraging the Arabs to oppose Zionism. The first joint act of Arab kings, with the exception of the Egyptian, was their appeal, at the initiative of the British, to the Arab Higher Committee in October 1936 to stop the Arab general strike in Palestine, in order to enable the Mufti to extricate himself honorably from the blind alley into which his policies had led. To the St. James Conference in London in 1939, which was designed to win Arab support for Britain in the approaching world conflict at the expense of the Jews, the representatives of Saudi Arabia, Iraq, Yemen, Transjordan, and this time also Egypt were invited. The British initiated the formation of the Arab League, which was founded in 1945 after lengthy preparatory talks; their purpose was to assure themselves a monopoly of political and economic influence in the region after the war. Among the British statesmen there were some who also saw in this new concept of "unite and rule" and in the broad framework of a coalition of states a ray of hope for the integration and advancement of the Jewish National Home. The Arabs, however, regarded the League primarily as a tool against Zionism. The opposition to Jewish aspirations in Palestine was always an important unifying force for many Arab factions and personalities including Nasser.

With all its importance the anti-Zionist aspect should not be considered the only unifying factor among the Arabs. The aspirations for Arab unity, though far from realization, have profound historical and emotional roots in Arab life, and have received strong encouragement from the rapid development of modern means of communication and from the trend toward comprehensive blocs of states which is prevalent throughout the world today. Egypt could not disregard the growth of pan-Arab aspirations in Syria and Iraq between 1940 and 1955. In accordance with Egyptian policy, unchanging since the days of the pharaohs, the Cairo government is determined that any loose or tight league of neighboring states, should it arise, must be subject to Egyptian hegemony. The rivalry between Cairo and Baghdad is ancient, and its prime object is usually Damascus. In the decade following World War II, there was a possibility that an Arab union of the Fertile Crescent under the leadership of Nūrī Sa'īd and the Hashimite dynasties would come into being without Egypt and with a clear-cut Western orientation. Egypt was able to take the wind out of the sails of this movement by placing herself at the head of the all-Arab movement under the slogan of neutralistic opposition to ties with imperialists. This, too, Nasser understood well.

Another important reason for his turn to Arabism at the end of 1953 was the realization that his group had no quick remedy for curing the terrible distress of the Egyptian people. The social and economic problems confronting the Egyptian government are objectively among the most difficult of any country in the world. After their first year in power, the officers clearly understood that they had not been and would not be able to perform miracles. In order to strengthen and vindicate their regime they sought to direct the attention of the population more to matters of foreign policy, and it became clear that it was easier to achieve impressive successes in this sphere than in raising the standard of living of millions of fellaheen. In relation to her neighbors Egypt was always the most powerful country, but her resources alone could not satisfy the needs of her population. Every strong government in Egypt has invariably displayed aspirations of expanding and overrunning the adjacent countries.

Shortly after becoming aware of their limited ability to solve Egypt's internal problems, the Free Officers were forced to reconcile themselves to an additional disappointment: The dream of Nile unity faded away. Sudan achieved her independence, largely thanks to Egypt; she then made it clear that she wanted friendship, but by no means union, with Cairo. Memories of decades of Egyptian rule in the past century have not yet been forgotten in Sudan. The fact that the Nile water flows from south to north means that normal relations between the two countries are very desirable for Sudan, but are vital for Egypt, especially at a time when she is pinning her economic future on the construction of the High Dam at Aswan. After even Naguib suffered a serious failure at Khartoum in March 1954, union with Sudan was eliminated from the agenda, and Cairo's interest turned more intensely to her Arab neighbors in Asia.

The ideology of three circles, with emphasis on the Arab circle, thus constitutes a distinct turning point in Nasser's political orientation and consciousness, but it did not come like a thief in the night; it was a station on a long road.

How did the doctrine of the circles develop into the ideology of Arab nationalism?

In the final part of *The Philosophy*, the terms "Arab nationalism", "Arab unity" and "Arabism" *('urūba)* had not yet been mentioned. The Arabs outside of Egypt hardly appear as living figures in the doctrine of the circles. Their struggles, leaders and masses remain pale, nameless shadows. They are still on the periphery of the circle and an object of Egyptian policy. For many months after the book's appearance, Arab ideology remained only an incidental matter in the pronouncements of Egypt's leaders and apparently in their consciousness as well. Arabism, to the extent that it was mentioned in 1954, only appeared in statements directed to listeners outside Egypt. That is what Nasser proclaimed on July 4, 1954 on the first anniversary of the broadcasting station "Voice of the Arabs": "Brothers in glorious Arabism! In the name of Allah, the Supreme, the Almighty, in the name of eternal Arabism, and in the name of the one Arab nation, I send you an Arab greeting from Arab Egypt."[26] This was perhaps the first time that one of the leaders of modern Egypt explicitly mentioned Arab unity by name. But it is extremely doubtful whether or not Arab consciousness was at that time for Nasser a value with which he identified himself.

Only on rare occasions is it possible to get a glimpse of a man's soul, but one occasion did arise. On October 26, 1954 a member of the Muslim Brethren attempted to assassinate Nasser during his speech in Alexandria. Hearing the shots, Nasser threw himself to the ground; when he realized that the bullets had missed, he rose to his feet and shouted excitedly, "You men, the first orthodox caliphs all died martyrs' deaths for Allah, and I, too, am prepared to die a martyr's death a thousand times for Allah and for Egypt."[27] These are sincere words, the words of a brave man; and what were the associations which instantaneously came into his mind in the face of death? The first Islamic caliphs, Allah and Egypt. Islam and Egypt are the values of his spontaneous self-identification and his inspiration.

Nevertheless, the shift to Arab ideology continued by stages. The Egyptian constitution of June 1956 begins with the words "We, the Egyptian people," and establishes in the first paragraph, "Egypt is a sovereign, independent, Arab state, a democratic republic, and the Egyptian people is part of the Arab nation."[28] Membership in the Arab nation is emphasized, but the foundation is still the Egyptian people. The terms "Arab nationalism" and "Arab unity" are not used. In two semi-official publications which appeared in 1956, *The Spirit of the Constitution*[29] and *Three Years of the Egyptian Revolution*[30]—each consisting of more than 200 pages—, these two terms do not appear.

However, in Syria and other Arab countries, Cairo's Arab philosophy

[26] *Taṣrīḥāt*, 68.
[27] *Al-Jumhūriyya*, 27 October 1954.
[28] 'Abd al-Qādir Ḥātim, (ed.), *Rūḥ al-dustūr*, Cairo (1956), 201.
[29] *Ibid.*
[30] *Al-thawra al-maṣriyya fī thalāth sanawāt*, Cairo (1956).

and propaganda and Egypt's international political achievements evoked strong echoes. The signing of the evacuation agreement at the end of 1954, Nasser's appearance as one of the three central figures in Africa and Asia at the Bandung Conference in the spring of 1955 together with Chou En-Lai and Nehru, Egypt's success in withstanding pressure to join the west in the Cold War, and Egyptian anti-imperialist neutralism, the arms transaction and collaboration with the Soviet Union in constructing the Aswan High Dam, nationalization of the Suez Canal and the political victory over Britain, France and Israel after the attack in Sinai and Suez in 1956 (the military defeat was skillfully obliterated)—all these developments raised Egypt's estimation in the eyes of the Arabs. It is no wonder, then, that this political success also had a reciprocal influence on Egypt's leaders. Furthermore, after Shīshaklī's overthrow in February 1954, Syria also adopted neutralism and the momentum of the pan-Arab Syrian Ba'th party mounted; the ideological influence of the Ba'th spread far beyond the borders of Syria.

Thus, in 1957, and more pronouncedly after the union with Syria in 1958, the slogan of Arab nationalism became a basic principle and the crowning glory of official ideology, in the sense of its being the source of everything.

A characteristic expression of the ideology of Arab nationalism was given in Nasser's speech on "Algeria Day" on November 1, 1960.[31] He develops a historiosophy of Arab nationalism: It has been in existence for centuries. It was always attacked by imperialism, which invariably operated according to a "planned technique," and Arab nationalism always had the upper hand. "In the 13th century,[32] the imperialist Crusades were launched against Syria, Palestine, Egypt and the Arab lands in northwest Africa. In that battle the monarchs of Europe joined forces to subjugate the Arab nation. And what was the result? This defenseless Arab people rose up, and arming itself with faith in national unity and in Arab unity, it succeeded in taking the kings of Britain and France prisoner and purging all Arab soil of the aggression of Crusader imperialism . . . At that time Louis IX advanced on Egypt; but Louis IX was defeated in Egypt and taken prisoner, losing his army. After paying a ransom, he went to the Maghreb—the Arab states in northwest Africa—for the purpose of making himself master of the western part of the Arab world, and there, too, he suffered defeat. In Syria and Palestine the armies of Europe united in order to destroy Arab nationalism. They captured Palestine and Jerusalem

[31] *Al-Ahram*, 2 November 1960.

[32] The principal Crusades occurred in the 12th century. Nasser's knowledge of history is not accurate.

and built fortresses in Syria, believing that in this way they had overcome Arab nationalism and established a permanent domicile for imperialism. And what was the outcome? A union between Egypt and Syria came into being . . . The Arab armies and the Arab peoples united . . . Eighty years after the conquest of Jerusalem the Arab people had not forgotten its land and its rights . . . and succeeded in making Palestine again an Arab country, because it believed in its God and in its right to liberty and life, believed that unity is the way to power and the way to life . . . The Crusades have never ended . . . We met them in Egypt in Napoleon's invasion. Palestine, too, was the goal of French invasion in Napoleon's time, and so was Syria. But the Arab people rose . . . And thus the chain of imperialist invasions and Arab victories continued: The British invasions in Egypt in 1801 and 1807, the conquest of Algeria by the French in 1830 , the British occupation of Egypt in 1882, and after that the Balfour Declaration, the establishment of the State of Israel and the tri-power attack in 1956. From the Crusades to the war in Algeria the struggle between imperialism and the Arab nationalism never ceased. And what is the result? Arab nationalism always won because of Arab unity. And what conclusion can be drawn from all this? Just as it emerged victorious from all past battles, so Arab nationalism eventually will be triumphant in all the battles in which it is engaged today, in Algeria, southern Arabia and Palestine."

The historical concept of this speech describes and interprets the facts quite freely. But that is not important. What is essential is the emphasis on Arab nationalism elevated to supreme importance, expanded in significance to become the key for true understanding of the Arabic-Islamic past and applied as the answer to all problems in the present. It is the pivotal point of everything in every speech and article by Nasser and his associates of that period. It is the alpha and omega of every philosophy, the criterion of liberation and enslavement, of progress and reaction. In his book which appeared in 1954 he had not yet mentioned it. But in a speech at Damascus in 1960 he proclaimed, "It was not we who invented Arab nationalism; we inherited it from our fathers and our fathers' fathers."[33] Now it appears as the prime motive for the actions of the Arabs, including the Egyptians, for hundreds of years in succession.

The emphasis on the Crusades deserves special attention. The war between the Arabs and Crusaders is recalled as an analogy inspiring hope and certainty in the struggles of the present. We have already found mention of the Crusades in Ṣabbāgh's writings. Ṣabbāgh and Nasser were neither original nor exceptional in reviving the memory of the Crusades or in

[33] *Al-Ahrām,* 19 October 1960.

regarding relations between Arabs and the West in its light. It occupies a conspicuous place in Arab political thinking. "The memory of the Crusades is still alive, and has been rekindled by recent developments and is growing."[34] Many sketches broadcast on the Egyptian radio glorify the wars and, of course, the victories of the Ayyubids and the Mamelukes over the Crusaders. Saladin is the hero of the first cinemascope motion picture filmed in Egypt in 1963, and his eagle is the new emblem of the state.

In the debate over Israel with Bourguiba, Arif declared in 1965: "History repeats itself. This Holy Land was in the past the aim of the Crusader imperialists. But the unity of the Arab nation became an eternal fact, and the battle of Hattin is strong proof of this unity. The homeland of Arabism and Islam succeeded in uniting the Euphrates and the Nile, it defeated the invaders, and Palestine returned to the Arab nation."[35]

The analogy of the Crusaders and the modern enemies of the Arabs is of outstanding importance in Arab anti-Israeli reasoning. Against the argument that the stubborn refusal to recognize the fact of Israel's existence is unrealistic and futile, the adherents of the uncompromising anti-Israeli position retort: The Crusader states also existed here for a century and more, and when the time came, after the Arabs had completed their preparations and launched their attack, they were defeated and passed out of existence as if they had never been. This analogy is not only used in Arab propaganda directed to the outside world. Its main importance is its function as an argument to convince the Arabs themselves to accept as reasonable and useful politics what is obviously an utterly absurd, unrealistic approach. It explains to the Arabs various courses adopted by their leaders which sometimes seem amazing. In making use of the example of the Crusades, it is possible to explain to extremists that a realistic approach and refraining from warlike adventures do not mean peace with Israel in the long run, and to moderates that stirring up constant hatred does not mean the carrying out of provocative hostile acts at any time.

Actually, the analogy does not hold water. Comparison of the Crusader states with Israel disregards the basic differences between these two historical phenomena which only have the geographical location in common. However, the fact is that the analogy continues to reappear often and occupies an important place in Arab ideology. In the historical consciousness of political movements it is not the memory or the knowledge of the past as it really was which is the determining factor, but of the past as it lives in popular traditions and in legends. Ahad ha-'Am discussed this in his

[34] Wilfred C. Smith, *Islam in modern history,* Princeton 1957, 101, 106.

[35] *Al-Jihād,* Jerusalem, 3 May 1965.

essay, *Moses*. And who can understand better than a Zionist how strong inspiration stemming from a revival of past memories and glories and from historical analogy can be?

Nasser's Arab philosophy achieved its great triumph with the establishment of the union of Egypt and Syria in 1958. Even in the light of the fact that the union ended before it was four years old, the greatness of the event should not be disregarded. Two countries united of their own free will and at the initiative of the smaller one; millions regarded the UAR as the realization of an ancient dream, and throughout the Arab world soared the hope and belief that it would be the nucleus of complete Arab union. However, the bearers of the idea were not able to rise to the grandeur of the occasion, and the idea of unity could not abolish real differences. Achieving Arab unity was as difficult as calling for it was easy. In Syria, where it attained its greatest triumph, Nasser's philosophy also suffered its greatest defeat. The dissolution of the UAR in the autumn of 1961 may have been fortuitous at the time, but it was essentially inevitable. Arab union in a centralized political pattern consisting of a single circle with the only center in Cairo is impossible. This fact was again demonstrated on the failure of the triple Egyptian-Syrian-Iraqi federal union in the spring of 1963. The Middle East and the Arabs can attain unity only on the basis of polycentrism and the acknowledgment of the region's fundamental pluralism.

As the facts changed, so, too, did Nasser's ideology. In 1960 it seemed that the Arab nationalist ideology of "the political revolution and the social revolution for the sake of the Arab revolution,"[36] as he stated in a speech in 1960, was the final formulation of his philosophy. And, indeed, he often emphasized that the goals had not changed. After the dissolution of the UAR, in a speech on "Union Day" on February 22, 1962, he posed the question "Why are we celebrating the day of union?. . . There are people who say, 'Leave the Arabs to themselves and let us stay by ourselves.'" But he replied with emphasis "Our Arabism and the Arabism of Egypt are not transitory but a stable, permanent thing. I said it on the day of separation and I repeat it now, five months later. Egypt's Arabism will remain, and Arab unity will continue to be our goal."[37] The consciousness of belonging to the great Arab nation and of over-all Arab solidarity has remained a permanent element in Egypt's national consciousness. However, the sudden and artificial abolition of Egypt's individuality has not lasted. Between 1958 and 1961 Egypt was, as it were, only a geographical

[36] *Al-Ahrām,* 18 October 1960.
[37] *Ibid.,* 22 February 1962.

term. Now it again became the primary element of national identification preceding Arabism.

After the secession of Syria, talk of Arab nationalism progressively diminished in Egypt. Nasser once again speaks of Egypt and in her name. True, this is an Arab Egypt striving for Arab unity. He did not return to the opinions and statements of 1952 but the tune of 1958 was no longer audible in 1964. Let us take a look at his speeches on July 22 of 1962, 1963 and 1964, at celebrations commemorating the day of the revolution. In 1962 he said, "The Syrian people is the conceiver of the idea of unity, and the Syrian army was always the devoted soldier fighting imperialism . . . The dissolution of the union does not really point to failure. We decided not to interfere in Syria because we rely on the Syrian people. We learned a lesson from the union but have no regrets at all from it, since Egypt has always believed in Arab nationalism." Referring to the army, he spoke of the Egyptian army" which is "part of the Egyptian people," and adressing the army which was the advance guard of the revolution in 1952, which fought the tri-power aggression in 1956, and whose men died to confine Israel inside her borders, he said, "The Egyptian people will not forget what you have done and thanks you and your commander, 'Abd al-Ḥakīm 'Āmir, on this great day on which Egyptian missiles made by Egyptian hands were launched . . . These missiles first of all reflect the character of the Egyptian people which expressed its wish for a change of values."[38] A year later, in 1963, he again emphasized, "We are an Arab people standing for Arab nationalism and union and we shall continue to work for nationalism and union. Each one of us will be an emissary to himself and others and the standardbearer of nationalism and union." The true expression of the recognition of this mission is the "Egyptian army" fighting in Yemen. For "the people of Egypt believes firmly and sincerely in union. It is ready for union in all stages, beginning with a union of goals and ending in full legal unification. When I hear people arguing that the people of Egypt is not of Arab extraction and lacks all Arab characteristics, I recall when I was in my first year in high school; at that time, schools would participate in demonstrations and call for Arab union whenever something happened in Egypt or Beirut." At this point he alluded to reservations concerning over-all Arab nationalism or its rejection which had in the meantime been heard in Egypt. Nasser dissociated himself from such ideas, but he saw a need for debating them and even taking them into consideration. At the end of the speech, after a long bitter argument with the Syrian Ba'th, he stressed a decisive reason for Arab nationalism—it is necessary for the

[38] *Ibid.*, 23 July 1962.

"liberation of Palestine"—and he concluded, "It is the union of the Arab world which will defend Arab soil and Arab nationalism."[39] One year later, in 1964, when he delivered a short speech at midnight after lengthy greetings by African leaders, who were then attending a conference in Cairo, the term "Arab nationalism" was no longer mentioned.

On other occasions in 1964, for instance, during the long speech in honor of the sixth anniversary of the union with Syria on February 22, which was entirely devoted to Arab affairs, the term "Arab nationalism" no longer appeared; the same holds true for the long programmatic speech at the opening of the National Assembly on March 26. According to the provisional constitution of March 1964 of the United Arab Republic, the name of which was not changed, the president must be "the son of two Egyptian parents." When the achievements of the regime were discussed in 1964 the "Egyptian man" was sometimes mentioned along the lines of the "Soviet man." The term "Arab nationalism" did not appear in *The National Charter* of 1962, the great programmatic document of the regime, as if the concept had never existed. However, on other occasions it is mentioned.

The active interference of Nasser's Egypt in non-Egyptian Arab affairs did not end with Syria's secession from the UAR. The most overt and costly Egyptian intervention of this sort was the intervention in the civil war in Yemen. But the chain of success after success, which distinguished Nasser's policies and influenced his ideology until 1958, has been broken during the sixties, and failure followed failure. Sallāl's regime could be upheld only through the presence of more than fifty thousand Egyptian soldiers. After the Six-Day War, Egypt was forced to withdraw all her troops from Yemen, and even before the last Egyptian soldiers left, Sallāl, the Egyptian stooge, was deposed.

In the imagery used by Nasser in his book it may be said that the hero in search of a role was forced to return to his Egyptian homeland after wandering in the Arab world. But he came back a different man than when he left. On his travels he established ties, made a name for himself and acquired experience. His horizons have broadened and his long-range aspirations have grown. He has become more realistic and also more ambitious. From the point of view of abstract logic, there is contradiction here; in political acts this constitutes Nasser's constant dilemna. His views are not and never have been the pure ideological system of a thinker who constructs his theories at a desk or in a discussion group of writers; they are signposts along the road of political struggles.

[39] *Ibid.*, 23 July 1963.

At the end of 1961 the National Union was disbanded and replaced by the Arab Socialist Union as the mass organizational base of the regime. The first conclusion reached by Nasser from the UAR's dissolution was to shift the emphasis from nationalism to socialism. In a conversation with Syrian leaders in 1963 he explained, "We discovered new things. In the past we thought that achieving socialism is more difficult than attaining the goal of union; however, now we believe that it is harder to realize union than any other aim of the Arab nation . . . I took it for granted that the liberation of one Arab country would naturally bring about its closer association with the free countries and lead to union with them, but now I believe that liberation is not union. Liberation must precede union."[40]

In the first few months following the secession of Syria, Nasser indulged in a great deal of self-criticism. He admitted that many middle-class and even feudal elements had infiltrated the National Union and had transformed it into a tool of reaction. From now on, the hegemony of the working people must be assured—fellaheen, wage earners, laborers, office workers, members of the liberal professions and soldiers, together with the "national capitalists"—with the exception of the "exploitative capitalists."

This technique of self-criticism is a convenient stratagem for taking the wind out of the sails of the opposition and for making certain that whoever failed yesterday should be able to continue in power tomorrow without being discredited by his failures; he washes his hands of his own mistakes and opens for himself a new credit account for the future. Admitting errors is certainly not a pleasant job. However, criticism is not so dangerous if it is not made by an opponent, and the culprit himself is, as it were, his own judge.

Moreover, as M. Kerr has pointed out,[41] the nature of his self-criticism was such as to throw all moral responsibility on to Nasser's opponents or over to his followers: "I confess that I was foolish enough to trust you." The same spectacle repeated itself in June 1967 when he made Marshal 'Āmir and the commanders of the armed forces the scapegoats for the defeat in the Six-Day War.

While it would be extremely naive to disregard the expediency of self-criticism, Nasser's behavior after the breakdown of the union with Syria cannot be seen in this aspect alone. It also showed that he was capable of learning from failure and of reaching new, courageous conclusions. The consequences of his policies in the Arab world, in Syria and in Egypt itself, taught Nasser in 1961 that only through socialism could he and his country progress.

[40] *Al-Kifāḥ,* Beirut, 23 September 1963.

[41] Malcom Kerr, *The Arab cold war 1958–1964*, London 1965, 36.

When the Free Officers rose to power their ideology contained no reference to socialism. There were socialists among them; however, all the leftists among the Free Officers were dismissed between 1952 and 1954. In the declarations of the leaders of the group, no mention was made of socialism—not because it had yet to be discovered, but because they were opposed to it. They rejected every variety of socialism and communism both in the domestic and in the international sphere. In a conversation with a western correspondent in September 1954 Nasser said, as a compelling argument against Israel, that "the Zionists are serving communists since they are attempting to stir disorders and prevent an improvement in relations between Arabs and the west."[42] Neither in *The Philosophy of the Revolution* nor in the 1956 constitution does "socialism" appear.

Although they were not socialists, the Free Officers aspired to social changes and not only to a change of the political regime from 1952 on. One of their first actions was agrarian reform. In *The Philosophy* Nasser writes: "We are going through two revolutions, not one revolution. Every people on earth goes through two revolutions: a political revolution by which it wrests the right to govern itself from the hands of tyranny, or from the army stationed upon its soil against its will, and a social revolution, involving the conflict of classes, which settles down when justice is secured for the citizens of the united nation. Peoples preceding us on the path of human progress have passed through two revolutions, but they have not had to face both simultaneously; their revolutions in fact were centuries apart in time. For us, the terrible experience through which our people are going is that we are having both revolutions at the same time. This terrible experience stems from the fact that both revolutions have attendant factors which clash and contradict violently. To be successful, the political revolution must unite all elements of the nation, build them solidly together and instill in them the spirit of self-sacrifice for the sake of the whole country. But one of the primary features of social revolution is that it shakes values and loosens principles, and sets the citizens, as individuals and classes, to fighting each other . . . We are caught between the millstones of the two revolutions."[43]

These statements are not distinguished for their clear thinking or formulation. Both the passion of a sincere aspiration to transform society and the typical petty-bourgeois fear of a class war are reflected in them. Later in the chapter Nasser writes that this situation "demanded the existence of a force set in one cohesive framework, far removed from the conflict

42 *Taṣrīḥāt,* 126.

43 Nasser, *Liberation,* 39–41; Arabic, 25–26.

between individuals and classes, and drawn from the heart of the people: a force composed of men able to trust each other; a force with enough material strength at its disposal to guarantee a swift and decisive action. These conditions could be met only by the army."[44]

So—a coup d'état instead of a revolution, a military dictatorship to prevent a class war, and social reforms instead of socialism.

Nasser's talent lies in his readiness to learn and to reach new conclusions. He does not change his aims, but he is prepared to proceed toward them by different and varying ways. He is neither a doctrinaire nor an opportunist. He explained his approach: "We reached our ideologies as a natural outcome of our experience . . . We did not indulge in theories in search of our life, but devoted our life to the search for theories. This absolute freedom in facing nature was the best way for us to reach the stage of preparing laws. The freedom of action preceded the ideologies and so the ideologies were the product of nature. We extracted our ideologies from the details of the events we passed through, and did not permit any ideology to force itself on us."[45]

Thus Nasser advanced toward socialism step by step. As far as is known, the first time he mentioned the term was in April 1955 when he proclaimed "The Revolution aims at creating socialist society without class distincttion."[46] However, that was only a sporadic expression. After that, more than two and a half years passed without socialism figuring in his declarations. The socialist slogan was mentioned in his speech at the convention for cooperation in December 1957. The goal of the revolution was defined as the creation of "a cooperative, democratic, socialist society" which would be "free of economic, social and political exploitation."[47] This meant the gradual abolition of the immense differences in property and income, primarily by increasing production and the peaceful coexistence of capital and labor and of the state cooperative and private sectors of the conomy. Nasser repeatedly emphasized the principle of "equality of opportunity." He did not overlook the existence of classes, but he nevertheless continued firmly to reject the idea of a class war. In 1960 he proclaimed that peace and cooperation between classes does exist: "we achieved it for the first time in history."[48] But two years later, in 1962, he said that all previous talk of a cooperative, democratic socialist society was "only words."[49]

[44] *Ibid.,* 42; Arabic, 27.

[45] *MER* 1960, 467.

[46] *Wheelock,* 53.

[47] *Al-Ahrām,* 6 December 1957.

[48] *Ibid.,* 29 July 1960.

[49] *Ibid.,* 31 May 1962.

And even before that, in giving reasons for the nationalization decrees of July 1961, he asserted that, in practice, development until then had actually led to the bourgeois elements' becoming strong and wealthy at the expense of the workers.

Arab socialism after the summer of 1961 is "scientific socialism." In contrast to previous doctrines it advocates a clear preference of state economy over private economy, mounting state supervision and interference in all sectors, and the reduction of large incomes by restrictions and taxations. At the same time it emphasizes that Arab socialism does not entirely negate the private ownership of the means of production, and that "national" private capital, in contrast to "exploitative" capital, enjoys state protection and the freedom of action in extensive spheres.

In the chapters on officers as heads of state we shall discuss Arab socialism as it is being realized in practice; here we shall confine ourselves to ideology.

In answer to the question what led him to shift the ideological emphasis from Arab nationalism to Arab socialism, Nasser's own oft-repeated reply may be accepted: All the activities of the 1950's—including the limited agrarian reform, the nationalization of the Suez Canal and the expropriation of the property of foreigners—did not basically raise the standard of living of the masses, while the middle class strengthened its position and increased its property and income. As a result of this, the social gap did not diminish but grew. The middle class itself displayed little initiative in developing basic enterprises and found ways of investing its capital and making profits in speculative, non-productive activities. There were no visible prospects of the country's developing at the necessary speed in the desired direction under private, capitalist initiative.

Chapter six of *The Charter* of 1962 bears the highly significant title: "On the Inevitability of the Socialist Solution," and explains: "The socialist solution to the problem of economic and social underdevelopment in Egypt—with a view to achieving progress in a revolutionary way—was never a question of free choice. The socialist solution was a historical inevitability imposed by reality, the broad aspirations of the masses, and the changing nature of the world in the second half of the 20th century. The capitalist experiments to achieve progress correlated with imperialism. The countries of the capitalist world reached the period of economic drive on the basis of investments they made in their colonies . . . Gone are the ages of imperialist piracy, when the people's wealth was looted to serve the interests of others with neither legal nor moral control. . . . Scientific socialism is the suitable style for finding the right method leading to progress. No other method can definitely achieve the desired progress . . . Work aimed at expanding the base of national wealth can never be left to the haphazard ways of the exploiting private capital with its unruly tendencies. The redistribution of the surplus national work on the basis of justice can never be accomplished through voluntary efforts based on good intentions, however sincere they may be."[50]

These statements show how the shift to socialism stemmed primarily from a recognition of Egypt's internal economic and social problems. Outside influences provided a second source for the turn to socialism. Egypt's international orientation developed from anti-imperialism, which also wished to preserve a tie with the West, to militant neutralism from the time of the Bandung Conference, and from it to a close association with the communist states. The Soviet Union became the chief military and political support of Nasser's Egypt in his international and inter-Arab policies, and especially in his provocative enmity against Israel.

It has sometimes been said that Tito's Yugoslavia has exerted special influence on shaping Nasser's socialism. This opinion draws an analogy from the Egyptian-Yugoslav rapprochement in international policy to a closer understanding regarding socialist outlook. It is true that both countries have declared that they do not identify themselves with either of the world economic and military blocs and act accordingly, which is the source of their special friendship in international politics. However, there are no indications of special Yugoslav influence on either the ideology or practice of Arab socialism. The most conspicuous and unique feature of Yugoslav Marxism—the self-management of enterprises owned by the workers—does not exist in Egypt. Trends of decentralization and autonomy receive no encouragement there whatsoever; on the contrary, Arab socialism, like every Egyptian form of government, is supremely centralistic. Whoever looks for recognizable signs in Arab socialism of the influences of special ideologies and slogans borrowed from international social thinking can find a similarity in the distinction drawn by Arab socialism between "national" and "exploitative" private capital to the difference outlined in German National-Socialist doctrine between "creative" and "cumulative" capital. However, it is also possible to see here the influence of the distinction between the compradorean bourgeoisie and the national bourgeoisie in communist theory.

Nasser was driven to socialism by the developing climate of opinion among Egyptian intellectuals and workers. Although he does not permit freedom of opinion and expression, his ears are turned to the murmurings of the population. It is certain that class tension and class consciousness

[50] *The Charter,* Cairo 1962, 43–5.

are growing and deepening in Egypt and that socialist views are crystallizing. Whoever has watched audience reaction to his public speeches—and no one pays more attention to it than Nasser himself—realizes that he receives particularly strong ovations whenever he attacks feudal landlords and capitalists and talks about the rights and aspirations of the laboring classes. Whether he wanted to or not, he has had to meet some of the socialist demands of the people, and the best method was to take the lead. Those who claim that the growth of socialist consciousness in Egypt is the result of his indoctrination are wrong. He is not stirring up a class war; he wants to channelize energy in directions which he considers constructive and to restrain it. He is interested neither in preserving the status quo nor in strengthening capitalist elements.

Thus the ideology of Arab socialism has not been and cannot be as consistent and radical as that, for example, of Castro in Cuba. While he acknowledges the necessity of socialism and nationalization, Nasser always defends the sanctity of private property and the private ownership of the means of production in important sectors of the conomy. The 1962 *Charter* explicity states "The people's control of the means of production does not necessitate the nationalization of all means of production or the abolition of private ownership or the mere touching of the legitimate right of inheritance."[51] In Arab socialism as an ideology the function of private capital is only of secondary importance. But in Arab socialism as a political system in actual practice its place and power are still very great.

The same applies to religion. One of the conspicuous contradictions beween Arab socialism and Marxism of all persuasions is the emphasis on the identity of the Arab socialist outlook with the principles of Islam and belief in Allah. Nasser has tried hard to sever the historic-political bond between Islam and reaction both in explanatory discussion and in legislative activity. At the same time, he always ensured that his views and programs would receive the stamp of approval from the official interpreters of Islam. Every large meeting at which the President speaks begins with the reading of a chapter from the Quran. Nasser's devotion to Islam is much more than a matter of ritual; it stems from a faith deeply rooted in his heart. He and his companions are sincere believers.

The basic element in the development of the social views of Nasser and his group is conviction that the high road to the liberation of Egypt from her backwardness and poverty is industrialization. In a speech on November 12, 1964, he emphasized, "In the days of Muḥammad 'Alī—150 years ago—the agricultural area of Egypt was four million feddans and its population

[51] *Ibid.*, 45.

numbered five to six million. In 1952, it was six million feddans and our population 22 million. Today, in 1964, we have the same six million feddans, but we have reached the 30 million mark. Every year we increase by 700,000 people. We are not self-sufficient, and for this reason the High Dam is a question of life and death for us . . . In this way we shall have an additional million feddans, and we shall increase them until they become a million and a half, and we shall progress from basin to permanent irrigation—and what comes after that? Will this limited wealth satisfy us as the population grows? By no means. We have no other way but to become an industrial state and as soon as possible."[52] "Industry is the backbone of all progress," as a leader in *al-Jumhūriyya* put it.[53]

At first they thought of advancing industrialization by speeding up capitalistic development. This was apparently the view common to Naguib the conservative, Jamāl Sālim the socialist, and Nasser the nationalist. One of the first acts of the officers' government announced on July 30, 1952 was a change in the law of corporations: Instead of 51 per cent of the stock specified by the previous law, only 49% had to be in the hands of Egyptian nationals.[54] This change, which was to make it possible for foreign capital to own a majority share in Egyptian companies, had been prepared long before, but the officers would not have been in a hurry to put it into effect if they had not approved of its aim of attracting foreign capital. Two weeks later the agrarian reform law was published. It, too, was designed to advance industrialization. In the official explanation of the law it was pointed out that "one of the principal aims" of the plan is "to direct every new investment to land-reclamation and to commercial and industrial enterprises."[55] The new government wanted to compel Egypt's rich to stop dealing in land speculation which was convenient, immensely profitable and subverted the development of the Egyptian economy, but to invest their capital in industrial development schemes. Another motive for spurring industrialization was the desire to increase the country's military power, a factor to which an officers' government is especially sensitive.

However, the Egyptian capitalists were not blessed with initiative and were not interested in, and perhaps incapable of, advancing industrialization. The capital that could no longer be used for speculating in land was partially diverted to speculation in urban lots and apartments for rent, and a part of it was smuggled out of the country. In the five years after the

[52] *Al-Ahrām,* 13 November 1964.
[53] *Al-Jumhūriyya,* 27 April 1961.
[54] *Hamizrah,* vol. 4, 20.
[55] *Ibid.,* 20.

coup, from 1953 to 1957, total Egyptian investments amounted to E£ 515 million. Of this sum only E£ 43 million was invested in industry, while building absorbed more than five times this figure, about E£ 245 million, nearly one half of the total investment. Sixty per cent of all the new buildings were erected in Cairo in 1957.[56] In 1956 Nasser complained in a conversation with a guest, "We have no capitalists, we have only speculators except for one man, Aḥmad 'Abbūd."

In all these matters Egypt is not unique among underdeveloped countries. However, problems affecting all these countries appear there in greater intensity: The paucity of natural resources, the dimensions of the population increase, "the revolution of rising expectations" among the masses, and the soaring ambition of the leaders—all these add immediacy to the challenge of development. The clock of history seems to tick faster in Egypt than in most of the other countries in the Middle East and Africa, and the race against time demands greater speed. There was no authority outside the government to initiate and direct the development and planning needed. Disappointment in private initiative led the leaders to the conclusion that the control of capital should be taken out of the hands of the capitalists. Whether this is called socialism or etatism, the emphasis on industrialization remains. Here Nasser moves with the spirit of the times. Most contemporary schools both of socialism and capitalism agree that the basic difference between advanced and backward countries lies in their degree of industrialization, and that backward people can emerge by developing industry. Industrialization is considered to be the take-off to self-sustained economic progress which in due course will close the gap between the underdeveloped and the advanced nations.

Arab socialism hopes to merge state industrialization and planning and the achievement of social justice with the preservation of the sanctity of private capital and private ownership of an important part of the means of production, especially in agriculture. It wants to effect a compromise between the classes without abolishing the class system. The ideological expression of this contradiction is the negation of Marxism. The defensive dissociation from Marxism reflects the fears of the petty-bourgeois, the son of a minor official and the grandson of a peasant, of the ever-present threat of proletarization; the apprehension of the high-school student who considers himself an intellectual lest he may have to work and live like an ignorant laborer; and the conceit of the academic or the officer who stresses the difference between someone like himself and the mass of the

[56] Dieter Weiss, *Wirtschaftliche Entwicklungsplanung in der Vereinigten Arabischen Republik*, Köln 1964, 67, 133.

people who labor with their hands or the inferior men under his command. When he thinks of socialism, it is the socialism of doing something *for* the workers, but not *of* or *with* the workers—a socialism that will redeem them without allowing them to liberate themselves. The hatred of capitalism which threatened the petty-bourgeois with proletarization and that appeared in Egypt in the figure of the British governor, the French banker and the Jewish department-store owner leads him to nationalistic anti-imperialism and socialism.

Nasser is a pragmatist; confronted with a challenge he is often ready to come to new conclusions. The more he realizes that socialism without socialists cannot solve the increasingly difficult problems of Egypt, the more he may be prepared for a new shift in direction, requesting more help from people with Marxist ideas and following their advice or taking socialist steps which he has thus far avoided, e.g., a far-reaching expansion of agrarian reform and the establishment of state or cooperative farms similar to the kholkhoz or the sovkhoz. These are still open questions and possibilities. His principal aspirations are political national greatness and Egypt's independence and hegemony in her spheres of influence—while social goals remain of secondary importance. Economic and social activities are designed to serve political ends, and so they are easily changed as the need arises or in the light of experience.

A second basic element in Nasser's outlook is his passionate hatred of imperialism and the West, first of Great Britain, later of the USA. His forehead still bears the scar made by a bullet fired by a British police officer when, at the age of 18, he took part in a students' demonstration. The wound healed a long time ago; the British have evacuated Egypt and their prestige throughout the world has declined. But the scar remains engraved on Nasser's forehead. A mixture of extremely rational motives and profound, irrational vengefulness add suspicion and bitterness to his hatred of the West.

The same holds true for his hatred of Israel. Nasser's pronouncements for years made it increasingly clear that his enmity does not stem from a controversy over a certain specific question, be it as important as the refugee problem, but from the very existence of a Jewish community in Palestine as an independent national body. Neither does he disdain to couple his hatred of Israel and Zionism with vile anti-Semitic propaganda. He is not satisfied with virulent attacks on "world Jewry" which stands behind Zionism. Since 1954 there has been a steady increase in the dissemination of anti-Semitic literature comparable to the racialist agitation of the French anti-Semites during the period of the Dreyfus affair and of the German Nazis in Hitler's time. And it is not the ragpickers who perform this despicable work. The President himself has sung the praises of the most infamous of anti-Semitic abominations, the *Protocols of the Learned Elders of Zion.* In an interview which he granted on September 28, 1958 to R.K. Karanjia of India, he said, "I wonder if you have read a book called *Protocols of the Learned Elders of Zion;* it is very important that you should read it. I will give you a copy. It proves beyond the shadow of a doubt that three hundred Zionists, each of whom knows all the others, govern the fate of the European continent and that they elect their successors from their entourage." This disgraceful citation was not included in the edition of Karanjia's book which came out in England, but it does appear in the Bombay edition and is included in the official Egyptian publication, *President Gamal Abdel Nasser's speeches and press interviews during the year 1958.*[57]

In 1963 a new approach to the Israel problem, more realistic and cautious, became apparent in Nasser's policies and speeches. At the Arab summit conferences in 1964 and 1965 he openly took the lead in opposing immediate war over the operation of Israel's national irrigation project and vigorously rejected the Syrians' irresponsible activism. His propagandists in enlightened world opinion praised him, and his Arab enemies attacked him for this moderation. He himself, however, repeatedly emphasized that his basic attitude towards Israel had not changed one iota. On many occasions he expressed his conviction that the Palestine question would be solved only by war. He did not refrain from imputing to Israel the most sinister intentions; he even said in a radio broadcast to millions of listeners—and he perhaps believed what he said, and certainly was aware of the inflammatory meaning of his words—that "the Jews intend to conquer Mecca and Medina."[58] His moderation was not rooted in any hidden yearning for peace; it was a current manifestation of self-control in order to prepare for the future crushing attack. A simple explanation can be found for his moderation from 1963 to 1966: When scores of thousands of Egyptian troops were pinned down in Yemen, a war with Israel would have been downright suicidal. If in the fall of 1962 he could have known that in 1966 his best troops would still be far away in the south of Arabia, it is quite possible that he would have listened to those of his friends who opposed that adventure from the very beginning.

Nasser's realistic attitude towards Israel from 1963 until the spring of 1967 is not to be regarded as only a function of the involvement in

[57] *President Gamal Abdel Nasser's speeches and press interviews during the year 1958,* Cairo (1959), 30.

[58] Radio Cairo, 22 July 1965; *al-Ahrām,* 23 July 1965.

Yemen. Actually, it was already noticeable several years previously. In his discussions in 1959 with the activist Syrian Baʻthist leaders in the UAR government—the details of which were published during the 1962 controversy—Nasser established a clear, considered position: The liquidation of Israel is a long-range matter and requires lengthy, thorough preparations; a premature showdown in view of Israel's strength would only lead to a new disaster like the one in the 1948 war.

But Nasser's self-control and realism broke down in May 1967. His basic hostility towards Israel proved to be stronger than any sober consideration, emotion prevailed over reason, and he plunged Egypt and her allies, Jordan and Syria, into the disaster of the Six-Day War. His own reasoning during the previous years should have taught him that the outcome would be certain defeat for Egypt. The actual result was even more catastrophic.

As the disaster in Palestine in 1948 exposed the intrinsic weakness of Fārūq's regime, so the disaster of 1967 revealed ruthlessly that republican Egypt was, after all, not so different from its forerunner despite the differing philosophies of the two regimes.

5. THE OFFICERS AND THE BA‘TH

WHILE THE Egyptian officer politicians were greatly influenced before their accession to power by the Muslim Brethren, the Syrian officers received inspiration and guidance from the Ba‘th party. They collaborated with it from the beginning of the 1950's, and its importance constantly grew. Ideologically and politically, the Ba‘th also exerted considerable influence on an important part of the Iraqi officers from about 1955, as well as on Jordanian officers. Even Nasser's philosophy drew inspiration from it in the middle 1950's. The Ba‘th was the 'best man' at the 1958 Egyptian-Syrian union and at the conclusion of the agreement for a federal union among Egypt, Syria and Iraq in 1963. On the other hand, it was accused of being the principal separatist factor, bearing a great deal of the responsibility for the failure of efforts for union. The Ba‘th always had rather large cadres of active members, but there was no social group in which it so succeeded in acquiring adherents as among army officers, especially in Syria.

What brought so many officers into the Ba‘th and with such fervency? The Ba‘th gave the officers a number of things to which they aspired without being able to achieve them themselves; it fulfilled or pretended to fulfil some of their desires.

First of all, the Ba‘th gave, or promised to give, a systematic, comprehensive political ideology. Among the hundreds of Syrian officer politicians there was not a single group or individual capable of developing and formulating a comprehensive political outlook based on definite principples in accordance with which it would determine unambiguous positions on current questions. They had opinions and aspirations but no program. A systematic political doctrine was their heart's desire, and they found it in the Ba‘th. Michel ‘Aflaq knew how to make speeches and write on all topics in a philosophically erudite fashion conveying an impression of profundity. The Ba‘th has a detailed "constitution," *The Constitution of the Socialist Arab Renaissance Party,* which defines "fundamental principles," "general principles," and programs for "the party's internal policy," "economic policy," and "social policy."[1] The Ba'th was one of the first parties in the Arab world with such a platform.

Little attention is devoted to the content of Ba'thist ideology, with the exception of its principle slogans. "No ideology is so imperfectly known in the Middle East and the West as that of the Ba'th."[2] Its central idea is the panegyrizing of pan-Arab nationalism and Arab unity. The call for Arab unity was the slogan which captivated the Syrian officers. Syria had always been the center of pan-Arab aspirations; particularist ideas were less acceptable there than anywhere else in the Arab world. The Ba'th platform of 1953 is headlined by the declaration, "One Arab nation with an eternal mission." The "first principle" of the "fundamental principles" establishes: "The Arabs are one nation, and it is its natural right to live in a single state and to be free to direct its own destiny." The second principle defines the "personality of the Arab nation, . . . characterized by virtues which are the result of its successive rebirths," etc. The third principle declares, "The Arab nation has an eternal mission which reveals itself in ever new and complementary forms in various periods of history and which aims at the renewal of human values, the acceleration of man's progress and the fostering of harmony and cooperation among nations." This ideology, "this synthesis of the ideas of the national, liberal school of the beginning of the 19th century and the totalitarian, nationalist notions of the 20th century,"[3] does speak in the style of scientific political theory, but it is "a kind of mystical nationalism."[4] In Ba'thist ideology socialism is a secondary corollary, albeit an important one, of Arab nationalism which alone is the supreme "eternal" value.

Let us quote from 'Aflaq's speech at a reception given by the Ba'th for the representatives of the Arab labor unions in Damascus in March 1956:[5] "Yesterday I addressed a group of students at the university in Beirut and a number of them asked me, 'Why should we bother now or later about socialism before achieving Arab unity? Won't the struggle for socialism make the union of our countries difficult and divide our efforts? Won't unity, when it is attained, be a guarantee of the realization of whatever the Arab people seeks of freedom, justice and prosperity?'—I must point out that the same question was put to me ten years ago in another form by the

[1] *Dustūr ḥizb al-ba'th al-'arabī al-ishtirākī,* Damascus s.a.; English in Sylvia G. Haim, *Arab nationalism, an anthology,* Berkeley and Los Angeles 1964, 233–241. The date of the platform's adoption is not clear. It was presumably in 1953.

[2] Jean-Pierre Viennot, 'Le Ba'th entre la théorie et la pratique', *Orient,* no. 30, 1964, 13.

[3] Yitzhak Oron, 'Mifleget ha-tehiya ha-aravit ha-sotzialistit', *Hamizrah,* vol. 9, 250.

[4] Bernard Lewis, *The Middle East and the West,* London 1964, 65.

[5] Mīshīl 'Aflaq, *Fī sabīl al-ba'th,* Beirut 1963, 216–7.

rulers and their parties and aides when they doubted whether activity for socialism and Arab unity was justified before their liberation from foreigners was completed. I answered the students in Beirut that Arab unity is not a matter of political activity, negotiation and agreements between governments, but an act of revolution and struggle conducted by that people which alone needs it and is devoted to its demands. Thus, the struggle for Arab unity will not be realistic and victorious unless it merges with the struggle of the masses of the Arab people for their vital rights and the raising of their standard of living. We must know that the enemies of unity are imperialism and Israel, which only exists for the purpose of impeding unity and causing it to fail, and internal reactionary interests and whatever there is to be found in our society of disease, fanaticism, ignorance and backwardness. It is impossible to conquer this large, frightening crowd of enemies only by government action, especially when we know that the governments still represent for the most part those interests opposed to unity. Therefore, it is imperative that the entire people assume the burden of unity see in it its daily bread, and the liberation of its homeland from the foreigner, risk its life for it, for it is the path to freedom and human dignity. When we linked unity to socialism, we did not act unthinkingly or in haste, but we saw that that is the only way for unity to become a dynamic, living fact in our lives, that it should be the demand of every worker eager for his bread, a raise in pay, and medical care for his children, and the demand of every poor, exploited fellah when he insists on the restoration of his right in what he has created and the elimination of oppression and slavery from his shoulders. That is how we made Arab unity a realistic, living demand becoming part and parcel of the lives of the Arab people in the circumstances of their daily lives, and the simplest thing in their lives, which is their material needs."

These words are characteristic of 'Aflaq's thinking; many more like them could be cited. They reveal the mystique of Arab unity and the relativist, almost cynical, attitude to socialism; and they show his evasion of a clear position regarding the day-to-day affairs of workers and farmers. In this respect there is no fundamental difference between 'Aflaq and his opponents and enemies within the Ba'th. The more Ba'thist theory descends from the eternal heavens of absolute Arab values to the vale of tears of pressing class problems, the vaguer it becomes. In the case of 'Aflaq himself, the obscurity does not stem from a failure to understand matters but precisely from a knowledge of them. From 1928 to 1932 he was a student in Paris where he read much of the works of Marx and for a time was also close to the Communist Party, or perhaps a member of it. However, for many Syrian army officers and large circles of petty-bourgeois elements, it was just the combination of contradictions which exerted a great attraction—the combination of nationalist fanaticism and social radicalism, of socialism and anti-communism, of prophesying in scientific language and anti-Marxism, of hatred of capitalist exploitation and opposition to the workers' freedom to strike, of stressing the humanitarian content of Arab nationalism and preaching passionate hatred of Israel, and of the negation of clericalism and communal fanaticism together with a vigorous emphasis on the essential and historical bond between Arabism and Islam. Ba'thist thought is full of inconsistencies and even contradictions. Perhaps it was just this multifariousness—which is actually confusion—which made this party so attractive to army officers in search of an ideology.

It was not only an ideology that the officers found in the Ba'th. It fulfilled another of their wishes—ties with an organized, active group in all Syrian towns and in numerous villages embracing laborers, fellaheen, office workers, teachers and merchants from all communities. Just as it was one of the first Arab bodies to formulate a platform, so the Ba'th was one of the first that knew how to organize a political party with branches, members and institutions—a party along European lines which was active the year round, not only during election time, and which achieved an impressive representation in parliament.

In those critical years between 1945 and 1955 when the political opinions and affiliations of many Syrian officers were forged, there was also another party which proposed a systematic, comprehensive political ideology and a well-organized political framework—the Syrian Social Nationalist Party, the SSNP. Why, it may be asked, did this party not serve as the political rallying point of the officers? And indeed, around 1950 numerous Syrian officers were influenced by the SSNP or joined it. But the race between the SSNP and the Ba'th was conclusively won by the latter. The SSNP was eliminated altogether and the Ba'th became the most decisive and sometimes the ruling party in Syria. What was the determining advantage of the Ba'th? Certainly not the clarity of its ideas or the orderliness of its organization. It was the force of its appeal to Arab national sentiment and fanaticism against the SSNP's Syrian nationalism, the victory of pan-Arabism, deeply rooted in Islamic traditions, over the radically secularistic outlook of the SSNP. The chief ideologists of both the Ba'th and the SSNP in their formative years, Anṭūn Sa'āda and Michel 'Aflaq, were both Christians; but while Sa'āda stressed the anti-clerical aspects of his ideology, 'Aflaq was always most cautious in this respect, and, moreoever, laid considerable emphasis on the historical anchorage of Arab nationalism in the glorious past of Islam. A further reason—also a very important one, but compared with the former, secondary only—was the Ba'th's embracing of socialist theories and slogans as opposed to the SSNP's overt Fascist doctrines.

With its ideological and organizational dispositions the Ba'th was able to move the officer politicians out of the isolation of their narrow military framework and into the broad horizons of inter-Arab and international contacts. In the Arab world the Ba'th stressed its adherence to the ideal of Arab unity; to the workers' movements and leftist parties throughout the world it appeared as the great Arab non-communist, anti-imperialist, independent socialist party, and its spokesmen were able to participate in many international forums.

Although it is also possible to point to the common social background of most of the Syrian officers and the Ba'th leaders, this fact, true as it may be, is not enough to explain the special attraction of the Ba'th for the officers. For the SSNP and the Muslim Brethren, which also gained many adherents in Syria after World War II, also developed from the same background. In the competition for the minds of the officers the Ba'th had the upper hand as a result of its ideological and political uniqueness.

There were varying degrees of allegiance between the officers and the Ba'th. Some, like Ḥamdūn in Syria and Windāwī in Iraq, conducted themselves as regular party members, regarding themselves as the party's emissaries in the army and acting in accordance with its directives and instructions. Others, and they were always the more numerous, tried to evade a clear-cut choice between party loyalty and adherence to the group of officers with whom they worked; when they could no longer vacillate, a minority, like Qanūt and Aḥmad Ḥasan al-Bakr, decided in favor of the party, while most of them preferred loyalty to the officer group and abandoned the party. There were others, also numerous, who were influenced by the Ba'th, collaborated with it and supported it, and were supported by it, without identifying themselves with it organizationally or joining it as members; such a person was Sarrāj, who was at one time very close to the Ba'th. Until the fall of 1963 Arif was in the same category; he was not as close to the Ba'th as Sarrāj, but he made more use of it. As a result, Arif was his country's president in 1964 and Sarrāj, a fugitive in exile.

Naturally, the limits of these groups are not sharply defined, and there were always numerous officers who wandered from one to the other. The unstable opinions of the officers and the inconsistency of the Ba'th's political positions coupled with widespread lust for power and passion for intrigue led to constant clashes.

The Ba'th's strong influence among the Syrian army officers began during the hated dictatorship of Shīshaklī and grew steadily between his ousting at the beginning of 1945, in which the Ba'thist officers played an important role, and the union with Egypt at the beginning of 1958, which also came about to a great extent at their initiative. During those years bonds with the Ba'th also multiplied among Iraqi and Jordanian officers. The internal contradictions in Ba'thist ideology did not interfere with the rise of its prestige, and may even have aided it, so long as the officers were only officers, despite their frequent meddling in politics, and so long as the civilian Ba'thist leaders were only members of parliament or party workers and propagandists.

However, when the officer politicians and the leaders of the Ba'th came to power, each with the other's help, or when they thought they had acceded to power, personal, organizational and ideological differences and contradictions quickly erupted and the whole relationship came apart at the seams. This occurred after the establishment of the UAR in Syria in 1958 when Nasser also took steps to hasten the decline of the Ba'th in Iraq in 1963 and again in Syria from 1964 on. The Ba'th was never a united party, either ideologically or organizationally, and whenever it was in power, its internal personal and political conflicts were intensified. In the opinion of Muḥammad Ḥasanayn Haykal, the Ba'th's struggles "recall the quarrels of the Mafia gangs of Sicily and America who join forces for the purpose of taking plunder and then fight each other to the death in dividing the spoils."[6] Nobody in the whole Middle East speaks so much about unity as the Ba'th leadership, and nobody does so much to deepen conflicts and to increase discord. When Arif and Barazānī came to an agreement in February 1964 to stop the fighting between the Iraqi army and the Kurds, the Syrian Ba'thists, who call themselves socialists, were the only body in the Arab world which came out against the cease-fire.[7] In their hatred of Israel they try to outdo all the others. However, in inter-Arab relations also they have become incomparably quarrelsome. The same applies to internal party life. The *Constitution* proclaims that the Ba'th is "a universal Arab party and branches will be founded in the rest of the Arab countries, and it does not concern itself with regional politics except in relation to the higher interests of the Arab cause. The headquarters is for the time being in Damascus. It can be transferred."[8] The history of the party was otherwise: an uninterrupted series of unions, splits into rival factions, and divisions. A Lebanese newspaper in March 1964 headlined an article on the history of the Ba'th with the statement "Ten Splits in Ten Years."[9] In the following period the internal splits and struggles in the Syrian Ba'th became even more frequent and more violent. They

[6] *Al-Ahrām,* 22 November 1963.
[7] Viennot, 24.
[8] Haim, 234.
[9] *Al-Anwār,* Beirut, 3 March 1964.

were not limited to mere discussions or vilifications; they reached the stage of arrests and shootings.

It was no wonder that the mutual attraction of the Ba'th and the Syrian officer politicians is so great. Birds of a feather flock together. Theoretically the authority of the party leadership, in which civilians have always been the majority, is paramount, and the officers are servants of the party. The rule, however, has nothing to do with the facts. The Ba'th would never have come to power in Syria without the army. Each faction which succeeded in overcoming its rivals for a certain period did so mainly as a result of the victory of its officer group over the others, and naturally these officers are loyal and subservient only to those politicians who do their will. The real meaning of the precept of the "ideological army," which became official doctrine in 1963, is not the education and indoctrination of the army in a certain spirit, but the predominance of a certain party faction by means of the army. As far as the army as a military force is concerned, this led only to a lowering of its professional standards. The poor performance of the Syrian army in the war against Israel in June 1967 gave evidence of this.

These remarks are not meant to imply that ideological developments and groupings were of no consequence at all in Ba'th party life. The intensity of ideological inquiry and theorizing has always been most remarkable in the Ba'th. But our concern here lies less with the development of the party's ideology than in the elucidation of why the Ba'th alone made such deep inroads in the Syrian officer corps, and why it, and no other party, came to power there. In these important respects the decisiveness of the army as a factor of power, as the possessor of the monopoly of institutionalized violence, cannot be overlooked.

PART SIX

OFFICERS AS HEADS OF STATE AND ARAB SOCIALISM

"All revolutions up to the present day have resulted in the displacement of one definite class rule by another; but all ruling classes up to now have been only small minorities in relation to the ruled mass of the people. The ruling minority was thus overthrown; another minority seized the helm of state in its stead and refashioned the state institutions to suit its own interests. This was on every occasion the minority group qualified and called to rule by the degree of economic development."

F. Engels, 1895.

"Those who conquer by the sword are doomed to be overcome by those who conquer with the plough, and finally to give place to them."

Atatürk, in a speech at Izmir, 1923.

1. THE GREAT CHANGE

We began our discussion by asking the question whether or not the accession of army officers to power by coups d'état constitutes the "natural course" in the contemporary history of the Arab nations in the Middle East.

Should rule by officers be regarded as a historical necessity?

Is the officer class that social group which is destined as well as able to bring about the fundamental, revolutionary changes required for the rapid advancement of Arab society?

The answers to these questions will be, to a large extent, determined by the actions of the officers as heads of the Arab states, by their achievements or failures.

The starting point for elucidating these questions had to be a description and analysis of what actually happened, how the officers struggled for political power, how they carried out their coups and how they fought for the continuity of their governments. Then the patterns of these coups could be examined, their characteristics defined and some comparisons drawn with developments in other regions. The next issues to be examined were the influences of history, of the Islamic heritage as well as the precendents established by the role which army officers played in the Arab Awakening under Ottoman rule. Then the enquiry went into the examination of the sociological background and composition of the Arab officer class, and the ideological motivations of the officer politicans. Yet the final criterion for evaluating their role in history must be what they did and achieved as heads of state.

On the face of it, one should be able to draw up a balance sheet of successes and failures. However, what is to be judged an achievement? And if one can point to a distinct achievement, can one also prove that another regime would not have realized it or would have failed at the same task? The experimental method employed in the natural sciences cannot be applied in a historical and sociological enquiry; it is impossible to isolate a single factor and examine its activity by itself.

Moreover, the success of a revolution should not be judged by the amount of immediate benefits granted to most of the population. By this criterion all the great revolutions in history could be regarded only as disasters. All brought in their wake, and sometimes for a lengthy period, a great deal of suffering, privation and loss of life and liberty for many and not only for the classes which were displaced. Nevertheless, each marked the beginning of a new period of progress and a volcanic upsurge of creative forces. But the question always arises: What is the price which the revolutionary generation must pay for a better future? How much have the fathers sacrificed so that their sons may be blessed? And who has the right to demand the fathers' sacrifice even without their consent and against their will? And in the name of what principle?

There is no escaping the perennial question of the end and the means, and no sin so debases a revolution as disregarding its significance. How many horrible crimes, from the Inquisition to Stalin, were committed on the pretext—and what is perhaps more terrible, in the belief— that the end justified the means? But there is a reciprocal bond between the end and the means, and even more than the end, which exists only in the intentions of the doers, affects the means, do the means—the actual deeds—influence the final outcome. Is it possible to educate a man to independence by exacting obedience or to guide a people to a free life by force? Is it possible to stimulate the creative initiative of a community by fiat, by issuing orders on all matters small and large, even if the decrees themselves are beneficial? "No way leads to any other goal but to that which is like it."[1] If there is aught to be learned from history, this is surely the outstanding lesson.

It is clear then that we cannot pass simple judgment.

Nevertheless, we shall try to isolate as far as possible some principal features and courses of action that characterize the regimes of army officers in some Arab states in the second third of the twentieth century. We shall furnish examples from those countries that have for years been molded by the acts of officer politicians: Egypt, Syria, Iraq and Sudan. These are also the leading Arab states in the Middle East. It is not the purpose of this chapter to present a general survey of the political development of these countries under officer rule; its aim is to examine the particular and characteristic lines of action of this type of regime.

From one basic point of view the rule of officers brought about a revolutionary change in Arab society: It eliminated the power of the big landowners. In Egypt, Iraq and Yemen this was personified by the abolition

[1] Martin Buber, 'Dialogue', in *Between man and man,* London 1961, 51.

of the monarchy. The proclamation of a republic represents much more than a constitutional change. The kings were the heads and representatives of a class and their deposition marked the end of its domination. The great difference between the periods of Fārūq and Nasser and those of 'Abd al-Ilāh and Qassim and Arif is certainly not the distinction between dictatorship and the rule of law honoring human freedoms. Nor is it the difference between a state headed by a corrupt man and an honest one; not all the monarchs were corrupt and not all the military dictators are honest. The great transformation is the change in ruling classes.

The transposition of classes in Arab society did not begin with the officers' coups and would have occurred without them, as is happening in countries where there is no officers' regime—Jordan, Lebanon and Tunisia. However, it is clear that in Egypt, Iraq and Syria the coups hastened the process and even changed its direction to such an extent that the different quantity became a new quality. But it should not be taken for granted *a priori* that whatever changes occurred were always only beneficial. The history of peoples should not be regarded as a steady march toward progress in which every step goes forward and only the rate of advance changes. The systems abolished by the officers were not worth preserving. But this does not automatically imply that the new ones are better or the only ones desirable or possible at this time.

The Arab officer politicians did not chart new goals. Their principal objectives are the three traditional aims of Arab nationalism: Independence, unity and progress. In modern Arab history independence was, chronologically speaking, the first aim, and the Arab countries had already gone a considerable way toward attaining it long before the appearance of the officer class as a prospective candidate for power. Indeed, the attainment of independence and sovereignty was a preliminary condition for the accession of the officers to power. A military coup of nationalist officers is impossible under a foreign army occupation. Egypt, Iraq and Syria would have fortified their national independence even without the military dictatorships, perhaps more slowly, perhaps at the same speed. Neutralism—Nasser's trump card—was not invented by officer politicians. During the Wafd regime Egypt had already adopted a neutralistic policy in 1951, in the Korean War. The rise of Soviet power and influence in the Middle East was not a result of Arab military coups. British military bases in Egypt were reduced before 1952, and even without the officers' coup, British troops would not have remained there for many more years. An attempt was made to nationalize oil resources in Iran in 1951 by a government not composed of officers. British command of the Jordanian army was eliminated and Algeria attained independence without the lead of officers.

The second aim of Arab nationalism, Arab unity, was given precedence in the Arab press and diplomacy during the era of the military dictatorships. Among the ruling officers there were several men, such as Bakr Ṣidqī, Shīshaklī, Qassim and ‘Abbūd, who were quite indifferent to the idea of Arab unity. Far more were enthusiasts about unity, regarding it as the crowning point of their aspirations—these included Ṣabbāgh, the Syrian Ba‘thist officers, Arif, and, heading them all, Nasser and his group. However, the sum total of the officers' contribution to Arab unity was negative. Both those who had reservations about it and those who wished to promote it added almost nothing to Arab brotherhood and only sharpened the existing differences. Unity cannot be achieved through coercion, through the military tactics which the officers took into politics—orders, regimentation and centralization. It is impossible to administer the affairs of two countries as a brigadier commands two battalions. Arab unity can be realized only as a process, not as a revolutionary operation, only through gradual accommodation based on tolerance and mutual consideration, on brotherhood and not on a lust for power: and the officer politicians are not endowed with these characteristics. They are to be credited with the Egyptian-Syrian union of 1958, the greatest act of unification in modern Arab history, and they are responsible for the Syrio-Egyptian rupture of 1961, which not only rendered that union completely null and void, but also dealt a crushing blow to the force of the idea itself.

The third aim, social progress, became a recognized, accepted aim of the Arab national movement only after World War II, during the period of numerous military governments, and the officer politicians became its strongest exponents. While the Egypt of 1965 would undoubtedly differ from the Egypt of 1950 even without Naguib and Nasser, the social changes more than any other are associated with Nasser's name, and he and his group have left their stamp on them. The summation of these attempts and aspirations is the Egyptian version of "Arab socialism." It is also the model of various movements outside Egypt.

What is this Arab socialism?

It sources and motives have already been discussed in the chapter on Nasser's philosophy. At this point we shall clarify a number of basic principles of Arab socialism as a pattern of social and political life as it actually exists and develops.

Whether or not Arab socialism is true socialism is a moot point; this is a relatively unimportant question liable to lead us into the blind alley of scholastic haggling over the definition of socialism itself without shedding any light on the nature of the concrete phenomenon which interests us. Anyone can call himself a socialist if he wishes; and many who call themselves socialists argue that they are the only true ones, and that all others who do not adhere to their brand of socialism bear its name in vain. British labourites deny the socialist nature of the soviet regime; communists are not prepared to regard the Israeli kibbutz as a form of socialist achievement, and so on, *ad infinitum*. To ask whether the Egyptian regime is socialism or etatism would not contribute anything substantial toward understanding it; it would interest only those bothered by the problem as into which terminological cubbyhole a particular phenomenon should be filed. Etatism can be defined as "a politico-economic system advocating the state's far-reaching intervention in the life of society, particularly its economic life, through the establishment of economic enterprises under state ownership and the direction of private economic interests, determining their functions and modes of activity."[2] According to this definition the distinction between etatism and socialism rests on two basic tenets, for socialism, in contrast to etatism, "demands the nationalization of *all* the means of production and their *transference to society"* and "predicts the withering away of the state." With regard to the withering away of the state, it may be concluded that socialism in the middle of the 20th century exists only in books, and that the Soviet Union is at least as etatist as Egypt. As for nationalization and the extent of socialization, Egypt is still at the crossroads. Eighteenth century Prussia and Atatürk's Turkey were distinctly etatist, for the state developed the basic branches of the economy as a foundation on which the private capitalist economy could flourish. Such tendencies also exist in Egypt, but there is no certainty that they will prevail. Contemporary developing states in general and Egypt in particular cannot be compared with Prussia, Japan or Turkey in earlier periods.

The Egyptian leaders themselves do not contend that they have already achieved socialism. They stress that socialism is their goal and they are headed in its direction. In November 1964 Nasser explained, "I must make this clear. We have not become a socialist state and we cannot say today that we are a socialist country. We are in a transition phase from capitalism to socialism. Socialism does not mean the nationalization of a number of enterprises and that's all. By no means. Socialism means that we shall build a society of prosperity and justice . . . Despite socialist transformations and activity, the old-time capitalist still exists, the old oppressor is still with us. The situation has not budged. Social ties have changed. Today we are in transition from exploitative capitalism to socialism. At this stage, socialist society cannot eliminate all the vestiges of capitalism and feudalism. We said that we have liquidated feudalism but not the feudal

[2] *Enziklopidia le-mada'e ha-hebra* (Hebrew), vol. 1, Merhavia 1964, 119.

lords. There have been people and societies which destroyed feudalism and killed off the feudal lords. We have wiped out feudalism, but the feudal lords exist. Are they satisfied? Of course not. Those from whom a single feddan or ten feddans have been taken away cannot help being hostile to the revolution and socialism. When we say that we have liquidated feudalism, we ought to know that the feudal lords still exist, that they are all friends of one another. We have eliminated exploitative capitalism, but the capitalists exist. We have eliminated reaction but the reactionaries exist. They exist, and not in museums and prisons. At the convocation of the National Assembly, we released everybody in prison and also amnestied persons who were communists and Muslim Brethren. Everyone was accorded the opportunity of becoming integrated into the new society, but the feudal lords, capitalists, and reactionaries exist and are lying in wait, for every blunder . . . We also inherited the bureaucracy from the old regime. We still require a long period of development."[3]

The question is what is Nasser doing for the full realization of Arab socialism? Whom is he enlisting, on whom is he relying in the struggle to set up a regime of prosperity and justice?

The few reactionaries who were under arrest were released and rejoined their numerous compatriots who had never been in prison and who—the Muslims at least—had never stopped working in their businesses and jobs, although their authority was reduced and their profits diminished. The communists and socialists who were released (and these were only some of the total arrested; others could not be freed as they had been tortured to death) were set free on condition that they served the regime as officials or newspapermen, placing their talents and experience at its disposal and defending it against its critics.

Karl Marx's great historical and revolutionary achievement was the synthesis of the abstract idea of socialism and the concrete class war of the workers and of forging them into a single force of thought and action. There were socialist ideas before Marx and also a fighting workers' movement. He united them into a single organism like the body and soul that cannot live one without the other. After Marx, socialism, however radical, when dissociated from a workers' movement, becomes only parlor-communism; and a workers' movement which is not socialist, be it as pugnacious as the labor unions in the United States, turns into a support of the capitalist system. Arab socialism seeks a new road. It wishes to abolish capitalism without acknowledging the primacy of the working class. It recognizes the existence of the class war but wishes to implement

[3] *Al-Ahrām,* 13 November 1964.

social justice without allowing the workers to wage their class war themselves. It wishes to achieve inter-class harmony while preserving private ownership in a large part of the means of production.

Egyptian social legislation in matters of health, education, protection of workers' rights against unjust dismissal and in old age, high progressive taxation on incomes and high salaries and similar regulations no doubt constitute great progress in comparison with the recent past. There is, however, no socialism in any of these measures. They are similar in nature, though limited in scope, to the practices of the welfare states of western Europe, which aim not at a basic change of regime but, on the contrary, assurance of its continuation by eliminating its more inhuman outgrowths. And the much publicized distribution of a fourth of the corporate profits among the Egyptian workers as provided by the law of July 1961 is only an illusory compensation for their meager wages. Of the total 25 per cent distributed, five per cent is invested in social services and housing, ten per cent in building dining halls, showers, etc., in factories, and only ten per cent is paid out to the workers in cash at different rates proportional to their basic wages in a sum not exceeding fifty Egyptian pounds per annum. In other words, the distribution of a fourth of the profits only amounts to a fulfilment of the employer's elementary obligations plus the payment of a 13th month's wage to the worker, with no basic changes in working conditions or wages. Moreover, as economic difficulties mounted in Egypt, this payment was reduced. According to a presidential decree of July 1965, every worker and office employee would receive a bonus on account of the past year equal to 15 working days in a sum not exceeding E£35. In view of the rise in prices, especially of foodstuffs, E£ 35 in 1962 were not worth more than half of E£ 50 in 1962.

The worker is the object of Arab socialism, but not its subject; he is an important, favored object, but neither an active nor independent factor. The labor union is a tool of the state and like all other organizations is directed from above; in the absence of the freedom of independent association there is no real value in the regulation requiring at least half of the delegates to the National Assembly to be workers or peasants. Workers' representatives on the governing boards of companies who are not the emissaries of active workers' committees serve as an instrument for blunting and distorting the workers' demands and quickly become management's spokesmen against them—in Egypt as in other countries. Since the brutal suppression of the workers' strike at Kafr-el-Dawār by the new officers' government in 1952, much has changed. "Revolution" and "socialism" have become slogans of the regime. But the hostile attitude toward an independent workers' movement remains.

Arab socialism promises to abolish class distinction but has no intention of a general abolition of private ownership of the means of production. "Non-exploiting" and "national" private capital continues to be active in profit-making.

There are two, actually three, sectors of the Egyptian economy: Public, private and mixed public-private. This is not the place for a statistical enumeration of the scope of each sector. Numerous official figures are published which upon examination sometimes reveal striking contradictions. Itemization and concealment, relevant discussion and propaganda, plans and facts are all indiscriminately sprinkled through recent Egyptian statistics. We can only try here to understand the general trend.

The public sector embraces most branches in which considerable investment is necessary and which will not yield immediate profits. These are chiefly development enterprises and basic industries, key branches for directing the economy, such as banking and foreign trade, and social services, e.g., health insurance. Private capital maintains ownership in branches that provide certain, quick profits: Rural and urban land which has been and will continue to be the principal national possession in Egypt is in private hands. Agriculture is entirely private. Agricultural cooperatives deal with the purchase of seeds, marketing, improving varieties, destroying pests and other praiseworthy objectives, but do not engage in production. The million feddans of desert to be transformed into good arable land after the completion of the Aswan High Dam will be divided among individual holdings. Building trades, housing, apartment rentals, wholesale trade, hotels and places of entertainment belong to private capital.

The state provides most of the new investment and also controls most of the branches deriving benefit from them. The rural and urban consumers, however, buy most of their necessities—food, housing, and clothing—from the private sector of the economy; according to the deputy prime minister for supply, the public sector provided only $11\frac{1}{2}$ per cent of all consumers' goods in 1964.[4] Most of the profits resulting from economic activity accrue to private individuals.

The following is the breakdown of the gross national product for 1962–63.[5] The figures are in millions of Egyptian pounds.

Of the six branches with the highest product—agriculture, industry, trade, transport and communications, personal services and construction—which together account for 80 per cent of the gross national product, the

[4] *Ibid.*, 1 December 1964.

[5] Charles Issawi, *Egypt in revolution*, London 1963, 117, quoting *al-Ahrām*, 30 June 1962.

private sector accounts for more than 90 per cent in agriculture and personal services; nearly 80 per cent in trade and construction; more than 50 per cent in industry; and 25 per cent in transport and communications. Capital gains, private business and entrepreneurs are limited by law (e.g., no individual may possess more than E£ 10,000 in stock or receive an annual salary exceeding E£ 5,000, including all kinds of special payments), by directing a large share of supply and marketing through cooperatives and

EGYPTIAN GNP FOR 1962–1963 (in million E£)

	Public Sector	*Private Sector*	*Total*
Agriculture	28.5	440.7	469.2
Industry	156.5	201.9	358.4
Electricity	11.2	6.8	18.0
Construction	21.0	70.0	91.0
Transport and communication	92.9	30.7	123.6
House rents	—	78.0	78.0
Public utilities	3.6	—	3.6
Trade	30.5	116.0	146.5
Finance	30.8	—	30.8
Education	57.7	13.3	71.0
Health	11.9	2.0	13.9
Social services	4.7	0.5	5.2
Culture and recreation	2.7	13.7	16.4
Security, justice and defense	81.0	3.1	84.1
Other government services	25.1	—	25.1
Personal services	1.2	97.8	99.0
TOTAL	559.3	1,074.5	1,633.8

by stringent control and supervision. But this is where the trouble lies: Bureaucracy has increased by leaps and bounds with the expansion of the state's economic activity; and with it, the endemic plague of Egyptian bureaucracy—inefficiency and corruption. An authoritative, cautious investigator, Issawi, wrote in 1962, "There is the question of the efficiency of the bureaucracy, a matter of supreme importance in any modern state and one which is absolutely vital for a country embarking on socialism and planning. From the 1920's on, the level of the Egyptian civil service has been steadily declining, a process stimulated by the growth in its number, the constant increase in its functions, and the relative deterioration in its social and economic status due to inflation. In the last few years the decline in efficiency seems to have been arrested, and perhaps even reversed, but the growth in numbers has been accelerated and there is no sign that Parkinson's law is about to be disproved in Egypt . . . An example was recently given in the press: officials have found it prudent to start action on their pension a full year before retirement; for one single form of the many in their file requires the signatures of forty-seven different officials . . . For a long time to come, the bureaucracy is likely to absorb a very large amount of the energy generated by the plans."[6] The Egyptian press is full of complaints and cartoons about the inflation of the civil service, the swelled-headedness of the civil servants and the paucity of their talent and honesty. And if Issawi wrote in 1962 that the process of decline may have been reversed, in the autumn of 1964 when the supply crisis became a problem of prime concern it was no longer possible to avoid exposing the evils of the bureaucrats whose efficiency and honesty had continued to deteriorate in the interim. Numerous cases of faulty planning and implementation, embezzlement, theft and bribery were disclosed and publicly denounced. Problems of supply were the central topic in every Egyptian household, in the discussions of the National Assembly and in the activities of the government.

The following two analyses of the factors in the crisis supplement rather than contradict each other.

Avraham Ben-Tzur points out the internal contradictions in the government of the Egyptian officers; "[It is] an attempt to secure the participation of opposing elements which are in the long run irreconcilable. Thus, they have tried to combine large-scale economic development with a huge military build-up, an arms race and an expansionist policy; to carry out general economic planning based, on the one hand, on a public, etatist sector and the nationalization of the principal means of production, and, on the other, on leaving private property and initiative a clear field in vital spheres of the economy; to implement bold social reforms for the masses but without allowing them really to participate and at the same time persecuting their revolutionary, ideological cadres—the socialist and communist left . . . The crisis is undoubtedly not one of growth but of method, and reflects three factors: a. The arms race and high military expenditures; b. Indiscriminate jumbling of socialist and capitalist systems; c. Etatism resting on corrupt bureaucracy."[7]

Muḥammad Ḥasanayn Haykal in 1964 did not disregard the veils of bureaucracy which has quantitatively been growing with the rapid development of the state's economic activity and qualitatively continues to stagnate on the old moral and administrative level. Nor does he shut his eyes to the burden of military expenditure, which, in his opinion, is unavoidable in view

[6] Issawi, 74–5.

[7] Avraham Ben-Tzur, 'Ha-mashber ha-kalkali be-mitzrayim', *Basha'ar,* no. 64, Tel Aviv 1964, 38–40; Avraham Ben-Tzur, *Ha-sotzializm ha-'aravi,* Tel Aviv 1965, *passim.*

of the threat of Israel, the withdrawal of Syria from the UAR, and the war in Yemen. At the same time, he stresses the inflationary pressures created by great development enterprises and the rapid population increase. The present bears the burden of future expenditure just as "the embryo in its mother's womb sucks the mother's blood, and until the age of 20 at least, until he is ready to stand on his own feet, constitutes a heavy burden for his father . . . one billion Egyptian pounds were thus far invested in great enterprises, huge dams, improving the soil, and reclaiming the desert. In addition to this billion, which we paid out of our own money, we have invested 200 million pounds borrowed from other countries . . . these are not grants but loans that have to be repaid . . . the development program has opened new horizons and created employment for numerous working hands which had been suffering from complete idleness in the towns and from disguised unemployment in the country. According to accurate statistics, more than a million jobs have been created in the last four years. This means that a million workers have entered the market of organized consumption, some for the first time in their lives. They have become partners in this market, but their work or the work of a large proportion of them has not increased the productivity of the market. Let us take the Aswan High Dam for example. In the Aswan region an average of 25,000 workers a day are employed throughout the year. Three times that number of workers are employed away from that region on transport lines to the High Dam, production centers serving it, e.g., cement and iron plants, and the centers of technical services required by the dam, such as planning, coordinating and administrative operations. Thus 100,000 persons are employed in the construction of the High Dam and receive regular, high wages. Some have for the first time entered the cycle of consumption. And this has occurred without the addition of merchandise or power to the market. The soil to be reclaimed by the High Dam has thus far not even produced a single orange or grain of wheat. This means that the quantity of merchandise offered for sale has not increased to the same extent that the demand has grown." [8]

Egypt's problems, irrespective of government or regime, are difficult. The country does not possess abundant natural resources; its soil and the water of the Nile are already exploited to a very great extent, and it is only possible to develop additional sources of livelihood and revenue by tremendous effort and expense. On the other hand, the population is increasing with mounting rapidity. Just for the purpose of maintaining the present standard of living it is necessary to produce food, clothing, housing, schools,

[8] *Al-Ahrām*, 27 November 1964.

hospitals, etc., for three quarters of a million more people each year. Michel Abū Jawda, a Lebanese journalist, has aptly described the chief worry of Egypt's leaders: "Egypt's natural increase is like the Nile itself which needs a high dam to control it. Thus far the Nile seems to have been 'tamed,' while the natural increase goes on flowing uninterruptedly." [9] The government is encouraging birth control, but a decline in the rate of natural increase cannot be expected until the middle of the seventies at the earliest. In the meantime the rise in the standard of health has decreased infant mortality (which is still high) and led to cures for sterility and a decline in the number of miscarriages; and every rise in the standard of living in town and country leads to earlier marriage. An additional rise in the rate of natural increase is expected in the coming years.

These circumstances force on every Egyptian government the need for sweeping changes, otherwise it will collapse in chaos. But no revolution or development project can bring immediate solutions, and new problems arise at the same time. In the light of their objective difficulties and unlikely prospects of success in the near future and as a consequence of the internal contradictions and the inconsistency of their system, the officers who have been ruling Egypt since 1952 have been driven to expend their energies and to seek grandiose victories outside their country; but in the Arab, Middle Eastern, African and world arenas as well, successes have alternated with failures, and the ambitious efforts abroad have themselves overstretched the capacities of the state and added to the seriousness of the internal problems.

[9] *Al-Nahār,* Beirut, 8 May 1964.

2. THE RULING ELITE

A new elite has arisen in the states ruled by officer politicians, especially in Egypt.

Who is this new Egyptian elite?

First of all, it should be pointed out that it is Egyptian. Egyptians now govern Egypt. In the light of history this is truly novel. Naguib and Nasser were the first Egyptians in nearly 2,500 years to rule the land of the Nile. From the times of Cambyses and Alexander the Great, throughout the reigns of ancient Persia, Hellenism, Rome, the Byzantine Empire, the Arabs, Mamelukes, Turks and the British until the middle of the 20th century—the rulers of Egypt have always been foreigners. The dynasty of Muḥammad 'Alī was Turkish. Its founder and his son Ibrāhīm were Turks on both their fathers' and mothers' side, and their native tongue was Turkish. Their descendants, khedives and kings, down to Fu'ad, Fārūq's father, were all sons of Turkish fathers, and their mothers Circassian slaves of the harem. The court vernacular was Turkish, social and family ties were mostly with Istanbul and the way of life was based on the tradition of the Ottoman aristocracy, even after Turkey herself had become a republic. Europeans from various countries were the proprietors and directors of the modern branches of the economy which began to develop in the second half of the 19th century—industry, transport, foreign trade, banks and insurance companies. Egyptians penetrated these branches of economy slowly, although from the 1920's there have been constant and deliberate efforts to Egyptianize economic life. But in 1951 the annual report of the joint-stock companies in Egypt still showed that of 1,406 directors only 35 per cent were Muslim or Coptic Egyptians; 18 per cent were Jews, mainly of foreign nationality, for few of the members of the old native Jewish community were rich; 30 per cent were European; eleven per cent Syrian and Lebanese; eight per cent were Greek and Armenians.[1] The struggle for Egyptian mastery of Egypt was more than a fight against

[1] Charles Issawi, *Egypt in revolution*, London 1963, 89.

direct or indirect British rule. The fact that Arabic-speaking Egyptians now head the country constitutes a fundamental historic change.

One segment of the elite, most of the big landowners and their political representation, the party leaders and the members of parliament, had for generations been Egyptian. This elite no longer has power either. Landowners are no longer men of substance whose opinions are decisive in the villages, and party politicians are not important in the cities any more. The rich have not become poor just as the poor have not become rich, but they no longer become rich as easily as they did formerly, and power has slipped out of their hands. For this the agrarian reform is responsible.

Agrarian reform had three goals at first—social, economic and political. The social objective was to improve the lot of the fellaheen. The economic aim was to compel the capitalists to invest their capital in industry rather than land speculation. How far these goals were achieved will be discussed later. The political objective was to smash the political domination of the landowners, and this was certainly achieved. The Egyptian agrarian section of the old upper class was eliminated as a ruling elite even before the liquidation of its foreign industrial and financial section.

The new political and social elite is evident in the composition of the successive Egyptian governments. For the purpose of analyzing some aspects of its composition we shall regard all the governments since the secession of Syria from the UAR until the government of Nasser's premiership of June 1967, after the defeat of the Six-Day War, as a single entity, irrespective of changes in personnel. Who are the men who filled the principal governmental posts?

Those who participated in more than one of these governments are listed only once; if they occupied different positions they are mentioned in their highest post, even if it was not the latest.

The structure of the elite is pyramidical. The apex is occupied by one personage, head and shoulders above the rest of the people in stature and talent, and more so in prestige and power. Nasser lays down policy, enacts and executes laws. He appoints and dismisses civil and military leaders, all responsible to him. His personality cult has no equal in our time except that of Hitler, Stalin and Mao. During the 1965 "election campaign" when he was about to be elected to the presidency for a third term, the weekly *Akhbār al-Yawm* printed in the box of "The day's pearl of wisdom" a verse from the Quran which, of course, refers to the Prophet, "Verily, those who swear allegiance to thee do but swear allegiance to God."[2] When on June 9, 1967, he was compelled "to assume the entire respon-

[2] *Akhbār al-Yawm*, Cairo, 13 March 1965; Quran, 48, 10.

sibility," as he said in his speech on radio and television, for the catastrophic defeat of Egypt's army and politics, and "to give up completely and finally every official post and every political role," the popular reaction was fundamentally different from the reaction to the resignation or dismissal of any other military or civilian leader. The mass demonstrations demanding his return to the presidency were partly engineered by his staff—but only partly. They would never have attained their extent and intensity if so many Egyptians had not felt a deep-rooted adherence to Nasser as their leader. The father image emerges not only when a strong personality, of the type which Max Weber called charismatic, wishes to impose his authority—it is created also by the desire of all those who yearn to be led and guided, and that yearning is especially strong in moments of crisis. For many Egyptians on June 9 and 10, 1967 loyalty to Nasser was the last and only faith left over from a crumbling political belief-system.

Nasser's power and the faith in his authority reached their apogee in the spring of 1958 after the nationalization of the Suez Canal in 1956, the retreat of the Israelis, the British and the French from Egyptian soil in 1957, and the union of Egypt and Syria in February 1958. From then on it has been declining, beginning with the non-accession of republican Iraq after the coup of July 1958 to the union with Egypt and Syria, followed in 1961 by the secession of Syria, the failure of Egypt's war in Yemen, the growing economic difficulties of Egypt, the disaster of the Six-Day War in 1967 and its aftermath. But so far he has survived all these adversities and all his adversaries.

The second level of the pyramid of Egypt's ruling elite, in descending order, consists of nine personalities: The vice-presidents, prime ministers and the speaker of the National Assembly. Four of them have been on the top during the whole period considered, from autumn 1961 to summer 1967: Zakariyyā Muḥī al-Dīn, 'Alī Ṣabrī, Ḥusayn Shāfi'ī and Anwar Sādāt. The fifth, Muḥammad Sidqī Sulaymān, rose to top rank only in 1966. Four other vice-presidents were eliminated at different times: 'Abd al-Laṭīf Baghdādī was for some years practically the first among the vice-presidents and the president's official deputy during his visits abroad; in March 1964 he was suddenly forced to resign. Together with him disappeared Kamāl al-Dīn Ḥusayn. In January 1966 Ḥasan Ibrāhīm's resignation was announced. And the Six-Day War brought with it the resignation, its acceptance and finally the suicide of Nasser's closest friend, until then his first deputy and deputy commander in chief of the armed forces, Marshal 'Abd al-Ḥakīm 'Āmir. Some months later Zakariyyā Muḥī al-Dīn was also relieved from all his posts; on June 9, 1967, in his resignation speech, Nasser had still nominated him as his successor.

The third level of the pyramid consists of those who served in the different governments until June 1967 as deputy premiers; their position can be compared to that of cabinet ministers in other countries. In the four governments since September 1962 thirteen men served in this capacity. Under them were the ministers who were actually the directors-general of the ministries. They are 42 in number.

Of these 65 men. 63 are Muslims. A Copt, Dr. Kamāl Ramzī Astīnū, was deputy premier for supply and internal commerce until September 1966; in the following government of Muḥammad Ṣidqī Sulaymān he was no longer included. In his stead another Copt served in the next cabinets, for the first time, Kamāl Henrī Abādīr, as minister of communications. Thus, in the successive Egyptian governments of the sixties, each comprising 30 or more ministers, there was always only one Copt; in the Egyptian population as a whole, one in approximately 14 people is a Copt. This detail is indicative of the general situation. The times when the Copt, Makram 'Ubayd, was deputy prime minister have passed. The economic and public position of the Copts—the oldest and most deeply rooted of the country's communities—has been growing weaker. The exclusion of foreigners is accompanied by discrimination against Egyptian Christians. The percentage of Copts in the Ministry for Foreign Affairs both as diplomatic representatives and clerical employees has dropped from more than six per cent in 1952 to less than three per cent in 1959. Of the 400 members of the National Assembly appointed in September 1960 there were only 13 Christians. Islam, as a religious community, reigns supreme.

Twenty-seven of the 65 members of the governing group are officers., i.e., men who received their vocational training and made a career in the army and who only took off their uniforms after they or their comrades had seized power by military coup. Almost all were born between 1917 and 1920. In 1940 they were second-lieutenants and in 1952 majors and colonels. The figure 27 out of 65, i.e., 42 per cent, is proportionately high, but does not yet completely reflect the supremacy of the officers. The ten men at the apex of the pyramid are all officers. When in September 1966 Muḥammad Ṣidqī Sulaymān was appointed prime minister, he was presented as an engineer and his civilian profession was widely publicized. He indeed excelled as an engineer and administrator (he was responsible for the construction of the Aswan High Dam) but his access to public life was as an officer, as other Egyptian premiers before him. After receiving his diploma as an engineer he served as an officer in the army from 1939.[5]

[3] Edward Wakin, *A lonely minority*, New York 1963, 45–6.

[4] *Ibid.*, 43; *al-Ahrām*, 19 July 1960.

[5] *Akhbār al-Yawm*, 10 September 1966.

In May 1948 he completed a course at the Staff College, the same one attended by Nasser, 'Āmir, Zakariyyā Muḥī al-Dīn and several other future leaders of republican Egypt.

Yet another rising star is Maḥmūd Yūnis, who is generally introduced as "the engineer, Maḥmūd Yūnis." He is an excellent engineer and outstanding administrator—and an officer politician. After studying engineering, he joined the army in 1937 where his talents attracted immediate attention. In 1942 he attended the Staff College, and in 1944 and 1951—then together with Nasser—became an instructor there. He joined the Free Officers, and after the coup, took the post of custodian of the royal family's property; from 1954 to 1956 he directed the Petroleum Authority.[6] In 1956, from the day of its nationalization, he became the chairman and managing director of the Suez Canal Authority, and it is largely to his credit that the Egyptian administration of the canal was an outstanding success. In September 1966 he was appointed deputy prime minister and minister for electricity, petroleum and mining.

So far only the peak of the Egyptian governmental pyramid has been discussed. Lower down, the percentage of officers becomes smaller, but is still very conspicuous. In the group of 65 members of government between 1962 and 1967, four out of 13 deputy prime ministers were officers, i.e., 31 per cent. Of the 42 ministers, 13 were officers, again 31 per cent.

It is worth noting that the proportion of officers among ministers, though fluctuating over the years, has not diminished. The following table shows the numbers and ratio of civilians to officers in Egyptian governments since 1952.

The penetration of the officers into positions of leadership does not stop at the level of cabinet minister; on the contrary, it begins there and continues throughout all branches of political and economic leadership and representation.

Of the 58 ambassadors and ministers who represented Egypt in the world's capitals in 1962, 25—nearly half—were former officers. Of the 73 ambassadors and ministers in the summer of 1964, 48—nearly two-thirds—were officers. This trend of officers occupying key positions is not weakening but growing stronger.

As to the economic sphere, a well-informed expert summarily stated in 1964 when discussing the nationalized enterprises: "The top positions are generally occupied by officers, whose qualifications are more their political reliability than their technical and economic proficiency."[7] The Egyptian socialist, Anwar 'Abd al-Malik, goes even further: "The

[6] *Middle East Forum*, Beirut, December 1962, 32–7.

[7] Dieter Weiss, *Wirtschaftliche Entwicklungsplanung in der VAR*, Köln 1964, 76.

officer corps is now organically integrated with the leading economic, administrative and political groups. All those who had to leave the armed forces, or who have elected to do so, have been appointed to the upper ranks of the non-military establishment."[8] His book on Nasser's Egypt is just entitled *Egypte, société militaire.*[9]

The large number of former officers in senior economic and political positions is not in itself evidence of an army-conducted regime. In every army the number of high-ranking officers is limited by the table of organization; not every captain reaches the rank of brigadier. In other hierarchic organizations, such as the civil service and the church, persons serving in intermediate grades keep the same post for many years before being retired. In armies officers often leave after having served for a number of years without receiving a promotion. At the age of 40 or 50, they must seek a new source of livelihood. The state and society regard themselves as obligated to them and morally bound to look after them and are also interested in making use of their administrative abilities and their experience as leaders of men. Sometimes these are personalities with established reputations and their joining the board of directors of a company or the parliamentary faction of a political party is excellent publicity. In many countries, therefore, numerous former officers are to be found in conspicuous positions in political and economic life. In 1960 officers constituted about a third of one per cent of the economically active males of the British population. However, retired officers comprised four per cent of the holders of high positions in industry and government service, nine per cent of the members of parliament, and 20 per cent of those whose names appeared in *"Who's Who in British Aviation."*[10] It is possible to cite examples from other countries, including Israel. No one, however, thinks that either England or Israel is functioning under a military government or is on the way to becoming a militaristic society, even though some regard such manifestations with concern. The essential distinction in Egypt lies in the entirely different dimensions of the phenomenon, which transform quantity to quality, and in the importance of the positions occupied by the officers. They not only constitute a high percentage of a rather large class of persons holding important posts but their ratio increases as one goes up the ladder of the decision-making hierarchy. Furthermore, in Britain the armed forces were reduced after World War II. This, coupled with the liquidation of British rule in India

8 Anouar Abdel-Malek, 'Nasserism and socialism', *The socialist register 1964*, New York 1964, 45.

9 Anouar Abdel-Malek, *Egypte, société militaire*, Paris 1962.

10 Philip Abrams in S.P. Huntington,(ed.), *Changing patterns of military politics*, New York 1962, 166–7.

and other possessions, added to the number of officers seeking employment and prestige outside the army. In Egypt, however, the officers seized key civilian positions as the army was expanding.

The group of men who have been in power since 1952 has persistently tightened its grip on the country. Today they control all key political positions and most of the prominent posts in administration, information, diplomatic representation and on numerous boards of directors of state-owned companies. This group is actually a professional coterie, small in number. In the spring of 1952 there were about 6,000 physicians in Egypt, more than 5,000 lawyers and 16,000 engineers, but officers of all ranks on active service in all the armed forces amounted only to about 4,000 in all. Of these, 2,500 men, about two-thirds, were still in service fifteen years later. Between 1952 and 1954 about 400 were cashiered and eliminated from all military and political positions for political reasons: The dismissed included all those who had held the rank of brigadier and above in 1952—with the exception of Brigadier Muḥammad Ibrāhīm—plus more than half of the colonels and some officers of lower rank. Tens of officers died. Those who took off their uniforms and entrenched themselves in government positions and pivotal points of the economy comprise a group of about 1,000 men: At its head stand a handful of Free Officer oldtimers around whom cluster peripheral hangers-on. These 1,000 officers provide the majority of the ministers, provincial governors, ambassadors, directors of companies and enterprises, newspaper editors and molders of public opinion in the new Egypt.

In Fārūq's time, if the daughter of a rich respected citizen of Cairo fell in love with a lieutenant, her parents did their best to dissuade her from the match. Now lieutenants have become the most sought-after suitors both by the girls and their parents.

It is superficial to assume that the officers fought for power and clung to it for the sake of power alone. But no less superficial is the view which disregards their overwhelming lust for power.

Officer rule in Egypt wears the guise of a constitutional, democratic form of government with secret, general elections. In 1956 the President, his deputies and the ministers, with the exception of 'Āmir, took off their uniforms. However, all this was only a fiction. The rulers of 1967 were essentially the same men who in 1949 were leaders of the Free Officers, in 1952 seized power in a military coup and in 1954 ousted Naguib. The source of their power was the army, which still remained their principal support. Their habits of thought and action remained those of the army officer. "It would be an insult to the effective training of the military, and to their indoctrination as well, to suppose that military officials shed their military character and outlook upon changing from uniform to mufti. This background is more important perhaps in the military case than in that of the corporate executives, for the training of the career is deeper and more total."[11]

A solitary soldier or a small group of officers entering civilian positions may adjust to habits of thinking and acting prevalent in the professional group in which they happen to find themselves. But this is not the case with respect to an entire group of officers which seizes control in a military coup, which continues to enlist new partners for directing the state and the economy from the ranks of its fellow officers, which honors the army more than any other institution and which maintains a dictatorship. A regime like this is government by army officers and the change in the uniform of its leaders does not alter the situation one whit.

The people know full well that the army is running the country and there are times when they are concretely reminded of the fact. In November 1964 a campaign was carried out against corrupt officials, merchants and storekeepers, and many were arrested by military police. Public criticism of the interference of the military police was voiced by Deputy Ḥilmī al-Ghandūr at a session of the National Assembly on December 2. "Things are happening which I cannot fathom. For example, when the transport service broke down, the army intervened to remedy the situation. This is fine, but strange. The army should intervene in order to protect the people from an enemy, but if it intervenes for the purpose of correcting mistakes, it is peculiar. Persons investigating the supply situation did not know how to carry out their duties—and so we brought in another authority [the reference is to the military investigators and police] which performed their function. We complain about companies, about what goes on in them, and about the presence of non-professionals on their directorates. One of them may be a doctor or a senior officer, but, first of all, he must be a trained man so that the company may be operated properly."[12] This restrained criticism was enough to elicit an immediate response from Prime Minister 'Alī Ṣabrī, "The army is part of the nation. It will do whatever it is capable of doing in times of peace and there is nothing wrong with it. The army is participating in strengthening the national economy; the army worked on the High Dam—without it we would never have been able to finish the work on time; it is the army which does the work in the New Valley where working conditions are very difficult; the army is in the towns, the villages and the schools engaged in construction work and repairing roads because it

[11] C. Wright Mills, *The power elite,* New York 1956, 285.
[12] *Al-Ahrām,* 3 December 1964.

has great possibilities which should be made use of in peace time. As for the Cairo General Transport Institution,—army workshops repaired a large number of immobilized buses, and it is neither strange nor wrong. The United States Navy carries out numerous construction jobs, especially in building ports. No one has said that it is wrong." The Prime Minister's reply did not explain why the army also acts in the capacity of a police force, and at the end of the session, al-Ghandūr once more took the floor in order to "clarify" his statements; these remarks were both in the nature of an apology and a repetition of his contention, "I admire and respect the army of which all of us are proud. It is the army which released me from prison in 1952. I was using the army as an example. Whenever something goes wrong, we call on the army. People are asking, 'What if something goes wrong in the field of education, shall we send out a division of troops?' Why don't we demand a report from everyone who makes a mistake before we turn to the army? . . . I mean that every institution should currently be able to stand on its own feet and manage its own affairs."[13]

The officers are masters, but they do not rule alone. An example of this can once again be taken from the composition of the government. Of the 65 top-flight officials mentioned, 38 are civilians. Of these, 20, more than half, have doctorates or are engineers. University graduates are becoming the leading partners of the officers. But this is not a realization of Plato's vision of a philosopher king. These are not doctors of philosophy, persons with an education in the humanities. In an article on *The Road to the Administrative Revolution,* M. Ḥ. Haykal reports that 45 per cent of the directors of large institutions and companies are engineers.[14] As in many other societies—particularly in the developing countries, but not in them alone—the emphasis of the intellectuals has shifted from the study of philosophy to that of physics, from literature and history to technology and economics. University graduates with a scientific education, engineers, the talented managers of former companies and economic and technical experts with initiative and resolution became the chief partners of the officers in power. This is the Egyptian version of the "managerial revolution." This phenomenon is shared by all countries, advanced or developing, socialist or capitalist, differing only in extent and tempo. Egypt is unique in this respect only insofar as she is ahead of the other Arab countries. The rise of the officer class and the rule of the military is accompanied by the advancement of technocrats and technocracy.

The Egyptian leaders are not blind to the dangers of corruption associated

[13] *Loc. cit.*

[14] *Al-Ahrām,* 13 March 1964.

with technocracy: Bureaucratization brings, on the one hand, rigid formalism and the avoidance of accepting responsibility and taking initiative. On the other, the cult of "getting things done" breeds the arrogance of people with know-how who extol efficiency but are contemptuous of basic social values. Once more, these dangers are not specifically Egyptian but have only come to the fore earlier and more extensively there than in other Arab countries; they are of deep concern to Egypt's leaders who launched broad public campaigns against them. To what extent they will succeed in overcoming the negative feature of the regime they introduced is one of the crucial tests facing the governmental system; in the final analysis, its solution is a function of the relationship between the leadership and the public, which we shall discuss later.

The bonds connecting the technocrats and the officers are strong and numerous. This phenomenon has already been discussed in the chapter on the Egyptian officer class. Frequently, officers, officials and professional men are brothers or cousins; socially they are members of the same class. In their approach to current problems and in their mentality they are very close to one another: They are usually more concerned with ways of carrying out tasks than with abstract reflections on objectives. And above all, officers and technocrats share identical interests and identical expectations of the future. From the point of view of origins, they can be brother-rivals, but where aspirations are involved, they are brother-comrades. They are dependent on one another and each can be secure in his own position only if the other is also firmly entrenched. They do not possess much property; their livelihood comes from salaries and their prestige from their share in the government. They do not own the means of production nor have they prospects of doing so. The enticement held out to them is not *proprietorship* but *collective control of the means of production* and the *power to determine their own salaries*. The realization of this aspiration is achieved by means of etatist nationalization, by the ownership of the state, in theory, but of the joint officer-technocrat-bureaucrat group, in fact. When the state is the principal capitalist and the owner of the leading economic development enterprises, the ruling class is that which exercises control over the administrative establishment—the officials—and over the forces of coercion—the police and the army. Such a regime can by no means be defined as capitalist in the traditional sense. In capitalist regimes the middle class accumulated property and capital *before* it took over political rule. In this case, the political seizure of power preceded economic domination.

A third group of the new Egyptian elite is a transformation of part of the previous elite. Tens of stockholders in financial and industrial enterprises in the early 1950's now serve on the boards of directors or as senior officials in the same enterprises after nationalization or as partners of the state in enterprises of joint public-private ownership. By comparison with the previous period their incomes have diminished, but they do not have to live on their salaries alone. They received ample compensation for their nationalized plants and shares of stock. They are significant factors in the economic life of the country, together with the "Nationalist capitalists" whose "capital does not involve exploitation" and who still maintain control of important parts of the national economy in light industry and wholesale and retail domestic trade. Politically, however, they have become powerless. Moreover, of the businessmen of the old regime, almost only Muslims have remained in important economic positions. Not only foreigners and Jews but also Coptic Egyptians have been eliminated from key positions. "In a list of several hundred persons who supplanted the middle class of the old regime in Egypt, we find that nearly half are officers, approximately a fourth are Muslim businessmen from the old regime, and about a quarter are technocrats and officials who passed from the service of private capital to that of the state." [15]

The social and political rise of the officer corps and the technocrats, together with the general trends of urbanization and industrialization are also bringing about a general shift in the ratio of town to country. The superiority of the town to the country is emphasized. But most of the Egyptians live in villages and work in agriculture, and the country's principal economic asset is its agrarian wealth.

Who rules the Egyptian village today?

To a large extent this was determined by the results of the agrarian reform: In its first stage in 1952 it limited the land permitted to a single proprietor to 200 feddans (1 feddan = 1.038 acres), and in 1961 it further limited the size of a single person's holding to 100 feddans. We shall consider here only a few striking features of this complicated reform, taking into account the fact that Egyptian statistics in recent years are not very reliable. The heads of the regime cite numerous statistics in their speeches, creating the impression that never was so much accurately planned and measured as in republican Egypt. However, examination of the data often shows irreconcilable discrepancies; and despite the spate of publicity, precisely the most fundamental matters are frequently concealed or ignored and ambitious projects confused with actual accomplishments. In general, Egyptian statistics were never accurate, and since 1952, when they became an obvious propaganda tool of the government, their reliability has diminished even more.

[15] Hassan Riad, *L'Egypte nassérienne,* Paris 1964, 227.

The last available official figures show the following changes in the distribution of landownership:[16]

LAND HOLDINGS IN EGYPT

Holdings ('000 *feddans*)	*Number of owners* ('000) 1952	1964	*Area owned* ('000 *feddans*) 1952	1964	*Change* *Figures* *owners*	*area*	*Per cent* *owners*	*area*
Less than 5	2642	2965	2182	3353	+323	+1171	+ 13	+ 54
5– 10	79	78	526	614	− 1	+ 88	− 1	+ 17
10– 50	69	90	1291	1342	+ 21	+ 51	+ 30	+ 40
50–100	6	6	429	392	=	− 37	=	− 9
100–200	3	4	437	421	+ 1	− 16	+ 33	− 4
over 200	2		1117		− 2	−1117	−100	−100
TOTAL	2801	3143	5982	6122	+342	+ 140	+ 12	+ 2

For the purpose of evaluating the influence and results of the agrarian reform, one must first of all consider the changes that would have occurred without it during the 12 years between 1952 and 1964. For even without the agrarian reform, if the previous developmental trends had continued at the same pace and direction as before, a number of changes would have taken place. The principal factors in recent generations were the Islamic inheritance laws which grant an equal part of the deceased's property to every male descendant, and which are thus responsible for the increasing fragmentation of holdings. On the other hand, the amount of arable land increased only in the most minute proportions, and some of the poor peasants inevitably became absolutely landless. In consequence, the increase in the number of owners of landed property always remained lower than the increase in the population in general and in the rural population in particular. The proportion of tiny plots in the total agricultural area grew and the number of landlords increased, but altogether at relatively low rates.[17]

The following table shows the developmental trends in approximately 12-year periods[18] and the results of the agrarian reform. The next to last column contains estimated figures for a hypothetical situation had the reform not taken place, and the final column shows the changes that occurred as a consequence of the reform.

[16] UAR Department of Statistics and Census, *Annuaire statistique 1944*, Cairo 1965, 43; Gabriel Baer, 'New data and conclusions about effects of Egypt's land reform' (in Hebrew), *Hamizrah*, vol. 16, 176–8.

[17] Gabriel Baer, *A history of landownership in modern Egypt, 1800–1950*, London 1962, 71–9.

[18] *Ibid.*, 224–5.

DISTRIBUTION OF AGRICULTURAL AREA/PERCENTAGES BY SIZE OF HOLDINGS

	1916	1929	1940	1952	1964	1964 *without reform*	*Real change*
Less than 1 feddan	7.9	9.8	12.4	13.0	54.7	40.7	+14.0
1– 5	18.7	19.7	20.1	23.4			
5– 10	9.7	9.8	9.8	8.8	10.1	7.2	+ 2.9
10– 50	20.6	20.5	20.6	21.6	21.9	22.1	– 0.2
50–100	43.1	8.4	7.9	7.2	6.4	6.7	– 0.3
100–200		7.8	7.5	7.3	6.9	7.0	– 0.1
over 200		24.0	21.7	18.7	–	16.3	–16.3
TOTAL	100.0	100.0	100.0	100.0	100.0	100.0	
Area ('000 feddans)	5452	5793	5841	5982	6122		
Owners ('000)	1720	2180	2491	2801	3143	3150	=

Thus, three facts stand out:

1) As a result of the laws and acts of agrarian reform, the ownership of nearly 1,200,000 feddans, i.e., of almost one fifth of Egyptian agricultural land, was changed.

2) The class of large landowners was liquidated both from the economic point of view and as regards their political control of the villages.

3) The lands which changed ownership belonged to two categories: Those taken over by the agrarian reform authorities and distributed to smallholders, and lands marked for expropriation according to the reform laws which were sold on the free market by their owners before the date of expropriation.

It is clear that lands in the second category, nearly a third of the lands which changed hands, were all acquired by previous landlords who were the only people with the capital and ability to purchase land.[19] But the rest also eventually became the property of previous landowners. From 1952 to 1964 the average area of landowners possessing less than five feddans increased from 0.9 to 1.1 feddan; of the holders of from five to 10 feddans, from 6.7 to 7.9 feddans. The process of excessive fragmentation of tiny plots was halted. But landless peasants did not become landowners. On the contrary, the total number of landowners in the Egyptian villages increased by 342,000 in the period from 1952 to 1964, a growth of 12 to 13 per cent,

[19] Bent Hansen and Girgis A. Marzouk, *Development and economic policy in the UAR (Egypt)*, Amsterdam 1965, 92; Gabriel S. Saab, *The Egyptian agrarian reform 1952–1962*. London 1967, 187–8; Saad M. Gadalla, *Land reform in relation to social development—Egypt*, Columbia, Missouri, 1962, 44.

while the total rural population increased by at least 25 per cent this period.

The medium landowners, owners of 10 to 100 feddans, succeeded in preserving their position and property. These well-to-do villagers do not share in the central political power, even to the tiny degree of the Muslim businessmen and stockholders who became the managers of nationalized enterprises. But on the local rural and provincial plane their influence has increased greatly, their holdings are flourishing and their position has become stronger. For some reason, sufficient attention has not yet been paid to the phenomenon that these are among the chief beneficiaries of the changes in the Egyptian village during both stages of the agrarian reform. These are also the "village notables" living in the village, who also lease their holdings or cultivate them with hired labor. These "notables" and "village bigwigs" owning several tens of feddans are the strongmen of the area who directly and harshly exploit the landless villagers. The huge surplus of virtually unemployed manpower in the Egyptian village—it is estimated that the number of those living on agriculture could be reduced by one half without harming the level of production—deprives the landless peasants of bargaining power in the labor market. Many of them do not even earn 10 piasters a day even in the time of Arab socialism.[20] And they are not even assured of regular employment the year round. The "notables" also dominate the village's social life. The *'umda,* the government's representative in the village, is selected from among their number or their associates. The status of the *'umda* has steadily been declining from the end of the last century, and during the past generation he has generally come from the class owning five to 20 feddans. The *'umdas* have not been changed with the institution of the new government. Before, they alternated between faithful service for the king or the Wafd, and today they serve the officers' government.[21] In the internal life of the villages they serve the interests of the "notables".

The class of village rich men—all owners of more than 20 feddans—comprises less than a quarter of a million out of a rural population of nearly 20 million. According to the figures of Hassan Riad, the average annual per capita income of members of families with holdings of 20 feddans or more amounts to E£ 789.5, i.e., 130–160 times the average annual income of five to six Egyptian pounds of members of landless families, who constitute nearly three quarters of the total rural population.[22] And let us

[20] *Al-Ahrām,* 29 May 1962.

[21] Gabriel Baer, 'The village shaykh in modern Egypt', in *Studies in Islamic history and civilization,* Jerusalem 1961, 121–153; Riad, 25–6.

[22] Riad, 19–20.

make no mistake about it—this is not in the days of Fārūq but under Nasser in the 1960's.

The village wealthy have preserved their position and riches during the period of the republic and have even enhanced them. Nor is it surprising, for the officers now in power are closely bound to them. In examining the origin of the officers it became clear that many of them are the sons and nephews of village men of substance. One need only cite the example of 'Abd al-Ḥakīm 'Āmir. Once more, strong ties of social origin connect a certain class whose position improved and property increased during the period of officer rule with the officers in power. The officers are loyal to the Arab tradition of powerful family solidarity.

The true position of the village rich is in fact much stronger than is revealed by official statistics. Many of the former large property owners succeeded in preserving their landed possessions. Taking advantage of various loopholes in the agrarian reform laws and through adroit legal subterfuge, a sizeable number managed to retain possession of large tracts of land. In many instances plots were sold to poor peasants through fictitious sales by means of carefully formulated agreements which actually leave to the purchaser only debts and obligations for years to come and to the seller all the practical rights and benefits.

In 1965 two correspondents of *Rūz al-Yūsuf* investigated such instances and cited complete details with names, figures and dates. One family possessed 1,364 feddans in 1965 and the other more than 25,000 feddans.[23] It is naturally impossible to determine how many instances of this kind there are. Several hundreds of thousands of feddans which appear in official statistics as the property of peasants with small holdings are in fact parts of large estates.

The social struggle in the Egyptian village, which becomes violent from time to time, is initiated by the landless poor or by tenants. This occurred in 1951, in 1952 on the eve of the officers' coup,[24] and again during the first half of 1966 as the general economic crisis in Egypt grew worse. The government and the leadership of the Socialist Union were forced to inaugurate a vigorous public campaign against the "remnants of feudalism." Special teams headed by Marshal 'Abd al-Ḥakīm 'Āmir investigated hundreds of cases and expropriated the property of tens of families. In the course of this campaign numerous cases of what was called the "smuggling" of land came to light, demonstrating the almost undisguised domination, economically and socially, of the families of the

23 *Rūz al-Yūsuf*, 22 February, 1 March 1965.

24 G. Baer, *Landownership*, 221; G.S. Saab, *Agrarian reform*, 13; Emīl Tūmā, *Thawrat 23 tammūz fī 'aqdihā al-awwal*, Haifa 1962, 25.

village strongmen. The following case is one of many examples published in *al-Ahrām*: "For example, in the village of Shabās al-Milḥ [in the Kafr al-Shaykh province] 15,000 people live on 3,600 feddans of land which constitute all the cultivated land in the village. Who owns this land? On the basis of the records of the village cooperative society the following peculiar data were obtained: 643 feddans belong to seven people who are members of the same family. This is followed by a long list of names, all of which end in the same surname, of people owning 1,378 feddans. Five hundred feddans of village land belong to two substantial landlords. On the other hand, 15,000 villagers own less than one half of the area of the village, which is 1,732 feddans. What is the status of the small peasant in this village? The peasant Muḥammad Khalaf answers frankly, 'The small peasant in a village like this has no place in the Committee of Twenty [of the Socialist Union], the village council, the cooperative society or even as a watchman as long as he does not enjoy the backing of the family which owns half of the village . . . The village *'umda*, the deputy *'umda*, the three shaykhs [the leaders of the village quarters], the Socialist Union Committee, the secretary-general and the assistant secretary are all members of the same family."[25]

The most serious and striking case in the struggle over the status of these "feudal lords" was the incident, in 1966, in the village of Kamshīsh in Minufiya province where a member of the landowning al-Fiqqī family murdered Ṣāliḥ Ḥusayn of the local committee of the Socialist Union who wanted to destroy the family's position in the village.[26] The authorities and the public appeared surprised and shocked. But it is doubtful whether the revelations were a real surprise. It may be correct to say that the situation had deteriorated to such an extent that it was no longer possible to maintain the prolonged conspiracy of silence that concealed what was really happening in the Egyptian village. For the clash of interests and classes in Kamshīsh was not new. Already in 1953 a detailed, illustrated article in *al-Muṣawwar*[27] told of assassinations, arrests and curfew in Kamshīsh. The background of the clashes was the exploitation and oppression of the villagers by the al-Fiqqī family. The article mentioned several members of the family and denounced their abuse of their position in the village. But no "revolution" took place there between 1953 and 1966.

The fifth and final class whose power and importance have grown considerably in the period of the republic has an entirely different character

[25] *Al-Ahrām,* 25 May 1966; *Hamizrah,* vol. 16, 179–195.

[26] *Al-Ahrām,* 5 May 1966; *Hamizrah, loc. cit.*

[27] *Al-Muṣawwar,* 14 August 1953.

from the other four. These are the skilled workers. There can be no doubt that their wages, working conditions and social benefits have greatly improved. Despite the fact that the labor unions are only a tool of the government and strikes are absolutely forbidden, the bargaining power of the skilled workers is considerable. In a country poor in natural resources, capital, and know-how, which is devoting tremendous energy to industrialization, the highly qualified skilled workman is a dear possession—dear in both sense of the term. Experts and advisers, grants and loans, machinery and armaments can be obtained in abundance from other countries, both from the East and West; the unskilled labor force is as vast and as cheap as sand at the seashore. Skilled labor is the bottleneck of development. It can not be brought from abroad nor can the tens of thousands of the simple, too simple, workers streaming in masses from the villages to the towns be educated and trained for the ever increasing requirements for skilled labor at the necessary speed and in the numbers required.

Hassan Riad's figures may be inexact, but we can accept them as approximating the facts and as an important clarification of several basic phenomena. According to these figures, the proletariat employed in manufacture and in enterprises of communication and their dependents comprises 790,000 persons,[28] more than three per cent of the Egyptian population. The average per capita income of this class is E£ 60.8—almost twice the average income of the general population, which is only E£ 34.1. This proletariat is one of the privileged groups. At least 80 out of every 100 Egyptians live on a lower income standard, and only 13 to 15 receive a higher income than urban workers. More than four million urban Egyptians and 18 million villagers live under worse, generally much worse, conditions than urban workers. "What undoubtedly characterizes the Egyptian proletariat is its position as a minority among the popular strata of the urban population and its relatively high standard of living. The proletariat scarecely represents 10 per cent of the urban population, and this proportion is not expected to increase in the near future, even assuming the country's rapid industrialization as a consequence of the demographic increase of the impoverished masses. The worker's average income is at least sixfold that of the lowest social group. An income of this size—E£ 60 per capita—is a decent livelihood in Egypt. Whoever calls the foreign observer's attention to this fact in order to show that this is not poverty, must not conceal the incomparably greater poverty of the destitute classes of the population."[29]

[28] Riad, 40–1.

[29] *Ibid.*, 45.

The average daily wage of the urban worker ranges from 50 to 60 piasters per diem. However those who benefit from the new government constitute only a part, albeit a growing one, of the working class as a whole. As among the entire Egyptian people so within the working class there exist extreme discrepancies in income. According to official figures from Egyptian sources which confirm most of the above, the average wage of 357 thousand employees in 861 industrial enterprises employing 50 workers and above, including the office personnel, amounted to E£ 171 per annum in 1962. The average income of 118.000 employees in Lower Egypt amounted to E£ 134 per annum, while 18,000 workers and office personnel in the Suez Canal region earned an average of E£ 292 per annum; of them, nearly 4,000 were employed in petroleum and gas plants and their average salary amounted to E£640 in 1961. On the other hand, 32,000 workers and office personnel in food industries employing at least 50 persons earned an average salary of only E£ 80 that year.[30] Most industrial workers live on a wage of 25 piasters, which, miserable as it is, is high compared with the income of most of the population; part of the urban workers and the mass of rural workers do not even earn this meager wage. The following describes the plight of one of the most underpriviledged groups of workers—and at the same time, one of the largest in number—in the summer of 1964, according to the economic supplement of *al-Ahrām*: "The Association of Tannery, Leather and Shoe Workers increased from 950 members in 1960 to 9,000 in 1964. However, the total number of workers in these trades is 120,000, which means that 111,000 workers are outside the trade union. Tannery workers suffer from harsh conditions more severe than those of other workers. They work almost naked, and no law for effective, systematic preservation of their health is observed. They work among acids and chemicals and have virtually no safety precautions, depending on how much additional expense the tannery owner wants to save. The result is that the vast majority of tannery workers is afflicted with various diseases, e.g., leprosy, tuberculosis, rheumatism and blindness. Despite this serious state of affairs, many tannery owners reduce production both in order to exert pressure on the workers and in order to trade in chemicals on the black market, instead of using them in the plant. Thus they accumulate disgraceful profits. Because their chemicals are sold on the black market. a number of tanneries are in operation for half a week only; the sole sufferers are the workers whose production is reduced and wages shrunken. The association made an effort to sign an agreement with the owners in order to assure the workers' rights, and after a campaign in the newspaper

[30] Issawi, 193; *Hamizrah,* vol. 13, 306, vol. 14, 55.

al-Jūmhuriyya in 1961, an agreement was concluded with 45 tanneries. But only two plants comply with the law . . . The worker's wage ranges from 25 to 120 piasters per day, depending on the workman's output. The leather workers are engaged in the manufacture of valises, belts, watchbands, whips, etc. The union members among them and those active on the committees of the Socialist Union come up against efforts to drive a wedge between them and the rest of the workers, to reduce their production and to exert pressure on them; the owners employ a large number of small boys in order to avoid paying the legal minimum wage."[31] This is followed by a description of the condition of the shoe workers, which is not very different. The survey goes on to relate that shoe workers generally work on a piecework basis in groups of three—an *usta* or skilled craftsman, a chief helper and a junior helper or boy. In a working day of 14 hours such a group makes on the average 40 pairs of shoes. The wage for a single pair ranges from eight to 10 piasters and is divided as follows: the *usta* receives four to four-and-a-half piasters, the chief helper three to three-and-a-half, and the boy one to one-and-a-half. "Actually," the article states, "these figures are misleading, giving the impression that each person earns a high wage. It must be kept in mind that the workmen pay for the leather and part of the raw materials; furthermore, the owners sometimes reduce production in order to exert pressure on the workers." The net profit the workshop owner makes on a pair of men's shoes amounts to 13 piasters and the retailer, 52 piasters. If the owner sells the shoes directly to the consumer, his profit amounts to more than 60 piasters—seven times the total wage of the three workers who made the shoes.

The tremendous discrepancies in working conditions and wages in the working class itself are striking. The skilled workers who earn more than E£1 in a working day of seven hours are the new class of workers, the new labor aristocracy.

In reaching the labor aristocracy we have come quite a way from the apex of the Egyptian pyramid; but from this level to the broad base of the tall pyramid the distance is still immense. All the various groups comprising the new ruling elite and its beneficiaries and hangers-on together constitute only a small part of the entire Egyptian people. For the great majority, much has not yet altered. Moreover, although the elite has changed, the social gap between it and the common people is the same. In the chapter summarizing his book, the Egyptian Marxist Riad stated in 1964, "Between the impoverished workers in town and village, on the one hand, and the rest of the classes, on the other, the abyss ten years after the

[31] *Al-Ahrām al-iqtiṣādī,* 15 July 1964, 52.

military coup remains as deep as it was in the past."[32] Probably not by chance the simile of the abyss is used by a French leftwing socialist who is generally most sympathetic towards Nasser's Egypt. Writing about different quarters of Cairo, Claude Estier remarked in 1965: "Just as Belleville is not Auteuil, Ataba is not Zamalek. But what in Paris is merely a difference in the standard of life, in measurable limits, between bourgeois and proletarian, is in Cairo a deep abyss between two worlds without the slightest common denominator. Of these two worlds, the more numerous one is directly at the other's service: Handymen, small artisans, domestic servants, watchmen of buildings are living on some piasters daily or some pounds monthly which they earn in serving owners of real-estate, diplomats and foreigners, intellectuals, high officials, managers of companies, etc. Generally, the lot of this innumerable crowd has till now scarcely improved."[33]

The highly developed UAR propaganda-machine has so far had much success in obscuring the bitter facts of Arab socialism's shortcomings—but mainly abroad, not in Egypt itself. Frustration is on the increase, and it finds odd ways of expressing itself. A typical instance occurred on May 1st, 1964, during Nasser's speech. A long stormy ovation greeted the President when he said: "We have fixed the minimum wage at 25 piasters. Is that a wage sufficient for a worker's happy life? I say—No! We must work toward the raising of this minimum wage in the future."[34] The turbulent applause was a demonstration of dissatisfaction with current conditions, and when he was able to proceed, Nasser hastened to add, "But, of course, compared with the past, 25 piasters are considered an achievement." Once more he interrupted himself and paused briefly, as if inviting further applause. But this time he was answered with silence. The hopes and demands for the future may be strong, but the evaluation of the present is a sober one. The granting or withholding of applause remains one of the few possible ways of conducting a demonstration.

We have dealt somewhat at length with Egypt, which serves as the model for the rest of the officer-ruled Arab countries. The main trends of development in Egypt are discernible in Iraq and Syria, too.

Taking as an example the composition of the Iraqi government of June 1964 we find that of its 20 ministers seven were officers and nine university graduates with doctorates. The intellectuals—those in uniform and in mufti—and the technocrats, the members of the salaried middle class, have

[32] Riad, 232.

[33] Claude Estier, *L'Egypte en révolution,* Paris 1965, 20.

[34] *Al-Ahrām,* 2 May 1964.

become the ruling elite. Their rise came about in two interrelated ways—by violence and by increasing the economic functions of the civil service which they control.

However, this is only the general course of development. Rival cliques of officers who keep changing are sometimes only competing factions in a single political and social group, and occasionally they embody conflicting social interests; at times, they advance the transformation of Arab society, and often enough, consciously or otherwise, serve the forces seeking to arrest the historical process.

The first modern officer politicians who seized power in Iraq and Syria, Bakr Ṣidqī and Ḥusnī Za'īm, aspired to modernization. Bakr Ṣidqī was influenced by the example of Atatürk, and the inspiration of Kemalist Turkey is also recognizable in Za'īm's secularization measures. However, the leadership of both was rapidly debased, the duration of their rule short, and their successors had other ambitions. The groups of officers who followed Bakr Ṣidqī in Iraq, especially Ṣabbāgh and the Golden Square, were indifferent to economic and social questions. They allowed the reactionary and feudal forces to continue exploiting the country, providing that they were permitted to conduct political affairs. 'Abbūd's attitude during his rule in Sudan from 1958 to 1964 was similar; of course, Sudan of 1960 differed greatly from Iraq of 1940—the relative power of the capitalistic factors was greater and the policy of politically subjugating and economically exploiting the African animistic south by the Muslim Arab north was one of the prime objectives of 'Abbūd and his group. Basically, however, the attitude of the military regime in Sudan to social questions consisted of granting a free hand to traditional and modern exploitative forces.

Even Shishaklī, although he contemplated political reform, adopted the line of minimal interference by the state in economic life. His rule was marked by capitalist prosperity in Syria. By not interfering he helped commercial and industrial capital to expand its power and profits. This state of affairs also continued after his fall, until 1957. UAR rule in Syria was in this, as in other respects, an important turning point. The beginnings of agrarian reform, the state's mounting activity, interference and supervision in economic life and, finally, large-scale nationalization were on the verge of bringing about far-reaching social changes. Among the reasons for Syria's secession from the UAR in 1961 was the desire to restore freedom of action and exploitation to private Syrian capital and initiative. But the Syrian regime set up by the secessionist army officers in 1961 lasted only one and a half years, and the coup of the Ba'th in March 1963 inaugurated a new period of socialism and nationalization.

The history of Syria's agrarian reform is extremely complicated and characterized by fluctuations and divergent trends. The issue is further complicated by the extensive diversity of land in Syria which had to be taken into account in the formulation and implementation of the laws. The laws themselves underwent frequent radical change. Expropriation, the restoring of land to previous owners, renewed expropriation and the distribution of expropriated land to individuals and cooperatives show even greater fluctuations. Moreover, official publications and figures on land reform are scanty and sometimes contradictory as well. Accordingly, only some of the most salient features can be outlined here.

In Syria, as in other Arab countries, agrarian reform was discussed and written about for a long time. However, concrete action was not taken until after the union with Egypt. But the reform law of September 1958 was patterned too much after the Egyptian law without sufficient consideration of Syria's special circumstances; furthermore, it imposed expropriations on a much larger scale than in Egypt. Whereas less than 10% of Egyptian agricultural land was slated for expropriation according to the laws of 1952, and an additional 5% by the law of 1961, Syria's agrarian reform law of 1958 decreed an immediate expropriation of 16% of the irrigated and plantation land and 30% of the rain-watered land. However, implementation of the law progressed slowly, primarily because of the stubborn passive opposition of the landowners. During the period of union only less than half of the dry-farming land and less than a quarter of the land under irrigation which had been slated for expropriation were expropriated, and of these expropriated lands only 22% were transferred to the new ownership of small peasants. The government which broke away from the UAR first of all suspended all agrarian reform measures, and in February 1962 enacted a new law which drastically altered the previous one. Among other things it greatly increased land quotas which the previous landlords and the members of their families were entitled to keep in the future as well. Numerous lands which had previously been expropriated and had not yet been redistributed were restored to their previous owners. The arrogant reactionary policy aroused such a ferment in Syria, which in any case lacked stability and was exposed to Egyptian subversion and propaganda, that the government was forced in May 1962 to abolish the law enacted in February and restore the one passed in 1958—but with various changes, in the spirit of the February law, favoring the large landowners. A positive change was to exempt the new owners from payment for the lands given to them, similar to a corresponding ruling then enacted in Egypt. It turned out that in any case the new owners could not have met these obligations. After May 1962 agrarian reform activities were again resumed in Syria.

Having once been started, the process of land distribution could not be stopped again absolutely. However, the tempo and scope of the agrarian reform program in Syria, which even during the period of strong Egyptian rule had been very limited, were reduced still more.[35] In 1963, when the Ba'th took over, agrarian reform received new impetus. The Agrarian Reform Law of June 1963 went further than the laws of 1958 in limiting the size of individual holdings,[36] and in 1965 and 1966, whenever more radical factions of the Ba'th assumed power, implementation of the laws was carried out more energetically.

The following table shows the first wave of large-scale expropriations after the promulgation of the first reform laws in 1958, the slowdown of agrarian reform activities until spring 1963—the table does not show land which after expropriation was returned to its former owner—and the new impetus from then on.[37] The general trend is most remarkable in the column of irrigated and plantation land.

EXPROPRIATION OF LAND ACCORDING TO THE AGRARIAN REFORM LAWS IN SYRIA (in dunams).

	Irrigated and Plantation Land	*Non-irrigated Land*	*Uncultivated Land*	*Total*
1959	114,470	3,260,420	1,792,110	5,167,000
1960	86,000	1,463,750	125,130	1,675,680
1961	92,190	1,182,490	57,300	1,331,980
1962	23,470	436,640	38,170	498,280
1963	40,010	415,350	23,180	478,540
1964	82,100	655,650	24,140	761,890
1965—first-half	71,430	634,730	35,070	741,230
TOTAL	510,470	8,049,030	2,095,100	10,654,600

The problems of Iraq are again different.

The term "feudalism" is often used to characterize the economic and social system in the Arab village—usually without proper clarification and

[35] Eva Garzoni, 'Land reform in Syria', *MEJ*, vol. 17, 85–9; Muhammad Diab, 'The economic system of the UAR', *Middle East forum*, vol. 37, no. 6, Beirut 1961, 18; *Progress in land reform,* a joint publication of the UN, the FAO and the ILO, New York 1962, 25–6, 87; United Nations, *Economic developments in the Middle East 1961–1963*, New York 1964, 26.

[36] *Hamizrah,* vol. 14, 237.

[37] *Ibid.*, vol. 16, 216, quoting *al-Ba'th,* Damascus, 19 December 1965.

frequently incorrectly. The Egyptian landlords in the period of the monarchy were agrarian capitalists and not feudal lords. However, the system which prevailed in most of Iraq during the monarchy can be termed feudal. Out of a total of 21,750,000 *masharas* of cultivated land (a *mashara* = 2,500 sq. meters, i.e., 2½ Palestinian-Syrian dunums), 17,750,000—70% of the total area—belonged to 3,619 owners, i.e., less than one half of one per cent of the total heads of agricultural households, More than half a million landless agricultural families lived in terrible poverty,[38] while two families in Amara Province owned more than 1,500,000 *masharas.* Without a revolutionary agrarian reform all of Iraq's development projects will be a drop in the bucket. Even in the period of Nūrī Sa'īd numerous large enterprises were planned and established which could have conferred a great blessing on the whole economy of the country; most of the large sums received as royalties from the oil companies were invested in the construction of dams, canals, bridges. roads, etc. However, since the government was not prepared to touch the question of agrarian ownership, the development projects could not provide the hoped-for results.

In Iraq, as in Egypt, the agrarian reform law was published a few weeks after the military coup, on September 30, 1958. But there is a great difference between both countries: In Egypt the fellaheen were the passive object of the government's activities, and the landlords displayed active opposition to the reform only in isolated instances in the fall of 1952; after that, they confined themselves to obstruction based on all kinds of legalistic stratagems. In Iraq, however, as soon as the monarchy was deposed, demonstrations were carried out by fellaheen who refused to pay rent and who seized portions of estates. On the other hand, the landlords marshaled factors subservient to their wishes in order to restore "their despoiled rights" and to terrorize the fellaheen. Additional complications were caused by the unclear legal situation with respect to the ownership, measurements and boundaries of many areas. Actually, during Qassim's period, confusion reigned in the Iraqi village. One of its consequences was a considerable decline in agricultural crops. In the four seasons preceding the summer of 1958 the average annual wheat crop amounted to 877,000 tons, but in the four subsequent seasons it dropped to 716,000.[39] In this latter period there were three years of severe drought and in the previous one, only one; but the losses caused by the drought could have been balanced by additional

[38] *Progress in land reform,* 26–7; Rony Gabbay, 'Ha-komunistim weha reforma ha-agrarit be-'Iraq', *Hamizrah,* vol. 11, 21.

[39] United Nations, *Economic developments in the Middle East,1958–59*, New York 1960, 53; *Economic developments in the Middle East, 1961–1963*, New York 1964, 94.

crops from large drainage and reservoir-construction projects finally completed in 1960.[40] The decrease in crops also continued in 1962 and 1963.[41] There is no doubt that the political disturbances played an important part in the great decline. The following official explanation was made to one of the amendments to the agrarian reform law in the summer of 1959: "So many suits have been filed with the magistrates courts responsible for dealing with disputes arising from agricultural relations that they cannot look into them quickly enough. This is the source of events which undermined security and led to the loss of numerous rights."[41]

In Qassim's period the initiative was generally in the hands of the fellaheen. The position of the landlords was thoroughly undermined. However, the actual benefits derived by the fellaheen were still limited: they lacked confidence in their ownership; litigation and violence were rife; there was a scarcity of experts, capital and seeds; and in addition to all these came the drought. The beginning of Arif's period of rule was marked by a large-scale reactionary counterattack in the rural areas as well as in the towns. This was followed by relative quiet, the tense quiet of terror.

Even after nine years of officer rule, it is still impossible to sum up the changes in Iraqi society. Published accounts are few, inexact and contradictory. According to Iraqi official publications, 7,020,123 *masharas* belonging to 2,351 owners were expropriated by May 1964; this figure includes state lands of various kinds which were temporarily given to farmers. Of these 2,022,035 *masharas* were distributed to 38,766 fellaheen, i.e., in plots averaging 52 *masharas*.[42]

To recapitulate: The changes in Iraq since 1958 have displaced the feudal lords from their political and social domination. But the situation of the fellaheen has not much altered. The beneficiaries, to the extent that anyone benefited, were the officers and the technocrats, and sections of the rural middle class.

And what holds true for Iraq is valid, *mutatis mutandis*, for Egypt and Syria too. The regime which call themselves revolutionary and which pretend to implement socialism have brought forth great changes in the composition of the ruling elite. But for the great majority of the people in villages and in towns the framework of life and social relationships remained quite unaffected and basically unchanged.

40 *Economic developments in the Middle East, 1959–1961*, New York 1962, 18.
41 *Al-Zamān*, Baghdad, 4 August 1958.
42 *Hamizrah*, vol. 16, 89–90.

3. THE LEADERSHIP AND THE "POPULAR BASE"

The greatest danger threatening every military dictatorship is a military coup d'état. Numerous military dictatorships in Latin America and in eastern Asia, in Iraq and Syria ended in this way; This was the fate of Bakr Ṣidqī and Qassim, of Za'īm and Shīshaklī and of Egyptian rule in Syria. The only security against this danger lies on basing the government on a broad public organization, i.e., a political party. The officer politicians scorn parties. But each one of them who has spent some time in power has felt the weakness resulting from the lack of organized public activity and has come to realize that indifference and passivity throughout the country may be almost as dangerous to the regime as an opposition or an underground movement; such a man then attempts to organize a party even though he does not call it such. Every political system in our time, in this period of mass communication and propaganda, strives for active mass support. Even the most powerful regime of terror cannot maintain its rule for any length of time if it does not have offshoots and partners in every social unit, in every professional group, in every village and family.

Just as army methods for transmitting instructions and information from higher to lower echelons are much more efficient than in reverse order, so it has become strikingly obvious in most instances that the officer politicians are much more capable of overthrowing governments than of governing countries. Their attempts to create basic, living, mass organization always fail. For it is in the nature of such an organization that a certain latitude must be given for the free expression of opinions and spontaneous association, and from that moment on, it begins to become a hotbed of opposition—so its wings are clipped again. Those who work with one hand to establish it, in the knowledge that they cannot do without it, strangle it with the other, in the justified apprehension that their creation is liable to rebel against them. This is the perennial dilemma of all officers' governments, and the longer they endure, the worse it becomes.

The "popular base", as it is called in the new Egyptian ideology, is necessary not only for the existence and security of the regime as such. It becomes essential if the leadership wishes to implement profound changes, as the Egyptian leaders aspire to do, in matters of ownership and production, social relations and spiritual life. Without people devoted to the ideology in every social sphere, it is impossible to increase productivity in factories, maintain cooperatives in the villages or impart a birth-control consciousness. No one is more aware of this than the leaders of the new Egypt themselves and they stress that "the indifferent ones are no less dangerous than the reactionaries and opportunists."[1] After Shīshaklī's fall in 1954 a Lebanese observer remarked: "If we record what Shīshaklī accomplished in the spheres of social and economic reform, and even in politics, we cannot but say that the cause for the crisis which befell him was his inability to find a permanent solid base for the regime which he established."[2] But the great dilemma has not been solved in Egypt either.

The Egyptian regime is called revolutionary. July 23, 1952 is considered the beginning of a new historical era no less than July 14, 1789, and November 7, 1917. But there is a basic difference between the French and Russian revolutions, on the one hand, when the masses rose up, and the Egyptian revolution, on the other hand, where the masses were passive. Lenin was the leader of an experienced, dynamic party. But Nasser and Naguib found themselves the vanguard of an army on the day after the coup—without an army. In his *Philosophy of the Revolution* Nasser wrote, "Then suddenly came reality after July 23rd. The vanguard performed its task and charged the battlements of tyranny . . . Then it paused, waiting for the serried ranks to come up in their sacred advance towards the great objective. For a long time it waited. Crowds did eventually come, and they came in endless droves—but how different is the reality from the dream! The masses that came were disunited, divided groups of stragglers. The sacred advance was stalled . . . We set about seeking the views of leaders of opinion and the experience of those that were experienced. Unfortunately, we were not able to obtain very much. Every man we questioned had nothing to recommend except to kill someone else . . . If anyone had asked me in those days what I wanted most, I would have answered promptly: To hear an Egyptian speaking fairly about another Egyptian. To sense that an Egyptian has opened his heart to pardon, forgiveness and love for his Egyptian brethren."[3] It is inconceivable for Mirabeau, Danton, Lenin or Trotsky to have written such words. Why was the Egypt of 1952 so different?

It is true that "The Land of the Pharaohs became the site of the most centralistic and united ancient state in history, and the most crystallized

1 Salāḥ Jawdat, *al-Muṣawwar,* Cairo, February 1962, quoted in *Orient,* no. 27, 176.

2 Ghassān Tuwaynī, *Manṭiq al-quwwa,* Beirut 1954, 93; *al-Nahār,* Beirut, 26 February 1954.

3 Gamal Abdul Nasser, *Egypt's liberation,* Washington D.C. 1955, 33–5; Arabic, 21–3.

of 'hydraulic' societies ... the centralism of control and management, and sometimes of ownership, in the economic sphere under the uniform authority of the state was likely to increase the function and importance of the government service to an unusual degree."[4] Wallace's observation of 80 years ago that "There is perhaps no people in the world more submissive to authority and more easily governed than the Egyptians" may be correct even today.[5] But neither was the Egypt of 1952 all degeneration and corruption as described in the *Philosophy*; without meaning to, Nasser becomes one of those who has nothing good to say about another Egyptian. There were certainly then in Egypt persons who strove for freedom and progress, devoted individuals and constructive forces. Although they were relatively few in number, disunited and scattered, the question was whether those coming to power would find them, stimulate them, and spur them on into action. However, for this the Free officers were neither prepared nor capable. Furthermore, these forces were first of all leftist elements—the progressive intellectuals and industrial workers. The Kafr Dawar incident indicates that long before the period of Arab socialism there were in Egypt conscientious workers ready for a struggle—and the same incident shows just how those officers turned against them. To the extent that they sought the aid of certain elements of the population, these were forces of the right, such as 'Alī Māhir and the Muslim Brethren. But the Free Officers had to break with them as well once they discovered their reactionary nature. For they really do wish to change Egyptian society and have constantly been searching for a broad political public champion of their ideas. Their experience has taught them that it is impossible to build socialism without socialists. But in the political climate of the regime, a dynamic, active public organization cannot grow or flourish even if the leadership itself desires to foster it. This is perhaps its most pressing problem—and all attempts to solve it have failed.

First the "Liberation Rally" was formed. In January 1958, five years after its establishment, it was dissolved because "traitors" had entered its ranks, and because it did not achieve its goals.[6] It was supplanted by the National Union, a complicated organization with a ramified structure[7] in order to assure "a people's government by the people,"[8] in the words of

4 Anouar Abdel-Malek, 'Nasserism and socialism', *The socialist register 1964*, New York 1964, 47.

5 D. Mackenzie Wallace, *Egypt and the Egyptian question,* London 1883, 138.

6 Shimon Shamir, 'Hamesh shanim shel irgun ha-shihrur be-Mitzrayim', *Hamizrah,* vol. 8, 277.

7 *MER* 1960, 478–83.

8 *Ibid.,* 484; *al-Ahrām,* 21 June 1960.

Kamāl al-Dīn Ḥusayn. At the end of 1961, after Syria's secession from the UAR, this was also dissolved since "reactionaries, the old feudal lords and the capitalists" had made themselves masters of it and occupied positions in most of its institutions and committees. In its place, the Arab Socialist Union was established. Preparations, discussions and elections to its institutions lasted from 1962 to 1963 with great pains being taken to avoid repeating previous errors. The regulation that at least 50% of the representatives in all its institutions must be workers or farmers is supposed to serve as the principal guarantee of its popular, revolutionary character. A worker is defined as a person who has the right to join a trade union. The experience of workers' movements throughout the world has taught that requiring workers to be represented on management boards often drives a wedge between them and the other workers, transforming them into management's representatives vis-à-vis the others. A farmer was originally defined as a person owning not more than five feddans of land; but later the definition was changed, and a farmer is anyone who possesses up to 25 feddans.[9] Actually, an owner of more than ten feddans is an employer and exploiter of hired labor. The Socialist Union is no more of a "popular base" than the other organizations which failed.

The dilemma of leadership which cannot realize its tasks without a public organization, on the one hand, and which cannot allow the existence of an independent body, on the other, is reflected in numerous accounts and articles in the Egyptian press. Here are a few examples: The correspondent of *Rūz al-Yūsuf* wrote the following after interviewing several people in the streets of Damietta: "Many people told me that numerous members of the district council of the Socialist Union should be dismissed. Several of them have previously been members of the 'Liberation Rally', then they went over to the National Union, and now they intend to take over the Socialist Union. This means that what will happen is simply a change in the label. People also claimed that the members of the district council are exploiters."[10] In the same weekly there are accounts of meetings conducted throughout the country for the purpose of "imbuing people with awareness." "In the village of Zerqā the brother of one of the prime ministers in the former regime sat in the first row. An engineer standing beside me told me that this man had prepared a sumptuous meal to which he was inviting the government representatives who had participated in the mass meeting of the Socialist Union. . . . In the village of 'Izbat al-Burj wealthy owners of fishing boats were sitting there who exploit the workers, and they

[9] Peter Mansfield, *Nasser's Egypt*, Penguin Books, 1965, 201.
[10] *Rūz al-Yūsuf*, 18 March 1963.

were the first to applaud every word uttered against reaction . . . In the village of Sa'ad landlords who possess large holdings in the vicinity were sitting up front at the meeting. These were the ones who had seized control of the National Union by means of an agreement among the big landowning families and without any elections at all . . . "[11]

In view of all these facts the search for a solution continues, for, "without a political organization, there is no guarantee for the continuance of the revolution," in the words of the headline to an article written by Khālid Muḥī al-Dīn in January 1965. He explains that the political organization must be "the pivot for the success of socialist policy." Its function is like that of the "nervous system in the human body." In dwelling upon questions of agriculture as a sphere of decisive importance, he writes, "We want cooperative agriculture which will lay the foundations of socialism in the villages. We want to develop large-scale agriculture which will at the same time eliminate the remnants of exploitative capitalism; but in attempting to implement this, we are confronted by two conflicts: a) Big landlords whose agriculture is based on exploiting the labor of others. The Revolution has reduced the harmfulness of this class by agrarian reform laws as well as by *The Charter* which pointed to the need for lowering the maximum holdings to 100 feddans per family, i.e., an average of 25 feddans per person. There is no doubt that the agricultural revolution and its continuance will arouse hostility and opposition among the landowners to whom the agrarian reform laws apply, and every revolutionary act will only be carried out at the expense of class interests, as the President has made clear in his speech. We do not hate the men of this class as such. We allow them and make it possible for them to merge with the ranks of the laboring classes—if they acknowledge the Revolution's laws and measures. But shall we content ourselves with enacting laws which are only honored superficially by the men of this class? Many of them are benefitting from errors in implementation. They are exploiting the advantages which the state is granting to agriculture for the purpose of consolidating their position. They will act in order to delay the revolutionary measures designed to help the small fellah and tenant farmer, and they will be the first to criticize mistakes in implementation. The conflict between the Revolution and village reaction will not be eliminated by publishing laws, and a long struggle will be necessary against the reactionaries and their activities and against the confusion created by their views. b) The second conflict, which is essentially quite different, is between the Revolution's desire for socialist progress and a number of the small farmers themselves. The

[11] *Ibid.*, 25 March 1963.

socialist revolution aspires to realize the interests of that class . . . There is no conflict of interests between socialist progress and the small farms. The conflict arises from other sources: The small fellah is by nature suspicious of any innovation. There is no doubt that society's intervention in order to convince the fellah of the advantages of large-scale, planned agriculture is based on strong motives and assures him that neither his rights nor his property will be harmed. However, the fellah is not easily convinced, and he is especially suspicious of persons sent by the government because of a complex which has been deeply rooted for generations. But large-scale agriculture means that large numbers of experts and technicians, including engineers, veterinarians, bookkeepers, etc., will stream to the villages . . . It happens that experts deal with problems by means of administrative machinery without any regard for the opinions of the fellaheen. And a wrong attitude towards the fellah only increases his suspicions . . . We must distinguish between these two kinds of conflicts and never confuse them. The first kind of conflict is the opposition of a group hostile to the socialist revolution, whereas the other consists of secondary conflicts among the masses with an interest in this revolution. Should we wish to translate these abstract terms into definite hypotheses and put them into actual practice in our everyday life, we shall arrive at the problem of a guiding political organization." On one side stand the "village notables" with the money and the say, while facing them are the small fellaheen to whom the law grants numerous rights, but they lack know-how and experience, so that their affairs are often ignored, "and more than once do they yield and are dragged along behind the notables either by force, willingly or because of traditional habits. The small farmers and agricultural workers still require training and practical political guidance . . . in order to be able to manage their affairs and properly protect their rights." And there is no solution to all these problems except the formation of nuclei of "politically aware individuals among the fellaheen themselves in each and every village."[12]

This article, like others which have been appearing in ever-increasing numbers since the summer of 1964, speaks the language of Marxism. While emphasizing that Arab socialism has no intention of harming the rich fellaheen who possess up to 100 feddans—"We are not hostile to the people of this class as such"—it stresses the existence and influence of class conflicts and calls on the small fellaheen and the village poor to carry on their class struggle. It leaves no room for the illusion that the fellaheen will be liberated unless they are led by an independent, politically conscious

[12] *Akhbār al-Yawm,* Cairo, 29 January 1965.

champion of their cause. However, how can this champion act when it is clear in advance and decreed from above that it is forbidden to object to the very property and position of the wealthy villagers who own tens of feddans? The dilemma remains.

The writer of this article is Khālid Muḥī al-Dīn, one of the veteran leaders of the Free Officers, who was already close to the communists in the early 1950's; in 1954 he was dismissed and fled to Switzerland. In December 1955 he returned to Egypt and in 1956 and 1957, during the Egypto-Soviet rapprochement and the Suez crisis, he once more took part in public life, although in roles of secondary importance—as editor of the daily *al-Masā'* and as a member of the National Assembly; in the summer of 1957 he visited China and was received by Chou En-Lai. In March 1959, during the acrimonious dispute between Nasser and Khrushchev and the campaign of mass arrests of communists and other leftists in Egypt, he was dismissed from his position as editor of *al-Masā',* arrested and imprisoned.[13] In 1961 he was free again, and at the end of the year he represented Egypt at the council of the Peace Movement in Stockholm.[14] In 1964, with Khrushchev's visit to Egypt and the strengthening of the friendly relations with the Soviet Union, he again rose to the top rank of the journalistic machine. His checkered career symbolizes the fate of the entire Egyptian left after 1952. Like him, many tens of leftists were arrested in 1959 and, like him, all of them—except those who had died after torture in concentration camps—were set free in 1964; many were permitted to serve in important posts in the fields of radio, book publishing and the press.

The activity of leftists was permitted as the result of various factors. One of them is the ever-increasing solidarity of Egypto-Soviet relations. Another is the Egyptian government's need of the former communists' services; it requires their talents and their experience. In view of the stupidity of the bureaucracy and the indifference of the masses, it does not want to give up the contribution they can make to Arab socialism. Moreover, the former and crypto-communists were to play an important role in the struggle for influence and power between two main factions, headed by 'Alī Ṣabrī and Zakariyyā Muḥī al-Dīn respectively, which unfolded in the middle of the sixties, and which became most intensive in the aftermath of the defeat in the Six-Day War in 1967. 'Alī Ṣabrī's faction, advocating radicalism in internal politics and all-out collaboration with the Soviet Union in external affairs, is relying on their support, and they, in turn, are interested in its victory.

[13] *Hamizrah,* vol. 7, 123; vol. 8, 299; vol. 9, 72; vol. 10, 207.

[14] *Al-Hamishmar,* Tel Aviv, 19 December 1961.

The leftists themselves are wondering what lies in store for them. They discuss at length whether they will really be allowed to influence state policy or only be exploited for ends which are not theirs; and they ask themselves whether a return to the suppressive measures and arrests of 1959 is not in the offing if they raise their heads a little too high. They generally tend to be optimistic about the answers to these questions; their assessment of the situation is that in relations with the Soviet Union, as well as in internal Egyptian social and political dynamics, Nasser has reached a point of no return. In any case, they prefer high-salaried positions on the editorial staffs of newspapers, with their comments appreciated even in Moscow, to sitting in concentration camps.

The authorities put the left exactly in its place. The position was clearly explained by Muḥammad Ḥasanayn Haykal. In an article in which he reminded the Egyptian communists of all their past mistakes and failures, he wrote, "I see no future for communism and the communists either in Egypt or in the Arab world. I do not say this because of a difference of opinion between communism and me but because I see—and I believe correctly—all of Arab reality and its historical process. However, my opinion of the future of communism and communists is one thing, and the struggle against them by means of the police and prisons is an entirely different matter. This does not mean that today I am demanding that communism and communists have a political party in Egypt as they do in the United States or Britain. What I mean to say, clearly and explicity, is that there is no longer any need, value or logic in any police action against communism and communists. And in my opinion, this means that the time has come to allow them to have their say, and that society should listen to them as much as it wants and reject what appears contrary to its wishes. Nevertheless, there are still instances which require resort to the law and, if necessary, to the police as well, in order to strike against communism and the communists if they do something which is against the basic principles of *The Charter*. For example: The attempt by communism or the communists to found an open or secret political party. This is against the free national will, which has established that political activity at the present stage should be entirely under the leadership of the league of the people's laboring forces and solely within their governing organization, which is the Socialist Union. An instance of this sort is against *The Charter* and the constitution and, therefore, the law is entitled and even required to intervene and strike back. Another example: An attempt by communism and the communists to impugn the message and precepts of religion. This, too, is against the elementary human faith in which our society, which respects religions and clings to their spiritual values and protects them, believes . . . Egyptian society is now able to take the matter of communism and the communists for granted . . . They can say whatever they please providing no activity will be against the principles and basic values in which the overwhelming majority of society believes and which it has placed above all law and justice."[15]

These statements were endowed with additional force by the President. At the National Assembly Aḥmad Sa'īd, the extremist nationalist propagandist, contended that the communists were given too much freedom and influence. Nasser pointed out his error: He threatened that anyone attempting to establish a communist organization would be arrested, "Even if we have to do it as in India [where communists were then arrested wholesale and without a trial]. Aḥmad Sa'īd spoke of the press and said that we are handing it over to the communists. When I appointed Khālid Muhī al-Dīn to *Akhbār al-Yawm,* it was in the knowledge that Khālid Muhī al-Dīn is part of the regime and not a part of the communists. I spoke with him and I am absolutely certain of what he told me. We will under no circumstances deliver the press to the communists, and we will not permit a single one of them to form an organization in the country. In my opinion, anyone who says he is a Marxist is free to do so. However, the establishment of a political organization is against the league of popular laboring forces."[16]

The meaning of these statements is clear: Marxist views are permissible, but whoever attempts to conduct organized activity accordingly is risking his life. Marxists are entitled, and even invited, to utilize the perfected tool of their thinking for explaining and buttressing government policy, but reaching independent, critical conclusions is absolutely forbidden. Marx said that the philosophers have only *interpreted* the world in various ways, while it was necessary to *change it*. Haykal and Nasser come and say to Marxists, "Interpret the world as much as you like, but do not attempt to change it."

Following the statements of Haykal and Nasser, the communists took an additional step towards their guided integration into the regime and announced the dissolution of their party. In 1961, during their imprisonment in the concentration camp of Abū Za'bal, the members of the various communist factions founded the United Egyptian Communist Party. Khrushchev then criticized Nasser. In 1964 he paid him an extended visit after which the Egyptian communists were released from prison—and from their party. In attempting to explain their program, they established the

15 *Al-Ahrām,* 29 January 1965.
16 *Ibid.,* 12, 13 March 1965.

primacy of foreign policy over domestic policy, and, in fact, mutual Soviet-Egyptian support in international relations took on new dimensions. From the beginning of 1965 there was no longer a contradiction between loyalty to Nasser and loyalty to the Soviet Union; the leftists only gave their explanations a nuance of their own. For example, when in the spring of 1965 a debate was conducted with Bourguiba on the questions of Arab-Israeli-West-German relations, the leftists attacked Bourguiba first and foremost because of his Western orientation, and only secondly because of his moderate attitude towards Israel, while others chiefly denounced him because of his deviation from the united Arab anti-Israel front. The difference remained one of emphasis; the Egyptian left did not reach, or did not want to reach, an independent position. When in 1967 the Soviets and the Egyptians together gave first place in their campaign of hostility to the vilification of Israel, the communists followed suit obediently and willingly.

The conference called by the leading Egyptian communist party (*Al-ḥaraka al-dīmūqrātiyya lil-taḥrīr al-waṭanī,* [Haditu], The Democratic Movement for National Liberation) on the eve of the presidential elections on March 14, 1965, for the purpose of disbanding itself, pointed proudly to the history of the party which "was the vanguard of the social and national struggle before the Revolution, participated in its emergence, and together with it conducted the fight against imperialism, aggression, exploitation and their reactionary plots, and against the threats of imperialism, its creation Israel, and Arab and international reaction."[17] At the same time, the 38 signatories of the resolution—who were still in "political isolation"—decided to "utilize our voting right and vote for Nasser" who "enriched revolutionary thought with new treasures," and to dissolve their independent political organization and join the Socialist Union as individuals. In April 1965 the other faction, the Egyptian Communist Party, adopted a similar resolution.[18]

The idyll did not last long. In October 1965, after the appointment of Zakariyyā Muḥī al-Dīn as prime minister, Khālid Muḥī al-Dīn was relieved of his duties as manager of *Akhbār al-Yawm.*[19] To be sure, Zakariyyā is Khālid's cousin and often saved him from worse harm than dismissal. At this time, economic difficulties and oppositional sentiment among the population mounted, but the communists, who had just proclaimed their absolute

[17] *Orient,* no. 34, 1965, 175–9 (the date is erroneously given as March 24, instead of March 14); Sāmī Dā'ūd, 'Ḥawla wiḥdat al-ishtirākiyyīn', *Al-Kātib,* Cairo, June 1965; *Al-Ittiḥād,* Haifa, 23 February 1962.

[18] Sāmī Dā'ūd, *loc. cit.*

[19] Arnold Hottinger, *Neue Zürcher Zeitung,* 2 November 1965.

identification with the regime, could no longer serve as an adress for them. What they had gained by obsequiousness they lost in influence. In the new wave of soul searching there were some who recalled that Peking, in contrast with Moscow, had never required the unreserved support of Nasser. But these were very few. When in 1966 and 1967 Soviet support for Egypt's policies became most massive and vociferous, the Egyptian communists were no longer able to play an independent role.

The swift military debacle in the Six-Day War of 1967 was as enormous as the gap between the proclamations of Egypt's leaders and the realities of Egyptian life. The defeat was the outcome and the reflection of the regime's inherent weakness. Haykal formulated the problem quite judiciously in one of his weekly articles in the summer of 1967: "It is not enough to have democracy of assent; what we are in need of is democracy of participation."[20] The following period was characterized by intensive efforts of Nasser to reorganize and revitalize the Arab Socialist Union. Enthusiastic speeches, criticism of past shortcomings, detailed new programs for organization and democratization, and new elections—all these were merely repetitions of what had already been done and what had already failed thrice. The illness has become has become more severe but it is not new, and so its diagnosis has been known for years; but no real progress in curing it can be seen.

The leadership has repeatedly attempted for more than fifteen years to organize and activate a "popular base" for the regime which would simultaneously be both dynamic and obedient. In this respect Egypt is unique. In Syria and Iraq the relations between the officer politicians and the broad public poses a perennial critical problem—but inversely to that of Egypt. The difference lies not only in the fact that in Egypt a united group has maintained a prolonged stable government, whereas in the other two countries we find the exact opposite of continuity, unity and stability. The problem in Egypt is how to establish a mass organization, while in Syria and Iraq it is how to curb the initiative and activity of parties, either of the right or the left, which regard themselves as full partners in governing the state, and which sometimes even fight the officers for hegemony.

The Free Officers' seizure of power in Egypt was accompanied by the crushing of all the traditional political parties. In Iraq and Syria, however, underground or opposition parties generally emerged together with the military coups, beginning with that of Bakr Ṣidqī. Only Ḥusnī Za'īm—and to a certain extent Shīshaklī—established and maintained his regime without ties or cooperation with a party organization.

[20] *Al-Ahrām*, 11 August 1967.

All the others were aided by parties and later fought them: In Iraq, beginning with Bakr Ṣidqī's ties with *al-Ahalī* until the affair with Arif and the Ba'th; in Syria, beginning with Ḥinnāwī's ties with the People's Party until the the partnership of Amīn al-Ḥāfiẓ and the Ba'th.

From the point of view of relations between government and citizens 'Abbūd's six years of dictatorship in Sudan were of a completely different character: He not only suppressed all public bodies, political parties and workers' organizations which had been active previously; he even thought that establishing a new public organization in their place was unnecessary and even fraught with danger. His was an open, exclusive military dictatorship. And it ended in a popular uprising and the extirpation of military rule. 'Abbūd wished to solve the dilemma of the officers' regime and the public base by treating it as if it did not exist—and it was solved by the total disappearance of the officers' government.

Common to all Arab regimes founded by officers' coups and headed by officer politicians is the unique complexity of the problem of relations between the group in power and the general public. In every case, whether the leadership seeks to stimulate public activity or to silence and paralyze it, the officers' regime is always confronted with the same predicament of having at one and the same time to look for support as well as to weaken it. This is the inherent dilemma of the government of officer politicians—the dilemma and not the dialectics, for in no case has it been solved; military rule has never brought about a synthesis of dictatorship and democracy. As relatively easy as the seizure of power is for those who control the state's organized machinery for violence, so is the job of maintaining it difficult.

CONCLUSION

THE OFFICERS AND THE ARAB REVOLUTION

"Then said all the trees unto the bramble: Come thou, and reign over us. And the Bramble said unto the trees: If in truth ye annoint me king over you, then come and take refuge in my shadow; and if not, let fire come out of the bramble, and devour the cedars of Lebanon."

Judges 9: 14,15

CONCLUSION: THE OFFICERS AND THE ARAB REVOLUTION

TWENTY NINE years passed between the appearance of Aḥmad 'Urābī on the political scene in 1879, and the Young Turks' revolution in 1908. After that victory of Ottoman officers another 28 years elapsed until the first officers' coup in an independent Arab country, that of Bakr Ṣidqī in 1936. An additional 28-year period, replete with coups of Arab officer politicians, passed and in 1964, for the first time in modern Arab history, a military dictatorship was toppled by a popular uprising, in Sudan. Three times after a span of a generation a new chapter began in the annals of officers' intervention in Middle-Eastern politics, and during each period the outlook of Arab nationalism changed. Its primary aim, national independence, was achieved, with one exception—it failed to prevent Jewish independence in Palestine. The political position of the Arabs in the world reached an importance unequalled for centuries. Concurrently with this growth and increase in power, social and political differentiation became progressively sharper in Arab society. Although the enhanced prestige of the Arabs in the international scene could have contributed to self-confidence, unity and stability, the factors undermining stability and self-confidence had a stronger effect. The penetration of capitalistic elements into the economy, the influence of new ideas, revolutions in Europe and Asia, the shrinking gaps in contact throughout the world—all these gave rise to an acute sensation of backwardness.

Arab nationalism was now permeated with an atmosphere of "the revolution of rising expectations." The second chapter (the most important one, after the first general introductory chapter) of the Egyptian *National*

Charter of 1962 is entitled: "The Necessity of the Revolution". The designation "revolutionary" has become the most sought-after honorary title among the Arabs.

The officer politicians believe that they are the liberators of revolutionary energy in the Arab nation; they are the ones who will lead the revolution to victory. In the words of M. Halpern, the army has changed its function "from Praetorian Guard to advance guard". It has become the advance guard by virtue of being "the instrument of the new middle class".[1] It is the middle class of non-proletarian wage-earners including persons—those employed as well as the unemployed with similar training and aspirations who seek employment—who are members of the liberal professions—university graduates, technicians, officials in governmental and private enterprises, teachers, officers, and the like. Halpern does not explain whether the army has become the instrument of this class out of a conscious intention; and if the question were asked, it would also be impossible to find an all-inclusive answer. At any rate, he regards the army as the unmistakable representative of this class and sees its rise as the expression of the historical trend of the class. "As the army officer corps came to represent the interests and views of the new middle class, it became the most powerful instrument of that class. The army's great strength being in the kind of men who joined it, the opportunities at their disposal and the weakness of competing institutions. In contrast to most Mid-Eastern political parties, armies are disciplined, well-organized, and able to move into action without securing the voluntary consent of their members . . . and are more prone to rebel against the status quo."[2] However, on acceding to power, the officers have become, thanks to their personal and group characteristics, the advance guard of the rising salaried middle class, and with it, of the whole of society. For this class is "the principal revolutionary—and potentially stabilizing force"[3] in the changes taking place in contemporary Middle-Eastern society.

Halpern points to the region on the socio-political map of the Arab world in which officer politicians should be sought. But his definitions should not be accepted without reservations. They are oversimplified generalizations, treating the officer corps "from Morocco to Pakistan" as being of a piece. They overlook the numerous fundamental differences in the officer corps of the various countries as well as within each of the armies—differences in origin and aims and conflicting ties, interests and outlook.

[1] Manfred Halpern, *The politics of social change in the Middle East and North Africa,* Princeton 1963, 253.

[2] *Ibid.,* 258–9.

[3] *Ibid.,* 51.

The one very important generalization which is correct is the fact that the officer corps does not represent the class which was the direct successor of colonial rule in the Arab countries: the large landlords and their intellectual hangers-on. The unbridled class interests of these feudalist oligarchs coupled with the sterile toughness of their intellectual and social conservatism had brought them into increasingly serious clashes with demands for national and social progress, and their governments have rapidly degenerated and collapsed. When the capitalist bourgeoisie largely consisted of foreign nationals and members of local minority groups, and organized, class-conscious forces had not yet crystallized among the workers and fellaheen, a power vacuum or stalemate came into being in which the officers could carry out their coups and seize control. However, the fact that the officer corps is not connected with the most reactionary class and that it seized power while engaged in a bitter struggle with it does not automatically ordain the officer corps as representing per se the best possible aspects of progress, as if it were taken for granted that it is the advance guard of all the forces which upon liberating themselves also set free all of society, that is the vanguard of that class whose class struggle serves the best historical interests of the entire nation, and the breaking of whose chains heralds liberty for all.

Many Arab officers and the large majority of those participating in coups are the representatives of the salaried middle class, of managers, officials and intellectuals. From these they derive their support. These are the forces which they set in operation and foster; their function is chiefly technocracy and bureaucracy, while supreme powers are left in the hands of the army command. Thus, in the long run, the rise of the officers constitutes an expression of the upsurge of these elements and the alimination of obstacles from their path. The officers, technocrats and intellectuals do not themselves have any prospects of owning the large means of production, and so they display no interest in having such enterprises transferred to their ownership. They are concerned with managing the economy, in controlling it and the state, and in seeing to it that the large means of production and key enterprises do not come under the ownership or control of another class. Accordingly, they are interested in having the state own the conomy, when the state is under their control. This is the source of the various forms of Arab etatism and socialism. The most serious rival of the salaried middle class is that part of the bourgeoisie which long before this had already embodied private initiative, established independent capitalist enterprises and amassed wealth—the recipients of government concessions and orders, the importers, merchants and bankers. The most active and successful members of this bourgeoisie were, until a few years ago, foreign nationals or citizens of the state belonging to minority groups, especially in Egypt, less strikingly in Syria, so that the war against them and the ideology serving them assume the form of aggressive nationalism.

But the Arab officer corps is not a single uniform group. It is not only the representative of the salaried middle class. Many officers have family and social ties with capitalists and businessmen and these are not discriminated against by the new regime. The officers permit and even encourage the former proprietors to share in the management of their enterprises after nationalization or to serve as capitalists in enterprises conducted under joint public and private ownership, with Muslims clearly preferred.

Particularly ramified and important are the ties of many officers with well-to-do farmers. Like office workers and intellectuals generally in the Arab world, many officers are of rural origin, the sons and brothers of village notables of all kinds—of the wealthy fellaheen with farms of several tens of feddans in Egypt and of several hundreds of dunams in Syria and Iraq. In contrast to the large urban absentee landlords, many of these wealthy notables live in the village itself; they are the village strongmen who exploit the hired agricultural laborers and the tenants directly, sometimes in the harshest fashion. The interests of this class conflict with those of the large landowners, competing with them for the acquisition of the plot of a small fellah who has gone into bankruptcy or has become a laborer. But the interests of these wealthy villagers conflict no less with the aspirations and demands of the poor villagers, the masses of small fellaheen and tenants, and the propertyless agricultural workers. The well-to-do farmers are prepared to agree to the nationalization of industrial enterprises, transport, irrigation, even to the expropriation of lands from large estates, especially when part of the expropriated land becomes theirs. However, where their own possessions are concerned, they firmly defend the sanctity of private property. Our discussion of the social origin of the officers in the Arab armies and their activities as rulers showed that a considerable number are connected with this village middle class, and that they have carefully protected the possessions and interests of the village strongmen. Furthermore, the position of the well-to-do farmers has grown stronger. The agrarian reforms which were introduced by the officers' governments eliminated the economic power and political influence of those who were above them in the village; and all the agrarian reforms have thus far stopped at a rather high ceiling of land ownership without adversely affecting the class of well-to-do farmers. Of the lands which were expropriated or on the verge of being expropriated from the large landlords, a large percentage came into the hands of these wealthy villagers. Their share in political power is not especially large, their initiative and activity in the dynamics of the economic changes are limited, but the interests of this class are protected and it constitutes one of the foundations of the military dictatorship.

There are undoubtedly conflicts between the interests of the well-to-do villagers, basically conservative, and the outlook and aspirations of the representatives of the urban and salaried middle class, the intellectuals and the technocrats, who stand or fall with the implementation of profound changes. Under the pressure of development needs, they may not leave the well-to-do farmers untouched for long. In Egypt, for example, should the agrarian reform be extended to include the lands of persons owning from 25 to 100 feddans, it would constitute an act of concrete revolutionary significance. However, thus far such measures have not been adopted, and the officers' governments have been relying on the common interests of the urban middle class and the village well-to-do.

The officers, technocrats, intellectuals and village rich men all oppose both the feudalism of the large landlords and the capitalism of private industrial and commercial investments. All this is clearly emphasized in the ideology of Arab socialism; this is the common denominator of many Arab socialist ideologies. Less stressed, but no less determined, is the joint opposition of the managers and well-to-do fellaheen to the aspirations of the workers and the village poor. They favor the active participation of large parts of the population in building the new social system; otherwise every program of modernization will fail. However, under no circumstances can they agree to the free organization of workers and fellaheen nor permit them to wage their own struggle for their interests. This is the ever-present dilemma of officers' regimes, their Achilles' heel. They are attempting to solve it by preaching democracy, on the one hand, and by tightening the dictatorship, on the other.

When all is said and done, the officers have the advantage over other candidates for power in their monopoly of institutionalized violence in an obedient, disciplined hierarchical organization; and the officer politicians have the advantage of not hesitating to utilize the instrument of violence of the state in the internal political struggle. The officers achieved power not because they were more adroit statesmen than their opponents, more profound ideologists or more moral. It suffices to have a look at the vicious criticism, sometimes accompanied by vicious deeds, of each one of these officers about the others in the course of their squabbles—Sabbāgh's remarks about Bakr Ṣidqī, Ḥinnāwī's vilification of Za'īm, Nasser on Naguib, Qassim on Arif and Arif on Qassim, and each one about everyone else. In recent years this criticism has become more exhaustive, and, from the denunciation of a certain man or government, has developed to the stage of complete negation in principle of the rule of the officer corps. Arab political thinkers themselves, to the extent they are able to express their views freely, are abandoning the doctrine of "the natural course" which postulates the rule of the officer corps as a necessary way-station on the road to progress. The Beirut *al-Hayāt* wrote a commentary on 'Alwān's attempted coup in Syria in 1963: "Last Thursday Damascus witnessed a new act in a Janissary performance: In broad daylight, after nightfall had served as their ally in previous coups, one of their groups slipped into the city and attacked the army headquarters and adjacent broadcasting station buildings in accordance with the tested tradition which bestows victory on whoever is first to broadcast communiqué No. 1 . . the modern Arab Janissaries are not a source of glory and pride as were the Ottoman. These days, after succesfully imposing their yoke on the population, they make no conquests, do not protect the country from misfortune and do not restore Palestine, but their cause is limited to efforts to seize power, to arbitrary acts, and to the abuse of citizens and laws, and the coups succeeding one another throw the country into an upheaval and hurt people." For added emphasis, this article appeared under the

زعين : — ما فهمان من هالصورة شي ؟
المواطن السوري : — ليش سيادتك فهمان الوضع حتى تفهم الصورة ؟!

"The situation in Syria" (the caption on the canvas).
Zv'ayyin (the Prime Minister):
"I cannot understand the meaning of this picture?"
The Syrian citizen (the painter):
"If Your Excellency understands the situation, you should also understand the picture!"
A cartoon in *Al-Hawādith* of Beirut, March 11, 1966.

headline, *The modern Janissaries*.[4] Demonstrators against Boumedienne in Algiers in June 1965 shouted in the same spirit, "We don't want the policies of the Arab East!" The unsuccessful civilian uprising in Syria against the military dictatorship in the spring of 1964, and the civilian revolt in Khartoum in October 1964 which destroyed the military dictatorship in Sudan are to be seen in the same light. Precisely in that country where in 1958 the seizure of power by the officer corps was described as the "natural course", and in which the most undisguised, and ostensibly the most stable, officers' government existed for six years, precisely there, the military dictatorship completely collapsed, overthrown by a civilian rebellion.

This is not to imply that the sole motivation of the officer politicians is a lust for power. They hold political views which they would like to put into practice—although the bare desire for power which characterizes all of them, without exception, should not be overlooked. They regard themselves as intellectuals imbued with a national mission. But in none of these do they differ essentially from other groups of intellectuals or politicians. Their decisive superiority is the physical power of a company of soldiers over a students' demonstration, the force of an order over a speech, the might of a tank over a ballot box.

The Islamic heritage and the tradition of the Arab national movement prepare the soil for military dictatorships, but, nevertheless, their legitimacy always remains doubtful, and upon seizing power, the officers generally devote considerable effort to finding public and legal justification for this usurpation and to creating the popular base which did not exist previously. The officer corps is not above or outside the class structure nor does it constitute a class of its own. An army which brutally interferes in the internal political struggles of a country can no longer demand for itself the right to stand above all contending groups.

Social background is no indicator of ideology. It was precisely the intellectuals, intellectuals in uniform too, who often produced the forerunners of revolutionary thought and organization and assumed the leadership of a rising oppressed class. The classic example is Karl Marx. Old Bolshevik leaders, headed by Lenin, were for the most part not the sons of workers or peasants. However, these revolutionaries sought and found the way to the people in whose name and in the name of whose historical mission they spoke; they not only guided it but also stirred it to action. Although they were the vanguard of the masses, in their own class they were a minority. The majority of the middle-class intellectuals of the generation of Marx and Lenin remained loyal to their class. Revolutionaries passing from one

[4] *Al-Ḥayāt,* 21 July 1963.

class to another are pioneers, the exception and not the rule. The same applies to Arab officers, the sons of well-to-do farmers and members of the middle class: Individuals developed radical views, and of these, more went to the extreme right than the left. However, tha majority remained, intentionally or as a matter of course, the representatives and the emissaries of the well-to-do middle class. No Marx or Lenin appeared among them.

The officer politicians boast of carrying out a revolution, and they have indeed been implementing far-reaching political changes. However, more than *carrying out* a revolution, they are *preventing* one. In advancing the industrialization of the Arab countries, they are spurring the growth of a workers' class, but they are largely preventing thc workers from waging their class struggle and their own revolution by bribing the labor-aristocracy, by dividing the workers, by diverting their feelings of solidarity to nationalist goals and, when all else fails, by brutal suppression. The same applies to the fellaheen.

In his book on the role of the military in politics, Finer cites an anecdote about Huey Long, the American leader and demagogue in the early 1930's. Asked by a newspaperman, if he thought there would be Fascism in the United States, Long replied, "Sure, but we'll call it anti-Fascism".[5] Thus military dictators call dictatorship "democracy". Ayūb Khan calls it "basic democracy" in Pakistan, Nasser once termed it "socialist-cooperative democracy"—but the content is the same. Whatever their good points in other fields, the governments of the Arab officers are all dictatorships. They have uprooted the seedlings of democracy which had begun to sprout in Egypt, Syria and Iraq. There is nothing easier than demonstrating that parliamentarism in those countries was defective. But what has supplanted it is neither less corrupt nor more stable and is not likely to liberate the constructive forces of the people nor inspire them to action. The remedies which critics of the party system suggest are worse than the disease.

It is easy to prove that Western parliamentarism is not suited to the peoples of the Middle East. Sometimes, the dictators cite reasons for opposing it and depriving the people of their rights which are identical with the arguments formerly advanced by the spokesmen of colonialism for depriving a people of its national independence; and the result is always suppression. About the Egypt of 1882 Cromer wrote, "What Egypt most of all required was order and good government."[6] In 1930 the British Simon Commission wrote about India: "We think that Indians have been apt to be led astray by keeping the British Parliament too closely in view."[7]

[5] S.E. Finer, *The man on horseback,* London 1962, 237.

[6] The Earl of Cromer, *Modern Egypt,* London 1908, vol. 1, 427.

[7] Quoted in Hugh Tinker, *Ballot box and bayonet,* London 1964, 11.

We have already cited Ayūb Khan's speech in Egypt that, "The first condition for progress is political stability. We, like you, borrowed Western parliamentarism. It did not work."[8] In almost the same words, Hermann Goering said at the end of his life in 1945, "But democracy just won't work with the German people." Nasser humorously said, "Democracy, democracy—that's utopia."[10] Further examples are not necessary.

No one would suggest the mechanical transference of political systems from distant countries to the Arab states. If the Arab peoples, as is argued by imperialistic rulers and Arab monarchists and militarists, have not yet matured for a democratic life, they should be educated for it; and there is no worse educational system than beatings and orders. You can only learn to swim in water. Dictators regard their people with contempt and suspicion; independent forces are regarded as factors leading to destruction and anarchy. Yet the Arab nation does contain creative forces which would bear a rich harvest, if only allowed to grow. In the last two generations a large number of excellent writers, thinkers, political leaders and communal workers were active on the Arab scene. However, from the moment the officer politicians seized power, they never encouraged them; under the regimentation of dictatorship creative forces are pulverized. For example, the writers of the best works in modern Egyptian literature published their important books before 1952. The crop of the last fifteen years is poor, and not by chance. Nasser is certainly a more positive figure than Fārūq. However, the writers and journalists who burn incense in the personality cult of the President are no more positive than the king's toadies. And prior to 1952, the government had neither the ambition nor propaganda techniques to determine what each person should think about every matter.

Discussing the struggles of the Iraqi people since 1920, Mahdāwī said in 1958, "What people's revolutions, movements, demonstrations, awakening and uprising lacked was a popular leadership with an excellent military supreme command."[11] And Sādāt wrote in 1956 about Egypt, "In 1952, the Egyptian revolution was in need of a new leadership . . . and where could the popular leadership of the Egyptian revolution have revealed itself? From where among the millions of enslaved Egyptians could have come the leaders who would turn their faces to the people and their backs to imperialism and the court? These were only the armed

[8] Radio Cairo, 7 November 1960.

[9] J.M. Gilbert, *Nuremberg diary,* New York 1961, 59.

[10] Aḥmad Abū al-Fatḥ, *Jamāl 'Abd al-Nāṣir,* Beirut (1962 ?) 257; French: Ahmed Abul-Fath, *L'Affaire Nasser,* Paris 1962, 239.

[11] *Maḥkamat al-sha'b, Muḥākamāt al-maḥkama al-'askariyya al-khāṣṣa,* vol. 18, Baghdad 1962, 7239.

forces."[12] Mahdāwī and Sādāt, both enemies, both say the same thing, and both are wrong. Besides the armed forces, there also existed in 1952 the workers of Kafr Dawar, and many intellectuals who were inferior to the officers only in respect of the means of violence at their disposal.

The national liberation of Egypt, Syria, Sudan and Iraq was achieved *before* the officers' coups. Their coups were only possible in countries where there was no longer foreign rule. The officers completed the task which their predecessors could not or would not finish; but there were others besides them also capable of doing so. In most countries, the actual achievements of officers' governments are negligible, and the benefits of the changes are offset by constant bloody upheavals.

The Arab officer politicians stand revealed as bad statesmen. They reverse Clemenceau's statement that war is too serious a matter for its conduct to be left only to generals, and contend that politics should not be left to politicians. But Finer is right when he says, "There is no good reason why generals, colonels, or majors should make good politicians, and a fair number of prima facie reasons why they should make very bad ones."[13]

By education and habit, officers tend to act through commands rather than persuasion, to exact obedience instead of encouraging cooperation, and it makes no difference whether they use violence or only threaten to use it. The other side of violence or the threat of violence is terror. Fear prevails in every country where officers rule and its grip extends to the cery top. Dictators not only impose terror; they themselves live in perennial fear that what they did to their predecessors could be done to them. A visiting statesman from a non-Arab country who happened to be a guest in one of the Arab capitals several years ago reported that, in the course of a conversation with the officer who was prime minister at the time, a car suddenly stopped in front of the office with a screech of brakes; the prime minister leaped up from his chair and rushed to the window with a drawn pistol. This incident taught the visitor more about the nature of the regime than lengthy explanations. And, as a matter of fact, that regime has long since been overthrown. Courageous people can answer, as King Ḥusayn did when asked if he were not afraid of being murdered, that it is a professional risk. But a whole people cannot prosper in an atmosphere of constant fear. Furthermore, it is worthwhile for rulers to take risks, even if they do not do so for a great ideal—for this they are amply rewarded. The people, however, receive only slight recompense, not worth the high price.

[12] Anwar al-Sādāt, *Quṣṣat al-thawra kāmila,* Cairo 1956, 85–6.

[13] Finer, 196.

Every Arab officer participating in a coup is regarded as a savior by a part of the population, and he succeeds in presenting this segment of the populace as if it were the whole. This part of the people may, later on, cheer some other officer who has displaced his predecessor in a coup, and denounce their former hero as an enemy of the people. It may be asked, how deep into the country's social and political structure do the changes penetrate? It sometimes appears that under the tissue of enthusiasm and terror the people continue to live as before; the vicissitudes of the coups are like storms raging in the streets of a city while inside the houses the citizens conduct their lives as usual; when the storm subsides, they go outside and resume their business as before.

It is instructive to compare the results of parliamentary elections in Syria and Sudan before and after the periods of military dictatorship. We shall cite a number of comparative figures of the results of four elections to the Syrian assembly and of two elections in the Arab provinces of Sudan (excluding the non-Arab south). Since the number of deputies often changed, the figures are given in percentages of the total deputies elected. It should also be emphasized that the figures cannot be considered accurate. No party lists appeared in any of these elections, and the party affiliations of many candidates were invariably unclear both to themselves and to their friends and opponents. However, for the sake of comparison, these figures are instructive.

The years when Za'īm, Shīshaklī and Nasser ruled Syria and 'Abbūd held sway in Sudan were only an intermezzo in their history, and just as soon as the dictatorships were eliminated, the life of the country and the parties resumed their previous courses as if nothing had happened. There is even room for the thought that in Egypt, too, the old constellations still exist, and during the ferment and crisis of 1965—in the face of economic distress and the defeat in Yemen—they emerged from their hiding places: A dangerous underground of the Muslim Brethren was revealed; and the funeral of Muṣṭafā Naḥḥās, the former Wafd leader who died in August 1965 at the age of 86 and seemed to have been forgotten for years, suddenly turned into a mass demonstration in Cairo with the number of participants estimated at thirty thousand.[14]

Naturally, the past cannot be restored, nor is this desirable. In all the Arab countries profound changes are taking place, and sometimes the traditional name of a party which has not changed since the 1940's expresses new and different contents in the 1960's. Manifestations of con-

[14] H.J. Andel, 'Ägyptische Opposition gegen Nasser', *Aussenpolitik,* Freiburg i. Br., January 1966, 46.

SYRIAN ELECTIONS
In percentages of deputies elected

Date	July 1947 Before 1st coup	Nov. 1949 During Hinnāwī's regime	August 1954 After Shīshaklī's overthrow	Dec. 1961 After dissolution of UAR
National Party	17	11	13	14
Liberals	14			
Opposition Independents	24			
Independents close to the People's Party		17		
People's Party		38	21	22
Ba'th		1	15	14
Syrian Social Nationalist Party (SSNP)		1	1	1
Muslim Brethren and the like	3	3	2	7
Communists			1	
Independents, tribal representarives and others	42	29	47	42
(Number of deputies)	(140)*	(114)**	(142)	(172)

* The Liberals and Opposition Independents later united to form the People's Party.
** Hinnāwī supported the People's Party.

SUDANESE ELECTIONS
—except for the southern provinces—
in percentages of deputies elected

Date	February 1958 Before 'Abbūd's coup	May 1965 After ousting of 'Abbūd
Umma Party	45	47
National Union Party	33	33
People's Democratic Party	22	2
Beja Tribes Congress		6
Muslim Brethren		2
Independents		10
(Number of deputies)	(130)	(156)

tinuity and their significance should not be overlooked, but neither should they be overrated. Nor should one be led astray by the noisy propaganda of the insurrectionists who present themselves as revolutionaries. The furrows they plow are not as deep as they pretend.

Nasser's regime differs from all other governments in the Arab world. It is headed by an outstanding leader, Egyptian prestige has risen in the world, and during a sufficiently lenghty period a stable government has crystallized. Arab socialism is being praised by the leaders of the Soviet bloc and by enthusiastic crowds throughout the Arab world. However, when stripped of the mantle of propaganda, its successes appear to be quite modest. The basic problems of the Egyptian people—economic, social and spiritual—have not yet been solved. Nasser's principal achievements, except for the very existence of the government, were matters of foreign policy.

Since its leaders adopted neutralism in 1955, Egypt has liberated itself from dependence on the West, acquired much support in the East and developed its bargaining power both in the East and West. The nationalization of the Suez Canal and the construction of the High Dam with the assistance of the Soviet Union, the arms purchases from the Soviet Bloc, the numerous visits of the heads of Asian and African states to Cairo, and, especially, the repulsing of the Israeli-Anglo-French attack in the fall of 1956 were all recorded as great Egyptian victories. But another triumph, which at the time appeared to be the greatest of all, the union with Syria, led to the staggering defeat of Syria's secession.

Egyptian activity in the sphere of foreign policy has demanded great sacrifices. A heavy burden of immense armaments expenditures has been imposed on the Egyptian people. On the other hand, their military usefulness per se was always small. The Egyptian accomplishments were achieved by diplomacy and propaganda and not by military force. The Egyptian army was defeated in Sinai in 1956 in a few days. The cessation of the attacks and the withdrawal of foreign troops from Egyptian territory and the Gaza Strip were the result of pressure brought to bear by the Soviet Union and the United States together. After seven years of additional intensified rearming, the Egyptian army was unable to achieve a decisive victory in Yemen, even after four years of fighting. In Sinai in June 1967 Egypt suffered the heaviest and swiftest defeat.

Nasser's politics did not succeeded in enhancing Egypt's military power; but they demanded a high price from the Egyptian people. The cost of the Egyptian international ambitions is paid for by the other Arab peoples as well. The Egyptian policy of expansion and domination has shaken the foundations of a number of other Arab countries, and not only pro-

Western and monarchical regimes. Cairo's intervention and subversion has plunged the entire Middle East into a maelstrom of perennial upheavals. It has introduced a new style in inter-Arab relations, the style of political gangsterism. There is almost no Arab state whose heads have not at some time been the objects of Egyptian incitement to murder, and occasionally not only of incitement. These politics are distinguished by a unique mixture of grandiose pan-Arab utopian aspirations and shrewd realism. Nasser knows that a number of objectives should not be stormed simultaneously. Each time, he trains his sights on another opponent against whom he concentrates his assault of propaganda, diplomacy and subversion; others are granted a respite until the proper time comes and are allowed to toy with the illusion that they have been spared his attacks. Willy-nilly, he and his comrades have had to make compromises with other Arab regimes. But there are no indications that they have altered their basic intentions. They renounce mastery by force only when they do not have the force to make themselves masters.

A comparison is in order between Nasser and Atatürk, the two outstanding leaders of two great Middle East countries.

There are great differences in time and national circumstances between Turkey and Egypt, between the 1920's and the 1950's, between the dissolute unbeliever and the devout Muslim and father of a model family, between the man who died more than 25 years ago, whose life's work can be reviewed from a perspective and the man still only halfway along the road he has taken. Until 1952, moreover, Nasser was still unknown to the public and appeared as an entirely new figure; he was one of hundreds of colonels, and was known only as an excellent officer in military circles and as a political activist among several groups of conspirators. Atatürk, however, was already a general and a pasha and famed as a national hero when he assumed the leadership of the national struggle after World War I; he was the commander of the division which repulsed the great British offensive against the Dardanelles in 1915—"the only striking success won by the Ottoman army during the war."[15]

But the similarities between the two leaders are just as striking as the differences: The family background of petty officials; both were orphaned in early youth—Atatürk, of his father, and Nasser, of his mother; adolescence in cosmopolitan port-cities, in Salonika and Alexandria, where national contrasts loom sharply: a military career after completing studies in high school; joining nationalist, revolutionary, underground movements at an early age; frontline experiences in the Balkan Wars, World War II and

[15] Bernard Lewis, *The emergence of modern Turkey,* London 1961, 239.

the Palestine War, and excelling in leadership and bravery. Both of them acceded to power and greatness and became dictators primarily because of the military power at their disposal. Both of them displayed uncompromising zeal for national independence, and both achieved it. And each was aware of his nation's backwardness and aspired to radical modernization.

Atatürk went farther than Nasser, much farther, in his cultural revolutionary ideas. He established secularism and the separation of the church and state as a basic principle and aspired to sever Turkish nationalism and culture from Islam and do away with supra-national Islamic feeling of solidarity. Nasser, on the other hand, relies on the close emotional and historical association between Islam and Arabism.

Nasser goes much farther in economic and social spheres. Atatürk's etatism was intended to build the foundation of a modern national economy by means of the state, so that, later, on, capitalistic entreprises operating on private capital could base themselves on it; and that is what happened. Arab socialism can achieve a similar result, but its intention is directly the opposite, and general trends of development in the second half of the century eliminate such a possibility.

Atatürk and Nasser doffed their uniforms after having overcome their enemies and proclaimed the establishment of regimes which would no longer be ruled by the army and would develop in the direction of democratic freedom. Kemalistic Turkey consistently followed this road from 1920 to 1960. In the Grand National Assembly of 1920 one out of every seven deputies was an officer; in the 1943 legislature—after the death of Atatürk—one out of every eight; in 1950 one out of every 20, and in 1958 one out of every 25. Among the 35 personalities who served as ministers in governments between 1920 and 1923 there were only nine officers.[16] And what is more important: Atatürk aspired to establish a multi-party regime. In 1946 the opposition Democratic Party was founded, and in the 1950 elections, which were really free, it defeated the Republican People's Party, Atatürk's party. In the 1950's there was a parliamentary regime with good points and faults. In May 1960, exactly ten years after the formation of the first government of the Democratic Party, a new military coup took place, and a new army officers' dictatorship headed by Gürsel came into being. But from 1961 Turkey experienced the gradual restoration of democratically elected civilian government and a multi-party system. Nasser, too, is constantly making efforts to broaden the base of the government and foster popular autonomous support for it,

[16] *Ibid.*, 360, 456; Dankwart Rustow, 'The army and the founding of the Turkish republic', *World politics*, Princeton, July 1959, 535, 550.

but democracy exists only on the surface. As the dictatorship became stabilized and more popular, it assumed gentler forms, but did not change its nature. In elections the regime only permits personal rivalry at low levels among those loyal to it, and the margins permitted in the possible outcome of presidential elections is that between 99 and 100 per cent in favor.

The greatest difference between the policies of Atatürk and Nasser is in international orientation. Atatürk completely rejected the Ottoman imperialistic tradition, pan-Islamic tendencies and the pan-Turanian ideology of the Young Turks. Just as, after World War I, he repulsed the Greek expansionist aspirations on the Aegean shore of Asia Minor with a desperate effort and complete success, so did he explicitly and consistently renounce every aspiration of political expansion and cultural influence among the Turkish-speaking peoples in Central Asia, even before Soviet rule there had become an unshakable fact. With secularism and the abolition of the caliphate, he abandoned every attempt to seek Turkish hegemony or influence in Arab countries in the name of tradition or Islamic solidarity. How different the mentality and policies of Nasser are requires no itemization. If Turkey were not the only one but the largest of a number of Turkish countries, similar to Egypt's position among the Arab states, Atatürk, too, might have developed an expansionist ideology and policy. This is merely a matter for speculation, and it must by no means be taken for granted. The facts are as follows: Inside the country, Kemalist Turkey adopted a policy of forced assimilation towards the Kurds with a planned brutality which was the harshest suppression of a minority in the Middle East between both World Wars; externally it kept aloof from the affairs of neighboring countries, the only exception being the annexation of the district of Alexandretta on the eve of World War II, but this was the absorption of a border region of great strategic importance containing a mixed population. At the same time, even tempting assurances of ascendant Nazi Germany could not entice Turkey to expansionist aspirations. When in July 1938 the German Foreign Minister von Ribbentrop spoke of necessary revisions at the expense of "the status-quo powers", the Secretary-General of the Turkish Foreign Office, Menemencioğlu, replied that "Turkey on principle is in no need of revisions . . . and did not want to return to Ottoman Imperialism."[17] There remains the striking difference between Atatürk's isolationist nationalist orientation and Nasser's pan-Arab interference in others' affairs whether he has been asked to or not.

The apologists for military dictatorship who regard it as a natural course

[17] Heinz Tillman, *Deutschlands Araberpolitik im zweiten Weltkrieg,* Berlin 1965, 440.

in contemporary Arab history, argue that these upheavals and injustices should be considered as the byproducts of a period of *Sturm und Drang* in the modern Arab world, the birth pangs of a new era. As far as they are concerned, the criticism of dictatorship is only the cowardice of the fastidious, and evaluations based on the well-being of the general population and the freedom of the individual in the present generation are only philistine antipathy to a major act of daring without which great deeds cannot be done. However, the magnitude of the sweep and daring in itself does not determine the quality of the goal at which they aim; criminals and tyrants have often displayed no less courage and persistence in their pursuits than the fighters for freedom and progress, but they did not cease being criminals and tyrants. The flowery expression "birth pangs" often serves as an excuse for injustice. In anticipating the birth of a new human being, one expects a healthy child who will grow up properly. However, social changes are not always, and as such, changes towards progress. In macro-history, which measures the annals of mankind in periods of centuries, the advancement of man and society is apparent; in the micro-history of a generation or two, progress alternates with regression, the happiness of peoples with their exploitation, man's honor with his degradation.

Dictatorship does not get rid of itself. After seizing power through coups, the officers usually promise—falsely—in their early communiqués that when the time comes, they will return to their barracks and hand the government over to elected representatives of the people. However, the liquidation of a dictatorship is much more difficult than its establishment, and its self-liquidation, infinitely harder. When did such an event occur in any kind of dictatorship—revolutionary, proletarian, military or Fascist? The continuance of a dictatorship generally means its strengthening, and its end, when its comes, is not produced from within, but from outside.

Attemps to escape from the jaws of dictatorship were made in 1964 in Syria and in Sudan. The merchants' strike at Hama in April 1964 was the first serious movement in years to shake the government without officers directing its course. The government, which understood its significance well, had sufficient reasons for adopting the most severe repressive measures. No government can withstand a political strike conducted by a large part of the population, if it does not succeed in breaking it early. The power of the political strike was demonstrated in the interception of the attempted putsch by Kapp in Germany in 1920, in the Indian national movement under Gandhi's leadership in the 1930's, in the strike of the Palestinian Arabs in 1936, and elsewhere.

The strike at Hama in 1964 failed, as did a similar strike in Damascus in January 1965. These were chiefly strikes by businessmen, inspired by the Muslim clergy and limited in their social base. Although they were directed against a government of political suppression, they lacked a progressive social impetus and did not gain the support of the workers, peasants or intellectuals. The demonstrations and strike in Khartoum in October 1964, which toppled and overthrew the Sudanese military dictatorship, were different in nature. This was a popular uprising with numerous and diverse supporters—workers and intellectuals, businessmen and office workers, northerners and southerners. It was hardly by chance that the most overt military dictatorship was the first to fall this way.

Military dictatorship is fundamentally opposed to the most fundamental needs of the contemporary Middle East—mutual respect and the spirit of cooperation among factors which, though different, are not in conflict with one another, in order to achieve common goals and to prevent the destructive struggles which are inevitable, if one factor should wish to suppress the others. The officer politicians strive for political and social regimentation, contrary to the basic conditions of the Middle East. They want to give society the shape and structure of a monolith. It is fine for tombstones to be monolithic, but not for living organisms.

Only national and political pluralism can serve as the foundation of freedom and prosperity in the Middle East, including a true Arab renaissance. In its national, linguistic, communal, religious and cultural composition, the Middle East is a pluralistic region. Arab nationalism constitutes one of the components in this mosaic, perhaps the most important one, a leading force with a great mission. However, when it appears with the demand that all other factors be assimilated into it and disappear or subordinate themselves to it, and especially when this nationalism fanatically strives to establish Arab-Islamic-Sunni-urban domination, it becomes transformed from a potentially stimulating, uniting base into a divisive, aggressive and destructive element. Will the Druze and Alawis in Syria agree to this kind of oppression? Under no circumstances will it be acceptable to the Kurds in the north-eastern territories of the Arab world, the Berbers in the western part, the animistic Negroes in its southern regions, the Israelis at its center, the Christians in Lebanon or the Shi'i in Iraq. Imperialistic Arab trends will hamstring the prospects of necessary cooperation among Arabs, Turks and Iranians. Arab nationalism, according to the version of centralized domination, is also undermining the growth of greater unity inside the Arab world itself. Nearly a thousand years ago al-Shahrastānī wrote, "Never was there an Islamic issue which brought about more bloodshed than the caliphate."[18] In the same way, it can be

[18] Quoted in Philip K. Hitti, *History of the Arabs,* London 1943, 139.

said today that there is no factor causing more dissension in the contemporary Middle East and among the Arabs themselves than the issue of Arab unity. Only the awareness of the pluralistic nature of the Middle East and the affirmation of its heterogeneity will make it possible to find real solutions to the problems of the region and its peoples. Only the pluralistic outlook, not for the purpose of making the best of a bad situation but in order to build the future on a sound foundation, can alone serve as the basis of fruitful coexistence and cooperation of the Arabs with Israel. The lengthy and hitherto constant efforts of the Arabs to deprive Israel of her independence and prevent her integration with the countries and peoples of the Middle East have been harming the Arabs themselves more than Israel. For they stem from the sterile principle of establishing a monolithic structure—sterile because it cannot be realized either in the relations of the Arabs with their neighbors or in inter-Arab relations.

Pluralism and military dictatorship are contradictory. The "natural course", as it were, of the domination of the Arab peoples' political, social and spiritual life by the officer corps leads into a blind alley. It is not the officer politicians who will guide the peoples in a spirit of tolerance to utilize their potentialities for the great future which awaits them.

APPENDICES

A. THE SOCIAL ORIGIN OF EGYPTIAN OFFICERS BEFORE 1952: ANALYSIS OF A SAMPLE

For the purpose of studying the social origin of the Egyptian officer class before the revolution, a sample group has been chosen. This group consists of the officers who fell in the Palestine War of 1948–49. As is customary in all countries, relatively comprehensive information about family and personal data has been given on those who died, particularly those killed in action.

After examining the details of this sample group and determining composition and scope, we can judge how far the sample is representative of the officer class of the period as a whole. The data provided by the list will then be analyzed.

The list is arranged according to the seniority of the officers in the service (column 4), that is to say, according to the dates on which they were commissioned as second-lieutenants on completion of their course at the military academy.

The ranks listed in column 5 are the ranks actually held by the officers at the time of their death. Literature on the subject will usually quote one rank higher, since, as in other armies, it is customary to award a posthumous promotion, both as a tribute to the fallen and as a means of augmenting the pension to this family.

Abbreviations

A	Asmā'; the Book of Names—see below, p. 488
'A.	'Abd
AF	Air Force
Aḥ.	Aḥmad
Art	Artillery
B	Batshatī's book—see p. 489
Cap	Captain (*yūzbāshi*; in AF *qā'id sirb*)
Cav	Cavalry—Armored Corps
Lt	Lieutenant (*mulāzim awwal*; in AF *ṭayyār awwal*)
Lt-Col	Lieutenant-Colonel (*bikbāshi*)
Col	Colonel (*qā'imaqām*)
Com.	Commissioned; Com. 27=Commissioned 1927
Diary	The Diary of Ṣalāḥ Badr—see below p. 490
Eng	Engineer Corps
fam.	family
Ḥāfiẓ	Ḥāfiẓ's books—see below, p. 490
Inf	Infantry
Mem.	The Memoirs of Nasser; see below, p. 490
Ob.	Obituary; if not otherwise stated—in *al-Ahrām*

M.	Muḥammad	R	Rāfi'ī's lists—see below, p. 489
Maj	Major (*ṣāgh*; in AF *qā'id asrāb*)	Sec-Lt	Second Lieutenant *(mulāzim thānī*; in AF *ṭayyār thānī*)
Med	Medical Corps		

THE EGYPTIAN OFFICERS WHO FELL IN THE PALESTINE WAR OF 1948

No. (1)	*Name* (2)	*Born* (3)	*Com.* (4)	*Rank* (5)	*Arm* (6)	*Family (sources)* (7)
1	Aḥ. 'A al-Azīz	07	27	Col	Cav	Son of brigadier in the army; son-in-law of Pasha; fam. of high officials (A, B, R, Ḥāfiẓ, Ob. 24 Aug. 48, 26 Dec. 62)
2	Aḥ. 'A. al-Salām 'Afīfī	13	33	Lt-Col	Inf	(A, B, R, Mem., Diary)
3	Aḥ. Fahmī Bayūmī	14	34	Lt-Col	Art	Son of brother of former army commander, M. Futūḥ Pasha (A, B, R, *al-Ahrām* 16 Jan. 49)
4	Aḥ. Fu'ād	18	37	Maj	Art	(A, B, R)
5	M. Wajīh Khalīl	19	38	Maj	Inf	Fam. of village notables, judge, Bey, officers and members of free professions (A, B, R, Ob. 22 July 49, 3 Apr. 66)
6	Filīb Buqṭur	18	38	Maj	Inf	Copt. His father was a 'property owner' (A, B, R, Ob, 23 July 48)
7	Shafīq Mu'awwaḍ	17	38	Maj	Inf	Copt (A, B, R)
8	Fu'ād Naṣr Hindī	17	38	Cap	Inf	Copt (B, R, Ob. 28 July 48)
9	Najīb 'A. al-Azīz Basyūnī	17	39	Maj	AF	Son of former senator; brother of army officers and *'umda*; son-in-law of Dr Maḥmud 'Azmī Bey, the renowned journalist (R, Ob. 30 Aug. 48, 18 Dec. 62)
10	'Izz al-Dīn al-Mawjī	14	39	Cap	Inf	Cousin of No. 45; son of brigadier (A, B, R, Ob. 3 July 48, 13 May 49)
11	Muṣṭafā Ṣabrī 'A. al-Ḥamīd	19	39	Maj	AF	(R)
12	M. 'Adlī Kafāfī	21	39	Maj	AF	Son of physician; fam. of officials and officers (R, Ob. 10 Nov. 48)
13	Ḥusayn Majdī	14	39	Cap	Art	(A, B, R)
14	'A. al-Mun'im Khulayf	19	39	Maj	Inf	His father and mother from families of religious clerks and learned men (A, B, R, Mem.)

No. (1)	*Name* (2)	*Born* (3)	*Com.* (4)	*Rank* (5)	*Arm* (6)	*Family (sources)* (7)
15	M. Ṣalāḥ Sha'bān	18	39	Cap	Art	Brother of engineer (A, B, R, Ob. 14 Jan. 49)
16	M. 'Alī 'Īsā	17	39	Maj	Eng	Engineer (A, B, R)
17	M. Samādūnī	15	39	Maj	Eng	Fam. of notables, property-owners, members of parliament and academics (A, B, R, Ob. 14 Jan. 49)
18	Aḥ. Jalāl	20	39	Maj	Cav	His father—'director of the offices of a royal princess' (A, B, R, Ob. 2 Jan. 49)
19	M. Jamāl Malash	21	39	Cap	Cav	Fam. of officials, merchants and advocates (A, B, R, Ob. 11 Dec. 48)
20	Al-Sayyid Abū Shādī	21	39	Cap	Inf	(A, B, R)
21	M. Sālim 'A. al-Salām	18	39	Cap	Art	Fam. of officials (A, B, R, Ob. 25 Aug. 48)
22	Muṣṭafā Rajab	16	39	Cap	Cav	Brother of official; relative of contractor (A, B, R, Ob. 19 Jan. 49)
23	Anwar Ṣiyaḥī	21	39	Cap	Art	(A, B, R, Ḥāfiẓ)
24	Maḥmūd Sāmī	18	39	Cap	Inf	His sister — teacher; among the relatives—a brigadier (A, B, R, Ob. 3, Nov. 48)
25	Ḥilmī 'Abduh	19	39	Cap	Inf	Copt. Son of village notable; among his relatives—members of free professions (A, B, R, Ob. *al-Miṣrī* 11 Dec. 48)
26	M. 'A. al-Ḥamīd Abū Zayd	18	39	Maj	AF	(B, R)
27	Sayyid 'Afifī Janzūrī	19	39	Maj	AF	(B, R, Mem.)
28	Anṭūn Jirjis	19	40	Cap	Inf	Copt (A, B, R)
29	Ibrāhīm Bakhīt	21	40	Cap	Cav	'The grandson of a pious and learned man' (A, B, R)
30	Muṣṭafā Kāmil M.	21	40	Cap	Cav	Fam. of officials of intermediate and high grades and senior officers (A, B, R, Ob. 15 July 48)
31	'Abd al-Ra'ūf 'Alī	21	40	Cap	Inf	(A, B, R)
32	M. M. Jalāl	22	40	Cap	Art	Fam. of high officials, army officers and physicians (A, B, R, Ob. 24, 27, 28 Oct. 48)
33	Ḥilmī Sulaymān	20	40	Cap	Inf	(A, B, R)
34	M. Muḥsin Ḥamad	22	40	Cap	Inf	(A, B, R; in A, p. 48, erroneously M. Muḥsin Muḥammad)

No. (1)	*Name* (2)	*Born* (3)	*Com.* (4)	*Rank* (5)	*Arm* (6)	*Family (sources)* (7)
35	M. ‘A. al-Mun‘im ‘Adīsī	18	41	Cap	Inf	After the death of his father he asked to retire from army service in order to manage his large estate (A, B, R)
36	M. Rif‘at Fahmī	20	41	Cap	Inf	Fam. of high officials (A, B, R, Ob. 17 Sept. 48)
37	Bayūmī Shāfi‘ī	20	41	Cap	Inf	(A, B, R)
38	Jalāl Ḥajjāj	19	41	Cap	Inf	Fam. of *'umda,* judges, high officials and officers (A, B, R, Ob. 28 Oct. 48)
39	M. ‘A. al-Raḥman Ismā‘īl	20	42	Cap	Inf	(A, B, R)
40	Ṣalāḥ Ibrāhīm	18	42	Cap	Inf	Son of Bey; brother of engineer (A, B, R)
41	Muṣṭafā Kāmil ‘Uthmān	22	42	Lt	Inf	(A, B, R)
42	M. ‘Izzat Ṭūlān	21	42	Lt	Inf	Fam. of village notables, high officials, academics and officers; relative of No. 66 (A, B, R, Ob. 26 July 48, 5 Mar. 53, 28 Mar. 63)
43	‘A. al-Mun‘im Ṣiddīq	20	42	Lt	Inf	(A, B, R)
44	M. Jamāl Khalīfa	21	42	Cap	Inf	Son of agricultural engineer; brother of army officers (A, B, R, Ḥāfiẓ, Ob. 20 Jan 49)
45	M. Ibrāhīm al-Mawjī	19	42	Lt	Inf	Cousin of No. 10; one of his relatives—a brigadier (A, B, R)
46	Ṣubḥī Ibrāhīm Fahmī	20	42	Cap	Inf	(A, B, R, Ob. 20 Jan. 49)
47	‘A. al-Majīd Abū-Zayd	18	42	Cap	Art	Fam. of merchants (A, B, Ob. 2 Jan. 49. The only one who is not mentioned in R)
48	Sa‘d Ḥanafī Ḥasan	22	42	Cap	Cav	Studied in U.K. (A, B, R)
49	Abū-Bakr Nazlāwī	18	42	Lt	Eng	His brothers-in-law—an army officer and a police officer (A, B, R, Ob. 23 July 48)
50	M. ‘A. al-Hādī M.	20	42	Cap	Eng	(A, B, R)
51	Muṣṭafā Abū Zahra	21	42	Lt	Inf	(A, B, R)
52	Sayyid Abū al-‘Alā	19	42	Lt	Inf	(B, R, Ob. 5 Jan. 49. A mentions his name on p. 69 as a lieutenant in the war, but not among the fallen)
53	Muṣṭafā Kamāl Zakī	22	42	Lt	Inf	Son of Bey; among the relatives—officials, a physician and a teacher (A, B, R, Ob. 22 July 48)

No. (1)	*Name* (2)	*Born* (3)	*Com.* (4)	*Rank* (5)	*Arm* (6)	*Family (sources)* (7)
54	Dr Ḥasan Ḥilwānī	15	43	Cap	Med	(A B, R)
55	Dr M. al-Sā'iḥ 'Adlī	17	43	Cap	Med	Son of police officer; brother of police officer, advocate and engineer; nephew of *'umda,* brother-in-law of police officers (A, B, R, Ob. 18 June 48)
56	Muṣṭafā Kamāl Naṣr	23	43	Cap	AF	(B, R)
57	'Alī Shākir al-Rūbī	23	44	Lt	Cav	Son of major-general (*liwā'*); famous fam. of army chiefs and big landowners (A, B, R, Ob. 9 Jan. 49, 14 June 49)
58	Sa'd Ṣādiq Duwaynī	23	44	Lt	AF	(A, B, R)
59	M. Jamāl Bar'ī	21	45	Lt	Inf	Son of former senator and big landowner; fam. of big landowners and high officials (A, B, R, Ob. 30 July 48, 3 Aug. 48)
60	Ismā'īl Muḥyī al-Dīn	20	45	Lt	Inf	(A, B, R)
61	'A. al-'Azīm Badīwī	20	45	Lt	Art	Family of village notables, teachers and officials (A, B, R, Ob. 23 Jan. 49)
62	Muṣṭafā Ḥamid Ḥamīd	21	45	Lt	Inf	(A, B, R, Diary)
63	Ṣāliḥ 'Aṭṭār	21	45	Lt	Art	Son of village notable; fam. of officials (A, B, R, Ob. 23 July 48)
64	'A. al-Salām Farīd	20	45	Lt	Cav	Son of lt.-col.; fam. of notables, academics, officials and titled persons (A, B, R, Ob. 1 Nov. 49)
65	Khalīl Jamāl 'Arūsī	21	45	Lt	AF	(B, R)
66	Mukhtār Sa'īd	22	45	Lt	AF	Son of brigadier; nephew of senator; relative of officials and officers, among them No. 42 (B, R, Ob. 1 Nov. 48, 26 Dec. 62)
67	Ḥasan Ismā'īl Yusrī	20	45	Lt	Inf	(A, R)
68	Aḥ. Jamāl Yūnis	21	46	Lt	Cav	(A, B, R)
69	M. Niḥād Ṭaha Fahmī	27	46	Lt	Cav	Fam. of officers, officials and *'umda* (A, B, R, *al-Ahrām* 21 Dec. 49, Ob. 12 Dec. 48)
70	'Alī Salām	22	46	Lt	Cav	(A, B, R)
71	M. Ṭaha 'Aṭ'ūṭ	23	46	Lt	Art	Fam. of merchants (A, B, R, Ob. 1 Nov. 48)
72	Anwar Ṭu'ma	22	46	Lt	Inf	Fam. of business clerks and officials (A, B, R, Ob. 29 Oct. 48)
73	Aḥ. Taysīr Bashīr	22	46	Lt	Inf	Son of physician (A, B, R, Ob. 18 June 48)

No. (1)	Name (2)	Born (3)	Com. (4)	Rank (5)	Arm (6)	Family (sources) (7)
74	Maḥmūd Fahmī Ḥāfiẓ	23	46	Lt	Inf	(A, B, R)
75	M. Anwar ʻAwaḍ Ḥasan	22	46	Lt	Inf	Son of village notable; among the relatives—officials, a druggist and a teacher (A, B, R, Ob. 25 Jan. 49)
76	Kamāl Aḥ. Shāfiʻī	21	46	Sec-Lt	Inf	Fam. of officials (A, B, R, Ob. 19 Jan. 49)
77	Ibrāhīm ʻA. al-Fattāḥ	?	46	Lt	AF	(R)
78	Ibrāhīm Maḥmūd Sālim	26	48	Sec-Lt	Inf	(A, B, R)
79	M. al-Sayyid Aḥ. Tawfīq Qarṭām	28	48	Sec-Lt	Inf	Son-in-law of *'umda* (A, B, R, *al-Miṣrī* 10 Feb. 49)
80	M. Sāmī Fakhr	28	48	Sec-Lt	Cav	Son of Bey; nephew of physician; his mother—from a rich fam. (A, B, R, Ob. 10 Jan. 49)
81	Yusrī Rāghib Fahmī	30	48	Sec-Lt	Inf	Copt; son of col.; brother of police officer; among the relatives—officials and *'umda* (A, B, R, Ob. 21 Oct. 48)
82	ʻAbbās Shirbīnī	?	48	Sec-Lt	Inf	Fam. of merchants (A, B, R, Ob. 30 Dec. 48)
83	M. Ṣidqī M.	?	48	Sec-Lt	Inf	Son of physician; nephew of Bey (A, B, R, Ob. 29 Dec. 48)
84	Shawqī Nīqūlā Damyān	?	48	Sec-Lt	Inf	Copt (A, B, R)
85	Basyūnī Maḥmūd Basyūnī	?	48	Sec-Lt	Cav	Grandson of contractor; the relatives—officials (A, B, R, Ob. 29 Dec. 48)
86	Ḥilmī ʻA. al-Qawī	?	48	Sec-Lt	Inf	Son of official (A, B, R, Ob. 10 Jan. 49)
87	Aḥ. ʻAwaḍ	?	48	Sec-Lt	Inf	Fam. of officials (A, B, R, Ob. 8 Oct. 48)

Composition and scope of the sample

We have consulted four lists of Egyptian officers who fell in the Palestine War.

1. The book referred to as Book of Names: *Asmā'al-ḍubbāṭ alladhīna ishtarakū fī ḥamlat al-jaysh al-miṣrī ilā Falasṭīn, māyū 1948–fibrāyir 1949* (Names of the officers who took part in the campaign of the Egyptian army in Palestine from May 1948 to February 1949). This book of 129 pages appeared in Cairo in 1949, without author's or publisher's name, as a presentation from the army to King Fārūq. It gives names and ranks of officers according to their units,

including Sa'ūdi and Sudanese units which operated in the framework of the Egyptian army, and also reserve and volunteer units, but it does not include air force or naval officers. In the list of fallen officers, by units, there appear the names of 70 regular officers of the Egyptian army, all of whom also appear in our list. One (No. 52 in our list) appears among the officers of his unit who returned home safely, although in fact he was killed. One officer (No. 8) who was killed is not to be found anywhere in the Book of Names. In addition to the fallen, 8 officers are listed as missing. Four of these, who were in fact killed, are mentioned in our list (37, 51, 59 and 67). The remaining four were prisoners-of-war in Israel or somehow found their way back to their units.

2. The book of Chaplain (*wā'iz*) Muḥammad 'Abd al-'Azīz al-Batshatī, *Shuhadā'-unā al-dubbāṭ fī ḥamlat Falasṭīn* (Our fallen officer heroes of the Palestine Campaign), which was published in Cairo in 1949 (152 pp.). This book gives biographical information on 81 officers who fell, mentioning particularly their personal merits and the battles in which they fought and fell, and in rare cases something about their families.

3. The book by the Egyptian historian, 'Abd al-Raḥmān al-Rāfi'ī, *Fi a'qāb al-thawra al-miṣriyya* (In the wake of the Egyptian Revolution). On pages 257–261 of the third volume which appeared in 1951 a list of 101 fallen officers is published which gives the officers' rank and date and place of death, but no other information. Rāfi'ī's book gives all the names which appear in the Book of Names, while Batshatī gives all but one (No. 47), the error possibly resulting from the similarity of the name 'Abd al-Majīd Abū-Zayd, the artillery captain, to that of Muḥammad 'Abd al-Ḥamīd Abū-Zayd (No. 26), the major in the air force. Of the names given only by Rāfi'ī but not in the Book of Names nor in Batshatī's list, four (Nos. 9, 11, 12 and 77) are in our list. The remainder, though listed by Rāfi'ī as fallen officers, were either prisoners-of-war in Israel who returned to Egypt in 1949 or were killed after the end of the war. The rest probably were not officers at all.

4. *Sijill al-khulūd* (Scroll of immortality), a book which gives the names of all Arab dead in the Palestine War, forms the sixth volume of the book *al-Nakba* (The holocaust) by 'Ārif al-'Ārif which was published in Sidon and Beirut in 1962. 862 Egyptian military personnel, including 101 officers with their rank, date of death and in most cases the place where they met their death, are listed on pages 133 to 171 in alphabetical order of their first names. On page 128 the author notes as his source 'the official printed notification, prepared by the Directorate-General of the armed forces at the Egyptian War Office', which he requested and received from 'Colonel Maḥmud Riyāḍ, Deputy Chief of the Palestine Administration Office in the above-mentioned ministry'. In fact, 'Ārif al-'Ārif's data are identical in almost every detail with those in Rāfi'ī's book which appeared eleven years earlier. Only No. 53 in our list, who appears in Rafi'ī's list, is not included in that of 'Ārif al-'Ārif.

In addition to these lists, a great deal of information on Aḥmad 'Abd al-'Azīz (No. 1) and on Muḥammad Jamāl Khalifa (44) and their families is to be found in the biographies *al-Batal Aḥmad 'Abd al-'Aziz* by Abū al-Ḥajjāj Ḥāfiẓ, a book of 475 pages which was published in Cairo in 1961, and *al-Baṭalān Jamāl Khalīfa wa-Nazīh Khalīfa*, by the same author, 135 pages, published in Cairo some years later. Captain Ṣalāḥ Badr, who was commander of 'Irāq Suwaydān, facing the kibbutz Negba which was encircled and cut off from 14 July until 9 November 1948, recorded in his diary brief remarks on a number of officers who were killed. The diary is preserved in the archives of the Israel Defense Army. A Hebrew translation, not accurate in all details, appeared in the weekly *Bamakhaneh* of 8 November 1960. Finally, Nasser makes mention of a number of fallen officers in his memoirs of the Palestine War, published in the Cairo weekly *Akhir Sā'a* in the issues of 9, 23 and 30 March and 7 April 1955.

Information on officers' families is drawn mostly from obituary notices in the Egyptian daily press, especially *al-Ahrām*. It is customary in such notices to mention a great many names of relatives, sometimes more than fifty, with their occupations or the positions they hold and also the family relationship to the deceased.

To what extent is the sample representative of the whole of the officer class?

Eighty-seven officers were, after all, only three per cent of the entire Egyptian officer class in 1948; 84 officers below the rank of lieutenant-colonel were 3.25 per cent of all the officers within the same span of ranks. Nevertheless, the sample may be regarded from several points of view as representative of the entirety of Egyptian officers of junior and intermediate rank.

The most important condition for obtaining a truly representative sample of a population is that it be composed of individuals drawn at random from all sections of this population, without bias and without objectives having been fixed beforehand. This condition is here fulfilled beyond any doubt. Apart from the fact that the information available on those who have fallen in battle is relatively greater than that for their surviving comrades, the fortuitous nature of the composition of the group is a prime reason for choosing it as a sample.

Many other points of view confirm that the sample is to a great extent, almost to an astonishing extent, representative of the junior and intermediate ranks of the officer class in general. Apart from the navy, which in 1948 was very small, all arms and branches of the Egyptian armed forces are represented in the list. The Copts in the list number seven, that is to say eight per cent. Of all Egyptian officers in 1948, about six per cent were Copts; of the junior and intermediate ranks—about seven per cent.

The objection may be raised that officers stationed in the combat area who alone suffered casualties are not representative of the entire officer class. Perhaps those who were sent to Palestine were of a different type from those who managed to secure comfortable postings nearer home. After all, it is by no means unknown in the history of warfare that those sent to the front differ greatly from those who sent them. However, we shall see that in the Egyptian army at the time of the 1948 war

The Book of Names lists 2,345 Egyptian officers, 145 of whom were reserve officers, 150 temporary officers (*ḍubbāṭ mukallafūn*), and 2,050 in the regular army, including the medical corps, but excluding the navy and the air force. Of the 168 graduates of the Staff College then serving in the army, 131 were in Palestine, i.e. almost 80 per cent. In Palestine there was no great distance between front lines and rear positions, and the scenes of action changed frequently and unexpectedly. Furthermore, the unit of the 'best families' was the (armored) cavalry corps, as it is in many other armies. In 1948 the officers in this unit numbered about 225, that is less than eight per cent of the entire officer corps. But among 87 officers who fell, 14 were from it, i.e. 16 per cent. This, of course, was primarily a result of the operational character of the unit. Nevertheless, the figure along with other facts shows that it would be wrong to assume that the officers in the privileged units attempted to avoid, or at any rate succeeded in avoiding, combat service. There must certainly have been such cases here and there, but they can only have been few. When they set out for the war, moreover, they thought they were off on an easy and victorious campaign from which they would soon return as glorious heroes. Thus the officers who were in Palestine may be regarded as presenting a faithful reflection of the whole Egyptian officer class.

A surprising fact is that, while captains in the sample numbered 28 and lieutenants 31, second-lieutenants numbered only 12. Yet here, too, is a reflection of a general phenomenon. In the entire Egyptian army in 1948 there were 550 second-lieutenants, 900 lieutenants and 650 captains. As in other armies, second-lieutenants were usually promoted to lieutenants after two years in the lower rank, while they served in the rank of lieutenant twice or three times as long, being promoted to the rank of captain only after four to six years as lieutenant. The particularly small number of second-lieutenants in the sample group is rather striking, nevertheless, but it has a simple explanation. The officers who were commissioned in 1946 were almost all full lieutenants by May 1948. The number of officer-training-course graduates in 1947 was unusually small, and for some reason officers commissioned in that year were not sent to Palestine. Those who were commissioned in 1948 completed their course only on 1 July, and those of them who were sent to the front arrived there after much of the heavy fighting was over.

The list is made up according to the years in which the officers were commissioned. The relatively small number of fatal casualties among officers commissioned in the years 1941, 1943, 1944 and 1947 claims one's attention. We have already seen the explanation as regards the year 1947. The small number of fallen who were commissioned in 1944 appears to be quite fortuitous. With regard to the other two years, the numbers again reflect the composition of the officer corps as a whole. Below are given the numbers of regular officers who served in the Egyptian army in 1948, excluding naval officers, by year of commission, showing comparison with the numbers in the sample group.

The progression by year in the following table is evident. The younger the graduates, up to the year 1946, the higher the percentage of fatal casualties. The ratio of front-line officers among those below the rank of major is consistently greater than that for senior ranks. By the summer of 1948 most of the graduates of 1939 were majors,

NUMBER OF OFFICERS SERVING IN 1948

Year of commission	*Total*	*In sample*	*Samples as % of the whole*
Before 1938	615	4	0.7
1938	180	4	2.2
1939	630	19	3.0
1940	315	7	2.2
1941	90	4	4.4
1942	330	15	4.5
1943	65	3	4.6
1944	160	2	1.3
1945	145	9	6.2
1946	200	10	5.0
1947	55	0	0.0
1948	225	10	4.4
Total	3010	87	2.9

and most of the 1940–42 graduates were captains. Those commissioned in 1947 and 1948 have already been discussed.

The various tests applied and comparisons drawn show that the list of fallen may be regarded as a representative sample of the whole Egyptian officer corps in its junior and intermediate ranks in the year 1948. Thus it is representative of four-fifths of the officer class in the last years of the monarchy, of the entire range of the officer class in the first years of the republic, and of all the officers of intermediate and senior ranks in the sixties.

Social origins

The sample provides details on family and social background of 54 out of 87 officers, i.e. 62 per cent. It is clear that most of them had come from well-to-do families or families of officers. The question arises whether those officers of whom we have no particulars come from the same social strata. Most of the information regarding the families comes from the obituary notices in the columns of *al-Ahrām*; perhaps the other officers came from poorer families who were not in the habit of putting announcements in that newspaper. However, it can be established with certainty that this is not the case. Sometimes, as in the cases of Nos. 8 and 44, the families published announcements without indicating names or occupations of members of the family. Moreover, not all the information we have on family background and origins is derived from obituary notices. In the cases of sixteen officers of the sample group regarding whom we saw no newspaper notices, we have clear indications or important information from other sources: Seven of them (Nos. 11, 26, 27, 56, 58, 65 and 77) were officers in the air force. All officers in the air force were of good education and from well-to-do families. Four others (Nos. 29, 48, 68 and 70) were officers of the (armored) cavalry corps, the crack unit officered by sons of the 'best families'. One of them, No. 48, studied for a time in England before entering the army. Others in this category include a doctor of medicine (No. 54), an engineer (No. 16), a son of a Bey (No. 40), the relative of a brigadier (No. 45) and one whose father was the owner of a large estate (No. 35). It is therefore clear that the absence of an obituary notice is no guide as to status.

On the other hand, the nature of the information in our possession does not enable us to define with any precision the position in society of each and every one of the surviving relatives of officers. A certain measure of exaggeration must also be taken into account. A relative described in an obituary notice as a merchant could well be, in fact, a petty shopkeeper, and so forth. From several other points of view, too, the classification of relatives cannot be exact, neither as regards social status and stratum, nor as regards occupational group. For example, a medical practitioner with the degree of doctor, holding the title of Bey and the rank of brigadier in the medical corps, could be listed under 'academics', under 'officers', or under bearers of titles such as Pasha or Bey. In such cases our rule for classification has been to choose the alternative which leaves the least room for ambiguity.

RELATIVES OF OFFICERS IN THE SAMPLE GROUP, BY OCCUPATION AND SOCIAL CLASS

Class	*Lower*			*Middle*			*Lower*				
Occupation / *Stratum*	*Lower*	*Middle*	*Upper*	*Lower*	*Middle*	*Upper*	*Lower*	*Middle*	*Upper*	*Totals*	*Per cent*
Officials (junior and intermediate grades)			8	56	40					104	30
Officers				18	21	14	9	4	1	67	20
Academics				9	32	6	3	2		52	15
Titled persons and members of parliament						8	12	6	3	29	9
Senior officials					10	10	5	2		27	8
Merchants and contractors			3	10	13	1				27	8
Village notables				2	7	13	2			24	7
Estate owners						1	4	2	1	8	2
Clerics			1	2	1	1				5	1
Totals			12	98	125	54	35	16	5	345	
Per cent			3	29	36	16	10	5	1		100

The descriptions of officers' relatives by occupation can be divided into nine groups. The largest group consists of officials of junior and intermediate grades, including teachers. Among 345 relatives of 54 officers, 104 such officials were relatives of 31 officers. This group includes government officials and clerks as well as clerks in commerce.

The second group consists of army officers, including a substantial number of senior officers, and some police officers. This group numbers 68 relatives of 29 officers of our sample group.

Third place is occupied by academics—doctors, lawyers and chemists—30 relatives of 30 officers. In fact, the number of academics is greater, but some of them are listed as senior officials, such as judges, and some as officers in the medical corps.

The fourth group consists of holders of titles of Pasha and Bey with no occupational description, and members of parliament and the senate. This group numbers 29 relatives of 19 officers.

Next come the senior officials—27 relatives of 20 officers.

Equal in number is the group of merchants and contractors, though these 27 were the relatives of only 11 officers.

The seventh group are the 'village notables', *'umdas* and *shaykhs*—24 relatives of 17 officers.

The eighth group are owners of large estates—though not of the largest in Egypt. They are 8 in number, relatives of 5 officers.

The smallest group is that of Muslim religious functionaries—only 5 in number, the relatives of 4 officers.

In addition to classification by occupation, we have tried to divide the relatives of officers into social classes and strata. Clearly, this classification cannot be an exact one, but the general picture which emerges seems to us to reflect social reality.

According to this classification, more than one-third of the officers' relatives belong to the middle stratum of the middle class, a little less than a third to the lower stratum of the same class, and about a quarter to the upper stratum of the middle class and the lower stratum of the upper class. Smaller proportions are accounted for by the middle and upper strata of the upper class and the upper stratum of the lower class. The masses of the lower class, that is to say, four-fifths of the whole population, are not represented at all.

According to another classification, about two-thirds (231) of officers' relatives belong to those social strata which are salaried employees (all the officials and clerks, the officers, the clerics and about half the academics). Most of the others (114) live on rents, usually from agricultural land. These are not exclusively village notablés and estate owners. Almost all who became Beys or Pashas, members of parliament or the senate, senior officials or senior officers, became also owners of land, as did successful lawyers and followers of other academic occupations. The category which is least represented among officers' relatives is that of the smaller or bigger capitalist-bourgeois employers and entrepreneurs. These are the merchants and contractors in our sample and perhaps a few of the academics, titled persons and members of parliament. Even though one may assume that in some cases the income derives from mixed sources—partly from salary, partly from property and partly from business—still the extent of the connection between the various income groups and the origins of officers' families is very clear.

This division has considerable significance. Not only are the officers themselves salaried employees, they also have, through social and family interests, strong and diverse connections with officials and other salaried employees, with academics and with medium landowners. Few are their connections with large estate owners on the one hand, and, on the other hand, with the capitalist groups of society in the proper sense of the term, i.e. with industrialists, artisans and traders.

There is also considerable significance in the fact that links between the officers and Muslim religious functionaries were very few indeed. Although in Egypt the *shaykhs* and *imāms* are much more numerous than the doctors, engineers, lawyers and all the other academics together, persons of modern-type education are represented among officers' families more than ten times as much as those of traditional Islamic education. The modernistic mentality of the Egyptian officer class as a whole is by no means accidental.

The three officers in the sample group who were sons and grandsons of Pashas (Nos. 1, 3 and 57) were also sons of officers' families, and the estate owners among the officers' relatives are also of military families; indeed, it was as such that they acquired their estates. A typical example is 'Alī Shākir (No. 57) of the distinguished al-Rūbī family. The founder of the family, 'Alī Pasha al-Rūbī, who was born around 1835, enlisted in the army as a private in the 1850's. In the 1870's we find him holding the rank of brigadier. Later he became a judge. During the 'Urābī revolt he returned to the army, played a chief role in the nationalist movement and was promoted to major-general. After the defeat he was sentenced to exile in Eritrea and Sudan, where he died in 1891. He laid the foundations of the large family estates in Fayyūm, the province in which he was born. The family and its descendants achieved position and wealth within the army and through military service, not the other way round. The more their possessions increased, the weaker became their connections with the army, and the fewer the number of officers in the family.

The sample group also throws light on the status of the various arms in the Egyptian army. It confirms and gives examples of the special place of honor held by the armored corps, which was formerly the cavalry corps and in fact was still called by that name until the middle fifties, and by the air force. Three officers of the sample group were sons of army brigadiers. Two of these (Nos. 1 and 57) were in the armored corps and the third (No. 66) in the air force. Of the two sons of senators, one (No. 9) was in the air force and the other (No. 59) in the infantry. The son of the director of the estate of a royal princess (No. 18) was in the armored corps. The young man whose parents had been able to send him to school in England (No. 48) was, on his enlistment, accepted into the armored corps. Thus, of seven of these privileged young men, four were in the armored corps, two in the air force and one in the infantry. Among the remaining 80 officers in the sample group, 60 were in infantry regiments, the artillery and engineers, 10 in the armored corps, 8 in the air force and 2 in the medical corps. Thus 86 per cent of the sons of the most privileged families were in the armored corps or air force, while among the others the percentage was 22.5 only.

Conclusion

The limitations, both quantitative and qualitative, of the sample are obvious. Nevertheless, biographical information on many other Egyptian officers of the same period is not at variance with the picture we receive from the review and analysis of the sample group; indeed, it confirms it.

To sum up, one may point out the following: The Egyptian officers at the time of the Palestine War were for the most part from well-to-do families, some from the wealthy and upper classes, some from the middle and lower-middle classes. Most came from families whose income was their salaries; many came from families whose revenues derived from rents, particularly from land; many others from families whose members engaged in the free professions; while only a few came from families of capitalists, industrialists and businessmen. There were no officers who were members of Egypt's top social 'aristocracy'; neither were there any from the great rural and urban masses.

The strata of officer origins cover quite a wide sweep. Nevertheless, all these strata cover no more than twenty per cent of the population of the country, a group whose standard of living is very much higher than that of the remaining eighty per cent of the mass of the people.

B. ARAB OFFICER RANKS

	United ranks[1]	Egypt until 1939 and from 1953 to 1957; Sudan until 1966	Egypt from 1940 to 1942	Egypt Air Force until 1958	Syria until April 1958
Second-Lieutenant	*Mulāzim*	*Mulāzim thānī*	*Mulāzim thānī*	*Ṭayyār thānī*	*Mulāzim*
Lieutenant	*Mulāzim awwal*	*Mulāzim awwal*	*Mulāzim awwal*	*Ṭayyār awwal*	*Mulāzim awwal*
Captain	*Naqīb*	*Yuzbāshī*	*Naqīb*	*Qā'id sirb*	*Ra'īs*
Major	*Rā'id*	*Ṣāgh*	*'Amīd thānī*	*Qā'id asrāb*	*Ra'īs awwal*[4]
Lieutenant-Colonel	*Muqaddam*	*Bikbāshī*	*'Amīd*	*Qa'id janāḥ*	*Muqaddam*
Colonel	*'Aqīd*	*Qā'im-maqām*	*Qā'im-maqām*	*Qā'id liwā' jawwī*	*'Aqīd*
Brigadier	*'Amīd*	*Amīralāī*	*Amīr alā'ī*	*Qā'id firqa jawwīyya*	*Za'īm*
Major-General	*Liwā'*	*Liwā'*	*Liwā'*	*Qā'id usṭūl jawwī*	*Liwā'*
Lieutenant	*Farīq*	*Farīq*	*Farīq*		*Farīq*
	Farīq awwal[2]	*Sirdār*[3]			
Marshal	*Mushīr*	*Mushīr*	*Mushīr*		*Mushīr*

NOTES:

1. The general trend towards uniformity in the names of military ranks seems to be spreading gradually throughout the different Arab armies. The united ranks were introduced in April 1958 into the army of the UAR and remained in use for the armies of Syria and Egypt after Syria's secession in 1961 as well. In April 1964 they were introduced into the Iraqi army, and in October 1966 into the Sudanese.
2. The rank of *Farīq awwal* was introduced in Egypt alone in January 1964; it appears also in the official Jordanian list of ranks of July 1966, but there was no officer of this rank.
3. *Sirdār* is not a rank but was the title of the Supreme Commander of the Egyptian Army from 1883 to 1924, who was always British.

	Lebanon	Iraq until April 1964	Saudi Arabia	Jordan until 1956	Jordan from 1956
Second-Lieutenant	*Mulāzim*	*Mulāzim thānī*	*Mulāzim thānī*	*Mulāzim thānī*	*Mulāzim thānī*
Lieutenant	*Mulāzim awwal*	*Mulāzim awwal*	*Mulāzim awwal*	*Mulāzim awwal*	*Mulāzim awwal*
Captain	*Naqīb*	*Ra'īs*	*Ra'īs*	*Ra'īs*	*Ra'īs*
Major	*Muqaddam*	*Ra'īs awwal*	*Wakīl qā'id*	*Wakīl qā'id*	*Ra'īs awwal*
Lieutenant-Colonel	*'Aqīd*	*Muqaddam*	*Qā'id*	*Qā'id*	*Muqaddam*
Colonel	*Za'īm*	*'Aqīd*	*'Aqīd*	*Qā'imaqām*	*'Aqīd*
Brigadier	*Za'īm awwal*[5]	*Za'īm*	*Za'īm*	*Za'īm*	*Za'īm*
Major-General	*Liwā'*	*Amīr liwā'*	*Liwā'*	*Amīr liwā'*	*Amīr liwā'*
Lieutenant-General	*Farīq*[5]	*Farīq*	*Farīq thānī*	*Farīq*	*Farīq*
General		*'Amīd*	*Farīq awwal*		*Farīq awwal*[2]
Marshal		*Mushīr*			*Mushīr*

4. This rank was introduced only in 1952.
5. The ranks *Za'īm awwal* and *Farīq* exist only in theory.

SELECT BIBLIOGRAPHY

Abbeg, Lily, *Neue Herren im Mittelost,* Stuttgart 1954.

Abdel-Malek, Anouar, *Egypte, société militaire,* Paris 1962.

'Abd al-Nāṣir, Jamāl, *Falsafat al-thawra,* Cairo (1954).

Abdul Nasser, Gamal, *Egypt's liberation*, Washington, D.C., 1955.

Abū al-Fatḥ, Aḥmad, *Jamāl 'Abd al-Nāṣir,* Beirut (1962).

Abu Jaber, Kamel S., *The Arab Ba'th Socialist Party*, Syracuse, N.Y., 1966.

Abul-Fath, Ahmed, *L'Affaire Nasser,* Paris 1962.

Agra, *Tseva'ot ha-'aravim be-dorenu,* Tel Aviv 1948.

Andrzejewski, Stanislaw, *Military organization and society,* London 1954.

Antonius, George, *The Arab awakening*, London 1938.

Al-'Ārif, 'Ārif, *Sijill al-khulūd, (al-Nakba,* part six), Sidon and Beirut (1962).

Asāf, Antūn, *Al-qā'id Muḥammad Najīb,* Cairo 1953.

Asmā' al-ḍubbāṭ alladhīna ishtarakū fī ḥamlat al-jaysh al-miṣrī ilā Falasṭīn, māyū 1948—fibrāyir 1949, Cairo (1949).

'Aṭiyyat-Allāh, Aḥmad, *Qāmūs al-thawra al-miṣriyya 1954*, Cairo 1954.

Al-'Auf, Bashīr, *Al-inquilāb al-sūrī,* Damascus 1949.

Ayalon, D., *L'esclavage du Mamelouk,* Jerusalem 1951.

Ayalon, D., *Gunpowder and firearms in the Mameluk kingdom,* London 1956.

Baer, Gabriel, *Population and society in the Arab East,* London 1964.

Baer, Gabriel, *A history of landownership in modern Egypt, 1800–1950*, London 1962.

Al-Bannā', Ḥasan, *Mudhakkirāt al-da'wa wal-di'āyya,* Cairo s.d.

El-Barawi, Rached, *The military coup in Egypt,* Cairo 1952.

Al-Barāwī, Rāshid, *Ḥaqīqat al-inqilāb al-akhīr fī Miṣr,* Cairo 1952.

Al-Batshatī, Muḥammad 'Abd al-'Azīz, *Shuhadā'unā al-ḍubbāṭ fī ḥamlat Falaṣṭīn,* Cairo 1949.

Be-'eyney oyev, Tel Aviv 1954.

Ben-Tzur, Avraham, *Ha-sotsializm ha-'aravi,* Tel Aviv 1965.

Berger, Morroe, *Bureaucracy and society in modern Egypt,* Princeton 1957.

Berger, Morroe, *Military elite and social change: Egypt since Napoleon,* Princeton 1960.

Birdwood, Lord, *Nuri As-Said,* London 1959.

Bleibtreu, Karl, *Der Militarismus im 19 Jahrhundert,* Berlin 1901.

Bretholz, Wolfgang, *Aufstand der Araber,* Wien 1960.

Bruneau, André, *Traditions et politique de la France au Levant,* Paris 1932.

Burns, L.M., *Between Arab and Israeli,* London 1962.
Caractacus [Frederick J. Snell], *Revolution in Iraq,* London 1959.
Carman, W.Y., *The military history of Egypt,* Cairo 1945.
Chaillé-Long, Charles, *My life in four continents,* 2 vols., London 1912.
Chamoun, Camille, *Crise au Moyen-Orient,* Paris 1963.
Cohen, Aharon, *Temurot mediniyot ba-'olam ha-'aravi,* Merhavia 1959.
Crabitès, Pierre, *The winning of the Sudan,* London 1934.
Cromer, The Earl of, *Modern Egypt,* 2 vols., London 1908.
Crozier, Brian, *The rebels: a study of post-war insurrections,* London 1960.
Daalder, H., *The role of military in emerging countries,* The Hague 1962.
Dann, Uriel, *Iraq under Qassem,* Jerusalem 1969.
Al-Darūbī, Ibrāhīm, *Al-Baghdādiyyūn,* Baghdad 1958.
Demeter, Karl, *Das deutsche Offizierskorps in Gesellschaft und Staat 1650–1945,* Frankfurt/M 1964.
Djemal Pascha, Ahmed, *Erinnerungen eines türkischen Staatsmannes,* München 1922 (English: *Memoirs . . .,* New York 1922).
Douin, G., *La mission du Baron de Boislecomte,* Cairo 1927.
Al-Dūrī, 'Abd al-'Azīz, *Al-judhūr al-tārīkhiyya lil-qawmīyy al-'arabiyya,* Beirut 1960.
Al-Durra, Maḥmūd, *Tārīkh al-'arab al-'askarī,* Cairo 1961.
Al-Durra, Maḥmūd, *Al-qadīyya al-kurdīyya wal-qawmiyya al-'arabīyya fī ma'arakat al'Irāq,* Beirut 1963.
Endres, F.C., *Soziologische Struktur und ihr entsprechende Ideologien des deutschen Offizierskorps,* Tübingen 1927.
Eppler, John W., *Rommel ruft Kairo,* Gütersloh 1959.
Estier, Claude, *L'Egypte en révolution,* Paris 1965.
Al-Fīl, Aḥmad 'Isā, *Sūrīya al-hadītha fī al-inqilābayn,* Damascus 1949.
Finer, S.E., *The man on horseback: the role of the military in politics,* London 1962.
Fischer, Sidney Nettleton, (editor), *The military in the Middle East,* Colombus, Ohio, 1963.
Frey, Frederick W., *The Turkish political elite,* Cambridge, Mass., 1965.
Gadalla, Saad M., *Land reform in relation to social development—Egypt,* Columbia, Missouri, 1962.
Gallman, Waldemar J., *Iraq under General Nuri,* Baltimore 1964.
Glubb, John Bagot, *The story of the Arab Legion,* London 1948.
Glubb, John Bagot, *A soldier with the Arabs,* London 1957.
Goren, Asher, *Ha-liga ha-aravit,* Tel Aviv 1952.
de Gontant Biron, Comte R., *Sur les routes de Syrie,* Paris 1928.
Grobba, Fritz, *Irak,* Berlin 1941.
Grobba, Fritz, *Männer und Mächte im Orient,* Göttingen 1967.
Gutteridge, William, *Armed forces in new states,* London 1962.
Ḥaddād, 'Uthmān Kamāl, *Harakat Rashīd 'Ālī al-Kaylānī,* Sidon 1950.
Haddas, George M., *Revolutions and military rule in the Middle East: the northern tier,* New York 1965.
Hadhihi al-thawra, kitāb al-'ām al-awwal, Cairo 1953.

Ḥāfiẓ, Abū al-Hajjāj, *Al-Baṭal Aḥmad 'Abd al-'Azīz,* Cairo 1961.
Ḥāfiẓ, Abū al-Hajjāj, *Al-Baṭalān Jamāl Khalīfa wa-Nazīh Khalīfa,* Cairo (1963).
Haim, Sylvia G., *Arab nationalism, an anthology,* Berkeley and Los Angeles 1964.
Halpern, Manfred, *The politics of social change in the Middle East and North Africa,* Princeton 1963.
Hamon Léo, (editor), *Le role extra-militaire de l'armée dans le tiers-monde,* Paris 1966.
Hansen, Bent and Girgis A. Marzouk, *Development and economic policy in the UAR (Egypt)*, Amsterdam 1965.
Harris, Christina Phelps, *Nationalism and revolution in Egypt—The role of the Muslim Brotherhood,* The Hague 1964.
Al-Ḥasanī, Al-Sayyid 'Abd al-Razzāq, *Tārīkh al-wizārāt al-'irāqīyya,* 8 vols., Sidon 1933–1955.
Al-Ḥasanī, Al-Sayyid 'Abd al-Razzāq, *Al thawra al-'irāqīyya al-kubrā,* Sidon 1952.
Hazīmat ṭāghīya, Damascus (1954).
Henderson, K.D.D., *Sudan Republic,* London 1965.
Hesseltine, William B. and Hazel C. Wolf, *The blue and the gray on the Nile,* Chicago 1961.
Heyworth-Dunne, J., *Introduction to the history of education in modern Egypt,* London 1938.
Heyworth-Dunne, J., *Religious and political trends in modern Egypt,* Washington, 1950.
Hill, Richard L., *A biographical dictionary of the Anglo-Egyptian Sudan,* Oxford 1951.
Hirscowicz, Lukasz, *III zesza i arabski wschód,* Warszawa 1963.
Hirscowicz, Lukasz, *The Third Reich and the Arab East,* London 1966.
Holt, P.M., *A modern history of the Sudan,* London 1961.
Hourani, Albert, *Arabic thought in the liberal age,* London 1962.
Howard, Michael, (editor), *Soldiers and governments,* London 1957.
Huntington, Samuel P., *The soldier and the state,* Cambridge, Mass., 1957.
Huntington, Samuel P., (editor), *Changing patterns of military politics,* Glencoe, IU., 1962.
Husaini, Ishak Musa, *The Moslem Brethren,* Beirut 1956.
Ibrāhīm, Muḥammad, *Majhūd Miṣr al-ḥarbī,* Cairo 1952.
Ingrams, Harold, *The Yemen,* London 1963.
Issawi, Charles, *Egypt in revolution,* London 1963.
Al-Jadda, 'Abd al-Raḥman, *Thawrat al-Za'īm al-Munqidh,* Baghdad 1960.
Janowitz, Morris, *The professional soldier,* New York 1960.
Janowitz, Morris, *The military in the development of new nations,* Chicago 1964.
Joesten, Joachim, *Nasser,* London 1960.
Johnson, John J., (editor), *The role of the military in underdeveloped countries,* Princeton 1962.
Johnson, John J., *The military and society in Latin America,* Princeton 1964.
Kautsky, John H., (editor), *Political change in underdeveloped countries,* New York 1962.

Kerr, Malcom, *The Arab cold war, 1958–1964,* London 1965.
Khadduri, Majid, *Independent Iraq,* London 1960.
Kīra, Kamāl, *Maḥkamat al-sha'b,* 2 vols., Cairo (1955).
Al-kullīya al-'askarīyya al-malakīyya, Baghdad 1950.
Kurd 'Alī, Muḥammad, *Al-Mudhakkirāt,* 3 vols., Damascus 1948–49.
Kurd Ali, Mohammad, *Memories, a selection,* Washington, D.C., 1954.
Lacouture, Jean and Simone, *Egypt in transition,* London 1958.
Landau, Jacob M., *Parliaments and parties in Egypt,* Tel Aviv 1953.
Laqueur, Walter Z., (editor), *The Middle East in transition,* New York 1958.
Larcher, M., *La guerre turque dans la guerre mondiale,* Paris 1926.
Lerner, Daniel, *The passing of traditional society,* Glencoe, Ill., 1958.
Lewis, Bernard, *The emergence of modern Turkey,* London 1961.
Lewis, Bernard, *The emergence of modern Turkey,* London 1961.
Lias, Godfrey, *Glubb's Legion,* London 1956.
Lieuwen, Edwin, *Generals versus presidents: neomilitarism in Latin America,* London 1965.
Longrigg, Stephen Hemsley, *Iraq, 1900 to 1950,* London 1953.
Mahāḍir, *slsāt mubāḥathāt al-waḥda,* Cairo 1963.
Maḥkamat al-sha'b: *Muḥākamāt al-maḥkama al-'askariyya al-khāṣṣa,* 22 vols., Baghdad 1958–63.
Makarius, Raoul, *La jeunesse intellectuelle d'Egypte au lendemain de la deuxième guerre mondiale,* Paris 1960.
Al-Mālikī—rajul wa-qaḍiyya, Damascus 1956.
Mannheim, Karl, *Ideology and utopia,* New York 1959.
Al-Marayati, Abid, *A diplomatic history of modern Iraq,* New York 1961.
Mardin, Şerif, *The genesis of Young Ottoman thought,* Princeton 1962.
Meahorey ha-pargod, Tel Aviv 1954.
Meyer-Ranke, Peter, *Der rote Pharao,* Hamburg 1964.
Mills, C. Wright, *The power elite,* New York 1956.
Moltke, Helmuth v., *Briefe über Zustände und Begebenheiten in der Türkei aus den Jahren 1835 bis 1939,* Berlin 1893.
Morsy, Hassan Ragab, *Die ägyptische Presse,* Hannover 1963.
Al-Munajjid, Ṣalāḥ al-Dīn, *Suriyā wa-Maṣr bayn al-waḥda wal-infisāl, wathā'iq wa-nuṣūṣ,* Beirut (1962).
Murphy, Robert, *Diplomat among warriors,* New York 1964.
Naguib, Mohammed, *Egypt's destiny,* New York 1955.
Najīb, Muḥammad, *Risāla 'an al-Sūdān,* Cairo 1954.
Al-Naqqāsh, Rajā', *Fī azamat al-thaqāfa al-maṣriyya,* Beirut 1958.
Naṣṣūr, Adīb, *Qabla fawāt al-awān,* Beirut 1955.
Nuseibeh, Hazem Z., *The Ideas of Arab nationalism,* Ithaca, N.Y., 1956.
Oduho, Joseph and William Deng, *The problem of the Southern Sudan,* London 1963.
Orga, Irfan, *Portrait of a Turkish family,* London 1950.
Orga, Irfan, *Phoenix ascendant,* London 1958.
Pawlikowski-Cholewa, A.V., *Die Heere des Morgenlandes,* Berlin 1940.
Qadiyyat al-thawra fī 7 sanawāt, Cairo 1959.

Quṣṣat al-thawra fīl-'Irāq wa-Sūriyā, Beirut (1963).
Al-Rāfi'ī, 'Abd al-Raḥmān, *'Aṣr Ismā'īl,* 2 vols., Cairo 1932.
Al-Rāfi'ī, 'Abd al-Raḥmān, *Al-thawra al-'Urābiyya,* Cairo 1949.
Al-Rāfi'ī, 'Abd al-Raḥmān, *Muqaddimāt thawrat 23 yuliyū 1952,* Cairo 1957.
Al-Rāfi'ī, 'Abd al-Raḥmān, *Thawrat 23 yuliyū 1952,* Cairo 1959.
Al-Razzāz, Munīf, *Ma'ālim al-ḥayāt al-'arabiyya al-hadītha,* Beirut, 1959.
Riad, Hassan, *L'Egypte nassérienne,* Paris 1964.
Rosenthal, Erwin J.J., *Islam in the modern national state,* Cambridge 1965.
Royle, Charles, *The Egyptian campaigns 1882 to 1885,* 2 vols., London 1886.
Russell Pasha, Sir Th.W., *Egyptian service, 1902–1946,* London 1949.
Saab, Gabriel S., *The Egyptian agrarian reform, 1952–1962,* London 1967.
Saab, Hassan, *The Arab federalists of the Ottoman Empire,* Amsterdam 1958.
Al-Ṣabbāgh, Ṣalāḥ al-Dīn, *Fursān al-'urūba fī al-'Irāq,* Damascus 1956.
Al-Sādāt, Anwar, *Quṣṣat al-thawra kāmila,* Cairo 1956.
Al-Sadat, Anwar, *Revolt on the Nile,* London 1957.
El Sadat, Anwar, *Geheimtagebuch der ägyptischen Revolution,* Düsseldorf 1957.
Safran, Nadav, *Egypt in search of political community,* Cambridge, Mass., 1961.
Sa'īd, Amīn, *Silsilat kutub tārīkh al-'arab al-ḥadīth,* 23 vols., Cairo 1934–1960.
Sansom, A.W., *I spied spies,* London 1965.
Ṣaqqāl, Fatḥ-Allāh Mīkhā'īl, *Min dhikriyyāt ḥukūmat al-za'īm Ḥusnī al-Za'īm,* Cairo 1952.
Schmidt, Dana Adams, *Journey among brave men,* Boston 1964.
Schmidt, Dana Adams, *Yemen: The unknown war,* London 1968.
Scalc, Patrick, *The struggle for Syria,* London 1965.
Al-Sharīf, Kāmil Isma'īl, *Al-ikhwān al-muslimūn fī ḥarb Falasṭīn,* Cairo 1951.
Al-Sharīf, Kāmil Isma'īl, *Al-muqāwama al-sirriyya fī qanāt al-Suways,* Beirut 1957.
Shawkat, Sāmī, *Hadhini ahdāfunā,* Baghdad 1939.
Shwadran, Benjamin, *Jordan, a state of tension,* New York 1959.
Shwadran, Benjamin, *The power struggle in Iraq,* New York 1960.
Smith, Wilfred C., *Islam in modern history,* Princeton 1957.
St. John, Robert, *The boss,* New York 1960.
Steffens, Hans v., *Salaam,* Neckargemünd 1960.
Tillmann, Heinz, *Deutschlands Araberpolitik im zweiten Weltkrieg,* Berlin 1965.
Tinker, Hugh, *Ballot box and bayonet,* London 1964.
Tully, Andrew, *CIA, the inside story,* New York 1962.
Tūmā, Emīl, *Thawrat 23 tammūz fī 'aqdihā al-awwal,* Haifa 1962.
Tuwaynī, Ghassān, *Manṭiq al-quwwa,* Beirut 1954.
Vagts, Alfred, *A history of militarism,* New York 1937 and 1959.
Vatikiotis, P.J., *The Egyptian army in politics,* Bloomington 1961.
Vatikiotis, P.J., *Politics and the military in Jordan,* London 1967.
Vaucher, Georges, *Gamal Abdel Nasser et son équipe,* 2 vols., Paris 1959 et 1961.
Vered, Yael, *Hafikha umilḥama be-Teyman,* Tel Aviv 1967.
Vernier, Bernard, *L'Irak d'aujourd'hui,* Paris 1963.
Vernier, Bernard, *Armée et politique au Moyen-Orient,* Paris 1966.
Vingtrinier, Aimé, *Soliman-Pacha,* Paris 1860.

Wakin, Edward, *A lonely minority, the modern story of Egypt's Copts,* New York 1963.
Wallace, D. Mackenzie, *Egypt and the Egyptian question,* London 1883.
Warriner, Doreen, *Land reform and development in the Middle East,* second edition, London 1962.
Die Wehrkraft des osmanischen Reiches und seiner Vasallen-Staaten, Wien 1871.
Weiker, Walter F., *The Turkish revolution,* Washington, D.C., 1963.
Weinstein, Adelbert, *Das neue Mekka liegt am Nil,* Wiesbaden 1958.
Weiss, Dieter, *Wirtschaftliche Entwicklungsplanung in der VAR,* Köln 1964.
Wenner, Manfred W., *Modern Yemen 1918–1966*, Baltimore 1967.
Wheelock, Keith, *Nasser's new Egypt,* New York 1960.
Al-Yāfī, 'Abd al-Fattāḥ, *Al-'Irāq bayna inqilābayn,* Beirut 1938.
Yamak, Labib Zuwiyya, *The ideological foundations, structure and organization of the Syrian Social Nationalist Party,* New York 1966.
Young, Peter, *Bedouin command,* London 1956.
Zeine, Zeine N., *The struggle for Arab independence,* Beirut 1960.

INDEX OF NAMES

Arabic patronyms have been treated as surnames. Titles have been mentioned only when necessary for identification.